THE SWORD OF LINCOLN

The Army of the Potomac

JEFFRY D. WERT

SIMON & SCHUSTER PAPERBACKS

New York London Toronto Sydney

SIMON & SCHUSTER PAPERBACKS
Rockefeller Center
1230 Avenue of the Americas
New York, NY 10020

First Simon & Schuster paperback edition 2006

SIMON & SCHUSTER PAPERBACKS and colophon are registered
trademarks of Simon & Schuster, Inc.

For information about special discounts for bulk purchases,
please contact Simon & Schuster Special Sales:
1-800-456-6798 or business@simonandschuster.com

DESIGNED BY PAUL DIPPOLITO

Manufactured in the United States of America

3   5   7   9   10   8   6   4   2

The Library of Congress has cataloged the hardcover edition as
follows:

Wert, Jeffry D.
The sword of Lincoln : the Army of the Potomac / Jeffry D. Wert.
p. cm.
Includes bibliographical references (p.) and index.
1. United States. Army of the Potomac. 2. United States—History—
Civil War, 1861–1865—Regimental histories. 3. United States—
History—Civil War, 1861–1865—Campaigns. I. Title.
E470.2.W46 2005
973.7'41—dc22
2004058467

ISBN-13: 978-0-7432-2506-9
ISBN-10:   0-7432-2506-6
ISBN-13: 978-0-7432-2507-6 (Pbk)
ISBN-10:   0-7432-2507-4 (Pbk)

*To Gloria,
with love*

⊰ CONTENTS ⊱

Preface and Acknowledgments   ix

Chapter One   "Things Look Very Mutch Like War"   1

Chapter Two   Bloody Sabbath at Bull Run   16

Chapter Three   An Army Born   32

Chapter Four   To the Peninsula   52

Chapter Five   Along the Chickahominy   74

Chapter Six   "If We Were Defeated, the Army and the Country
Would Be Lost"   98

Chapter Seven   "McClellan Has the Army with Him"   126

Chapter Eight   "Behold, a Pale Horse"   142

Chapter Nine   The Army's "Saddest Hour"   174

Chapter Ten   Winter of Transition   205

Chapter Eleven   "God Almighty Could Not Prevent Me from
Winning a Victory"   231

Chapter Twelve   "Big Fight Some Wears Ahead"   259

Chapter Thirteen   "An Army of Lions"   274

Chapter Fourteen   Virginia Interlude   310

Chapter Fifteen   "This War Is Horrid"   333

Chapter Sixteen   "A Sit Down Before the Wall of Petersburg"   368

Chapter Seventeen   "I Never Seen a Crazier Set of Fellows"   392

Abbreviations   417

Notes   421

Bibliography   497

Index   535

A rough-cut granite monument, with a bronze tablet, stands today, like a lonely sentry at its post, in the small central Pennsylvania village of Rebersburg. It commemorates a day in August 1862, when seventy-eight men stood in Rebersburg's main street and took an oath of allegiance to the United States of America. The bronze tablet lists their names and the names of others who followed later into the army. Before long, the original volunteers formed Company A, 148th Pennsylvania Volunteer Infantry.

There are many grander, more imposing Civil War monuments throughout the country. Few, if any, such memorials have meant more to me. A typical small Pennsylvania village, nestled in a narrow valley, Rebersburg was my hometown. As a boy, I read the names on the tablet, knew the ones who were family, visited their graves in the cemetery, and sat in the room where they held their monthly Grand Army of the Republic meetings. I understood little at the time, except that they seemed heroic to me.

It has been more than half a century since that time. With members from the other companies in the regiment, the 148th compiled an excellent unit history. On its cover is a red trefoil, denoting the regiment's service in the First Division, Second Corps, Army of the Potomac. The 148th was justly proud of its membership in the command. These soldiers had stood in the Wheatfield at Gettysburg, at the Bloody Angle at Spotsylvania, before the trenches at Cold Harbor, and on the final road at Appomattox.

Youthful memories recur. Mine have led me, as a historian, to the writing of this book. The story of the men of the 148th Pennsylvania and their comrades in the Army of the Potomac deserves a retelling. This book is not a detailed account of battles and campaigns. Other historians and scholars have written excellent, modern, and thorough works on the major engagements in the East. My book is more a study, based upon several major themes. It does, however, cover the army's entire story, from its early formative days to the last hours at Appomattox.

Created to defend Washington, D.C., the Army of the Potomac operated within the capital's looming shadow. The Northern populace focused its attention upon the army's successes and failures on a battlefield. In many ways, its fortunes defined the fortunes of Abraham Lincoln and his administration. No American army has been so closely identified with a president nor have any other army's operations been so intertwined with politics. Lincoln's relationship with the army and the impact of politics upon its operations comprise a major theme of this book.

The men who led the army remain some of the most controversial generals in American history. In the hands of Irvin McDowell, George B. McClellan, Ambrose E. Burnside, Joseph Hooker, and George G. Meade, the army compiled a record of more defeats than victories. The army's senior leadership was cursed with internal dissension, political intrigue, and ineptness at times. My book reexamines the army's leadership, from army command to corps, division, brigade, and regimental command.

An integral part of my narrative is the morale and attitudes of the common soldiers. Despite the frequent blunders of their commanders, the army's rank and file fought with a valor worthy of any army. I have allowed them to speak for themselves, for their words convey an immediacy that transcends time. It has been argued that a defeatism afflicted the army as it faced Robert E. Lee and the magnificent Army of Northern Virginia. I have found that not to be accurate, at least among the soldiers who bore the greatest sacrifice.

I have integrated the best of modern scholarship with primary sources. My interpretations and conclusions will differ from others', but history abounds with disagreement. The story of the Army of the Potomac deserves a recounting. History is always more than words cast on metal or sculpted in stone.

Any work of history results from the collective efforts of individuals. To them, I extend my deepest appreciation and gratitude. Their assistance, knowledge, and insight have made this a better book. All errors are solely, however, the responsibility of the author.

I wish to thank the archivists and librarians at the institutions cited in the bibliography for their unfailing patience and understanding.

Other individuals merit my particular gratitude and recognition:

Dr. Richard Sommers, Head of Patron Services and an incomparable source for manuscript material, and his excellent staff, United States Army Military History Institute; Julie Holcomb, archivist, Pearce Civil War Collection, Navarro College; interlibrary loan staff, Centre County (Pennsylvania) Library; and James Quigle, Head of Archives and Special Collections, Pattee-Paterno Library, Pennsylvania State University.

Russ and Budge Weidman, friends and fellow Civil War buffs, for their generosity, kindness, and assistance and sharing their home with me on a research trip to Washington, D.C.

Mary Lou and Blair Pavlik, fellow students of the Civil War, for sharing with me the letters of George Bronson.

Ted Alexander, Chief Historian, Antietam National Battlefield, and trusted friend, for reading my chapter on Antietam and offering his acute comments.

David Ward, a friend and fellow historian, for reading portions of the manuscript, sharing material with me, and challenging my conclusions.

Daniel Laney, a proud Texan, Civil War historian and preservationist, president of the Austin Civil War Round Table, and a cherished family friend, for reading the entire manuscript, editing passages, and reminding me constantly of the merits of the Army of Northern Virginia.

Nicholas Picerno, Sr., an avid Civil War collector, authority on the 1st, 10th, and 29th Maine, and a longtime and deeply valued family friend, for sharing items from his superb collection and for reading my Antietam chapter.

Robert Gottlieb, President, Trident Media Group and my agent, for all of his efforts on my behalf.

Bob Bender, my editor, for his unwavering counsel, expertise, and friendship; and Johanna Li, associate editor, for her constant kindness, assistance, and patience; and Fred Chase, copy editor, for his fine work.

Our son, Jason Wert, our daughter-in-law, Kathy Neese Wert, our grandchildren, Rachel and Gabriel Wert, our daughter, Natalie Wert Corman, and our son-in-law, Grant Corman, for their cherished love and support.

My wife, Gloria, without whom none of my work as a historian would be possible. Her love and devotion has sustained me and enriched my life beyond words. For these reasons and more, this book is dedicated to her.

Jeffry D. Wert
Centre Hall, Pennsylvania
March 25, 2004

THE SWORD OF
LINCOLN

Chapter 1

"Things Look Very Mutch Like War"

Henry L. Martin walked the streets of Washington, D.C., loitered at saloons, listened to rumors, and made calculations. To an observer, the nation's capital throbbed with excitement and activity as the reality of civil war seemed at its doorstep. Volunteers from nearly every Northern state spilled out of railroad cars, marched down Pennsylvania Avenue to the cheers of onlookers, and filled nearly every parcel of open ground with their campsites. It appeared as if the spring rains had brought forth gardens of white tents.

For a man like Martin, Washington was a good place to be during the months of April, May, and June 1861. A Southern sympathizer, if not a hired spy, who used the pseudonym "D. L. Dalton," Martin gathered information and forwarded it to Confederate president Jefferson Davis in Richmond, Virginia. In a letter to Davis, dated June 29, Martin estimated the number of troops in the district and across the Potomac River in Virginia at 80,000. He noted that the cry, "still they come," echoed from residents as more new regiments arrived.

Martin assured the Confederate president, however, that except for three or four regiments, the volunteer soldiers "are of the very dregs of creation, collected from cities." Their officers were generally "Sunday militia" types, who knew little or nothing about their duties. He claimed that Union General-in-Chief Winfield Scott did not trust the volunteers to stand and fight in an engagement, adding that the old warrior suffered from lumbago and could conduct meetings only while lying on a couch.[1]

There were others in the capital who shared Martin's sympathies and passed enciphered messages south to Richmond. Federal officers and government officials talked freely at parties and in barrooms about military matters. Astute listeners could collect a mass of information and funnel it through an amateurish spy network. They gleaned valuable details, and probably like Martin, submitted erroneous intelligence.[2]

Some things were, however, beyond these informants' knowledge and understanding. Perhaps most of them shared Martin's dim assessment of the volunteers. There were in each regiment unsavory individuals, maybe even "the very dregs of creation, collected from cities." But more of them were ordinary farm boys and laborers than citified clerks. Home meant more than just New York City, Boston, and Philadelphia. It meant villages and farmsteads in Maine, Vermont, New Hampshire, Massachusetts, Connecticut, Rhode Island, New York, New Jersey, Pennsylvania, Ohio, Indiana, Michigan, Minnesota, and Wisconsin.[3]

They were awkward on drill fields, rowdy in camps and on city streets, attired in a kaleidoscope of multicolored, ill-fitting uniforms, and spoke in various languages. They reflected the North's increasing diversity and its woeful militia system. As Martin accurately reported, Scott and fellow Regular Army officers despaired over the prospects of leading them into battle.[4]

Beneath the outward appearances, however, lay something deeper of inestimable value. Many had volunteered because of the excitement of the times, the lure of adventure, and the prospect of earning money. But most came forth from a sense of duty and a devotion to their country—a simple idealism. These motives would sustain most of them during the many dark months and years ahead.[5]

"With thousands of others," a Wisconsin volunteer explained to his parents, "I was so much excited at the thought of treason breaking out in our Old Union that I thought nothing but to be if possible the first to enroll my name amongst those of her defenders." A New Jersey man wrote home that Southerners had "insulted our flag and we must in sult thers," vowing that he intended "to stand by the Union and constitution of the states." "If I fall," wrote another soldier in words shared by many of his comrades, "I die in defence of the Flag I was born under and which I will die under."[6]

Whatever their motivations they had come forth in response to a call from the president of the United States. When they arrived in Washington, Abraham Lincoln welcomed them, stood on the rear por-tico of the White House, watching them parade past, and visited them in their camps. A tall man, he seemed as awkward as they were, as rough at being president in this crisis as they were at being soldiers. Like them, he understood what was at risk and would draw upon those beliefs time and again. They shared a resiliency, as yet unformed, that would sustain them and their cause through the long passage ahead. He would give definition in words to the struggle. They would give it in blood.[7]

Here, then, was the beginning. While tens of thousands of other Union volunteers flooded camps across the country, these men in the capital formed the nucleus of America's most star-crossed army. They would be cursed, even damned, with the burdens of defending Washing-ton, inept leadership, and a splendid opponent. Many thousands more were destined to join them, to know more defeats than victories, but finally to prevail. With them through it all was Lincoln, for if any army in the nation's history belonged to a president, it would be theirs. They numbered neither 80,000 yet nor were they "the very dregs of creation." In time, they would be the sword of Lincoln, the Army of the Potomac.

"WE ARE LIVING A MONTH of common life every day," recorded a New York City diarist on April 18, 1861. It did, indeed, seem as if people and events were being swept along by a fearful gale. Less than a week had passed since Confederate artillerists had opened fire on Fort Sumter, at Charleston, South Carolina, pounding the garrison into surrender two days later. On April 17, Virginia seceded, to be followed in days and weeks by three more Southern states. The new Confederate States of America would soon have eleven members, with its capital located in Richmond, Virginia, only a hundred miles south of Washington, D.C.[8]

Abraham Lincoln reacted to the outbreak of hostilities by asking loyal states for 75,000 ninety-day volunteers to suppress the rebellion.

The president had little choice, as the Regular Army numbered barely more than 16,000, with garrisons scattered in coastal forts in the East and in frontier outposts from Washington Territory to Texas in the West. Nearly forty percent of army officers either had resigned their commissions or would do so to join the Confederacy.[9]

The burden of mobilization fell upon Northern governors. In each state the executives had to rely initially upon militia companies. Unfortunately, in nearly every state, the militia had been neglected for decades. Monthly musters of companies had amounted to little more than social gatherings. "Mars on a holiday in the country, whopping and spitting powder and rum," as a Maine civilian described his local company's mock battle. "The rum kegs in the country grocery there were exhaustless." Connecticut's militia system was "a laughing stock for thirty years." Americans had been comfortable with the myth of the Revolutionary War minuteman.[10]

Well-armed and well-drilled militia units existed, and they were among the first to respond to Lincoln's proclamation. Massachusetts governor John A. Andrew had begun supplying his state's units with arms and ordering daily drills since January. Consequently, by the evening of April 15, four regiments had received instructions to report to Boston. They left the city for Washington two days later. In Pennsylvania, Governor Andrew Gregg Curtin had five companies, so-called First Defenders, on trains for the national capital on April 18. On that same day, the state commandeered the Dauphin County Agricultural Fairgrounds in Harrisburg for a training site, renaming it Camp Curtin.[11]

The security of Washington was the immediate priority of the Lincoln administration. With Virginia out of the union and with slaveholding Maryland's future course uncertain, the capital could be isolated. Only six weakly manned forts guarded the city. From the conflict's earliest days, the defense of the capital became paramount.[12]

Senator James Lane's Frontier Guard of 120 Kansas volunteers offered its services first to the government. Winfield Scott designated them as the president's bodyguard, billeting them in the East Room of the White House. On April 18, Pennsylvania's First Defenders arrived, followed the next day by the 6th Massachusetts. A mob had attacked the Massachusetts troops as they marched between railroad stations in Baltimore. Lincoln then decided to bypass Baltimore and detoured units to Annapolis, which troops occupied on April 21. By month's end, additional regiments from Massachusetts, New York, Pennsylvania, and Rhode Island had reached either Washington or Annapolis, bringing the total to 11,000 men.[13]

Behind these units, thousands more recruits were filling state camps or were en route to the capital. The firing on Fort Sumter had galvanized the North. "Change in public feeling marked," New Yorker George Templeton Strong wrote in his diary on April 15, "and a thing to thank God for. We begin to look like a United North." Strong believed a flag "decorated" every New York City cart horse. When the 7th New York marched down Broadway on the way to Washington, "the roar of the crowd was grand and terrible." From New England to Wisconsin, citizens gathered in "war meetings," enrolling recruits and signing pledges of support.[14]

The flood of volunteers overwhelmed state authorities. More than 13,000 New Yorkers filled seventeen regiments in response to Lincoln's proclamation, while nearly 21,000 Pennsylvanians enlisted in twenty-five regiments. Governors deluged the War Department for advice and assistance. On May 3, without legal authority, Lincoln asked for 42,034 volunteers to be mustered in for three years. Secretary of War Simon Cameron advised governors to accept only three-year units. Although New York authorities specified a two-year term of service for thirty-eight regiments, most governors complied with Cameron's request.[15]

So they came, piling onto steamers at New York City and Boston, and crowding into railroad cars from Maine to Minnesota. A New Yorker admitted that he and his comrades had "a rough old time" on board a ship, but "being all for glory, we are in high spirits." For those on trains, a few units rode "first class," while many traveled inside filthy livestock and freight cars. Hardships could not dampen their enthusiasm. "Many were confident that the war would last but for a few months," stated a Wisconsin volunteer, "and none anticipated remaining more than a year away from those happy homes to which so many were destined never to return."[16]

WASHINGTON, D.C., RAPIDLY assumed the appearance of an armed camp. Private James B. Flynn of the 3rd New Jersey wrote home in mid-

May, "things look very mutch like war here but there is so mutch military that it cant look other ways." In another letter he asserted, "I never would have thought their was as many tents in the United States as there is around our encampment." Campsites filled public grounds, and regiments bivouacked in the Capitol and at the Navy Yard. Soldiers lounged and slept in the House and Senate chambers, while flour barrels lined the hallways for a bakery in the basement.[17]

When the newcomers had an opportunity, they roamed the streets as sightseers. They visited the White House, Capitol, Smithsonian, and Patent Office and were impressed. "Washington is the prettiest place in the World," Private Flynn told his parents. "The Capitol is beyond the possibility of description," claimed a Pennsylvania chaplain. They had enlisted to save the constitution and the union, and before them were the imposing symbols, fashioned from granite, marble, and brick.[18]

A few of the soldiers found little, except for the public edifices, appealing about the city. One volunteer used a common expression of the time to describe it, "just no place at all." A lieutenant thought that Washington resembled "a half grown tree withered by the premature extraction of *sap*." A private could not believe that "hogs run around the street just like dogs."[19]

It was a colorful and diverse lot who roamed through the city. A civilian described the variety of uniforms as "a queer medley of costumes." Men dressed in the common blue pants and coats passed members of the 79th New York or "Cameron Highlanders," resplendent in tartan trews and Glengarry caps. Most colorful were the Zouave regiments, attired in variations of the French-style baggy red pants, blue jackets, and red fezzes. Vermonters wore state-issued gray uniforms, with green facings in honor of Ethan Allen and the Green Mountain Boys. By contrast, volunteers in the 1st Minnesota had poorly made uniforms that had become threadbare and shrunken, while soldiers in the 4th Pennsylvania were reportedly "the worst clothed troops that Pennsylvania had sent to the field."[20]

Although native-born Americans comprised a majority of the volunteers, a number of regiments reflected the increasing polyglot nature of Northern society. Units raised in metropolitan areas generally filled their ranks from ethnic groups. No regiment typified this diversity more than the 39ᵗʰ New York or "Garibaldi Guards," which had at least a dozen European nationalities and South Americans in its companies. Two regiments—the 9ᵗʰ Massachusetts and 69ᵗʰ New York—were primarily composed of Irishmen, who proudly carried green flags in honor of their homeland. Although the Irish had opposed Lincoln's election, allegiance to the Union, endorsed by the Catholic Church, brought them by the thousands into the army. With Germans, they formed the largest contingents of foreign-born troops.[21]

Regardless of their motivations, the color and cut of their uniforms, and their ethnic heritage, the volunteers enjoyed soldiering. The novelty of the experience had appeal. A Massachusetts recruit stated that he and his comrades "liked the kind of life that the army offered," especially the camaraderie in the camps. "We had everything an Irishman needs to make him happy," boasted a member of the 69ᵗʰ New York, "not the least of which is some good 'old rye.'" When Germans in the 5ᵗʰ New York State Militia established their campsite, they had "a lager beer cart going in about an hour." The volunteers seemed to take to nearly everything, except discipline. They were neither an army in name nor in fact.[22]

BREVET LIEUTENANT GENERAL Winfield Scott had been the foremost soldier in the land, a hero of the War of 1812 and the Mexican War. At six feet, five inches tall, he had towered physically and figuratively over the Regular Army. But in the spring of 1861, he was seventy-four years old, more ancient than the capital, his once magnificent frame reduced to a worn hulk by time and obesity. He neither could mount a horse unaided nor work long hours. He was proud and vain— "Old Fuss and Feathers" to his troops—but he still possessed a brilliant mind and a grim-eyed view of the impending nightmare. As Lincoln's chief military advisor, he predicted that it would require three years and incalculable manpower to suppress the rebellion.[23]

A native Virginian, Scott had an unbending loyalty to the Union. "I have served my country, under the flag of the Union, for more than fifty years," he stated. "I will defend that flag with my sword, even if my native State assails it." He and fellow Regular Army officers denigrated the fighting qualities of the enthusiastic volunteers. Time and training, Scott cautioned, would be needed before they could be fashioned into soldiers and sent forth into combat. "His object," confided Secretary of the Navy Gideon Welles of Scott, "seemed to be to avoid hostilities."[24]

The general's judgment was prudent. Carriage tours of camps—"He was a grim old giant, gorgeously appareled," wrote a sergeant of Scott— and reports from subordinates confirmed his assessment of the rawness and ill-discipline of the capital's new defenders. An army had to be created, and days of drill commenced.[25]

Although Lincoln and Scott enjoyed an excellent relationship, conferring often, usually at the general's residence, the president went against the general-in-chief's advice and appointed Major Irvin McDowell to brigadier general on May 14, with the intent of assigning him to command of the troops in the district. Scott had recommended fifty-seven-year-old Joseph K. F. Mansfield for the post. Secretary of War Cameron, Secretary of the Treasury Salmon P. Chase, and Ohio governor William Dennison had lobbied for McDowell, a forty-two-year-old Ohioan. When Scott learned of Lincoln's decision, he sent staff officers to McDowell to ask him to decline the appointment. McDowell refused.[26]

McDowell's selection was a surprise. Perhaps, despite Scott's endorsement, Lincoln considered Mansfield too old for field command of an army. As Brigadier General Montgomery Meigs, quartermaster general of the United States and a close advisor of the president, told his father, "No one in the army would have selected him [McDowell] as the first officer to be made a general." A West Point graduate and career staff officer, McDowell had never led even a company of troops in combat. When the war began, he was an assistant adjutant general on Scott's staff, with the task of mustering in and inspecting the volunteer regiments.[27]

The brigadier was an oddly proportioned man physically. He had a large body propped up by short legs. Although he did not drink coffee, tea, or alcohol, McDowell possessed a gargantuan appetite for food. Meigs described him as "fat," and another officer claimed "he had all the distinctive appearance of a marshal of the First Empire" of Napoleon. He spoke fluent French and enjoyed architecture, landscape gardening, and dancing waltzes.[28]

Secretary Chase confessed that McDowell could be "indifferent in manner" to other people. A staff officer who knew him well remarked, "he imagined himself on a higher plane" than "ordinary mortals." He was pompous, ill-tempered, opinionated, and punctilious. At his worst, McDowell could be arrogant and arbitrary. His own popularity mattered little to him. What he knew of war, he had acquired mostly from books. While Meigs thought him to be a "good, brave" man, he also regarded him as "commonplace."[29]

In the predawn darkness of May 24, hours after Virginians had approved their convention's ordinance of secession, thousands of Federal troops crossed the Potomac River into the Old Dominion. Colonel Elmer Ellsworth's 11th New York Fire Zouaves led the advance into Alexandria. A magnetic officer, the twenty-four-year-old Ellsworth had clerked in Lincoln's law office, and the president thought of him as almost another son. When the colonel saw a secessionist flag on the roof of the Marshall House, he entered the hotel, ascended the stairs, and tore it down. As he returned, the hotelkeeper met him with a shotgun and killed him. His death deeply grieved Lincoln, who held funeral ceremonies in the White House. The cause of the Union had its first martyr.[30]

The regiments in the operation belonged to the Department of Washington, now commanded by Mansfield. Additional units followed into Virginia. On May 27, the administration created the Department of Northeastern Virginia, which consisted of the portion of the Old Dominion east of the Allegheny Mountains and north of the James River. Lincoln assigned McDowell to command of it. The next day the general established his headquarters in Arlington, at the former home of Robert E. Lee. Weeks earlier, Lee had rejected an offer to command the Union army at the capital, resigned his commission, and volunteered his services to his native Virginia. In time, Lee would become the Confederacy's greatest general, and the Federals' nemesis in the East.[31]

McDowell immediately organized the regiments into three brigades. During the next six weeks, as more regiments arrived in Washington and were assigned to his department, he created additional brigades. By July 8, he had thirteen brigades assigned to five divisions, numbering more than 30,000 troops. McDowell now commanded the largest army in American history.[32]

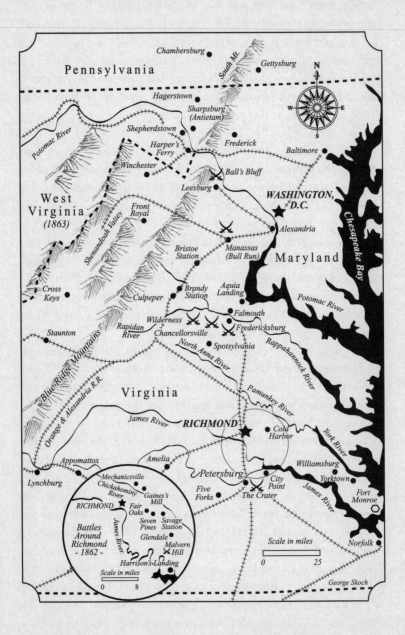

The division and brigade commanders were mainly Regular Army officers, recommended by Scott and McDowell. The majority had graduated from West Point, men who possessed a professional's "habit of mind," which citizen soldiers lacked. A primary factor in their appointment, however, was a simple matter—they were at hand. They were either on duty in Washington when the war began or arrived later at the head of a volunteer regiment. Lincoln selected three of them, basing his decision on political considerations or personal association. Five of the sixteen would be destined for corps command, three for army command, and only one, William T. Sherman, for greatness.[33]

The division commanders were Daniel Tyler, David Hunter, Samuel P. Heintzelman, Dixon S. Miles, and Theodore Runyon. As a group, they were an uninspiring lot. Although he still looked like a soldier, Tyler was sixty-two years old and had been out of the army for almost thirty years. Hunter had ingratiated himself to Lincoln by corresponding with the president-elect during the winter of 1861, and received an invitation to the inauguration. With an undistinguished record, he was available and was appointed by Lincoln. Miles and Runyon would play minor roles in the operations. Except for Heintzelman, the division commanders' association with the army would end after the forthcoming campaign.[34]

Heintzelman had spent his entire career in the army, distinguishing himself in Mexico and on the frontier. A grizzled and gnarled "old customer," he was army to the bone. He could be blunt in speech and unbending in discipline. He had the spirit of a warrior but lacked dash. An officer who met him in April confided in his diary, "I was much disappointed in him; could not see any signs of a great man."[35]

Several of the brigade commanders, however, would share the army's fortunes on future battlefields and would obtain higher rank and responsibility. To a man, they were West Pointers, but only one of them, Israel B. Richardson, had led troops in combat. Four of them—Richardson, Ambrose E. Burnside, Oliver Otis Howard, and Orlando B. Willcox— had left the army to pursue civilian opportunities and returned to service as colonels of volunteer regiments. William B. Franklin and Erasmus D. Keyes had been career staff officers, highly regarded by their superiors. But the best of the group, William Sherman, would be assigned to the West in September.[36]

McDowell completed the organization of his army by the second week of July. His units covered Arlington and Alexandria, with picket posts shoved west along the roads toward Centreville and Manassas Junction, where a Confederate force had been growing in strength since early May. At Manassas, the Manassas Gap Railroad and the Orange & Alexandria Railroad intersected. If the 18,000 Confederates, under Brigadier General P. G. T. Beauregard, could hold the junction, they could keep the Federals from advancing into the state's interior. To the west, across the Blue Ridge, Brigadier General Joseph E. Johnston's 11,000 men defended the Shenandoah Valley. [37]

At the northern end of the Shenandoah Valley stood an 18,000-man Union army, led by Major General Robert Patterson. A veteran of the War of 1812 and Scott's second-in-command in Mexico, the sixty-nine-year-old Patterson had been appointed to the command of the Department of Pennsylvania by his old friend shortly after Fort Sumter. His command consisted primarily of Pennsylvania regiments, whose duty was to guard western Maryland and protect the Keystone State. When the Confederates withdrew from Harper's Ferry in mid-June, Patterson sent his troops across the Potomac River and occupied the historic town. Long past his prime, Patterson seemed befuddled by the burdens of command.[38]

With Beauregard's command less than thirty miles from Washington, and its advanced detachments even closer, pressure mounted on McDowell to act. Although Scott believed that a Virginia campaign would be a mistake, he asked McDowell for a plan of advance in cooperation with Patterson on Leesburg. "McDowell was," wrote his chief of staff, "dominated by the feeling of subordination and deference to General Scott which at that time pervaded the whole army." Nevertheless, McDowell countered with a proposal for a move against Beauregard at Manassas.[39]

Lincoln, meanwhile, intervened. The clamor for action among the Northern people had been escalating since a New York *Tribune* headline proclaimed, *"Forward to Richmond! Forward to Richmond!"* on June 24. Other newspapers picked up the call, editorializing that the Confederate Congress should not be allowed to meet in Richmond on July 20. If the administration waited much longer to act against the Confederates, the terms of enlistment of ninety-day militia units would expire.

To Lincoln, the Federals must strike, both for military and political reasons.[40]

On June 29, the president met with the Cabinet, Scott, McDowell, and several generals. The discussion centered upon a movement by McDowell against the enemy at Manassas. The meeting crystallized at this early stage in the conflict the issues that would plague the Union's overall military strategy throughout much of the war. In a democracy at war with itself, politics would never be far removed from the battlefields.[41]

For weeks Scott had warned against a hasty offensive into Confederate territory with untrained troops and inexperienced officers. He had advocated a naval blockade of Confederate ports—which the president had implemented in his April 15 proclamation—and a concentration of Union might to seize the Mississippi River to split the Confederacy. The Federals should not undertake any major offensives into the Southern heartland, including Virginia. This, reasoned Scott, would minimize casualties on both sides and expedite reconciliation between the sections. Although the commanding general had predicted a lengthy conflict, he now argued that the war could be won by the summer of 1862. He believed, however, that his strategy would be politically unpopular in the North, stating that pro-Union voices "will urge instant and vigorous action, regardless, I fear, of consequences."[42]

McDowell shared Scott's concern about a strike against the Confederates with untrained troops and inexperienced officers. When he noted these matters at the meeting, Lincoln replied: "You are green. But they are green too. You are all green alike." McDowell also expressed his doubts about whether Patterson would act aggressively to keep Johnston's Rebels in the Shenandoah Valley and to prevent the Confederate general from reinforcing Beauregard at Manassas. In the end, Lincoln decided that they could not wait and ordered the forward movement. Without asking McDowell when he could advance, Scott designated July 8 as the date. But McDowell needed more time, and it would be more than a week later before the army marched.[43]

"IF EVER I GET A CHANCE to draw sight on a Rebel down goes his shanty," a 2nd Wisconsin corporal bragged to his brother. Many of his comrades shared his boast. There was an itch among the rank and file to meet the enemy and to settle the matter in one battle. As government officials and generals discussed strategy, soldiers bided their time with daily drills and camp chores. When on picket duty, they slept in their uniforms—"We don't calculate to be taken by surprize," remarked one of them. Daily skirmishes ignited between them and their opponents. It was not enough, however, to stop the itch.[44]

Sickness reduced their ranks, and drunkenness weakened discipline. "I found the Army with which we were to meet the enemy," reported a veteran army surgeon, "composed of the best, and also of the worst, material I had ever met with." Since the regiments had been "hastily collected," many of the volunteers had not received medical examinations upon enlistment. The summer heat, foul water, and unkempt camps sent hundreds of men on sick call or into hospitals.[45]

Both officers and men sought relief from duties with alcohol. Sergeant Andrew McClintock of the 1st Connecticut stated that the number of drunks in his regiment put the unit in a "very bad condition." The men, McClintock asserted, "are nearly all disheartened. They have lost nearly all the patriotism that should animate the Citizen Soldier."[46]

McDowell ordered frequent reviews of individual regiments and of brigades. Lincoln attended many of the parades and demonstrations. On one occasion, the 39th New York or Garibaldi Guards tossed flowers to the president, having plucked them from civilian gardens before the review. One soldier described a march down Pennsylvania Avenue, with Lincoln, Scott, and Cabinet members watching, as "a festive atmosphere."[47]

In fact, the president remained a nearly constant presence among the troops during this time. An acquaintance of Lincoln's remembered him as "eminently human," and the soldiers saw this in him. An officer recounted an incident when "a boy came by with a pail of water for us, and the President took a great swig from it as it passed." In another letter, the lieutenant wrote about Lincoln: "It is easy to see why he is so popular with all who come in contact with him. He gives you the impression of being a gentleman."[48]

It was the president's common touch that struck the men in the ranks. His reported homeliness elicited comments. A Massachusetts lieutenant thought that "he is ten times a homlier man than I expected he was," while another officer argued, "It is really too bad to call him one of the ugliest men in the country for I have seldom seen a pleasanter or more kind-hearted looking one and he has certainly a very striking face." In these early weeks, then, for many reasons, Lincoln established a bond with the common soldiers that would endure through the horrific tests to come. He cared about them and their welfare, seemed to be like them, whether watching them pass in review or sharing a drink with them from a pail of water.[49]

It fell to him, finally, to order them forth into battle. He knew they were "green," listened to the reports of their illnesses and discipline problems, but he and the country needed them to meet the enemy. It was what most of them also wanted, believing that the Union must be saved. Upon them a legacy had been bequeathed.

"I KNOW HOW STRONGLY American civilization now leans on the triumph of the Government," an officer, Sullivan Ballou, explained to his wife, "and how great a debt we owe to those who went before us through the blood and sufferings of the Revolution." He warned her that he might be killed in the forthcoming battle, but he assured her, "I am willing—perfectly willing—to lay down all my joys in this life, to help maintain this government, and to pay that debt." Within a week, Ballou would perish in the battle, fulfilling his share of the debt.[50]

A private in the 38th New York offered a similar view to his parents. "Don't feel sorry that one of your sons enlisted in this struggle for our rights and the rights of our forefathers who died for their country and made it free and now we are duty bound to protect it and keep it free, for without Union there cannot be Peace so down with Secession."[51]

Many, if not most, of them saw the approaching engagement as Sergeant Frank L. Lemont, a Maine volunteer, did. "It is generally believed that the contest will be a short and decisive one," Lemont assured his mother. "It is thought that it will be a comparatively bloodless one." They were, indeed, "green."[52]

Chapter 2

Bloody Sabbath at Bull Run

Bands played patriotic songs as Brigadier General Irvin McDowell's Union army marched forth under a "brilliant" afternoon sun on July 16, 1861. They moved in three long columns, heading toward Brigadier General P. G. T. Beauregard's Confederate troops, deployed behind Bull Run, roughly twenty-five miles southwest of Washington. The inexperience of the Federal officers and men slowed the pace. The day passed without incident until gunfire exploded near Fairfax Station. A brigade rushed to the scene, only to find the 39th New York shooting a farmer's flock of turkeys. In front of each column, Rebel pickets nipped at the Yankees and then fled.[1]

The advance resumed at daylight on July 17. As the day lengthened, however, problems mounted. Felled trees blocked roads, stalling the march. Hundreds of men abandoned the ranks, either straggling or foraging into the countryside. A soldier had predicted a week earlier that "the boys are all anxious to get further south, where they can have a chance to *forage* without fear of trespassing upon unionists. I pity the country they pass through, for I fear they would be more destructive than the tornado that has just passed through the West." As they had done the day before, Southern pickets receded before the Union columns.[2]

McDowell designated Centreville as the army's destination for July

18, which Brigadier General Daniel Tyler's leading division reached at 9:00 A.M. Without seeking McDowell's approval, Tyler ordered a reconnaissance of the Confederate position south of Bull Run. Colonel Israel B. Richardson's brigade led the movement, halting at Blackburn's Ford, where Brigadier General James Longstreet's Southerners guarded the crossing. Tyler oversaw the deployment of two batteries and sent skirmishers from the 1st Massachusetts down the slope. Sporadic cannon fire and musketry characterized the action until Richardson ordered the 12th New York toward the ford.[3]

Israel Richardson looked more like a disheveled farmer who had strayed into the area to watch the combat than a brigade commander. A West Pointer and Mexican War veteran, he had been farming in Pontiac, Michigan, when the war began. The townsfolk had come to regard him as "crazy" because he was decidedly unsocial. When he helped organize the 2nd Michigan, Governor Austin Blair had reservations about giving him a commission. Orlando Willcox had known Richardson in the old army and assured Blair that the "crazy" man was "as sound as a nut, but he was slouchly and slovenly." Willcox recommended him for the colonelcy, and the governor appointed him.[4]

A staff officer remembered Richardson as "a man of great determination and courage," who "dressed roughly and spoke and acted very brusquely." A private claimed that his men believed "he was one of them," with his rough manners and utter lack of pretense. A firm disciplinarian, Richardson evidently had difficulty controlling the 2nd Michigan while en route to Washington. The volunteers raided stores at each stop along the railroad, stealing "every thing movable." Telegraph operators wired ahead, warning merchants, who closed their businesses before the regiment arrived.[5]

When the 12th New York staggered before a volley and then fled to the rear, Richardson prepared to attack with his three other regiments. Although Colonel William Sherman's brigade had arrived for support, Tyler had seen enough and stopped the advance. Richardson, who had been known as "Fighting Dick," obeyed Tyler's order but believed his and Sherman's troops could have taken the ford. The Federals withdrew in good order under artillery fire. Casualties amounted to fewer than a hundred.[6]

Riding "in a covered hackney coach" and wearing "a hat of a Kaiser," McDowell arrived at Centreville late in the afternoon. He learned of the affair at Blackburn's Ford from Tyler, who claimed his division could whip the Rebels if allowed to renew the attacks. Upset with Tyler's disobedience of orders, McDowell rejected the idea. The unauthorized reconnaissance confirmed reports that the Confederates were in force behind Bull Run and would oppose a crossing.[7]

While quartermasters replenished depleted supplies, Union commanders spent July 19 and most of the next day examining the Confederate position behind Bull Run. Warrenton Turnpike, the main road, crossed the stream at Stone Bridge. Six fords, all guarded by the Rebels, lay to the east, or downstream from the bridge. McDowell's engineers, however, located an upstream ford at Sudley Church and a route to it during the reconnaissances. McDowell settled upon a turning movement beyond the Confederate left by Sudley Ford. Initially, he ordered the advance for 6:00 P.M., on July 20, but was dissuaded by his fellow generals, who cited the men's need for rest. At eight o'clock that night, he met with his division and brigade commanders.[8]

The generals stood around a large table, in "a great tent," lit by lanterns and candles, examining maps. Outside the tent, a group of civilians, including members of Congress, milled about. McDowell explained his offensive plan in detail but sought no opinions from his subordinates. Tyler's division would lead the advance on Warrenton Turnpike, demonstrating against the enemy at Stone Bridge and the lower fords. Colonels David Hunter's and Samuel Heintzelman's divisions would follow Tyler's, turn north before the bridge, cross Bull Run at Sudley Ford and a ford below it, and attack the Confederates. When they cleared Stone Bridge, Tyler would cross in support. The plan had merit, but McDowell overreached, relying upon novice officers and men, marching on "cart paths" at night, to reach their assigned positions in time.[9]

McDowell opened the council to questions, and a few of the generals, led by Tyler, voiced concern about the number of Confederate troops beyond Bull Run. They believed that Brigadier General Joseph Johnston's command had arrived from the Shenandoah Valley and had joined Beauregard's army. Before he had left Washington, Winfield

Scott had assured McDowell that Major General Robert Patterson either would keep Johnston in the region or follow him east if he left the Valley. McDowell had received no information from the War Department that Johnston had disappeared from Patterson's front. If the Federals were successful, he said, they would seize the Manassas Gap Railroad and prevent a junction of the Southern units. The army would advance at two o'clock the next morning. McDowell had no other choice—"Forward to Richmond" was a clarion call for action.[10]

Tyler and the other generals, however, were accurate in their assessment. Patterson, an encrusted old fossil, had failed miserably. When Beauregard had learned of the Union advance on July 16, he telegraphed Richmond for reinforcements. President Jefferson Davis ordered five regiments to Manassas and instructed Johnston to move there if he could elude Patterson. Johnston so baffled his opponent that Patterson retreated north as the Confederates hurried east. By July 20, three of Johnston's brigades, using the railroad for the final leg, joined Beauregard. Another brigade was expected the next day. Together, Beauregard and Johnston counted roughly 33,000 troops to oppose McDowell's 35,000. The two-day halt at Centreville for reconnaissance and resupply would be costly for the Federals. In fact, Beauregard issued orders for an assault on McDowell's left flank for the morning of July 21.[11]

During the day of July 20, McDowell asked the 4th Pennsylvania, whose ninety-day enlistments expired the next day, to extend them two weeks. A majority of men refused. A captain in the 4th Pennsylvania explained the regiment's decision as "the fact of the matter was, the men had been badly used. They had a right to their discharge." Their colonel, John F. Hartranft, stayed with the army and volunteered as an aide-de-camp on the staff of Colonel William Franklin. As the army marched toward battle the next morning, the Pennsylvanians left for Washington and home.[12]

The mood in the camps that night was one of both solemnity and confidence. Chaplains conducted religious services, and bands played sacred music. "I pray," a sergeant confided in his journal, "that I may have the strength & courage to carry me safely through or to die decently in a manner becoming an American soldier." Another soldier wrote to his parents, "it will be a great battle the greatest yet God only knows how it will end and who amongst us will stand the contest God can only disside." Private George Rollins of the 3rd Maine told his father later, "Troops never marched to battle more confident of victory than we."[13]

THE FIRST BATTLE OF BULL RUN or Manassas marked a passage for those who experienced it and for the entire country. Never before had so many Americans embraced such a storm. Never before had so many citizen soldiers faced combat's terrible testing. And never again would so many go forth with such naive illusions of glory. On a hot July Sabbath, Americans glimpsed the outlines of a fearful future.

Irvin McDowell's ambitious plan faltered from the outset. Daniel Tyler's division started late and slowed the march of the flanking column, comprised of Hunter's and Heintzelman's troops. The men's fatigue and lack of discipline compounded the difficulties. According to one of the soldiers, however, it was an impressive sight as the moonlight glinted off bayonets, looking "like an immense silver sea serpent."[14]

It was past 9:30 A.M., hours behind schedule, before the van of Hunter's division crossed at Sudley Ford. Colonel Ambrose Burnside's brigade of Rhode Islanders, New Hampshiremen, and New Yorkers stepped off first, advancing against three Confederate brigades on Matthews Hill. "We advanced double quick time yelling like so many devils," wrote corporal Samuel J. English of the 2nd Rhode Island. Their time had come, or as a lieutenant admitted to his wife afterward, "I never thought I had the bravery to stand on the field of battle but I did."[15]

For more than an hour, Matthews Hill seethed with musketry and cannon fire. "It was a whirlwind of bullets," claimed a Confederate. Hunter suffered a wound and relinquished command to Colonel Andrew Porter. Both sides clung to their lines, with charges and countercharges. Unlike the 4th Pennsylvania, the 71st New York, a three-month unit whose term of enlistment had expired on July 20, stood and fought. "We would not turn back on eve of a battle," asserted one of them. Many of the Federals wore uniforms that were in part or entirely gray, which added to the confusion.[16]

"Our men," stated one of Burnside's soldiers, "began to grow unsteady under the enemy's fire." He blamed it on their commanders, who "didn't seem to know what to do." Porter asked for help, while Burnside reported that his men were nearly out of ammunition. McDowell, who had joined the flanking column, ordered both Heintzelman's and Tyler's divisions across the stream.[17]

William Franklin's brigade arrived first, filing into line on Matthews Hill. A week earlier Franklin had written to his wife, "This is not precisely what I enlisted for [commanding volunteer troops], but I suppose it will all come right in the end." But it must not have seemed so to him as his brigade marched onto the field. The 5th and 11th Massachusetts, while still in column, opened fire, killing and wounding some of their own members.[18]

Hunter's regiments stabilized the Union line, and the Federals pressed forward. On their left, Colonel William Sherman's brigade, wading across Bull Run at an unnamed ford discovered that morning, closed on the Confederates' right flank. The Southerners abandoned Matthews Hill, spilled across Warrenton Turnpike, and fled up and over the crest of Henry House Hill, where they began to rally upon Brigadier General Thomas J. Jackson's five Virginia regiments. Confederate brigadier Barnard B. Bee, trying to re-form his ranks, shouted: "Look, men, there is Jackson standing like a stone wall! Let us determine to die here, and we will conquer! Follow me!" Upon Jackson's line in a pine thicket on the reverse slope of the hill, the Rebels prepared to make a stand.[19]

It was not yet noon when the Yankees cleared Matthews Hill. Victory appeared at hand as perhaps 18,000 Federals were south of Bull Run with only Confederate artillery in view on Henry House Hill. One coordinated assault would surely seize the height and sweep the Rebels from the field. All they needed were orders and leadership. Instead, McDowell sat passively, issuing no instructions for two hours. It would be left to his subordinate commanders and the men in the ranks. On a broad rise, around the home of eighty-five-year-old Judith Henry, for whose family the hill was named, the outcome of the battle would be decided.[20]

Whatever doubts the West Pointers and Regular Army officers had before the battle about the volunteers' willingness to fight and to die for

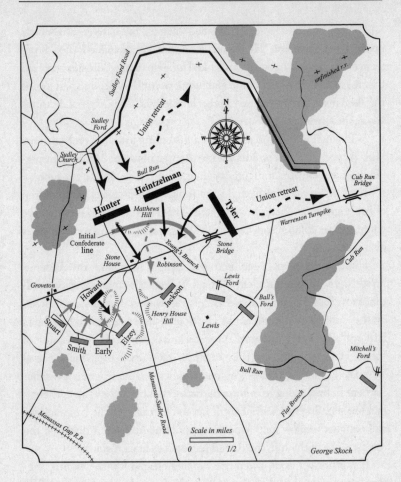

George Skoch

the cause should have been dispelled this Sunday afternoon on the slopes and crest of Henry House Hill. Time and again, regiments—sent in piecemeal—ascended the rise and gave of themselves. The struggle for Matthews Hill did not compare to the bloodletting on the land of the Henry family. A Virginian with Jackson spoke for thousands on both sides when he wrote his wife three days later: "I never expected to see you again. The balls was falling around me like hail and I don't see how I ever did escape for the men was falling around me like cornstalks."[21]

The 27th New York, followed by the 8th New York State Militia and 14th Brooklyn, went in first. They drove toward the hill's northeast crest and a small house owned by a family named Robinson. Confederate cannon and South Carolina infantrymen blasted them back in disorder. Behind them came Colonel Erasmus Keyes's 2nd Maine and 3rd Connecticut. "One howl passed along the line," boasted a Maine corporal, "& the bold boys of the 2d Me. dashed forward like lightning firing as fast as possible." The New Englanders passed the Robinson house and faltered before enemy fire. The volleys tore into the Yankee ranks, and as Keyes reported, "exposure to it of five minutes would have annihilated my whole line." Isolated, with no support in view, he ordered a retreat.[22]

With the repulse of Keyes's troops, a brief lull ensued—"an indescribable calm," in the words of a Northerner. McDowell then directed his chief of artillery, Major William F. Barry, to send two batteries to the open crest of Henry House Hill. Barry selected Captain James B. Ricketts's Battery I, 1st U.S. Artillery and Captain Charles Griffin's Battery D, 5th U.S. Artillery. When the captains received the order, they protested it, arguing that artillery would not be safe there without ample infantry support. The order stood, and the crews rolled forward. For the next two hours these eleven cannon would stand at the center of a maelstrom.[23]

The Union artillerists dueled with their Confederate counterparts for more than thirty minutes before infantry support arrived. On they came—the red-shirted men of the 1st Minnesota; the 11th New York Fire Zouaves, whose members shouted "Ellsworth!" in honor of their martyred colonel; the red-legged Chasseurs of the 14th Brooklyn, whose major implored them to "recollect your uniform, Brooklyn, and the Flag of your country"; and a battalion of United States Marines. Before long, the crest of the hill flashed again with cannon fire and musketry.[24]

The 1st Minnesota and Fire Zouaves deployed to the right of the batteries and advanced toward the woods held by the Rebels. A volley from Jackson's Virginians staggered the Federals. "It was a most damnable thing leading men in to such a place," grumbled a Minnesotan. Back they went, as if "swept back by a tornado." On the hill's slope, Confederate cavalrymen, under Colonel J. E. B. Stuart, plunged into the fleeing ranks, scattering the infantrymen. No regiments lost more men killed than the Minnesotans and the Fire Zouaves.[25]

Griffin now shifted two cannon farther to the right, and the combat escalated. The 33rd Virginia stormed out of the woods, overrunning the isolated guns. Within minutes, the 14th Brooklyn wrenched the cannon from the Virginians and kept going toward Jackson's line. Three times the Federals charged across the open ground into a wall of musketry and canister. They came within a few feet of the Rebel cannon during their final attack before being swept off the hill. The Brooklyn men had redeemed themselves after breaking earlier.[26]

From the pine thicket, a yell cascaded across the plateau, followed by a surging line of Confederates. Jackson's men advanced directly toward the Union line of cannon, withstood a wave of canister, and seized the guns, clubbing and shooting down the crews. Once again, the Southerners held the crest of Henry House Hill. From the low ground along Warrenton Pike, however, appeared more Union regiments. Men from Michigan, Massachusetts, and New York marched up the slope.[27]

The struggle for the Union artillery pieces took on a hellish symmetry—a back and a forth, an ebb and a flow, a maiming and a killing. The Northerners climbed up the hillside, were beaten back, and tried again. The carnage was "fearful," wrote a Virginian. Colonel Orlando Willcox fell with a wound and would be captured, along with battery commander Ricketts, who lay bleeding among his cannon. Watching the fighting, McDowell ordered in Sherman's brigade.[28]

The 13th New York led Sherman's attack, trailed closely by the 2nd Wisconsin, whose members emitted an "Indian war whoop" as they charged. The Wisconsin men went in without a field officer. Their colonel, S. Park Coon, whom the troops considered to be "a great drunken bloat," was serving as a volunteer aide on Sherman's staff. The regiment's lieutenant colonel and major had fled the battlefield earlier and reportedly were the first two officers to reach Washington that night.[29]

While the New Yorkers tried valiantly to recapture the cannon and failed, the Wisconsin troops were caught in a swirl of musketry and artillery fire. "Oh! It was dreadful," claimed a captain, "and I cannot see how not only myself, but any of us, escaped with life." Suddenly, from the rear, their comrades in the 69th and 79th New York mistakenly triggered volleys into the gray-uniformed Federals. A private in the regiment described the fury as "the most hellish shower of bullets you can imagine." Wounded men pleaded to be shot to end their agony.[30]

Like the other units before them, the two New York regiments encountered a "severe fire," in Sherman's words, recoiled, and charged again. Colonel James Cameron, brother of Secretary of War Simon Cameron, died at the head of his Highlanders of the 79th New York. Captain Thomas Meagher of the 69th New York twice rallied the men, imploring them to do so "in the name of Ireland." Joined by the 38th New York, the 69th New York retook Ricketts's guns and began rolling them off the crest.[31]

While Sherman's troops fought for the guns, McDowell sent Colonel Oliver Howard's brigade beyond the Confederates' left flank to Chinn Ridge, several hundred yards west of the Henry house. Howard's New Englanders—2nd Vermont, 3rd, 4th, and 5th Maine—opposed two Southern brigades and a pair of South Carolina regiments. It was an uneven struggle, but the Yankees "fought bravely and stood their ground manfully," until Howard ordered one wing of a regiment to change the position. His instructions, however, were misinterpreted as an order for a retreat by all of the troops. The Rebels pressed their rear, and by the time the Yankees reached Warrenton Turnpike, they had disintegrated into a "panic stricken" mob.[32]

To the east, the 8th and 18th Virginia swept across Henry House Hill, driving off the 38th and 69th New York and recapturing the Union cannon. The entire Union force south of Bull Run was now in flight toward Stone Bridge, Sudley Ford, and the farmer's ford used earlier by Sherman's and Keyes's brigades. "Until then," wrote McDowell's chief of staff of the Federals, "they had fought wonderfully well for raw troops."[33]

Several factors contributed to the ensuing rout—the contagious nature of a panic, the exhaustion of the troops, the inability of inexperienced officers to stem the tide, the Confederate pursuit, and the closing of the bridge over Cub Run by an overturned wagon. Undoubtedly, before most of the units reached Bull Run, it was a "scene of confusion and disorder." Regimental and brigade organization had disappeared. Men discarded equipment and arms. As groups of men tried to rally and to re-form ranks, the strong current of fleeing soldiers swept them along. "The plain was covered with retreating groups," reported McDowell, "and they seemed to infect those with whom they came in contact."[34]

The rout degenerated into a frenzied mob of men when a Confederate artillery round caused a wagon to upset on the Warrenton Turnpike bridge over Cub Run. Teamsters abandoned their wagons, and soldiers abandoned their senses. "Such a scampering you never did see," asserted a Union artilleryman. When a mounted officer galloped into the mass and yelled that the Rebels were "upon us," the Federals who heard him "started like a flock of sheep every man for himself and the devil take the hindermost." The New Jersey troops in Theodore Runyon's division tried to stop the flight, but their efforts failed. "The whole scene beggars all description," confessed one of their officers.[35]

Israel Richardson's brigade and Dixon Miles's division, held in reserve by McDowell to protect the army's left flank, covered the retreat. McDowell contemplated making a stand at Centreville, but by then most of the troops had passed through the village on the road to Washington. McDowell ordered a withdrawal. It did not matter, for he no longer commanded an army, mostly a rabble of demoralized men, stumbling through the darkness until exhaustion halted them. Hours earlier, the government had learned of the disaster at Bull Run in a telegram to the War Department from McDowell: "The day is lost. Save Washington and the remnants of this army."[36]

RAIN BEGAN TO FALL on July 22, and continued throughout the day. As the hours passed, the shards of an army—wet, muddy, and sullen—plodded across the Potomac bridges into Washington, or returned to their camps at Arlington and Alexandria. In the city, according to an officer who arrived on this day, "an intense excitement" raged, with "a thousand rumors" scurrying through the streets: "whole army totally routed—Washington being bombarded—Congress adjourned to Philadelphia." When a congressman asked Abraham Lincoln about the situation, the president confided, "It's damned bad."[37]

Irvin McDowell returned to his headquarters at Arlington. William W. Averell joined him and found the army commander, "at first completely broken in spirit." He "spoke but little." McDowell must have known that he would be blamed for the defeat as a clamoring public and politicians would demand a scapegoat. When Averell suggested that he could be captured by a few daring Confederates, he seemed to stir from his dark mood.[38]

The army commander soon learned that neither the president nor General-in-Chief Winfield Scott attributed the defeat to his generalship. Scott blamed himself for allowing politicians and newspaper headlines to force an offensive with an ill-prepared army. He and Lincoln assigned some of the blame to Robert Patterson, whose miserable efforts in the Shenandoah Valley resulted in his dismissal on July 22. This war would have few places for old men.[39]

Responsibility for the defeat ultimately rested with McDowell, however. Elevated to army command without any combat experience, he fashioned an attack plan far too ambitious and complicated for the army he commanded. Once the Federals drove the enemy off Matthews Hill and with the majority of his troops south of Bull Run, McDowell hesitated to act for two crucial hours. The units drifted without direction when a coordinated assault would have probably secured Henry House Hill. Instead, the Yankees charged in piecemeal assaults against a foe that was well led and on the defensive. Upward of twenty regiments and two battalions assailed the Southerners, but their numerical advantage was drained away in a series of disjointed attacks.

William Sherman argued later that the defeat resulted "not from a want of combination, strategy or tactics, but because our army was green as grass." Indeed it was. None of the army's senior officers had ever led this many troops on a battlefield. Like the rank and file, they were new to this. They managed to maintain tactical command and control only with one or two regiments at a time. They led men who were tired, if not exhausted, amid the confusion inherent in combat. William Franklin claimed afterward that the inexperience of regimental commanders forced brigade commanders "to act as field officers of all the regiments in their brigades." There had been an evident "want of combination" at the tactical level, but it was simply beyond the army's capability and training.[40]

Union casualties amounted to 482 killed, 1,126 wounded, and 1,836 missing, for a total of 3,444. Confederate losses exceeded 1,900 in killed, wounded, and missing. "I will own," Captain Clark S. Edwards of the 5th Maine confessed to his wife, "that after the Battle was over I sat down and shed a tear. Some of the Boys cryed as well as myself." A private told his sister, "I doe not like to write About it it was bad Enough to see it." They had been whipped and fled the field in a humiliating rout. They had reasons to cry and to refuse to write of the experience. Bull Run would haunt them for a long time.[41]

Sherman passed judgment on these citizen volunteers after the battle. "Our men are not good soldiers," he asserted. "They brag, but don't perform, complain loudly if they don't get everything they want, and a march of a few miles uses them up. It will take a long time to overcome these things, and what is in store for us in the future I know not."[42]

It could have hardly looked otherwise to a crusty West Pointer such as Sherman. They were not "good soldiers," at least not yet, and were certainly not well trained. They had not taken to discipline, had left the ranks on the march to Centreville to rest or to forage, had boasted of a swift, certain victory, and had grumbled about many things. The final image of them at Bull Run had been of panic-stricken men, discarding arms and gear, in a headlong and unstoppable rout.

There was something else to them, however. It could be found on Matthews Hill and on the slope and crest of Henry House Hill. They had demonstrated their courage, their willingness to sacrifice themselves for duty and for a cause. If they were not yet good soldiers, they were good men, with the makings of good soldiers. They had been defeated, but not destroyed. From Bull Run came a resolution, a renewed devotion to the Union. And so, too, came the beginning of one of the army's enduring characteristics—a resiliency in the aftermath of a defeat that approached defiance.

As Sherman noted, they required time to be drilled and disciplined into soldiers. For McDowell, however, his tenure as army commander could not weather Bull Run. A staff officer put it well in a letter after the battle about McDowell: "He exposed himself gallantly the other day, but was not *the great general* we should have had on that field. We wanted a man with a reputation. He had none." Lincoln needed "a man with a reputation."[43]

THE WAR DEPARTMENT telegram arrived at headquarters of the Department of the Ohio at Beverly, (West) Virginia, on July 22. Addressed to Major General George B. McClellan, its message was terse: "Circumstances make your presence here necessary. Charge [William S.]

Rosecrans or some other general with your present department and come hither without delay." Three days later, General Orders No. 47 came over the wire, announcing McClellan's official assignment to command of the departments of Washington and of Northeastern Virginia, with headquarters in the capital. On July 26, the general boarded a special train at Wheeling, and sped toward a rendezvous with destiny.[44]

From his privileged birth, George McClellan enjoyed fortune's favor. The son of a prominent Philadelphia surgeon and founder of Jefferson Medical College, he had attended private schools and the University of Pennsylvania until he accepted an appointment to West Point in 1842. At the academy, he excelled academically and socially. He had a "magnetic" personality, recalled a fellow cadet, and was "the most popular, if not most prominent, cadet in the corps." McClellan, added his friend, "was full of life and enthusiasm, had charming address and manners, and void of pretension, and a steadfast friend. . . . He was a leader and organizer, natural born."[45]

McClellan ranked second in the Class of 1846, which included future Civil War generals John Gibbon, Ambrose P. Hill, Stonewall Jackson, George E. Pickett, Jesse Reno, and George Stoneman. Appointed a second lieutenant of engineers, he served with Winfield Scott's army in Mexico, where he contracted malaria, a disease that would periodically afflict him. Engineering assignments marked his service until 1855, when he traveled to Europe as a member of a commission to study strategic and tactical developments on the continent. The three-man group observed operations during the Crimean War and visited several battlefields of earlier conflicts, including Waterloo. Less than a year after his return, McClellan resigned his commission, accepting the position of chief engineer of the Illinois Central Railroad, which retained Abraham Lincoln as one of its attorneys. On May 22, 1860, he married Ellen Marcy, daughter of Randolph B. Marcy, one of his former commanders. A. P. Hill, McClellan's academy roommate and future Confederate foe, had proposed marriage earlier to Miss Marcy, but her parents opposed the union.[46]

When the Civil War began, McClellan accepted a major generalcy of the Ohio volunteers from Governor William Dennison. On May 3, the War Department assigned him to command of the Department of the Ohio, which embraced the states of Ohio, Indiana, and Illinois, and western Pennsylvania and western Virginia. On May 14, through the efforts of Secretary of the Treasury Salmon Chase, he was promoted to major general in the Regular Army, ranking only below Scott. In Mexico, McClellan had railed against politically appointed generals, but now he owed his swift ascension in command to the intercessions of powerful political supporters.[47]

As department commander, he directed operations against Confederate forces in mountainous western Virginia, an area of strong Union sentiment. "Personally he was a very charming man," remembered a subordinate of McClellan's, "and his manner of doing business impressed every one with the belief that he knew what he was about." A skillful administrator, he implemented a strategy that resulted in minor victories at Rich Mountain and Corrick's Ford in mid-July. Congress voted a resolution of thanks to the general, and the Northern press hailed him as a hero, with one newspaper proclaiming him "the Napoleon of the Present War." With the defeat at Bull Run, McClellan appeared as a man who knew "what he was about."[48]

McClellan arrived in Washington on the afternoon of July 27. During the evening, he met with Winfield Scott, with whom he had clashed over strategy, authority, and troop numbers while department commander. The general-in-chief, thought McClellan, knew little about the city's defenses. The next day, he visited with the president and the Cabinet. He then officially assumed command of the departments of Washington and Northeastern Virginia.[49]

Later on July 27, McClellan wrote a letter to his wife, Ellen. "I find myself," he confided, "in a new & strange position here—Presdt, Cabinet, Genl Scott & all deferring to me—by some strange operation of magic I seem to have become *the* power of the land." He thought that if he could achieve "some small success now," he "could become Dictator," as in the ancient sense of a savior of the Roman republic. "But nothing of that kind would please me—*therefore* I *won't* be Dictator. Admirable self denial! I see already the main causes of our recent failure—I am *sure* that I can remedy these & am confident that I can lead these armies of men to victory once more."[50]

Three days later, after visiting Congress and receiving a crowd's admiring stares, he wrote again to his wife: "I began to feel how great the task committed to me. Oh! How sincerely I pray to God that I may be endowed with the wisdom & courage necessary to accomplish the work. Who would have thought when we were married, that I should so soon be called upon to save my country? I learn that before I came on they said in Richmond, that there was only one man they feared & that was McClellan."[51]

Chapter 3

An Army Born

SEVERAL MONTHS AFTER George McClellan arrived in Washington, he described the situation that had awaited him after Bull Run. "I found no army to command," he wrote, "a mere collection of regiments cowering on the banks of the Potomac, some perfectly raw, others dispirited by their recent defeat." "The troops," he added, "were not only undisciplined, undrilled & dispirited—they were not even placed in military positions—the city was almost in a condition to have been taken by a clash of a single regiment of cavalry."[1]

Although McClellan exaggerated the defenselessness of the capital, the lack of order and discipline was evident. Drunken soldiers stumbled through camps, absentee troops roamed the streets, "gangs of thieves" preyed on civilians, and foragers ransacked private homes and even churches. "The Capital was at that time," stated Colonel William Averell, "in a frightful state of misrule." A staff officer grumbled, "Good men are scarce and ignorance is plentiful in camp."[2]

McClellan acted initially to restore order in the city. He appointed Brigadier General Andrew Porter as provost marshal and assigned companies from three Regular Army infantry regiments to the duty. Porter's troops cleaned out saloons and other establishments of soldiers and herded them back to their units. In time McClellan imposed martial law in the capital, requiring all soldiers to have passes before entering the city. He also added to the provost command by using his headquarters detail, the Sturgis Rifles.[3]

Most importantly, the commanding general implemented a "systematic plan" to impose organization upon "a collection of undisciplined, ill-officered, and uninstructed men." He stated later "everything was to be created from the very foundation." The troops needed arms, ammunition, uniforms, and equipment. He began by moving regiments into new campsites and putting the men to work on felling trees and building works for the city's defenses.[4]

When McClellan assumed command, he had roughly 50,000 troops. From mid-August to early November, at least twenty-five new regiments joined the army, totaling more than 30,000 men. One or more of the units arrived each week during these months.[5]

As the recruits scrambled off the trains, their regiments were assigned to a Provisional Division, created by McClellan. He chose Brigadier General Silas Casey to command the division and to oversee the training. An author of a manual on infantry tactics, Casey was a fifty-four-year-old West Pointer and career soldier. A captain of one of the new regiments described him as "a fine looking, grey haired elderly man and I think our officer who knows his business."[6]

Casey had a formidable task before him. The officers in the new regiments knew as little about soldiering as the men in the ranks. The recruits complained constantly about their company commanders and field officers. A member of the 6th Wisconsin told his wife, "our Regimental officers are not very competent men." A paymaster informed the governor of Maine that all of the state's units "suffer from inefficiency and incompetency of officers." A New Yorker growled that his "officers did not work at all, as they knew little or nothing of how it should be done," while a Pennsylvanian put it bluntly about his major, "He knew no more of tactics than a pig does of French."[7]

Consequently, the camps of instruction reverberated daily with the shouts of orders and the tramp of men as they executed the various tactical evolutions required of Civil War soldiers. "Drill, drill, drill," wrote a colonel, "day in and day out, is the program." Several hours each day, the novice troops worked at squad, platoon, company, battalion, and skirmish drills. They fired at targets and learned to use a bayonet. Every evening the officers held a dress parade in each regiment. It was tiring, seemingly endless work that moved a Wisconsin volunteer to grumble, "For God's sake kill us off in battle, and don't do us to death as jack mules."[8]

When a regiment completed its initial training in a camp of instruction, it was assigned to a brigade, usually comprised, in part or in whole, of units that had been at Bull Run. Assignment to a brigade meant, however, more drilling, augmented with picket and guard duty and labor on fortifications. The daily routine went on from six o'clock in the morning until nine o'clock at night. A soldier in the 2nd Wisconsin called the work and drills "Damd hard business."[9]

Discipline and morale problems plagued the older regiments after Bull Run. The humiliation of the defeat worsened their attitudes. According to a lieutenant there were simply too many men who "think a soldier should never be called on to do duty, to march a long distance or to sleep out-doors." They continued to sneak out of camp to forage, to steal from civilians and fellow soldiers, and to fight each other with fists. An officer noted that one regiment had "two prevailing faults, uncleanliness and a tendency to drunkenness."[10]

The difficulty of imposing discipline upon the troops—both in the newer and older units—lay, in part, with the men's character. The regimentation of army life clashed with their individualism as Americans. The loss of freedom gnawed at them, and they bristled at compliance. "One of the most difficult things in the world for a genuine Yankee to do," explained a Maine private, "was to settle down, and become accustomed to the experience of a soldier's life. . . . Accustomed to be independent, the words go and come grated harshly upon his ear."[11]

They saw themselves as temporary soldiers, or as an Indiana volunteer put it, "We were in the army for business—that of putting down the rebellion, and not particularly for military display, and we expected to as soon as that was accomplished to return to our several homes, to our knitting, our plows, our shops, our counters, etc., and live in peace." While they remained steadfast in their devotion to the cause—their letters and diaries affirm this—they were citizens first, and they would be citizens again when the war ended. "The transformation from civilian to soldier," a historian has written, "was rarely completed."[12]

They had enlisted, above all else, because of their "love for the

Union," with its "ideals of liberty and democracy." Southerners had threatened their ideals, and their duty as citizens brought them into the army. "My *country* is in danger," one soldier told his wife, "human liberty at stake, shall I therefore falter in the discharge of my plainly laid outline of duty—No!" They bowed eventually to the discipline and to the demands of soldiering, but never entirely and never without complaint. The cause ultimately meant more to them than the hardships and sacrifices.[13]

The relationship between officers and enlisted men at the regimental level contributed to discipline problems. The rank and file saw their officers as social equals, acquaintances, or friends from civilian life. To obey orders or to accept punishment from one's equal proved to be a difficult transition. The men, wrote a major, "measure the individual, not the grade of his commission." They could be harsh in their judgment, as one private wrote of his major, "*Hell deserving red mouth puny damned stuck up.*" They learned, however, to obey orders from officers and to accept punishments if they were considered fair. One private offered his view: "it is better to be on good terms with the head officers than with drunken hogs."[14]

The process of turning citizens into soldiers required time. In October, Brigadier General George G. Meade, a West Pointer with a dim view of volunteers, wrote home about his brigade of Pennsylvanians: "They do not any of them, officers or men, seem to have the least idea of the solemn duty they have imposed upon themselves in becoming soldiers. Soldiers they are not in any sense of the word. Brave men they may be, and I trust in God will prove themselves; . . . I doubt if any of the numerous living beings around me realize in the slightest degree what they may have to meet."[15]

To his credit, George McClellan worked tirelessly at making them into soldiers. From his headquarters at the home of Navy Captain Charles Wilkes on Jackson Square, two blocks from the War Department, he attended to the smallest of details, conferred with generals, and then rode forth to inspect camps and to watch the training each day. "I do not *live* at all," he wrote to Ellen in late August. "Merely exist, worked & worried half to death. I have no privacy, no leisure, no relaxation, except in reading your letters & writing to you."[16]

McClellan's efforts gradually brought order, instilled discipline, and built morale. Examining boards removed 310 officers from service between August 1861 and March 1862. McClellan directed that "all work," except inspections, should be suspended on Sundays, as "we are fighting in a holy cause." When the 79th New York and three other regiments refused to do their duty because of various grievances in mid-August, the commanding general reacted swiftly and firmly. He took the flag of the 79th New York and court-martialed ringleaders in the units.[17]

The army commander understood the importance of pageantry in giving the men an identity and in fostering morale. Less than a month after he took command, McClellan held his first review. Joined by Abraham Lincoln, he watched eight infantry regiments, several companies of cavalry, and artillery batteries pass in review. The men cheered him and the president. More such displays followed almost on a weekly schedule. On September 12, he held a review of a division for the public. He also had units participate in sham battles, with cannon firing rounds and infantrymen triggering volleys. A New York private told his parents after being in one of them, that it was "a splendid sight."[18]

The rank and file noticed the transformation and credited it to McClellan. "You can hardly imagine the different aspect of things pertaining to the troops and the war generally since Gen. McLellan took command," Lieutenant Frank Lemont wrote to his parents on September 1. "Before everything went at loose ends." A chaplain told his wife that now "everything is intensely military." A staff officer declared: "Since Gen. McClellan took hold of them they have improved in every respect. Every day adds to their efficiency." At the end of September, McClellan informed a governor: "We have a splendid body of men. . . . I think that, as a mass, our Army is composed of the best men who ever formed an army" and were "becoming organized, disciplined, & well instructed."[19]

During these long days of drill, frequent reviews, imposition of discipline, and McClellan's constant presence, a bond developed between the general and the men in the ranks. "The truth is," noted a chaplain, "our magnificent army much needed a transcendent leader, and the crisis prompted us both to crave and expect one fit for the occasion—one whom we could afford to idolize." A corporal in the 18th Massachusetts affirmed, "The army, to the last man, so learned to love McClellan."

Another soldier described the depth of the bond between them: "In his hands I am willing to place my life and destiny, and blindly go where he may direct."[20]

"There is a soul to an army as well as to the individual man," stated William Sherman, "and no general can accomplish the full work of his army unless he commands the soul of his men as well as their body and legs." And so it was with McClellan during the summer and fall of 1861. He forged the army, gave it an identity, instilled in the men a belief in themselves that would go deep into the marrow of the army, and possessed its soul. It had been a daunting task, brilliantly accomplished. He came to love his creation, that "splendid body of men." George Meade, a future commander, admitted later, "the army made no essential improvement under any of his successors."[21]

ON AUGUST 17, the War Department merged the departments of Washington, Northeastern Virginia, and Shenandoah into the Department of the Potomac. Three days later, George McClellan assumed command of the new department and officially designated the units as the Army of the Potomac. With the department's creation, McClellan began the formal organization of the army.[22]

During the next three months as the army swelled in numbers, McClellan arrayed the infantry regiments into a dozen divisions. He had inherited five divisions from Irvin McDowell's army at Bull Run and reconstituted them and appointed their commanders. He gave McDowell a division, claiming later, however, that it was "one of my greatest mistakes" because McDowell "intrigued against me to the utmost of his power." Only Samuel Heintzelman retained divisional command after Bull Run.[23]

The other ten division commanders had either served under McDowell or had joined the army after Bull Run. Seven of them were West Pointers; one, Edwin V. Sumner, had spent more than four decades in the army; another, Nathaniel P. Banks, a former speaker of the House of Representatives and Republican governor of Massachusetts, owed his commission to politics; and one, Louis Blenker, had been a revolutionary émigré from Germany who had received a colonelcy of a volunteer regiment. William Franklin, Erasmus Keyes, and Blenker had commanded brigades at Bull Run, while Fitz John Porter, William F. Smith, and Charles P. Stone—fellow graduates of the academy's Class of 1845, a year ahead of McClellan—had held staff positions during the war's early months. Another West Pointer, Joseph Hooker, had left the army in 1853, amid rumors of "bad habits and excesses." He had been struggling to eke out a living when he received a commission as brigadier general.[24]

The final member of the group, George McCall, had brought his command with him to Washington after Bull Run. The response of Pennsylvanians to Lincoln's call for volunteers in April had been so overwhelming that the legislature created a "Reserve Volunteer Corps of the Commonwealth." The law authorized thirteen infantry regiments, one cavalry regiment, and a battery of artillery. By mid-July, recruits from across the state had filled the Reserve Corps and were sworn into Federal service. With the defeat at Bull Run, Governor Andrew Curtin began forwarding McCall's 15,000 troops to the national capital. Known eventually as the Pennsylvania Reserve Division, it was the only division in the army comprised of units from one state.[25]

These twelve men, except for Banks and Blenker, formed the core of the army's senior leadership for much of the next eighteen months. They were all professionals, with most of them having served under Winfield Scott in Mexico. Many of them shared McClellan's political and social conservatism and cautious military strategy. Seniority, prior associations with Scott and McClellan, and fortune's favor figured prominently in their selection. Only command's burdens and battle's testing would reveal their shortcomings. With McClellan, however, they fashioned the army's temper for a long time.[26]

At the brigade level, an influx of commanders, whose destinies would be closely linked to that of the army, arrived during the summer and fall. The newcomers included three Pennsylvanians—George Meade, John F. Reynolds, and Winfield Scott Hancock—a wealthy, one-armed veteran soldier from New Jersey, Philip Kearny; a former congressman and New York City politician, Daniel E. Sickles; and a host of West Pointers—John Sedgwick, Darius N. Couch, Isaac Stevens, William T. H. Brooks, John Newton, and William H. French. Several officers earned promotion to brigadier general for their conduct at Bull Run—Henry W. Slocum, Willis A. Gorman, James Wadsworth, and Thomas Meagher. Israel Richardson and Oliver Howard retained command of the brigades that they had led in the battle. Ambrose Burnside, one of McClellan's best friends, left the army to recruit units for an operation that he had proposed against Confederate defenses in North Carolina.[27]

Among the dozens of brigades organized at this time, several had distinctive compositions. In addition to the three brigades of the Pennsylvania Reserve Division, there were a brigade of five Vermont regiments, a 1st and 2nd New Jersey Brigade, the Excelsior Brigade comprised entirely of New Yorkers, and a brigade of Wisconsin and Indiana troops, Westerners whom their comrades said came from "way down beyond the sunset." The most colorful unit was, however, the Irish Brigade, which originally consisted of three New York regiments, recruited by Meagher, who became its commander. Each regiment carried a green flag, embroidered with an Irish harp, a sunburst, and a shamrock.[28]

A newspaperman described the Irish "as a party of mad fellows." Despite the icy reception and discrimination they had encountered upon their arrival in Protestant America in the 1840s and 1850s, they were among the most patriotic troops in the army, filling seven regiments by year's end. Like native-born Americans, they had enlisted to save the Union and the Constitution. To them, however, more was at stake. "America is Irlands refuge Irlands last hope," explained one of them. "Destroy this republic and her hopes are blasted! If Irland is ever ever free the means to accomplish it must come from the shores of America." Devout Catholics, they would be accompanied by a priest throughout the war. Some of them curiously wore "charms" around their necks "to keep off the bullets in battle."[29]

While the army's infantry units consisted almost entirely of volunteer troops, Regular Army batteries formed the foundation of the artillery. At Scott's insistence, the War Department limited the resignations of artillery officers to accept higher rank in infantry regiments, resulting in a core of capable and experienced officers. In turn, McClellan selected two excellent artillerists—Brigadier General William Barry and Colonel Henry J. Hunt—to organize the branch and to oversee the training.[30]

An academy graduate and Mexican War veteran, Barry proved to be "a superb administrator." Before the war, he, Hunt, and William French had co-authored a manual for artillery service. In the aftermath of the Bull Run defeat, he prepared a set of guidelines or principles for the reorganization of the field artillery. He prescribed a uniform caliber of guns in each battery, four to six cannon in each battery, and that four batteries—one Regular Army and three volunteer—be attached to each infantry division. McClellan chose the twelve-pound, bronze Napoleon as the primary field piece because of its usefulness in wooded terrain. The armament also included ten-pound, cast-iron Parrott Rifles and three-inch, wrought iron Ordnance Rifles. Napoleons had an effective range of up to 1,200 yards; the rifles, from 3,000 to 4,000 yards.[31]

Shortly after he assumed command, McClellan established Camp Barry on the road to Bladensburg, Maryland, east of the Capitol. Here Barry brought the batteries engaged at Bull Run for refitting and welcomed new units as they joined the army. The North enjoyed enormous advantages in manufacturing, wealth, and manpower that would be critical to the artillery. Foundries could forge cannon, skilled mechanics could man gun crews, and highly capable officers could direct the batteries in combat. The backbone of the army originated almost in the shadow of the unfinished Capitol dome.[32]

McClellan proposed one hundred field batteries for the army. As a part of this plan, he created an Artillery Reserve and assigned Hunt to command of it. Since his graduation from West Point, where fellow cadets nicknamed him "Cupid," Hunt had devoted his entire career to the artillery. A conservative Democrat, he believed that secession was a terrible mistake. Days after the firing on Fort Sumter, he warned Braxton Bragg, an old friend who would eventually command the Confederate Army of Tennessee, "Revolution devours her children, the plans and expectations of the leaders on both sides will fail them." He had no doubt, he told Bragg, that the North would ultimately prevail.[33]

Unlike Barry, who as chief of artillery was limited by McClellan to administrative duties, Hunt would have tactical control of the reserve batteries. He was blunt, even tactless at times, but with unquestioned integrity. He needed all the talent he possessed to find good officers, to train them and the crews, to secure cannon, and to accumulate the ammunition and gear for the batteries. By year's end, he had managed to organize and equip thirteen batteries. For Henry Hunt, that marked only a beginning.[34]

The organization of the army's third branch, the cavalry, suffered from bureaucratic myopia and McClellan's view of its role. When the conflict began, the army had only five mounted units—two regiments of dragoons, two of light cavalry, and a regiment of mounted riflemen. "The mounted service of the army," a historian has argued, "had been a stepchild of the military establishment from the start." After Fort Sumter, the War Department refused initially to accept volunteer cavalry regiments, despite offers from governors. This attitude soon changed, and on August 6, Congress authorized six cavalry regiments for the Regular Army, including the five antebellum units. Eight days later, McClellan appointed his former academy classmate Brigadier General George Stoneman as chief of cavalry.[35]

One of McClellan's worst failings as an army commander was his utilization of mounted units. He did not view them as an independent force nor did he seem to understand the tactical role of a unified cavalry command. As the volunteer regiments arrived, he dispersed them throughout the army, assigning each unit to an infantry brigade. The horsemen's role would be confined to headquarters duty and scouting. While the Confederates were consolidating their regiments into brigades that could undertake raids and screen their army's movements, McClellan impaired his mounted forces' tactical effectiveness. It was a policy that hampered Union cavalry operations for a long time.[36]

As summer's heat cooled into autumn's chill, then, McClellan's imprint upon the army was visible. Divisions and brigades had been organized, most with professionals in command. The drilling and training continued. Much work remained. If John Reynolds's words were accurate, the prospects for the rank and file were discouraging: "I begin to agree with somebody who, writing in one of the papers, said 'you, can not make soldiers out of volunteers.' . . . They are no better than those that went forward at Bull Run and if they go backwards as they did—we can hope for nothing from them in this war. They are under no discipline and with the officers they have can never be disciplined or drilled. I almost despair from what I have seen of them since I have been here, of our ever making an attack upon any of the positions the enemy may take up."[37]

McClellan, however, had no plans, even intentions, for an advance against the enemy, despite the presence of Confederate outposts nearly on the doorstep of Washington. Since their victory at Bull Run, General Joseph Johnston's troops had erected defenses at Centreville and pushed their picket posts and signal stations east beyond Fairfax Court House to Mason's and Munson's hills, where men with spyglasses could view the Capitol dome and even count windowpanes in Washington residences. Rebel skirmishers clashed with their Federal counterparts on the same ground the Confederates had held before the July battle.[38]

The enemy's proximity to Washington and its defiance formed the background of a dispute, which mounted in intensity and in consequences, between McClellan and the administration. At the most basic level, it was an argument over preparations and timing. At its most significant level, it defined the relationship between a popularly elected government in a struggle for its existence and the role of its premier army in that struggle. Its two central figures were the army commander and the president of the United States.[39]

When McClellan assumed command in the aftermath of Bull Run, he had to strengthen the capital's defenses and forge a weapon that could undertake field operations. He argued correctly that it would require time to accomplish both. On August 2, in a memorandum prepared at the request of Lincoln, he stated his strategic ideas and the requirements for victory. At the heart of the document was his assertion that the enemy had made Virginia "their battle-field—and it seems proper to make the first great struggle there." The Federal war aim should be a limited one—the restoration of Union, while adopting "a rigidly protective policy as to private property and unarmed persons, and a lenient course as to common soldiers."[40]

He had no doubt that victory would result only from the application of "overwhelming physical force." Such a force, "the main Army of Operations" or his army, would need 273,000 men in 283 regiments of infantry, cavalry, and engineers and 100 field batteries. "It is perhaps unnecessary to state," he concluded, "that in addition to the forces named in this memorandum strong reserves should be formed, ready to supply any losses that may occur."[41]

How deeply McClellan believed that he needed an army of such size is difficult to assess. He surely knew that the administration would need months, if not longer, to recruit, arm, and equip this "main Army of Operations," while also meeting the requests of commanders in other theaters. In turn, he would refuse to undertake a major offensive until he had an army of sufficient strength, armament, and training.[42]

McClellan supported his argument for a sizable army with inflated estimates of enemy numbers. On August 8, he reported that Johnston had at least 100,000 troops in front of the Federals. Five weeks later, he placed the figure at 170,000, while his department had barely 80,000 officers and men. At the same time, he called Allan Pinkerton, the head of a detective agency, to Washington to conduct intelligence operations. By the end of September, Pinkerton, who used the name E. J. Allan, had twenty-four agents in the field.[43]

Together, Pinkerton and McClellan submitted overestimates of Confederate strength, a pattern that would characterize McClellan's tenure as army commander. Pinkerton deliberately overstated the number of Rebels, and McClellan knew it. On October 4, when the agent reported Johnston's strength as 98,400, far less than the 170,000 that McClellan had stated earlier, the general did not forward this estimate to the War Department. "No other general," historian Stephen W. Sears has asserted, "exaggerated in such monumental proportions or for so long a period."[44]

His assessments of enemy numbers defy logic. His reports painted a portrait of a "vast machine" constructed by the Confederacy, although its white male population was only one-third that of the North. If the Lincoln administration could not marshal such manpower, how could the newly organized Davis government? McClellan, however, evidently believed his own reports, which provided him with a logical base for his strategic and command decisions. He could justify his unwillingness to advance against the Rebels until preparations had been completed. Likewise he justified his cautious tactics when he met the foe. But these overestimates could, however, cripple, if not paralyze, the army when an opportunity to strike arose.[45]

If the difficulties between McClellan and the administration had been only questions about numbers, readiness, and timing, they might have been resolved. But it went deeper than that, for McClellan had a record of quarreling with superiors and an abiding contempt for politicians. From his days at West Point through his years in the army, he had clashed "with *anyone* in authority," according to Sears.[46]

It is not surprising then that McClellan ignited a feud with Winfield Scott within days of his appointment. "The old man . . . cannot long retain command I think," he informed his wife on August 2. "When he retires I am sure to succeed him, unless in the mean time I lose a battle—which I do not expect to do." Six days later, after he had "a row" with Scott—most likely over the adequacy of the capital's defenses—he described the general-in-chief to Ellen: "I do not know whether he is a *dotard* or a traitor! . . . he is a perfect imbecile. He understands nothing, appreciates nothing & is ever in my way." Six weeks later, he wrote that Scott "threw down the glove & I took it up, I presume war is declared."[47]

His letters to his wife during these months contain a litany of his troubles and also harsh descriptions of Lincoln and Cabinet members. At different times, McClellan called the president "an idiot," "a rare bird," and "'the original gorilla,' about as intelligent as ever. What a specimen to be at the head of our affairs now!" Following a Cabinet meeting, he railed to Ellen: "I can't tell you how disgusted I am becoming with these wretched politicians—they are a most despicable set of men & I think [Secretary of State William] Seward is . . . a meddling, officious, incompetent little puppy." As for Lincoln, "The Presdt is nothing more than a well meaning baboon."[48]

McClellan's antipathy toward political leaders reflected a common opinion within the professional military. He and fellow officers had seen the pernicious effects, as they thought, of political interference with the army in Mexico. McClellan was contemptuous of and condescending toward them. In his thinking, he was a general beset with a numerically superior force in front and an ignorant and obstructive government in the rear. "It is perfectly sickening," he wrote in another letter to Ellen, "to have to work with such people & to see the fate of the nation in such hands."[49]

The army commander's disdainful attitude festered and worsened over time. He failed to understand that the conflict was fundamentally a political contest. Campaigns and battles would derive much of their significance from their impact on public opinion. The war had begun in a boiling cauldron of politics; its resolution rested on the steadfastness of the political will of Northerners and Southerners.[50]

As Henry Hunt said, "Revolution devours her children," and revolution was afoot in the land. Its shape remained undefined, but it could not be limited. Like a swelling current, it would scour and establish new courses. The war tested, as never before, the viability of America's experiment in democracy. And as never before, the military would be intertwined with politics. Blinded by his prejudices, McClellan refused to see that "the fate of the nation" rested "in such hands." He was a soldier breasting a powerful stream.[51]

Despite his private, belittling descriptions of Lincoln, McClellan enjoyed the support of the president during the summer and fall. Lincoln conferred frequently with McClellan, joined the general at reviews of the troops, worked tirelessly to recruit and equip the army, and even defended the commander when others complained about the army's inertia. He witnessed the disagreements between Scott and McClellan over the capital's security and strategy. A patient man, Lincoln accepted McClellan's argument for more men and more time.[52]

Lincoln, however, never lost sight of his greatest burden as president—to sustain his fellow citizens' will to wage war against the Confederacy for as long as it might require and at whatever its cost. He had tapped into the outpouring of nationalism after Fort Sumter and had exploited the new resolve after the defeat at Bull Run, but he knew that it would not endure without success on battlefields. The foundation of the Union cause resided at isolated farmhouses, on dusty village roads, and amid the bustle of city streets. Military inactivity or stalemate could erode away some of that foundation.[53]

While the Union war effort encompassed both the Eastern and Western theaters, most of the Northern press and populace focused on the Army of the Potomac. It had the primary burden of defending Washington. If the national capital fell, the Union cause would be no longer politically sustainable. In turn, the Confederate capital beckoned a mere hundred miles to the south as it had before Bull Run. Although Federal successes in the West ultimately led to the collapse of the Confederacy, the war's main battleground rested in Virginia. Here, the Southerners had their best opportunity to secure a favorable political settlement with battlefield victories. Here, too, the Army of the Potomac, with the shadow of Washington upon it, carried, more than any other Union command, the political will of the North.[54]

Military necessity and political reality bound Lincoln to the Army of the Potomac. His almost unremitting attention to its operations reflected this tie. Its fortunes would be his. The relationship between him and its commander would be a central theme of the war in the East. In George McClellan, he would find his most difficult subordinate. One of them believed the army belonged to him. The other knew it belonged to the country.

BY MID-OCTOBER the campsites of the Army of the Potomac extended for more than one hundred miles on both sides of its namesake river. Nathaniel Banks's division covered the northern end of the Shenandoah Valley on the Maryland side of the river. Upriver from Washington, Charles Stone's brigades guarded the crossings in the Poolesville, Maryland, area, while Joseph Hooker's command watched the Potomac River below the capital in southern Maryland. The bulk of the army manned the city's defenses at Arlington and Alexandria, with its pickets posted along the roads toward Centreville.[55]

During the preceding three weeks skirmishes between the opposing pickets had slackened as the Confederates abandoned their outposts and retired beyond Fairfax Court House. With far fewer men than McClellan credited him with, Joseph Johnston gradually withdrew his advance lines to his main defenses at Centreville. "It has become a common duty with us," wrote a Federal soldier during this time, "to go out 'hunting up a fight' and never getting into one."[56]

On October 19, Brigadier General George McCall's Pennsylvania Reserve Division conducted a reconnaissance up the Potomac River and occupied Dranesville, Virginia. The Pennsylvanians probed farther upstream the next day. McClellan, meanwhile, received a message from Banks that a signal station reported that the Rebels had retired from Leesburg. McClellan ordered Stone to conduct "a slight demonstration" along the river. In turn, Stone moved units to the river and sent scouts into Virginia, where they mistook rows of hay for a small enemy campsite near Leesburg. The erroneous report triggered a disaster.[57]

Four companies of the 15th Massachusetts crossed the Potomac in boats the next morning, with orders to destroy the camp. Landing at the foot of Ball's Bluff, they climbed up the steep hillside and filed into open fields. Instead of finding a handful of Southerners, the Yankees encountered troops from Brigadier General Nathan Evans's brigade, which still occupied the area. The Rebels pressed the Federals back, but "our men came bravely up to the scratch," wrote a Massachusetts private.[58]

It was as if a spark had lit a bonfire. The 20th Massachusetts joined their Bay State comrades, followed by a pair of cannon and companies from three regiments of Colonel Edward Baker's brigade. Baker had informed Stone of the action, and the division commander approved the crossing. Stone believed that McCall's division was moving on Leesburg; instead, McClellan had ordered it to withdraw from Dranesville. South of the Potomac, then, inexperienced Federal troops found themselves in a billowing fight with Southerners who had been at Bull Run.[59]

Confusion characterized the combat, with attacks and counterattacks between the opponents. The Rebels, however, had the best of it, pressing against the Union line. "Good God how our men did drop," exclaimed a 20th Massachusetts private. "They fell on both sides of me and I would not give 2 cents for my life that afternoon." When Baker was killed about 5:00 P.M., the Federal line unraveled. The Yankees fled toward the river, plunging down Ball's Bluff. From the crest, the Confederates raked the riverbank, where many of the Northerners were trapped.[60]

Lucky Yankees piled into the few twenty-five-foot-long boats, although one boat, filled with wounded men, upset and all aboard drowned. Those stranded on the bank either surrendered or tried to swim to Harrison's Island in the river. "I had to throw my gun and clothes in the river," wrote a private, "and swim for my life." Scores of men drowned or were shot by the enemy, slipping beneath the waters. Hundreds more were captured.[61]

The next day McClellan visited Stone and learned details of the disaster. More than nine hundred Federals had been lost, including 161 reported as missing and presumed to have drowned. McClellan blamed the martyred Baker, a former Illinois congressman and Oregon senator and friend of Lincoln. The debacle, McClellan notified his division com-

manders, "was caused by errors committed by the immediate commander—*not* Genl Stone." George Meade wrote his wife at the time that
McClellan must not have known of the situation at Ball's Bluff or he
would not have ordered McCall's division away from Dranesville. But
the recriminations from another Union defeat had not been stilled.[62]

Less than two weeks after Ball's Bluff, probably on October 31,
McClellan submitted a lengthy report to Secretary of War Simon
Cameron. A friend of and advisor to the general, Edwin McM. Stanton,
helped him prepare the draft. The army, McClellan stated, could either
prepare winter quarters or advance against the enemy at Centreville. "If
political considerations render the first course inadvisable the second
alone remains," he wrote. If the latter course were to be adopted, his
army would require reinforcements from Union forces in other sections
of the country. "The enemy have a force on the Potomac not less than
150,000 strong well drilled & equipped, ably commanded & strongly
intrenched." He had slightly more than 76,000 officers and men who
could be used in an offensive. But "the infantry regiments are to a considerable extent armed with unserviceable weapons."[63]

"The nation feels, & I share the feeling," McClellan reminded the
secretary, "that the Army of the Potomac holds the fate of the country
in its hands. The stake is so vast, the issue so momentous, & the effect
of the next battle will be so important throughout the future as well as
the present, that I continue to urge, as I have ever done since I entered
upon the command of this army, upon the Govt to devote its energies &
its available resources towards increasing the numbers & efficiency of
the Army on which its salvation depends."[64]

His "fixed purpose" was, concluded McClellan, not "to expose this
government to hazard by premature movement." If Cameron and Lincoln expected a forward movement before cold weather set in, it was
not to be. McClellan would not risk the army and "the fate of the country" by a premature advance. Unwilling to be moved by "political considerations," he remained determined to have an army that when it
advanced, would go forth irresistibly.[65]

Ironically, at this time, McClellan's "war" with Winfield Scott had
ended. The dispute had festered and worsened during the previous
weeks. The general-in-chief's failing health had been evident to anyone

who saw him. On October 18, Lincoln and the Cabinet accepted his resignation. Scott preferred Henry W. Halleck as his successor, but the president appointed McClellan to the post on November 1, telling the general, "you will, therefore, assume this enlarged duty at once, conferring with me so far as necessary."[66]

A downpour fell through the "pitch dark" skies on the early morning of November 2, as Winfield Scott boarded a train for West Point. The hero of two wars, he was now, as an enlisted man described him, a "long ago soldier." No one from the White House or Congress was there to see him off, only McClellan, members of his staff, and a detail of cavalrymen. "I saw there," McClellan wrote to his wife, "the end of a long, active & ambitious life—the end of the career of the first soldier of his nation—& it was a feeble old man scarce able to walk." The train finally pulled away from the station, and the "long ago soldier" departed Washington as the rain pelted his car.[67]

Eleven days later, Lincoln, accompanied by Secretary of State William Seward and John Hay, one of his secretaries, made an unexpected evening visit to McClellan's headquarters. The president had habitually stopped in unannounced to see the general. The practice galled McClellan, who confided to Ellen once that he went elsewhere to work and "to dodge all enemies in shape of 'browsing' Presdt etc."[68]

On this night, McClellan was attending an officer's wedding, so the visitors decided to wait his return. About an hour later, the general-in-chief entered the house and was told by an orderly that his guests were waiting for him in the parlor. McClellan went directly upstairs. Thirty minutes later, the orderly informed Lincoln and the others that the general had gone to bed for the night. The three men left, with Hay afterward calling it "unparalleled insolence." Lincoln, however, seemed not to be offended as he returned the next evening to confer with the man he had so recently promoted to general-in-chief.[69]

A RAW, COLD WIND blew across the muddy fields near Bailey's Crossroads, Virginia, outside Washington. Patches of snow pockmarked the ground, and a drizzling rain came with the wind. Throughout the morning of November 20, long columns of Union soldiers filed into place on the fields—infantry and cavalry regiments and batteries of artillery. Officers aligned the regiments in two-company fronts and tried to straighten the ranks. Reviews had been routine since August, but this one included a majority of the army, upward of 75,000 men, who covered at least two hundred acres of ground, "a perfect sea of heads as far as the eye could reach."[70]

All morning they stood in the ranks and waited as hundreds of spectators ringed the fields. At 1:00 P.M., General-in-Chief George McClellan, President Abraham Lincoln, and Cabinet members appeared. Cannon fire announced their arrival. With McClellan and Lincoln in the van, the official party rode past the rows of men. The troops took off their hats and cheered, with many amused by the ungainly president on horseback. "His long legs were well clasped around the body of his horse," a lieutenant wrote of Lincoln, "his hair & coat tails horizontal. He looked as though he was determined to go through if it killed him but he would be most almighty glad when it was over." It took them an hour to cover the distance from one end to the other.[71]

Now, it was the men's turn. On they came, each regiment in column of divisions, two companies abreast, passing in review. "It was by far the grandest thing I ever saw," asserted a participant. When the 49th Pennsylvania reached the reviewing stand, Colonel William H. Irwin halted the regiment and began drilling the troops, stopping each unit in their rear. Brigadier General Winfield Scott Hancock, Irwin's brigade commander, rode up and "in very forcible language" placed Irwin under arrest. Hancock ordered the Pennsylvanians forward, and the review continued.[72]

Through the afternoon and into the evening they marched—New Yorkers, Pennsylvanians, New Jerseymen, New Englanders, and Westerners from "way down beyond the sunset." They had come together as one, a moving river of men. "The display was grand and imposing in the extreme," as a soldier described it in his diary. If they had not been certain before, they could see now that each man was a part of something much larger than his company or regiment, or even division. Rank upon rank, they were an army, taking hours to pass in review.[73]

"I was completely satisfied & delighted beyond expression," McClellan enthused to his wife, calling it "The Grand Review." He was proud of the army and deservedly so. As he watched, he saw his creation, the army that held the country's destiny in its hands. When they were ready, he would send them forth to meet the enemy, not until then. But for the present, near a small Virginia crossroads, as an officer stated, "In the realization of all observers, even of the most experienced officer, the army was born that day."[74]

Chapter 4

To the Peninsula

RAIN FELL SEEMINGLY every day on the winter camps of the Army of the Potomac during December 1861. "If it rains much longer," joked a soldier, "Abe will be obliged to furnish us canoes in order to get around camp." Drilling slowed as the men kept dry and warm in their huts, which they had built by placing tents on three-foot-high log frames banked with dirt. "The encampments," recalled a Federal, "were laid out with the regularity of streets."[1]

Camp life took on a monotonous routine. The men enlivened the tedium by sneaking off to forage, which brought a stream of complaints from local civilians. A New Yorker explained their attitude about the practice: "we would not let a Secesh chickin go to the Rebels if we can get our hands on it." While in their huts, they amused themselves with dice and card games when they had money. They bought peaches, cured in jars of whiskey, from sutlers. A private confessed to a friend, "he has had a great many 'peaches' lately which has been a cause of filling up the guard house." A chaplain grumbled, "Every camp is a place where Satan's seat is."[2]

The men complained and cursed about many things. The poor quality of their rations moved Private Miles Peabody of the 5th New Hampshire to tell his brother, "We have been obliged to eat stuff that you would not think fit to give to the hogs and if I was at home I would not eat it but we have to eat it or starve." A staple of their diet was hard-tack, a thick, square cracker made of unleavened flour. A sergeant called it "a great institution. You might soak a biscuit in a cup of coffee six weeks, then you would have to have a good set of teeth to eat it. This kind of bread I suppose was made to *keep*."[3]

The closeness of life in small huts, aggravated by the miserable weather, brought forth strings of oaths. "Officers swear at the men," stated a New York sergeant, "the men swear at the horses and at each other and at the officers." Another enlisted man noted: "Army life reveals character. Ther's little hypocricy. Everyone shows out just what he is."[4]

Diseases thrived in the conditions. Typhoid fever, pneumonia, and diarrhea sent thousands on sick call or into hospitals. Surgeons treated the last ailment with oak bark tea and opium. An outbreak of smallpox in Washington kept men out of the city. The rate of illness in the army approached 10 percent.[5]

Few men celebrated Christmas. Snow fell for several hours that day, and homesickness contributed to the somber mood. "The camp is uncommonly still," a soldier recorded in his diary. A German immigrant serving as a fifer in the 7th Wisconsin offered another explanation for the silence in the camps: "Here Christmas pleasures are very rare. It is because Americans do not have any *gemutlichkeit* [generosity]. Americans are a materialistic people, and are interested only in making money and raising hell."[6]

As winter's grip deepened after Christmas and New Year's Day, the weather worsened. The men filled letters and diaries about the mud, rain, and snow. "It has not been pleasant more than a half dozen days since the first of Jan.," a soldier wrote near the end of February, adding that "you cannot imagine what *mud* is until you have lived in Va." A lieutenant claimed, "The streets of Washington are perfect rivers, and unless a person can swim, it is very dangerous for short persons to attempt to navigate them."[7]

Despite the mud and the long days and nights, most of them retained their morale. One soldier related that few recruits joined the regiment during the winter, moving his comrades to remark, "All the

Fools have enlisted." That sentiment, however, did not prevail. Private James T. Miller, a Scottish immigrant in the 111th Pennsylvania with a family at home, typified the majority view, "i feel that the cause in which i am inlisted is one of the most just and holy that mortal man ever engaged in." Another soldier declared, "I never want to return to the quiet Scenes of home, until every fabric of Rebel Ingenuity is pulled down, and their Treacherous Architects, be made to suffer the penalty of their Crimes."[8]

They also had impatience with the army's inactivity. "There is considerable discontentment in the army here," asserted a sergeant, "the boys say they enlisted to fight not to lay around here in the mud." A Pennsylvanian told his wife in mid-January, "i long to have it commence so we can tell how it is a going." For the veterans of Bull Run, it was a matter of atonement. "It will be a disgrace to the United States," declared Corporal Horace Emerson of the 2nd Wisconsin, "to close this war before the Army of the Potomac redeemed themselves our Regiment would rather go out to Manassas alone than to go back to Wisconsin and have it said that we was in two Battles and retreated both times would it not be a disgrace."[9]

A New Yorker blamed the army's commander, George McClellan, for the failure to advance against the enemy. "He seems to be acting very queer about the war," he wrote of the general-in-chief, adding that he was "losing the confidence I once had in that man." In another letter, the private said, "I cannot for my part see what they can be waiting on."[10]

The rank and file's desire for action corresponded to a mounting chorus in newspapers and in Congress for an offensive strike. McClellan described it later as "that impatient and unceasing clamor—inevitable among a people unaccustomed to war." In his defense, the weather hampered, if not precluded, a major movement. On December 20, the general was stricken with typhoid fever. For three days he was critically ill, and it would be three weeks before he returned to duty. His illness "paralyzed work" at headquarters.[11]

Abraham Lincoln heard the "impatient and unceasing clamor." During the late summer and fall, the president had wrestled with the public's demands for an offensive movement and McClellan's argument that the army needed more time. He patiently accepted the general's cautious strategy, but his mood darkened after the new year. There was military stalemate in the East and the West, and Lincoln's patience was draining away.[12]

On January 10, the president met with generals Irvin McDowell and William Franklin. With McClellan still confined to headquarters with his illness, Lincoln wanted to discuss plans for an offensive. Cabinet members William Seward and Salmon Chase sat in on the meeting. Franklin testified that the president "was in great distress over the condition of the country." Lincoln "complained that he was abused in Congress for the military inaction . . . that there was a general feeling of depression on account of the inaction; and that, as he expressed it, the bottom appeared to be falling out of everything." He said that he would like "to *borrow* the Army of the Potomac for a few weeks, and wanted us to help him as to how to do it."[13]

More discussions followed. When McClellan learned of them, he came to a White House conference on January 13. "Looking exceedingly pale and weak," McClellan listened as Lincoln explained why he had called the earlier meetings. When Chase asked if he would reveal his plans for the army, the general refused, unless ordered to by the president. "No general fit to command an army," he remarked, "will ever submit his plans to the judgment of such an assembly." Then he added, "There are many here entirely incompetent to pass judgment upon them; . . . no plan made known to so many persons can be kept secret an hour."[14]

Lincoln pressed McClellan if he had devised an operation, and the general said that he had. "Then, General, I shall not order you to give it," responded the president. Franklin wrote later that someone said quietly, "Well if that is Mac's decision, he is a ruined man."[15]

McClellan had made a critical and fateful mistake. He should have, at least, taken the president into his confidence. Lincoln seemed unable to make McClellan understand that the administration politically needed a victory, even a modest one and preferably near the capital. By his silence, McClellan appeared obstinate and unwilling to have his plans interfered with or questioned, even by the commander-in-chief. A few days later, Lincoln told Assistant Secretary of the Navy Gustavus Fox that now "he must take these army matters into his own hands."[16]

While these meetings transpired, Lincoln accepted the resignation of Secretary of War Simon Cameron. The Pennsylvanian's administration of the War Department had been plagued with charges of blatant patronage, malfeasance, and corruption. Cameron had created a host of critics and political opponents. When he released a report to the press, without the president's knowledge, about arming slaves, Lincoln maneuvered Cameron into submitting his resignation. Lincoln then nominated him as minister to Russia.[17]

Lincoln's choice for Cameron's successor surprised many people. Edwin McM. Stanton had been a lifelong Democrat, James Buchanan's attorney general, a confidant of McClellan's for the past several months, and a private critic of the administration. Cameron, however, had recommended Stanton, who had been serving as a special counsel to the War Department. Lincoln held few personal grudges, and in Stanton he found a superb administrator.[18]

Stanton possessed a brilliant intellect, a fierce honesty, and a belligerent temperament. He could not abide fools and favor seekers. Individuals who dealt with him soon discovered that he was "opinionated, implacable, intent, and not easily turned from any purpose." A newspaperman wrote that his fellow members of the press hated the secretary "as they do Original Sin, for he is inexorable as death and as reticent as the grave." Fifty-seven years old, stout, and asthmatic, he worked long hours, with his industriousness transforming the War Department. Two weeks after he took office, a member of the Sanitary Commission wrote of him, "At lowest estimate, worth a wagon load of Camerons."[19]

Before long, Lincoln and Stanton established an "excellent working relationship" that over time became "a warm friendship." Lincoln learned that the secretary had a deep and unflagging faith in the cause of the Union. While Stanton attended to the workings of the department, the president could devote his efforts to overseeing the armies. Lincoln explained later how their relationship worked: "I want to oblige everybody when I can; and Stanton and I have an understanding that if I send an order to him which cannot be consistently granted, he is to refuse it. This he sometimes does." Lincoln affectionately called him "Mars."[20]

Many of the army's ranking officers seemed to welcome Stanton's appointment. George Meade wrote home, "Every one seems relieved at the change in the War Department." A staff officer informed his father, "The Army is delighted with the appointment of Stanton as Sec. of War." McClellan described it as "a most unexpected piece of good fortune." For the general, it must have seemed propitious. He and Stanton had formed a close association during the previous months, and he knew of the secretary's censorious views of the Lincoln administration.[21]

The cordial relationship between the general-in-chief and the secretary of war, however, deteriorated rapidly. McClellan wrote later, "It at once became very difficult to approach" Stanton, and "our personal relations at once ceased." Although a Democrat, Stanton saw the need for more radical measures if the rebellion were to be suppressed. He had endorsed Cameron's proposal for the use of African-American soldiers. He also recognized the necessity, politically and militarily, of an advance by Union armies. It was probably inevitable that the pair would clash, and sooner rather than later.[22]

The dispute that would arise between McClellan and Stanton was set amid mounting arguments as to the nature and purpose of the conflict. McClellan and most of his senior generals believed that the prosecution of the war should be limited to the Confederate armies. Union forces should not confiscate Southern civilian property, including slaves, nor should freedmen and escaped slaves be enlisted in Federal service.[23]

George Meade explained the conservative view of the military when he wrote at this time that the Rebels must be compelled "to return to their allegiance under the old Constitution and agree that the will of the majority will govern. Here, however, is our great danger, and it lies in the effort that the ultras [Radical Republicans] are making to give a character to the war which will forbid any hope of the Southerners ever yielding as long as there is any power of resistance left in them. I still trust, however, in the good sense of the mass of the people to preserve us from a condition from which I fear it would take years to emerge."[24]

McClellan understood the connection between his military strategy and the political aims of the war. His cautious approach underlay his belief that by creating a powerful, if not irresistible, army, the Confederacy could be subdued swiftly and with limited bloodshed. If the political purposes assumed a revolutionary character, the struggle would be long and fearful in its costs and consequences. McClellan, however, had failed to appreciate the political impact of military inactivity and the difficulties it caused Lincoln.[25]

The president had acted in the past to limit the confines of the conflict. Now, he faced increasing pressure from within his own party for military action and a redefinition of the war's goals. The "ultras" referred to by Meade had been gaining influence and power in Congress. They welcomed the revolution, still undefined, that the war had unleashed.[26]

When the Thirty-seventh Congress convened in December 1861, both houses created a Joint Committee on the Conduct of the War (JCCW), whose purpose was to examine "the causes of the disasters that have attended the public arms." Comprised of seven members— five Republicans and two Democrats—the committee lacked real authority. Nevertheless, through the influence of its chairman, Senator Benjamin Wade of Ohio, and a fellow Republican, Senator Zachariah Chandler of Michigan, it assumed a powerful role through its investigations and its political beliefs.[27]

Wade and Chandler had been outspoken critics of both McClellan and Lincoln. The inactivity of the army during the fall had been intolerable to them, and McClellan's policy of conciliation to the Rebels was inimical to their beliefs. They dismissed a cautious military strategy, believing that war meant going forth and meeting an enemy on the battlefield. More importantly, they measured a general's competence by his political ideology. They wanted to crush the rebellion and the South's slavocracy, and if a general held different views, a majority of the committee members questioned his patriotism and commitment to the cause. Throughout its existence, the committee focused its attention on the Army of the Potomac.[28]

The nature of the committee's investigations became evident before long. Although it failed to learn McClellan's plans for the army, despite securing his testimony and that of other generals, the committee examined the disaster at Ball's Bluff. The members heard from Charles Stone and subordinate officers. Soon after the battle, McClellan had assured

Stone and the army's generals that Colonel Edward Baker, not the division commander, had been to blame for the bloody fiasco. The JCCW found otherwise, and solicited Stanton to order Stone's arrest as a traitor. The secretary directed McClellan to remove the general from command and place him in arrest.[29]

A conservative Democrat like McClellan, Stone had returned fugitive slaves to Virginia and allegedly had met mysteriously with Confederate officers. Stone testified again before the committee, but the members refused to reveal the specific allegations made against him. McClellan, meanwhile, had Allan Pinkerton conduct an investigation, and on the testimony of a dubious witness, submitted a report to Stanton that condemned Stone. The secretary of war ordered Stone's immediate arrest, which was executed in February. Without charges ever being filed against him, Stone would spend six months in prison.[30]

The army's officers grasped the import of Stone's arrest. "I must believe," wrote Meade, "he is the victim of political malice." Brigadier General Philip Kearny declared, "Stone has been militarily killed under a false pretense." Unfounded accusations against an officer who held political views contrary to powerful politicians could result in terrible retribution.[31]

The president, meanwhile, had stayed out of the Stone affair. He had not welcomed the creation of the JCCW, sensing that its motives were to discredit the administration and its military policy. When its members recommended that Irvin McDowell replace McClellan, Lincoln ignored them. He had urged McClellan to testify before the committee, but that had done nothing to allay Wade's and Chandler's complaints about the general and the commander-in-chief.[32]

As the committee ended its investigation of Ball's Bluff, Lincoln decided, in the words of Gustavus Fox, to "take these army matters into his own hands." On January 27, he issued President's General War Order No. 1, directing "the land and naval forces of the United States" to undertake "a general movement" against the Confederates on February 22, George Washington's birthday. In a special order four days later, he directed the Army of the Potomac to advance on Joseph Johnston's Rebel army at Centreville. His purpose was to stir his generals into action, and as he told a friend, to "threaten all their [Confederate] positions at the same time with superior force, and if they weakened one to strengthen another seize and hold the one weakened."[33]

McClellan came to the White House four days later to protest the president's order for a general movement. For some time, he and Lincoln had been discussing the general's so-called Urbanna Plan. With Johnston's Confederate army in the Centreville-Manassas area and with enemy batteries on the Virginia shore closing the lower Potomac to commercial river traffic, McClellan had proposed a turning movement by the army down the Chesapeake Bay to Urbanna at the mouth of the Rappahannock River. If successful, the Federals would render both Johnston's position and the artillery emplacements untenable. Instead of a bloody confrontation near Bull Run again, the Union army could by maneuver place itself between Johnston's forces and Richmond. The Confederate general would have no choice but to abandon his defenses. In turn, the Yankees would have a shorter route of advance on the enemy capital.[34]

The plan demonstrated McClellan's commitment to a war of maneuver with limited casualties. It also revealed the general's grasp of strategic possibilities. At the meeting, McClellan offered to submit in writing his objections to a February 22 advance and the rationale for his Urbanna proposal. He did so four days later in a twenty-two-page document sent to the War Department. He assured the president that Washington's defenses would be fully manned—Lincoln's primary concern—and if his plan were approved, "I regard success as certain by all chances of war."[35]

February rains and McClellan's opposition to an offensive against Johnston at Centreville insured that the Army of the Potomac would not be in motion by Washington's birthday. Elsewhere, however, Union forces scored victories—in North Carolina, McClellan's old friend Ambrose Burnside seized Roanoke Island, giving the Federals an excellent naval base on the Atlantic coast, and in Tennessee, Brigadier General Ulysses S. Grant's army, with river naval support, captured forts Henry and Donelson, which led to the fall of Nashville. At last, the administration and the Northern people had victories to cheer about after a winter of stalemate.[36]

While these events were transpiring, tragedy struck at the White

House. The Lincolns' twelve-year-old son, William, or Willie as he was affectionately called, died of typhoid fever on February 20. The couple had lost another son, three-year-old Edward, in 1850. Willie had been the president's favorite, a boy he had doted on almost from his birth. His death devastated his parents. For a long time, Lincoln wept privately. Mary Lincoln could not attend the funeral and refused, ever again, to enter Willie's bedroom.[37]

While the Lincolns mourned their son, McClellan met with a dozen generals at headquarters on the morning of March 7. He and his staff had become convinced that there were plots to have McClellan removed as general-in-chief and commander of the army. "From all I can learn," wrote George Meade, "McClellan's star is rapidly setting, and nothing but a victory will save him from ruin." The recent Union victories in Tennessee and North Carolina had magnified the army's inactivity.[38]

McClellan had brought twelve of his senior commanders together to unveil his Urbanna Plan and to seek their approval. Only Irvin McDowell, Samuel Heintzelman, Edwin Sumner, and John Barnard opposed the movement. McClellan had indicated to them that if they did not support the plan, he could be replaced as commander. From headquarters the generals went to the White House, where Lincoln and Stanton questioned them about the proposal. Barnard stated later that if the president "got an intelligent reason, or any reason from any officer . . . for going to Urbanna it is more than I heard." At the same time all of the generals agreed that the infantry divisions should be organized into corps.[39]

The generals returned again, without McClellan, to the White House on the next day. Lincoln informed them that he approved the Urbanna movement, but Washington must be securely defended, only two corps would move until the Confederate batteries were eliminated, and it must begin by March 18. The president also announced that he had authorized the creation of five infantry corps and had selected the army's senior officers—McDowell, Sumner, Heintzelman, Erasmus Keyes, and Nathaniel Banks—as their commanders. He expected, Lincoln said, the generals' full support for the offensive.[40]

Lincoln had made the decision about the corps and their commanders without consulting McClellan. The general-in-chief was clearly displeased by the president's order, arguing later that he wanted to wait to appoint the commanders until they had proven themselves in the field. The army, however, needed corps organizations, and Lincoln had received advice earlier from Stanton and some generals to create them. McClellan was particularly galled by Lincoln's refusal to discuss with him his selection of commanders.[41]

McClellan's relationship with McDowell, Sumner, Heintzelman, and Keyes—Banks was on the upper Potomac and not in close contact with the army—had been strained, if not hostile, for some time. According to division commander William Smith, the generals "looked on McClellan as a boy." Smith asserted that McDowell was "hounded by the defeat at Bull Run," and "the three others had no claim to their positions except by seniority and senility." In a letter, Meade believed that the "enmity" between McClellan and the generals resulted from McClellan's "failure to conciliate them, and the injustice they considered his favoritism to others has been to them. So long as he had full swing, they were silent, but so soon as others had shaken the pedestal he stood on, they join in to lend their hands."[42]

On the day after Lincoln's order had created the corps, March 9, the strategic situation changed in Virginia. During the morning, the administration received news of the destruction wrought by the CSS *Virginia* on the Union fleet at Hampton Roads off the Virginia Peninsula. The day before, the ironclad vessel had sunk two wooden frigates and grounded a third. Even as Lincoln and the Cabinet discussed the prospects of the *Virginia*'s ascent of the Potomac, the USS *Monitor*, another ironclad, dueled with the Confederate ship. That duel ended in a draw and eliminated further danger to Federal ships and the capital.[43]

At Centreville and Manassas, meanwhile, Joseph Johnston's Confederate troops abandoned their winter quarters and marched south. Like McClellan, Johnston had been feuding with his president over strategy. With only 48,000 officers and men, the Southern general believed that his positions at Centreville were vulnerable to an attack from McClellan's nearly 100,000 troops. He had discussed the situation with President Davis, who left the decision with Johnston but thought that a withdrawal should occur only under compelling circumstances.

Instead, without informing Davis beforehand and concluding that McClellan was preparing an advance, Johnston ordered a retreat to beyond the Rappahannock River. As the Southerners headed away, they destroyed huge stockpiles of foodstuffs, much to the infuriation of Davis. By March 12, the Rebels had crossed the Rappahannock and filed into new defensive positions.[44]

McClellan learned of the Confederate evacuation that night and ordered a pursuit for the next morning. "Well, the Army of the Potomac," a soldier scribbled in his journal on March 10, "is at last in motion . . . [and] the Van Winkleish sleep apparently broken." The column stretched for fifteen miles. Hundreds, perhaps even thousands, abandoned the march to forage.[45]

The Yankees entered Centreville and Manassas Junction on March 11. "We expected to find masked batteries, entrenchments, etc.," wrote one of them, "but saw nothing of the kind." They took notice of the graveyards next to the former campsites. A member of the 19th Indiana thought "that they lived better than we did last winter."[46]

What caught the attention of the men and a throng of civilians, who had accompanied the army, were logs, painted black to look like cannon from a distance. They would be dubbed derisively "Quaker guns." A Pennsylvanian growled that "it is sickening" to have been intimidated by them for months. A lieutenant noted in his diary, "we are satisfied the enemy's strength has been greatly overestimated," while a civilian diarist recorded, "We have been humbugged by the rebels."[47]

Johnston's withdrawal to beyond the Rappahannock doomed McClellan's Urbanna movement. The Confederates had also abandoned their artillery emplacements on the lower Potomac, clearing the river for Union shipping. For McClellan, the open river meant that he could move the army directly down the Potomac to Fort Monroe on the Peninsula. With the fort as a base of operations, the Federals could advance directly on Richmond from the southeast.[48]

As the army started back from Centreville on March 12, McClellan read in the newspapers that the president had relieved him the day before of his duties as general-in-chief, retaining him as commander of the Department of the Potomac and of the army. A staff officer of McClellan's wrote that Lincoln's decision "was mortifying in its method" to the general. "We shall now see how great Mr. Lincoln's military talents are," stated an artillery officer. "The whole thing is plainly the result of the radical influence on the President."[49]

Lincoln had come to the conclusion that the burdens of general-in-chief would be too much for McClellan as he personally directed the campaign against Richmond. In his order, Lincoln wrote that this change in command would remain in effect "until otherwise ordered," which indicated that McClellan might reassume his post after the campaign had ended successfully. When McClellan learned of the president's thinking, he thanked Lincoln "most sincerely for the official confidence & kind personal feelings you entertain for me." To a friend, McClellan declared, "*The President is all right*—he is my strongest friend."[50]

Privately, meanwhile, Secretary of War Stanton approached Brigadier General Ethan Allen Hitchcock with an offer of command of the Army of the Potomac. Hitchcock had been Winfield Scott's chief of staff in Mexico, but he was now sixty-three years old and unwell. The old soldier wisely declined the proposal. Evidently, Lincoln knew nothing of Stanton's almost desperate action, and arguably he would never have replaced McClellan with Hitchcock. The episode revealed Stanton's distrust of and disbelief in McClellan's generalship.[51]

The time had passed for such last-minute machinations. Lincoln had approved the Peninsula Campaign, having been assured of Washington's security. He had directed Quartermaster General Meigs to oversee the transportation of the army and the mountains of matériel to Fort Monroe. McClellan had outlined in a report his thinking about the operation, noting that "we shall fight a decisive battle" before Richmond, as the Confederates understand "that it involves the fate of their cause." The campaign's "ultimate object" would be the capture of the Confederate capital. After nine months of preparation and controversy, the Army of the Potomac prepared to launch an offensive campaign unparalleled in size and in logistical requirements in the nation's history.[52]

Before the army started forth, McClellan issued an address to his soldiers. "For a long time I have kept you inactive," he began, "but not without purpose: you were to be disciplined, armed and instructed; the formidable artillery you now have, had to be created; other armies were to move and accomplish certain results. I have held you back that you might give the deathblow to the rebellion that has distracted our once happy country." They were "now a real Army. . . . The period of inaction has passed. I will bring you now face to face with the rebels, and only pray that God defend the right."

"My fate is linked with yours," he stated, "and that all I do is to bring you, where I know you wish to be,—on the decisive battlefield. It is my business to place you there. I am to watch over you as a parent over his children; and you know that your General loves you from the depths of his heart." Many privations and a worthy opponent await them, but "we will share all these together; and when this sad war is over we will all return to our homes, and feel that we can ask no higher honor than the proud consciousness that we belonged to the ARMY OF THE POTOMAC."[53]

ALEXANDRIA, VIRGINIA, "IS ALIVE with soldiers & every house, nook & corner, is full of them," a Pennsylvanian recorded in his diary during the third week of March. The river town had been selected as the point of embarkation for the army, and it throbbed with activity. The government had chartered slightly more than four hundred vessels—steamboats, schooners, ferryboats, side-wheelers, canal boats, transatlantic packets, barges, and even excursion boats—at a cost of $24,300 per day, or roughly $3 million today. They filled the Potomac, "a perfect forest of masts & smoke stacks."[54]

The first contingent of troops, members of Samuel Heintzelman's Third Corps, began filing down to the wharves and boarding the vessels on the evening of March 16 and on the morning of March 17. Bands played and cannon boomed as the ships turned into the current and headed south. A soldier remembered his departure a few days later, "The sun had come out and shone on the white steamers crowded with blue uniforms or the red ones of the Zouaves—glistening muskets and bayonets and the white sails of the sailing vessels, while the smoke of the saluting guns from Fort Lyon gave an impressive and fine effect."[55]

Few of the men enjoyed the downriver trip. "In no place," recalled a sergeant, "is the life of a soldier so hard as on a transport." They were crammed below decks "like cattle" and drank "miserable" whiskey. A Regular Army captain wrote that their steamer, the *Knickerbocker*, "came to us dirty and musty, crusted with grease, dirt and tobacco-juice, long past her days of gilding, brussels carpeting and mirrors." Many crowded the decks to view Mount Vernon as they passed George Washington's impressive home.[56]

At last, the "long grey walls" of Fort Monroe came into view. To the west lay the ruins of Hampton, a village burned by Confederates the previous summer to prevent its occupation by the Federals. Here, the troops disembarked and marched inland. Offshore, the *Monitor* bobbed in the water, drawing loud cheers from the Yankees when they recognized its low silhouette. "Utter confusion at the wharves" marked the disembarking. McClellan had appointed Heintzelman to command the units until he joined them. "We are bound by General McClellan's instructions," Heintzelman noted in his journal, "not to make any demonstration that will indicate our ulterior object."[57]

More transports arrived, unloaded their cargo, headed north, and returned later with another load. In roughly a month, the government shipped more than 100,000 men, nearly 15,000 horses and mules, 1,224 wagons and ambulances, 44 artillery batteries, and enormous stockpiles of equipment, pontoons, ammunition, forage, and foodstuffs. Quartermaster and commissary officers established depots at Fort Monroe, Cheeseman's Creek, and Ship Point. A British observer with the army described it as "the stride of a giant."[58]

The steamer *Commodore*, with McClellan and staff onboard, docked at Fort Monroe on the afternoon of April 2. McClellan met with the senior generals, who had preceded him, and the naval commander. The James and York rivers framed the Peninsula. Before McClellan had left Washington, he knew that the *Virginia* prowled the James and Confederate shore batteries closed the York to the Union fleet. An enemy infantry and artillery force manned defenses at Yorktown. He hoped to capture the historic village by maneuver, but he knew that he might have to conduct a siege. He ordered the troops to march on Yorktown on April 4.[59]

The Yankees marched early that day, slogging through mud on two roads. The pace was slow, hampered by felled trees and destroyed

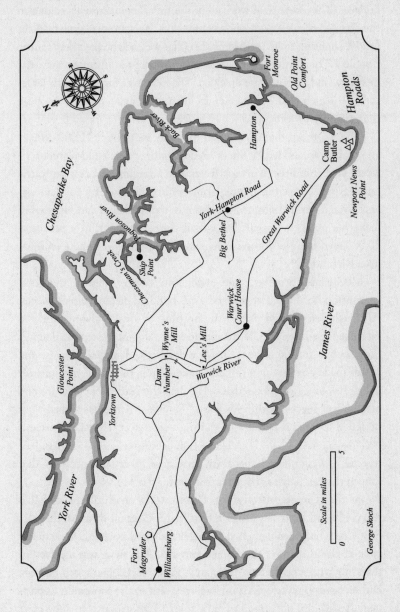

Chesapeake Bay

Back River

Fort Monroe

Old Point Comfort

Hampton Roads

Hampton

Camp Butler

York-Hampton Road

Big Bethel

Great Warwick Road

Newport News Point

Poquoson River

Cheeseman's Creek

Ship Point

Warwick Court House

Warwick River

Wynne's Mill

Lee's Mill

Dam Number 1

James River

Gloucester Point

Yorktown

York River

Fort Magruder

Williamsburg

Scale in miles

0   5

George Skoch

bridges. "They kept us at work all of the time," complained a soldier in the 38th New York, "made our advance slow the scarcity of grub made us feel like fighting them the first chance that we had and pay them for the trouble." The van of the columns reached the Confederate lines the next day, and skirmish fire crackled. "The enemy's force is much larger than we anticipated," wrote Heintzelman. McClellan ordered the siege train from Fort Monroe.[60]

The Southern force amounted to barely more than 11,000 officers and men, commanded by Major General John Bankhead Magruder. Its works lay behind the Warwick River, extending from Yorktown to the James River. Known in the old army as "Prince John" for his flamboyance, Magruder had situated the defenses well and used various ploys to make his numbers appear larger than they were. Within a few days, 20,000 men from Johnston's army joined Magruder, with more en route from Richmond.[61]

McClellan, however, had with him seven infantry divisions, amounting to 53,000 men, and one hundred field artillery pieces. Although defective maps and the hostility of local civilians hindered intelligence efforts, McClellan should have, at least, tested the enemy's lines with a reconnaissance in force. Swamps, dammed streams, and woods made any assault a difficult undertaking, but he seemed unwilling to risk even a minor setback. He "had the golden opportunity of a magnificent success within his grasp," Peter S. Michie has argued, "but he failed to seize it because he did not perceive it. He failed to see it because he was characteristically non-aggressive as a commander." Instead, he committed the army to a siege, a critical decision that shaped the campaign's character from its outset.[62]

As the Federals probed the Southern works on April 5, McClellan received word from Washington that Major General Irvin McDowell's First Corps had been detached from the army and assigned to the newly created Department of the Rappahannock. "The news was received in the army with stupefaction," declared one of McClellan's staff officers. Earlier, Louis Blenker's division had been sent to the Mountain Department. In all, this amounted to more than 50,000 troops. "It is the most infamous thing that history has recorded," McClellan averred to his wife.[63]

Before McClellan had departed for the Peninsula, he had submitted a list of troops responsible for the defense of the capital. Lincoln and Stanton examined the figures and found over-counting and double-counting by the general. McClellan had included Nathaniel Banks's command, which was posted in the Shenandoah Valley and recently constituted into the Department of the Shenandoah. McClellan stated that 18,000 officers and men manned Washington's forts and an additional 55,500 covered the approaches to the city.[64]

By Lincoln's and Stanton's calculations fewer than 27,000 troops were in the defenses and at Manassas. The president "was justly indignant" when he discovered the disparity. "My explicit order," Lincoln reminded McClellan, "that Washington should, by the judgment of all commanders of army corps, be left entirely secure, had been neglected. It was precisely this that drove me to detain McDowell."[65]

McClellan protested against the decision immediately. From that time and for the rest of his life, he convinced himself that the administration had undermined his campaign from its outset and would continue to do so for its duration. It would become his justification for the campaign's ultimate failure. In his mind, he had become a victim of political machinations within the government. He expressed his beliefs well in a letter to Ellen within a few days: "History will present a sad record of these traitors who are willing to sacrifice the country & its army for personal spite & personal aims. The people will soon understand the whole matter & then woe betide the guilty ones." It would be a continuous refrain in his private letters and official correspondence.[66]

As he so often did, McClellan refused to see or to admit his responsibility. He had been less than forthright with Lincoln and had failed to explain clearly to the president the strategic implications of a move to the Peninsula. With the Federals on the Peninsula, Joseph Johnston's Confederate army would have to abandon its Rappahannock River line to confront the Northerners before Richmond. The withdrawal would reduce the threat to Washington. For months, however, McClellan had been inflating the enemy's numbers and military prowess. If the Rebels were so numerous and so capable, could they not oppose McClellan while striking at the vulnerable capital?[67]

Lincoln would not, could not, jeopardize the security of Washington. He believed firmly that if the Confederates seized the national capital their independence would be assured. Whether McClellan had offered a full explanation of his plans or not, neither Lincoln nor Stanton seemed to appreciate the strategic implications of the movement to the Peninsula. In less than a month, McClellan had shifted the conflict from Washington to Richmond. He had reduced the danger to the former city and increased it to the latter. Unfortunately, the president believed that McClellan had been less than honest with him, while the general believed that he had been betrayed by the administration. Like a festering wound, the dispute poisoned the Peninsula Campaign.[68]

By retaining McDowell's corps, Lincoln gave himself flexibility in its use. When the government learned of Johnston's withdrawal from the Rappahannock during the second week of April, Lincoln ordered McDowell to Fredericksburg, Virginia, midway between the two capitals. From there, McDowell could cover the overland approaches to Washington, and if the opportunity arose, cooperate with McClellan as he neared Richmond. As a department commander, however, McDowell remained under Lincoln's direct authority, not McClellan's. The president acquiesced to McClellan's constant urgings for more troops by sending William Franklin's division from McDowell to the Peninsula.[69]

Before Franklin's troops arrived, Lincoln had pressed McClellan for action at Yorktown. With the Federals on the Peninsula, Northern newspapers were already predicting the end of the war. Lincoln began his frank letter to the general by noting, "Your dispatches complaining that you are not properly sustained, while they do not offend me, do pain me very much." Continuing, he wrote:

> I think it is the precise time for you to strike a blow. By delay the enemy will relatively gain on you—that is, he will gain faster by fortifications and re-enforcements than you can by re-enforcements alone. And once more let me tell you it is indispensable to you that you strike a blow. I am powerless to help this. You will do me the justice to remember I always insisted that going down the bay in search of a field, instead of fighting at or near Manassas, was only shifting and not surmounting a difficulty; that we would find the same enemy and the same or equal

intrenchments at either place. The country will not fail to note, is now noting, that the present hesitation to move upon an intrenched enemy is but the story of Manassas repeated.

I beg to assure you that I have never written you or spoken to you in greater kindness of feeling than now, nor with a fuller purpose to sustain you, so far as, in my most anxious judgment, I consistently can. But you must act.[70]

McClellan did not respond directly to the president's sincere dispatch. Instead, he wrote privately to his wife: "The Presdt very coolly telegraphed me yesterday that he thought I had better break the enemy's lines at once! I was much tempted to reply that he had better come & do it himself." McClellan refused to be goaded into an attack. Yorktown would be reduced by a siege.[71]

"IT WAS A DREARY, cheerless, miserable existence for man and mules in front of Yorktown," remembered Corporal James A. Wright of the 1st Minnesota. From April 5 to the end of the siege a month later, the men built corduroy roads to haul up the heavy siege artillery, felled trees, dug ditches, constructed works, and served on picket and guard duties. They lacked vegetables and fresh meat. It rained two days out of every three. "The place is," grumbled an officer, "a perfect Paradise for fleas and woodticks." They bore it patiently, however, "though often at the expense of profanity."[72]

Picket duty was miserable and dangerous as the Union works edged closer to the Confederate lines. The Federals rotated in and out of the advance posts every three days, serving for twenty-four hours at a time. A Pennsylvanian described a man's experience at the front: "his shoes are soaked through and through and his feet are damp and cold; . . . his garments are all dripping with wet, and that if he rests it must be upon the ground; . . . that his food is hard crackers and raw pork, with, perhaps, a cup of coffee." Officers even forbade the men to smoke their pipes.[73]

As the siege progressed, the arrival of Johnston's entire army brought Southern numbers to 70,000, facing slightly more than 100,000

Northerners. Many of them had never been in such close proximity to their opponents for such a length of time. They commented about the "zish" of a bullet through the air and the particular sound of an artillery shell, which a New Yorker described as "a hum like twenty thousand bumble bees." Familiarity with the distinctive noises lessened fears. "We have got a little used to the rebel shell," a corporal wrote home, "so that we do not crouch and cringe quite so much when one comes hissing over. When one of them bursts, just before reaching us, the pieces that fly and scatter make the awfulest buzzing you ever heard."[74]

The siege operations proceeded methodically and slowly. The rains and wretched roads brought the movement of heavy-caliber cannon from Fort Monroe to Yorktown to a crawl. When he had the guns in place, McClellan planned to assail the enemy works with these artillery pieces and naval guns. He assigned Brigadier General Fitz John Porter to oversee the work. Calling him "Director of the Siege," McClellan sent all orders through Porter and conferred with him daily.[75]

Among the army's senior leadership, division commander Porter had emerged as McClellan's most trusted subordinate, or as a headquarters staff officer said, his "favorite general." The two men had known each other since their years at the academy, where Porter was in the class ahead of McClellan's. A native of New Hampshire, with his father, uncle, and cousin in the navy, Porter had distinguished himself in Mexico and in various posts before the war. He shared McClellan's social and political conservatism and endorsed the commanding general's cautious strategy. A handsome, even-tempered man, Porter was, according to an aide, "not a man who talks much," noting "one can rely on what General Porter says."[76]

McClellan's appointment of Porter rankled the brigadier's superior officers and elicited much grumbling. Third Corps commander Samuel Heintzelman related in his journal: "The conduct of General McClellan is causing great dissatisfaction in this Army, particularly about General Porter. No less than three generals report to me about it, and one of them this morning was afraid his name would have to be changed to Porter before he would be able to do anything." A clerk at headquarters asserted that most of the army's ranking generals "never go to McClellan's headquarters to consult about the military situation." A critic of McClellan,

Brigadier General Philip Kearny, thought, however, that Porter was one of the army's "superior generals." When William Franklin arrived with his division, he and Porter comprised McClellan's inner circle.[77]

McClellan's and Porter's efforts neared completion during the first week of May. McClellan expected to open fire on the Confederate works on either May 5 or 6. On the morning of May 4, however, the Yankees awoke to deserted Rebel lines. During the night, Joseph Johnston had pulled his army away from the muzzles of Union cannon. All night the Southerners plodded through the darkness, an ordeal of mired artillery pieces and wagons shouldered out of the muck by infantrymen. Rebel cavalrymen rimmed the rear of the columns on two roads. A rear guard halted at Williamsburg while the army's main body proceeded up the Peninsula.[78]

The Federals greeted the abandoned works with cheers and the music of bands. Some members of the army were disappointed that the Rebels had escaped unpunished, but that seemed not to be the prevailing view. McClellan ordered cavalry units and two infantry divisions in pursuit. Although it had taken the army a month to seize Yorktown and to open the Peninsula for an advance, McClellan had accomplished it with minimal casualties. On May 3, he penned a familiar complaint to Ellen: "I feel that the fate of a nation depends upon me, & I feel that I have not one single friend at the seat of Govt—any day may bring an order relieving me from command—if such a thing should be done our cause is lost."[79]

Chapter 5

Along the Chickahominy

JOSEPH HOOKER AND PHILIP KEARNY shared the spirit of warriors. A fire burned within each man, stoked by personal ambition, aggressiveness, and confidence. To them, warfare favored the bold, and they had chafed under George McClellan's cautious generalship. Outspoken and faultfinding, they had failed to hide their criticisms of the army commander. In an army confined to a narrow road, Hooker and Kearny followed another path, toward a rendezvous of kindred souls.[1]

With much in common, they were, in many ways, starkly different men. A native of Massachusetts, the forty-seven-year-old Hooker was an academy graduate, Class of 1837, and a Mexican War veteran. While on garrison duty in California in the 1850s, he cultivated "bad habits and excesses"—too much liquor and too many women. He left the army, failed at business, and amassed gambling debts and legal problems. When the war began, Hooker traveled east, and despite Winfield Scott's effort to stall an appointment, he received a brigadiership. McClellan then assigned him to divisional command. Among his fellow officers, stories of his California years had preceded him.[2]

Tall and strikingly handsome, Hooker possessed an engaging personality and polished manners. He loved to talk, savored army gossip, and seldom hesitated to criticize fellow officers. His enemies—there would be a host of them—regarded him as "thoroughly unprincipled." An "all-consuming" ambition and undoubted self-confidence drove Hooker. War intoxicated him and offered salvation for a troubled life. As a gambler, he liked the odds.[3]

Unlike Hooker, Kearny had a renowned reputation in the army. A wound had cost him his left arm in Mexico, and his exploits in the war had moved Scott to call him "the bravest man I ever saw, and a perfect soldier." An inheritor of vast wealth, he had been tainted by an adultery scandal, which led officials of his native New York to refuse him a commission when the war began. He had lived, however, for nearly a decade in New Jersey. Consequently, the state's governor offered him a brigadiership of volunteers and command of the 1st New Jersey Brigade, which had been in the army at Bull Run. In turn, President Lincoln approved the appointment, and Kearny joined the army.[4]

Shortly after Kearny assumed command of the brigade, he wrote, "I am shocked at the conditions I have found . . . but those wild lads are in for an even greater shock." He instituted strict discipline and oversaw countless hours of drill. The general, an officer soon complained, "was hell bent to perfect the brigade . . . even if he had to run us all into the ground to do it." Private Charles Hopkins of the 1st New Jersey declared, "Some swore, some prayed—not very reverently—to be delivered from the thraldom of Phil Kearny." The men marveled at his ability to string together colorful expletives—a "fluent vocabulary of wrath." A private admitted, "I'd sooner be caught in the jaws of a lion than to be a shoulder strap the general find[s] botching his job."[5]

At a review, Kearny had confided to an officer "his ambition is to have the best brigade in the service." In time, his imprint was indelible, and the men "idolized" him. When the government failed to meet the brigade's needs, he purchased the items himself, spending "a mint of money on them." For his own comfort, he outfitted a wagon with carpet, upholstered furniture, and a chest of chilled French wine. He hired a Parisian chef to prepare his meals.[6]

Kearny had a volatile, prickly demeanor. He could be both flattering and icily gruff to people. Ambition consumed him almost as much as it did Hooker. He asserted to his wife in April 1862, "I can command this entire army, as easily, and as perfectly as my now small command."

Although self-assured, he reacted swiftly and heatedly to a real or perceived slight upon his reputation. Privately, he called McClellan "this ass . . . so powerful with figures, but weak with men." Kearny was preeminently a man of action and bristled under McClellan's strategy.[7]

In March 1862, McClellan offered Kearny command of a division, but the brigadier declined when he could not take his New Jersey brigade with him. McClellan wrote after the war that he had not given Kearny one of the first divisions the previous summer because "I had not sufficient confidence in his brains." Finally, when Major General Charles S. Hamilton was relieved of command of a Third Corps division in a dispute with Samuel Heintzelman, Kearny accepted command on May 3, a day before the Federals entered Yorktown's deserted works.[8]

It was this pair of men, the army's most aggressive fighters, who led the Union pursuit on May 5, 1862. Hooker's division marched in the van as torrents of rain pelted the ranks and turned the roads into "pudding." Before 6:00 A.M., the Yankees found Confederate General Joseph Johnston's rear guard, deployed east of Williamsburg in Fort Magruder and a series of other earthen redoubts. Major General James Longstreet's division manned the works and occupied the old colonial capital. Longstreet had orders to delay the Federals until the army's wagons had passed safely up the Peninsula. A Union artillery officer wrote of Hooker on this day, "His great idea was to go ahead quick until you ran against the enemy, and then fight him."[9]

A Massachusetts private told his mother in a letter that it was "a terrible morning for a fight." It never improved. The rain poured down, saturating the ground, soaking uniforms, and fouling weapons. For nearly twelve hours, the opponents slugged it out. The combat began with an artillery duel and escalated into bloody infantry attacks and counterattacks. Hooker's men went in, recoiled, pounded back Rebel charges, clung to the muddy ground, and used up their ammunition. Hooker and Longstreet fed all of their brigades into the battle and summoned reinforcements.[10]

The Union high command left Hooker's troops isolated and unsupported until late in the afternoon. With McClellan still at Yorktown, directing another operation, Edwin Sumner commanded the pursuit of three corps. He seemed unmoved by the sounds of the combat and unable to get additional units to advance to the field. Third Corps commander Heintzelman wrote in his journal that Sumner "behaved so strangely." McClellan stated to his wife after the battle, "Sumner had proved that he was even a greater fool than I had supposed & had come within an ace of having us defeated."[11]

Finally, Sumner instructed Kearny to march to the action. The van of Kearny's column arrived about four o'clock as many of Hooker's fought-out men streamed to the rear. Kearny spurred his horse to the front to draw enemy fire and locate their lines. When he met Heintzelman, he exclaimed, "General, I can make men follow me to hell." He brought forward five regiments, shouting to them to "give the steel don't wait to shoot." One of Kearny's men admitted to his family, "At first my heart failed me but I kept up courage, trusting in God and my bayonet, soon forgot all and was as cool as ever."[12]

Michiganders and New Yorkers charged across the muddy ground, stabilizing the Union line. Kearny watched the attack from his horse as calm "as if he was reviewing his troops." A lieutenant in the 2nd Michigan wrote afterward: "A good deal has been said abt brave men in the late fight. I saw some but none like Gen. Kearney." The division commander ordered Federal cavalry on the left to charge, but they stayed put. The combat before Fort Magruder finally subsided. A Southerner remarked later "it was the prettiest fight I ever saw."[13]

The battle's final action occurred on the Union right, where five regiments, under Brigadier General Winfield Scott Hancock, assailed the Rebel flank. Like Hooker and Kearny, Hancock seemed to own a battlefield. McClellan called him a "superb presence." The thirty-eight-year-old Pennsylvanian and West Pointer had already become renowned for his physical bearing—"the best looking officer in the army," in the view of many. His unbending discipline and his rich vocabulary of fiery oaths only enhanced the image. "Hancock," declared a fellow general, "always swore at everybody," and according to one of his men, he "reached the highest degree of perfection in cursing at his volunteer troops."[14]

Hancock's men overran a redoubt before repulsing a spirited assault by Brigadier General Jubal A. Early's Virginians. The Yankees unleashed a furnace of musketry, shattering the Southern ranks. It was a needless assault and a bloody slaughter. Darkness ended the combat, with Longstreet's troops retiring into the night. In his telegram to the War Department, McClellan declared that Hancock's "conduct was brilliant in the extreme." To Ellen, he wired, "Hancock was superb." It was this latter description that was made public, and the tall, neatly attired brigadier had a nickname, "Hancock the Superb."[15]

Union casualties approached 2,300, out of 14,600 engaged; Confederate losses exceeded 1,800, out of 12,500 engaged. Hooker's and Kearny's troops sustained the most casualties, nearly 2,100. The 70th New York of the Excelsior Brigade lost 330 in killed, wounded, and missing, the highest of any Federal regiment. Hancock's regiments suffered only 126 casualties. For a rear guard engagement, Williamsburg had been a bloody affair.[16]

Besides Hancock, brigadier generals Hiram G. Berry and David B. Birney earned the praises of their superior officers. Both men commanded brigades under Kearny. Heintzelman wrote that Berry's "energy saved the battle at Williamsburg." A rough-hewn Mainer, Berry was, in the words of a fellow officer, "a plain, straight-forward man, tall and broad-shouldered" with "very little of a military air." He looked more like "an honest farmer" than a general. A businessman and politician, he had led the 4th Maine until his promotion to brigadier.[17]

Like Berry, Birney had no prior military experience and had entered service as colonel of a volunteer regiment, the 23rd Pennsylvania. The son of the noted abolitionist James G. Birney, the brigadier was a thin, dignified, somewhat aloof man. A private described him graphically: "He reminds me of a graven image and could act as a bust for his own tomb, being utterly destitute of color. As for his countenance, it is as expressionless as a Dutch cheese." Kearny said of him after the battle, "His genius of command was especially conspicuous on this day."[18]

McClellan's commendation of Hancock and failure to praise Hooker, Kearny, and their troops ignited a furor within the Third Corps. In Hooker and Kearny's collective judgment, Hancock and his men had done little, or as Kearny argued, had driven only "a paltry few of the enemy, with a *pittance* of a loss." The uproar began when the Philadelphia *Inquirer* published a copy of McClellan's telegram on May 10. Hooker and Kearny deluged Heintzelman with complaints. "The telegraph does us grave injustice," the corps commander wrote. Heintzelman discussed it with McClellan, who sent a second telegram the next day, noting the contributions of Heintzelman's command.[19]

Hooker's and Kearny's performances merited official recognition. Kearny confided to a friend that McClellan had made him "the marked victim of his indirect injustice." As for Hooker, Kearny wrote privately: "Joe detests Little Mac [the troops' nickname for McClellan] worse than a kid hates sulphur and molasses. . . . He cannot abide sight, taste or smell of McClellan." Ironically for Hooker, he became known to the public after Williamsburg as "Fighting Joe Hooker." Allegedly a typesetter for a New York City newspaper earlier had headlined a story with "Fighting—Joe Hooker." Although Hooker disliked the nickname, it stuck. In the end, Williamsburg's aftermath only intensified Hooker's and Kearny's dislike of the army commander.[20]

In McClellan's estimation, however, the engagement had nearly been a defeat because of the bungling of Sumner, Heintzelman, and Keyes. He had remained at Yorktown during the fighting—assured by Sumner that it was proceeding well—until an aide reported, "General you have three old women in the advance." McClellan rode to the scene "like a rocket" and arrived at Sumner's headquarters as the combat began to subside. He ordered up reinforcements and undoubtedly fumed about his senior generals' mishandling of the battle. On May 8, he wired Secretary of War Stanton, "I wish either to return to the organization by Divisions or else be authorized to relieve incompetent Commanders of Army Corps."[21]

Lincoln responded to McClellan's telegram on May 9, granting him authority to dissolve the corps. The president then wrote him a private letter: "I think it indispensable for you to know how your struggle against it [the corps organization] is received in quarters which we cannot entirely disregard. It is looked upon as merely an effort to pamper one or two pets, and to persecute and degrade their supposed rivals. . . . I am constantly told . . . that you consult and communicate with nobody but General Fitz John Porter, and perhaps General Franklin. . . . Are you strong enough, even with my help—to set foot upon the necks of Sumner, Heintzelman, and Keyes all at once? This is a practical and very serious question for you."[22]

McClellan heeded Lincoln's advice. Instead of dismantling the corps, he created two provisional corps, the Fifth and Sixth, assigning Porter and Franklin, respectively, to command. Porter's Fifth Corps consisted of his own division and Brigadier General George Sykes's division of Regular Army units, while the Sixth Corps included Franklin's and William Smith's divisions. Brigadier General George W. Morell succeeded Porter, and Brigadier General Henry Slocum replaced Franklin in division command. The reorganization left Heintzelman and Keyes with two divisions in each corps. McClellan's action only exacerbated the ill feelings and jealousies within the army's senior leadership. Franklin admitted that before the new corps were organized he had "purposely kept away from [army] HdQrs for days together in order to silence slanderous tongues."[23]

McClellan issued the order for the new corps on May 18, nearly a fortnight after the Federal pursuit up the Peninsula had resumed. During those intervening days, the army had plodded along on the miserable roads, averaging about six miles a day. More rain churned up more mud. A feeble effort by Franklin to interdict the Confederate retreat at Eltham's Landing on the York River on May 7 failed. Three days later McClellan wired the War Department that he expected "a life and death contest" near the Confederate capital and required "every man that the Department can send me."[24]

For the men in the ranks, the march up the Peninsula became a wretched crawl with sickness and a shortage of food. They cursed the mud—"If sacred things are the things mostly damned by profane lips," grumbled a New Yorker, "then the soil of Virginia may be entitled to the name and all the honors." Commissary and quartermaster details strained under the difficulties of supplying the troops over the horrible roads. Hundreds left the ranks ill with typhoid fever, malaria, diarrhea, and scurvy. Typhoid or camp fever, "the damned disease," was "much more feared than Rebel bullets," asserted a private. Many probably shared the view of a surgeon, who wrote his wife, "I shall feel that every step towards Richmond is so many steps towards home, for I anticipate that that will be the end of our journey."[25]

As the pursuit proceeded, McClellan issued strict orders about respecting Southern civilians' private property and against pillaging. The troops, however, ignored the proclamation, roaming through the countryside and removing pieces of furniture and other items from houses. They found many deserted residences, except for "very bitter" women and slaves. The plight of bondsmen evoked sympathy among some of the Yankees. The slaves, wrote a signal corpsman, "are in miserable condition & the huts they live in would not be considered up north fit for animals." A lieutenant explained the soldiers' attitude: "Our men are becoming vindictive & revengeful very fast at the sight of their dead comrades & dislike even to help bury the enemies' dead."[26]

Advance elements of the army approached the Chickahominy River on May 17. The stream, northeast of Richmond, coursed in a southeasterly direction across the Peninsula to the James River. Two days earlier Johnston's Rebels had crossed it, the last natural barrier between the Confederate capital and the Yankees, and burned the bridges behind them. During their withdrawal, the Southerners had abandoned Norfolk and scuttled the CSS *Virginia*, the *Monitor*'s ironclad foe. With the *Virginia* gone, the James lay open to the Union navy. On May 15, however, Confederate batteries on Drewry's Bluff, eight miles downriver from Richmond, repulsed a pair of gunboats. As McClellan's troops reached the Chickahominy, the enemy retired behind fieldworks only three miles from the city.[27]

During the next week the Federals deployed along the Chickahominy. The army's Volunteer Engineer Brigade, comprised of the 15th and 50th New York regiments, began repair of the destroyed bridges and construction of new spans. It was a daunting task, as the contrary river rose swiftly and flooded bottomlands after rainstorms. "This d____d Chickahominy" was how an engineer officer described it. But within days, the New Yorkers had erected two trestle bridges at the site of Bottom's Bridge. Upriver, soldiers from two Second Corps regiments built a pair of spans, with one of the units using grapevines to lash trees together. They finished what came to be called the Grapevine Bridge and the other one on May 30. By mid-June the Federals had ten bridges across the stream, which a general called "one of the most formidable obstacles that could be to the advance of the army."[28]

While the engineer regiments labored at bridge building, other details put up piers at White House on the Pamunkey River, where McClellan had established the army's main supply depot. The single-track Richmond and York River Railroad ran from White House across the Peninsula to the capital. Crews repaired it and had trains running by May 24, and it would serve as the army's main lifeline for the next five weeks. With roughly 100,000 men and thousands of horses and mules, the army needed about 700 tons of food and forage daily. This gargantuan appetite placed "almost unbearable demands" upon commissary, quartermaster, and ordnance bureaus. They managed to sustain the army, but a shortage of fresh vegetables resulted in mounting cases of sickness. At one point, more than 25,000 troops were on sick call.[29]

Although the size of his army stretched the limits of his logistical departments, McClellan had kept urging the War Department for more troops. Still convinced he faced a numerically superior foe, he wired Stanton and Lincoln with his requests, stating in one to the president, "I beg that you will cause this Army to be reinforced without delay by all the disposable troops of the Government." Privately, he described the administration as "those hounds in Washington," and told his friend Ambrose Burnside: "The Government have deliberately placed me in this position. If I win, the greater the glory. If I lose, they will be damned forever, both by God and men."[30]

On May 18, McClellan received a telegram from Stanton notifying him that the president had directed Irvin McDowell to join McClellan from Fredericksburg by an overland march. McDowell would start south as soon as a division from Nathaniel Banks's department joined him. McDowell was instructed to "hold yourself always in such position to cover the capital of the nation against a sudden dash of any large body of the rebel forces." In turn, McClellan should extend his right flank to the north and west to link up with McDowell. On May 24, however, Lincoln canceled McDowell's march as events in the Shenandoah Valley upended Federal plans.[31]

The Confederate offensive in that region owed its genesis to a possible union between McClellan and McDowell. General Robert E. Lee, military advisor to Jefferson Davis, believed that if the two Federal commands combined, Richmond's defenders could be crushed between an anvil and hammer of Northern might, and the capital would fall. Working with Major General Thomas J. "Stonewall" Jackson, Lee saw an opportunity to disrupt Union operations with a strike in the Shenandoah Valley. Jackson started forth on May 3, and for the next six weeks baffled his opponents, advanced to the Potomac River, and fought four successful engagements. Jackson's brilliant campaign altered the strategic balance in Virginia.[32]

With Jackson's "foot cavalry" near the Potomac, Lincoln reacted to the threat by halting McDowell—as Lee had hoped—and issuing orders to bag the Confederates. He also prodded McClellan, "I think the time is near when you must either attack Richmond or give up the job and come to the defence of Washington." The president's plan to capture Jackson's force failed, however, because of inept Federal generalship. The consequences of his decision to redirect McDowell's troops were far-reaching.[33]

For his part, McClellan viewed Jackson's operations correctly as a diversion. On the day he learned of Jackson's attack on Banks's troops, May 24, units of the Fourth Corps crossed to the south side of the Chickahominy, followed by the Third Corps. The Federal advance pushed forward to Seven Pines, a crossroads named for the loblolly pine trees at the junction. The Second, Fifth, and Sixth corps remained north of the river. McClellan stated later in his report that he held back the three corps to protect his supply line and to be in position to cooperate with McDowell when the latter resumed his overland advance.[34]

It was a dangerous division of the army. The fickle Chickahominy was prone to a rapid rise after a heavy rainfall, which could isolate the Third and Fourth corps, whose forward lines were within six miles of Richmond. Characteristically, McClellan would blame the administration for the campaign's eventual outcome, attributing it to the separation of the corps along the river.[35]

Was McClellan's assessment fair or was he, once again, shifting responsibility to others for his own failings? At first, Lincoln reacted to Jackson's movement to the Potomac by insuring Washington's safety. When he concluded, as McClellan had, that it was a diversion, he tried to punish, even capture, Jackson's army. Before the Valley campaign had ended, he notified McClellan that he would reinforce him with five regiments from Baltimore and the Pennsylvania Reserve Division from McDowell's command. Unquestionably, had Lincoln released most of McDowell's force, perhaps 30,000 men, it could have posed a dire threat to the Confederate capital. But what assurance did he have in risking his own capital's security that McClellan would take the offensive upon

McDowell's arrival? When he had recently urged McClellan to "either attack Richmond or give up the job," the army commander replied, "the time is very near when I shall attack."[36]

During the final week of May, as a recurrence of malaria put McClellan in bed, he seemed optimistic about the prospects, writing to Ellen: "My men are in such excellent condition & such good spirits that I cannot doubt the result. I feel that we must beat the rebels & I hope end the war." His mood brightened even more when on May 27 units of the Fifth Corps attacked a small Confederate force at Hanover Court House, north of Richmond. The Rebels fought stubbornly, but Porter's numerical advantage prevailed, driving the enemy to the west. McClellan described it as "a glorious victory" to the War Department.[37]

The officers and men shared McClellan's sanguine view. A Pennsylvania private called Richmond "the Doomed City." A New York private assured his parents that the city's defenders "will shurly git a flogin there for Mccleland is a long headed buger." Lieutenant Colonel Patrick R. Guiney of the 9th Massachusetts declared to his wife: "The Army of the Potomac tramples on the hills of Virginia with all the pride and conscious power of a God upon Olympus. *We cannot be beaten.*" Although the men believed they would ultimately prevail, "they don't anticipate much childs play."[38]

In the "Doomed City," meanwhile, Joseph Johnston's time had run out. Like McClellan, he had been in conflict with his administration over strategy since he had abandoned Yorktown. Earlier, when the Cabinet discussed the possible evacuation of Richmond, Lee exclaimed, with uncharacteristic fervor, "Richmond must not be given up; it shall not be given up!" As the Federals edged closer, pressure on Johnston mounted to strike the enemy. He settled on an attack on the isolated Union Third and Fourth corps south of the river in the Seven Pines–Fair Oaks area. He planned it for the morning of May 31. During the night of May 30–31, as if ordained, a thunderstorm lashed the region with heavy downpours and rapidly swelled the Chickahominy, further endangering the two isolated Federal corps.[39]

MISUNDERSTANDINGS, JAMMED ROADS, and confusion delayed the Confederate assault until after noon on May 31. Johnston's plan targeted the Union troops at Seven Pines and Fair Oaks Station on the Richmond and York River Railroad, a mile northwest of the former village. Roads led from Richmond through each place, and the Southerners followed them. Johnston had committed twenty-three of the army's twenty-seven brigades to the offensive, amounting to 42,000 men.[40]

Ahead of the oncoming Rebels lay Brigadier General Silas Casey's Fourth Corps division. The command was the army's worst division, comprised of inexperienced regiments that had been organized from the Provisional Division before the campaign began. Two days earlier, an inspector reported that the unit had been seriously weakened by sickness and straggling, lacked discipline and efficient officers, and neglected assigned duties. "The men are," he wrote, "generally good material." It counted probably 3,600 in the ranks when Major General Daniel Harvey Hill's Confederate division spearheaded the assault.[41]

After the battle, McClellan wired the War Department that Casey's division "gave way unaccountably and discreditably." Within the army his report became accepted as true. In fact, except for Casey's pickets, his men fought stubbornly behind fieldworks and an open redoubt— subsequently called "Casey's Redoubt." The Federal troops held on, unsupported, for an hour. Eventually, corps commander Erasmus Keyes reinforced them with Brigadier General Darius N. Couch's division.[42]

Earlier in the day Keyes and Couch had examined the corps's lines at Seven Pines. According to Couch, Keyes did "nothing" in preparation for a possible assault, as he did not share "my anxiety." When the combat erupted, Keyes "was much more engaged in looking after his personal effects . . . than his command." He failed to notify Casey that he was sending reinforcements and then ordered Couch's regiments in piecemeal. He alerted Samuel Heintzelman, whose Third Corps lay behind Couch's division, and sent a message to Second Corps commander Edwin Sumner, whose units were posted north of the river. Keyes's performance exposed his unfitness for corps command.[43]

Couch's regiments extended Casey's lines north toward Fair Oaks. When Confederate general Harvey Hill coordinated his attack with all of his four brigades and additional Confederate units came in on his left flank, however, the Southerners overran the Union works and drove Couch's and Casey's men rearward. A Federal described the combat as "one continual sheet of Flames all along our line."[44]

Philip Kearny's Third Corps division, meanwhile, arrived north of Seven Pines. Heintzelman—"a weak old fool" in Kearny's words—parceled out the division's brigades, sending one north toward Fair Oaks, assigning one as a reserve, and leaving Kearny only with Brigadier General Charles Jameson's regiments to meet the charging enemy. The one-armed Kearny rode at the front of the brigade, with a sword in his one hand and the reins of his bridle in his teeth. He shouted to Jameson's Pennsylvanians and New Yorkers: "Hurrah! Boys. Let us at 'em." He had begun calling his troops the "Fighting Division," and he led part of it into the ranks of Rebels.[45]

Jameson's men hit the enemy line with "great impetuosity" but suffered a repulse. Kearny had his bay horse shot from under him. To the north, Colonel Micah Jenkins's South Carolinians scoured Nine Mile Road, which ran between Seven Pines and Fair Oaks, clear of Yankees. The Union Fourth Corps's position at Seven Pines had been swept away to the east. North of Fair Oaks, a third Confederate division had collided with regiments from Couch's division and troops from the Second Corps. The killing and maiming continued.[46]

At 2:30 P.M., Edwin Sumner had received an order from McClellan to cross the Chickahominy and move to the support of Keyes. The previous night's storm, however, had churned the stream into a raging current and had swept away one of the bridges, leaving only the Grapevine Bridge in place. When an engineer officer warned Sumner not to attempt a crossing, he ignored him. He was, remarked a comrade, "not a man to reason with."[47]

At sixty-five years old, Sumner had been in the army for more than four decades. He had earned the nickname "Bull," some said for his booming voice, others because he rushed into action like "a bull in a china shop," and a few claimed that he received it because musket balls allegedly bounced off his thick skull. He was of a singular, stubborn bent of mind, whose narrow focus on a battlefield limited his usefulness at corps command. He had not done well directing the battle at Williamsburg. But on this day he had a direct order, a clear mission, and he would go to the fighting.[48]

Sumner's face, thought a lieutenant, seemed to be "burning with enthusiasm" as he sent his troops across the span. The men's weight stabilized the damaged bridge, and Brigadier General John Sedgwick's three brigades joined Couch's units near a house that belonged to a family named Adams. Sedgwick's division had been Charles Stone's command, with survivors of the Ball's Bluff debacle in the ranks. It had been eight months since that humiliation, a long time to wait for redemption.[49]

Supported by four batteries, the infantrymen deployed into line as the ranks of a Confederate brigade cleared the tree line. Couch's men had repulsed one assault before this second Rebel line appeared. Union cannon exploded and rifles flashed in a volley. A Federal artillery officer described the charge as "the grandest sight I ever witnessed. . . . I never expect to witness another as beautiful a fight if I live to be as old as Methuselah." The Southerners reeled and staggered to the rear. In the dark woods, Joseph Johnston crumpled in the saddle, hit by a bullet and shell pieces.[50]

When the combat had ended, Israel Richardson's Second Corps division joined Sedgwick and extended the line south in the woods toward Seven Pines. The Federals now had five divisions in place—those of Sedgwick, Richardson, Couch, Kearny, and Hooker. During the night, McClellan issued instructions "to hold firm and repulse every and any attack" on June 1. To the west, Major General Gustavus Smith succeeded Johnston and ordered a renewal of the attack.[51]

The Southerners came on soon after daylight toward the Union brigades of Oliver Howard, William French, and Thomas Meagher of Richardson's division. The fighting raged along a section of the railroad between Fair Oaks and Seven Pines. Thick smoke and rifle flashes filled the woods as the opponents battled each other in thrusts and counterthrusts. Howard described the enemy's fire as "rapid, well-directed, and fatal." Alabamians, Virginians, and Louisianans fought men from Pennsylvania, New York, and New Hampshire. A Federal private stated, "we did not think of the danger we were in but of little else then to load and fire as fast as possible."[52]

In the Federal ranks, Fighting Dick Richardson rode along the front, sending regiments in to bolster the line and rallying troops. Dressed as usual in nondescript clothes, the general seemed to be everywhere. His appearance on horseback had often evoked laughter from his men. He always took "hold of the mane with one hand to keep from falling off," according to a lieutenant. But his troops regarded him "as one of them; he had their confidence and affection, and they willingly followed him."[53]

Several of Richardson's subordinates and regiments distinguished themselves in the action. Brigade commander Howard skillfully led his command, despite having two horses shot from under him and suffering two wounds. He relinquished command after a bullet shattered a bone in his right arm, which necessitated amputation below the elbow.[54]

A native of Maine, Howard was renowned for his religious piety. He conducted frequent prayer meetings and church services in the brigade and "bedeviled his staff" to participate. While a cadet at West Point, he greeted young women by asking "if she had reflected on the goodness of God during the past night."[55]

Colonel Edward E. Cross of the 5th New Hampshire succeeded Howard. The tall, strapping Cross possessed a fiery demeanor worthy of his New Englanders. Before he led them in an attack, he exclaimed: "Charge them like hell, boys! Show 'em you are damned Yankees." When he fell wounded, the 61st New York's Colonel Francis Barlow took command. Like Cross, the native New Yorker and Harvard graduate plunged into combat with ferocity. His men had hated him initially for his harsh discipline, but they eventually adapted to this tough, icy, and earnest man. On this day, as he reported, his regiment "calmly and faithfully performed its duty."[56]

At a critical point in the fighting, a pair of New York regiments, the 69th and 88th, charged across the railroad and "fought like tigers." They belonged to the Irish Brigade, a command recruited and organized in New York City by Thomas Meagher during the previous fall. Originally a three-month unit, the 69th New York had fought at Bull Run, where Meagher, one of its captains, had rallied its ranks twice. Upon the regiment's return to New York, it was reorganized into a three-year command and became a part of Meagher's new brigade, comprised initially of the 63rd, 69th, and 88th. In time, a regiment of Irishmen from Boston and one from Philadelphia joined its ranks.[57]

Meagher was as colorful a fellow as the men he led. A native of Ireland, he had been deported from his homeland and shipped to Australia after his involvement in the 1848 rebellion against England. Escaping from the penal colony, he arrived in America in 1852, received a hero's welcome, and became one of the most famous and outspoken advocates of Irish independence. His appointment to a brigadiership resulted from his performance at Bull Run and his standing in the Irish community. A soldier offered another explanation, "They were most excellent soldiers in a fight, but it took a man of iron character and great tact to command them, and he was the right man in the proper place." Meagher possessed, however, the "besetting sin" of "intemperance."[58]

Shortly after the Irishmen entered the fighting, the combat ended about mid-morning. Its final action occurred near Seven Pines, where units from Hooker's and Kearny's divisions repulsed an attack by Brigadier General George Pickett's Virginia brigade. The woods and open fields around Seven Pines and Fair Oaks now resembled, in the words of a sergeant, "a graveyard." Total casualties exceeded 11,000—Union losses reported at 5,031 killed, wounded, and missing, and Confederate at 6,134. The two-day battle was the bloodiest to date in the East, with a 13 percent casualty rate among the units engaged. Union field hospitals looked "like a perfect butcher's shambles." Heintzelman confessed in his journal: "I am getting used to the amputations and groans. I hear them all the time."[59]

Had problems not plagued the Confederate offensive—miscommunication, units jammed up on the same road, failure between Johnston and wing commander James Longstreet to coordinate attacks, and Johnston's wound—the Union Third and Fourth corps could have incurred a severe defeat. The wooded terrain, stubborn resistance, and Sumner's aggressive action to cross the river spared the Federals. Although Johnston had taken advantage of the divided Union army, McClellan placed the blame on Casey's division, a criticism that infuriated the brigadier's men. In his report, McClellan stated that Casey "had failed to infuse proper morale in his troops." Casey defended his command from "the unmerited aspersion" by arguing that his men fought for three hours "without re-enforcement of a single man at my first line." By implication, he attributed this failure to Keyes.[60]

McClellan, who was still weak from the effects of malaria, did not come to the battlefield until after the fighting had ended on June 1. He had reached his judgment about the conduct of Casey's troops from an interview with Heintzelman, who also repeated a false report that an officer "found more men bayoneted and shot within their shelter-tents than outside of them." Consequently, on June 7, McClellan consolidated Casey's three brigades into two and redesignated it as the Second Division. Sixteen days later, he relieved Casey of command and ordered him to the supply base at White House. The brigadier was eventually assigned to the training of new troops, a duty he performed for the remainder of the war.[61]

On June 2, McClellan issued a proclamation to the army. "I have fulfilled at least a part of my promise to you," he began; "you are now face to face with the rebels, who are at bay in front of the Capital. The final and decisive battle is at hand." He praised their conduct in the campaign's engagements and then concluded: "Soldiers! I will be with you in this battle and share its dangers with you. Our confidence in each other is now founded upon the past. Let us strike the blow which is to restore peace and union to this distracted land. Upon your valor, discipline and mutual confidence that result depends."[62]

ON THE DAY OFFICERS read McClellan's proclamation to the troops, Sergeant Charles E. Perkins of the 2nd Rhode Island wrote a letter to his sister. The army commander, thought Perkins, "wants to save all the men he can. . . . I like to go slow and sure for I know what it is to go in a hurry and come back in a hurrey for I remember I went to buls run once and came back agane and I don't want to see eney more such cind of work."[63]

Perkins must have been satisfied as operations continued "to go slow and sure" throughout June. Many of his fellow soldiers, however, found little to cheer about with each passing day. They had to endure a steady diet of salt pork and hardtack, which the men called "bullet proof hardbread" and "Uncle Sam's pies." Visits by sutlers, with their various food items and other wares, were, scoffed a private, "almost as rare as those of angels." Private A. W. Stillwell of the 5th Wisconsin described the month as "digging, entrenching, mortifying, and dying in the Chickamoniny swamps."[64]

Cases of typhoid, malaria, and dysentery reached "almost an epidemic," overwhelming the medical staffs. Symptoms of scurvy appeared because of the lack of fresh vegetables. "The life of the men is *horrible*," Major Thomas W. Hyde of the 7th Maine wrote home. "We have averaged one death per day ever since we came out." A hospital steward confessed to his wife, "to get an idea of the true state of the army sufferings you must visit the hospitals and witness the sufferings of its inmates all kinds of diseases prevail and death in its most hideous forms is of daily occurrences." A 38th New York sergeant declared that with the increasing illnesses and deaths, "All seem to complain of the unnecessary delay in opening the battle, and if things go on much longer, there will be no army to fight with."[65]

During the month, McClellan shifted all of the corps, except the Fifth, south of the Chickahominy. The Federals pushed their lines closer to the enemy's works, and clashes between skirmishers, bolstered by exchanges of artillery fire, occurred almost daily. Duty on the skirmish or picket lines took more men's lives. "Line fighting is barbarous," asserted a captain, "but skirmishing is savage—nay, devilish." He believed that to take deliberate aim at another man and shoot him was unchristian. A Massachusetts soldier recalled these weeks at the front: "Picket-life in White-oak Swamp was diversified, and full of incident. Some regiments when engaged in this duty were as quiet as when in camp. Others would begin to fire the moment their men were posted, and keep it up for twenty-four hours, until they were relieved."[66]

A unit particularly good at this deadly work was the 1st United States Sharpshooters. Recruited, organized, and commanded by Colonel Hiram Berdan, a renowned antebellum marksman, the regiment had a distinctive reputation in the army. A member qualified for the command by putting ten shots in a ten-inch target at two hundred yards. The men wore dark green uniform coats—"green breeches" as they were called—and carried Sharps breechloading rifles, "a very superior weapon especially for skirmishers," according to Berdan. The colonel was not a popular officer with the men, who claimed he never fulfilled recruitment promises. They called themselves "Unfortunate Soldiers Sadly Sold."[67]

The enemy remained to the Yankees, as a Pennsylvanian put it, "traitors and demons to the best of governments." Private David Archer of the 20th Indiana, a unit that joined the army during June, bluntly wrote, "I think that the old devil is in me and I don't think that I will ever get it out until I get to kill a god damn Rebel and then I can die with a clear conscience." They feared death, but as a lieutenant said, "It seems that the thought that one was doing his duty would over balance all other considerations."[68]

It was this steadfastness to duty and to country that sustained them. The 2nd Michigan's Lieutenant Charles B. Haydon expressed their attitude well in a June 14 letter: "The courage & spirit of the men is however unbroken. The nearer they approach death the stronger is their hatred of Secession & the dearer is the sight of the true flag. The soldier who lives on two cups of black muddy coffee & a few squares of hard tack per day, who endures the scorching heat & the damp and chills of night, who drags his weary limbs through [mud] or dust to days of toil & nights of watching finds no fault with McClellan. He would give his life for him or for the cause he upholds."[69]

They wanted, however, to have it settled, sooner rather than later. One soldier declared that the swiftest way to have peace was "if General McClelan would take this armey and mach in to the City of Washington and kill every sun of a bich in the White House, this War would end soon." He also admonished his friend at home, "when eney of the Ablinishenist comes in to the store, take your gun and shoot them." In contrast, an army wag started a rumor that Lincoln and Davis had met privately to discuss peace, but "Old Abe said that Jeff should buy the drinks and Jeff thought Abe ought to buy it."[70]

Whenever McClellan appeared in their camps or rode along the lines, the men greeted him "with the wildest enthusiasm." One soldier stepped out of the ranks as he passed one day and exclaimed to him, "you are the only one of the whole crowd of Genls that is worth a damn." The bond between "our little Mac," a favorite expression for him, and the men was undeniable. They believed that with him in command, said an officer, "We are bound to get Richmond and in Richmond they know it." To Ellen, McClellan boasted: "I think there is scarcely a man in this whole army who would not give his life for me & willingly do whatever I ask. I have tried them more than once & whenever I am near they never fail me."[71]

On McClellan's rides among the troops, a cloud of staff officers, couriers, and cavalry escorts accompanied him. It appeared more like an entourage of glittering uniforms than a working staff. A member of it argued later that the men around the general "were the most ungallant, good-for-nothing set of martinets that I have met with. . . . Not a man among them was worth a damn as a military advisor—or had any show of fire or boldness. A self-indulgent and timorous policy seemed to pervade the whole surrounding and the General." A regimental commander stated, "At headquarters they had but one bell, and consequently only one sound was heard—praises of McClellan."[72]

The staff had, however, some highly capable, if not excellent, department heads. Brigadier General Stewart Van Vliet overcame a gargantuan task as chief quartermaster, ably assisted by Colonel Rufus Ingalls. Brigadier General John Barnard was the army's chief engineer, and Brigadier General Andrew A. Humphreys acted as chief of topographical engineers. Colonel Charles P. Kingsburg oversaw the army's ordnance needs. Finally, Colonel Henry F. Clarke served as chief commissary. The army could not have been sustained on the Peninsula without their services.[73]

Although Brigadier General Randolph Marcy, McClellan's father-in-law, served as nominal chief of staff, Brigadier General Seth Williams ran headquarters. Described as "the workingman of McClellan's staff" and as "General Mac's head man," Adjutant General Williams was a native of Maine and a West Pointer. A "stumpy red beard framed his broad face and bald head." Congenial, quiet, and modest, he had the perfect temperament for the position. He was, said a fellow officer, "a master of the minuest details of every department and an indefatigable worker." When he spoke, he "cuts off his words and lisps them, and swallows them, and has the true Yankee accent into the bargain." If someone had business at headquarters, they usually dealt with this remarkable aide.[74]

At headquarters, meanwhile, caution prevailed. As he had before Yorktown, McClellan continued to rely on pushing his works closer to the enemy's and bringing up artillery to pound the Confederates. He reiterated to Washington "my inferiority in numbers" and his need for reinforcements. The War Department sent him nine regiments from the garrison at Fort Monroe and transferred George McCall's Pennsylvania Reserve Division from Irvin McDowell's department to the army. When these units arrived, McClellan had about 115,000 present for duty, with at least 90,000 effectives or men available for battle. His opponent counted about 70,000 officers and men in the Richmond defenses, with Stonewall Jackson's command of 18,000 in the Shenandoah Valley.[75]

McClellan's deliberateness gave the Confederates an opportunity to seize the initiative, a vital element in any campaign. He could have shifted the entire army south of the Chickahominy, using the James River as his supply route. He also could have placed the army north of the Chickahominy, maintaining his base at White House, and maneuvered against Richmond from that direction. Instead, he kept Porter's Fifth Corps, reinforced by McCall's division, isolated north of the stream at Mechanicsville. If a daring foe struck Porter and drove his corps beyond the river, the army's right flank would be unhinged and its supply line vulnerable.[76]

In McClellan's mind, his difficulties could be ascribed to the "insane folly behind me." To a staff officer he complained, "The President is opposing him and has written insulting letters or has not answered his communications." George Meade wrote that McClellan "talked very freely of the way in which he had been treated and said positively that had not McDowell's corps been withdrawn, he would long before now have been in Richmond." These familiar rings echoed with a hollowness.[77]

He confided to his wife other reasons for his caution. In a letter of June 22, he stated: "I must not run the slightest risk of disaster, for if anything happened to this army our cause would be lost. I feel too that I must not unnecessarily risk my life—for the fate of my army depends upon me & they all know it." A day later, he confessed to her: "every poor fellow that is killed or wounded almost haunts! My only consolation is that I have honestly done my best to save as many lives as possible & that many others might have done less towards it." It was a prescription for strategic and tactical inertia.[78]

One of McClellan's greatest failings as a general was his lack of appreciation for the weapon he had created. Publicly and privately he had praised the rank and file's devotion to duty and willingness to sacrifice themselves for him and for the cause. But his actions belied his words. There was mettle if not iron will to them, and there would be over time a resiliency that sustained them. McClellan never fully understood this. His unwillingness to risk their lives endangered them more. Before long, however, he and they would learn the consequences of his generalship.

On June 12, Confederate Brigadier General J. E. B. Stuart and twelve hundred cavalrymen started forth on a raid to locate the Union army's right flank north of the Chickahominy and to map the road network between that stream and the Pamunkey River. In four days, Stuart's troopers gathered the intelligence, burned supply wagons and two schooners, destroyed Tunstall's Station on the Richmond and York River Railroad, and rode around the entire Union army, all at a loss of one man. Richmond newspapers hailed Stuart and his men as heroes. For the Federals, it was a humiliating embarrassment. McClellan's policy of parceling out his cavalry regiments to infantry commands and as headquarters escorts left the army with no combined force to interdict and to punish the raiders. It was the new commander of the Confederate Army of Northern Virginia, Robert E. Lee, who had ordered what came to be known as "Stuart's Ride."[79]

When Joseph Johnston had fallen wounded on the evening of May 31, Gustavus Smith had succeeded him. But Jefferson Davis replaced Smith the next morning with Lee, his military advisor. Winfield Scott had regarded Lee, his former staff officer, as the finest soldier in the Regular Army and had offered him command of the Union army after Fort Sumter. Lee rejected it and went with his native Virginia and then the Confederacy. His decision had cost his family its Arlington estate, a sacrifice that a Union soldier thought made Lee "a damd fool" to give up such a home. During the war's first year, Lee had conducted a failed campaign in western Virginia and had overseen the construction of coastal defenses in Georgia and South Carolina, before being ordered to Richmond by Davis. Lee was fifty-five years old when he assumed temporary command of the army. Its officers and men expected Johnston to return.[80]

During the early days of the Peninsula Campaign, McClellan heard a rumor that Lee had replaced Johnston as commander of the army. McClellan sent the information on to Lincoln and then wrote, "I prefer Lee to Johnston—the former is *too* cautious & weak under grave responsibility—personally brave & energetic to a fault, he yet is want- ing in moral firmness when pressed by heavy responsibility & is likely to be timid & irresolute in action." McClellan could not have been more mistaken about a man.[81]

More than any other Confederate general, Lee understood that the Confederacy could not win a long, protracted war. Once the might of Union manpower and matériel was unleashed against the seceded states, the South was doomed to defeat. He dismissed the chimera of intervention by Great Britain and France on the side of the Confeder- acy. He also believed that behind the Union host lay the will of the North's populace to withstand the casualties, sacrifices, and defeats. If that will endured, the South faced certain defeat.[82]

The Confederates must, thought Lee, take the offensive and accept the risks in such a strategy. With the offensive, Lee could dictate opera- tions and acquire and retain the strategic or operational initiative in the East. If Southerners adopted a passive defensive posture, a slow, inevitable death would result. Time pressed against the Confederacy, and Lee planned to stay the darkness by audacity.[83]

Lee would use maneuver, particularly the turning movement, to overcome his opponent's numerical superiority. He sought not to inflict a crippling defeat upon the Federals, but a fatal one. He possessed an apti- tude for warfare, an exceptionable ability to discern strategy and tactics amid war's inherent confusion. When Davis selected Lee to command the army, the conflict in the East followed a different fork in the road.[84]

With gifted subordinates, such as Stonewall Jackson, James Longstreet, Richard S. Ewell, A. P. Hill, D. H. Hill, John Bell Hood, and others, Lee infused his army with an élan and aggressiveness, which contrasted starkly with the mind-set of the senior leadership of the Army of the Potomac. In time, Lee and his generals forged the army into a formidable weapon, unmatched by any other Confederate army. When Lee unsheathed his sword, it changed the war.

For McClellan and the Army of the Potomac, time ran out during June's final week. Using the intelligence obtained by Stuart, Lee ordered Jackson's command from the Valley to Richmond. The Confederates would strike Porter's corps at Mechanicsville and roll up the Union army's right flank. A few days before the Southerners advanced, Philip Kearny wrote to a friend, "McClellan himself will be deceived— killed into procrastination, until the enemy having matured his plans, and massed his troops, will find us in a position, where disaster will be irretrievable."[85]

Chapter 6

"If We Were Defeated, the Army and the Country Would Be Lost"

THE SOUND WAS EERIE — many men who heard it described it as "infernal," as if it came from the bowels of hell. A high-pitched "ki-i," the yell was emitted from the throats of Confederate soldiers on the attack. During the final week of June 1862, this fearsome screech rolled across the woodlots and bottomlands of the Virginia Peninsula, heralding the rise of Southern arms in the East. When the Seven Days Campaign ended on July 1, the "Rebel Yell" echoed across a changed landscape of war.[1]

Ironically, after weeks of slow, methodical Union steps toward Richmond, the overdue reckoning began with an advance by the Federals on June 25. With Fitz John Porter's Fifth Corps north of the Chickahominy, isolated from the rest of the army, George McClellan wanted to shorten the distance to Porter by seizing Old Tavern, a crossroads village. If the Yankees occupied the intersection, they could also move heavy cannon closer to the enemy works.[2]

Joseph Hooker's Third Corps division led the reconnaissance-in-force, colliding with Major General Benjamin Huger's Confederate brigades. The Rebels resisted stubbornly, and Philip Kearny's troops and units from the Second and Fourth corps joined Hooker's men. A Union lieutenant described the enemy as "wretches . . . with their tall hats and brown coats, looking as if they would like to cut our livers out." The fighting at Oak Grove lasted until sunset. In the end, Huger's men held their works. Before the combat had ended, McClellan learned of an approaching whirlwind.[3]

McClellan sent a telegram to Secretary of War Edwin Stanton at 6:15 P.M., June 25, stating that several runaway slaves or "contrabands" had reported that Stonewall Jackson's command was at Hanover Court House, north and west of Porter's position near Mechanicsville. He estimated enemy strength around Richmond at 200,000, and remarked, "I am inclined that Jackson will attack my right and rear." If that were to occur, "this army will do all in the power of men to hold their position and repulse any attack." But if the outcome resulted in "a disaster" for the army, "the responsibility cannot be thrown on my shoulders. It must rest where it belongs," with the administration in Washington.[4]

Stanton forwarded the telegram to Abraham Lincoln. The president was surely tired of reading another such dispatch from McClellan. He replied the next day, noting that the general's assertion as to being overwhelmed by superior numbers and as to the responsibility for it "pains me very much." Continuing, "I give you all I can, and act on the presumption that you will do the best you can with what you have, while you continue, ungenerously I think, to assume that I could give you more if I would. I have omitted and shall omit no opportunity to send you re-enforcements whenever I possibly can."[5]

After he had wired Stanton, McClellan visited Porter's headquarters across the Chickahominy and approved the general's dispositions to meet an assault. He instructed his other corps commanders to clear the ground in front of their works. If the enemy attacked, they should "fight behind the lines." Before he slept, he telegraphed the War Department: "Every possible precaution is being taken. If I had another good Division I could laugh at Jackson. The task is difficult but this Army will do its best & will never disgrace the country. Nothing but overwhelming forces can defeat us."[6]

At McClellan's order, then, the Army of the Potomac awaited the coming storm. It had been brewing for ten days, since Jeb Stuart's ride

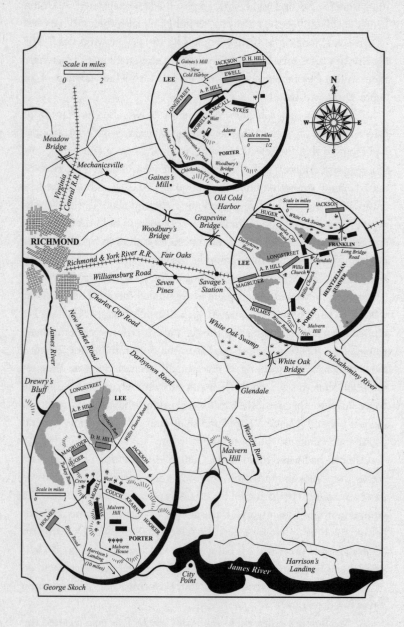

George Skoch

around the Federal army. General Robert E. Lee had met with his senior generals, including Jackson, on June 23, when it was decided to strike Porter's corps near Mechanicsville and roll up McClellan's right flank. Jackson's troops, en route from the Shenandoah Valley, would initiate the offensive, followed by three of the army's other divisions. Lee gambled that his opponent would not exploit the Southerners' weak position south of the Chickahominy, where more than 70,000 Federals opposed fewer than 30,000 Confederates. Lee scheduled Jackson's attack for 3:00 A.M., on June 26.[7]

Porter's roughly 30,000 Northerners manned a strong defensive position east of Mechanicsville behind Beaver Dam Creek. Earthworks strengthened their lines, while to their front open fields stretched west from the swampy creek bottom and steep banks. George McCall's division of Pennsylvania Reserves stood behind the fieldworks, supported by two additional divisions. Sixteen cannon braced the infantry lines. Cavalrymen patrolled Porter's right flank, watching for the arrival of Jackson's troops. If the Confederates attacked frontally, they would plunge into a cauldron of artillery fire and musketry.[8]

The Pennsylvanians had been with the army barely a week, coming from Irvin McDowell's department. Except for the minor affair at Dranesville the previous December, they had been spared from the combat. Three West Pointers—John Reynolds, George Meade, and Truman Seymour—commanded McCall's brigades. On this day, Reynolds's and Seymour's men held the earthworks, with Meade's in reserve.[9]

At six feet tall, darkly complexioned, with "piercing, penetrating eyes," Reynolds was an impressive man. McClellan described him as "remarkably brave and intelligent, an honest, true gentleman." He said little, greeted most individuals with a smile, and eschewed the infighting among fellow officers. As a general, he worked indefatigably. Although he believed that the administration interfered inordinately into army affairs, he kept his own counsel. He was popular with both his fellow Pennsylvanians and fellow generals. "His look and manner," thought one of his men, "denoted uncommon coolness."[10]

It was not until about three o'clock in the afternoon when the Rebels moved to the attack against the Federals. Lee's plan called for

Major General A. P. Hill's division to initiate the assault once Jackson made contact with one of his brigades. But Jackson's column of weary men, harried by Union horsemen, was hours overdue and finally went into bivouac three miles from Porter's flank. With his patience drained and without Lee's blessing, Hill advanced against the Yankees. When Lee learned that Hill had acted without Jackson, he allowed the attack to proceed.[11]

The Southerners never had a chance. Union artillery crews and the Pennsylvanians erased the charges with gales of canister and rifle fire. "The conduct of the troops, most of them for the first time under fire," stated Reynolds of his volunteers, "was all that could be expected." A gunner declared that the enemy was left "laying sweltering in their own blood." It was a simple matter for the Northerners—load, fire, and repeat the procedure. The enemy dead and wounded reminded a Union officer of "flies in a bowl of sugar." Lee's losses approached 1,400; Porter's, less than 400. The Fifth Corps commander claimed later that only 5,000 of his men had been seriously engaged in the repulse of the enemy assaults.[12]

McClellan had joined Porter as the fighting subsided. Jubilant at the result, he issued a dispatch to the army, announcing the victory. South of the river, the troops cheered the news "until it seemed as though pandemonium had broken loose." Officers granted permission for bands to play music for the first time in weeks. It had been a good day for the army, and its members celebrated.[13]

Despite the exultant tone of his message, McClellan faced critical decisions. He had lost the strategic initiative to Lee. If he wanted to retake it, he either could heavily reinforce Porter and make a stand north of the Chickahominy or he could assault the Confederate lines south of the river. Lee had predicated his risky offensive on the belief that McClellan would not strike the weakened defenses in front of Richmond. For McClellan to assail the works, he would have to incur risks, tactics uncharacteristic to his temperament and beliefs.[14]

Earlier in the day, McClellan had instructed Porter to send his wagons and heavy artillery south of the Chickahominy and had directed officers at White House to forward supplies to the front and to prepare to abandon the supply base. During the night, he ordered Porter to withdraw to a stronger defensive position at Gaines's Mill and stressed to the general "the absolute necessity of holding the ground." By these actions, McClellan took preliminary steps for the abandonment of the three-month campaign. An officer assessed the consequences of McClellan's decisions: "He went over to the right and did the very thing necessary for defeat in either case, by ordering his troops to stay there and receive the attack, and letting his troops on the left remain idle."[15]

Porter withdrew from his position at Beaver Dam Creek at daylight on June 27, moving southeast four miles to a plateau behind Boatswain's Swamp. When the Fifth Corps reached the site, Brigadier General George Morell's division filed right into line behind the morass. With a "long white beard," Morell looked more like a biblical prophet than a general, but he was a no-nonsense soldier, clearheaded, and devoted to duty. To his right, Brigadier General George Sykes's brigades of Regular Army and volunteer regiments deployed. Like Morell, Sykes was old army, a tireless and methodical soldier, who "enforced discipline like a machine." His Regulars believed, as one of them put it, "We are the Commanding General's hope and pride, the 'old guard,' etc." Behind Morell's ranks and the "old guard," McCall's Pennsylvanians formed the reserve.[16]

When Lee had the enemy—"those people," he called the Federals—reeling, he pressed the attack. He took the offensive initially to save Richmond and then to "crush" or destroy McClellan's army. With Porter in retreat and with Jackson's troops at hand, Lee ordered his divisions forward in pursuit. By 1:00 P.M., the Rebels had located Porter's corps behind Boatswain's Swamp. The Southerners shifted into battle lines, moving in for the kill.[17]

Confederate artillery crews opened fire on the Northerners. Union officers ordered the soldiers to lie down, and in the words of a New Yorker, "there was not a man in the line that could complain of being too thin at this particular time." Behind the shelling came gray-clad infantrymen, A. P. Hill's Light Division, which had been bloodied the day before. Across the fields and into brush-lined swamps, the Rebels charged, "their piratical flag waving defiantly in the breeze." On the plateau, rifles flashed. Within minutes, the Battle of Gaines's Mill escalated into a fearfulness worse than any prior engagement in the East.[18]

A Pennsylvanian wrote that the combat was "as terrible as human beings can make it." Officers shouted at the men to "give 'em hell," as the Rebels ascended the rise and plunged into the Federal ranks. Men clubbed each other with their rifles. A Union corporal admitted later, "I had a most sincere desire to be somewhere else." The Yankees hammered the Southerners back only to see them come on again. A Berdan Sharpshooter remembered that the flag of the 4th Michigan, posted near the center of the line, had "the stars almost blotted out with blood, and bullet holes exceeding the number of stars."[19]

Along Sykes's front, no troops fought better than the small brigade of two volunteer regiments, the 5th and 10th New York, under Colonel Gouverneur K. Warren. Sykes asserted later of the 5th New York, "*I have always maintained it to be the best volunteer organization I ever knew.*" Recruited in the New York City area by Colonel Hiram Duryée, a wealthy businessman, the members adopted the name Duryée's Zouaves. They soon received the nickname the "Red Devils." When Warren succeeded Duryée in command, they became renowned in the army for their discipline and proficiency in drill. They believed that they were as good soldiers as the Regulars in their division.[20]

Warren was a fellow New Yorker and a graduate of West Point. A physically small man, with a swarthy complexion and intensely black eyes, Warren possessed a keen intellect, read widely, and had been an excellent engineer in the antebellum army. He was inordinately proud, even arrogant, and disdainful toward men whom he regarded as inferior to him. His closest friend was Andrew Humphreys, McClellan's topographical engineer. Warren had visited army headquarters frequently during the weeks on the Peninsula. Few questioned his ability as a soldier.[21]

On this afternoon, Warren led the 5th New York in a riveting counterattack. "The artillery," Warren wrote subsequently, "which had been firing stopped on both sides, and the whole armies were spectators." The Red Devils smashed into the 1st South Carolina Rifles and drove them back. The Zouaves were, declared a Regular, "the peers of any troops on that hard-fought field." Captain John W. Ames of the 11th United States told his parents afterward that the counterattack of the New Yorkers haunted his sleep. Every night, he wrote a week later, he saw a

Zouave, with his arms around a comrade, who was "fairly a dead man, walking in his living friend's support." Ames admitted, "the horrors of sudden, accidental, bloody death are here so much augmented and multiplied."[22]

As the afternoon lengthened, Jackson's men came onto the field and assaulted Porter's position. The corps commander had committed the Pennsylvania Reserves and wired McClellan: "I am pressed hard, very hard. About every Regiment I have has been in action." Without reinforcements, "I am afraid I shall be driven from my position." McClellan had already ordered Brigadier General Henry Slocum's division across the Chickahominy and two Second Corps brigades.[23]

Slocum's men went in as Confederate attacks mounted. Screeching their "ki-i," announcing that hell was coming with them, Texans, Georgians, and Alabamians cracked the Union center. Blue-coated ranks splintered, but a Yankee believed that the day's "most desperate fighting" occurred at this time. At places along the lines, the "slaughter" was hand-to-hand.[24]

Regimental commanders tried to rally their men, refuse flanks, or re-form ranks. Colonels Jesse Gove of the 22nd Massachusetts and John W. McLane of the 83rd Pennsylvania were killed. The Pennsylvanians belonged to the brigade of Brigadier General Daniel Butterfield. Earlier in the action, he had urged McLane's volunteers: "Boys, if they come upon you again, I want you to give it to them! *You are just the boys that can do it.*" Now, he shouted to them to use the bayonet, as he grabbed the regimental colors and waved them at the enemy. Butterfield suffered a wound, but after the war his conduct would earn him a Medal of Honor. The 83rd Pennsylvania and 22nd Massachusetts lost more men killed or mortally wounded than any other Union regiments on the field.[25]

Several Federal units held firm against the Confederate surge. Artillery crews poured canister into the attackers' ranks, and infantry regiments triggered volleys. The 4th New Jersey and 11th Pennsylvania Reserves, advancing together, counterattacked, but were soon surrounded, forcing hundreds to surrender. An ill-advised, even suicidal, mounted charge by the 5th United States Cavalry bought time for some cannon to be saved. As thousands of Yankees streamed toward the river, the Irish Brigade and William French's brigade from the Second Corps arrived and helped stabilize the rear guard line, preventing a headlong rout. Darkness ended the battle.[26]

The Yankees crossed the Chickahominy throughout the night. By daylight, the withdrawal had been completed and the bridges destroyed. In the confusion, John Reynolds and a staff officer became lost, stranded in a swamp. Confederate pickets discovered them the next morning, and Reynolds would spend the next several weeks in a Richmond prison before being exchanged.[27]

"Yesterday was a terable day for us," wrote Lieutenant Colonel Robert McAllister to his wife on June 28, "one of the hardest fights of the war." The Federals had lost twenty-two cannon and had incurred 6,837 casualties in killed, wounded, and captured. Eight regiments, or one sixth of the units, lost more than two hundred men. The casualty rate was nineteen percent. In turn, they inflicted 8,700 losses on their opponents, or a fifteen percent rate. The combined casualties made Gaines's Mill one of the bloodiest single days of the war and the costliest of the Seven Days Campaign.[28]

In his letter home, McAllister added, "The brave boys fought to the last." The Federals had made a valiant stand for roughly seven hours, despite being outnumbered three-to-two. Porter, Sykes, Morell, McCall, Slocum, and brigade commanders performed ably, shifting units and bringing forward reserves. Porter "had every reason to expect that McClellan would send him ample re-enforcements," a biographer of the army commander, Peter Michie, has argued. But McClellan sent only Slocum's division to Porter in a timely manner. Thousands of troops stood idle south of the river while the Fifth Corps and Slocum's three brigades fought desperately to hold their position. McClellan never rode personally to the battlefield, where one third of his army was engaged. In contrast, Lee accompanied his troops, ordering the assaults at Gaines's Mill.[29]

During the night McClellan met with his senior generals. The army's options had been reduced to two—it could assault the Confederate lines south of the Chickahominy or retreat down the Peninsula. An offensive could salvage the campaign and perhaps carry the Federals into Richmond while the bulk of Lee's army was north of the river.

Convinced that he was outnumbered, McClellan could not intellectually or emotionally, or both, order such a gamble. Confronted with one of the most crucial decisions of his career, McClellan informed his subordinates that the army would abandon the supply base at White House and withdraw to the James River, where a new depot would be established. The campaign, begun three months ago and with such high prospects, was to be given up. "If we were defeated," he said to the group, "the Army and the country would be lost."[30]

On this night McClellan defined himself as a general. He failed the army and the cause to which he was devoted. Here, a handful of miles from the enemy's capital, as historian John T. Hubbell has argued, "The army was not beaten, but the general was, most completely." As another historian, Archer Jones, has concluded, "McClellan had lost his nerve when confronted with his first really big engagement." In fairness to McClellan, he believed deeply that a defeat would doom the Union. But he refused to do what Lee had dared—to follow a risky path to an uncertain destination. It is the measure of the man and of the general.[31]

In his mind, characteristically, others had forced the decision upon him. He sent a telegram to Stanton after he had met with his corps commanders. McClellan attributed the defeat to his lack of numbers. If he had 10,000 more men, he could "gain the victory tomorrow." He then concluded: "I feel too earnestly tonight—I have seen too many dead & wounded comrades to feel otherwise than that the Govt has not sustained this Army. If you do not do so now the game is lost. If I save this Army now I tell you plainly that I owe no thanks to you or any other persons in Washington—you have done your best to sacrifice this Army."[32]

When the telegram came into the War Department, a telegrapher deciphered it and showed it to Colonel Edward S. Sanford, head of the telegraph office. Sanford ordered the general's final sentence be deleted and the message recopied. Although McClellan naturally believed that his telegram had been copied in full, neither Stanton nor Lincoln learned of his insubordinate and false allegation. The president replied, "Save your Army at all events. Will send re-enforcements as fast as we can. . . . I feel any misfortune to you and your Army quite as keenly as you feel it yourself. If you have had a drawn battle, or a repulse, it is the price we pay for the enemy not being in Washington."[33]

At the meeting with his generals, McClellan told them, "We will have a difficult retreat to make." The movement entailed the passage of approximately 100,000 men, more than 300 cannon and heavy siege guns, 3,800 ambulances and wagons, and a herd of cattle. Although the army had to march only about fifteen miles to the James River, few roads ran south, and the army would have to cross White Oak Swamp. As the Federals marched, Lee's army could be expected to press their rear and try to interdict the retreat. Four roads followed an east–west course, and the Rebels could use these avenues to strike the Union column's flank. While McClellan had chosen the safer option, the withdrawal was a dangerous undertaking.[34]

The retreat, or "change of base" as McClellan preferred to call it, had begun before he met with his generals. Erasmus Keyes's Fourth Corps had been ordered to start for White Oak Swamp. The engineer regiments marched with the corps, and at daylight on June 28, began rebuilding White Oak Bridge and constructing a new one upstream at Brackett's Ford. Porter's Fifth Corps and the wagon train followed Keyes. Wounded men who could walk left the large hospital at Savage Station and hobbled along among the wagons. At White House, troops destroyed vast stockpiles of supplies. As the smoke blackened the sky, the Federals marched away. Behind them came Confederates, who extinguished the flames. "It did not take them so long to put out the fire," grumbled a sergeant, "as it did us to make it."[35]

The Second, Third, and Sixth corps guarded the Chickahominy crossings and covered the approaches from the west. After dark, the men in the three corps started southeast toward the bridges over White Oak Swamp. Samuel Heintzelman noted in his diary that the troops marched in "good order." During the day, Philip Kearny had issued 150 rounds of ammunition and directed officers to have each man in the division sew a patch of red cloth on his cap. Kearny told his brigade commanders that they were "the rear guard of all God's creation."[36]

When the rank and file learned of the army's destination, they reacted with both disbelief and anger. A sergeant declared that he "never thought this Army *never* could never" retreat. A member of the 15th Massachusetts recorded in his diary on June 28, "Every one was blue and thought we were defeated." A lieutenant contended that McClellan's decision was "in the judgment of most of us, without sufficient cause." Another soldier described June 28 as "*Blue Saturday*. This day never to be forgotten."[37]

North of the Chickahominy, Lee searched for evidence of McClellan's next move throughout the morning of June 28. Unconvinced that his opponent would abandon the supply base at White House, Lee sent Jeb Stuart's cavalry and infantry units east toward the Richmond and York River Railroad. When these commands reported that the Federals had destroyed the railroad bridge over the Chickahominy and dust clouds indicated a southward march by the Yankees, Lee concluded that McClellan was retreating either down the Peninsula or toward the James. He issued orders for a pursuit early on June 29. "Though not certain," as Lee wrote to Jefferson Davis, he believed the enemy was retreating toward the James, and "the whole army has been put in motion on this supposition."[38]

North and south of the Chickahominy, the Confederates marched on June 29. Lee sent the divisions of James Longstreet and A. P. Hill back across the river to interdict the Union withdrawal on the next day. While these troops headed south on a "forced march," Lee directed the commands of John Magruder, Benjamin Huger, and Theophilus H. Holmes to advance east, to gnaw at the enemy's columns, and to slow the Federal march. Stonewall Jackson received instructions to repair the bridge, to cross the Chickahominy, and in Lee's words, "to push the pursuit vigorously" against the Northerners' rear units.[39]

A Union quartermaster described the march on June 29 in his diary as "the grandest 'skedaddling' ever I saw." The heat was, insisted a soldier, "almost insupportable; there was not a breath of air." Exhausted men fell from the ranks in droves, joining the able-bodied wounded who plodded along with the wagons. Cavalry escorts had to remove men who had collapsed in the roadbed. "Many of the boys had not a mouthful to eat," recounted a private. "I had nothing but hard bread, the sight of wich became sickening." A lieutenant wrote afterward, "we have lived on excitement and a few crackers."[40]

Keyes's Fourth Corps and Porter's Fifth Corps continued to lead the retreat toward the James River. Marching most of the day and through the night, the Fourth Corps reached the James River by daylight on June 30. Behind it, the Fifth Corps halted on Malvern Hill, which dominated the surrounding terrain. A foul-up had left George McCall's division of Pennsylvania Reserves in bivouac near a crossroads named Glendale, where three roads intersected. During the evening of June 29, Henry Slocum's division of the Sixth Corps reached Glendale, which had to be held if the other three corps and wagons were to pass safely to the James.[41]

Those commands—the Second, Third, and Sixth corps—closed on Savage Station throughout June 29. For a second day, they guarded the army's rear and western flank north of White Oak Swamp. At Savage Station, the Federals had the forward supply base for the army and a hospital with thousands of sick and wounded men. Unwilling to have the Rebels seize the vast amount of supplies, McClellan ordered the base's destruction.[42]

Second Corps troops carried out the task. Although a lieutenant declared, "we had a sort of savage joy in seeing the destruction which would keep our rations from the enemy," most men who witnessed it were dispirited by the action. A Pennsylvanian recalled that there was "enough hardtack on one pile at that place to reach from Philadelphia to Pittsburg." The detail dumped mounds of coffee and sugar on the ground, smashed whiskey barrels, and lit fires. "In a few seconds," attested an onlooker, "the fire became a seething furnace of white heat." Men scattered to avoid the flames.[43]

As a final act, the men ignited boxcars of ammunition and sent them down the tracks toward the destroyed bridge over the Chickahominy. When the engine and cars hurtled off the rails, the ammunition exploded in a terrific blast, shattering windows in nearby houses and rocking the ground. The pall of smoke at Savage Station and the deafening explosion must have made the Yankees feel that, as one of them jotted in his diary, "Everything seems to be going wrong with our side."[44]

Most disheartening to the Federals was the decision to leave behind their sick and wounded comrades to the Confederates. At least 2,000, and perhaps as many as 3,000, patients filled the hospital. One of the unfortunate men was heard to cry out: "O my God! Is this the reward I deserve for all the sacrifices I have made, the battles I have fought, and the agony I have endured from my wounds?" Their fate would rest with the kindness and generosity of the Southerners.[45]

Late on the afternoon, west of Savage Station, a Confederate battle line suddenly appeared. The troops belonged to Magruder's command and were trying, as Lee had directed, to hit the Union flank. The Rebels triggered a volley, "before we were aware of their presence," according to a Federal soldier. On came South Carolinians, Georgians, and Virginians, advancing along the railroad and Williamsburg Road. On the tracks, a specially mounted cannon hurled shells toward the Northerners.[46]

The surprise resulted from confusion among the Union corps commanders. Second Corps commander Edwin Sumner thought that the Third Corps was still to his right and rear. Its commander, Samuel Heintzelman, however, had continued the march toward White Oak Swamp without informing either Sumner or William Franklin of the Sixth Corps. When Sumner learned of Heintzelman's absence he was furious, but he reacted quickly to the Rebel assault. According to a sergeant who saw him, he "was as cool as pigs in clover."[47]

Sumner rushed back two brigades. The Confederates were so close that the Federals heard their officers issue orders. The woods exploded with musketry. Corporal James Wright of the 1st Minnesota, which had been sent into the action, described combat's fearful randomness: "The safe or unsafe place on the fighting line is about as difficult to pick out beforehand as it is to tell where and when the next bolt of lightning will strike. One of the incalculable and surprising things connected with battles is the irregular, uncertain, disproportionate, and eccentric way that losses occur in action."[48]

While fortune favored the Minnesotans on this afternoon, to their left Brigadier General William Brooks's Vermont Brigade of the Sixth Corps met a wall of rifle and artillery fire. The 5th Vermont plunged ahead almost into the Southerners' ranks. Then combat's indiscriminateness struck the New Englanders as if it were a bolt of lightning. "Thirty men of the Fifth Vermont," recounted a surgeon, "were found lying side by side, dressed in as perfect a line as for dress parade, who were all stricken down by one discharge of grape and canister from the enemy's battery." In all, seventy-two Vermonters lay dead or mortally wounded, and 116 wounded, the greatest loss sustained in an engagement by any of that state's regiments in the war.[49]

Additional Union regiments filed into line, and the fighting intensified. Officers reported that rifles became fouled and unserviceable from the rapid discharges. The thick woods filled with smoke, adding to the confusion. A Confederate called the Yankees' fire "dreadful." Federal counterattacks stabilized their lines, and darkness ended the engagement. A South Carolinian declared afterward: "I do hope never again to be a participant in such a terrible battle. It was heart-rending indeed."[50]

While the Battle of Savage Station raged, McClellan once again rode away from the fighting. Army headquarters had been at the railroad depot until the afternoon of June 29. McClellan had alerted the corps commanders of the possibility of an attack and then headed across White Oak Swamp. For a third time, the commander had either removed himself from a battlefield or did not go to the sound of combat until it had ended. It might have been as historian John Hubbell has claimed, "he had distanced himself physically and psychologically (even spiritually) from his army." Undoubtedly, he relinquished active field command and burdened his corps commanders with the management of the retreat.[51]

Once across White Oak Swamp, McClellan met William Averell, whose horsemen picketed the roads to the west. Averell reported that his videttes had not seen Confederate troops. "The roads will be full enough tomorrow," responded the commander. "Averell, if any army can save this country, it will be the Army of the Potomac, and it must be saved for that purpose." McClellan continued on to Glendale and issued orders for the Second and Sixth corps to cross White Oak Swamp during the night.[52]

When Sumner received the orders at Savage Station, he refused to obey them, storming that they had won a victory and he would not abandon the field. Franklin said that he would obey and start the Sixth Corps south. When a second message arrived, threatening Sumner with arrest, the stubborn corps commander relented. The Second Corps filed into columns and followed Franklin's troops.[53]

For the men on the march, it was a wretched night. A thunderstorm blew in, dumping rain on the exhausted, hungry Northerners. "The horrors of that night's march no one can imagine," remembered a Pennsylvanian. "Men declared that they could go no further, and I saw them take their guns from their shoulders, break the stocks off, and sit down by the roadside, to be taken prisoners in a few hours. Wagons, artillery, cavalry and infantry blocked the road, and the wounded were endeavoring to get on with the moving mass. How much further to go? Some said one or two, some four or five miles. It was impossible for regiments to keep together—we would become separated before we knew it, but all tried to follow the same road." Lieutenant Colonel Theodore Dodge of the 101st New York confided in his journal, "I should like to know the meaning of all these movements—they are very incomprehensible."[54]

By the morning of June 30, seven divisions and a brigade of the Union army lay at or around Glendale, where Charles City, Long Bridge, and Quaker roads intersected. If the Confederates seized the crossroads, the Federal army could be divided and vulnerable to piecemeal destruction. The defense of Glendale on this day was vital to the passage of the army to the James River.[55]

McClellan conferred with Sumner, Heintzelman, and Franklin and oversaw the deployment of the units, before riding away with his staff. "Why he left was an enigma," stated one of Heintzelman's headquarters clerks. McClellan expected a Confederate assault—"The roads will be full enough tomorrow," as he predicted the day before—and still he fled from another battlefield. It was, as historian Hubbell declared, an "inexplicable and inexcusable" decision. McClellan went to Haxall's Landing on the James, where he boarded the gunboat *Galena* and had dinner, while at Glendale, his army struggled for its survival.[56]

The burden of command fell upon the three corps commanders. Heintzelman noted in his journal that Sumner remained angry about the Third Corps's march away from Savage Station and "avoided speaking to me." The Federal position formed a reverse L, with William Smith's and Israel Richardson's divisions and a Fourth Corps brigade, under Franklin, covering their rear, or base of the L, at the White Oak Swamp crossing. The main Union line extended from north to south, from Charles City Road to Long Bridge Road, manned by the divisions of Henry Slocum, Philip Kearny, George McCall, and Joseph Hooker. Eighteen batteries supported the infantrymen. In all, about 55,000 Yankees waited.[57]

Before noon the Charles City and Long Bridge roads were "full enough." Since the previous morning, it had been Lee's plan to interdict the Federal retreat, and he had expected more than Magruder's troops to be engaged at Savage Station. He now directed his units toward Glendale and the opportunity to sever, if not destroy, his opponent's army. He ordered Stonewall Jackson to cross White Oak Swamp and to assail the Union rear. From the west, Benjamin Huger's three brigades were to attack along Charles City Road, while the divisions of James Longstreet and A. P. Hill were to charge on Long Bridge Road. If his subordinates fulfilled their roles, nearly 70,000 Rebels would assault the Yankees.[58]

"With great suddenness and severity," wrote a Confederate staff officer, the Battle of Glendale erupted. In its intensity and bloodletting, it rivaled Gaines's Mill. While Huger's feeble attack stalled quickly before Slocum's troops, Longstreet's Rebels charged with ferocity toward McCall's Pennsylvanians. These Fifth Corps men had been encamped near Glendale because of the previous night's countermarch. It was fortuitous for the Federals that they were available, but as the unit's historian claimed, "Most of the men were fitter subjects for the hospital than for the battle-field."[59]

"The fire of hell was let loose upon us," exclaimed a Pennsylvania captain, as shells and canister from Confederate batteries swept in upon their ranks. Behind them, gray-coated infantrymen charged. In front of the Keystone State volunteers, six Union batteries blasted the Rebels. The deployment of cannon in front of infantry was faulty. In turn, the Southerners drove toward the inviting targets. A furnace of artillery and rifle fire blew across the ground into the ranks of both attackers and defenders. Sergeant Michael Miller of the 1st Pennsylvania Reserves swore to his wife that bullets "flew in every Square inch of air around me except the little Space I stood in." A comrade asserted, "To believe any man desires to go into battle, is to believe him a fool."[60]

Longstreet hurled more troops into the fury. His men overran some of the batteries, clubbing and shooting the Union crews. Colonel Seneca G. Simmons, who had succeeded John Reynolds in brigade command after the general's capture, was killed. Another brigade commander, George Meade, suffered bullet wounds in the right forearm and in his side. An officer who witnessed Meade's wounding wrote of the general, "He did not fall from his horse—only winced a little and rode slowly to the rear." He would not return to the army for seven weeks.[61]

No Federal troops had fought more valiantly or suffered more than these Pennsylvanians during the campaign. They had little left, and their ranks began to crumble under the enemy onslaught. McCall tried to rally the men and found himself a prisoner. When taken to the rear, McCall met Longstreet, a former subordinate of the Union general. Longstreet offered his hand to his old friend. McCall refused it, remarking: "Excuse me, sir. I can stand defeat but not insult."[62]

Before he was captured, McCall had met Kearny, who was leading regiments of his division to the support of the Pennsylvanians. Accounts of his men are universal in their praise of Kearny's conduct during the campaign. Kearny seemed tireless to the troops as he "rode along from front to rear, from rear to front, alive to the welfare of his men." They remarked about "his armless sleeve flapping up and down," riding with his horse's reins in his mouth, and his confident words to them. A New Yorker believed that he looked "like a Knight errant of old," as they trudged through the night from Savage Station. They had learned, as a lieutenant put it, "he would go into a fight, as an eater would go to a banquet." They had also heard that the Rebels called him "the one armed devil on the white horse."[63]

When Kearny ordered his men into an attack, he liked to tell them to "go in gaily." Whether he used the phrase on this day is unknown, but few, if any, of his troops would have thought of gaiety at this time. "The Rebels were as thick as blackberries," wrote a lieutenant. Toward them came three Confederate brigades, Southerners from Alabama, Mississippi, Louisiana, and South Carolina. The opposing lines stiffened and hammered each other. A soldier in the 20th Indiana claimed, "We fired so rapidly that our guns were too hot to hold."[64]

Colonel Alexander Hays and the 63rd Pennsylvania typified the Union resistance. A West Pointer, Hays had left the army after the Mexican War to hunt for gold in California and then to build railroads in his native Pennsylvania. Elected colonel of the regiment in August 1861, he proved to be "a most kind-hearted and patient man with a private soldier." He possessed an "impetuous, even fiery" personality, and like Kearny, a passion for battle. On this day Hays and his men saved a Union battery with a counterattack. Kearny called it "this most heroic action," and Hays's brigade commander, Hiram Berry, declared "that I have not in my carreer in military life seen better fighting or work better done."[65]

Additional Federal units came up in support of Kearny, sealing the breach where McCall's Pennsylvanians had been broken. As the 15th Massachusetts charged, Sumner shouted to its members: "Go in, boys, for the honor of old Massachusetts! I have been hit twice this afternoon, but it is nothing when you get used to it." On the left, Hooker's troops unleashed volleys into the attackers. Two days earlier, Private William C. Wiley of the 70th New York had complained in a letter home, "It seems as if General McClellan has no other Division in his Army but Hookers." Another soldier admitted later that he had had "a dread of it at first," but "I wanted to go in and give the Rebs a try, but it was awful work."[66]

The Union lines held. A Confederate artillerist contended, "[N]owhere else, to my knowledge, [occurred] so much actual personal fighting with bayonet and butt of gun." At places, the combat had been hand-to-hand, and volleys had been triggered into foes at less than a hundred yards. Although imprecise, casualty figures are estimated at 3,500–3,800 in killed, wounded, and missing for the Federals, and 3,500–3,700 for the Confederates. Adjutant Robert Taggart of the 9th Pennsylvania Reserves recorded in his diary that night: "When will it end. . . . It is terrible. Yet this is war. Heaven interpose."[67]

Glendale had offered Lee his finest chance to inflict a crippling, if not fatal, defeat upon McClellan's army. Instead of coordinated assaults, Longstreet's and Hill's divisions bled and died virtually alone against five Union divisions. They had fought "for all they were worth," but Federal reserves proved decisive. Huger had performed miserably, but most critically, Jackson had done little to execute his orders. His mysterious conduct has been controversial ever since. For whatever reasons, he failed Lee and the army. E. Porter Alexander, a Confederate artillery officer and the army's finest chronicler, stated it bluntly: "never, before or after, did the fates put such a prize within our reach."[68]

McClellan, who had witnessed none of the fighting, wired the War Department that night, saying in part: "My Army has behaved superbly and have done all that men could do. If none of us escape we shall at least have done honor to the country. I shall do my best to save the

Army." Hours later, he sent a second telegram, requesting 50,000 additional troops. "With them," he avowed, "I will retrieve our fortunes. More would be well, but that number sent at once, will, I think, enable me to assume the offensive."[69]

Lincoln responded to both dispatches in separate messages. He advised the general: "Maintain your ground if you can; but save the Army at all events, even if you fall back to Fortress-Monroe. We still have strength enough in the country, and will bring it out." As to his request for reinforcements, the president stated, "When you ask for fifty thousand men to be promptly sent you, you surely labor under some gross mistake of fact." The government had barely 60,000 troops in the other departments in Virginia and in Washington's defenses. The idea, said Lincoln, "is simply absurd."[70]

At the time McClellan telegraphed the War Department, he issued orders to the troops at Glendale to withdraw to Malvern Hill. For a second night in a row the men trudged through the darkness. "We did little more than drag ourselves along," said a soldier. A comrade likened it to "a funeral procession." Hooker's division remained at the crossroads as a rear guard until nearly daylight. Hooker's men watched Rebels, with lanterns, search for missing friends. He stated in his report, "The unbroken, mournful wail of human suffering was all that we heard from Glendale during that long dismal night."[71]

When Hooker's division arrived, the Army of the Potomac stood reunited on Malvern Hill. The height rose 150 feet above the surrounding terrain. The open crest extended one and a half miles in length and three-fourths of a mile in width. The ground sloped to the north and northwest, with the hillsides cleared for several hundred yards. An extensive field of ripened grain and shocks of harvested wheat lay beneath the northwestern crest. Ravines and marshes protected the flanks. The position had "elements of great strength," wrote Porter.[72]

McClellan, Porter, and the army's senior generals directed the deployment of the infantry and artillery. The army commander reportedly told a subordinate that the army was "in no condition to fight without 24 hours rest—I pray that the enemy may not be in condition to disturb us today." The army's chief topographical engineer, Andrew Humphreys, who personally posted units, stated later: "Never did I see a man more cut down than Genl. McClellan was. He was unable to do anything or say anything." When McClellan had finished riding along the lines about nine o'clock in the morning, he and staff members departed for Haxall's Landing, where he reboarded the *Galena* and steamed downriver to Harrison's Landing, to examine the campsite for the army. Porter acted as unofficial commander in his absence.[73]

McClellan's abandonment of the army as it awaited another probable battle—the campaign's final showdown—constituted a dereliction of duty unparalleled in the annals of the Civil War. Was he so depressed, as Humphreys indicated, or did he lack the moral courage to command the army in battle where young men were killed and maimed? Whatever the reason or reasons, for a third time McClellan deserted the troops whom he claimed he loved. Hooker told a brigade commander months later that McClellan was drunk on the *Galena*, but no other account substantiates Hooker's allegation. A lieutenant put it cynically, "McClellan was on the James River protecting the gun boats, and composing a scolding letter to the president—probably." He declared that Little Mac was "a fearful incompetent."[74]

By mid-morning on July 1, an imposing array of artillery batteries and infantry ranks held the crest of Malvern Hill. This would be a memorable day for Union gun crews, and 171 of them stood beside their bronze and iron cannon. Colonel Henry Hunt, commander of the Artillery Reserve, supervised the placement of the batteries. No one in the army knew his business better than Hunt. "I regarded him as the best living commander of field-artillery," McClellan wrote of Hunt. "He was a man of the utmost coolness in danger, thoroughly versed in his profession, an admirable organizer, a soldier of a very high order."[75]

Infantrymen called an artillery battery a "brass band." Hunt expected each commander of a brass band to fire deliberately and to assess the accuracy of each shot. The discharges from the brass bands should possess a kind of rhythm, a fearful music of shells and canister. With sweeping fields of fire, Hunt and the gun crews anchored the Union position.[76]

As the pieces rolled into place, Heintzelman located one of his Third Corps batteries. Returning later, he discovered that Kearny had moved it. He "rode brim full of wrath" to his division commander. "You countermand another order of mine," stormed Heintzelman, "and I will have you arrested, Sir." Kearny shot back, "Arrest my ass, God Damn you," and then spurred away. An onlooker claimed that Heintzelman smiled.[77]

The Fourth Corps division of Darius Couch and the Fifth Corps division of George Morell defended the hill's northern crest, covering the likely approaches of Confederate assaults. To Morell's left, George Sykes's division of the same corps held the western hillside. On the right, the Third and Second corps guarded the army's eastern flank. The Sixth Corps extended the line south to Turkey Creek. Its commander, William Franklin, had accompanied McClellan to Harrison's Landing. A soldier asserted about their position on Malvern Hill, "I could hardly conceive any power that could overwhelm us."[78]

The van of the Army of Northern Virginia came into view of the Yankees about midday. Unwell and ill-tempered, Lee had ordered the pursuit. Perhaps he still believed that he could inflict a punishing blow on the retreating Federals before they reached the protection of Union gunboats on the James. During the previous night, D. H. Hill, who had questioned a local civilian about Malvern Hill, told Lee and Longstreet, "If General McClellan is there in force, we had better let him alone." Longstreet laughed and jokingly replied, "Don't get scared now that we have got him whipped."[79]

It took hours for the Southerners to deploy, slowed by inaccurate maps and the dense woods and swamps. Confederate artillerists opened the action, inducing a blizzard of fire from the massed Union batteries. With fewer than thirty cannon in action, the outmatched Rebel pieces soon fell silent under the hammering. Along the edges of the armies, opposing skirmish lines dueled. Berdan's Sharpshooters covered a portion of the Union front. In their distinctive green coats, these soldiers were deadly at such work. Brigadier General Alexander Hays later called them "the damdest thieves and the damdest fighters."[80]

While on reconnaissance with Longstreet of the army's left flank, Lee received an erroneous report that the enemy was withdrawing. Earlier Lee had designated Brigadier General Lewis A. Armistead's brigade to initiate the assault. When a second message arrived, stating that Armistead was making progress, Lee instructed John Magruder to "press forward your whole command and follow up Armistead's success." The army was committing to a bloodbath—the Yankees had only shifted units; they had not begun a retreat.[81]

On this July afternoon, war's terrible magnificence could be seen on the slopes of Malvern Hill. Before the battle had ended, men in fifteen Confederate brigades dressed ranks, stepped forth, screamed their yell, and charged into a maelstrom. It was not a complicated engagement— waves of hot iron, belched from cannon, and torrents of lead, spat from muskets, tore into human flesh. The words of the defenders and the attackers relate a grievous story of valor and of death.[82]

A Massachusetts private stated that the Southerners "rushed on in great numbers, seemingly regardless of consequences." He was con- vinced that they had to be "full of whiskey" to keep coming. An artillery lieutenant said that even after they had been repulsed, "they advanced again with grim, hard-set resolution." Union gunners had orders to aim at the feet of the Rebels and not to sponge their pieces between rounds, which increased the accuracy and rate of their fire. An infantryman declared that the Northerners *"mowed down the grey jackets like grass." "Hell with all its horrors,"* Private William Wiley of the 70th New York told his folks, *"cannot be worse than a battlefield. All the bad passions of men are excited to frenzy and each trying to be as destructive as possible.* The Rebels fought like a set of demons."[83]

Confederate accounts speak of the carnage that engulfed them. One soldier described the enemy artillery fire as a "perfect hailstorm of shell, grape, canister." A Georgia lieutenant wrote "that a tempest of iron and lead" swept over them, "cutting down every living thing." He added: "Oh what a terrible consuming fire is man's passions when it has full sway. Nothing but a kind Providence saved any of us alive." A Virginian swore, "At no other time did I so realize the horrors of a battlefield."[84]

Major General Lafayette McLaws, a Confederate division com- mander, contended later that he never saw so many men panic under the withering fire. "It was but a slaughter pen." In a postwar letter, McLaws confided: "As for Malvern Hill, who is going to tell the truth about it, the whole truth. If I [were] ever to write what I saw . . . I would be denounced by our own people as a calumniator." D. H. Hill, who had warned Lee of the position's natural strength, said afterward, "It was not war—it was murder."[85]

After four hours, the butchery ended. At times, the Confederate assaults nearly reached the Union lines. Federal officers had to call up reserves to stabilize the ranks. Each man in several blue-coated regiments expended more than one hundred rounds of ammunition, while artillery crews discharged thousands of rounds. The casualty figures revealed the grim reality of the Southern defeat. Lee's losses exceeded 5,000. Northern casualties amounted to slightly more than 2,000. The dominance of Henry Hunt's artillery crews was undeniable on this day. Hill believed that more than half of the Rebel killed and wounded resulted from the "tempest of iron" spewed forth from Union cannon.[86]

McClellan returned to Malvern Hill from his downriver trip as the combat waned. He examined part of the Union line, but not the sector that was still engaged. He then headed back to Haxall's Landing. During the evening he sent instructions to Porter to withdraw from Malvern Hill to Harrison's Landing. As the army prepared to march, McClellan boarded the *Galena* for the night.[87]

Porter objected to the retreat order, suggesting that the Federals might even consider an advance on Richmond after the victory. Couch, who had distinguished himself in the battle, noted in his diary when he learned of the withdrawal, "I felt somewhat as Sumner had done the night before after his hard fought victory, I not knowing the plans of the Commanding General." A member of Heintzelman's staff declared that the order "produced great dissatisfaction and excitement in the ranks . . . but more so from the general officers, who now knowing the real cause for the movement, were loud in their protestations against the order. [They] denounced McClellan as a coward or traitor! General Kearny protested against the movement vehemently."[88]

The Yankees began to file off Malvern Hill before midnight. They left their wounded comrades on the battlefield—"an indelible disgrace," thought an officer. They marched, once again, through the night. Rain began falling on July 2, as they slogged through mud "over shoe tops" until they arrived at Harrison's Landing. They were hungry and "utterly exhausted." According to a colonel, officers and men "were in a sad plight," reminding him of "a shipwrecked crew."[89]

Lee wrote in his official report, "Under ordinary circumstances the Federal Army should have been destroyed." He attributed the enemy's "escape" primarily to "the want of correct and timely information." Inaccurate maps, inadequate staff, and the wooded terrain hampered, if not crippled, the army's offensive operations. Subordinates failed Lee at critical times, resulting in headlong assaults at Mechanicsville, Gaines's Mill, Glendale, and Malvern Hill. The campaign cost the army more than 20,000 men, or nearly thirty percent of its strength. Lee "was deeply, bitterly disappointed" that they had missed opportunities to destroy the Federals. But his bold gamble had saved Richmond and redirected the war in Virginia. It had been a stunning achievement.[90]

THE FOURTH OF JULY WAS, wrote a Maine captain, "a holy day." In the camps of the Army of the Potomac at Harrison's Landing, bands played "Hail Columbia," "Yankee Doodle," "The Star-Spangled Banner," and other patriotic songs. Fireworks arced into the air. "It was a lively scene," added the captain. George McClellan visited the troops, inspiring "the soldiers with a new vigor." When he appeared among the men of the 2nd Michigan, they "cheered most heartily for country, cause & leader." But a 5th New Hampshire lieutenant offered a contrasting view of the day, "not much enthusiasm, but we fired a salute by the way of keeping up appearances." A quartermaster sergeant admitted, "we are all pretty well haggard out."[91]

They tried to make sense of the ordeal through which they had passed. A Pennsylvanian argued, "I don't call it a defeat." A Maine volunteer comforted himself with the knowledge: "no Bull Run's & scenes which we repeated! No panics, and stampedes, were here witnessed!" A member of the 38th New York informed his cousin that they had been outnumbered two-to-one and that McClellan "deemed it wiser to retreat to the James River where our Gun Boats would be a great help to us." A 20th Indiana private concluded simply that they had "roused the real critter and we are both here."[92]

They had indeed met "the real critter" on five battlefields, but held the ground on four of them when the fighting had ended. On scant rations and few hours of sleep, they had executed a dangerous movement—a retreat in the presence of an opponent—across difficult terrain. Their casualties amounted to, by one count, 1,734 killed, 8,062 wounded, and 6,053 missing or captured, for a total of 15,849, nearly 5,000 fewer than their foe. As McClellan told them, in part, in a Fourth of July proclamation: "Your conduct ranks you among the celebrated armies of history. No one will now question that each of you may always say with pride: 'I belonged to the Army of the Potomac!'"[93]

Many, if not most, of them concluded that they had been "compelled" to retreat by superior enemy numbers. It has been argued by historians that as a result of the campaign's outcome a defeatism characterized the army's attitude. Historian Gordon Rhea has concluded that the Federals "expected to be defeated, and this caused a form of 'institutional timidity.'" Historian Stephen Sears termed it "an inferiority complex." The contemporary letters and diaries of the rank and file belie this conclusion.[94]

"The retreat was," a lieutenant noted in his diary, "conducted superbly." Another lieutenant wrote his brother less than a week after Malvern Hill, "the successful accomplishment of the movement by us . . . is one of the greatest feats in military history." An artillery officer declared in a July 4 letter, "The Army is in as good condition today as it has ever been and there is no symptom of demoralization in it." On the same day, Sergeant Frank Young of the 15th Massachusetts scribbled in his diary, "the troops are anxious for another fight." Finally, a Maine soldier averred to his mother on July 6: "I will venture to say that considering the numbers the Army will fight better to day than it would one week ago. Experience has given us confidence. And unless the enemy bring superior numbers against us he cannot whip us."[95]

In their estimation, they had accomplished what had been required of them. They had not made the decision to retreat, to destroy the supplies, or to abandon wounded and sick comrades. While some of them saw that the withdrawal meant a strategic defeat, their primary view encompassed the fields of battle. On them they had held their own. In the end, it was as one of them stated it, "McClellan was whipped." It was the army, not its commander, who made the safe passage from the Chickahominy to the James.[96]

The conduct of the men and their commanders saved the army. Nothing more could have been asked of Fitz John Porter and the Fifth Corps. They bore the brunt of the fighting at Mechanicsville, Gaines's

Mill, and Malvern Hill. The Pennsylvania Reserves incurred one fifth of the army's casualties. Once the retreat began, the burden of command rested with Edwin Sumner, Samuel Heintzelman, William Franklin and their division and brigade commanders. At Savage Station and Glendale, their troops repulsed the Confederate assaults, preventing a piecemeal destruction of the army. Unlike their opponent, they deserved better from the army commander.[97]

"It is considered generally," wrote Colonel Francis Barlow in a July 4 letter, "that McClellan has been completely outwitted and that our present safety is owing more to the severe fighting of some of the Divisions than to any skill of our General." Many other field officers and generals shared Barlow's judgment. An aide at Third Corps headquarters related that the "fighting generals" had "a profound contempt for General McClellan's fighting qualities, and several officers high in command denounce him without stint." They accused him of indecisiveness, even timidity. "He is beaten before the battle is fought," declared Colonel Regis de Trobriand. "He foresees only defeat; he dreams only of the excuses necessary to throw the responsibility on some one else."[98]

Apparently no officers criticized McClellan more than Kearny and Hooker. During the retreat, Kearny allegedly damned McClellan as "a coward and a traitor" and personally confronted him "with language so strong that all who heard it expected he would be placed under arrest." Following the campaign, the brigadier asserted in a letter, "the fearful error of McClellan's [was] want of heart." Hooker contended that McClellan "never gave birth to a soldier like idea or act or adopted those of others." To Hooker, McClellan missed the opportunity of the campaign when he refused to attack the Confederate lines south of the Chickahominy when the bulk of Lee's army was north of the river.[99]

Except for the reported Kearny incident, the criticism or discontent simmered beneath the surface. McClellan had many defenders, and whenever he appeared among the troops, they cheered him. The fact remained, however, that the campaign exposed his failings as an army commander. Characteristically, he attributed the campaign's outcome to authorities in Washington, with their failure to reinforce him and his need to divide the army along the Chickahominy as he awaited the possible advance of Irvin McDowell from Fredericksburg. He argued rightly that the "true defense of Washington" lay on the Peninsula. He had demonstrated strategic aptitude when he chose it as the route of advance on Richmond. But when the critical test came, when "the real critter" appeared before him, he failed as an army commander.[100]

Convinced that he faced a horde of Rebels and consumed by the belief that the Union cause rested in the salvation of his army, McClellan surrendered the strategic and tactical initiative to Lee. It would be two years before the Federals retrieved it in Virginia. Most critically, McClellan fled responsibility, abandoning the army to its fate, particularly at Glendale and at Malvern Hill. His decisions to ride away from impending battles constituted a dereliction of duty. Perhaps he was so haunted by the sights of dead and maimed men, or as historian Russell F. Weigley has concluded, he "was simply and continually frightened by war, which is not so mysterious a condition." McClellan was "never a warrior." The contrast between him and Lee could not be more compelling. Only one army had a leader who had proved himself worthy of leading it into the carnage of war.[101]

The Seven Days Campaign resulted ultimately in foreclosing the Peninsula as an avenue of advance on Richmond by the Federals. It would limit strategic options for the next two years. The Union failure to capture the Confederate capital, predicted an aide of McClellan, "is destined to be followed by the effusion of seas of blood." A lieutenant believed that now the conflict would be "a war truly to the knife!"[102]

Corporal James Wright of the 1st Minnesota thought of the campaign as it affected him and his comrades. "Each day of the Seven Days added a full year to our ages," he remembered, "and the whole campaign left us ten years older than we began it. I am sure that every man of the company *felt* that, practically, that was true. They '*looked it*' anyway, and not one of them was the rollicking noisy boy he was before. And he *never was afterwards*."[103]

Chapter 7

"McClellan Has the Army with Him"

THE STEAMER *Ariel* ARRIVED at Harrison's Landing on the evening of July 8, 1862. George McClellan came on board and "grasped" the hand of President Abraham Lincoln. The two men had not seen each other in more than three months. The president had traveled from Washington to meet with the army's senior generals, to assess the army's condition, and to discuss its future operations. Lincoln's visit would last less than twenty-four hours. Behind it, however, lay swelling currents that would reshape the conflict's course.[1]

While on board, Lincoln and McClellan conferred. It might have been at this time or later that night when the president asked the general a series of questions. Lincoln wanted to know the size of the army—about 80,000—the health of the men in the camp, and the location of the Confederate army. If McClellan "desired," could he "remove the army safely" from the Peninsula, asked Lincoln. As the president recorded it in a memorandum he prepared of his visit, McClellan replied, "It would be a delicate & very difficult matter."[2]

They left the boat together and rode into the army's camps, where cannon saluted the president's arrival. McClellan had the army readied for a review, and he, Lincoln, and a swarm of staff officers passed before the ranks. "Although a novel affair," noted a lieutenant in his diary, "was a magnificent scene. Thousands of muskets flashed in the moon-light." The troops cheered and applauded the "Grand Old Man," as a New Yorker called Lincoln. "It made us feel better all around," wrote an artillery officer. "If our good and noble President loves his army as well as it loves him he must have a good big heart." A Pennsylvanian thought that Lincoln looked "weary and sad."[3]

The next morning Lincoln met with the army's five corps com-manders, without McClellan present. On the critical question of whether the army could be withdrawn safely from the Peninsula, except for Fitz John Porter, they agreed that it could be done. Porter, Edwin Sumner, and Samuel Heintzelman believed, however, that it would be a mistake to do so. "I think we could," declared Sumner, "but I think we give up the cause if we do it." Heintzelman said, "it would be ruinous to the country," while Porter asserted, "move the Army & ruin the coun-try." Erasmus Keyes and William Franklin agreed that it could be accomplished. When Lincoln had finished the interviews, he reboarded the *Ariel* and headed for Washington.[4]

During the visit, McClellan handed the president a letter in which the army commander presented "my general views concerning the existing state of the rebellion." Both men had agreed earlier that at some point the general could offer his advice on military policy and affairs. McClellan decided the time was now. He described it to his wife as "a strong frank letter." If Lincoln "acts upon it," he told her, "the country will be saved."[5]

The "Harrison's Landing Letter," as it has come to be known, repeated McClellan's conservative views on the prosecution of the war. "The time has come," he stated, "when the Government must determine upon a civil and military policy, covering the whole ground of our national trou-ble." He opposed the confiscation of private property of Rebels and the "forcible abolition of slavery." "A declaration of radical views, especially upon slavery," he claimed, "will rapidly disintegrate our present Armies." The power of the North should be concentrated upon Confederate armies, not "to the subjugation of the people of any state." He recom-mended the appointment of a general-in-chief, but "I do not ask that place for myself." He would serve the president "in such position as you assign me and I will do so faithfully as ever subordinate served superior."[6]

Although McClellan did not state it forthrightly, he feared, most of all, that the conflict would become a social and political revolution. At all costs, the Union and the Constitution must be preserved, but individual rights must remain inviolate. The specter of arbitrary arrests, pillaged property, and freed bondsmen chilled McClellan. Unfortunately for the general and fellow conservatives, his letter was but a recurring echo, growing fainter as louder and more strident voices found an audience in Washington and in the North.[7]

The failure of the army's campaign on the Peninsula resulted in the acceptance by Lincoln, political leaders, and Northern civilians of the necessity for a grimmer prosecution of the war. McClellan's cautious tactics and conciliation policy toward the Southern people had not brought victory, but defeat. A determined enemy had to be met by an iron resolve. Philip Kearny expressed this changing attitude in a letter to a friend: "This war is no longer one of mild measures, when McClellan wrecked us at Richmond, our last chance for a Union party in the south ceased. Peace with the rebels on their own terms would only mean time to recommence."[8]

No one understood the necessity for a redirection of Union policy better than Lincoln. "Things had gone on from bad to worse," he explained subsequently, "until I felt that we had reached the end of our rope on the plan of operations we had been pursuing, that we had about played our last card, and must change our tactics, or lose the game!" For several weeks he had been preparing a draft of a proclamation that would emancipate the slaves. He had been pressed by Radicals in Congress and some Republican governors to act. He had tested the sentiment in the Cabinet. When Congress passed the Second Confiscation Act on July 17, Lincoln decided to present his proposal to the Cabinet, believing that Congress lacked the constitutional authority to abolish slavery in individual states.[9]

When the Cabinet members gathered at the White House on July 22, Lincoln informed them that he "had not called them together to ask their advice, but to lay the subject-matter of a proclamation before them." As commander-in-chief, he said, he planned to emancipate "all persons held as slaves" in states or parts of states under Confederate authority on January 1, 1863. He was taking this step "as a fit and necessary military measure."[10]

Several of the members raised objections, particularly to the timing of the announcement. They expressed concern about its impact on the fall elections and on relations with foreign governments. Lincoln adjourned the meeting, leaving the matter unresolved. That night Thurlow Weed, a powerful New York Republican and a political ally of Secretary of State William Seward, visited the president, arguing that the act would alienate the border slave states. In the end, Lincoln decided to wait to issue it until his armies had won a battlefield victory. When the time came, Lincoln would give redefinition to the war.[11]

While Lincoln wrestled with the momentous issue of emancipation, he and Congress took additional measures. On April 3, Secretary of War Stanton had optimistically, and unwisely, closed recruiting offices. Following the Seven Days Campaign, however, the War Department reopened them, and Lincoln called for 300,000 three-year volunteers. On July 17, Congress enacted a militia act, enrolling all male citizens between the ages of eighteen and forty-five for future draft calls by governors. The law also granted the president authority to summon militia units into Federal service for nine months, which Lincoln did on August 4, asking for 300,000 nine-month troops. Once again, the burden of implementing the calls and meeting the quotas fell upon governors and state legislatures. Eventually, however, 510,000 men volunteered under these two calls, the overwhelming majority in three-year regiments.[12]

Lincoln and Stanton also implemented organizational and department changes in the East. On June 26, the War Department had consolidated the troops in the Mountain, Shenandoah, and Rappahannock departments into the Army of Virginia. Lincoln selected Major General John Pope as commander of the new army. An 1842 graduate of West Point and career soldier, the forty-year-old Pope belonged to a distinguished family and was related by marriage to Mary Todd Lincoln's Kentucky family. Appointed a brigadier in June 1861, he had won a pair of minor victories on the Mississippi River in the spring of 1862. Brash, outspoken, and aggressive, Pope arrived in Washington during the final week of June.[13]

Pope recounted later that Stanton told him that the administration had been "greatly discontented" with McClellan's operations. The "general object" of Pope's army was to cover Washington and to aid

McClellan. The secretary stressed that Pope should "have in mind always the safety of the Capital." In his memoirs, Pope contended, "I was offered command of a forlorn hope under the most unfavorable conditions possible for success."[14]

To augment Pope's force, the administration created the Ninth Corps, drawing divisions from the departments of North Carolina and of the South. Lincoln appointed McClellan's old friend Major General Ambrose Burnside to command. By the first week of August, Burnside's units were disembarking at Aquia on the Rappahannock River and marching toward Falmouth. With the Ninth Corps's arrival, Pope could count nearly 60,000 troops under his direction. Eventually, two of the corps's three divisions joined Pope's army, posted along the Orange & Alexandria Railroad in central Virginia.[15]

As a final act, two days after his return from the Peninsula, Lincoln named Major General Henry Halleck as general-in-chief. McClellan had proposed that the position be refilled and evidently suggested Halleck to the president. A year before, Winfield Scott had recommended Halleck for command of the Army of the Potomac, but Lincoln had favored McClellan. Since then, the forty-seven-year-old academy graduate had led the Department of the Mississippi. Under his overall command, Pope and Ulysses S. Grant had scored victories along the Mississippi, Tennessee, and Cumberland rivers. To Lincoln, Halleck appeared to be a successful departmental commander.[16]

A man of "gigantic intellect," in Grant's words, Halleck had written *Elements of Military Art and Science* and had received the nickname "Old Brains." As Lincoln would learn, Halleck was more comfortable with the theory of warfare than its execution. A capable administrator, he was a cautious individual who avoided responsibility. He possessed little skill in cultivating personal relationships. A journalist described him as a "cold, calculating owl," with a stare that could "make all rogues tremble, and even honest men look about them to be sure they had not been up to some mischief."[17]

In time, Halleck infuriated just about everybody he worked with, from the secretaries of war and of the navy to a cast of generals. Stanton called him "probably the greatest scoundrel and most bare-faced villain in America." The navy chief, Gideon Welles, thought him to be "good for nothing." In Halleck, however, Lincoln found the kind of officer he wanted, a chief of staff who could handle the mountains of paperwork, act as an intermediary between generals and the president, and sign removal orders in his name, not Lincoln's. Both of them regarded the security of the capital as paramount and agreed that the objective of Union forces in the East was Robert E. Lee's army, not territory.[18]

Soon after Halleck arrived in Washington, Lincoln sent him, Quartermaster General Montgomery Meigs, and Burnside to the Peninsula to discuss with its senior leadership a withdrawal of the army. Lincoln had become convinced that McClellan would not attack the Confederates. The president had told a friend, "If by magic he could reinforce McClelland [sic] with 100,000 men to-day, he would be in an ecstasy over it, thank him for it, and tell him that he would go to Richmond tomorrow, but then when tomorrow came he would telegraph that he had certain information that the enemy had 400,000 men, and that he could not advance without reinforcements."[19]

The three generals visited the army during the last days of July. McClellan, Sumner, and Heintzelman renewed their arguments against a withdrawal, while Keyes and Franklin favored it. Privately, McClellan had been confiding to his wife and close friends that he continued to be a victim of the administration's "inveterate persecution." He blamed Stanton primarily and accused him of "magnificent treachery & rascality." He expected to be removed from command. Other officers believed that it would be only a matter of time before he was replaced.[20]

While on the visit, Meigs heard "officers of rank" discuss "a march on Washington" to "clear out those fellows." When Burnside learned of it, he exclaimed, "Flat treason, by God!" Halleck dismissed it as "camp talk." It was evident, however, that McClellan enjoyed enormous popularity with the men in the ranks. Meigs informed his wife: "McClellan is the only one of our generals commanding who seems to have won the fervent affection of the troops. They cling to him with love and confidence even through the fatal delays & these terrible retreating combats." Meigs thought this devotion made McClellan a greater threat to the administration than the Confederates.[21]

The soldiers' letters and diaries during these weeks reveal the depth of their attachment to Little Mac. A few critical remarks about his generalship arose, but they were a minority. Private John Faller of the 7th Pennsylvania Reserves wrote that whenever McClellan appeared among the men, they "jump up and cheer him as long as he is in sight." Another soldier claimed that the "enthusiasm for him now . . . amounts to wildness." They believed that the army had been outnumbered during the Seven Days Campaign and attributed that to government officials who withheld reinforcements. A New Yorker insisted in mid-July, "Let no one think the army have lost confidence in their general, for he is a hundred fold more popular today than ever before among the rank and file."[22]

The dissatisfaction with McClellan's generalship, when found, rested among ranking officers. But the three generals from Washington found an army plagued with sickness and the usual grumbling about food and officers. A sergeant complained, for instance, "Our ofisers hant got eney more feeling for a man than a boy has for a potato." A surgeon noted that during July, "Sickness became almost universal," while another doctor described the death rate as "fearful" from fevers and diarrhea. Private Patrick K. Fowler of the 5th New York summarized the men's complaints amid the stifling heat and hordes of flies, "Glory consists of being half starved, naked, and worked like negroes, knocked around generally while our officers are in their tents, drunk or gambling or endeavoring to find more hard work for us."[23]

Before Halleck, Meigs, and Burnside departed for Washington, the general-in-chief offered McClellan two choices for operations—a reinforcement of 20,000 troops and an advance on Richmond or a withdrawal from the Peninsula. As Lincoln might have predicted, McClellan wired the next day, July 30, that Lee had been reinforced and that he would need at least 50,000 more men.[24]

On August 3, Lincoln met with the Cabinet, discussing emancipation and generals. The president told the members that he was "pretty well cured of objections to any measure except want of adaptedness to put down the rebellion." On that day, Halleck telegraphed McClellan: "It is determined to withdraw your army from the Peninsula to Aquia Creek. You will take immediate measures to effect this, covering the movement the best you can." Halleck stated later that when it came to the Army of the Potomac, Lincoln told him that he would "run that machine himself." Unquestionably, the decision had been the president's.[25]

Lincoln had hesitated to remove McClellan from command despite urgings for that action from Stanton and Secretary of the Treasury Salmon Chase. Meigs must have informed him of McClellan's popularity with the troops. Halleck indicated that the president and others wanted him to order the general's removal, but he refused "to do what they are afraid to attempt." It would seem, however, that Lincoln would have ordered it done if he wanted to replace McClellan. If McClellan refused to fight with the army, Lincoln would send its units to Pope, who might achieve a victory.[26]

McClellan objected to the order, telling Halleck "that it has caused me the greatest pain I ever experienced." For the next two weeks, the general stalled, sought intelligence on a possible attack on Petersburg, ordered a reconnaissance-in-force to Malvern Hill, which gave the appearance of an advance, and kept warning Washington of the demoralization in the army if it were sent from the Peninsula. He and other generals had only contempt for Pope and seemed unmoved with the need to reinforce his army expeditiously. It required time to withdraw the army, but the first units did not march for Fort Monroe and Newport News until August 14, ten days after he had been directed to "take immediate measures" to leave the region.[27]

"Thick clouds" of dust smothered the columns as they marched down the Peninsula. Porter's Fifth Corps embarked on transports on August 20, followed the next day by Heintzelman's Third Corps. While Porter's troops went to Aquia, and then on to Falmouth, the Third Corps, trailed by the Sixth and Second corps, traveled to Alexandria, where the final contingent of infantry units unloaded on August 28. Only the Fourth Corps remained behind on the Peninsula at Fort Monroe.[28]

During these two weeks, as the Army of the Potomac retired from the Peninsula, the strategic situation in central Virginia raced toward a climax. On August 11, three days before the van of McClellan's army started the march down the Peninsula, Lee began shifting troops from in front of Richmond to Gordonsville. A month earlier he had sent Stonewall Jackson to the region, with the orders, "I want Pope to be suppressed." Jackson attacked Pope's vanguard at Cedar Mountain on

August 9, and after a hard-fought engagement, held the battlefield at nightfall. Calculating correctly that McClellan would evacuate the Peninsula, Lee gambled that his reunited divisions could strike Pope before elements of the Army of the Potomac could unite with Pope's Army of Virginia.[29]

Once Lee's forces merged, operations accelerated. When the Confederates failed to trap Pope's Federals between the Rapidan and Rappahannock rivers, Lee sent Jackson's wing of the army on a broad movement around the Yankees' right flank. On August 26, Jackson's foot cavalry struck Pope's supply base at Manassas Junction on the Orange & Alexandria Railroad. The jubilant Rebels ransacked the stores of foodstuff and equipment and then torched the mounds of matériel.[30]

With his supply line severed, Pope ordered his army north in pursuit of Jackson, who concealed his troops near the old Manassas or Bull Run battlefield. Late on the afternoon of August 28, Jackson assailed some Federal brigades at Groveton or Brawner's Farm. By the next morning, blue-coated units—including Heintzelman's Third Corps, Porter's Fifth Corps, and two divisions of the Ninth Corps—had closed on the old killing ground along Bull Run or were en route. To the west, Lee and James Longstreet's wing began filing into position on Jackson's flank. Lee and his army had executed a brilliant maneuver, an offensive masterpiece. A reckoning was at hand.[31]

GEORGE MCCLELLAN STEPPED off a boat at Alexandria on the night of August 26. Upriver in Washington, "unfounded rumors" fed fears of the imminent appearance of a resurgent Confederate Army of Northern Virginia. "Our rulers seem to be crazy," a cavalry officer told his father from the capital. "The air of this city seems thick with treachery; our army seems in danger of utter demoralization. . . . Everything is ripe for a terrible panic, the end of which I cannot see or even imagine." He asserted in a second letter the next day, "it requires good courage not to despair of the republic."[32]

Into this atmosphere came McClellan, accompanied only by his staff. He was a general without a defined command. The Third and

Fifth corps were marching to join John Pope, while the Fourth Corps had stayed behind at Fort Monroe. The Sixth Corps had preceded him to the river town, and the Second Corps would arrive on August 28. As Pope's Federals and Robert E. Lee's Rebels moved toward a climactic battle at Bull Run, McClellan and General-in-Chief Henry Halleck became embroiled in a dispute over the use of the two corps at Alexandria. McClellan's actions and the motivations behind his decisions ignited a furious controversy within the administration then and have stained his reputation since.[33]

Between August 27 and August 30, McClellan and Halleck burned the telegraph wires between their headquarters in a series of exchanges and met personally for three hours. Nevertheless, the generals worked at cross-purposes. Halleck was consumed with the urgent need to reinforce Pope, while McClellan viewed the security of the capital as the primary concern. Consequently, neither corps reached the battlefield at Bull Run in time to aid Pope's army.[34]

Throughout the crisis, McClellan appeared as his own worst enemy. When Lincoln asked him for "news from direction of Manassas Junction," he used an unfortunate expression in his reply: "I am clear that one of two courses should be adopted—1st to concentrate all our available forces to communicate with Pope—2nd to leave Pope to get out of his scrape & at once use all our means to make the Capital perfectly safe." Then, he halted the march of William Franklin's Sixth Corps at Annandale on August 29, a direct violation of Halleck's orders.[35]

McClellan had often used the "scrape" phrase, and most likely, thought nothing of the word's dark import. When the president read the message, he reacted angrily, believing that the general "wanted Pope defeated." With Halleck providing copies of the dispatches between the two men, four Cabinet officers, led by an irate Secretary of War Stanton, signed a letter accusing McClellan of incompetence and deliberate disobedience of orders. Secretary of the Navy Gideon Welles refused to join the others, unwilling "to denounce McC. for incapacity, or declare him a traitor."[36]

Unquestionably, McClellan had acted with his habitual caution, delayed the execution of Halleck's orders, and offered reasons or excuses for not expediting the movement to Pope. He regarded the latter general as a "fool" and admitted to his wife on August 28 that Pope was "in a bad way." But his reluctance to rush Franklin's troops toward Manassas seemed reasonable to him at the time. Like Halleck and Lincoln, he wrestled with conflicting information from the front. One report placed Stonewall Jackson's Rebels between Pope's army and Washington. If accurate, that situation would constitute a serious threat to the capital. McClellan lacked adequate cavalry for scouting, could not resupply depleted artillery ammunition, and contended that Franklin's and Sumner's men were in no condition "to accomplish much" if force marched to Manassas. He acted judiciously in not starting Franklin before Sumner arrived at Alexandria on August 28. Ultimately, McClellan should not be blamed for the consequences of Pope's woeful generalship at Second Bull Run.[37]

An indication of the extent of Pope's failure came from an aide of McClellan's early on the morning of August 31. In a telegram to Halleck, McClellan stated that the staff officer "reports our army as badly beaten. Our losses very heavy." Although Pope denied the decisiveness of the defeat in a dispatch to Halleck—"The enemy is badly crippled. . . . Do not be uneasy. We will hold our own here."—his army had barely survived destruction. At no other time in the war would Lee and the Army of Northern Virginia come so close to crushing an opponent, to shattering a Union army into pieces.[38]

For two days, August 29 and 30, Pope had hurled his units, including troops from the Third and Fifth corps, in piecemeal attacks against the Confederates, posted behind an embankment of an unfinished railroad. Pope ignored reports and protestations from his generals that Lee's army had been reunited. Throughout the campaign, he had either misinterpreted intelligence or misjudged Lee's intentions. He and his army paid dearly for his myopia when late on the afternoon of August 30, James Longstreet's Confederate divisions counterattacked. Only the stout resistance by some Union commands saved Pope's army from a crushing defeat. Longstreet insisted afterward that the victory was Lee's most masterful triumph of the war. The Southerners had suffered fewer than 8,500 casualties, while inflicting nearly 14,000.[39]

The remnants of Pope's army retreated during the night of August 30–31 to Centreville. They met Franklin's troops, who taunted them with whether this was "the new road to Richmond." According to one of Pope's men, some members of the Sixth Corps "in plain English expressed their delight at the defeat of Pope and his army."[40]

Reinforced by Franklin's and Sumner's corps, the army stayed at Centreville until the afternoon of September 1, when Pope learned of a Confederate movement around his right flank. He dispatched units to block the enemy and started the rest of the army east toward Washington. The detached troops collided with Jackson's men at Chantilly. For two hours, in a violent thunderstorm, they fought each other to a standstill. Early in the action, Brigadier General Isaac Stevens, a Ninth Corps division commander, was slain. And near the combat's end, Philip Kearny accidentally rode into the Rebel ranks. As he spurred away, he was shot and killed instantly.[41]

Kearny's death stunned the officers and men of his division. Private William Wiley of the 70th New York thought that it was only "a dream" and Kearny still lived. A lieutenant stated after the war that he was "the only one for whom I have shed a tear." Although he had not particularly distinguished himself at Second Bull Run, Kearny, more than any other general in the Army of the Potomac, embodied a warrior's temperament. He had been an inordinately ambitious man, a difficult subordinate, a self-promoter, and a caustic critic. But combat had inflamed his soul, and he possessed a fighting spirit sorely lacking in the army. "The country has lost much when he died," declared Colonel Regis de Trobriand in a letter.[42]

Volunteers from the 57th Pennsylvania retrieved his body under a flag of truce the next morning, with five companies of the regiment escorting it to Washington. He had belonged to them, and they to him. A sergeant professed to his parents that the division's "battle cry will bea remember Kearny and they will fight for they loved him for they knew him to be true for he took every advantage to save the men and to whip the rebel." They wore proudly the *"red diamond"* patches or badges he had created for them. Even after his death, claimed an officer, Kearny's soul "animated" the division. If so, he marched in good company.[43]

On the same day the Pennsylvanians carried Kearny's body homeward, Lincoln gathered Cabinet members for a meeting at the White House. When he had learned of the defeat at Bull Run, Lincoln told

Hay, "Well John, we are whipped again, I am afraid." The secretary thought, however, that the president seemed "defiant." The next day, September 1, Lincoln and Halleck met with McClellan, who admitted to Ellen that he came to the War Department as "mad as a March hare." Lincoln directed him to assume command of the Washington defenses and the garrison troops. He also informed McClellan that he had learned that Army of the Potomac officers were not cooperating with Pope and wanted it stopped.[44]

Lincoln had based his statement about a lack of cooperation on a message, dated September 1, that he had read from Pope. In it, Pope declared, "I think it my duty to call your attention to the unsoldierly and dangerous conduct" of "many" officers of the Army of the Potomac. He did not identify them by name but called them "mere tools or parasites" whose "example is producing . . . very disastrous results." In his judgment, the only course left was to "draw back this army to the intrenchments in front of Washington, and set to work in that secure place to reorganize and secure it. You may avoid great disaster by doing so."[45]

If Lincoln had doubts about Pope's ability to retain command of the army, this dispatch probably dispelled them. An evident crisis of leadership and infighting cursed the army. The president no longer trusted McClellan, describing him as the "chief alarmist and grand marplot of the Army." He called the general's dispatches as "weak, whiney, vague, and incorrect." He confided to Hay about McClellan: "Unquestionably he has acted badly toward Pope! He wanted him to fail. That is unpardonable."[46]

Lincoln had endured many long, difficult days and nights since his inauguration. The unprecedented burdens of the office, worsened by personal grief over the death of his son Willie, had worn him down. The spring prospects of the capture of Richmond had vanished. Events had compelled him to withhold his Emancipation Proclamation, and he knew that the Cabinet seethed with division over command of the army. Despite his efforts, he appeared helpless to will a battlefield victory. Recently, abolitionist leader Wendell Phillips had proclaimed him publicly to be "a first-rate second-rate man."[47]

About this time, perhaps even on the night of September 1, Lincoln searched for an explanation for the desperate crisis. He put his thoughts on paper, only for himself: "In the present civil war it is quite possible that God's purpose is something different from the purpose of either party. . . . I am almost ready to say this is probably true—that God wills this contest, and wills that it shall not end yet. . . . He could have either *saved* or *destroyed* the Union without a human contest. Yet the contest began. And having begun He could give the final victory to either side any day. Yet the contest proceeds."[48]

If it were so, if "God's purpose" required a continuance of the struggle, of the sacrifice, of the loss of more lives, then it would be. As a bleak fatalism darkened Lincoln's thoughts, a grim realism guided his decisions. For army commander, "we must use what tools we have," he told Hay. "I must have McClellan to reorganize the army and bring it out of chaos. McClellan has the army with him." The restoration of McClellan to command, in the assessment of historian Stephen Sears, "surely made this the most agonizing military-command decision that Lincoln had to make during the war."[49]

At seven o'clock on the morning of September 2, with Halleck accompanying him, the president came to McClellan's residence on H Street in Washington. Lincoln offered him command of the Army of the Potomac and Pope's Army of Virginia, merged into the former one. His immediate duty would be to reorganize the army and to defend the capital. After Lincoln and Halleck departed, McClellan informed his wife of the news. He said that he faced "a terrible & thankless task," explaining that he assumed "it reluctantly—with a full knowledge of all its difficulties & of the immensity of the responsibility. I only consent to take it for the country's sake & with the humble hope that God has called me to it—how I pray he may support me!"[50]

Lincoln announced the reinstatement of McClellan to the Cabinet at the midday meeting. "There was a more disturbed and desponding feeling than I have ever witnessed in council," recorded Gideon Welles in his diary. The president insisted that he alone was responsible for the decision, admitting that McClellan had the "slows," but he had done what "seemed to him best." The four members who signed the letter of "remonstrance" against the general presented it to Lincoln. According to Welles, Stanton possessed an "implacable hostility" to McClellan. The president read the document "in deep distress," telling his department heads that he respected their "earnest sincerity." But no one, he added, "could do the work wanted as well as McClellan." He revealed the torment he had gone through over the decision when he said that at times "he felt almost ready to hang himself."[51]

It was done—there would be no reconsideration for the present. Earlier, Salmon Chase had grumbled to Welles: "Conversations . . . amounted to but little with the President on subjects of this importance. It was like throwing water on a duck's back." A few days later, Welles wrote in his diary that Lincoln would not have McClellan publicly disgraced, although he had been "more offended" with the general than ever before. "From what I have seen and heard within the last few days," the navy secretary added, "the more highly do I appreciate the President's judgment and sagacity in the stand he made."[52]

On the road from Centreville, meanwhile, came the army. A lieutenant in one of the capital's forts thought that the troops looked "more like a mob than disciplined soldiers." A 7th Wisconsin officer claimed that the army had been "scattered from hell to breakfast." Beneath the outward appearance simmered a contempt for Pope and a hatred of McDowell, who allegedly had signaled the enemy during the battle with his "mystic white hat." An utterly false accusation, embellished by camp talk, it moved the men to damn him as "the *traitor.*" As for the army commander, "We suffered more in 14 days that we was under Pope," declared one member of the Pennsylvania Reserves, "than we did all the time on the Peninsula." Colonel Gouverneur Warren insisted to his brother, "A more utterly unfit man than Pope was never seen."[53]

McClellan rode out of the city to meet the troops, halting on Munson's Hill. He had put on his dress uniform, with a yellow sash and sword. As the van of the army approached, Pope and McDowell joined McClellan, who informed the pair of generals that he was now in command of the army. Months later, Brigadier General David Birney claimed to a friend that McClellan "was so pleased with *Popes defeat!*" McClellan then discussed briefly where troops should be posted. The generals exchanged salutes, and Pope and McDowell rode on.[54]

Brigadier General John Hatch had overheard the conversation, and hurrying back to his brigade, shouted, "Boys, McClellan is in command again; three cheers!" The men yelled in response. And then the news rolled back along the ranks, pushed rearward in a swelling thunder of voices—"Little Mac is back." "They were perfectly wild with delight," a brigadier wrote of his troops, "hauled their caps in the air and showed the greatest enthusiasm." A staff officer boasted, "Such cheers I never heard before. The effect was like magic on the whole army." A gunner, who witnessed it from a fort, remembered it as "the greatest ovation" he had ever seen given any general."[55]

Never before and never again would the army give such an embrace to a general. The depth of their emotions could not be denied. "A Deliverer had come," exclaimed one of them. "Our army is now in the best of spirits," Sergeant Charles T. Bowen of the 12th United States Infantry told his wife that night, "for our little McClellan is at our head once more & we cant be whipped under him." Captain Hiram S. Wilson of the 93rd New York explained in a letter their intense feelings for McClellan: "I am ready to lay down my life at any time at his bidding. and you may rely upon it the whole Army of the Potomac feels the same way. The Government now sees that he is the onely man that can crush this Rebellion." A chorus of tens of thousands of voices had affirmed Lincoln's choice.[56]

Chapter 8

"Behold, a Pale Horse"

"THERE IS A GENERAL FEELING that the Southern Confederacy will be recognized & that they deserve to be recognized,"
observed Union Brigadier General Marsena Patrick on September 6. A
brigade commander under John Pope, Patrick had shared the army's fate
at Second Bull Run and had witnessed the battlefield prowess and fighting spirit of the Confederate Army of Northern Virginia. These Southerners carried with them their country's best hope for independence, a
prospect even closer, perhaps, than Patrick surmised.[1]

On the day Patrick penned his observation, the final contingent of
Robert E. Lee's army was crossing the Potomac River at White's Ford,
upstream from Washington, into Maryland. Bands had struck up "Maryland, My Maryland," as the men waded through the neck-high water. A
young boy, watching the unbroken columns pass, said the Rebels "were
the dirtiest men I ever saw, a most ragged, lean, and hungry set of
wolves." An army staff officer told his father in a letter, "I never expect
as long as I live to witness so imposing a spectacle." Silence pervaded
the ranks because "it was a time of great feeling." "I felt," he exclaimed,
"I was beholding what must be the turning point of the war."[2]

In the aftermath of the victory at Bull Run, Lee saw an opportunity
to strike another decisive blow against the Federals. "The present," he

stated to President Jefferson Davis on September 2, "seems to be the most propitious time since the commencement of the war for the Confederate Army to enter Maryland." He admitted that an offensive beyond the Potomac was "attended with much risk," but it would spare Virginia temporarily from the conflict's ravages, allow the Rebels to gather supplies and recruits, and possibly force the enemy into an engagement. If the operation proceeded well, Lee planned to extend the movement into Pennsylvania. It was a bold undertaking, a calculated gamble that offered a compelling outcome.[3]

By nightfall on September 6, the Confederates had encamped in and around Frederick, Maryland, where they stayed until September 10. Although the physical hardships of long marches and the attrition of combat losses had taken their toll during the past three months, the army possessed a redoubtable fighting spirit. As it rested at Frederick, it was not yet the splendid combat force it was destined to be, but the recent victories had heightened morale and had tempered it, like a sword of the finest steel that had been fired, hammered, and honed into a lethal weapon.[4]

The initial news of the Confederate movement toward Maryland reached Washington on the afternoon of September 4, from a signal station on Sugar Loaf Mountain in Maryland, thirty miles upriver from the capital. Additional reports confirmed the enemy's crossing of the Potomac but contained conflicting information as to Lee's numerical strength and destination. Dispatches warned of an advance on Washington and Baltimore, even on Harrisburg and Philadelphia, Pennsylvania. On the day the Southerners bivouacked at Frederick, a Union lieutenant recorded in his diary, "The possibilities of a disaster to our arms at this juncture are so momentous that every man feels the necessity of doing his utmost."[5]

Lee's portentous movement into Maryland, possibly even beyond into Pennsylvania, brought urgency to George McClellan's efforts to restore morale in the ranks and to implement organizational changes in the army. It was a challenge eminently suited to his skill as an administrator and organizer. His restoration to command had been enough to rekindle the troops' morale—"The army *loved* him and confided in him, and new spirit was infused into the army on knowing that he again commanded it," declared a captain. As Abraham Lincoln told his Cabinet members at a meeting, he had reinstated McClellan "to defend the city, for he has great powers of organization and discipline; he comprehends and can arrange military combinations better than any of our generals."[6]

Within a week McClellan integrated John Pope's units into the Army of the Potomac, assigned dozens of new regiments that had flooded into Washington in response to the president's July and August calls for troops, and started the army in pursuit of the Confederates. That he accomplished so much in such a brief time testifies to his executive ability. With justification, he confided to Ellen, "The fact is that commanding such an army as this—picked up after a defeat, is no very easy thing." Arguably, McClellan rendered the Union cause no more valuable service than during these critical days.[7]

The army's infantry corps underwent organizational changes that would comprise its command structure for a year. Pope's three corps were incorporated into the army with new numerical designations and two new commanders. Major General Franz Sigel's First Corps of the Army of Virginia became the Eleventh Corps and was assigned to the capital's defenses south of the Potomac. Pope's Second Corps was redesignated the Twelfth Corps and would march with the army. McClellan relieved its commander, Major General Nathaniel Banks, assigning him to command of Washington's forts and garrisons. When John Sedgwick declined command of the corps, Major General Joseph Mansfield assumed the post. A grizzled career soldier, Mansfield joined the corps on September 15.[8]

Irvin McDowell's Third Corps received the new designation as the First Corps. McClellan wanted, however, nothing to do with its commander. He wrote to Ellen about McDowell, "I simply regard him as a scoundrel a liar & fool. . . . I have the most thorough contempt for him." As a successor, McClellan recommended Joseph Hooker. He told his wife that Hooker could revitalize the corps and "soon bring them out of the kinks, & . . . make them fight if anyone can." Neither man liked the other. Hooker, said an artillery officer who knew him well, "has no love for McClellan," but no general deserved corps command more than Hooker.[9]

In a postwar letter to one of his former staff officers, Hooker alleged that McClellan approached him personally with an offer to be the army's chief of staff. According to Hooker, he declined because "I did not want my fortunes to be identified with his no further than was necessary." Since no contemporary evidence has been found to support this claim, it seems difficult to accept as factual. It made little sense for McClellan to assign one of his finest combat officers to a staff position. Like McClellan, Hooker would demonstrate executive talent, but the men's personal relationship would have almost precluded such a close professional relationship. Hooker was "in capital spirits" when he received the corps command.[10]

The influx of new regiments and recruits for the veteran units augmented the army's strength. By September 6, thirty-six newly organized regiments had arrived in Washington, with more en route. They came from all of the New England states, New York, New Jersey, Pennsylvania, Ohio, Indiana, and Michigan. Pennsylvania alone supplied nearly one third of the units, including ten nine-month commands. They had been recruited, organized, and equipped so rapidly that they had received little training. Many of the volunteers did not even know the manual of arms. "They are extremely green and excite much comment and ridicule," scoffed a veteran. "They are truly Band box regiments."[11]

McClellan parceled out twenty-four of the new regiments to the army corps and assigned the others to the capital's defenses. Eighteen of the units would march with the army in the forthcoming campaign. He also created an entire new division comprised of Pennsylvanians— seven new regiments and one that had been on provost duty in Alexandria. McClellan selected a Keystone State native, Brigadier General Andrew Humphreys, the army's former topographical engineer, as its commander. A West Pointer, the fifty-one-year-old Humphreys was an officer of much promise and talent, described as "a man of broad and liberal views, of commanding intellect, and of the highest personal honor."[12]

McClellan also reassigned Darius Couch's Fourth Corps division to the Sixth Corps and formed a third division for the Second Corps, under William French. This command had been Louis Blenker's and had served in the Shenandoah Valley. During the Second Bull Run

Campaign John Reynolds's Pennsylvania Reserves had been detached from the Fifth Corps. Now, McClellan placed it in Hooker's First Corps. Unfortunately for the division, the administration bowed to the demands of Pennsylvania governor Andrew Curtin for an officer to direct the commonwealth's defense. Curtin wanted his fellow Pennsylvanian Reynolds for the duty. Although McClellan and Hooker opposed it, Reynolds was ordered to Harrisburg. "A scared Governor," growled Hooker, "ought not to be permitted to destroy the usefulness of an entire division of the army, on the eve of important operations." George Meade succeeded Reynolds.[13]

Additionally, the commanding general revamped the artillery and cavalry branches. He implored the War Department to increase the efficiency of Regular Army batteries and to create new ones. "There is no more important arm of the military service than the regular artillery," he stated. In turn, he relieved William Barry as chief of artillery, replacing him with Colonel Henry Hunt. Barry had been an excellent organizer and administrator, but he could not direct batteries on a field of battle as Hunt had done at Malvern Hill.[14]

Few, if any, men in the army equaled Hunt as an artillerist. Hunt, said an officer, "stands very high, as one of the best artillery officers in the Army, especially as to the handling of light batteries." During the forthcoming campaign, Hunt issued a lengthy set of instructions to his subordinates. His plan was to bring precision and discipline to the killing power of batteries.[15]

The cavalry consisted of a dozen regiments organized into a division of five brigades. Brigadier General Alfred Pleasonton commanded the division. Two years ahead of McClellan at West Point, Pleasonton had led only a regiment on the Peninsula, but had been jumped from major to brigadier in July. A sprig of a man physically, he dressed fancily and strutted like a gamecock. He had a way of inflating his exploits. An officer who had served with him noted, "He is unpleasant in his manners, ignorant of his duties and very arbitrary." He soon proved to be a miserable intelligence officer, overestimating by tens of thousands the strength of Lee's army.[16]

The War Department completed the reorganization by assigning Ambrose Burnside's Ninth Corps to the army. When McClellan

President Abraham Lincoln, the Confederacy's most formidable foe. Because the Army of the Potomac was charged with the defense of Washington, D.C., Lincoln paid close attention to it and constantly interfered with commanders and their operations. (UNITED STATES ARMY MILITARY HISTORY INSTITUTE [USAMHI])

A lithograph of Secretary of War Edwin McM. Stanton. Abrasive, opinionated, and highly capable, Stanton clashed frequently with army commanders but was one of Lincoln's finest Cabinet members. (USAMHI)

Major General Irvin McDowell, the army's first commander, whose ill-prepared troops suffered defeat at First Bull Run on July 21, 1861. McDowell's subsequent career as a corps commander was controversial and mediocre. (USAMHI)

Brigadier General Samuel P. Heintzelman, first commander of the Third Corps. His service in the Peninsula Campaign was undistinguished. (USAMHI)

Postwar view, looking north toward the Henry and Robinson houses on Henry House Hill. The most intense combat of the First Battle of Bull Run, July 21, 1861, occurred across this ground. (USAMHI)

Members of the 114th Pennsylvania or Collis' Zouaves. The regiment was one of several Zouave units in the army. Zouaves favored French army–style uniforms. Regimental band stands alongside the formation. (USAMHI)

An infantry regiment of the 96th Pennsylvania Infantry on drill in camp. Regiments drilled as weather permitted during winter months. (USAMHI)

Major General George B. McClellan, who assumed command of the army after First Bull Run in July 1861, and whose legacy extended well beyond his removal in November 1862. (USAMHI)

Brigadier General Seth Williams, the army's assistant adjutant general. The workhorse of the staff, the quiet and congenial Williams attended capably to the details at army headquarters. (USAMHI)

Major General Fitz John Porter, first commander of the Fifth Corps and close confidant of George B. McClellan. Porter's career ended in a court-martial over his performance at Second Bull Run. (USAMHI)

Brigadier General Henry J. Hunt, the army's artillery chief. Hunt was the finest artillerist in the war. Testament to his skill and leadership can be found at Malvern Hill and Gettysburg. (USAMHI)

A typical artillery battery in typical formation, with gun crews at their posts. (USAMHI)

Major General Henry W. Halleck, general-in-chief of Union armies, "Old Brains." Halleck served as liaison between the army's generals and Abraham Lincoln. (USAMHI)

Brigadier General Philip Kearny, commander of a Third Corps division. The one-armed Kearny embodied the army's fighting spirit in 1862. Killed at Chantilly on September 1, 1862. (USAMHI)

General Robert E. Lee, commander of the Army of Northern Virginia. Under Lee's generalship, his army bested the Army of the Potomac on many of the war's bloodiest battlefields. Lee's 1864–1865 confrontation with Ulysses S. Grant pitted the conflict's two greatest generals against each other. (USAMHI)

Postwar view of the sunken road or "Bloody Lane" at Antietam. Union Second Corps troops charged it from the ridge in left background. (USAMHI)

President Abraham Lincoln, Major General George B. McClellan, and headquarters staff at Sharpsburg (Antietam), Maryland, October 1862. "Little Mac" McClellan was the army's most popular and controversial commander. His contentious relationship with Lincoln defined the army's operations from the summer of 1861 to the fall of 1862. (NATIONAL ARCHIVES [NA])

Major General Ambrose E. Burnside, who replaced the popular McClellan as army commander. Burnside led the army to its "saddest hour" at Fredericksburg, and in the luckless "Mud March." (USAMHI)

Major General Joseph Hooker, the army's fourth commander. Hooker restored the army's morale and organized the cavalry corps in the winter of 1863, and then led it to defeat at Chancellorsville in the spring. (USAMHI)

Postwar view of Fredericksburg, Virginia, from Marye's Heights. Across this ground Union troops charged the hill in a series of futile and bloody assaults. (USAMHI)

appointed Burnside as a wing commander, Major General Jesse Reno led the corps. With Samuel Heintzelman's Third Corps and Sigel's Eleventh Corps posted in the capital's forts, McClellan's field army contained six infantry corps, sixty-three batteries of artillery, and a division of cavalry. When all of the troops joined the march, the army counted 95,000 officers and men.[17]

John Pope, meanwhile, filed a preliminary report on his operations, specifying charges against Fitz John Porter, William Franklin, and Charles Griffin, a brigade commander under Porter. Lincoln ordered that the generals be relieved from duty and a court of inquiry formed. When McClellan learned of the president's decision, he requested that the order be suspended "until I have got through with the present crisis." Lincoln passed McClellan's letter on to Halleck, who restored the generals to command. A New York diarist upon reading Pope's published report wrote: "Jealousies exist among our generals beyond doubt, though one would think them impossible in a time like this. Their existence is a fearful source of weakness and paralysis."[18]

At last, like a lumbering beast, the Army of the Potomac filled Maryland roads in search of the Confederates. A brigadier called the army "a crippled nation's *defenders*." Uncertain about Lee's location and intentions, McClellan consolidated the corps into three wings—led by Franklin, Sumner, and Burnside—and advanced on a broad front, covering Washington and Baltimore. Pleasonton's cavalrymen rimmed the infantry columns' fronts, searching for the Rebels and gathering information. On September 9, Pleasonton reported the number of Confederates in Maryland at 110,000. Two days later, it had grown to 120,000, while their actual numbers probably exceeded 50,000.[19]

The Federals crawled on the roads toward Frederick during the march's initial days. The men in the new regiments fell out of ranks in droves and foraged through the countryside. When a private asked a general where the 118th Pennsylvania, a new unit, was, the brigadier replied, "Certainly, my man, everywhere between here and Washington." They scoured the farms for food "like a cloud of locusts, as thick and as destructive. . . . A crop of soldiers kills out any other crop in the quickest possible time." By nightfall on September 11, the Yankees had closed to within six miles of Frederick.[20]

Throughout September 11, Jeb Stuart's Confederate cavalrymen receded to the north and west before the Union advance. As the horsemen withdrew, the final contingent of Lee's infantry and artillery had left Frederick. When Lee crossed into Maryland, he had expected the Federal garrison at Harper's Ferry, Virginia, to abandon the place to avoid capture. McClellan had recommended an evacuation, with the troops joining his army. Halleck opposed the idea, directing the 13,000-man force to defend the garrison. Consequently, Lee decided that he had to capture Harper's Ferry to eliminate the threat in his rear.[21]

On September 9, in Special Orders No. 191, Lee divided his army into five segments. Stonewall Jackson's command and three divisions would advance on Harper's Ferry from three directions. A fourth segment, Longstreet's wing, would cross South Mountain, west of Frederick, and march north toward Hagerstown, Maryland. Finally D. H. Hill's division would follow Longstreet, halting on the west side of the mountain at Boonsborough and acting as a rear guard. It was an audacious gamble, predicated on the belief that the subjugation of Harper's Ferry could be accomplished in three days and that McClellan's army still lay more than twenty miles from Frederick. Lee had, as historian Joseph L. Harsh has argued, "put at risk his campaign in Maryland and possibly even the safety of his army."[22]

Within three days, however, Lee's timetable had unraveled. None of the units had closed on Harper's Ferry. Still worse, behind the Confederates, the van of Burnside's wing had entered Frederick on September 12. The next day, thousands more of the Yankees marched into the town to a boisterous welcome. American flags hung from houses, and women and children crammed the sidewalks, waving and cheering. "It seemed more like a review," wrote a sergeant, "than the march on the war path."[23]

McClellan and his staff rode into Frederick on the morning of September 13, weaving their way through the throngs of civilians, who pressed against his horse to shake his hand and to hold up children for the general to kiss. Before noon, he was handed a copy of Lee's Special Order No. 191, which had been discovered by a soldier in the 27th Indiana in a field outside town. This copy was addressed to Confederate general D. H. Hill and had been wrapped around three cigars. Who lost it has remained a mystery.[24]

When McClellan received the copy, he was speaking to a group of local citizens. Stopping to read it, he exclaimed, "Now I know what to do!" One of McClellan's aides was familiar with the handwriting of the Confederate staff officer who had penned the order from their service together in the antebellum army and attested to the document's authenticity. At noon, McClellan wired the president: "I have the whole Rebel force in front of me but am confident and no time shall be lost. . . . I think Lee has made a gross mistake and that he will be severely punished for it. The Army is in motion as rapidly as possible. I hope for a great success if the plans of the Rebels remain unchanged. . . . I have all the plans of the Rebels and will catch them in their own trap if my men are equal to the emergency. . . . Will send you trophies."[25]

The discovery of the "Lost Order" has been regarded as one of the most significant intelligence finds in American military history. It confirmed reports that Lee had divided his army, but it did not reveal Lee's strength. From Frederick, where four Union infantry corps lay in its vicinity, McClellan had the bulk of his army closer geographically to elements of Lee's scattered forces than they were to each other. Only the barrier of South Mountain, less than fifteen miles west of Frederick, separated the Yankees from the Rebels. Two main gaps, Turner's and Crampton's, lying nearly ten miles apart, notched the mountain's spine and provided avenues of march for the Northerners. The possibilities of saving the Harper's Ferry garrison and of destroying a portion of Lee's army beckoned to the west, across looming South Mountain.[26]

Much has been written about McClellan's response to the information in the order. When the circumstances demanded boldness, it has been argued, he acted with characteristic slowness. Certainly, Lee had lost the strategic initiative to his opponent, but that had occurred the day before, when his plans for capturing Harper's Ferry had been delayed and when Burnside's column had entered Frederick. When McClellan read Lee's order, he knew that the campaign's course had shifted in his favor. Did the Union commander, with his timid generalship, then fritter away this fortuitous discovery? Had he been given a realistic chance of destroying Lee's army piecemeal?[27]

McClellan spent the afternoon of September 13 seeking further corroboration of the order's details. He knew from the sounds of gunfire that the Harper's Ferry garrison had not surrendered. He sent a copy of the order to Pleasonton and directed him "to ascertain whether this order of march has thus far been followed by the enemy." The cavalry officer's troopers were clashing with Stuart's men in the valley east of South Mountain. When Pleasonton reported in the early evening that the enemy had apparently followed the specified routes, McClellan decided to advance on the two gaps the next day. He would attack the Confederates west of Turner's Gap at Boonsborough, and would try to relieve the beleaguered garrison through Crampton's Gap.[28]

Although McClellan had assured Lincoln, "The Army is in motion as rapidly as possible," it did not advance for eighteen hours after he had been handed the Lost Order. His efforts to seek additional intelligence during the afternoon seemed reasonable. But the situation clamored for action, even a limited movement. A possible, if not probable, engagement with the Confederates loomed ahead to the west. With minimal risk, he could have marched his infantry westward, closer to the South Mountain gaps. The army's good fortune required of its commander not rashness, but aggressiveness.[29]

Ultimately, however, what seemed to beckon beyond South Mountain was not attainable. At no time, unless Lee chose to stand and give battle, could McClellan have crippled a contingent of the Rebel army. With Stuart's cavalrymen screening the rear, the commands still in Maryland could have eluded their pursuers and recrossed the river into Virginia, joining the troops already south of the Potomac. "No matter who commanded it," Harsh has concluded, "the Army of the Potomac did not have the discipline, the officers, or the legs to outrun the Army of Northern Virginia." Whether there would be an offer of battle in Maryland rested not with McClellan, but with his opponent.[30]

Lee learned in separate dispatches from Stuart and Hill on the night of September 13 that the Federals knew of the division of the army and were approaching the South Mountain gaps. Stuart reported that the enemy was moving to the relief of Harper's Ferry, while Hill concluded, from the number of campfires visible in the valley below the crest, that McClellan's main force lay opposite Turner's Gap. The initiative, a critical factor in a campaign, now belonged to his opponent.[31]

The Confederate commander could either defend the mountain passages until the siege of Harper's Ferry had ended or start his units in Maryland for the Potomac fords, abandoning the campaign. From its inception, this offensive strike into Northern soil had been a bold enterprise. Lee had gambled further when he had fragmented his army. He had risked much. He would risk more. The Rebels would stand and fight on South Mountain. He issued the orders. Hours later a second dispatch arrived from Stuart at army headquarters in Hagerstown. In it, Stuart stated that a civilian had informed him that McClellan had in his possession a document that contained plans for the Confederate army.[32]

SOUTH MOUNTAIN ROSE thirteen hundred feet above the valley floor on its eastern side. Heavily wooded, its face creased with hollows and ravines, it was an imposing sight. Splotches of mountain laurel, intertwined among the trees, choked the rocky ground. A handful of pastures and farmers' fields, framed by rail and stone fences, pockmarked the curtain of green. Amid its natural beauty lay a terrible place if a determined foe chose to make it a battleground. Here, on the early morning of September 14, 1862, gray-coated men waited.[33]

The Battle of South Mountain began at nine o'clock on the morning of September 14, when troops of the Union Ninth Corps advanced to the attack. Smoke rose above the treetops as streams of fire flashed from muskets and cannon. From this time until after nightfall, the eastern slope of South Mountain reverberated with the sounds of combat and the shouts of warriors. The "sides of the mountain seemed in a blaze of flame," declared a Northerner. Before the fighting ended, thirteen Confederate brigades and seventeen Federal brigades had been drawn into the struggle.[34]

The combat centered upon two gaps—Turner's, where the old National Road crossed the mountain, and Fox's, a mile to the south, where the Old Sharpsburg Road angled over the crest. Here, D. H. Hill's 6,000 Confederates held the ground against 20,000 Federals throughout much of the day. Wing commander Ambrose Burnside directed the Union attacks, funneling Ninth Corps units to Fox's Gap and bringing up Joseph Hooker's First Corps to assail Turner's Gap. But the stubborn resistance of the defenders, the wooded terrain, the steepness of the slope, and confusion hampered the attackers. Hill shifted his brigades and regiments deftly and used the advantages of the terrain. The afternoon arrival of James Longstreet's eight brigades bolstered the defenders and added vital reinforcements.[35]

In Fox's Gap, the Ninth Corps kept pressing forward against the beleaguered defenders. The corps's well-liked acting commander, Major General Jesse Reno, fell mortally wounded, dying within an hour after a bullet had torn into his side and exited through his abdomen. To the north at Turner's Gap, it was not until mid-afternoon before the First Corps attempted "to turn the enemy's left and get in his rear." It had taken time for Hooker to bring up his three divisions, align them in an assault column, and ascend the mountain. When they advanced, the veterans moved steadily and relentlessly against the Confederate flank. Only the timely appearance of Longstreet's final units allowed the Rebels to hold on until nightfall.[36]

Down below, along National Road, a single Union brigade advanced into the gorge of Turner's Gap. Like most of the units in Hooker's corps, this brigade had belonged to John Pope's Army of Virginia. It differed from others in the army by being composed of Westerners, the 2nd, 6th, and 7th Wisconsin and 19th Indiana. Each member wore the black, standard Regular Army or so-called Hardee hat, with its high crown and wide brim. The headwear had been the idea of the commander, Brigadier General John Gibbon, who had wanted his men to have the appearance and discipline of Regular troops. That task had been a struggle for Gibbon.[37]

Gibbon had assumed command of the brigade in May 1862, months after the four regiments had been placed together. A West Pointer in the class behind McClellan's, Gibbon was old army to the soul. A private wrote, "you'll just feel that you hadn't better call him Johnnie." He ordered hours of drill and imposed a strict discipline upon the Westerners, who universally hated him. They resisted the efforts of "the old tyrant" to turn them into Regulars. They complained loudly when they had to pay for their new hats and long frock coats. More than anything, they complained about not meeting Southerners in battle. Only the 2nd Wisconsin had been at First Bull Run, and its members wanted another chance.[38]

Their chance had come at last at Brawner's Farm on August 28. For more than an hour, standing in open fields, almost alone, they fought four Confederate brigades, at times with their ranks less than a hundred yards apart. When the 2nd Wisconsin saw the Rebels, some of them shouted, "Come on, God damn you." "A roaring hell of fire" marked the battle lines. A member of the brigade explained later their valor and their willingness to stand under such a fire: "When we went down to the Potomac in '61, we were the only Western soldiers in the entire army, and we would have died rather than dishonor the West." Gibbon, however, had earned their respect.[39]

On this September afternoon, the Westerners advanced into the darkened woods along National Road. Alabamians and Georgians blasted them. If Gibbon's men were not well known in their army, these Southerners knew who they were because of Brawner's Farm, calling them "damned black hats." Both sides maintained an "incessant and forcible" fire, but the Yankees kept coming, and gained ground. Whether it was because of South Mountain or Antietam, three days later, McClellan conferred the name "Iron Brigade" upon the Westerners.[40]

The deepening blackness finally ended the combat. The Confederates still clung to Turner's Gap and National Road, their route of escape. Their stalwart defense had given Lee another day. He ordered them off the mountain. Through the night—"a bad night," in the words of a staff officer—they filed down the western slope to Boonsborough, leaving behind the dead and wounded, who lay abandoned and "dying by inches." The engagement had cost the Southerners 1,950 casualties, the Northerners 1,800. Confederate cavalrymen formed a picket line on the mountain as the last infantry unit passed to the rear.[41]

To the south, at Crampton's Gap, McClellan's plan for the successful relief of the Harper's Ferry garrison had been thwarted by a handful of Confederates and wing commander William Franklin's lackluster generalship. McClellan had instructed Franklin to attack the pass if he found it defended and to move against Lafayette McLaws's Confederate command, which held Maryland Heights above Harper's Ferry. "I ask of you at this important moment all your intellect the utmost activity that a general can exercise," wrote McClellan. The purpose was, he added, "to attack the enemy in detail & beat him."[42]

Franklin had his troops on the march by daybreak. Halting them after only three miles, he decided to wait for Darius Couch's division to overtake his column, a violation of McClellan's specific instructions. Three hours passed before Franklin resumed the advance without Couch. Passing through Burkittsville, the Federals formed a battle line in front of Crampton's Gap. A Southerner in the pass noted: "As they drew nearer, the whole country seemed to be full of bluecoats. They were so numerous that it looked as if they were creeping up out of the ground." It had taken Franklin ten hours to cover eight miles and deploy his units.[43]

In the gap, backed by artillery, 1,200 infantrymen and dismounted cavalrymen crouched behind stone walls. Jeb Stuart had misjudged Union movements on this day, pulling out a brigade from Crampton's to cover approaches to the south. Outnumbered ten-to-one, the gap's defenders stalled the Federals for two hours. Eventually, however, Union numbers prevailed, despite the arrival of four Confederate infantry regiments. When a brigade shattered the Southerners' right flank, the defenders panicked and fled in a rout. Nightfall prevented a pursuit, and the Yankees bivouacked in the pass. Any chance of lifting the siege had been foiled by the stout resistance of a small Rebel force and Franklin's uninspired performance.[44]

IT HAD BEEN MORE than two months since members of the Army of the Potomac had awakened with the belief that they had won a battle. Daylight on September 15 revealed that the enemy had fled off South Mountain to the west during the night. Morale among the Federals was high. An officer in the Pennsylvania Reserves remembered, "The consciousness that we had by sheer hard fighting, beaten the enemy and driven him from his strong positions filled me to overflowing and gave me confidence that we would finally win and the country be safe."[45]

The pursuit began shortly after first light. Through Turner's and Fox's gaps and down South Mountain the Yankees marched. The columns stretched for miles, back across the crest and into the valley below. When Captain George H. Nye of the 10th Maine passed a group of Confederate prisoners, he thought "they were the scaliest looking set of mortals my eyes ever beheld." At the mountain's western base, the Northerners entered Boonsborough and then turned west on the road to Sharpsburg, Maryland. The leading units halted at Keedysville, midway between the two villages.[46]

About one o'clock in the afternoon, cheers resounded along the ranks as George McClellan and his staff rode past the troops. Captain Nye declared in a letter the next day: "the cheering that greeted him was one continual roar. Satisfaction and confidence seemed stamped upon his countenance. He passed through the lines bearheaded. He is a noble looking man." A Second Corps veteran joked: "No fight to-day; Little Mac has gone to the front. Look out for a fight when he goes to the rear."[47]

McClellan knew already from a signal station that the Southerners had halted behind Antietam Creek outside Sharpsburg, evidently preparing to make another stand. Late in the afternoon, he received confirmation of the fall of Harper's Ferry, where the garrison had surrendered that morning, handing to the Confederates 13,000 prisoners, 73 cannon, thousands of weapons, and hundreds of wagons. At five o'clock, McClellan proceeded to Keedysville and viewed the enemy ranks on bluffs west of Antietam Creek. The line of bluffs ruled out a frontal assault, but McClellan thought that a turning movement beyond the Rebels' left flank to the north offered the possibility of success. It was, however, too late in the day to accomplish much.[48]

Three days earlier, McClellan had written to his wife, "my only apprehension now is that secesh will manage to get back across the Potomac at Wmsport [Williamsport, Maryland] before I can catch him." From what he had seen from Keedysville, his apprehension should have been assuaged. It appeared as if the Confederates intended to fight behind Antietam Creek.[49]

When Lee crossed Antietam Creek early on the morning of September 15, he had pointed to the bluffs and remarked to a group of men, "We will make our stand on those hills." With that decision, he had taken the most dangerous gamble of the campaign. After the war, he explained, "it was better to have fought in Maryland than to have left it without a struggle." When his scattered divisions had been reconcentrated, however, he would count barely 40,000 men in the ranks. The campaign's hardships had taken a severe toll on the troops, with thousands of them having disappeared into the countryside, heading for Virginia. A tactical victory would garner few results, while a defeat risked the destruction of the army, with its only escape route lying three miles to the west across one ford on the Potomac River. Lee had asked much of his army during the past three months, and now he would ask even more.[50]

With a population of more than 1,300 inhabitants, Sharpsburg lay in a bend of the Potomac River, which allowed Lee to post each flank near the stream. Less than a mile to the east, Antietam Creek flowed south, spanned by four stone bridges. Bluffs jutted above the creek on both its banks. A ridge extended north from the village, ending in wooded knolls and ravines, which could conceal bodies of troops. Hagerstown Turnpike followed the ridge, its roadbed framed by rail fences. Outcroppings of stones, fields of corn, and hollows offered the Rebels additional concealment and protection. No natural eminence dominated the terrain, but the ravines, hollows, sunken farmers' lanes, and woodlots could make it an awful killing ground.[51]

The Confederate line lengthened throughout the day as three divisions from Harper's Ferry arrived. Most of the infantrymen had tramped through the night with only a few hours rest, in stark contrast to the march routines of their opponents. By early afternoon, Lee's ranks extended for two and a half miles in a rough, inverted L-shaped line. Stonewall Jackson assumed command of the left wing—the base of the L, north of town, along Hagerstown Pike. James Longstreet led the units on the right wing, which manned the heights west of Antietam Creek. The position's major advantage was that it expedited the movement of units from one wing to the other along interior lines.[52]

McClellan surveyed this landscape and the Confederate lines throughout September 16. He had at hand most of the army—First, Second, Ninth, and Twelfth corps and two divisions of the Fifth Corps, in all about 60,000 officers and men. The Sixth Corps remained in Pleasant Valley, protecting the army's flank and rear toward Harper's Ferry. Late in the day, McClellan directed William Franklin to join the army with two of the Sixth Corps's three divisions.[53]

During the morning McClellan considered an attack on this day only to rule it out. The position before him he described as "one of the strongest to be found in the region of the country, which is well adapted to defensive warfare." In the end, McClellan settled upon an initial assault against Lee's left flank, the base of the inverted L, north of Sharpsburg. As this attack progressed, McClellan expected Lee to shift units to bolster his lines, which would give the Federals an opportunity to assail his weaker right flank and then the center. Unfortunately, McClellan did not meet with his corps commanders to clarify their roles or to issue written orders. Joseph Hooker, whose First Corps would begin the offensive, testified subsequently that he "had been assured that, simultaneously with my attack, there should be an attack upon the rebel army in the centre and on the [Union] left the next morning." If Hooker is to be believed—and that is doubtful—it indicated the "complicated and confusing" plan ordered by McClellan.[54]

Hooker's three divisions began moving north and west on the afternoon of September 16, crossing Antietam Creek upstream from the Confederate center. Southern batteries shelled the column and skirmishers gnawed at its edges. When the Federals halted, they lay less than a mile beyond the Rebel positions. During the night, Joseph Mansfield's two Twelfth Corps divisions forded the stream and moved up in support. On the army's opposite flank, Ambrose Burnside's Ninth Corps shifted into position for tomorrow's attack. Finally, McClellan instructed Edwin Sumner to have the Second Corps ready to advance before daylight and held the two Fifth Corps divisions in reserve along the army's center. For the first time in McClellan's career, the Army of the Potomac prepared to launch a major offensive against the Army of Northern Virginia.[55]

"The camp was ominously still this night," recalled an officer. "We all knew," recorded a soldier in his diary, "we were on the eve of a great battle." Members of the Second Corps received eighty rounds of ammunition, a certain indication of "sharp work the next day." Private James J. Maycock of the 132nd Pennsylvania, a new Second Corps regiment, confessed in his diary, "from this time I am determined by the grace of God to live closer to the Lord." At the far end of the Union line on the Joseph Poffenberger farm beside Hagerstown Turnpike, the Westerners of John Gibbon's brigade were told that they "will have the honor to open the battle at dusky dawn." When one of them heard it, he growled, "To Hell with your honors!"[56]

A drizzling rain fell, followed by fog, which filled the woodlots, hollows, and ravines. It was as if ghosts had gathered, flitting across the placid fields and pastures, to whisper warnings of the impending terribleness. If it were so, no one heeded their cries.[57]

NEARLY THREE WEEKS AFTER the Battle of Antietam, Surgeon William Child of the 5th New Hampshire wrote a letter to his wife. "When I think of the battle of Antietam it seems so strange who permits it," he said. "To see or feel that a power is in existence that can and will hurl masses of men against each other in deadly conflict—slaying each by thousands—mangling and deforming their fellow men is almost impossible. But it is so—and why we can not know."[58]

To Child and many of his fellow men who either participated in or witnessed the staggering carnage, the battle understandably surpassed comprehension. Never before in America had a single day been drenched in so much blood. Lieutenant Frank A. Haskell of the 6th Wisconsin likened the sound of the fury to "a great tumbling together of all heaven and earth." The musketry and artillery discharges were, professed Haskell, "a roaring hell of fire." Nothing compared in the veterans' memory to the convulsion that engulfed them. The sky seemed, thought a soldier, to touch the ground, like a veil of "leaden hued hazy vapor which wrapped everything in its folds."[59]

The fighting began at daylight with the advance of the Union First Corps. Moving south along the axis of Hagerstown Turnpike, the Federals headed toward a plateau east of the roadbed and opposite a whitewashed brick German Baptist Brethren or Dunker church. The farm of David R. Miller lay midway between the church and the Northerners' campsites. South of Miller's farmhouse, a twenty-acre field of ripening corn—the Cornfield—stood east of the pike. Beyond it, a forty-acre, wedge-shaped pasture extended to the intersection of the turnpike and Smoketown Road, opposite the church. A stand of trees, East Woods, sprawled for eight hundred yards along a section of Smoketown Road, while a more extensive woodlot, West Woods, ran for nearly fifteen hundred yards from the Cornfield's northern edge south to beyond Dunker Church. Eight hundred yards due west of the Miller farm buildings, Nicodemus Heights rose, a natural platform for Confederate artillery. This benign ground encompassed less than two square miles, and within its confines, men turned it into a slaughterhouse.[60]

Mounted on a pale horse, Joseph Hooker led his nearly 9,000 soldiers toward the Cornfield and into East Woods—eight brigades in three divisions, men from New York, Pennsylvania, Massachusetts, Wisconsin, and Indiana. Waiting for them in the rows of corn, behind rock ledges and among the trees, were Stonewall Jackson's foot cavalry—5,000 Virginians, North Carolinians, Alabamians, Georgians, and Louisianans in six brigades. The pop of skirmishers' rifles heralded the reckoning. Combat was, in Lieutenant Haskell's judgment, a simple matter, "the killing of men; the hunting to kill men, and being hunted to be killed."[61]

Within minutes, the hunters and the hunted met in an explosion of savagery. From Nicodemus Heights and the plateau east of Dunker Church, Confederate artillerists unleashed waves of shellfire, answered by Union gunners north of the Miller farm. The volleys of musketry clipped off cornstalks, tore bark from trees, and leveled men by scores and hundreds. One of John Gibbon's black-hatted Westerners told his family, "I could not tell wether I killed any or not as they fell so fast . . . but I know I tried as hard as I could to kill some of them." He was not alone, on either side. Private Hugh C. Perkins of the 7th Wisconsin exclaimed in a letter, "The Rebs fight like mad men."[62]

An officer believed that when a man stood in combat, amid a stream of "hissing bullets," he could hear the "whisper of eternity." On this morning, it must have sounded like a shout. Their words testify to the grim reality. "It was never my fortune to witness a more bloody, dismal battlefield," reported Hooker. "I thought I had seen men piled up and cut up in all kindes of shape," a Yankee confided to his family, "but never anything in comparison to that field." A Virginian called the Cornfield "those corn acres of hell," while a New Yorker thought the enemy dead in it looked "like sheaves of grain tossed together by a reaper."[63]

It was as if a howling ill wind had found this place and kept sweeping more men into it. Jackson sent in reserves, and the Union Twelfth Corps joined Hooker's troops. The ground consumed men. Confederate Brigadier General John Hood, an intrepid fighter, swore, "It was here that I witnessed the most terrible clash of arms, by far, that has occurred during the war." One of his regiments, the 1st Texas, lost 82 percent of its members, a rate unmatched by any regiment on either side in any battle of the war. Twelfth Corps commander Joseph Mansfield fell mortally wounded, dying the next day. He had been with the corps for three days.[64]

Mansfield was shot while he rode with the 10th Maine in East Woods. One of its officers, Captain George Nye, revealed weeks later in a letter to his wife that as the order came to advance, he thought only of their daughter who had died. "When I went into the fight at Antietam," he wrote, "I never expected to leave the field alive. None knew my thoughts but the one above. I thought of what our Darling use to sing 'Pray on the field of Battle.' . . . The splinters were flying from the fence and trees, but I felt no fear—I knew not but what the next bullet would send me where Georgie dwelt and why should I fear? She met death bravely—should not I? Death had no terrors for her—why should it for me? She hoped to welcome me in the other world."[65]

"I do not see how any of us got out alive," declared a survivor. Everywhere, it appeared, was awash in dead and wounded men. In three hours of combat, engaging approximately 27,000 troops, nearly 8,700 had been killed, wounded, or captured, a staggering casualty rate of almost one-third. The carnage stunned even the veterans. "The absolute worthlessness of human life no where was so evident as here," professed a Union sergeant. An artillery private wrote home, "You can imagine what effect war has on men when you see them standing in the midst of dead and dying men, some begging to be carried off and others crying for water."[66]

The 10th Maine's Captain Nye, who had found courage in the memory of his deceased child, reacted differently to the slaughter around him. "I looked more calmly on the field of carnage," he admitted to his wife, "than I could a few years ago to have seen a sheep killed. The finer feelings of man is stunted at such time—and I felt when I saw our boys taking in prisoners that there was a quicker way to dispose of them."[67]

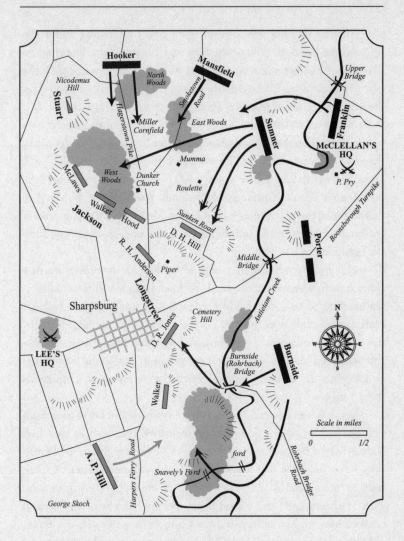

George Skoch

The wind stilled momentarily, and silence settled in across the fields. It lasted only a handful of minutes, like a curtain lowered between acts of an American tragedy. When it lifted, and the terrible gusts resumed, Major General John Sedgwick's Second Corps division appeared—three brigades, 5,200 officers and men. With it rode corps commander Edwin Sumner, who had been ordered by McClellan to cross Antietam Creek and to support the First and Twelfth corps. Before him, Sumner saw the wreckage of three hours of combat and a gap between the battered ranks of the First and Twelfth corps. Ignoring the advice of Brigadier General Alpheus Williams, who succeeded the fallen Mansfield, and believing that he had to strike at once to retain the initiative, Sumner instructed Sedgwick to advance into the gap.[68]

It was a critical mistake, arguably the worst tactical decision by a Union general on the field. Had he waited for his trailing two divisions, the entire Second Corps, 15,000 men, and Brigadier General George S. Greene's Twelfth Corps division of 1,500 troops could have launched a coordinated assault. Although Confederate reserves were hurrying to this sector of the battlefield, such a Union attack held the potential of crushing Lee's center and unhinging his entire line. Instead, Bull Sumner fashioned a disaster.[69]

In his rush to act, Sumner stacked Sedgwick's three brigades in a column, with seventy-yard intervals between brigades. This tactical formation limited the command's firepower to a single brigade and left both flanks vulnerable. Sumner compounded the faulty alignment by not posting skirmishers to the front. Finally, the sixty-five-year-old general abdicated his duty as a corps commander by personally leading the attack. On a day in which tragedy touched so many units, it embraced these Yankees.[70]

They deserved better. "The men were veterans and knew their business," stated a colonel. Some of the regiments had been at First Bull Run, others at Ball's Bluff, and all except one had fought on the Peninsula. John Sedgwick had led them since the previous winter. A Connecticut native and West Pointer, Sedgwick was a physically stout man, with "a cheery soul" and a kind heart. No one who knew the general disliked him, and an officer described him as "a very mild, courteous, old fashioned rustic gentleman." When duty permitted, he spent hours playing solitaire. Staff members thought of him as "a kind father." McClellan said he "was thoroughly unselfish, honest, and true as steel."[71]

Sedgwick and his veterans cleared East Woods, angled south, and then wheeled toward the Dunker Church and West Woods. At army headquarters east of the creek, an officer watched and exclaimed later, "With flags flying and long unfaltering lines rising and falling as they crossed the fields, it looked as though nothing could stop them." In succession, each of the three brigades plunged into West Woods north of Dunker Church. Suddenly they were hit with, reported a brigade commander, "the most deadly fire it has ever been my lot to witness." They had stumbled into a rapidly forming trap. Earlier, Lee had ordered reserves to Jackson's support, and now these troops were racing to join Jackson's men. When they arrived, they ringed West Woods and shredded the Yankee ranks.[72]

Caught in a cauldron of hellfire, Sedgwick's men fell by the hundreds. "For a time the loss of life was fearful," recalled a member of the 20th Massachusetts. "We had never before seen anything like it." A staff officer contended, "It was impossible for an officer to sit on horseback under the terrible fire." Sedgwick was hit with two bullets, one of which broke his wrist bone. When the left flank regiments disintegrated and with Confederates closing on their rear, Sumner rode into the ranks, shouting, "Back boys, for God's sake move back, you are in a bad fix." A sergeant admitted: "It was every man for himself. We all run like a flock of sheep." Most of the Federals poured from the woods, streaming for East Woods, where officers eventually restored order. The fight in West Woods had lasted all of twenty minutes.[73]

In that time, Sedgwick's division lost 2,200 men killed, wounded, and captured, a grievous casualty rate of forty-two percent. On this bloodiest of days, no Union division sustained more losses, and two of its brigades ranked first and second, respectively, among the army's forty brigades. The 15th Massachusetts left more of its members on the ground than any other regiment in the army. It never should have been, and blame for it rested squarely with Bull Sumner.[74]

HISTORY KNOWS IT AS Sunken Road or Bloody Lane. Before armies came to Sharpsburg, it was little more than a lane used by farmers to haul grain to a grist mill on Antietam Creek. It began on Hagerstown Pike, approximately six hundred yards south of Dunker Church, and ran east before angling southeast to the creek. Over the years, the farmers' loaded wagons had worn away the roadbed, creating a natural trench for men who filled such places. On the morning of September 17, 1862, it marked the center of the Confederate line, where the inverted L bent west. About ten o'clock in the morning, this day's bloody work came to the old road and stayed for three terrible hours.[75]

When Edwin Sumner accompanied John Sedgwick's troops, the Second Corps commander left his oncoming two division commanders, William French and Israel Richardson, without direction. French and his three brigades arrived shortly after Sedgwick began his advance. The forty-seven-year-old French was known as "Old Blinky" or "Old Blink Eye" because of an affliction that made his eyes blink excessively when he spoke. His division had been organized only a week earlier and consisted of ten regiments, seven of which had never been in combat before. Without instructions, French turned his division south, marching it until he halted it in the fields of the William Roulette farm, north of Sunken Road.[76]

Approximately 2,500 Rebels manned the roadbed. French had 5,700 officers and men, but he negated his numerical advantage by sending one brigade in at a time. When the Federals reached the crest of a low ridge that lay in front of Sunken Road, D. H. Hill's veteran infantrymen and artillery crews hit them with musketry and cannon fire. The Yankees staggered under the blasts but clung to the ridge, returning the fire. French added a second brigade and then his final brigade to the action.[77]

An 8th Ohio soldier described the fighting as "unabated fury." His regiment had advanced into it with "heads downward as if under a pelting rain." The inexperience of most of the Federals caused confusion and increased casualties. "It was difficult work the men were given," noted an officer of the 130th Pennsylvania, "they hardly knew what was wanted of them." Some of them shot mistakenly into the ranks of other Federals. Major William Houghton of the 14th Indiana, a veteran outfit, admitted, "I saw my brave boys fall like sheep led to the slaughter," but "the men yelled like demons and fought like infuriated mad men." For an hour the Northerners held the ridge without support. Finally, at eleven o'clock, the leading unit of Israel Richardson's division, the Irish Brigade, arrived and formed on the left of French's division.[78]

With shouts of "Faugh a Ballagh, Faugh a Ballagh!"—"Clear the Way"—the Irishmen charged. When they topped the ridge's crest, Hill's

Confederates unleashed a volley that stopped the Federals. The musketry sang along the slope before Sunken Road. By now, more Southern troops had joined Hill's men, and losses mounted rapidly on both sides. The 63rd New York lost sixteen color-bearers. Like French's troops, the Irishmen hugged the ground and fired. One of them argued that amid the smoke and deafening noise "there is no such thing as taking shure aim in the battle field." Officers gathered up cartridges from dead and wounded men as the combat passed another hour.[79]

At this point, Brigadier General John Caldwell's brigade moved to the attack on the Irishmen's left. Their advance had been delayed when no one could locate Caldwell. Told that the brigadier was behind a haystack, Richardson growled, "God damn the field officers!" and ordered the troops forward at the double-quick. These men were as fine as any combat troops in the army. The brigade also had two of the best regimental commanders in Colonel Francis Barlow of the 61st New York and Colonel Edward Cross of the 5th New Hampshire. Before they advanced, Cross, who had tied a red handkerchief around his head, addressed his fellow New Hampshiremen: "Men, you are about to engage in battle. You have never disgraced your State. I hope you won't this time. If any man runs I want the file closers to shoot him; if they don't, I shall myself. That's all I have to say."[80]

Caldwell's five regiments came in on the right flank of the Rebel line. On the ridge in front, Richardson's last brigade, under Colonel John R. Brooke, the Irishmen, and some of French's units charged. In Sunken Road, some Confederate troops misinterpreted an order and withdrew. Barlow's 61st New York plunged into the gap. Almost in an instant, it seemed, the Rebel position disintegrated, with its defenders streaming south. The Yankees swarmed into the roadbed, where the enemy dead and wounded "lay as thick as autumn leaves . . . into which they seemed to have tumbled." Knots of Southerners waved white handkerchiefs. Union officers pushed forward the attack, across the road and into a cornfield. The hinge in Lee's line at Sharpsburg had been snapped.[81]

The impetus of the Union assault, however, spent itself among the cornstalks. Hill rallied about two hundred Rebel infantrymen and counterattacked. Four Southern cannon, one manned by members of Longstreet's staff, fired canister. Another group of Confederates charged the 5ᵗʰ New Hampshire on the Federal left. Cross tore a cartridge apart, smearing gunpowder on his face, and shouted to his men: "Put on the war paint! Give 'em the war whoop!" The men emitted an Indian cry and repulsed the Rebels, who had closed to within fifteen feet. Nearby, Barlow fell seriously wounded from a round of canister. Finally, Richardson ordered a withdrawal, and the Yankees retired to the ridge above Sunken Road.[82]

On the ridge, Richardson instructed officers to re-form ranks and to prepare to renew the advance. His and French's casualties had exceeded 3,000, but Fighting Dick Richardson was an aggressive soldier. Confederate batteries continued to fire on the Federals, and before Richardson could order the troops forward, a piece of iron struck him in the body. A detail of soldiers carried him across the creek to the Philip Pry house, where the general lay in an upstairs bedroom for nearly seven weeks. His wife and his sister came to nurse him, but he succumbed on November 3. One of his men wrote home when they heard the news of his death, "I felt as if my best friend was gone."[83]

Before long, William Franklin and two Sixth Corps divisions— 9,000 officers and men—came onto the field. McClellan had ordered Franklin across Antietam Creek in response to Sumner's pleas for reinforcements. At the time, the battered ranks of the First, Second, and Twelfth corps stretched from north of the Miller farm, through East Woods, to the Sunken Road. Stonewall Jackson had refashioned a line in West Woods, but among the Union corps there must have been nearly 15,000 troops still in the ranks. They had been through a terrible ordeal, but so, too, had Jackson's men. With Franklin's divisions, the Federals possessed a clear, if not decisive, numerical advantage.[84]

The disaster that had befallen Sedgwick's division in West Woods had evidently drained away Sumner's fighting spirit. Despite Franklin's uncharacteristic urging to renew the attacks, Sumner refused, because, in Franklin's retelling, "if we failed there the day would be gone." The disagreement between the two generals brought McClellan across Antietam Creek for the first time. It was between 2:30 and 3:00 P.M. when he arrived. Sumner stated his argument vigorously about the troops' unsteadiness and the danger to the army of a repulse. McClellan accepted Sumner's judgment and canceled the assault. Serious action on this part of the battlefield ceased, and McClellan's original battle plan had been abandoned.[85]

McClellan then recrossed the creek and returned to army headquarters. He would never know, nor would history, if one more assault would have brought a crowning victory. He would never know because he could not bring himself to ask of his men what Lee and his subordinates had required of their men all day. Too many of the Federals lay dead and dying in the Cornfield, in East and West woods, along Hagerstown Turnpike, and on the ridge above Sunken Road to question their courage or their willingness to sacrifice themselves for the cause. If he had asked again, they would have gone forward and bled more for their country. When it had mattered the most, on terrible fields of battle, McClellan had never been worthy of them.

Before he departed or earlier, McClellan assigned one of Franklin's brigade commanders, Winfield Scott Hancock, to command of Richardson's division. Hancock had been readying his troops for the attack when the order came. Franklin wrote later of his subordinate, "I never met a man who, as a general officer, while under my observation, combined so well as he did the prudence which cherished the lives of his command, with the dash which was his distinguishing characteristic." Continuing, Franklin said, "to be under his command, to know him . . . was to have a complete military education." Hancock hurried ahead of his staff to his new command. The Pennsylvanian reined up on the ridge above Sunken Road, dismounted, and began an association that would, in time, define the Second Corps.[86]

ON A DAY STEEPED IN DRAMA, Antietam's final act ended in a fitting climax. At the time George McClellan suspended offensive operations on the northern section of the battlefield, the Union Ninth Corps started an advance from the army's left or southern flank toward Sharpsburg and Robert E. Lee's rear. It was the culmination of a long and frustrating day for these soldiers and their commander, Major General Ambrose Burnside.[87]

At daybreak, the Ninth Corps lay back from Antietam Creek behind hills opposite a triple-arched stone span, which local folks called

Rohrback Bridge (today, Burnside's Bridge). At seven o'clock, McClellan instructed Burnside, who believed that he was still acting as a wing commander, to prepare to assault the bridge. At the bridge's western end, a bluff abutted the bank, held by four hundred Georgians of Brigadier General Robert Toombs's brigade. The Georgians covered the eastern approaches to the bridge. Although the creek could be crossed at almost any point, army engineers reported to Burnside that a passage could only be effected at bridges and fords.[88]

In an order dated 9:10 A.M., McClellan directed Burnside "to make the attack." Burnside passed the message on to Brigadier General Jacob D. Cox, whom Burnside had assigned to field command of the corps. Cox acted at once. From 10:00 A.M. to 1:00 P.M., however, the Georgians beat back with withering gunfire a series of Union attempts to carry the bridge. The 11th Connecticut went in first, lost a third of its men and all its field officers, and retired. A member of the regiment wrote home that night, "I do not know the name of the creek, but I have named it the creek of death." Both the 2nd Maryland and 6th New Hampshire tried twice and were repulsed. Finally, about one o'clock, the 51st New York and 51st Pennsylvania, whose members were promised all the whiskey they wanted by their brigade commander if they secured the bridge, darted down to the creek and rushed across the span. By then, however, most of the Georgians had abandoned the bluff, retreating toward the town.[89]

Earlier, Cox had sent Brigadier General Isaac Rodman's division downstream to force a crossing at Snavely's Ford, located about one-third of a mile below the bridge. Rodman advanced methodically, evidently assuming that the shallows would be heavily protected. John Walker's division had held the ford until Lee pulled it out to reinforce Jackson's troops. When Rodman approached, a small force of infantry and cavalry and a battery guarded it, which the Yankees swatted aside. Rodman marched upstream, triggering the Georgians' withdrawal from the bluff at the time the New Yorkers and Pennsylvanians seized the bridge. With the bridge cleared, Cox funneled three brigades, about 5,000 men, across it, joining Rodman's 5,700 troops. To the north, their Second Corps comrades had overrun Sunken Road. Lee's army faced another crisis.[90]

Then, Cox halted the advance, asking Burnside for more ammunition and Brigadier General Orlando Willcox's division. The delay lasted for two hours, and it was not until three o'clock when roughly 8,500 Federals, in two lines, rolled forward. Confederate defenders slowed the onslaught but could not stop it across the undulating terrain. Within an hour, the Northerners had driven enemy batteries from Cemetery Hill at the southeastern corner of Sharpsburg and neared the village's edge. Their left flank, however, dangled unsupported, and from the southwest toward it came the van of A. P. Hill's Confederate division. Hill's command had been left in Harper's Ferry to gather up the spoils and to parole prisoners. Ordered to rejoin the army that morning, Hill's veterans arrived as their fellow Southerners teetered on defeat. Union signalmen had discovered their approach, but the message apparently never reached Burnside or Cox.[91]

Brigadier General Maxcy Gregg's South Carolinians smashed into Rodman's left flank and the 16th Connecticut, another new regiment, whose members had received little instruction and drill. "The devils [Rebels] advanced till our very noses touched theirs," asserted a sergeant in the 16th Connecticut. The South Carolinians lashed the ranks of the novice Federals, who fled rearward, carrying with them a regiment next in line. More of Hill's units charged, and Cox's line unraveled. Rodman fell with a mortal wound. Cox ordered a withdrawal to the bluffs and hills on the western side of the creek. Sputtering fire from skirmishers and sporadic cannon fire ended the Battle of Antietam, as Northerners would name it because of the creek, or Sharpsburg, as Southerners would call it for the town.[92]

When the sun set on September 17, Americans had suffered the bloodiest day in their history. Although figures conflict, casualties amounted to or exceeded 23,000: approximately 10,800 Confederates, 12,500 Federals. More than 3,700 were either killed or mortally wounded, with another 18,300 wounded. On a battlefield of less than a thousand acres, the dead and maimed covered seemingly every square foot of ground. The survivors described the overwhelming carnage. In typical words, a Union surgeon noted in his journal, "The dead in rows—in piles—in heaps—the dead of the brute and of the human race mingled in mass." Similarly, a sergeant told his father, "On some portions of the field they are lying so that you can step from body to body." And a captain thought the battlefield "was like a Dead House."[93]

Both armies slept on the battlefield amid the horrors. Lieutenant Robert G. Shaw of the 2nd Massachusetts wrote that while he lay within feet of twenty corpses, "The crickets chirped, and the frogs croaked, just as if nothing unusual had happened all day long." Many, if not most, of the troops must have expected a renewal of the fighting with another day's sunrise. In fact, McClellan had ordered William Franklin to attack Nicodemus Heights at dawn. He also sent dispatches to Andrew Humphreys at Hagerstown, and Darius Couch on Maryland Heights, to march their divisions through the night to join the army. Later, when informed of a critical shortage of artillery ammunition, McClellan suspended Franklin's assault.[94]

At Confederate headquarters, Lee anticipated a Union offensive against his thinned ranks. During the night, he compacted his lines into an arc around Sharpsburg, with 25,000 to 30,000 men in the line. Lee's defiant stand reflected his unwillingness to abandon the field, admitting a tactical and strategic defeat, and his belief in the prowess of his army. In his report, Lee praised the conduct of his men on September 17, saying that "nothing could surpass the determined valor with which they met the large army of the enemy, fully supplied and equipped, and the result reflects the highest credit on the officers and men engaged." In time, he regarded the battle as the army's finest hour and rightfully so. His willingness to imperil the army and to defy the enemy for another day rested upon his faith in those he led.[95]

The Federal offensive never came. With the arrival of Humphreys's and Couch's divisions during the morning, McClellan had with him roughly 60,000 troops, with more than half of them unbloodied by the previous day's combat. His concerns for the shortage of long-range artillery ammunition and the combat efficiency of the First, Second, and Twelfth corps were legitimate. It appears that the counsel he received from Edwin Sumner, Fitz John Porter, Ambrose Burnside, and others warned about the consequences of a repulse. He and his senior generals remained convinced that Lee's numbers equaled or exceeded their rank and file. McClellan refused, as he explained later, "to hazard another battle with less than an absolute assurance of success." At some time during the day, he fell ill with a recurring case of dysentery and confined himself to his tent. Late in the afternoon, he issued orders to Franklin to attack on the next morning. By then, however, the Rebels were gone.[96]

The Confederates recrossed the Potomac River into Virginia during the night of September 18–19, ending the Maryland Campaign. When he learned of the enemy's departure, McClellan telegraphed Washington, "We may safely claim a complete victory." Late in the afternoon, a detachment dashed across the river, scattering Lee's small rear guard and capturing two cannon. Their success prompted McClellan to order Porter to follow up the next morning with two divisions. The result was a one-hour engagement known as the Battle of Shepherdstown. It would have been of slight consequence, except for the fate that struck the 118th Pennsylvania.[97]

Members of a Philadelphia banking firm, the Corn Exchange, had recruited and organized the 118th Pennsylvania, paying each volunteer a bounty of two hundred dollars. Known as the Corn Exchange Regiment, the unit had joined the Fifth Corps while on the march through Maryland. Veterans jeered the newcomers as "The $200 boys from Pennsylvania." At Shepherdstown, they were armed with defective rifles and were left isolated on a bluff, facing A. P. Hill's oncoming Southerners. The Rebels hit the Pennsylvanians with an "appalling" fire. "The rush of bullets," declared a captain, "sounded like a hurricane." Hill's veterans swarmed around the Yankees, who fled precipitously toward the river. They had lost more than a third of their numbers in a matter of minutes. The taunts about their bounties quieted.[98]

ON THE MORNING OF September 18, George McClellan wrote to his wife, Ellen: "The general result was in our favor, that is to say we gained a great deal of ground & held it. . . . The spectacle yesterday was the grandest I could conceive of—nothing could be more sublime. Those in whose judgment I rely tell me that I fought the battle splendidly & that it was a masterpiece of art." As time passed, he never wavered in his belief that Antietam had been his finest achievement of the war, or as he told his wife the next day, he had "with a beaten and demoralized army defeated Lee so utterly & saved the North so completely."[99]

His conduct of the battle had been, however, far from "a master-piece of art." Historian Russell Weigley has argued, in fact, that McClellan "directed it as a model of how not to fight a battle." Dis-jointed assaults characterized the Union offensive, giving Lee and his generals the ability to shift units to counter the threats. In contrast to Lee's deft personal direction of his army, McClellan kept himself removed from the ebb and flow of the action on the crucial northern end of the battlefield. He never sensed the urgency, even crisis, on the field. His presence might have brought order and would have, almost certainly, inspired the troops. But he never seemed to be in his element in the boiling cauldron of combat. Instead, he viewed, as well as he could, the engagement's progress through a telescope.[100]

In fairness, he did not have such subordinates as Stonewall Jackson and James Longstreet. A Confederate staff officer described Longstreet's performance as "magnificent," which applied equally to Jackson's. Joseph Hooker and Alpheus Williams, who replaced a fallen Joseph Mansfield, led the First and Twelfth corps, respectively, with skill. Sec-ond Corps commander Edwin Sumner, however, failed miserably, caus-ing the West Woods debacle and losing control of his divisions. On the other flank of the army, Ambrose Burnside displayed a lack of energy and of tactical imagination. The Ninth Corps plodded through the day when an hour's time became a precious commodity.[101]

McClellan and his generals could have inflicted a decisive, if not devastating, tactical defeat upon Lee's army. To do so would have required aggressiveness, even daring, at critical junctures. But within the Union army's senior leadership those attributes were rare. Twice on September 17, and again throughout the next day, McClellan could have ordered bold strikes. All of the actions incurred unknown risks, which were unacceptable to McClellan. Writing of Antietam, an early biographer of the general concluded, "it can not with justice be held that he displayed those rare qualities that belong *per se* to the few men that are entitled to be called great commanders."[102]

McClellan had taken, however, a dispirited army after Second Bull Run, reorganized and reinvigorated it, marched it in pursuit of Lee, and if he had not won a tactical victory at Antietam, he had stopped the Confederate incursion into Northern soil. In itself, it had been a commendable achievement. The significance of Antietam as a strategic victory for the North transcended the battlefield. Lee's failure to win or to extend the movement into Pennsylvania seriously affected the Confederate government's diplomatic efforts to obtain foreign recognition and intervention. And ironically for McClellan, his greatest moment led to an expansion of Union war aims, a policy he had vigorously opposed.[103]

On the morning of September 19, McClellan wired General-in-Chief Halleck: "Our victory was complete. The enemy is driven back into Virginia. Maryland & Penna. are now safe." Halleck passed the news on to Abraham Lincoln. Three days later, at a Cabinet meeting, the president announced that he was issuing the Emancipation Proclamation, with its promise of freedom to slaves held in Confederate territory after January 1, 1863. He admitted that he could not measure the public's reaction to the decision, but he had set a course and would not change it. Later, he remarked to a group of serenaders: "I can only trust in God I have made no mistake. It is now for the country and the world to pass judgment on it."[104]

Newspapers carried word of Lincoln's act to the army. In time, they would offer their views on its meaning and how it would affect them and the cause. For the present, they wrote about prayers, about their weariness of war, and about the horrors they had just endured. Like others, a Pennsylvanian thought of the future: "I cant see how it even will be settled, the Rebels is bound to fight as long as a man left and we will do the same. We both think we are right."[105]

Chapter 9

The Army's "Saddest Hour"

A RAILROAD ENGINE HISSED and clanged to a stop in Salem, Virginia, on the evening of November 7, 1862. From the cab stepped Brigadier General Catharinus P. Buckingham, a War Department officer. Borrowing a horse, he rode with an escort through the season's first snowfall fifteen miles to Orleans and the headquarters of Major General Ambrose Burnside. The Ninth Corps commander was eating dinner when Buckingham joined him. The brigadier handed Burnside an order. Dated November 5, General Orders No. 182 read, "By direction of the President of the United States, it is ordered that Major-General McClellan be relieved of command of the Army of the Potomac, and that Major-General Burnside take command of the army."[1]

Burnside objected at once, arguing that neither he nor any other general could command the army. He valued his long-standing friendship with McClellan, who had helped him out of financial straits before the war. He had refused the command when it was offered after Second Bull Run. Buckingham explained, however, that McClellan was finished, and if Burnside did not accept it, it would be tendered to Major General Joseph Hooker. Disliking the ambitious Hooker, Burnside discussed it with his staff. With their encouragement, he accepted reluctantly. He confided to a fellow officer the next morning, "I don't feel equal to it."[2]

Burnside returned with Buckingham to Salem, where he boarded the engine and rode to Rectortown, the site of army headquarters. It was eleven o'clock at night when the pair of generals walked into McClellan's tent. McClellan was sitting at a desk, writing a letter to his wife. Buckingham handed him a copy of the order. He read it and then said, "Well, Burnside, I turn the command over to you." Burnside asked him if he would remain for one or two days so they could confer about the army's deployment and the military situation. McClellan agreed.[3]

It had been seven weeks since Robert E. Lee's Army of Northern Virginia had forded the Potomac River into Virginia after the Battle of Antietam. For much of that time, McClellan kept his army in the vicinity of Sharpsburg, where it recovered from the campaign's hardships and staggering casualties. Stragglers, recovered wounded men, recruits, and detachments replenished ranks, and the War Department forwarded dozens of new regiments to the army. These additional troops amounted to about 40,000, bringing the total present for duty to approximately 135,000 by October 20. On this same date, Lee reported 68,000 present for duty with the Confederate army.[4]

The Federals suffered from shortages of shoes, clothing, and blankets. A brigadier wrote on October 2 that the army "is not in condition to take the field at present. Our men are tired out, and they are out of clothing, discipline, every thing that goes to make efficient soldiers." It was probably not as bleak as the general painted it, but artillery chests needed to be refilled, cavalry mounts lacked horseshoes, and thousands of men were barefoot. McClellan, however, did not notify the government of these shortages until nearly mid-October.[5]

Abraham Lincoln saw for himself the condition of the army when he visited it at Sharpsburg, on October 1–4. The president toured portions of the battlefield, walked through the hospitals, talking with the wounded and sick patients, and reviewed the troops. Except for the long hours of waiting for him to appear at the reviews, the rank and file enjoyed seeing Lincoln. Afterward, they commented on his ordinary attire—"looks like some old farmer," said one of them—and his apparent weariness—"He looks tired and worn out," thought a cavalryman.

A member of the 19th Indiana jotted in his diary, "altogether he is the man to suit the soldiers." They began to call him "Father Abraham."[6]

The soldiers' response to his visit pleased Lincoln, who sensed their affection for him. His reception, thought a private, "shows that the army has not lost a jot of confidence in their commander-in-chief." Their comments on the Emancipation Proclamation were, at this time, relatively muted. The overwhelming majority of them had not enlisted to abolish slavery but to uphold the Constitution and to save the Union. Perhaps they believed that the edict would not be implemented on January 1, 1863. For the present, those who wrote about it viewed it as a pragmatic measure that could shorten the conflict. Lieutenant Robert Robertson of the 93rd New York expressed well the common sentiment: "I did not and I presume two thirds of the officers did not come out to fight for slave emancipation, but if it becomes a military necessity, we will do it. In the Army we attach little, if any, importance to the proclamation. It is no doubt intended to bring the South to their senses, & end the war sooner, & in that light it is a good idea."[7]

It was altogether different with the army's ranking officers. Before he had left Washington, Lincoln had heard tales of a conspiracy to march the army to the capital and to intimidate civilian officials, and of a "game" or plan to continue the bloody stalemate until exhaustion led to a compromise, with slavery untouched. The plots seemed to have emanated from brash-talking members of McClellan's staff. McClellan might have overheard or listened to the talk, but disloyalty to the government was not one of his failings. Although Lincoln dismissed them as "staff talk," he removed from the service one unfortunate major who spoke of the "game." "I wanted an example," said Lincoln.[8]

The discontent with the president centered upon the Emancipation Proclamation and his meddling in army affairs. The majority of the army's generals, particularly the career officers, were socially and politically conservative. They believed that abolition would increase Southern resistance and feared that granting freedom to slaves could ignite, as McClellan put it, a "servile war." None of them, including McClellan, chose, however, to risk their careers with public opposition to the policy. A brigadier might call the president "Dictator Lincoln" in a letter to his father, but the dissidents kept such opinions private.[9]

The level or intensity of disgruntlement is difficult to assess. John Gibbon declared to his wife, "if this contest is going to end in an abolition war *I cannot remain in the service*." But Gibbon and like-minded generals stayed when it became "an abolition war." After Lincoln returned to Washington, McClellan issued a public proclamation to the army, reminding officers and men of the military's relationship to "the Civil Authorities of the Government." "The remedy for political error if any are committed," stated McClellan, "is to be found only in the action of the people at the polls." It was the army's duty to carry out "all measures of public policy." Ironically, while opposition to the emancipation policy continued to simmer, its successful execution depended upon the military successes of Union armies.[10]

During Lincoln's stay with the army—he called it "General McClellan's body-guard"—he and McClellan conferred privately at length. Afterward, McClellan wrote his wife that the president acted "very kind personally," telling him, "I was the best general in the country, etc., etc." Neither man left a written record of their conversations, but subsequent correspondence between them indicate that Lincoln urged the general to undertake offensive operations during the favorable autumn weather. He spoke of McClellan's "over-cautiousness." When Lincoln returned to Washington, he informed a friend that he had warned McClellan that he would be "a ruined man if he did not move forward, move rapidly and effectively."[11]

On October 6, the president directed McClellan to "cross the Potomac and give battle to the enemy or drive him south. Your army must move now while the roads are good." McClellan resisted, however, the president's orders. He held the army in Maryland until the final week of October, citing shortages in supplies and ammunition and the need for reinforcements. McClellan's telegrams echoed with a familiar ring. When the general complained that his cavalry mounts were "absolutely broken down with fatigue and want of flesh," Lincoln wired, "Will you pardon me for asking what the horses of your army have done since the battle of Antietam that fatigue anything?"[12]

In Washington, meanwhile, pressure increased on Lincoln to remove McClellan. Halleck, Secretary of War Stanton, and Republican members of Congress argued for the general's dismissal. Like Lincoln, they saw that Northern unity was eroding and Democrats were flailing the administration over the Emancipation Proclamation and the recent suspension of habeas corpus for individuals who interfered with the recruitment of troops and other war measures. Democrats hoped to exploit the divisions in the North with gains in gubernatorial and congressional elections, which were being held in October and culminating on November 4.[13]

In the capital, politicians and administrative officials who opposed McClellan received support from Joseph Hooker. Recovering from his Antietam wound, Hooker welcomed senators, representatives, Cabinet members, and even Lincoln to his quarters, giving advice on military affairs and on McClellan. Secretary of the Treasury Salmon Chase wrote in his diary after a visit that Hooker "was very free in his expressions about McClellan." According to Chase, the general downplayed the army's attachment to McClellan and claimed that he had reconciled himself to the withdrawal from the Peninsula once he learned that "it was a plan for getting rid of McClellan." Word of Hooker's machinations reached his fellow generals in the army. Ironically, after Antietam, McClellan had recommended him for the brigadier general vacancy in the Regular Army caused by the death of Joseph Mansfield.[14]

In mid-October, McClellan and the army suffered a major embarrassment when Confederate cavalry commander Jeb Stuart and 1,800 troopers raided into southern Pennsylvania. In three days, the Rebels captured hundreds of horses and dozens of prisoners, eluded Union pursuers, and recrossed into Virginia, with a loss of only two men. McClellan explained his own cavalry's failure to interdict the raiders to "how greatly service suffers from our deficiency in the Cavalry Arm." Blame for that, however, rested with McClellan, who had done little to organize his mounted units into an effective force. George Meade predicted correctly that the Confederate raid "will be a mortifying affair to McClellan, and will do him, I fear, serious injury."[15]

On October 26, the Army of the Potomac began crossing the Potomac River at Berlin, Maryland, into Virginia. It took the army, however, six days to complete the return to Virginia. The men carried with them ten days of rations, but soon roamed through the countryside, stripping farms of animals and foodstuffs. Foraging became widespread. "A mania seized the troops for killing sheep," recalled a Second Corps officer. They seemed to believe that the Emancipation Proclamation and confiscation acts passed by Congress were a license to forage. Southerners, explained a staff officer, "deserved to have their property taken, we all felt." A private declared, "There is no order against it, the officers *encourage it* and the law allows it but still it looks hard."[16]

By the end of the first week of November, the army covered a swath of Virginia, east of the Blue Ridge and north of the Rappahannock River in the Warrenton area. McClellan had his headquarters at the small village of Rectortown, where Burnside and Buckingham found him on the night of November 7. Lincoln had waited to issue McClellan's removal order until after the results of the midterm election had come in. While the Democrats gained thirty-four seats in the House of Representatives, elected governors in New York and New Jersey, and secured majorities in the Illinois and Indiana legislatures, the Republicans picked up five Senate seats and held their majority in the House. But Democrats heralded the election as a victory, and the results encouraged the Confederates.[17]

According to a friend, Lincoln "was the last man to yield to the necessity of McClellan's removal. . . . He wished to give him every chance." But McClellan had squandered his final "chance." As Lincoln put it, he was weary of trying to "bore with an auger too dull to take hold." The president explained his decision to John Hay: "I began to fear he was playing false—that he did not want to hurt the enemy. I saw how he could intercept the enemy on the way to Richmond. I determined to make that the test. If he let them get away I would remove him. He did so & I relieved him." He also believed from his visit that "I am stronger with the Army of the Potomac than McClellan."[18]

Lincoln gave further insight to his thinking at this time when he spoke to a group from the Sanitary Commission. "They [Northerners] have got the idea into their heads," he stated, "that we are going to get out of this fix, somehow by strategy. General McClellan thinks he is going to whip the rebels by strategy; and the army has got the same notion. They have no idea that the war is to be carried on and put through by hard, tough fighting . . . and no headway is going to be made while this delusion lasts." McClellan's removal was, in part, a move toward a grimmer conflict.[19]

When the army learned of the President's action, "the news broke upon us like a thunder clap," exclaimed a captain. "Gen. McClellan was the father of the Army of the Potomac," stated an artillerist in his diary. In their letters and diaries they used strong words to describe their own and their comrades' reactions: "great dissatisfaction," "infernal outrage," "bitter feeling," "one continuous growl," "greatest indignation," and "swear and damn." One lieutenant compared it to "a funeral of some dear friend." Around some campfires, soldiers swore that they would not fight "under any other general than 'Little Mac.'" One enlisted man blamed Stanton, Halleck, politics, and "the God——d ____ abolitionists" for McClellan's dismissal.[20]

The most vociferous grumbling centered in the units that had been with McClellan on the Peninsula. Although some officers and men proposed a march on Washington to force the administration to reinstate McClellan, there was, said a member of one of the old regiments, no "danger of mutiny." Most of the troops concluded "that we were fighting for the country, and not any individual," declared a captain. A 6th Wisconsin soldier explained, "[I] am not a McClellan man, a Burnside man, a Hooker man, i am for the man that leads us to fight the Rebs on any terms he can get."[21]

The army's generals reacted with both opposition and acceptance. George Meade contended that the action "proves conclusively that the cause is political." John Gibbon believed "that the Govt. has gone mad. It is the worst possible thing that could have been done." Conversely David Birney insisted that McClellan and his "Clique . . . have been weighed & weighed and found wanting." A rumor circulated that Andrew Humphreys had declared that the army should march to the capital and "throw Lincoln & his Cabinet in the river & McC power." When Winfield Hancock heard such talk he responded, "We are serving our country, and not any man." Although John Reynolds thought Lincoln's decision was "unwise, injudicious," he wrote, "the prevailing spirit, with few exceptions, is obedience to the powers that be—and determine to do all they are capable of under the new chief."[22]

After he had received the order from Buckingham, McClellan finished his letter to his wife. "I was very much surprised," he wrote. He reassured her that he was not worried, "I have done the best I could for my country—to the last I have done my duty as I understand it." He admitted that he had "made many mistakes," but no "great blunders." He also told her, "I know in my innermost heart she [the country] never had a truer servant."[23]

McClellan then prepared an address, dated November 7, and had it issued as a broadside to the army: "In parting from you I cannot express the love and gratitude I bear for you. As an Army you have grown up under my care. In you I have never found doubt or coldness. The battles you have fought under my command will proudly live in our Nation's history. The glory you have achieved, our mutual perils & fatigues, the graves of our comrades fallen in battle & by disease, the broken forms of these whom wounds & sickness have disabled—the strangest associations which can exist among men, unite us still by indissoluble tie. Farewell!"[24]

He moved his headquarters to Warrenton, where he hosted a party for officers on the night of November 9. "A feeling as deep as I have ever seen," wrote Marsena Patrick, hung over the occasion. McClellan told one group of participants: "I feel as if the Army of the Potomac belonged to me. It is mine. I feel that its officers are my brothers, its soldiers my children. This separation is like a forcible divorce of husband and wife." They drank champagne and offered toasts. McClellan made one, saying, "The Army of the Potomac, God bless the hour I shall be with you again."[25]

Early on the morning of November 10, outside Warrenton, officers and men of the First, Second, and Fifth corps formed ranks in a final review for McClellan. They had to wait for two hours or more before he appeared, accompanied by Burnside, corps commanders, and staff members. Cannon announced his arrival, and then "a melancholy silence" swept the ranks. They presented arms in a salute, as tears trickled down the cheeks of these veterans. Although he indicated otherwise to Ellen, accounts note that tears welled in his eyes. Some of the regiments broke the stillness with cheers, but the depth of feeling toward him seemed to fill every breath they took. *"I cannot account for it,"* marveled a private, *"but his presence was magical."* When he rode away for the last time,

Colonel Edward Cross stated, "He carried the hearts of the army with him." The men filed back to their camps, and as one of them wrote, "The Army of the Potomac has just returned from its funeral."[26]

Little Mac—he would always be Little Mac to the men—boarded a special train for Washington on the morning of November 11. Members of his personal staff accompanied him. He had been in command of the army for slightly more than fifteen months. He claimed rightfully that he had created it and had given it its identity. As he said, it "belonged to me. It is mine." For nearly another year, the army seemed to belong to him in spirit. Many veterans yearned for his return and repeated every rumor that had him coming back to them. Those numbers, however, dwindled over time. No general haunted the army's soul more than McClellan.[27]

He remains the most controversial commander of the Army of the Potomac. A modern biographer of the general, Stephen Sears, has concluded that he was "inarguably the worst" of the army's commanders, a man "possessed by demons and delusions." Historian Russell Weigley has argued: "He was never a warrior. He was a cautious, timorous man . . . who was simply and continually frightened by war, which is not so mysterious a condition." He unquestionably refused to take risks and overestimated his enemy's numbers and prowess, which justified in his mind his cautious approach. In the judgment of Alexander K. McClure, a powerful Pennsylvania Republican politician, McClellan believed that Lincoln, Stanton, and Halleck "deliberately conspired to prevent him from achieving military success." The general's private thoughts to his wife revealed his disdain, even contempt, for civil authorities. He deeply resented Lincoln's meddling and came to loathe Stanton. His attitude had a corrosive effect on him and many of the army's senior generals.[28]

At the core of his caution lay his deep belief that if the army were destroyed the cause would be lost. It was a reasonable judgment on his part, but it tethered him as a general. He either was blinded to or refused to see that link between the army's need to act and the political pressures on the administration. He led the army to crests of roads, looked ahead and saw indefinite risks, and turned them into well-worn paths. He never had the faith in his creation that it did in him. It was arguably his greatest failing as a general.

When he boarded the train on that November morning, the war had passed him by. His concept of limited warfare was insufficient to meet the demands of this war. Now as Lincoln saw it, the war would be won only by "hard, tough fighting." What Lincoln had feared, "a remorseless, revolutionary struggle," was at hand. More than George McClellan rode in that railroad car.[29]

"POOR BURN FEELS DREADFULLY, almost crazy," wrote George McClellan of his old friend Ambrose Burnside. McClellan added of Burnside in his letter, "I am sorry for him."[30]

Abraham Lincoln had considered both Burnside and Hooker for the post but settled upon the safe choice. Although a friend of McClellan's, Burnside had avoided the political bickering within the army and had served capably and selflessly during the Second Bull Run Campaign, funneling units from McClellan's army to John Pope's. His fellow generals liked the personable thirty-eight-year-old native Rhode Islander and knew him to be honest, patriotic, cautious, and open to advice from others. They knew also that he could be obstinate, even intensely so. Division commander Alpheus Williams observed, "he is not regarded by officers who know him best as equal to McClellan in any respect."[31]

The army's rank and file, except for members of his Ninth Corps, knew little about Burnside. "Burnside may be just as smart a man and smarter than Mc.," asserted a sergeant, "but we Soldiers don't think so." A lieutenant noted in his dairy, "Burnside's name is not associated with any great deeds." He would have to earn their confidence, while he contended with, said a soldier, "all this festering and formenting" from McClellan's removal. "Burnside is a good man," stated Colonel Robert McAllister of the 11th New Jersey, "but he is to be tried on a large scale. If he fails, the results will be disastrous."[32]

The officers and men were, however, willing to meet the enemy on a battlefield. "We came here to fight," declared a lieutenant. "We expected and wanted to fight weeks ago." They understood that they faced a formidable opponent. The Confederates, wrote a private, "have a splendid army for *Dash* and *Bravery*." A staff officer thought similarly but contended, "In fair, open fighting, we are their superiors, and in an equal pitched battle have beaten and will most generally beat them."[33]

Still, an undercurrent of doubt flowed through the ranks, expressed well by Captain Charles Haydon of the 2nd Michigan: "No one seems to have any heart for the war except Lincoln, some of the lower officers & the privates. We have fought well & are willing to fight till the last man falls. Still nothing is done. We are fooled, beaten, bamboozled, out-flanked, hoodwinked & disgraced by half our numbers. . . . Hell & furies it is enough to drive a man mad if he has one particle of regard for his country."[34]

Active operations were nearer than they knew when Burnside assumed command. With the order appointing him, Burnside received instructions from Halleck to "report the position of your troops, and what you propose doing with them." Burnside responded in a dispatch sent on November 9. He planned to concentrate his corps at Warren-ton and "then make a rapid move of the whole force to Fredericksburg, with a view to a movement upon Richmond from that point." He also proposed to organize the corps into three wings—right, left and center. A move to Fredericksburg, which lay halfway between Washington and Richmond on the Rappahannock River, would protect the national capital and offer the most direct overland route to the Con-federate capital.[35]

Three days later, Halleck, Quartermaster General Montgomery Meigs, and Brigadier General Herman Haupt, superintendent of rail-roads, visited Burnside at Warrenton to settle upon a line of operations. Burnside reiterated his belief that he was "not fit" for army command. At the time, Burnside had the bulk of the army's 135,000 officers and men with him. To the south, beyond the Rappahannock and Rapidan rivers in the Culpeper area, General Robert E. Lee had Lieutenant Gen-eral James Longstreet's First Corps, with Lieutenant General Stonewall Jackson's Second Corps posted to the west beyond the Blue Ridge in the Shenandoah Valley. When united, the Army of Northern Virginia counted 78,000 in the ranks.[36]

In their discussions, Halleck argued for an advance south against Longstreet's corps, and then to Gordonsville, a railroad junction. Haupt asserted, however, that the Orange & Alexandria Railroad could not handle the army's supply needs. Burnside repeated his plan for a march to Fredericksburg, where he would cross the Rappahannock on pontoon bridges. If the Federals moved expeditiously, they could turn Lee's right flank and force the Confederates to give battle between the river town and Richmond. Halleck relented, provided the president approved the movement. He would have the pontoons forwarded to Fredericksburg. Richmond was, said Burnside, "the great object of the campaign."[37]

While Burnside awaited Lincoln's decision, he organized the corps into wings, assigning two corps to a Grand Division. The Second and Ninth corps formed the Right Grand Division, under Major General Edwin Sumner. Major General William Franklin commanded the Left Grand Division, which consisted of the First and Sixth corps. The Third and Fifth corps comprised the Center Grand Division, led by Major General Joseph Hooker. Burnside also created a Reserve Grand Division of the Eleventh Corps, deployed south and west of Washington, and of the Twelfth Corps, which garrisoned Harper's Ferry, which the Federals had reoccupied after Antietam. Major General Franz Sigel commanded this reserve force.[38]

By this time, Hooker had recovered from his Antietam wound and rejoined the army. He succeeded Fitz John Porter as commander of the Fifth Corps. Lincoln's order that had removed McClellan from command also relieved Porter of his position. Porter had been McClellan's closest confidant and one of the army's outspoken critics of the administration and the emancipation policy. Before he departed for Washington, his former corps held a review for him. As he rode past his veterans, a band played "Auld Lang Syne" and the men presented arms. He boarded a train to a fate far different from McClellan's.[39]

On November 17, the War Department charged Porter with disobedience of orders during the Battle of Second Bull Run and ordered his arrest. John Pope, who blamed Porter for his failures as commander of the Army of Virginia, had preferred the charges. Porter defended himself vigorously against Pope's accusations before a court-martial board, selected by Edwin Stanton. Biased and false testimony and Porter's indiscreet condemnations of Pope doomed the corps commander. The court found him guilty and cashiered him from the army on January 21, 1863. In 1879, another board exonerated Porter, but it would be another seven years before he was restored to the rank of colonel in the Regular Army. His worst crime had been his close association with McClellan.[40]

Two days after Porter left the army, on November 14, Halleck wired Burnside: "The President has just assented to your plan. He thinks that it will succeed, if you move very rapidly; otherwise not." Lincoln's approval had been given reluctantly, believing that Lee's army, not Richmond, should be "the great object of the campaign." Burnside acted immediately, concentrating his units and issuing orders for the march for the next day. His aggressive actions contrasted sharply with McClellan's habitual delays in reaction to the president's orders.[41]

On November 15, troops of Sumner's Right Grand Division filled the roads east toward Fredericksburg, followed the next two days by Franklin's and Hooker's wings. A soldier described the movement as "some of the hardest marching on record." Rain fell, making the roads "as slippery as grease." A soldier claimed that they suffered from a lack of rations and "what we got we begged it of the people Along the rhode." The army's vanguard reached Falmouth, opposite Fredericksburg, on November 17. Here, Burnside expected the pontoons to be waiting for the army.[42]

It would seem that fate or the gods had cursed the Army of the Potomac, even savoring its misfortunes. Burnside had stolen a march on his opponent. All that was needed for the Federals to secure Fredericksburg and the hills west of it was the pontoon train. General-in-Chief Halleck had failed to oversee a prompt execution of his orders. An orderly at Burnside's headquarters wrote, "A train of pontoon boats on wagons have been moving about like uneasy ghosts from point to point as if seeking but unable to obtain a desirable location." It was not until November 25, slowed by the rains, when the pontoons arrived at Falmouth. By then, however, Confederate troops manned the hills west of Fredericksburg, beginning to post artillery batteries and to dig fieldworks. Burnside's plans had been wrecked.[43]

With the enemy—James Longstreet's divisions—evident on the hills beyond Fredericksburg, Burnside had to recast his operations. Before the Confederates had arrived, Sumner had urged a crossing of the river upstream from the town. But with the Rappahannock swelling from the rain, Burnside refused to risk the isolation of one or two corps south of the river. Reconnaissance parties, meanwhile, scouted for favorable crossing points. Wherever the Federals looked, enemy troops appeared across the river. Sumner warned Burnside not to attempt a passage opposite the town, as the Confederates could fill every house and building with riflemen.[44]

At Lincoln's request, Burnside joined the president and Halleck on a steamer at the mouth of Aquia Creek on the evening of November 26. The three men discussed operations that night and the next morning. With the pontoons available, Halleck recommended an attack as soon as possible. Lincoln, however, said that the decision should be Burnside's, remarking, as the general related, "the country will wait until he [Burnside] is ready." With winter weather approaching, Burnside understood that the president expected a movement. He "felt compelled to attack somewhere."[45]

Burnside returned to the army on November 27, Thanksgiving Day, "a cheerless day" to a Maine soldier. Since their arrival at Falmouth, the Federals had been on reduced rations, living mainly on hardtack, which was "so full of bugs and worms that you have to eat without looking to make it go down." Fortunately for them, the first engine reached Falmouth on November 26, on a railroad built by Haupt's construction crews. Barges, loaded with supplies, floated down the Potomac River to Aquia Landing, where details transferred the goods to railroad cars. Before long, twenty trains clanged over the tracks between the landing and Falmouth each day. The army had a secure supply line.[46]

Tents soon covered the hills and fields around Falmouth. Two soldiers paired up, or "pooled their issues," forming a tent with each man's shelter half. An army wit concluded, "the tent was invented by some preacher who was desirous of getting the boys on their knees occasionally and thought this was a sure way." Officers resumed drills, and regiments felled trees to corduroy roads. On December 1, some of the regiments received five months' pay, or "'Fat' thing," in army slang. New regiments arrived, as raw and as untrained as those who had joined the army before Antietam.[47]

The men's mood darkened as the days passed without a movement. *"I am at a loss to understand why we are at a standstill,"* wrote Private Walter Carter of the 22nd Massachusetts, *"idle and allowing the rebs to fortify and gain strength."* Colonel Patrick H. O'Rorke of the 140th New York noted, "a very despondent feeling pervading" the ranks, with "the new regiments . . . rapidly taking their tone from the old ones." The 70th New York's Private William Wiley told his brother: "Everything seems to be at a standstill. I have been around the troops a good deal and I find that there is a good deal of grumbling and dissatisfaction at the thin way things are going on. The men as a general thing are anxious and willing to move or fight if necessary. They want to finish the war up this winter and get home." A sergeant grumbled that the Yankees and Rebels "water our horses in the river at the same time."[48]

Reconnaissance parties continued to search for possible crossing sites. After a two-hundred-mile march from the Shenandoah Valley, Stonewall Jackson's wing had reunited with Lee, and by December 3, Confederate units covered nearly thirty miles of the river. Burnside attempted a crossing at Skinker's Neck, downriver from Falmouth, on December 5. When the Yankees encountered a Southern division, they abandoned the effort.[49]

At noon, on December 9, Burnside held a council of war with his senior generals. Convinced that only a surprise movement would succeed, Burnside told them the army would cross at Fredericksburg, arguing that the enemy "did not expect us to cross here." It appeared from the Skinker's Neck expedition that Lee's units were widely scattered. If the Federals could move swiftly, they could assail Lee's divided army. To Burnside, it was either here or no place else. The administration expected a movement, and he would comply. Burnside remarked afterward, "when once convinced of the correctness of my course, all the influence on the face of the earth cannot swerve me from pursuing it."[50]

That night Edwin Sumner gathered together his division and brigade commanders to inform them of Burnside's plan. "A plain, free talk" ensued "in which words were not minced." Acting Second Corps commander Major General Darius Couch and division commander Winfield Hancock voiced the loudest opposition to the crossing. The majority of the generals believed that it was "rashness" to undertake such a movement. "Sumner seemed," remembered Couch, "to feel badly that the officers did not agree to Burnside's mode of advance. That noble old hero was so faithful and loyal that he wanted, even against impossibilities, to carry out everything Burnside suggested."[51]

Burnside learned of the opposition among Sumner's officers and summoned them to headquarters on December 10. He seemed particularly incensed with Hancock's objections. Burnside should have been wary of his plan if a fighter such as Hancock thought it rash. Their duty was, Burnside said, "to aid me loyally." Later that day, one of the officers wrote to his mother: "To-morrow, if our present plans are carried out, the great battle of the war will commence. . . . I have little hope of the plans succeeding. I do not think them good,—there will be a great loss of life and nothing accomplished. I am sure we are to fight against all chances of success."[52]

Brigadier General Daniel Woodbury, commander of the engineer brigade, and his officers selected three sites for the pontoon bridges— one each at the upper and lower ends of Fredericksburg, and a final one a mile downstream below Deep Run. The 50th New York Engineers would construct three spans opposite the town, while the 15th New York Engineers and the United States Engineer Battalion would erect one each at the downriver site. The bridges would extend from 400 to 440 feet in length, based upon their locations. To protect the engineer troops, Brigadier General Henry Hunt added more batteries to those deployed on Stafford Heights, which overlooked Fredericksburg on the Union side of the river. By two o'clock on the morning of December 11, Hunt had in place 147 cannon.[53]

Shielded by a heavy, cold fog and predawn darkness, the engineers began the difficult work. Minutes after five o'clock, hundreds of enemy rifles flashed from houses and buildings in Fredericksburg and from along its riverbank. Fifteen hundred Mississippians of Brigadier General William Barksdale's brigade occupied the town, having dug rifle pits, notched loopholes in structures, and barricaded streets. The engineer troops abandoned the bridges, fleeing to safety. Some of Hunt's cannon opened on the Mississippians, hurling solid shot into the residences and public structures. So it would be for the next seven hours at the two sites in town. The Mississippians beat back repeated attempts by the engineers to finish the work. Union infantry added their fire as protection, but Barksdale's veterans could not be budged.[54]

In frustration, Burnside directed Hunt to unleash his artillery's fury upon the town. Union cannon erupted in a thunderclap of flame and smoke. Solid shot and shells gouged holes in buildings, toppled chimneys into yards and streets, and ignited fires. Townsfolk who had not fled earlier huddled together in cellars. Walls of residences collapsed in rubble, and fires spread throughout the town. A watching infantryman wrote later: "the most beautiful Sight that I ever beheld was presented to our view. Whole squares of Buildings on Fire at a time and when they would Fall in it would look like so many Camp fires the whole city was lighted by the flames." A sergeant counted eight blocks of Fredericksburg on fire at the same time.[55]

The bombardment lasted an hour. When Hunt's gunners ceased firing, the Mississippians emerged from their shelters and resumed blistering the unfinished bridges and opposite bank with musketry. At last, using a proposal of Major Ira Spaulding of the 50th New York Engineers, volunteers from the 7th Michigan and 89th New York piled into boats to be ferried across the river to secure a bridgehead. A Michigander called the mission a "forlorn hope," while a New Yorker claimed, "Not a man that got into the Boats expected to land alive."[56]

The two regiments were carried across the river under musketry from the Rebels. Scrambling onto the bank, the Yankees fanned out and returned the enemy's gunfire. Engineer troops raced onto the bridges to finish the spans, while more infantrymen crossed in boats. For the next three hours, the foes engaged in a vicious house-to-house, street-to-street fight in Fredericksburg. Barksdale's Mississippians fired from behind barricades, sprung ambushes on the Federals, and launched small counterattacks. Regiments from three Union brigades battled the Confederates. The combat continued in the darkness until the Southerners retreated. Their stalwart defense cost them nearly a third of their numbers but had given Lee an entire day to regroup his units. The frustrating day had ruined Burnside's chances, if they ever existed, to surprise his opponent.[57]

Burnside suspended his original plan to cross the army that day, postponing it to the next morning. A headquarters orderly noted on December 11, "The health of the Army is excellent and they are in fine spirits anxious for a fight to *finish up the work and go home*." A New

Yorker who had fought in Fredericksburg's streets had a different attitude, telling his parents: "I don't know which side did get licked and I
don't care a dam do you. I wish that one side or the other would lick so
that I could get out of this."[58]

Fog clung again to the ground on the morning of December 12. It
would be early afternoon before it dissipated, and through it marched
the Army of the Potomac. Steadily, in columns that stretched for miles,
more than 70,000 Yankees filed across the pontoon bridges. Confederate artillerists greeted them with sporadic cannon fire, answered by
Union gunners on Stafford Heights. A Southern prisoner, most likely a
Mississippian, drawled to a group of marchers, "Never mind, Yanks, you
chaps will ketch hell over there." As he crossed the river, Lieutenant
Augustus D. Ayling of the 29th Massachusetts recalled a memorized
stanza about the Battle of Waterloo from Lord Byron's "Childe Harold's
Pilgrimage":

> *Ardennes waves above them her green leaves,*
> *Dewey with nature's tear drops, as they pass;*
> *Grieving, if aught inanimate e'er grieves,*
> *Over the unreturning brave.*

Ayling confided in his diary, the "lines haunted me all day and seemed
to be ominous."[59]

Members of the Second and Ninth corps—Sumner's Right Grand
Division—entered the rubble of Fredericksburg. Debris littered the
streets, and dead men still lay where they had fallen the day before, with
pigs ripping apart the flesh. Then, inexplicably, discipline evaporated in
a frenzy of looting and pillaging. These veteran soldiers swarmed into
abandoned houses and businesses, seizing "just what we were a mind
to," boasted a private. They grabbed books, bed linen, petticoats, bon-
nets, children's dolls, food, and furniture, which they hauled into the
streets and smashed to pieces. Groups rolled flour barrels outside,
opened them, built fires from pieces of furniture, and made fritters.
Some men blew open a bank vault only to find worthless scrip inside it.
Members of the 8th Ohio discovered a cache of Scotch ale, and others
found casks of brandy and bourbon. Soon hundreds of drunken soldiers

staggered through the streets. "The Boys had high time," declared a Maine private.[60]

Private Roland E. Bowen of the 15th Massachusetts told his mother, "we stole or destroyed everything in the City, great was the ransacking thereof." A Second Corps brigade commander, Colonel Oliver H. Palmer, described the rampage to his wife: "The whole town was pillaged utterly ripped to pieces. Even furniture apparel &c scattered I never before saw a city sacked and pillaged and have no desire to see another. The spectacle is to me a sad and heart sickening one. The government should have taken the property and not allowed sacking & pillaging, by private soldiers." They rationalized the wanton destruction by blaming the Rebels for using it as a defensive position. Whatever impelled them, including officers, their actions stained the army's record.[61]

While the Federals ransacked Fredericksburg, Burnside crossed the river and conferred with generals about an attack on the Confederate position. His initial plan had been predicated on a swift passage of the river and subsequent assaults before Lee could concentrate his units. "The delay in laying the bridges had rendered some change in the plan of attack necessary," he explained. The evidence indicates that Burnside never reconsidered the wisdom of assaults although he had lost the vital element of "surprise," giving Lee nearly two days to mass his army.[62]

Lee's lines extended a distance of roughly eight miles, from north of Fredericksburg to Hamilton's Crossing. James Longstreet's corps covered three hills—Taylor's, Marye's, and Telegraph (or Lee's, as it was known afterward). His front ended beyond Deep Run, where Stonewall Jackson's divisions lengthened the front to Hamilton's Crossing. Jackson's ranks manned the wooded Prospect Hill, west of the Richmond, Fredericksburg and Potomac Railroad tracks. Jeb Stuart's cavalry and horse artillery guarded the army's right or southern flank. The Southerners had widened an old logging path into the so-called Military Road, which could expedite the transfer of units from one portion of the line to another.[63]

At the center of the Confederate position rose Marye's Heights, two hills joined by a swale or saddle. "Brompton," the Marye family mansion, graced its crest. Below the brow, the slope bristled with cannon, protected by pits. At the heights' base ran a sunken road, edged by two stone walls. Between the roadbed and Fredericksburg lay an open plain dotted with a few houses, gardens, and a small brick store. Five hundred yards from the stone walls, a millrace or canal, fifteen feet in width, sliced through the plain. The millrace was a natural barrier for any assault force to cross, and the Federals closed the gates to it at a paper mill on December 12, reducing the depth of the water to about three feet. Finally, the ground's contour was flush with the top of the eastern stone wall, making a natural trench invisible to the Yankees.[64]

During an inspection of his lines, Longstreet met with E. Porter Alexander, a gifted artillery officer. Longstreet suggested to Alexander that he place more guns on Marye's Heights. Alexander replied: "General, we cover that ground now so well that we will comb it as with a finetooth comb. A chicken could not live on that field when we open on it." The Army of Northern Virginia had never defended finer killing ground.[65]

Burnside, however, looked at Jackson's lines on wooded Prospect Hill. He reconnoitered the ground with Left Grand Division commander William Franklin and corps commanders John Reynolds and William Smith. The three generals proposed an attack on the position, to begin at dawn so the troops could deploy under the cover of darkness. Burnside seemed to agree—at least the subordinates thought that he had. He promised to send orders and rode away. Returning to headquarters after midnight, Burnside waited nearly six hours before issuing the orders. By then, it was too late for Franklin to advance at dawn.[66]

First Corps division commander John Gibbon asserted later that Burnside's "characteristic defect was to trust too many things *to chance*, exemplified by a favorite expression of his, 'Trust to luck.'" What he planned for his army on December 13 required more than luck. Before the sun set on this day, fields blue with dead and dying men would affirm Burnside's admission that he was "not fit" to command the army. Fortune's favor must have been elsewhere.[67]

MID-NINETEENTH-CENTURY AMERICAN culture enshrined courage. With duty, honor, and religion, it defined the attributes of manliness. Amid combat's fearful carnage, it was a harsh standard for an individual to uphold. But if Americans chose to worship this most valued mark of a man, there was an altar with the word Fredericksburg chiseled upon it.[68]

Years after the war, a member of the Iron Brigade declared that why men went forward into battle "cannot be easily explained." He conjectured that it might have been, in part, the security a soldier found in the close ranks of a battle line, with men touching elbows and striding with a common step. A Maine veteran thought that a man faced death by self-denial. "He simply takes his chances," wrote the former soldier, "always believing that as an individual he is immune. . . . To him it is always the man in the next rank who is to be the victim."[69]

Both of these veterans had been on some of the conflict's worse battlefields. They had witnessed bravery and cowardice and could offer only a partial explanation for what impelled men to do what they had seen and done. Perhaps the ideas of courage, duty, and honor had seeped into the marrow of men; perhaps an abiding religious faith steeled them; and perhaps devotion to a cause stilled their fears. For whatever reason, or all of them, men clung to these ideas and beliefs. Without deeply held beliefs, they could not have answered the summons that brought them onto the ground before Marye's Heights and Prospect Hill.

The Union offensive began with muddled orders from Ambrose Burnside to William Franklin. Brigadier General James A. Hardie of Burnside's staff delivered a pencil copy of the order to Franklin's headquarters at 7:30 A.M. Franklin had been awake all night, waiting for the directive to initiate the army's main assault against Stonewall Jackson's position. His mood had soured badly and his willingness to undertake an attack had waned by the time Hardie arrived. Then he read a poorly worded and vague, even contradictory, instruction "to seize, if possible," the heights with a division, "taking care to keep it well supported and its line of retreat open." He also learned that Edwin Sumner's Right Grand Division would advance against Marye's Heights.[70]

Franklin neither asked Hardie about Burnside's intentions nor telegraphed headquarters for clarity. Burnside wanted Franklin to deliver the army's main attack, but the orders directed him to "seize" the heights, not to "carry" them, which implied a more forceful action against a defended position. In turn, Franklin interpreted them in the narrowest sense, assigning one division to the effort. He had authority over roughly 60,000 troops but used less than one fourth of them directly against Jackson's 35,000 infantrymen and fifty-four cannon. Later in the day, when Burnside directed him "to make a vigorous attack with his whole force," he said that it could not be done. A historian of the battle, George C. Rable, has concluded fairly, "the force of the attack depended on Franklin's understanding and judgment, and that general had never shown much imagination or aggressiveness."[71]

Burnside thought that a full-scale assault by Franklin on Jackson would force Lee to shift units to his endangered right, weakening his position on Marye's Heights. When he issued his orders to Franklin, Burnside instructed Edwin Sumner to ready his Right Grand Division troops for an attack on the Confederates' formidable lines on Marye's Heights. They would advance once Franklin's men had become engaged. In Burnside's mind, then, the army would assail the enemy at two points, with Franklin initiating and conducting the primary assault. Instead, his confusing orders and Franklin's stubborn reaction to them triggered a tragedy. Both generals, particularly Franklin, had ample time to seek clarification because it took the entire morning to implement the orders. Valor would have to compensate for leadership. It would not be enough.[72]

Franklin assigned John Reynolds's First Corps to the attack. Reynolds had tried in vain to persuade Franklin that the orders reflected the previous night's discussion with Burnside for a major assault. Franklin respected Reynolds as a soldier but would not be swayed. Reynolds selected recently promoted Major General George Meade and the Pennsylvania Reserves for the duty. Meade protested against it, arguing that it would be like the piecemeal attacks at Antietam. Franklin cut him off: "That is General Burnside's order." Franklin admitted to his wife later that he "never thought" it would succeed.[73]

It was not until 1:00 P.M. when Meade's 4,500 Pennsylvanians charged. They had been delayed one hour by a single Confederate cannon, directed by Major John Pelham of Jeb Stuart's horse artillery. Then Union cannon pounded Prospect Hill for two more hours. When

Southern counterfire slackened, Meade's veterans stepped out. "This was a fearful moment," Sergeant Jacob Heffelfinger wrote afterward in his diary. To Lieutenant Robert Taggart, "The undertaking seemed like madness."[74]

Confederate artillerists and infantrymen punished the Pennsylvanians, whose ranks began to fray. Regiments intermingled ranks, but the Federals kept coming, across the railroad tracks and into the woods below Prospect Hill. "With wild yells," they surged into a six-hundred-yard gap of swampy ground in the Rebel lines that had been left unfilled by Jackson and division commander A. P. Hill. They shredded the ranks of one Southern brigade and blasted another one with volleys at close range. Meade's men clung to their gains against mounting enemy numbers.[75]

Reynolds ordered in John Gibbon's division. A staff officer described Gibbon later as "cool as a steel knife, always, and unmoved by anything and everything." His three brigades advanced to the right of Meade and seized a section of the railroad. By now, Hill had rallied his troops, and with Major General Jubal Early's division, counterattacked. The Southern assault was powerful and unrelenting, regaining the lost ground and sending Meade's and Gibbon's troops rearward. A Yankee contended that "coming in was rough but giting out was rougher." Brigadier General David Birney's Third Corps division and Union artillerists repulsed the pursuing Southerners, and the combat frittered away into skirmish fire.[76]

"I do not recollect of ever feeling so discouraged over the result of anything we ever undertook to do," wrote one of Meade's Pennsylvanians. Lieutenant Taggart, who thought it "madness," exclaimed, "I am sick at heart at this." Captain David Porter of the 11th Pennsylvania Reserves put it bluntly in a letter: "The boys fought like heroes. They were too brave. . . . We were butchered like so many animals." Casualties in the division exceeded 1,850, while Gibbon lost more than 1,250, a combined rate of nearly forty percent.[77]

Reynolds wrote in a private letter that Meade's and Gibbon's men had "faltered and failed" in their "attack of the wooded heights." What more he had expected of them is difficult to fathom. Fellow division commander Abner Doubleday, who witnessed the assaults, confided in his journal that the troops had been "sacrificed" by Franklin. In Doubleday's judgment, Franklin had more than 50,000 troops "standing still and doing nothing." Meade related that after the battle he told Burnside that the army commander should have "impressed" upon Franklin the importance of an attack on the army's left. It had been as Franklin had thought—no assault could succeed. His actions had fulfilled his belief.[78]

THE NAMES OF FREDERICKSBURG'S streets evoked its colonial past as a river town founded by English settlers—William, George, Caroline, Princess, Sophia, Frederick, and Hanover. Since the early morning of December 13, thousands of Union troops, officers and men of the Union Second and Ninth corps, had jammed these narrow avenues, waiting for orders to advance. Two of the streets, Frederick and Hanover, ran west from near the river to the base of Marye's Heights, paralleling each other. As the day approached noon, lengthened through the afternoon, and on into evening's twilight, ribbons of blue-uniformed men followed them toward a waning day's sun, toward a stone wall, toward hell.[79]

Ambrose Burnside's instructions to Right Grand Division commander Edwin Sumner directed him to "push a column of a division or more along the Plank and Telegraph roads [Frederick and Hanover streets], with a view to seizing the heights in rear of the town." Sumner should make the preparations but wait until Burnside sent a second order to begin the attack. In turn, Sumner forwarded the directive to Second Corps commander Darius Couch, who designated William French's division to lead the initial assault, supported by Winfield Hancock's division. At eleven o'clock, Burnside issued the attack order, having been informed that William Franklin's advance on the army's left was progressing. Within thirty minutes, three Union regiments from French's command—the 4th and 8th Ohio and 1st Delaware—cleared Fredericksburg's western edge to dislodge Confederate skirmishers along the millrace.[80]

The snap and pop of rifle fire signaled the beginning. The Federals pressed ahead, dislodging the Rebels from behind the millrace. The 8th

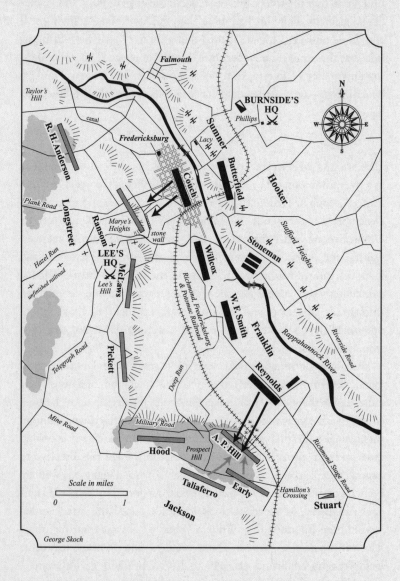

George Skoch

Ohio filed across a bridge where Hanover Street spanned the waterway. The Southerners had removed the planks, forcing the Ohioans to step on the stringers. The 4th Ohio and 1st Delaware joined their comrades in a ravine west of the millrace, formed a battle line, and charged. Rebel cannon opened on them. Confederate artillerist E. Porter Alexander wrote afterward, "I never conceived for a moment that Burnside would make his main attack right where we were the strongest—at Marye's Hill."[81]

From behind the stone wall, Brigadier General Thomas R. R. Cobb's Georgians leveled their rifles as officers shouted, "Get ready Boys—here they come!" A colonel directed his troops, "Men, if you do shoot, shoot low." A sheet of flame flashed from above the wall, as a volley of musketry blew into the Federal ranks, leveling scores of men from Ohio and Delaware. A second volley, and then a third, toppled more. The Yankees either scrambled for cover behind two houses and the brick store or flattened themselves on the ground. They could go no farther before such gunfire and artillery blasts. It was a harbinger of the insanity that was about to engulf this field.[82]

Behind them appeared their comrades in the division. Brigade commander Colonel Oliver Palmer had encountered French as his men marched up a street. French gave Palmer instructions and then said goodbye. French, noted Palmer, "preferred to stay in town behind the buildings and it was just about as proper for him to do so as it would have been for me but he could do so being a Division commander with less impunity. There he remained during the fight." French admitted that he had not reconnoitered the ground before he sent in his command.[83]

The three brigades came up Hanover Street, crossed the millrace at the bridge, aligned ranks in the ravine, and ascended the slope in succession. From the stone wall, a rooster crowed, trained by the Georgians to announce such times. Adjutant Frederick Hitchcock of the 132nd Pennsylvania averred, "I do not expect ever again to face death more certainly than I thought I did then." The Southerners opened fire and "mowed us down like cutting grass," testified a New Yorker. Ranks splintered, with the men either hugging the earth or shielding themselves behind the buildings. A private told his wife "man cant stand before the batters and trenchments." French implored of a staff officer: "Adjutant, where is my division? Tell me where my men are. My God, I am without a command!"[84]

Before long, Winfield Scott Hancock's division—three brigades, seventeen regiments, some of the army's finest soldiers—advanced to the attack. Hancock was, remarked a staff officer, "a kind of meteor on the battle-field." He had directed his brigade commanders that if one line "should fail the other should pass on and over and so on until the works of the enemy were carried." He told an officer, "we were going to have a severe struggle [and] scarcely a pigeon could live through it." Tall and physically imposing, Hancock always wore a clean white shirt beneath his uniform coat as if he were going to a wedding or funeral. On this day, it would be the latter.[85]

As Colonel Samuel K. Zook's brigade cleared the town, Alexander's gunners of Marye's Heights saw them and opened fire. Across the mill-race and up the slope, avoiding French's survivors, they marched. The Georgians' rooster crowed a second time. Volleys from the Georgians slammed into the Federals, whose line quivered as if some unseen force had lifted it up and shaken it. One of Zook's aides stated, "the losses were so tremendous that before we knew it, our momentum was gone, and the charge a failure." "Just then," as a lieutenant put it in his diary, "there was no romance, no glorious pomp, nothing but disgust for the genius who planned so frightful a slaughter."[86]

Into the carnage now marched the Irish Brigade, with its green flags unmistakable above the blue-coated ranks. Each officer and enlisted man wore a sprig of a boxwood in his cap, given to them by aides of Brigadier General Thomas Meagher. The Irishmen prided themselves on the rumor they had heard that the Rebels feared them the most "for they fight more like devils than humans." An eyewitness described their advance as "an unforgettable sight." Enemy gunners unleashed canister into their ranks. As the iron slugs hit, a soldier recounted that he saw "red flashes in the white gloom of a pearly powder cloud." Still, they came, sheltered briefly by a swale 150 yards from the wall. As they had done at Antietam, they shouted, "Faugh a Ballagh"—"Clear the Way." The Georgians stood and squeezed a volley. "A blinding fire of musketry met them in the face. It staggered the line for a few seconds."[87]

At less than fifty paces, the Irishmen and the Georgians exchanged volleys. "It was simply madness to advance as far as we did," declared an Irish private, "and an utter impossibility to go farther." They fell back to the shelter of the swale and clung either to the ground or fled into town. In their written accounts, almost to a man, they used the words "slaughtered" and "slaughter pen" to describe what they had passed through before the stone wall. Their dead lay closer to the Confederate line than any other Union command. A month later, in St. Patrick's Cathedral in New York City, a requiem mass was held for the souls of the slain Irishmen.[88]

Brigadier General John Caldwell's six regiments followed the Irishmen. The Rebels opened fire, and "on all sides men fell like grass before the scythe," wrote a 5th New Hampshire man. Colonel Edward Cross of the regiment collapsed unconscious to the ground from a shell burst. Caldwell suffered two wounds and left the field. Hancock rode up to the ranks, urging them forward. But, as a soldier contended, "no line could stand their fire." Lieutenant Charles A. Fuller of the 61st New York recalled: "A soldier lay nearby where I ought to have stood. A shell had gone through his body, and in its passage had set fire to his clothing and there his corpse lay slowly cooking. There was no time to do anything."[89]

Hancock wrote a few days later, "Our troops fought with the greatest determination and died with the utmost devotion." A newspaperman witnessing the assaults claimed, "It was not war, it was madness." Still, the army's senior commanders continued the assaults. Couch committed his final division; Sumner ordered in the Ninth Corps; and Burnside sent the Fifth Corps across the river. A historian of the Second Corps asked years later, "Will posterity believe that such a battle was fought under such orders?"[90]

In succession, came the divisions of Oliver Howard, Samuel D. Sturgis, Charles Griffin, Andrew Humphreys, and George W. Getty. And in succession, the gray-coated defenders ripped apart their ranks. At one point in the fighting, Lee expressed concern to Longstreet about whether his troops could hold the line. "General," responded Longstreet, "if you put every man now on the other side of the Potomac on that field to approach me over the same line, and give me plenty of ammunition, I will kill them all before they reach my line."[91]

The words of the Federals recount the horror and futility of it all. "Our very footsteps are implanted in blood and gore," wrote a New Yorker as he and his comrades charged. A soldier, who had gone in earlier, shouted a warning to a passing regiment: "It's no use, boys; we've tried that. Nothing living can stand there; it's only for the dead." A Massachusetts private swore that when the enemy's musketry and cannon fire hit their line it began "moving *sideways*, as though breasting a 'blizzard' or wind and hail-storm in bluff old New England." Wounded men clogged the ground, and their "cries and shrieks could be heard above the roar of battle." "Flesh and blood," asserted a corporal, "could not face the decimating fire and leave a live man to tell the story, and the line grew thinner and thinner until it practically melted away altogether."[92]

A regimental colonel called the slope before the stone wall "the gates of hell." The Confederate fire was so withering that the dead "seemed to be kept constantly in motion from the kick of the rebel bullets striking them." Some of the slain had been, recalled a sergeant, "mashed into one complete jelly, their remains stringing over a distance of five yards." "It was not a battle," insisted a Yankee, "it was a wholesale slaughter of human beings."[93]

Between 35,000 and 40,000 Federals had charged Marye's Heights— six full divisions and part of another one, comprised of eighteen brigades with eighty-five regiments. Their casualties exceeded 7,000 in killed, wounded, and missing. Of the eighteen regiments in the army that sustained the highest losses on this day, a dozen had participated in the attacks. Such sacrifice could be understood and accepted if it made sense, but not on this day, not against the Confederate position. Five days later, a captain conveyed this in a letter: "The mad attempt to storm their position by an infantry attack on Saturday resulted in an unavailing slaughter. . . . According to all I could learn, it could have had no other result."[94]

WITNESSES AT ARMY HEADQUARTERS noted that "a painfully anxious feeling" pervaded the place and that Ambrose Burnside showed "evidences of great nervous exhaustion" throughout the day. He had not slept the night before and could not hide the strain upon him during the battle. After dark, he met with Edwin Sumner, Joseph Hooker, and William Franklin, informing them that the army would renew the attack the next morning, with him personally leading his old Ninth Corps. All three of the generals opposed the idea, with Hooker speaking "ungentlemanly and unpatriotly." Another officer thought that his words bordered on "insubordination." Burnside ended the meeting.[95]

The army commander crossed the river and spent a few hours discussing the situation with other subordinates. Returning at 3:00 A.M., he wired the president, "We hope to carry the crest today." His delusion persisted until Sumner convinced him later in the morning that the attacks would fail. When Burnside held another council at noon, he heard the same argument from other generals and canceled his plan. Stubbornly, however, he waited another day until he ordered a withdrawal. According to an aide, "he choked & his tears ran as he gave the order to evacuate."[96]

For the army on the field, the two nights and days were harrowing ordeals. At night, temperatures sank below freezing, with "bitter, raw north winds." During the day, particularly in front of Marye's Heights, any movement brought fire from the Southerners. Men used whatever protection they could find, including the corpses of comrades. An officer said that they were "unable to eat, drink, or attend to the calls of nature." They negotiated an informal truce for a few hours with the Rebels and gathered up wounded men. Unknown numbers had died from exposure. One of those still alive shouted as they carried him away: "All right now! I shall not die like a dog, in the ditch."[97]

On the night of December 14–15, the aurora borealis or northern lights brightened the darkened sky. "The heavens were filled with long streaks of pale yellow light then blended together and turned to blood red," an onlooker wrote. Southerners viewed it as an omen, a celestial affirmation of their victory. Perhaps the lights radiated from the campfires of Fredericksburg's fallen, a gathering of the souls of former enemies. And, perhaps, as the colorful display tinted into "blood red," it was their warning of what the future held.[98]

The Army of the Potomac filed across the Rappahannock, shielded by darkness, on the night of December 15–16. The Federals left behind in Fredericksburg many of the wounded—"The city is filled with the pieces of brave men who went whole into the conflict," wrote a lieutenant. By eight o'clock in the morning, the rear guard had crossed over. Once the army reached Falmouth, bands filled "the air with requiems for the dead." When Burnside rode past a regiment, the members watched in silence. "They had no bad words to offer him," stated an officer, "nothing but pity."[99]

The Battle of Fredericksburg cost the Union army 1,284 killed or mortally wounded, 9,600 wounded, and 1,769 captured or missing, for a total of 12,653. Confederate losses amounted to 595 killed or mortally wounded, 4,061 wounded, and 653 captured or missing, or 5,309 in total.[100]

Among the Federal dead were brigadiers Conrad F. Jackson and George D. Bayard. Jackson had fallen with his Pennsylvania Reserves, while Bayard, a cavalry officer, was sitting under a tree at Franklin's headquarters when a shell crushed his thighs and tore into his abdomen. He was to be married on December 18, at West Point, to the academy superintendent's daughter. Before long, uncounted waiting brides heard similar news. Fredericksburg was, concluded Lieutenant Colonel St. Clair A. Mulholland of the 116th Pennsylvania, "the saddest hour that the army of the Potomac ever knew."[101]

Chapter 10

Winter of Transition

FREDERICKSBURG'S GRIM REALITY cast a pall across the North. As newspapers reported the details of the defeat and the casualty figures, the initial shock boiled over into anger. In New York City, a diarist noted, "The general indignation is fast growing revolutionary." The furor and grief, however, extended far beyond the cities to the villages of New England, into the coal-mining towns of Pennsylvania, and on to the farming communities of Indiana, Illinois, and Wisconsin. It was not just the defeat but also the apparent senselessness of the slaughter that fueled the reaction.[1]

In Washington, divisiveness and acrimony walked the streets. "Political factions are fuming, too bitter for the interests of our country," Brigadier General Alexander Hays, who served in the city's defenses, told his wife. It was reported that supporters of George B. McClellan were "jubilant" over the outcome and were lobbying discreetly for his reappointment to command of the army. Democrats blamed the administration for the defeat, accusing it of pushing Ambrose Burnside into an unwise battle. Radical Republicans were outraged and feared that the bloody debacle might delay the official issuance of the Emancipation Proclamation, scheduled for January 1, 1863. They passed a Senate resolution that authorized an investigation into the reasons for the defeat.[2]

The defeat, the casualties, and the billowing controversy deeply affected Abraham Lincoln. Associates of the president and visitors to the White House commented on the sadness that seemed to have enveloped him. A newspaperman noted of Lincoln, "His hair is grizzled, his gait more stooping, his countenance sallow, and there is a sunken, deathly look about the large cavernous eyes." Lincoln exclaimed during a meeting that if he heard more bad news, it would make him "crazy." In the army at Falmouth, a rumor circulated that "Uncle Abe" was "on the verge of lunacy." To a friend, he confessed, "If there is a worse place than Hell, I am in it."[3]

Pressures on the president mounted during the year's final two weeks. A delegation of Republican senators demanded the resignation of Secretary of State William H. Seward. At Falmouth, members of the Joint Committee on the Conduct of the War interrogated Ambrose Burnside and the army's senior generals. The committee had come ostensibly to investigate the Fredericksburg defeat and current conditions in the army. Unofficially, they were there to gather damaging testimony, which they hoped would show that the administration pressured Burnside into the disaster.[4]

In the army, William Franklin and Sixth Corps commander William Smith worked to undermine Burnside's authority and to have him removed from command. Without Burnside's knowledge they submitted a letter to Lincoln proposing another campaign on the Peninsula and implying that someone other than Burnside should direct it. Lincoln rejected the plan in a letter to the generals.[5]

On December 30, brigadier generals John Newton and John Cochrane secured an interview with the president. They had been granted leaves of absences by Franklin to "see influential people, and try to have things made right." It was believed, however, that Franklin had sent them. In their meeting with Lincoln, the generals expressed opposition to Burnside's plan for another offensive across the river. "Mr. President," stated Newton, "the army has no confidence in General Burnside; that is the whole trouble down here."[6]

Newton and Cochrane surely knew that their conduct amounted to insubordination. Newton admitted that they were in "a very delicate position." At one point in the discussion Lincoln remarked that he thought that they meant "to injure General Burnside." They denied it, replying that only patriotism motivated them. Lincoln thanked them for the information, and the generals departed. He then telegraphed Burnside, "I have good reason for saying you must not make a general movement of the army without letting me know."[7]

Burnside traveled to Washington on the year's final day. Two days of discussions ensued at the White House, with Lincoln, Secretary of War Edwin Stanton, and General-in-Chief Henry Halleck. Angered when he learned of the visit of the two generals, whom Lincoln would not identify, Burnside submitted his resignation. The president refused to accept it. Most of the talk centered on Burnside's proposed offensive movement, which he admitted had been opposed by his Grand Division commanders. The conference ended without a resolution on the army's operations.[8]

During the discussions Lincoln had asked for Halleck's opinion about a resumption of operations. The general-in-chief, however, would neither sanction it nor disapprove it. Obviously frustrated, Lincoln wrote afterward to Halleck, "If in such a difficulty as this you do not help, you fail me precisely in the point for which I sought your assistance." He directed Halleck to visit the army, to confer with its generals, and "in a word, gather all the elements for forming a judgment of your own, and then tell General Burnside that you do approve or that you do not approve his plan. Your military skill is useless to me if you will not do this."[9]

Lincoln's letter incensed Halleck. The general-in-chief's policy had been, as he had stated in the past, "that a General in command of an army in the field is the best judge of existing conditions." He tendered his resignation, writing, "I cannot perform the duties of my present office satisfactorily at the same time to the President and to myself." Unwilling to have another crisis among his advisors, Lincoln rescinded the order with the notation, "Withdrawn, because considered harsh by Gen. Halleck." The general-in-chief, however, had failed Lincoln when the president wanted his advice at a critical and contentious time. His reliance on Halleck's counsel diminished. Eventually, Lincoln referred to him as "a first-rate clerk."[10]

Lincoln intimated to a friend during these grueling days: "They

[Radical Republicans] wish to get rid of me, and I am sometimes half disposed to gratify them. We are now on the brink of destruction. It appears to me the Almighty is against us, and I can hardly see a ray of hope." But he withstood the storms. He did not accede to the demand for Seward's resignation. The Joint Committee on the Conduct of the War had been thwarted when Burnside accepted personal responsibility for Fredericksburg and denied that the administration had prodded him into a battle. Lincoln had weathered one of the darkest periods of his presidency.[11]

To Burnside, meanwhile, he wrote, "I do not yet see how I could profit by changing the command" of the army. He respected the general's honest patriotism and fighting spirit and stood by the beleaguered general. The extent of demoralization among the troops and their lack of confidence in Burnside he knew of only from disgruntled generals. He attributed part of the dissension and insubordination to supporters of McClellan within the officer ranks. Without an obvious successor, Burnside was retained and given another chance.[12]

Lincoln saw, however, that neither Burnside nor any other general in the army seemed to grasp a truth about Fredericksburg. There was, he told a secretary, an "awful arithmetic" to the conflict. The disparity in casualties between the Federals and Confederates in the battle had been staggering. But in Lincoln's reckoning, if the two armies fought each other every day for a week and sustained a similar casualty rate, the Rebels would be wiped out, and the Army of the Potomac would still be "a mighty host." According to his secretary, the president asserted, "No general yet found can face the arithmetic, but the end of the war will be at hand when he shall be discovered."[13]

During the morning of January 1, Lincoln welcomed a river of guests to the president's annual New Year's Day reception at the White House. He stood in the receiving line for hours, shaking countless hands before walking upstairs to his office. Shortly, Secretary of State Seward and his son, Frederick, joined Lincoln, bringing with them the final copy of the Emancipation Proclamation. "I never, in my life, felt more certain that I was doing right, than I do in signing this paper," he said to them. He took up a pen, steadied his hand after the many handshakes, and firmly signed the document. His signature granted freedom not to all slaves but only to those in states and portions of states still held by Confederate forces. Believing he lacked the constitutional authority, Lincoln exempted slaves in the loyal Border states of Delaware, Maryland, Kentucky, and Missouri. But the act sounded the death knell of the institution. It also authorized the acceptance of African-Americans into military service. The burden of reclaiming rebellious territory and bringing freedom to bondsmen and bondswomen now rested with Union armies.[14]

LIKE A HOUSE, WROTE Colonel Oliver Palmer to his wife on December 16, an army needed a foundation. A house could not be expected "to stand upright after its foundation was removed." Nor could an army "stand upright," he stated, "unless there is confidence in the leaders." Fredericksburg had removed the army's foundation. "There is no disguising the fact that confidence in Burnside is gone," Palmer believed. "There is scarely an officer of intelligence here but that feels it. It is a most deplorable state of things."[15]

In his letter, Palmer related that during the battle he had felt trapped in "an insane dream world or ticket to the wicked wilderness of such wastes of human life." A brigade commander, Palmer was not alone in feeling that Fredericksburg had been a nightmare of senseless carnage. The rank and file believed that they had been slaughtered for no explicable reason. Their anger and bitterness spilled over into their letters and diary entries. They used words such as "butchered" and "murder" to describe what had happened to them. They believed, as a captain declared, "No men could have fought better or shown more bravery than did ours in these repeated charges."[16]

They blamed the defeat and bloodshed squarely on the army's leadership and authorities in Washington. While they did not spare Burnside from harsh criticism—"there was no more Generalship in putting us in to the fight than there was to the bull that bunted the engine," wrote a 17th Maine private—they cursed the administration, notably Stanton and Halleck, for pushing Burnside into a battle. A captain called the officials "our true enemies, those blood stained scoundrels in Washington." A Pennsylvania officer professed later in his diary: "I believe the battle of Fredericksburg first gave me a insight into the manner with which the war was prosecuted. The Army of the Potomac is merely a political machine. We are moved forward and backward to suit the political situation."[17]

Officers and men alike filled their letters and diaries with expressions of their desire to have McClellan in command again. They argued, as a lieutenant put it, "McClellan would not have led us there— he knew better." A 2nd Maine soldier told his mother, "I for one should like to know what the people of the north think of *little Mac* now." Lieutenant Colonel Clark Edwards wrote bluntly, "I honestly believe the removal of Mc has made Thousands of Widows and tens of Thousands of orphan children." [18]

It was an army adrift, yearning for the past and despairing of the future. "I feel like a man in a ship with a crazy pilot and rocks ahead," contended a soldier. "Gaily we sail on . . . going swiftly, going surely to the Devil." A New York private insisted, "One thing is sure, and I would almost stake my life on it, and that is that another such disaster such as Fredericksburg, and the Army of the Potomac will not fight any more."[19]

If Fredericksburg were the army's "saddest hour," the weeks after the engagement were its darkest night. "A settled gloom pervaded the camps of the Army of the Potomac," remembered a chaplain, "and increased as the weary days wore away." The demoralization resulted from more than Fredericksburg's "foul murder" and the "blundering Generals or Imbecile fools" who led them. Inadequate rations, a resurgence of sickness, and the lack of pay contributed to the plunging morale. Even the bleak landscape around their winter camps at Falmouth blackened their mood. "The country all around here is and never was good for anything," wrote a Michigan soldier, "and it had been run to death and skinned in the bargain."[20]

"I have at no time seen it so depressed," wrote a surgeon of the morale in his veteran regiment. They reacted bitterly when they learned of Christmas and New Year's parties at various headquarters, where officers feasted on turkey, chicken, roast beef, ham, bread, and cakes, washed down with whiskey and cognac. In contrast, the men in the ranks passed a cheerless holiday season, dining on hardtack and salt pork. Some German troops "manufactured Xmas trees" by hanging pieces of hardtack and salt pork on them. Many of the troops lacked overcoats and blankets because of bureaucratic bungling. They believed that quartermaster officers and army contractors were enriching themselves at the expense of their suffering. A cavalryman damned them, claiming that these thieves "would *steal the coppers from a dead soldier's eyes* after cheating him out of his *daily bread* while living."[21]

Insubordination pervaded the camps, and desertions escalated. A New York soldier noted that desertions "are of daily occurrence in almost every Regt." When units received their back pay, more men fled. "There is no honor in this war as it is now being carried on," explained a sergeant of deserters' attitudes, "& consequently no dishonor in leaving it." By the end of January 1863, official rolls listed 25,363 men as deserters.[22]

They yearned for peace. A staff officer estimated that three fourths of the army wanted the war ended. A lieutenant told his wife: "This thing is played out. The whole army is disheartened and want peace on some terms." A man in the 6th Wisconsin grumbled: "The paper's all say that the soldiers are aching to fight, but the papers are notorious liars. We were never so fast to have the war brought to a close."[23]

Their hopes for an early cessation of hostilities were based, in part, on their growing belief that the Confederacy could not be conquered. Sergeant John W. St. Clair of the 6th Wisconsin expressed a common view: "the south never will give up they air hard boys they fite well." They noticed the "jolly time" in the Rebels' camps across the Rappahannock River at Christmas. Men from both armies traded goods with their opponents, especially Southern tobacco for Northern coffee, and even visited each others' camps for meals. The Yankees learned that their foes were as sick of the war as they were. But the Confederates, concluded a lieutenant, "are *certainly better led* & have I believe more heart in the cause."[24]

In the midst of the army's dissension and despair came the news of the president's signing of the Emancipation Proclamation. While a majority of the men believed that slavery had brought on this terrible scourge, they had not volunteered to fight for its abolition but "to restore the Constitution and the laws." Although they sympathized with the sad plight of slaves and contrabands or runaways, they possessed, in general, a deep racial prejudice against African-Americans. The proclamation portended a social equality with freedmen that they viscerally opposed. A New Hampshire soldier expressed this common attitude when he wrote home, "I did not come out here to shed my blood for the sake of raising the niggers on an equal footing with the whites."[25]

Thousands of the New Englander's comrades shared his sentiment. Many of them declared that they were "*not* fighting for the nigger." A Pennsylvanian stated in a typical view, "I wish the Niger was in Hell and all the Stiff Abolishonist with them." Regiments adopted resolutions against the proclamation, and officers and men faced courts-martial for outspoken opposition to it. Extreme voices clamored that they would rather have the North defeated than freedom given to the slaves.[26]

Opposition to emancipation was not, however, universal within the army. Historian William C. Davis has concluded that "a general approval" of the policy was more widespread than the disaffection with it. Many of the officers and men who wrote about it and approved it saw it as a practical act that would weaken the South and thus shorten the war. "It seems to be generally admitted by intelligent men," wrote an orderly, "that it is a wise and necessary measure if we are *going ahead* with the war." They understood that abolition would stiffen Southern resistance, and as Captain Thomas Osborn said, the proclamation "precludes the possibility of any settlement except by absolute subjugation, and even that carried to the last extremity."[27]

Acceptance of emancipation eventually prevailed in the army. Vocal opposition subsided as more soldiers saw it as a necessary war measure. The men's patriotism also overrode objections to it. An Indiana captain who was against the proclamation conveyed this shared devotion to the cause when he wrote, "I go for my country, *right* or *wrong*." Probably few of them, however, would have agreed at the time with Colonel Theodore B. Gates's prediction, "President Lincolns emancipation proclamation will take its place among the most important papers of the age & will by & by stand side by side with our Declaration of Independence."[28]

On the day after the proclamation went into effect, January 2, a Michigan soldier recorded in his diary a joke that was being repeated from hut to hut, "that Jeff Davis gives us 60 days in which to get out of

Va." But as the days passed, rumors circulated about another movement across the river. The news was unwelcome to the discontented troops. "Some of the boys," wrote Private J. B. Tarleton of the 13th New Hampshire, "are most crasey for fear we shall to giv those rebs another hack."[29]

Since his return from Washington on New Year's Day, Burnside had worked on another strike at Robert E. Lee's Confederates. Although William Franklin described his commander as "inefficient and indecisive to the last degree," Burnside seemed determined to undertake an offensive despite continual opposition to it by his senior generals and the troops' demoralization. He saw personally the rank and file's attitude at a review when an officer ordered the veterans to give him three cheers and "not a man opened his mouth." Burnside admitted to Lincoln, "there is much hazard" in "another crossing of the river." But stubbornness was one of Burnside's defining characteristics as a man and as a general.[30]

When General-in-Chief Halleck approved the operation, Burnside finalized plans for a crossing at Banks's Ford on the Rappahannock, upriver from Fredericksburg and beyond Lee's left or western flank. Engineers examined the site, and pontoon trains were readied. Lincoln had read Halleck's letter to Burnside and added an endorsement: "I approve this letter. I deplore the want of concurrence with you in opinion by your general officers, but I do not see the remedy. Be cautious, and do not understand that the Government or country is driving you."[31]

Burnside designated 1:00 P.M., January 20, as the commencement of the movement, led by the Grand Divisions of Franklin and Joseph Hooker. On the day before, with the orders issued, Colonel Charles S. Wainwright, First Corps artillery chief, visited the headquarters of Franklin. In his diary, Wainwright wrote that Franklin's and Smith's staff members "are talking outrageously, only repeating though, no doubt, the words of their generals." Wainwright thought that Burnside "may be unfit to command this army; his present plan may be absurd, and failure certain; but his lieutenants have no right to say so to their subordinates." Franklin's denunciation of the movement, asserted Wainwright, "has completely demoralized his whole command," and "Smith and . . . Hooker are almost as bad." The artillery officer believed that the generals deserved "to be broken" in rank.[32]

Captain Henry L. Abbott of the 15th Massachusetts reported that when Burnside's orders were read at evening parade on January 19, men in his regiment and the 42nd New York "hooted" and shouted, "put him out, put him out." But the next afternoon, the army marched, angling north and west toward the ford. "Everything went off very well," stated George Meade. About nine o'clock at night, however, a winter storm blew in, lashing the countryside with downpours. "It was a terrible night," said a New York private. "It rained incessantly all night, and the mud, I think, without doubt was over two feet in places."[33]

The rain poured down during the next day as the troops struggled through the mud, which seemed to suck up everything. "Our position was like that of liliputions in a great mud pile," claimed a soldier. The men tried to shoulder forward mired wagons and cannon. They called such strenuous work, *play horse*. Captain Francis A. Donaldson of the 118th Pennsylvania wrote, "the whole army that day was in a state of heaving, as it were, or to be more explicit, it reminded me of workmen lifting a heavy stone." He heard "prodigious blasphemy."[34]

Conditions worsened on January 22. Across the river, Rebels held up signs with large painted letters: "BURNSIDE STUCK IN THE MUD." The army had come to a standstill. Exhausted, soaked men could no longer move the vehicles out of the mire. Dead horses and mules were strewn along the roads. When some units received a whiskey issue, a brawl erupted among troops in four regiments. Finally, Burnside canceled the movement, ordering the troops back to their camps.[35]

The return march was, recalled a 7th Wisconsin veteran, "a living Hell, but I pacified myself that I would keep my vow with Govt (and Father Abraham) and do the right thing to the bitter end. It was tough medicines tho." Thousands of his comrades, however, thought other-wise and deserted in droves. It was more an armed, sullen, furious mob than an army as they plodded through the mud. Lieutenant Dayton E. Flint of the 15th New Jersey spoke for many: "The Army of the Potomac is no more an army. Its patriotism has oozed out through the pores opened by the imbecility of its leaders, and the fatigues and disappoint-ments of a fruitless winter campaign." Flint believed, "It is only a sense of honor and self-respect and an adherence to their oath to support and obey those over them that keep them from deserting enmasse."[36]

Almost to a man, they blamed Burnside. When the army commander passed a group of soldiers during the movement—which newspapers dubbed the "Mud March"—he was greeted with "hooting and yells." A 24th Michigan soldier insisted: "There has got to be a change soon in the affairs in general. It can't last long this way." A sergeant noted in his diary that if Burnside and Halleck heard "the deadly threats" spewed out around campfires, "they would not trust their precious carcasses in reach of a soldiers rifle, very soon." Meade confided to his wife: "I never felt so disappointed and sorry for any one in my life as I did for Burnside. He really seems to have even the elements against him."[37]

Burnside soon learned that more than the "elements" seemed to have conspired against him. Accompanying the army was New York *Times* editor Henry J. Raymond, who had spoken with the newspaper's army correspondent, William Swinton, and various officers. Raymond informed Burnside of an effort, centered in Franklin's grand division, to have McClellan restored to command, of the generals' lack of confidence in him, and of Hooker's outburst to Swinton "about the absurdity of the movement." Hooker had called Burnside "incompetent" and an "imbecile." Seething with anger, Burnside prepared General Orders No. 8, dated January 23.[38]

General Orders No. 8 was a stunning document, an act of reprisal, even of desperation. Burnside ordered that Hooker be dismissed from the service, accusing him of "having been guilty of unjust and unnecessary criticisms of the actions of his superior officers" and "as a man unfit to hold an important commission during a crisis like the present." Burnside also directed that generals William Brooks, John Newton, and John Cochrane be dismissed from the service. Brooks had been under arrest for insubordination, and Burnside had learned that Newton and Cochrane had been the two generals who had met with Lincoln. As for Franklin and Smith, the army commander ordered them relieved from duty, along with Ninth Corps division commander Samuel Sturgis, a brigade commander, and Franklin's chief of staff.[39]

When an officer cautioned Burnside that he needed the president's approval to execute the order, the general wired Lincoln that he was coming to Washington, with "some very important orders, and I want to see you before issuing them." Lincoln met with Burnside on the morning of January 24. Burnside handed Lincoln General Orders No. 8 and his major general's commission. Either the president endorse the order, said Burnside, or accept his resignation. He could no longer command the army with these generals in it. Lincoln replied that he wanted to consult with his advisors and told Burnside to return to the White House the next day.[40]

That night at a reception, Lincoln learned directly from Henry Raymond of the newspaper editor's recent visit to the army. Raymond repeated the conversations he had had with officers and particularly talked about Hooker's interview with Swinton and the general's declaration, "Nothing would go right . . . until we had a dictator, and the sooner the better." Lincoln replied, "That is all true—Hooker does talk badly; but the trouble is, he is stronger with the country to-day than any other man."[41]

The next morning, Lincoln summoned Stanton and Halleck to the White House. The president had not consulted with either the secretary of war or the general-in-chief before telling them that he had accepted Burnside's resignation and had appointed Hooker to command of the army. He had made the change, Lincoln explained, because of "the unfortunate state of existing circumstances" within the army. When Burnside arrived at ten o'clock, Lincoln informed the general of his decision. He refused, however, to accept Burnside's resignation of his commission and granted him a thirty-day leave of absence. He told the loyal soldier that he still needed his services to the Union.[42]

Lincoln also moved to rid the army of its most disgruntled troublemakers and the last members of the McClellan clique. In the order that removed Burnside and appointed Hooker, the president relieved William Franklin of command. Franklin had been at the center of the effort to discredit Burnside, and his close association with McClellan made his motives suspect. Within two weeks, Sixth Corps commander William Smith was removed and reassigned to duty in the West. Ironically, on the day the order was issued, January 25, the army learned that Fitz John Porter had been cashiered from the service.[43]

The president's actions marked a passage within the Army of the Potomac. His primary purpose had been to restore the army's morale and appoint a commander who might earn its confidence. Although he could not alter the rank and file's devotion to Little Mac and numerous generals' admiration for their former commander, he could and did eliminate, except to those blinded by myopia, the idea that he would turn again to McClellan. In Hooker, Lincoln had one of McClellan's foremost critics in the army now in command. Furthermore, Lincoln affirmed that it would be the president, not an army commander, who would shape Union war aims. There would be no turning back from his commitment to the restoration of the Union and the emancipation of slaves. Lincoln had wrested some, but not all, ghosts from the army.[44]

The War Department also accepted "at his own request" Edwin Sumner's relief from duty. The sixty-six-year-old Sumner did not wish to serve under Hooker and had been plagued by health problems. In fact, the career officer would be dead within two months. His finest day with the army had been at Fair Oaks, on May 31, 1862, when he pushed his Second Corps troops across the flooded Chickahominy River. Conversely, his rash actions at Antietam had resulted in the West Woods disaster. Artillery chief Charles Wainwright offered a fair assessment of Sumner: "The old soldier was as honest as the day, and simple as a child. The fault was not so much his, as of those who put him and kept him in such a place. . . . He was one of those whom every one must hate to find fault with: yet whose removal from the command of a corps was generally looked on as a relief."[45]

Burnside relinquished command of the army to Hooker on the morning of January 26. After he had written a farewell address to the officers and men in which he asked them to "be true in your devotion to your country and the principles you have sworn to maintain" and to give "your full and cordial support and co-operation" to the new commander, Burnside and his staff departed. He had been the most unfortunate commander of the army, a general who had been cursed by succeeding its most popular leader and a man who believed he was unfit for the post. His tenure had been marked by bitter animosity among his subordinates and a fearful, if not needless, sacrifice of life. A firm patriot, he lacked the power of personality and will to direct recalcitrant generals. He had been willing to fight the enemy, but the terrible slope before Marye's Heights stands as his legacy.[46]

To be sure, the untimely arrival of the pontoons had forced him to alter his plans and to give battle against a superb opponent in an almost impregnable position. Franklin's failure during the battle to launch a major assault as Burnside expected crippled any chance the Federals had of breaking the Confederate lines. After the engagement, Burnside proved to be a poor administrator, failing to fill the physical needs of the troops, which worsened their demoralization after the defeat. When fortune again conspired against him during the Mud March, the army stood on the verge of mutiny, marked by an increasing stream of deserters. He had lost that critical bond between a commander and the men in the ranks. If Lincoln had acceded to his demand for the removal of generals, it is very doubtful that he could have restored the morale and led the army into another battle.[47]

Perhaps, in the end, Burnside was his own worst enemy. George Meade respected Burnside's willingness to accept responsibility for his decisions and for his "determination and nerve." But, thought Meade, Burnside "wanted knowledge and judgment" and "that enlarged mental capacity which is essential in a commander." "Another drawback," contended Meade, "was a very general opinion among officers and men, brought about by his own assertions, that the command was too much for him. This greatly weakened his position."[48]

ABRAHAM LINCOLN HAD TAKEN a chance with the appointment of Joseph Hooker. He had heard the stories of the general's alleged sordid reputation, with his fondness for liquor and women, including prostitutes. The president probably knew of the enmity between Hooker and General-in-Chief Henry Halleck, which was deep and long-standing. He knew of Hooker's harsh criticisms of his superiors and the administration. Within the army, his vanity, boastfulness, and open condemnation of fellow generals had endeared him to few officers. Inordinate ambition seemed to define the man, who shamelessly courted newspaper correspondents, senators, and representatives, enhancing himself by undermining others. His self-assurance struck many as arrogance.[49]

No other general in the army, however, had the stature of Hooker. He had endeared himself to Radical Republicans with his condemnation of McClellan. A handsome man, he possessed a commanding physical presence. On battlefields, he had been aggressive and energetic, with unquestioned personal bravery. He enjoyed the respect and popularity of the troops who had served under him. Some fellow officers questioned his judgment and prudence, thinking that he might be too rash as an army commander. What few recognized was that he had a talent for administration and an eye for capable subordinates.[50]

When Lincoln met with Hooker, he handed the general a private letter. In it, the president praised Hooker's bravery, skill, self-confidence, and observed that "you do not mix politics with your profession." Then, Lincoln went to the heart of the matter. While Burnside commanded the army, "you have taken counsel of your ambition, and thwarted him as much as you could, in which you did a great wrong to the country." Continuing: "I have heard, in such a way as to believe it, of your recently saying that both the Army and the government needed a Dictator. Of course it was not *for* this, but in spite of it, that I have given you the command. Only those generals who gain successes, can set up dictators. What I now ask of you is military success, and I will risk the dictatorship."

Lincoln pledged the administration's support. But Hooker should realize, he warned, "the spirit which you have aided to infuse into the Army, of criticizing their Commander, and withholding confidence from him will now turn upon you. I shall assist you as far as I can, to put it down. Neither you, nor Napoleon, if he were alive again, could get any good out of an army, while such a spirit prevails in it." Finally, "And now, beware of rashness. Beware of rashness, but with energy, and sleepless vigilance, go forward, and give us victories."[51]

It was a remarkable letter, unlike any given to a recently appointed army commander in the annals of American military history. With it, however, Lincoln set the tone for the relationship between him and Hooker, which would become frank and cordial. Like others, Hooker must have seen on the president the strain of the past several weeks. His despondency had deepened, the hollowness and lines around his eyes more pronounced. A visitor to the White House noted in his diary: "I observe that the President never tells a joke now."[52]

Lincoln had passed through a terrible period—Fredericksburg's casualties, the crises in the Cabinet and in the Army of the Potomac, and the firestorm of protest against his Emancipation Proclamation. Elsewhere, Ulysses Grant's campaign against Vicksburg, Mississippi, had led to a bloody repulse at Chickasaw Bluffs, on December 29, 1862. Only in Tennessee, as the old year passed into the new, could the Federals claim a military victory at Stones River. William Rosecrans's army had withstood Confederate assaults and held the field. For the present, Lincoln had to be patient with Hooker as he restored morale and prepared the army for spring operations.[53]

MEADE THOUGHT HOOKER would have to achieve "impossibilities" to satisfy the Northern people. "This army is in a false position," wrote Meade, "both as regards the enemy and the public." Colonel Patrick Guiney of the 9th Massachusetts noted at this time: "The army seems dreary and partially dead. We want a good shaking up of some kind." The prospects for the future appeared dire to Brigadier General Alexander Hays, "Unless this war takes a new phase, within six months, with traitors at home, and the almost indomitable courage and perseverance of the Rebels, we will be forced to acknowledge their independence."[54]

With self-confidence and energy, Hooker began the overhaul of the army, the "good shaking up," at once. On February 5, he disbanded the Grand Divisions and readopted the corps organization as the army's largest command structure. For the first time in the army's history, Hooker organized the mounted units into a cavalry corps. With the transfer of the Ninth Corps to the West, the army's command structure now consisted of seven infantry, an artillery, and a cavalry corps.[55]

The commanders of the seven infantry corps reflected the command changes that the army had undergone during the previous weeks and months. Gone from the army was every man, except for one, who either had led a corps on the Peninsula or had served in John Pope's Army of Virginia. They had owed their rank and posts to seniority in the Regular Army, to political influence, and to McClellan's favoritism. The final vestiges of leadership, which extended back to First Bull Run, had been removed. Now, for the most part, their successors had earned the commands through merit. The army had passed a divide at the senior command level.[56]

Five of the major generals had commanded a corps before Hooker replaced Ambrose Burnside—John Reynolds, First Corps; Darius Couch, Second; George Meade, Fifth; Franz Sigel, Eleventh; and Henry Slocum, Twelfth. Reynolds and Couch had led their corps at Fredericksburg, while Burnside had appointed Meade after the battle. All three of them held conservative views, opposed McClellan's removal, but had avoided the internal bickering and had kept their comments private. They were, said an officer, "first-rate men."[57]

Sigel's and Slocum's corps had been posted elsewhere in Virginia, and were not with the army at Fredericksburg. A politically powerful figure in the German-American communities, Sigel had held corps command under Pope during the Second Bull Run Campaign. His Eleventh Corps, remarked a staff officer, "is like a German settlement." The troops' proud boast was "I fights mit Sigel." But the general complained that his undersized corps was not worthy of his stature and asked to be relieved of command in February.[58]

Weeks later, to the surprise of the officers and men in the Eleventh Corps, Hooker assigned Oliver Howard, a Maine Yankee who had lost an arm at Fair Oaks and had led his division against Marye's Heights, to the predominantly German units. It was not a good fit. Howard's religious piety—they began calling him "Old Prayer Book"—clashed with the German "freethinkers." They soon resented his attempt "to make a Sunday School class of a military organization." Their choice had been Major General Carl Schurz, who, like Sigel, had been a revolutionary émigré from Germany. Schurz had held temporary command of the corps, enjoyed high standing among his fellow Germans, but lacked the capability for corps command.[59]

A West Pointer, Slocum had led a volunteer regiment at First Bull Run, commanded a division on the Peninsula, and had been rewarded with the Twelfth Corps in October 1862. A physically small man, who dressed rather elegantly, Slocum possessed intelligence, ability, and a combative disposition. With his corps deployed south of Washington until February 1863, he had been spared from the internal turmoil among the generals. Like Reynolds and the other professionals, he kept his own counsel in political matters.[60]

Like Slocum, John Sedgwick owed his promotion to command of the Sixth Corps to his battlefield conduct. Wounded at Glendale and again at Antietam, he had been cited for gallantry in the latter engagement. Although his division had been routed in West Woods, the fault had been more Edwin Sumner's than Sedgwick's. The Sixth Corps was the army's largest and had been William Franklin's and then William Smith's former command. In time, the likable and unassuming Sedgwick would become one of the army's most popular generals. To his troops he was "Uncle John."[61]

The most colorful and most controversial new corps commander was Major General Daniel Sickles. He was a man who had seized life by the throat and choked all he could out of it. Before the war, he had been a New York City lawyer, Tammany Hall Democratic politician, confidential secretary to James Buchanan when the future president served as minister to Great Britain, and a congressman. He was quick-witted, willful, brash, and ambitious, with pliable morals and principles. A fellow attorney described him as "one of the bigger bubbles in the scum of the profession, swollen and windy, and puffed out with fetid gas." Elizabeth Blair Lee, daughter of Major General Francis P. Blair, Jr., remarked of Sickles, "he has no sense & nobody ever thought he had."[62]

In 1852, at the age of thirty-two, Sickles married sixteen-year-old Teresa Bagioli. Seven years later, while a member of Congress, Sickles shot and killed Philip Barton Key, his wife's lover and son of Francis Scott Key, the writer of "The Star-Spangled Banner." Defended by a team of lawyers led by Edwin Stanton, Sickles pleaded temporary insanity, the first defendant to do so in an American court, and was acquitted.[63]

When the war began, Sickles recruited the 70th New York before receiving a brigadiership from the administration in September 1861. The president had welcomed the services of this former Democratic congressman, despite his notorious personal reputation. Members of the Senate, however, thought otherwise and only after Lincoln had renominated him was he confirmed in May 1862. While he waited for the commission, Sickles commanded fellow New Yorkers in the Excelsior Brigade in Hooker's division, earning their respect and affection. "It is no fable about the men of this Brigade thinking a great deal of the General," wrote a member. Following the Peninsula Campaign, he returned to New York to recruit for the brigade and missed the battles of Second Bull Run and Antietam.[64]

When Sickles rejoined the army before Fredericksburg, he assumed command, as senior brigadier, of Hooker's former division of the Third Corps. Hooker's subsequent assignment of the corps's commander, Brigadier General George Stoneman, to the newly created cavalry corps, left Sickles as the corps's ranking officer. His appointment to the command was temporary, but Lincoln had nominated him for a major generalcy. Professionals within the army attributed his rise to his skill "as a political maneuverer." Few men, however, questioned his personal bravery.[65]

Sickles's promotion resulted from Hooker's most important and far-reaching organizational change—the formation of a cavalry corps. For nearly two years Union mounted units had been parceled out to infantry commands and had been no match for Jeb Stuart's Confederate horsemen. Stuart's raids in the rear of the Federal army had embarrassed the Yankee troopers and had demonstrated the superiority of the Southerner's horse soldiers. Recently, during the week between Christmas and New Year's, Stuart's veterans had struck between Washington and the Union army at Falmouth, and had escaped virtually unharmed. Hooker took the initial step in rectifying George McClellan's and Ambrose Burnside's neglect of the mounted arm.[66]

Stoneman's appointment to command of the corps brought the forty-year-old New Yorker back to the mounted units. He had served as McClellan's chief of cavalry, but his duties had been limited to administrative control. Now he would have tactical command and was promoted to major general in March 1863. He was, stated a cavalry officer, "the very best selection that could have been made in the whole army. We are glad to get him again and he is glad to come back to his old position." Captain Charles Francis Adams of the 1st Massachusetts Cavalry declared: "Stoneman we believe in. We believe in his judgment, his courage and determination. We know he is ready to shoulder responsibility, that he will take good care of us and won't get us into places from which we can't get us out." A severe case of hemorrhoids plagued Stoneman and made his time in the saddle excruciatingly painful.[67]

Stoneman's mounted corps consisted of three divisions of volunteer regiments and a Reserve Brigade of Regular Army units, twenty-six regiments and three companies in all. Brigadiers Alfred Pleasonton, William

Averell, and David McM. Gregg commanded the divisions, while John Buford led the Reserve Brigade. Pleasonton seemed to owe his position more to self-promotion than to demonstrated skill as a cavalryman. He had performed poorly as a reconnaissance officer during the Antietam Campaign. A career horse soldier, Averell was guided by the principles of careful preparation and cautious tactics in an arm that favored the bold. Unlike Pleasonton, Gregg was a self-effacing man, who was, in the words of an officer, "brave, prudent, dashing when the occasion required dash, and firm as a rock." His troopers called him "Old Reliable."[68]

The four regiments of Regulars went to John Buford. A Kentuckian and West Pointer, Buford had led a brigade under Pope and had served as chief of cavalry under McClellan in the fall of 1862. He did not "put on so much style as most officers." A staff officer said later of Buford, "We certainly had no cavalry officer to equal him, and I doubt whether he had many superiors in any respect." Although his rank entitled him to a division, he preferred command of the Reserve Brigade, and the Regulars wanted him.[69]

Stoneman inherited a command that had been misused, lacked an identity, but possessed a smoldering fighting spirit. Hooker expected Stoneman to act aggressively and to confront Stuart's vaunted horsemen. The cavalry chief secured single-shot, breechloading carbines for each trooper, instituted daily drills, ordered the study of mounted tactics by commissioned and noncommissioned officers, and saw to the replacement of worn-out horses. As Hooker explained later, his and Stoneman's efforts had a clear purpose: "Whenever the state of the roads and of the [Rappahannock] River permitted, expeditions were started out to attack the pickets and advance posts of the enemy, and to forage in the country he occupied. My object was to encourage the men, to incite in their hearts, by successes, however unimportant they might be, a sentiment of superiority over their adversaries."[70]

When Hooker assumed command, his primary duty was "to incite" the hearts of the entire army. His appointment elicited mixed opinions from the rank and file. A New York officer described the troops' mood at the time: "An entire army struck with melancholy. Enthusiasm all evaporated—the army of the Potomac never sings, never shouts, and I wish I could say, never swears." When they learned of Hooker's replacement of Burnside, "no two men agree or have the same opinion of the same man or the same thing," claimed a private. They adopted a wait-and-see attitude about Hooker, or as a colonel put it, "It is to be hoped the right man will be found by & by." The crux of it was, in the words of Private James Miller of the 111th Pennsylvania, "we don't care so much who commands so that we winn."[71]

Hooker addressed the two most pressing concerns, desertion and the men's physical wants, energetically. A soldier swore that deserters "had the good wishes of the whole regiments, almost without exception. Men here attach no disgrace to desertion." Hooker ordered the army's provost marshal, Brigadier General Marsena Patrick, to hunt down deserters and to tighten the cordon around the army. Patrick was, said an orderly, "a terror to evil doers," and succeeded in stanching the flood. Hooker also directed that regimental officers keep accurate records and implemented a system of furloughs that proved to be enormously popular. Soon, there was "a continual stream of officers and men going home and returning from leave." In March, President Lincoln announced an amnesty policy for deserters.[72]

The unprecedented desertion rate resulted from the Fredericksburg defeat, the Mud March, and Burnside's neglect of the men's welfare. Scurvy, diarrhea, typhoid fever, and a smallpox outbreak sent thousands of men to hospitals. Frequent snowstorms increased the illnesses and caused a scarcity of firewood. Some days were "cold enough to freeze a fellow." Throughout the weeks, the men had lived on hardtack and salt pork, a recipe for more sickness. A 2nd Wisconsin corporal said that to make the rations palatable, they soaked the hardtack in water and then fried it in pork fat until browned. "We call the thing a *Son of a bitch*."[73]

Hooker's reforms were widespread and effective. He systematized the medical department under the supervision of the competent medical director Dr. Jonathan Letterman. He improved sanitation by rotating campsites and having latrines placed away from water sources. He required the issuance of regular provisions of vegetables and had bakeries built to provide the troops with soft bread four times a week. When officers announced the measures, the men cheered. Within weeks, sick rolls had been reduced, and by April, scurvy had virtually disappeared. A veteran contended that Hooker "is a good man to feed an army for we have lived the best scince he took command that we ever did scince we have been in the army." On the final day of February, the men mustered for four months' pay, which silenced another complaint.[74]

One of Hooker's enduring acts was the creation of badges for individual corps. His original intent was to reduce straggling and shirking during a battle. With each officer and man wearing the badge on his cap, he could be returned more rapidly to his unit. Each corps received a distinctive symbol: First, sphere; Second, trefoil; Third, diamond; Fifth, Maltese cross; Sixth, Greek cross; Eleventh, crescent; and Twelfth, star. The color of the badge for the First Division of each corps was red; for the Second Division, white; and, for the Third Division, blue.[75]

The troops received the badges, made initially of either cotton or flannel, in mid-April. Members of Philip Kearny's former division of the Third Corps had been wearing proudly their "Red Patch" for months. In time, the army's rank and file took equal pride in their badges, which gave them a unit identity. Eventually, metal badges replaced the cloth ones. Years later, when members prepared regimental histories, they frequently adorned them with the corps badges.[76]

The army commander also resumed drills and held reviews to rekindle a common bond. At each review the men turned "out in their best dress with every gun and sword in the best order." The grandest review occurred during the first week of April, when President Lincoln, Mrs. Lincoln, and their son Tad visited the army. For three days, the presidential party—"Father and Mother Abraham," in a lieutenant's words—gazed upon the might of the Army of the Potomac. The men noticed the President's thinness and weariness. One soldier thought he looked "so cadaverous, or so like one lately from the tomb." Private William Wiley of the 70th New York wrote of the president, "I really pitied him, and today I have a greater love and respect for him than I ever had before."[77]

The Lincolns visited hospitals, and Hooker hosted a dinner for them and corps commanders. Tad Lincoln, who celebrated his tenth birthday during the visit, seemed to enjoy himself thoroughly, riding on a pony beside his father at the reviews. Mrs. Lincoln's presence in the army elicited remarks from the soldiers, with a cavalry private writing in his diary, "A woman looks so queer in camp it looks as if the army was going to move." Before Lincoln departed, he told Hooker and Darius Couch, "Gentlemen, in your next battle *put in all your men*."[78]

By the time of the Lincolns' visit, the fighting spirit of the army had been restored. Hooker's attention to the men's basic needs and reforms had dispelled the dark shadow of demoralization. One soldier believed that Hooker's management had been "almost magical." It had been a simple matter to a sergeant in the Irish Brigade: "old fighting joe has an eye to the welfare of this army. It is given up that this army was never so well supplied with food and clothing as it has been since he took command of it." He was the finest administrator in the army's history, and the men's confidence in him equaled, if not exceeded, that of McClellan.[79]

The weeks after Fredericksburg had marked the nadir of the army's morale. It had boiled to the surface in the despair found in their letters and diaries, acts of insubordination, and the rampant desertion. Beneath the evident demoralization, however, lay one of the army's defining characteristics, resiliency. They had passed through Fredericksburg's slaughter, endured serious shortages of food and clothing, and witnessed a reshaping of Union war aims with the Emancipation Proclamation. They had clamored for a change in commanders and fled the ranks by thousands. But the majority stayed, steeled by a belief in a cause that transcended their sufferings and defeats and by a commitment to duty and to each other.

To Sergeant Robert B. Goodyear of the 27th Connecticut it was "a holy cause." If the Federals did not succeed, Goodyear told his wife, "a long night of tyranny and barbarism" would follow, and "all the hope and confidence of the world in the capacity of men for self government will be lost." The defeats, the casualties, and the hardships, argued an officer, "could not dishearten or sour the loyal men of our army. . . . Men knew it all; knew that they stood with one foot in the grave all the while; and for this were better men and better soldiers." They prayed for the end of "*this mad-handed demon of war*," but were committed to crushing "this most causless and damnable rebellion." A staff officer declared tersely, "I could not be out of such a war as this."[80]

Few soldiers, if any, expressed more clearly their devotion to the cause and what it meant than an Irish immigrant, Sergeant Peter Welsh of the 28th Massachusetts. America was, wrote Welsh, "my country as much as the man born on the soil" and his stake "in the maintenance of the government and laws and the integrity of the nation as any other man." The conflict's outcome extended beyond this country's shores. "This war with all its evils with all its errors and mismanagement is a war in which the people of all nations have a vital interest. this is the first test of a modern free government in the act of sustaining itself against internal enemys and matured rebellion. all men who love free government and equal laws are watching this crisis to see if a republic can sustain itself in such a case. if it fails then the hopes of millions fall and the desighns and wishes of all tyrants will succeed."[81]

THE MEMBERS OF THE Irish Brigade celebrated St. Patrick's Day, March 17, 1863, with "athletic contests of the Irish type." Before an audience of many of the army's generals, civilian guests from New York City, and thousands of troops from other units, the Irishmen competed in foot, sack, hurdle, and horse races and climbed a greased pole. The contests proved to be one of the highlights of winter camp until cannon fire from up the Rappahannock River suddenly brought the festivities to an end. Generals scattered to their commands, and the men were ordered to their posts.[82]

The artillery discharges came from a cavalry engagement northwest of Falmouth at Kelly's Ford on the river. Three weeks earlier, four hundred Confederate horsemen, under Brigadier General Fitzhugh Lee, had crossed the Rappahannock and attacked Union mounted pickets near Hartwood Church, before returning to the south side of the river. Angered by the incursion, Joseph Hooker berated his cavalry chief, George Stoneman: "We ought to be invincible, and by God, sir, we shall be! You have got to stop these disgraceful cavalry 'surprises.' I'll have no more of them."[83]

When reports placed Lee's troopers near Culpeper Court House, Hooker directed William Averell to cross the river and to assail the enemy. With 2,000 horsemen, Averell rode south, splashing through Kelly's Ford on the morning of March 17. Although outnumbered nearly three-to-one, the Southerners met the Yankees with a charge. The fighting lasted for four hours until the Federals repulsed a final Confederate attack. Instead of pressing his advantage, Averell acted cautiously, returning to the north side of the river. Total casualties amounted to a little more than two hundred. The most grievous loss sustained by the Confederates was the mortal wounding of Major John Pelham, Jeb Stuart's chief of horse artillery and a hero of Fredericksburg. Known as the "Gallant Pelham," the twenty-four-year-old Alabamian had been one of the Confederacy's most renowned heroes.[84]

The engagement at Kelly's Ford marked a beginning for the Army of the Potomac's mounted units. They had taken the battle to their opponents and had held their own in "a square, stand-up, cavalry fight." The Federals "are in great spirits over the affair," bragged a trooper. Captain George N. Bliss of the 1st Rhode Island Cavalry explained the reason for the men's reaction: "At last our regiment has had the opportunity so long wished for of meeting the rebel cavalry in a fair field fight and the result has far surpassed our expectations." Averell's lackluster performance, however, brought a rebuke from Hooker, who had wanted the brigadier to act more aggressively and to penetrate deeper into the enemy's lines.[85]

The clash between Averell's and Lee's veterans heralded the approach of active operations when spring rains slowed to showers and roads dried in the warmth. Within days of Kelly's Ford, a 24th Michigan soldier wrote, "We do not know where we will go but expect to go down, and whisper kind words in the rebs ears." From the time he had replaced Ambrose Burnside, Hooker had been making preparations and formulating plans for a spring offensive against Lee's Army of Northern Virginia. Hooker's insistence on boldness from the cavalry was based, in part, on the need to screen his preliminary movements and to gather information on Lee's dispositions.[86]

In a major reform of intelligence-gathering activities, Hooker had created a Bureau of Military Intelligence, led by Colonel George H. Sharpe of the 120th New York. Sharpe built a network of spies, who soon supplied Hooker with accurate information on Lee's numerical strength and the unit composition of the Confederate army. The agents' reports contrasted starkly in their detail and preciseness with Allan Pinkerton's inflated estimates for McClellan. By the time Hooker advanced, he had better intelligence on his opponents' numbers and dispositions than any previous commander of the army.[87]

Although Hooker enjoyed a numerical advantage over Lee of two-to-one, the Union army contained upward of fifty two-year and nine-month regiments whose terms of enlistment would expire in April, May, and June. The two-year units from New York and Maine had come into the service during the war's initial weeks, while the nine-month Pennsylvania and New Jersey units had been organized in August and September 1862. This amounted to about 37,000 troops or roughly one third of the army's infantrymen.[88]

On March 3, Congress passed a conscription act, more than a year after Confederate legislators had enacted a similar measure. The law established the principle of a national draft, calling for the enrollment of all eligible men between the ages of twenty and forty-five. It would take time to implement the act and for recruits or conscripts to enter the service. Authorities expected that many of the veterans in regiments whose terms were to expire would reenlist but not before they returned home and collected a bounty, which could amount to hundreds of dollars. These troops' determination to go home was evident when the 1st New York mutinied after the War Department extended its term of service from date of enlistment to date of muster into the army.[89]

Hooker had planned to begin an offensive by the beginning of April, weeks before any regiment left the army, but inclement weather canceled those plans. At mid-month, another rainstorm mired the cavalry in its tracks and flooded the Rappahannock before Stoneman's horsemen could mount a raid in the Confederate rear. More rain fell a week later, postponing a movement until April's final days. Hooker planned to cross the river and to outflank Lee's lines. On April 27, Hooker issued the orders for the army to march the next day.[90]

Hooker commanded a powerful force as he readied it to march. He counted 135,000 officers and men present for duty in the infantry, artillery, and cavalry corps. Weeks earlier, as recounted in a letter, Hooker had allegedly boasted to a colonel "that he was just as sure that he was a going to whip the rebs as he was a living man. He said all he was afraid of was that they would run before he got a chance to fight." So with the peach and cherry trees in blossom, a self-assured Fighting Joe Hooker led his army toward Robert E. Lee's legions. A Union soldier had described Virginia to his family as "the greatest slaughter pen and the largest burying ground in America." It awaited.[91]

Chapter 11

"God Almighty Could Not Prevent Me from Winning a Victory"

LOCAL FOLKS KNEW IT AS THE Wilderness, a seventy-square-mile swath of Virginia that lay north and west of Fredericksburg. For decades inhabitants had felled the stands of stunted oak, hickory, cedar, and pine for charcoal to fuel iron furnaces and factories. Dense snarls of undergrowth choked the ground, and small streams meandered through it, their paths marked by ravines and bogs. A scattering of dwellings and small farms, with cleared fields, dotted the area. It could be a forbidding place, a region of darkened woods and gnarled ground.[1]

A network of narrow roads wound through the woods, while two main roads, Orange Turnpike and Orange Plank Road, cut through the thickets, connecting Fredericksburg to the Virginia Piedmont. The Turnpike and Plank Road merged for a distance of two miles before separating again at Chancellorsville, where a large brick house sat in a seventy-acre clearing. In 1816, George Chancellor had built the residence, opened a tavern, given the site its name, and looked to the future. His dreams of prosperity and of a village never materialized, and Chancellorsville settled into a slow decline. All but time had seemed to pass by Chancellorsville until the final days of April 1863, when the Army of the Potomac came toward it.[2]

At mid-month, the army's commander, Joseph Hooker, had learned from a Union spy that only a thin Confederate force guarded the region beyond the left flank of Robert E. Lee's Army of Northern Virginia. He reported that the Rebels watched fords on the Rappahannock and Rapidan rivers, but "are very much scattered," with no "standing troops" or large numbers of men in the area. Hooker seized upon the intelligence, substantiated by other reports, to fashion a bold and "innovative plan" for a broad turning movement, which would bring the army upon the Southerners' flank and rear. In conception, it compared to Lee's strike around John Pope's army during the Second Bull Run Campaign in August 1862.[3]

Hooker assigned the Fifth, Eleventh, and Twelfth corps, about 43,000 officers and men, to the flanking column. While they marched toward crossings on the Rappahannock and Rapidan rivers, the First and Sixth corps would prepare for a crossing of the Rappahannock below Fredericksburg. His remaining infantry corps, the Second and Third, would act as a reserve to augment either of the two forces. Finally, Hooker ordered George Stoneman and six brigades of cavalry to ride south in a raid against Lee's railroad connections to Richmond, and if the Rebels retreated from their Rappahannock line, to block their passage. Hooker calculated that Lee would have to give battle or would have to abandon the works his army had held for six months. Hooker's plan required coordinated movements across a wide landscape.[4]

The members of the Fifth, Eleventh, and Twelfth corps started from their winter encampments on April 27. Obsessed with secrecy, Hooker had selected these troops for the turning movements as their camps were far removed from enemy picket posts. "The men were in the best of spirits," insisted a New York sergeant, "singing and jesting, enjoying the change of being relieved from the monotony of the camp." The march proceeded well, slowed only by a cumbersome supply train. By nightfall on April 28, the three corps had arrived opposite Kelly's Ford on the Rappahannock and bivouacked. In two hours, engineers had a pontoon bridge across the river.[5]

The Federals filed over the bridge the next morning, heading for Germanna and Ely's fords on the Rapidan. By late afternoon, the Eleventh and Twelfth corps reached Germanna Ford, with the Fifth

Corps at Ely's. Recent rains had swelled the river "to a torrent," but the Yankees plunged in, joining hands as they crossed. The crossing proceeded into the night as large bonfires lighted the ford. "The shadows of the men on the water and the . . . fires all combined to make a most weird picture."[6]

Below Fredericksburg, meanwhile, blue-coated troops had secured lodgments on the Confederate side of the river. As they had done on December 11, 1862, troops piled into pontoon boats and rowed across in the face of Confederate rifle and artillery fire. Spilling out of the boats, the Yankees scattered the Rebels, and engineers erected five bridges. Two divisions filed over the spans and deployed. That night a soldier recorded in his diary, "We expect to meet the enemy tomorrow, when the ball will be opened & the union army will *show* old Jeff Davis that the last Fredericksburg battle did not in the least discourage our troops."[7]

The Union flanking column resumed the march on the morning of Thursday, April 30. By mid-afternoon the three corps had arrived at Chancellorsville. The corps commanders—Henry Slocum, George Meade, and Oliver Howard—conferred. They had turned the enemy's left flank without encountering any serious resistance. An exultant Meade urged a continuation of the movement eastward to "get out of this Wilderness." But Slocum, the senior officer, had orders from Hooker "that no advance be made from Chancellorsville" until troops from the Second and Third corps came up. Slocum, described by a staff officer as "slow, careful," rejected Meade's proposal. That night, Meade wrote to his wife, "We are across the river and out-manaeuvered the enemy but are not yet out of the woods."[8]

Meade's concern was well founded, but the Army of the Potomac had executed an offensive movement new in its history. Confederate artillerist Colonel E. Porter Alexander argued after the war, "On the whole I think this plan was decidedly the best strategy conceived in any of the campaigns ever set on foot against us." That night at Chancellorsville, "the general hilarity in the camps was particularly noticeable."[9]

Hooker and his staff clattered into Chancellorsville that evening. The army commander could not have been more pleased with the army's movements. He was overheard declaring, "God Almighty could not prevent me from winning a victory tomorrow." He issued a proclamation to the troops that read in part, "It is with heartfelt satisfaction the commanding general announces to the army that the operations of the last three days have determined that our enemy must either ingloriously fly, or come out from behind his defenses and give us battle on our own ground, where certain destruction awaits him."[10]

Hooker had learned from Colonel George Sharpe of the Bureau of Military Intelligence that Lee's army numbered 54,600 officers and men, a figure just 1,600 fewer than its actual strength. By nightfall of May 1, Hooker would have roughly 78,000 officers and men and 31 batteries with him at Chancellorsville and about 40,000 infantrymen and artillerymen around Fredericksburg. His plans for the next day were to "assume the initiative" with an advance toward Fredericksburg. If the enemy retired before them, he directed Sixth Corps commander John Sedgwick to move against the Confederates from his position below the town and "when you strike let it be done to destroy."[11]

Despite the buoyant, if not cocksure, mood at army headquarters, a disquietude simmered beneath the surface. "We cannot understand *how* they," wrote Provost Marshal Marsena Patrick of the Confederates in his diary, "are so blinded and that is all that makes us afraid some deep plan is laid for us." Like Hooker, Patrick believed that the enemy either had to retreat or suffer "a terrible licking." The Yankees were, noted the brigadier, "quietly awaiting developments."[12]

Those "developments" had been brewing for a day. Hooker's offensive threatened Lee's entire Rappahannock line. The Confederates could either abandon it, withdrawing to a new defensive position farther south, or confront the mighty Union host. Lee knew the long odds against his outnumbered army. First Corps commander James Longstreet and two infantry divisions had spent the winter in southeastern Virginia, gathering critically needed supplies and could not be expected to rejoin the army in time. If Lee were to stand and to give battle, he would have to do it with 56,000 troops, against Hooker's 120,000.[13]

With characteristic boldness, Lee chose to move against the Federals. During the day on April 30, based on reports and personal reconnaissance, Lee concluded, as he told an aide, "the main attack will come from above," that is, from Chancellorsville. He then summoned Stonewall Jackson to army headquarters. Jackson concurred with Lee's judgment about the enemy's operations. They decided to leave Major General Jubal Early's division and another brigade, 12,400 men, to hold Marye's Heights behind Fredericksburg, and to protect their rear. With the rest of the army, fewer than 44,000 in the ranks, Lee and Jackson would move against the Yankees at Chancellorsville.[14]

In a dispatch to Richmond, Lee explained his decision: "I determined to hold our lines in rear of Fredericksburg with part of the force and endeavor with the rest to drive the enemy back to the Rapidan." He began shifting troops in that direction during the day to reinforce Major General Richard H. Anderson's division, which had fortified a ridge roughly three miles east of Chancellorsville. Jackson, meanwhile, readied his units to march at first light on May 1. With a spirit and celerity rarely witnessed in the Union army, Lee's legions took the initial stride in the most storied campaign in the annals of the Army of Northern Virginia.[15]

UNION BRIGADIER GENERAL Alpheus Williams stated that at Chancellorsville, on the morning of May 1, he had never seen troops "more anxious to meet the enemy." The men in the ranks sensed that their flank movement had given them an edge over their vaunted foe. They had listened to the words of their commander, Joseph Hooker, that the enemy "must either fly ingloriously" or face "certain destruction." When they saw him on this morning, they cheered, for he had brought them here. For this hard luck army, fortune seemed to have turned, with victory beckoning to the east, beyond the Wilderness.[16]

The march began minutes before eleven o'clock—nearly 30,000 men, six divisions and more than two dozen cannon, moving in three columns. While George Meade and two Fifth Corps divisions angled north to secure Banks's Ford on the Rappahannock, the corps's third division, under Major General George Sykes, followed Orange Turnpike eastward. On Sykes's right, Henry Slocum's Twelfth Corps started forth on Orange Plank Road. Ahead of them, dismounted Union cavalrymen skirmished with Confederate infantrymen. The most recent reports from signal stations across the river indicated that one, perhaps two, enemy divisions were dug in on a ridge, Hooker's objective for the day.[17]

To Sergeant Charles Bowen of the 12th United States Infantry in Sykes's division, their purpose on this day was to find the Rebels "& see if we could not coax them out of their holes." Before long, Bowen and his comrades on the Turnpike encountered their foes, who poured "out of their holes." Sykes hurried his brigades into line, and a fierce engagement ensued. More Confederate troops arrived, pressing forward and against both flanks of Sykes's line. On the Plank Road, the Twelfth Corps had not cleared the Wilderness when the van of Stonewall Jackson's oncoming column appeared. Confederate artillerist Colonel Porter Alexander remembered that when he saw Jackson's troops arrive he knew then "We were not going to wait for the enemy to come & attack us in those lines, we were going out on the warpath after them."[18]

At Chancellorsville, Hooker received reports that the troops on the Plank Road were indeed Jackson's and that Sykes's division was being pressed hard with no support at hand. He issued orders for Sykes and Slocum to disengage and to withdraw and for Meade to countermarch to Chancellorsville. It was about two o'clock in the afternoon, and Hooker had ceded the tactical initiative to his opponent. It might not have been as dramatic as Porter Alexander recalled, "in a moment all was changed" with Jackson's appearance. The Battle of Chancellorsville would not be fought on open ground but within the Wilderness, a place that held secrets.[19]

A relentless enemy, Jackson had his Southerners pursue the retiring Federals on the Turnpike and the Plank Road. Sykes's men fought a rear guard action, assisted by troops from Major General Winfield Scott Hancock's Second Corps division. Sykes's and Hancock's veterans halted on a ridgeline, known locally as McGee's Hill and located slightly more than a mile east of the Chancellorsville clearing. Hooker, however, ordered them off of it, and the Confederates seized the position. When Hooker countermanded the earlier dispatch, it was too late. That night, Hooker told a staff officer that the army would assume the defensive.[20]

It appears that Hooker's decision to retire into the Wilderness brought protests from his senior generals. Slocum was allegedly "very much vexed" by the retreat and went to Hooker and asked for permission to attack, which was denied. This seems doubtful, as his overcautious morning advance had left Sykes isolated. His corps's casualties for the day amounted to ten killed and wounded.[21]

In a postwar letter Second Corps commander Darius Couch argued that Hooker had "lost confidence in his ability to maneuvre so large an army in the presence of the enemy" and preferred to offer battle "where he was partially enveloped and hidden by woods." It is claimed that when Meade saw that they had lost McGee's Hill, he growled, "My God, if we can't hold the top of the hill, we certainly cannot hold the bottom of it." He and Third Corps commander Daniel Sickles urged a resumption of the offensive on May 2.[22]

Couch's assertion that Hooker's self-confidence deserted him in the face of the enemy's unexpected aggressive attacks seems overstated. A historian of the campaign, Stephen Sears, has argued that with Sykes under mounting assaults and with Jackson's arrival on the field, Hooker "made a most prudent decision." At the time, Hooker's order for a withdrawal had merit. Nevertheless, Hooker's self-proclaimed combativeness recoiled before enemy onslaughts. He knew from intelligence reports that he retained numerical superiority with ample reserves for counterattacks. Instead, he responded with caution, not unlike George McClellan in similar circumstances.[23]

The burdens of command on a battlefield, at least on this day, apparently dampened Hooker's fighting spirit. According to one of Meade's staff officers in a contemporary letter: "Hooker was at a loss to know what to do, and left everything to his Corps Commanders. This I saw myself. The line was established without any suggestions from him." Meade believed that Hooker discovered that it was one thing for a subordinate, as Hooker had done, to "talk very big," and "quite a different thing, acting when you are responsible" for the entire army.[24]

The consequence of Hooker's decision was to place the Federals within the confines of the Wilderness, an awful battleground. He testified later that when he entered the region: "I was not prepared to find it an almost impenetrable thicket. It was impossible to maneuver." Still, he made it his chosen battlefield upon which he would wage a defensive fight. But the impenetrable thickets limited the army's range of vision, negated its artillery superiority, confining batteries to open spaces, and compromised its numerical superiority. With most of his cavalry units on the raid with George Stoneman, he lacked an adequate mounted force to guard the flanks and to discover enemy movements. Jeb Stuart's aggressive Rebel horsemen commanded the edges of the armies. Finally, Hooker had relinquished the tactical initiative to Lee, an ominous proposition.[25]

It did not take Lee long to exploit the initiative. Before nightfall on May 1, he had determined to strike the Federals' right flank. Jeb Stuart had located the Yankees' flank on Orange Turnpike, west of Chancellorsville. A member of Jackson's command, who had lived in the area, confirmed that the Confederates could follow a road network that would lead them to the Turnpike and beyond Union lines. With Stuart's cavalry controlling the roads, the column of troops could march behind a screen of horsemen. Jackson's units would comprise the attack force and would move early the next morning.[26]

Lee and Jackson shared a bivouac site that night, with both generals up early on May 2. Members of Jackson's staff had secured a local guide for the march, and the troops were readied. When Lee asked Jackson, "What do you propose to go with?" Jackson replied, "With my whole command." That left Lee with the divisions of Richard Anderson and Lafayette McLaws, about 16,000 men, to keep the enemy's attention and to oppose any assault. "Well, go ahead," Lee said. Around a small campfire in the darkened woods of the Wilderness, Lee and Jackson committed the army to one of the war's most daring gambles.[27]

Around Chancellorsville, meanwhile, "the sound of the ax broke the stillness of the night." The Yankees dug rifle pits, cut down trees for field-works, and cleared the ground in front of them, using branches to create abatis. By the morning of May 2, the line ran south for two miles from the Rappahannock to Chancellorsville, where it bent west for three miles along Orange Turnpike. Meade's Fifth Corps manned the ground from the river to the Chancellor House, where the Second Corps divisions of Winfield Scott Hancock and William French were posted. Slocum's Twelfth Corps continued the line west, holding an elevated, open clearing known as Fairview. On its right, Brigadier General David Birney's Third Corps division covered Hazel Grove, another open rise, with Sickles's other two divisions in reserve behind Birney. Howard's Eleventh Corps troops completed the line along the turnpike. The Twelfth, Third, and Eleventh corps units faced south. As Stuart's troopers had discovered, Howard's right flank hung unprotected in the air.[28]

Hooker rose early on May 2, and conducted a reconnaissance of his lines. At one point in the morning, he remarked to Marsena Patrick that his plans "all were working admirably and . . . believed the game was all in our hands." He anticipated an assault from the enemy. In his tour, he had discussed with Howard the vulnerability of the flank, and according to a postwar account, told Howard "to prepare to meet the enemy from the west." Hooker had expected that John Reynolds's First Corps would be on the field and bolster the army's right flank. But the courier carrying the dispatch became lost, and Reynolds's troops would not arrive until well after nightfall.[29]

By mid-morning, Hooker had been alerted to a movement of Confederate troops across the Union front. Lookouts in trees at Hazel Grove had spotted Jackson's men as they turned south at an intersection at Catherine Furnace, located a mile and a half southwest of Chancellorsville. Hooker informed Howard and Slocum of the reports, instructing them to take protective measures against an attack from the west and to push forward their pickets. After noon, Birney's Third Corps troops advanced toward the furnace and bagged nearly three hundred Georgians, who had been guarding the crossroads. Sickles reported that they had seen wagons "still moving south." "I think it is a retreat," stated Sickles. His dispatch added to a growing belief at army headquarters that, indeed, the enemy was withdrawing. Twelfth Corps division commander Alpheus William recalled, "the old story of a flying enemy was repeated to me."[30]

Howard assured Hooker, "I am taking measures to resist an attack from the west." In fact, the one-armed general did virtually nothing. At the least, he should have refused or bent back his right flank units, facing them to the west and erecting fieldworks. Instead, he sent a Signal Corps detail farther to the west on the Turnpike with orders to watch for enemy movements. He also ignored division commander Carl

Schurz's concerns about the position and late afternoon reports from the pickets, who claimed that Rebel troops were massing in their front. Dark clouds of an impending storm were billowing, a foreboding danger unseen by Howard despite the signs. His miserable, if not inexcusable, generalship left his corps vulnerable to a formidable enemy.[31]

To the rest of the army, the German members of the Eleventh Corps were the "damned Dutch." Native-born Americans regarded them as poor soldiers and worse fighters. It was an unfair aspersion, but morale in the corps did not match that in other commands. In command less than a month, the unpopular Howard had done little to renew the men's spirit. By early evening then on May 2, these Federal soldiers were around campfires, cooking and eating supper. Hours before, Brigadier General Alexander Schimmelfennig, a former ensign in the Prussian army, warned a staff officer that if the Rebels "should come in our flank we will be in a hell of a fix."[32]

It was about 5:30 P.M. when Stonewall Jackson turned to Brigadier General Robert E. Rodes, commander of his leading division, and said, "You can go forward then." The Confederates stepped out, three battle lines deep, roughly 30,000 officers and men, aligned on both sides of Orange Turnpike. Ahead of them, deer and other forest creatures scampered toward the camps of the Eleventh Corps, unlikely harbingers of the oncoming fury. Then the Southerners appeared, "yelling like devils let loose." Volleys swept into the surprised Federals. Union regiments at the far end of the line shattered, with many of the men fleeing without firing a shot. The 54th New York and 153rd Pennsylvania managed to fire one or two volleys before being raked with frontal and flank fire. They ran rearward.[33]

Historic images of a headlong rout of the "damned Dutch" distort the truth. Undoubtedly, hundreds, even thousands, of them fled quickly, "like a parcele of sheep." Alpheus Williams, who witnessed their flight, declared that it was "the first really frightened mass of men I ever saw." But various units formed islands of resistance, slowing the Confederate avalanche until they were outflanked. Carl Schurz aligned the 82nd Ohio, 58th New York, and 26th Wisconsin to meet the Rebels, and they fought stubbornly, sustaining casualties of 40 percent of their numbers. On a rise near the intersection of the turnpike and Plank Road, Captain

Hubert Dilger's six Napoleons of Battery I, 1st Ohio Light Artillery unleashed canister into the enemy ranks, retreated as the Southerners closed, unlimbered, and blasted the attackers again. When Howard saw his fleeing troops, he grabbed a flag, putting it under his one arm, and rode into the mass of men, rallying hundreds of them.[34]

Army headquarters at the Chancellor House knew nothing about the disaster on its right flank because of an acoustic shadow until Eleventh Corps fugitives came running down the Plank Road. Hooker rode at once toward the action. He directed Twelfth Corps artillery on Fairview to be turned on the attackers and sent in his old Third Corps division, under Major General Hiram Berry. A soldier in Berry's division asserted later that the order tried "the nerves of the most experienced veterans."[35]

Union cannon, Berry's counterattack, and a stand by Alpheus Williams's Twelfth Corps division blunted the Confederate assault. By then, however, the force of Jackson's attack had spent itself. Disorganization in the ranks and nightfall prevented further efforts. The Southerners had inflicted more than 2,400 casualties on the Eleventh Corps, including 1,000 prisoners, captured nine cannon, and seized a mile and a half of Union works along the Turnpike and Plank Road. When they halted, they lay close to the high ground of Fairview and Hazel Grove. Oliver Howard, whose ineptness contributed to the fate of his corps, declared subsequently: "I wanted to die. . . . That night I did all in my power to remedy the mistake, and I sought death everywhere I could find an excuse to go on the field."[36]

The closeness of the opposing lines and the play of shadows in the moonlit woods sparked outbursts of musketry and cannon fire for hours. About nine o'clock, under orders, Williams's division undertook an effort to retake fieldworks along Orange Plank Road north of Fairview. It ended, as Williams put it, in "a mess." Joseph Knipe's brigade collided with a brigade of North Carolinians, lost more than two hundred men as prisoners, and stumbled back. In one exchange of gunfire, a volley from the 18th North Carolina accidentally wounded Stonewall Jackson, who had ridden forward between the lines with a small party of officers on a reconnaissance. A litter detail carried Jackson to a field hospital, where a surgeon amputated his left arm.[37]

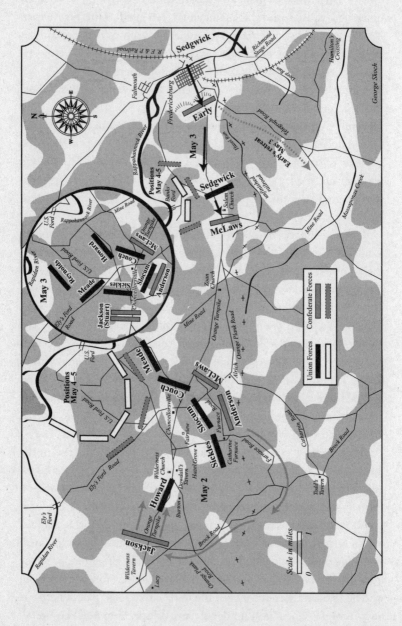

A Massachusetts battery takes a break from war. In times of relaxation, soldiers wrote letters and mended clothing. (USAMHI)

Wartime view of a sutler's store. Sutlers sold personal items to soldiers, who considered these businessmen thieves because of their inflated prices. (USAMHI)

Major General Oliver O. Howard, commander of the Eleventh Corps, whose troops, the "damned Dutch," fled at Chancellorsville. Religiously devout, Howard was called "Old Prayer Book." (USAMHI)

Major General Daniel E. Sickles, commander of the Third Corps at Chancellorsville and Gettysburg, where his unauthorized movement jeopardized the army's position on July 2, 1863. The colorful and notorious Sickles was popular with common soldiers and disliked by fellow generals. (USAMHI)

Major General George G. Meade, the army's fifth and final commander. Meade won the Battle of Gettysburg but failed to prevent the escape of the Confederates into Virginia, causing a rift with Lincoln. Meade served as commander of the army longer than any other general. (USAMHI)

Major General John F. Reynolds, the army's popular First Corps commander. At Gettysburg, on July 1, 1863, Reynolds had his finest day as a general, choosing to offer battle west of the town, but was killed instantly on McPherson's Ridge at mid-morning. (USAMHI)

Brigadier General George A. Custer, commander of the Michigan Cavalry Brigade and Third Cavalry Division. At age twenty-three, the dashing and colorful Custer was the army's youngest brigadier when appointed in June 1863. The "Boy General" proved to be one of the most capable mounted leaders. (USAMHI)

Postwar view, looking southwest, of the ground on Cemetery Ridge defended by the Union Second Corps on July 2 and 3, 1863. The Nicholas Codori farm, with its postwar barn, is in the background. (USAMHI)

Cavalry soldiers in winter camp. The log huts usually housed four to six men and were the centers of their lives during winter months. (USAMHI)

A company of Pennsylvania Reserve troops, standing for inspection. (USAMHI)

Lieutenant General Ulysses S. Grant, general-in-chief of all Union armies. In the spring of 1864, Grant accompanied the Army of the Potomac and directed its operations against Lee's Confederate army. Grant accepted Lee's surrender at Appomattox Court House, Virginia, on April 9, 1865. (USAMHI)

Major General Gouverneur K. Warren, the army's topographical engineer and commander of the Fifth Corps. Warren was removed from corps command at Five Forks on April 1, 1865. (USAMHI)

Major General Philip H. Sheridan, commander of the Cavalry Corps. "Little Phil" Sheridan joined the army in spring of 1864 as cavalry chief and served until assigned to command of the Army of the Shenandoah in August 1864. (USAMHI)

Major General George G. Meade (seated at center) and members of the headquarters staff of the Army of the Potomac. The size of the staff contrasted sharply with the smaller staff of General Robert E. Lee at the Army of Northern Virginia. (USAMHI)

View of the Wilderness. Armies fought the battles of Chancellorsville and the Wilderness in this heavily wooded and difficult terrain. (USAMHI)

View of the "Bloody Angle" at Spotsylvania, where some of the war's most fearful combat occurred on May 12, 1864. (USAMHI)

Major generals Winfield Scott Hancock, seated, and left to right: Francis Barlow, David B. Birney, and John Gibbon. Photograph taken in 1864, when the three generals served as division commanders in Hancock's Second Corps. Hancock's finest hour came at Gettysburg on July 2 and 3. He was the army's best corps commander. (USAMHI)

Major General Andrew A. Humphreys, the army's chief of staff and commander of the Second Corps. Humphreys was one of the army's best executive and combat officers. (USAMHI)

Wartime view, 1865, of a pontoon bridge across the James River. Pontoons were used by both armies to cross rivers. (NA)

1864 or 1865 view of Fort Sedgwick at Petersburg. Called "Fort Hell" by soldiers, the earthwork was typical of the fortifications during the siege of the Virginia city. (USAMHI)

About midnight, near Hazel Grove, David Birney's Third Corps division went forward on a similar mission. Like Williams's men, they were hit with a sudden blast of musketry. "Everything was in a perfect uproar" at once, remembered Private Frederick Townsend of the 17th Maine. A fellow Mainer declared, "we were mortally scared," and they bolted rearward. "Discipline was a dead letter." He claimed that Brigadier General J. H. Hobart Ward's horse trampled two soldiers in the brigadier's race to safety. After this, it quieted. They could hear "the plaintive tones of a whip-poor-will," mingled with "the cries of the dying and wounded."[38]

Although Hooker expected Lee to renew his attacks on May 3, the Union commander had an enticing opportunity to reverse the army's fortunes. He knew from intelligence reports that Lee's bold strike had left only the divisions of Richard Anderson and Lafayette McLaws to confront the Federals east of Chancellorsville. In the wake of Jackson's assault, the wings of the Confederate force remained separated, with the Union Third and Twelfth corps between them. By daylight on May 3, John Reynolds's entire First Corps would be at hand, and with George Meade's Fifth Corps and two Second Corps divisions, Hooker counted more than 40,000 troops available for a counterassault either against Jackson's left flank or Anderson's and McLaws's commands.[39]

In his report, the army's topographical engineer, Gouverneur Warren, stated that Hooker planned to hold the front against Jackson's force, and "the whole of the rest of our force was to be thrown upon his left at dawn of day." In turn, Rebel captives said that only a token force remained at Fredericksburg in front of John Sedgwick's Sixth Corps. Based upon that information, Hooker dispatched orders to Sedgwick "to move at once" and be at Chancellorsville by daylight. If Sedgwick arrived in time, the Federals could crush Lee's divided wings. He sent Warren to Sedgwick to act as a guide for the nighttime march.[40]

During the night, Hooker shifted Meade's Fifth Corps into position along Ely's Ford Road, less than a mile northeast of and perpendicular to Jackson's left flank. Reynolds's three First Corps divisions formed on Meade's right flank, extending the line northeast to the Rappahannock and at a right angle to Meade's alignment. If Hooker planned to include Reynolds's troops in an assault, they were improperly placed. With reliable knowledge of enemy numbers and the composition of each wing of

Lee's forces in front of him, the advantage rested with Hooker. As Warren wrote, May 3 "promised a decisive battle." Indeed, it would be. But when dawn arrived, it was Lee, not Hooker, who attacked.[41]

The Southerners advanced at daylight against the Union-held breastworks, which extended from Hazel Grove to north of the Plank Road. A New Yorker wrote of the Rebels that suddenly "the whole woods in front of us seemed to be full of them." The Yankees triggered volleys, blasting the Confederates back. But this was a day in which these men refused to be denied. The Confederates shrieked "like devils" and charged again. "It is astonishing how these creatures will fight," marveled Private John W. Haley of the 17th Maine. It was the most intense combat of the battle. Alpheus Williams described the musketry as "incessant."[42]

Lee had assigned his cavalry commander, Jeb Stuart, to command of Jackson's corps. The volley that had wounded Jackson also struck down his senior division commander, A. P. Hill. Stuart shared Jackson's warrior spirit, and he pressed the assaults, committing all of his units to the attacks. Relentlessly, the Southerners closed the vise around the bluecoated defenders.[43]

Early in the action, Hooker directed Daniel Sickles to withdraw his Third Corps units from Hazel Grove to Fairview. Hooker had learned that Sedgwick would not arrive from Fredericksburg and wanted to contract his lines. Sickles rightfully objected to abandoning the high ground, but Hooker held firm. It was one of Hooker's most critical mistakes of the battle. Confederate artillerist Porter Alexander rolled seventeen cannon onto the rise. Before long, these crews pounded Fairview and the plateau around Chancellorsville, which became "a hell of fire."[44]

A few minutes after nine o'clock, a Confederate round shot split a porch pillar of the Chancellor house. A piece struck Hooker, knocking him senseless for at least thirty minutes. When he awoke, he "seemed rather dull," symptomatic of a severe concussion. The fog in his head cleared enough for him to relinquish command to Couch, with instructions to withdraw the units to a line he had designated on a map. With him was Meade, who urged that he be given permission to counterattack with his and Reynolds's corps. Hooker said no.[45]

It was now ten o'clock, and the Confederate surge had carried over Fairview and toward the Chancellor house. Their cannon bombarded the collapsing Federal ranks. "The getting away was worse than stay-ing," insisted Alpheus Williams. A line of Union batteries at Chancel-lorsville opposed the oncoming enemy, but the Federal artillery had been poorly handled all day. Before the campaign had begun, Hooker relegated artillery chief Henry Hunt to administrative duties. Hunt was at Banks's Ford on this day, instead of on the battlefield, where his matchless prowess with artillery was desperately required. Hooker would restore him to tactical command of the batteries that night.[46]

As their comrades streamed past the Chancellorsville clearing, Winfield Scott Hancock's Second Corps division held the plateau. Confederate artillery on Fairview and Hazel Grove raked the area. Han-cock steadied the ranks by riding along the line "amidst this rain of shells utterly indifferent, not even ducking his head when one came close to him." A lieutenant who saw him stated, "General Hancock is in his element and at his best in the midst of a fight." At such times, admitted Private Henry Meyer of the 148th Pennsylvania, a unit in its first battle, the fury "possesses a wonderful potency for separating chaff from wheat in a regiment."[47]

Pressed on two sides, Hancock's men finally retired. They had saved some cannon and prevented the capture of many of their comrades in other units. Colonel Nelson A. Miles of the 61st New York commanded the division's skirmish line and suffered a grievous wound. His conduct would earn him a Medal of Honor. In the confusion of the withdrawal, orders never reached the 27th Connecticut and 145th Pennsylvania, which were nearly surrounded and lost 350 men as prisoners. With Han-cock's retirement, the Union line formed a giant U, with both flanks resting on the Rappahannock and with U.S. Ford on the river secured.[48]

Five hours of combat had exacted more than 17,000 casualties from both sides. Thirty-two Federal regimental commanders or successors had been killed, wounded, or captured. The most grievous loss was the mortal wounding of division commander Hiram Berry, a popular and capable general who had first distinguished himself at Williamsburg. But the attacking Confederates had sustained the majority of casualties. "The Rebels fought desperately," professed a Yankee. "They had evi-dently made up their minds to conquer or die and die they did." But as the Northerners filed into a new position, the Southerners swarmed onto the Chancellorsville plateau. When Robert E. Lee rode in, they cheered him. Their desperate charges and willingness to die had given him one of his most brilliant battlefield victories.[49]

UNION MAJOR GENERAL John Sedgwick was an officer ill-suited for the role assigned to him in the Chancellorsville Campaign. Appointed a wing commander, Sedgwick directed operations of his Sixth Corps and John Reynolds's First Corps below Fredericksburg. His orders specified that if the Confederates retreated toward Richmond, he should pursue them, and if they marched to oppose the Federals at Chancellorsville, he should "attack and carry their works at all hazards." The duty required of Sedgwick alertness, initiative, and flexibility amid fluid circumstances. Unfortunately, caution and deliberateness characterized his generalship.[50]

From April 29, when his forces crossed to the enemy side of the Rappahannock, through May 2, Sedgwick held his troops in place. Observers in balloons kept him informed of enemy movements from their lines behind Fredericksburg to Chancellorsville. The Southerners who remained in front of Sedgwick manned the hills and ridges along a six-mile front. They numbered less than half of Sedgwick's 24,000-man Sixth Corps. Artillery fire and skirmishing marked the action. Sedgwick ordered weak demonstrations, but undertook no attacks, despite seeing most of the remaining defenders pull out and march west on May 2.[51]

To be sure, Sedgwick wrestled with telegraphic breakdowns—the wire between Chancellorsville and Falmouth had been strung on lances—lost couriers, and conflicting orders. Joseph Hooker shifted the First Corps to Chancellorsville on May 2, under the mistaken belief that Sedgwick had recrossed the river. Nevertheless, Sedgwick squandered an opportunity to strike the weakly held works on May 2. He finally stirred into action when Hooker sent him a peremptory order to seize the town and to attack the Rebel lines. Hooker sent Gouverneur Warren to Sedgwick to make certain the general acted. Warren confided subsequently to Hooker that he believed Sedgwick would not have moved against the enemy had Warren not been present.[52]

It was minutes after ten o'clock on the morning of May 3 when ten

Sixth Corps regiments in three attack columns advanced at the double-quick toward Marye's Heights. Jubal Early's ranks had been stretched so thin that only eight cannon crews and 1,200 Mississippians manned the hill when the Yankees appeared. The Southerners opened fire, lashing the heads of the columns. Casualties mounted among the blue-coated soldiers, but in the words of a staff officer, "Sedgwick's men could not be stopped, they were for blood."[53]

The attackers, as "if moved by a sudden impulse," poured over the infamous stone wall at the base of the hill and wrenched it from the Mississippians. Up the slope they went, seizing the eight cannon and hundreds of prisoners. The assault had taken less than thirty minutes, but at a cost of more than six hundred in killed and wounded. Early managed to gather up his scattered units and retreat south away from Fredericksburg.[54]

With the road open to Chancellorsville, Sedgwick hesitated to advance westward until he had consolidated his divisions. His orders required a rapid march, but caution owned the soul of Uncle John. By the time the Sixth Corps resumed its march, Lee had dispatched a division from Chancellorsville to oppose the Federals. Five Confederate brigades held the wooded terrain around Salem Church, three miles east of Chancellorsville.[55]

Two brigades of Brigadier General William Brooks's Union division advanced on the enemy position about four o'clock. Some of Brooks's troops had received bounties to enlist, and as they went in, he allegedly called them "two hundred dollar sons of bitches." Bounty men or not, they charged with spirit, breaking through a section of the Rebel line. "We fired as fast as we could," claimed a Yankee, "and Johnny Reb done the same." But the Confederates rallied, counterattacked, and repulsed the Federals. Brooks's men streamed to the rear.[56]

In all, Sedgwick had committed only 4,000 troops to the attack. Evidently, he and his other generals underestimated enemy strength. The assault cost Brooks more than 1,500 casualties, or roughly 40 percent of those engaged. Southern losses amounted to less than half their opponents'. The Sixth Corps "rested on their arms," along and north of Orange Plank Road.[57]

Sedgwick endured a long and difficult night of May 3–4. His chief of staff recounted that the general "scarcely slept." He paced, listened to the sounds through the darkness, and tried to sleep. In his report, Sedgwick said that he heard enemy reinforcements move into position. His corps was miles away from the main body of the army, with the Rebels between them. If the Confederates retook the heights at Fredericksburg, his troops would be boxed in on three sides. "The night was," said his aide, "inexpressibly gloomy."[58]

At daylight on May 4, Sedgwick shifted his divisions, forming a broad U-shaped position, with both flanks on the Rappahannock. The only instructions he received from Hooker came in a dispatch from Warren, who directed him to remain on the defensive unless the Federals attacked at Chancellorsville, "look well to the safety of your corps," and to cover his retreat route at Banks's Ford. They were not reassuring words to a general of Sedgwick's temperament.[59]

Contrary to what Sedgwick believed, Lee had not sent additional units out the Plank Road during the night. But the Rebels were coming on the morning of May 4. Jubal Early's veterans reoccupied a vacant Marye's Heights—John Gibbon's Union Second Corps division had been ordered to occupy Fredericksburg, not the high ground to the west—and then turned toward Sedgwick's corps. From Chancellorsville, Lee sent three brigades. In all, the Southerners massed three divisions, or more than 20,000 troops, against the Sixth Corps.[60]

It took the Confederates most of the day to deploy for an assault. It was not until six o'clock before they charged Sedgwick's line. The fighting centered on the Union left, held by Brigadier General Albion P. Howe, a native of Maine and a West Pointer known for his "unsociable disposition." The combat was fierce at points. One Federal soldier remarked afterward, "I no more expected to get out of that place alive than I expected to fly." Blue-jacketed artillerymen and Howe's veterans repulsed the attacks, carried out by only four Rebel brigades. Under the cover of darkness, Sedgwick compacted his line toward Banks's Ford.[61]

Throughout the day, Sedgwick sent a stream of telegrams to Hooker and the army's chief of staff, Major General Daniel Butterfield, who had stayed at Falmouth during the campaign to coordinate communications and movements between the two wings. The tone of his dispatches revealed a general overwrought with the dangers in front of him. Hours before the Rebels attacked he insisted, "The enemy are pressing me hard." Fifteen minutes later, he asked Hooker, "Can you help me strongly if I am attacked?" He reported that deserters placed the number of troops opposed to him at 40,000. Despite the repulse of the Confederates, he was committed to a withdrawal of his corps across the river.[62]

At 1:00 A.M., on May 5, Butterfield directed Sedgwick to cross the Rappahannock. Sedgwick received the order an hour later and replied, "Will withdraw my forces immediately." At 1:20 A.M., Hooker countermanded the order, but the dispatch did not reach Sedgwick until 3:20 A.M. By then, it was too late to stop the crossing at Banks's Ford. By daylight, the Sixth Corps had filed to the north side of the river, and the pontoon bridges had been cut loose from the south bank.[63]

The next day, May 6, Sedgwick wrote to his sister, "I am perfectly satisfied with the part my corps took in it, and their conduct was admirable." Indeed, the Sixth Corps troops had fought well, but their commander had restricted their role in the campaign. Hooker had expected much more from them, but he had misjudged Sedgwick's capability for an independent command that required aggressiveness. In his letter to his sister, Sedgwick warned her to "believe little that you see in the papers. There will be an effort to throw the blame for the failure on me, but it will not succeed. My friends here will do me justice."[64]

Unfortunately for the army, Sedgwick's performance typified one of the curses that plagued its senior leadership. He was "perfectly satisfied" with minimal performance. There was no urgency in his movements, no pressing desire to go to the sounds of battle at Chancellorsville. While Lee, Stonewall Jackson, and their subordinates sought a reckoning, despite the odds, Sedgwick searched only for obstacles that prevented him from fulfilling his primary mission. The contrast between the differing mind-sets characterized the great divide between the two armies. A firm admirer of George McClellan, Sedgwick shared his former commander's approach to battle. It had crippled McClellan, and it crippled Sedgwick.[65]

MONDAY, MAY 4, PASSED in relative quiet at Chancellorsville. When Lee decided to concentrate the day's operations on Sedgwick's Sixth Corps, he believed that Hooker would keep his troops behind their fieldworks in the Wilderness. Lee rode to the Salem Church area to oversee the attacks and left Jeb Stuart with the mission of masking their numerical weakness and of responding aggressively to any enemy movement. The wooded terrain concealed gaps in the Southern ranks, and Stuart purposefully moved troops into and through openings to fool the Yankees. Deserters crossed into Union lines with tales of the arrival of Longstreet's two divisions from Petersburg.[66]

Along the opposing lines, Confederate pickets and artillery crews maintained an active fire at the appearance of Yankees. Federal pickets probed ahead and ignited skirmishes, which escalated into a spasm of intensity and then receded. During one action, a Rebel sharpshooter killed Brigadier General Amiel W. Whipple, a Third Corps division commander. When Private John Haley of the 17th Maine heard of Whipple's death, he was astonished. "How any bullet ever pierced General Whipple's armor of dirt is a mystery of mysteries," exclaimed Haley. "I considered him perfectly safe from any missile weighing less than a ton, having a casing of dirt of unknown thickness supposed to be invulnerable."[67]

Lee's calculation that his opponent would not assume the offensive at Chancellorsville proved correct. In fact, Hooker expected the Southerners to resume their attacks on his lines. The previous night he had asserted to Colonel Charles Wainwright that if Lee did assail the Federals, "let him look out." The statement amounted to nothing more than braggadocio on Hooker's part. On May 4, he appeared tired and undoubtedly still suffered from the effects of the concussion. Reconnaissances by two Union brigades constituted the extent of advances. One brigade pushed ahead to a section of Southern works and met a gale of canister and musketry.[68]

At midnight, Hooker and Chief of Staff Daniel Butterfield met with corps commanders John Reynolds, Darius Couch, Daniel Sickles, George Meade, and Oliver Howard. Hooker summarized the situation at Chancellorsville and read to them John Sedgwick's dispatch that he would begin a withdrawal. He reminded them that his primary mission was to protect Washington and not to jeopardize the army. The sporadic outbursts of gunfire during the day showed a "want of steadiness" among some of the troops, and that concerned Hooker. He and Butterfield then departed to allow the generals to express their views freely.[69]

Meade seemed to take the lead in the discussions. "I opposed the withdrawal with all my influence," he told his wife. He "considered this army had already too long been made subservient to the safety of Washington" and argued for an advance on May 5. As was his habit, Reynolds said little but agreed with Meade before going to sleep. Howard voted against a retreat and for an offensive, while Sickles favored a withdrawal. Sickles believed that success in attacks was "doubtful," stating, "a defeat would endanger Washington. The uncertainties are against us." He was, however, "astonished" that Hooker placed the decision upon them. Unwilling to make a stand, Couch was counted as in favor of a retreat.[70]

When Hooker and Butterfield rejoined the group, the army commander asked each general for his opinion—three-to-two against a withdrawal. The army would retreat, announced Hooker, and he would take responsibility for the decision. As the generals left, Reynolds grumbled, "what was the use of calling us together at this time of night when he intended to retreat anyhow?" Twelfth Corps commander Henry Slocum arrived as the meeting ended. Before Meade departed, Hooker said to him "in the most desponding manner," according to Meade, "that he was ready to turn over to me the Army of the Potomac; that he had enough of it, and almost wished he had never been born."[71]

"Like everyone else who knew the state of affairs," recorded Wainwright in his diary for May 5, "I expected this would be a busy day with a good deal of hard fighting." Hooker "had assured" the artillery officer "that he would make Lee smart today." Instead, wrote Wainwright, "Today, like yesterday, has passed without moving a foot." Hooker started the artillery reserve batteries and wagons for U.S. Ford and had his engineers map out a new defensive position closer to the crossing site. His opponent, meanwhile, planned to assault the Yankees in their works, but it took time to countermarch the troops around Salem Church and to deploy for the attack. Then at four o'clock in the afternoon, a storm blew in, unleashing sheets of rain.[72]

Three hours later, shielded by the night, Union infantrymen and artillery crews abandoned their works and started toward U.S. Ford. Many of the officers and men reacted with surprise when the order came to retreat. By now, the road and woods were "one vast sea of mud & water." At the ford, engineer troops labored to secure the pontoon bridges from the swiftly rising river, which had overflowed its banks. The columns halted, and "troops got mixed up & lost from each other."

It was not until after 1:00 A.M. on May 6 when the engineers deemed the bridges safe for troops and cannon. A large bonfire brightened the darkness, the signal for the crossing to begin.[73]

Alexander Webb, one of Meade's staff officers, declared, "We all prayed that the bridges might be washed away rather than have that order carried out." Marsena Patrick claimed that many generals were "perfectly astonished at the retrograde movement." "There is," he added, "a feeling of universal disgust & indignation." When the march was delayed until engineers anchored the bridges, there seemed to be talk of remaining in place and awaiting enemy attacks. According to an aide, Reynolds told Meade, "General I will remain with you if there is any battle to be fought we will fight it together."[74]

When the engineers had finished their work, Hooker, who had crossed hours earlier, reiterated his retreat order. The columns filed across, and by about seven o'clock on the morning of May 6, the Federals had returned to the north side of the Rappahannock River. They were wet, sullen, even bitter. A campaign that had begun with high hopes and early successes had ended in defeat amid rain and mud. Expressing a common view, a captain professed, "I recrossed with a heavy heart, and . . . I felt tears rolling down my cheeks."[75]

John Reynolds summarized the Chancellorsville Campaign in a letter home, "We did not effect much more by our crossing than to be slaughtered and to slaughter the Rebels." The bloodletting or "butchering," in a private's word, had been indeed staggering. The casualties of more than 21,000 on May 3 had been exceeded for a single day only by Antietam's carnage. A recent tabulation placed Union losses at 1,694 killed and mortally wounded, 9,672 wounded, and 5,938 missing or captured for a total of 17,304. Confederate losses amounted to 1,724 killed and mortally wounded, 9,233 wounded, and 2,503 missing or captured, for a total of 13,460. The Battle of Chancellorsville ranks behind only Gettysburg and the series of battles at Spotsylvania as the costliest of the war in the East.[76]

NEWSPAPERMAN NOAH BROOKS visited the White House on May 6, and wrote afterward that he had never seen Abraham Lincoln look "so broken, so dispirited, and so ghostlike." While the fighting raged at Chancellorsville, Lincoln had spent hours at the War Department, awaiting news from the army. Secretary of the Navy Gideon Welles said that the President was "constantly up and down" during these days. Joseph Hooker had kept Lincoln and the War Department deliberately uninformed of the campaign's progress until May 3. Then, at 1:00 P.M., on May 6, Chief of Staff Butterfield wired that the army had recrossed the Rappahannock.[77]

The dispatch stunned Lincoln. According to Brooks, "Had a thunderbolt fallen upon the President he could not have been more overwhelmed." Another visitor was with Brooks when Lincoln said to them: "My God! My God! What will the country say! What will the country say!" At four o'clock, the president and General-in-Chief Halleck boarded a steamer for the army.[78]

Lincoln and Halleck spent less than a day at Falmouth. It was reported that the president "said he had come down to enquire for himself as to the condition of affairs." When he spoke with Hooker, he learned of the general's plans for the campaign and the mishap that had befallen Hooker on May 3. Ultimately, Lincoln blamed no one for the defeat, and decided to give Hooker another chance. The president thought, however, that the defeat's "effect, both at home and abroad, would be more serious and injurious than any previous act of the war."[79]

A week after his visit, on May 14, Lincoln wrote to Hooker. In the letter, he stated: "I must tell you I have some painful intimations that some of your corps and Division Commanders are not giving you their entire confidence. This would be ruinous, if true; and you should therefore, first of all, ascertain the real facts beyond all possibility of doubt." Lincoln must have learned of this from Halleck, who had met with the corps commanders while they were at Falmouth. Halleck discovered that "a great dissatisfaction" existed among the generals about Hooker's conduct of the campaign. Couch wanted to take the matter up personally with the president, but the others refused. Newspapermen heard of the dissension and printed the story.[80]

The "great dissatisfaction" with Hooker extended throughout the army. Unlike Fredericksburg, the outcome of the Chancellorsville Campaign defied understanding among the rank and file. The prevailing conclusion was that Fighting Joe had been "outgeneraled" by Lee. "There is no doubt that what we were completely out Generaled," stated Lieutenant Frank Lemont of the 5th Maine in a representative letter. "Our men fight just as well as the Rebels and are just as brave." Fifth Corps staff officer James Biddle asserted: "I am nothing of a General, but why we did not whip them I do not see. . . . We never gave our men a chance."[81]

It was this sense that Hooker had never given his veterans "a chance" that gnawed at the army. The First and Fifth corps had been virtually unengaged. No commander of the army had entered upon a campaign with better intelligence on his opponent's numerical strength and unit composition than Hooker. He knew that he outnumbered Lee by more than two-to-one and was kept posted throughout the operations with additional reports. Nevertheless, from the time Lee reacted aggressively on May 1, Hooker recoiled from ordering counterstrikes.

Alexander Webb thought that when confronted with Lee's audacity, Hooker "lost himself very suddenly." Contrary to postwar allegations, Hooker never said that he had lost confidence in himself. How long and to what extent the effects of the concussion he suffered on May 3 clouded his judgment cannot be assessed. Whether he would have approved Meade's request for a counterattack against the Confederates' left flank had he not been knocked unconscious remains unanswerable. It would appear, however, from his decisions on May 4 and 5 that Hooker's combative spirit had been drained away. Tactical circumstances and numbers favored the Federals almost until the army retreated.[82]

George Meade insisted *"Hooker never lost his head."* His "objection" to Hooker's generalship was "that *he did not and would not listen* to those around him; that he acted deliberately on his own judgment, and in doing so committed, as I think, fatal errors." Unfortunately for Hooker, his refusal to accept the counsel of others only increased the burden of command upon himself. Perhaps he had come to recognize that responsibility for an entire army had been too much for him when he blurted out to Meade "that he had enough of it, and almost wished he had never been born."[83]

Hooker, however, attributed the defeat to the failings of Oliver Howard, John Sedgwick, and George Stoneman. No subordinate officer served Hooker and the army more poorly than Howard. On May 2, the one-armed Eleventh Corps commander did not comply with Hooker's orders and ignored mounting evidence of an attack against his vulnerable flank, which resulted in the disaster that befell his command. Howard's performance amounted at least to negligence of duty.[84]

To the rest of the army, the Eleventh Corps had disgraced itself and bore responsibility for the defeat. They cursed and scorned Howard's men. A Pennsylvania corporal wrote on May 10, "i can tell you that for the present we think very little of the dutch sons of bitches that used to brag that they fight mit Sigle and i don't know but they might have fought well with Sigle but they did not fight worth shit under Howard." Captain Henry Abbott of the 20th Massachusetts averred, "Every man in Sigel's [Howard's] Corps ought to be hauled off the face of the Earth." Although some of the regiments and batteries had resisted until outflanked, the entire corps suffered the denunciations. Writing on May 7, a staff officer in the corps contended, "a spirit of depression and lack of confidence manifests itself everywhere."[85]

As John Sedgwick had predicted, he became one of the scapegoats for the defeat. Artillery officer Charles Wainwright noted that Hooker in a conversation with First Corps officers laid "the whole blame on General Sedgwick." The army commander "was very bitter against 'Uncle John,' accusing him of being slow and afraid to fight; also of disobeying orders directly." According to John Gibbon, Sedgwick confronted Hooker about the accusations, and "a stormy scene" ensued, with Sedgwick arguing that reports about his conduct of the Sixth Corps "were a pack of 'lies.'" While Hooker had justifiable complaints against Howard and Sedgwick, he took no official action. One of Sedgwick's aides claimed, "The army—so far as we could learn, the whole army—stood to endorse the General, and to uphold him even against Hooker."[86]

It was a different matter for Cavalry Corps commander George Stoneman. Ordered to conduct a mounted raid in the rear of Lee's army to sever the Confederates' supply lines and to harass any retreating columns, Stoneman and his 7,400 officers and men spent ten days operating in the region between Fredericksburg and Richmond. The Union troopers damaged two railroads, burned captured supply wagons, foraged throughout the countryside, and clashed with Rebel cavalrymen. The raid, however, had minimal effects on enemy operations. But for the Federal horsemen, it enhanced morale and confidence. Never before had the army's mounted units conducted such a raid into enemy territory.[87]

In his report, Stoneman declared that the raid's "primary object" to cut the Confederates' communications between Richmond and Fredericksburg "was fully complied with and carried out." But Hooker thought otherwise, telling Secretary of War Edwin Stanton: "the raid does not appear to have amounted to much. . . . My instructions appear to have been entirely disregarded by General Stoneman." Hooker's accusation was unfair, but Stoneman asked for and was granted a medical leave on May 20. He had suffered excruciating pain from hemorrhoids during the raid. He never served again in the Army of the Potomac.[88]

Hooker offered command of the Cavalry Corps initially to Winfield Scott Hancock, who reluctantly agreed to accept it. When Second Corps commander Darius Couch asked to be relieved of duty, Hancock as senior division commander succeeded Couch. Consequently, Hooker appointed Alfred Pleasonton to temporary command of the mounted units. A cavalry officer accused Pleasonton of "intriguing" against Stoneman and seeking his removal. Hooker had preferred John Buford for the post, but Pleasonton's commission as brigadier general predated Buford's. It would have been better for Hooker and the army had he pressed for Buford's appointment.[89]

The dissension between Hooker and his senior generals seethed for weeks after the battle. Couch left the army on a leave of absence after he told Lincoln that he could no longer serve under Hooker. When Couch spoke to the president, he recommended Meade as a replacement for Hooker. In June, Couch was appointed commander of the Department of the Susquehanna.[90]

In private letters, Sedgwick and Hancock claimed that each of them had been approached about command of the army. Most likely, Halleck or an intermediary for the general-in-chief made the unofficial offers to the generals. Halleck's personal antipathy toward Hooker was well known, but if he had contacted Sedgwick and Hancock, he did so without Lincoln's approval. Howard heard a rumor that Daniel Sickles was to succeed Hooker. "If God gives us Sickles to lead us," bewailed Howard, "I shall cry with vexation & sorrow and plead to be delivered."[91]

Lincoln did, however, meet with John Reynolds about command of the army on June 2. For some time, Reynolds had complained privately about interference from Washington with the army's operations. Lincoln told Reynolds that he was reluctant to remove Hooker, as "he was not disposed to throw away a gun because it miss fired once; that he would pick the lock and try it again." Evidently, the president inquired under what conditions Reynolds would accept command. He would need a "free hand" from Washington authorities, replied the general, but he did not want the post. The two men left it at that.[92]

The general who had emerged from Chancellorsville with an enhanced reputation and the most likely successor to Hooker was George Meade. Perhaps sensing Meade as a threat, Hooker claimed falsely that the Fifth Corps commander had approved of the retreat. Meade possessed a volcanic temper and confronted Hooker about his charge, and the two generals "had words." His fellow corps commanders, however, had expressed a willingness to serve under Meade as army commander. Meade confided to his wife when he heard that Couch had recommended him to Lincoln, "I do not desire the command."[93]

Meade staff officer Alexander Webb described the failures of generals as "the *sore the running sore*" of the army. He added: "Our men are splendid. They will do anything they are told to do." As Webb recognized, here lay the army's true core. At Chancellorsville, for yet another time, they deserved more from the commander and certain generals. A modern historian, Russell Weigley, has concluded, "Whenever the soldiers of the Army of the Potomac were given a fair chance to fight, they did so with tenacity and ferocity, and with their army's customary tactical skill at every level save that of the highest headquarters."[94]

It was the rank and file's resiliency in the aftermath of another defeat that so defined its character. A newspaper correspondent insisted that the army "never failed to respond to any demand made upon it, and it was ready to renew its courage at the first ray of hope." Writing after Chancellorsville, a staff officer described the army as "something of the English bulldog. . . . You can whip them time and again, but the next fight they go into, they are in good spirits, and as full of pluck as ever.

They are used to being whipped and no longer mind it. Some day or other we shall have our turn."[95]

Chancellorsville also demonstrated to them the formidable opponent that was the Army of Northern Virginia. "The Southern army is disciplined—as machines—and are certainly more efficient than ours," declared Lieutenant William Blodgett of the 151st Pennsylvania. The 6th Wisconsin's Lieutenant Colonel Rufus Dawes professed, "I do not think the Rebellion is to be crushed here, unless we may *annihilate* the great army in front of us."[96]

Chancellorsville had been a brilliant victory for the Confederates. Against daunting odds, "their heroic courage overcame every obstacle of nature and art, and achieved a triumph most honorable to our arms," Robert E. Lee stated in his report. To Lee, however, the battle was barren of the decisive defeat that he had planned to inflict upon the Federals. He was furious when he learned that the Yankees had recrossed the Rappahannock during the night of May 5–6. He knew that with time they would return.[97]

The battle had cost Lee's army dearly, and the results did not compensate for the lengthy casualty lists. Perhaps no price could be calculated for the loss of Stonewall Jackson, who died on May 10. When Lee learned of his death, he said, "I do not know how to replace him." He never would, but the army had to go forth without him—and go forth it would.[98]

Chapter 12

"Big Fight Some Wears Ahead"

THE RECKONING BEGAN with a trickle of men in gray and butternut on the march, the leading edge of a floodtide destined to follow. June 3, 1863, was "a beautiful bright" day, and elements of the Army of Northern Virginia headed away from Fredericksburg, Virginia, moving up the Rappahannock River. Ahead, at the end of many roads, awaited a rendezvous unique in American history. For the Army of Northern Virginia and for its foe, the Army of the Potomac, a fateful trumpet sounded.[1]

The Confederates' victory at Chancellorsville had given General Robert E. Lee the strategic opportunity to carry the war in the East beyond the Potomac River for a second time. When he presented his plan to President Jefferson Davis and the Cabinet, Lee argued that the offensive would spare Virginia from further ravages for weeks, garner a harvest of foodstuffs and livestock, and disrupt Union operations for the summer. But in Lee's thinking, there was more to it. He was going north for a settlement, for a victory on free soil that might compel the administration in Washington to open negotiations on a political resolution to the conflict. Despite his army's achievements, time pressed hard against the Confederacy. It must be stayed, and to do that, Lee looked north.[2]

By the end of the first week of June, Lee had gathered the bulk of his army—now organized into three infantry corps under James Longstreet, Richard Ewell, and A. P. Hill—at Culpeper Court House. The halt at Culpeper was intended to be brief before the Rebels filled the roads north and west to the Shenandoah Valley, their route into Maryland and Pennsylvania. A cocksureness permeated the army's ranks. Weeks earlier, Lee had stated: "There never were such men in any army before & never can be again. If properly led they will go anywhere & never fail at the work before them."[3]

Across the Rappahannock, meanwhile, Major General Joseph Hooker had learned of the Confederate march upriver as early as June 4. Initially, Hooker thought that Lee intended to turn the right flank of the Union army as he had done during the Second Bull Run Campaign, either by interposing his army between Washington and the Federals or by crossing the Potomac River. To counter the enemy's movement, Hooker telegraphed Washington, proposing that he cross the Rappahannock and "pitch into" Lee's rear.[4]

When Abraham Lincoln received the telegram, he saw the flaw in Hooker's plan at once. While the Federals could become bogged down in assaults against the Confederate works at Fredericksburg, Lee would be free to roam through northern Virginia and to threaten the Union capital. Lincoln replied within the hour, "In one word, I would not take any risk of being entangled upon the river, like an ox jumped half over a fence and liable to be torn by dogs front and rear, without a fair chance to gore one way or kick the other."[5]

For the present, Hooker deferred to Lincoln. He tested the Southern works at Fredericksburg with a reconnaissance in force and found Hill's veterans in them. On June 7, based on a dispatch from Brigadier General John Buford that placed all of Jeb Stuart's Confederate cavalry in Culpeper County, Hooker ordered Brigadier General Alfred Pleasonton "to disperse and destroy the rebel force assembled in the vicinity of Culpeper." Pleasonton would have the entire Cavalry Corps with him and two infantry brigades—in all, 8,000 troopers, 3,000 infantrymen, and four artillery batteries. Intelligence reports did not indicate the presence of enemy infantry units in the area.[6]

The blue-jacketed horsemen splashed across the Rappahannock at dawn on June 9—the right wing under Buford at Beverly Ford; the left wing under Brigadier General David McM. Gregg at Kelly's Ford. Shots from Rebel pickets rang out in the morning's shadowy light. To the rear, their comrades scrambled from beneath blankets or left breakfasts uneaten as they rushed to mount horses or to man cannon. The Yankees had surprised Jeb Stuart's veterans and were coming. The Battle of Brandy Station, the largest cavalry engagement of the war, had begun.[7]

The fighting ignited on Buford's front in a swirling melee of sabers and pistols, marking the pattern of mounted combat on this day. In this initial clash, a Virginian shot and killed brigade commander Colonel Benjamin F. Davis. A darkly handsome man, "Grimes" Davis, as he was known, had grown up in Mississippi, graduated from West Point in the same class as Stuart, and remained loyal to the Union. During the Antietam Campaign, Davis had led the cavalry regiments at Harper's Ferry out of the town in a daring escape before the garrison surrendered. He was universally respected within the army, with John Gibbon writing, "I regard his death as *the greatest loss this army has met with in a long time*."[8]

While Buford pushed forward from Beverly Ford, Gregg's troopers advanced from the southeast. By late morning, the combat moved toward high ground, known locally as Fleetwood Hill. Stuart's men resisted fiercely, but these Federals had been waiting a long time to meet their renowned foes on a battlefield. On this day Yankees in the 2nd, 6th, 8th, 9th, and 10th New York, 1st, 6th, and 17th Pennsylvania, 1st Maine, 2nd Massachusetts, 8th Illinois, 1st New Jersey, and 1st Maryland challenged the Confederates as never before. Charges and countercharges flowed up, over, and back down Fleetwood Hill. As a Southerner remembered, it "was a great and imposing spectacle of squadrons charging in every portion of the field—men falling, cut out of the saddle with the saber, artillery roaring, carbines cracking—a perfect hurly-burly of combat."[9]

Only by the grimmest tenacity and courage did the Southerners cling to Fleetwood Hill. Stuart's subordinates shifted units, rallied broken regiments, and hurled every man they could into the struggle. Buford and Gregg directed their commands as Pleasonton watched from the rear. The Rebels might have been swept from the field had Colonel Alfred N. Duffié, at the head of the Second Division, acted aggressively and moved to the sounds of battle. Ordered to guard the Union left flank, Duffié rode into Stevensburg, four miles south of Brandy Station, took hours to brush aside an outnumbered enemy force, and when ordered by Gregg to join him, used a roundabout route, instead of the direct road, to Brandy Station. His troopers arrived to join in the Federal withdrawal.[10]

Pleasonton ordered the retreat late in the afternoon, and by nine o'clock, every Federal had recrossed the river. Stuart's men held the field, and he claimed a victory. Confederate casualties exceeded 400, while Union losses amounted to 484 killed and wounded, and 372 captured. That night, in typical boastful fashion, without basis in fact, Pleasonton informed Hooker that Stuart was to have started on a raid, but "you may rest satisfied he will not attempt it." He had failed, however, in his primary mission of wrecking Stuart's command.[11]

The importance of Brandy Station rested not in its impact on Confederate operations but in its effect upon the Union cavalrymen who had been given a chance to show their mettle. Major Henry McClellan of Stuart's staff declared afterward that the engagement "made the Federal Cavalry." Unquestionably it heralded a new reality. No longer would Stuart's cavalrymen ride unchallenged. Writing of his regiment, a member of the 1st Maine Cavalry could have been speaking for all the regiments engaged at Brandy Station: "The battle aroused its latent powers, and awoke it . . . to a new career. It became self-reliant, and began to comprehend its own possibilities. It became inspired with an invincible spirit that never again forsook it."[12]

LED BY RICHARD EWELL'S Second Corps, the Confederate march resumed on June 10 toward the Blue Ridge Mountains and beyond into the Shenandoah Valley. Four days later, Ewell's veterans routed a Union force at Winchester, capturing supplies, wagons, cannon, and nearly 4,000 prisoners. On June 17, the vanguard of the Southern invasion forded the Potomac into Maryland. Behind Ewell, Longstreet's First Corps had entered the Valley, with A. P. Hill's Third Corps nearing the Blue Ridge gaps. Jeb Stuart's cavalrymen manned the mountain passes, screening the infantry units. At one point, Lee's army stretched for one hundred miles across the Old Dominion.[13]

During most of this week of rapid Confederate movement, Hooker held the Army of the Potomac along the Rappahannock. Viewing Lee's operation as a raid, Hooker proposed again to Lincoln a "rapid advance on Richmond" by his army. Lincoln rejected the plan once again, writing: "I think Lee's army, and not Richmond, is your sure objective point. If he comes toward the Upper Potomac, follow on his flank and on his inside track, shortening your lines while he lengthens his. Fight him, too, when opportunity offers. If he stays where he is, fret him and fret him."[14]

By the evening of June 13, Hooker had become convinced from reliable reports that Ewell's and Longstreet's corps were in the Shenandoah Valley. He informed Washington that the army would be moving north along the Orange & Alexandria Railroad, placing it between the Rebels and the capital. Hooker issued the orders for the march, and by the next morning, the roads of central Virginia filled with living ribbons of men in blue.[15]

The march rapidly turned into an ordeal they remembered for years. It had not rained in more than a month, and thick clouds of dust enveloped the columns as the sun burned the air. Men drained their canteens, and water was scarce. Hundreds collapsed from sunstroke. "Strong men wilted down as though blasted by something in the air," exclaimed a sergeant. Entire regiments fell out of the ranks, and ambulances overflowed. All of them most likely would have agreed with a New Hampshire soldier's words, "Hardest marching I ever had on account of the heat and want of water."[16]

By June 17, the army corps sprawled across northern Virginia, west of the capital. When they finally halted, a New York private, echoing a common feeling, confessed, "I think I could have slept if I had stood on my head." Lice infested their uniforms. But as soon as they could, they roamed into the countryside, where "the men had good foraging—chickens, pork, beef and vegetables." A Pennsylvanian offered one explanation for the foraging: "Those Virginians had, as they thought, gone out of the Union. We were out to whip them into the Union again. We were laboring and suffering for their benefit, and it was proper they should board us part of the time."[17]

The march had been stopped as Hooker grappled with conflicting information about the enemy's whereabouts. He had learned of the disaster at Winchester, and "vague rumors" placed Ewell's Confederates in Pennsylvania. Chief of Staff Daniel Butterfield remarked, "We cannot go boggling around until we know what we are going after." Provost Marshal Marsena Patrick believed, however, that Hooker "acts like a man without a plan and is entirely at a loss what to do, or how to match the enemy, or counteract his movements."[18]

Seeking better intelligence, Hooker sent Pleasonton's cavalrymen toward the gaps of the Blue Ridge. When the Federals reached Virginia's Piedmont, they encountered their old adversaries in Stuart's cavalry, who were guarding the mountain passages. First at Aldie on June 17, then at Middleburg on June 19, and finally at Upperville on June 21, the opponents clashed in a series of mounted charges and dismounted fighting. The Yankees showed the same grit and valor as they had at Brandy Station, pressing their attacks against the Rebels. Stuart's troopers prevented the Federals from entering the gaps, but Pleasonton reported to Hooker that Lee's entire army was in the Shenandoah Valley.[19]

Pleasonton's information was accurate, except for Ewell's corps, which had crossed the Potomac into Maryland, with a cavalry brigade and infantry division edging into Pennsylvania. By June 27, Longstreet's and Hill's commands had entered the Keystone State, with Ewell's leading elements moving toward the Susquehanna River. The beauty and richness of the country amazed the Southerners, who reaped a bounty from the larders of the farmers.[20]

Reports of a swelling tide of Southerners in Pennsylvania finally brought a reaction from Hooker. On June 25, he started the army north into Maryland. For three days, the Yankees trudged ahead in forced marches. Crossing on pontoons at Edwards Ferry, they moved toward Frederick. Thousands of men straggled, unable to stand the pace. One soldier saw a dead man along the road and grumbled that these marches will "soon kill all of us." By nightfall of June 27, most of the corps had closed on Frederick. "Our army," wrote a surgeon on this day, "is like a large serpent—it has to gather itself into a coil when preparing to strike a blow." A New Yorker predicted, "Big fight some wears ahead."[21]

In Washington, meanwhile, Lincoln responded to the mounting crisis. Pressed by Pennsylvania governor Andrew Curtin, Lincoln issued a proclamation calling for 100,000 militia volunteers from Pennsylvania, Maryland, Ohio, and West Virginia, to serve for six months or until the emergency had passed. The president also answered Hooker's pleas for reinforcements—since Chancellorsville, nineteen nine-month and two-year regiments had left the army—by assigning 15,000 troops from two departments to the army.[22]

The troops that joined the army consisted of three infantry brigades, two artillery batteries, a cavalry division, and two brigades of the Pennsylvania Reserve Division. Few, if any, divisions in the army had sustained more losses in the 1862 campaigns than the Pennsylvanians. During the previous winter, the War Department had assigned them to the capital defenses to recuperate and to refill the ranks. When they received the order for two of the three brigades to rejoin the army, "The boys did not like leaving at first," wrote one of them. "All got pretty well corned." As they marched up Pennsylvania Avenue en route to Frederick, they joined in a chorus of *"McClellan give us McClellan."*[23]

In the midst of the flood of alarms from Pennsylvania and the uncertainties surrounding Lee's movements, Lincoln faced another command crisis in the army. Early on the afternoon of June 27, Hooker wired General-in-Chief Halleck, requesting, "that I may at once be relieved from the position I occupy." At issue was a dispute between Hooker and Halleck over the 10,000-man garrison at Harper's Ferry. Hooker wanted the place abandoned and the troops sent to his army; Halleck wanted it held. Hooker had been working on a scheme to unite the Twelfth Corps and a cavalry regiment with the garrison to operate against the Confederates' supply line in the Shenandoah Valley. He gave up the ill-conceived plan on the day he sent in his resignation.[24]

The mutual antipathy between the men only aggravated the professional disagreement. Hooker had refused to keep Halleck informed of the army's operations until Lincoln intervened and ordered him to report directly to Halleck. In turn, Halleck had been unwilling to issue orders to Hooker. But it was Hooker, not Halleck, who precipitated the crisis with his resignation. Apparently Hooker thought he could force Halleck into backing down and ceding control of strategy to him. The general-in-chief responded to Hooker's telegram by notifying him that he had forwarded his request to the president.[25]

Lincoln acted upon receipt of the telegram. To change commanders of the army at such a crucial phase in the campaign was, as an officer would argue, "a very dangerous experiment on the eve of battle." While Hooker had not conducted operations aggressively during the past two weeks, he had kept the army between Washington and the Rebels, his primary duty. If Lincoln did not know it with certainty, he must have thought that Hooker had not won back the confidence of his senior generals. Stanton and Halleck had been pressing for his removal for some time. Lincoln issued the order that night.[26]

The next day Lincoln explained his decision at a Cabinet meeting. As Secretary of the Navy Welles recorded it in his diary, Lincoln said, "he had, for several days as the conflict became imminent, observed in Hooker the same failings that were witnessed in McClellan after the Battle of Antietam. —A want of alacrity to obey, and a greedy call for more troops which could not, and ought not to be taken from other points. He would . . . strip Washington bare."[27]

Joseph Hooker's tenure as commander of the army had lasted almost exactly five months. It was a position that he had coveted and had shamelessly worked to obtain. He had assumed command with the troops' morale at its nadir, instituted reforms, and restored their fighting spirit. His lasting achievement was the creation of a cavalry corps whose prowess and role would continue to increase after he was gone. Then, there was Chancellorsville and the bitter controversy with his corps commanders. Perhaps, Lincoln had done Fighting Joe a favor, for now he would not have to meet Robert E. Lee on another battlefield.

BRIGADIER GENERAL JAMES Hardie arrived at the headquarters of the Fifth Army Corps outside Frederick, Maryland, about two o'clock on the morning of June 28. Traveling by special train from Washington, Hardie carried with him the order that assigned Major General George G. Meade to command of the army. Led into Meade's tent, Hardie greeted the suddenly awakened general by saying he brought "trouble." For a moment, Meade thought that he had been removed from command.[28]

An aide of Meade's wrote that the appointment came as "a complete surprise to General Meade." Written by General-in-Chief Halleck, the direct order left Meade with little recourse but to accept the duty or resign his commission. The selection of Meade had been the president's, not Halleck's. Lincoln knew that Meade enjoyed the confidence and respect of most of the army's corps commanders, who had argued for weeks that he should succeed Hooker. As Welles put it in his diary, "His brother officers speak well of him, but he is considered rather a 'smooth bore' than a rifle."[29]

Born in Cádiz, Spain, into a prominent Philadelphia merchant family, the forty-seven-year-old Meade had been a professional soldier for nearly three decades. His promotion from brigade commander in the Pennsylvania Reserve Division to corps command had been earned on battlefields. Like his close friend John Reynolds, Meade had admired George McClellan, but had avoided the army's internal politics and intrigues, venting his complaints privately in letters to his wife, Margaret. He possessed ambition but had never allowed it to consume him as Joseph Hooker had. Within a day of his appointment, he confided to Margaret, "Dearest, you know how reluctant we both have been to see me placed in this position, and as it appears to be God's will for some good purpose—at any rate, as a soldier I had nothing to do but accept."[30]

Lincoln had risked much on a man he barely knew. Friends and fellow officers of Meade knew him as an honest and straightforward man who was thorough and painstaking in his attention to duties. His temper could be, and often was, explosive. There was a cold, even irascible, edge to him, particularly when occupied with army business. He was demanding of himself and of aides and subordinates. A future staff member asserted, "He will pitch into himself in a moment, if he thinks he has done wrong; and woe to those, no matter who they are, who do not do right."[31]

When demands on his time slackened, Meade could be cordial and outgoing with friends and staff members. The rank and file who served under him seldom witnessed this side of the man, whom one officer described as "grumpy, stern, severe." Physically, he lacked the commanding presence of a Winfield Scott Hancock or the darkly handsome stature of Reynolds. Meade was a tall, thin man, with brown hair and beard liberally sprinkled with gray. His face, thought a newspaperman, "is colorless, being of a ghostly pale," and "his nose of the antique bend." He wore eyeglasses, which elicited the nicknames "Old Four Eyes" or "Old Goggle Eyes" from the troops.[32]

An aide observed, "as for clothes, General Meade was nowhere." Another officer remarked, "it would be rather difficult to make him look well-dressed." His large, black slouch hat seemed to be the distinguishing feature of his attire. Meade reminded a captain of "a good sort of a family doctor," while a corporal thought "he might have been taken for a Presbyterian clergymen, unless one approached him when he was mad." A less charitable soldier called him "a damned old goggle-eye snapping turtle."[33]

What mattered, however, was that Meade was "a thorough soldier, and a mighty clear-headed man," with "extraordinary moral courage." When the news of Meade's appointment circulated, the army's senior leadership welcomed it. John Gibbon told his wife, "I now feel my confidence restored & believe we shall whip these fellows." Meade's son, George, who served on his father's staff, exclaimed to his mother: "I never saw such universal satisfaction, everyone is delighted. Reynolds, Slocum, & Sedgewick have all given in and behaved very well, as far as I know." Artillery chief Henry Hunt and chief engineer Gouverneur Warren expressed doubts about the wisdom of Lincoln's action, with Warren calling it an "extraordinary change at such a time."[34]

In the lower ranks, Hooker's removal and Meade's appointment received a mixed reaction. Few men knew much about Meade, and like Hunt and Warren wondered about the change's timing. A rumor raced through the army that McClellan had replaced Halleck. Another one had Meade in command only until Little Mac joined the army, which one officer claimed would be greeted with "a shout of rapture and glorious exultation." A New York surgeon expressed the common reaction to Meade: "All were willing to try him, and hoped for the best."[35]

Accompanied by Hardie, Meade rode to army headquarters at Frederick, where Hooker greeted them and received his removal order from Hardie. Hooker treated Meade generously, and the two generals, joined by Chief of Staff Butterfield, discussed the military situation for hours. Hooker remarked that enemy operations "had occupied two hours of his time each day, Washington had required the remainder." Meade decided to retain the headquarters staff. Late in the afternoon, after preparing a final address to the army, Hooker rode away. When Meade saw his son, he said, "Well, George I am in command of the Army of the Potomac."[36]

In the appointment order, Halleck stated, "Considering the circumstances, no one ever received a more important command; and I cannot doubt that you will fully justify the confidence which the Government has reposed in you." He assured Meade that he "will not be hampered by any instructions from these headquarters." The president had granted Meade authority over "all forces within the sphere of your operations," including militia troops in Pennsylvania and the Harper's Ferry garrison.

As for the current operations, Halleck wrote: "Your army is free to act as you may deem proper under the circumstances as they arise. You will, however, keep in view the important fact that the Army of the Potomac is the covering army of Washington as well as the army of operation against the invading forces of the rebels. You will, therefore, maneuver and fight in such a manner as to cover the capital and also Baltimore, as far as circumstances will admit. Should General Lee move upon either of these places, it is expected that you will either anticipate him or arrive with him so as to give battle."[37]

It was the paramount burden that all of Meade's predecessors had borne—the security of Washington must not be compromised, while seeking a battle with the Confederates. But none of them had confronted such a looming, if not immediate, crisis. Brigadier General Alpheus Williams, writing on June 29, conveyed what was at stake for Meade and the army: "we run a fearful risk, because upon this small army everything depends. If we are badly defeated the Capital is gone and all our principal cities and our national honor."[38]

From Hooker and Butterfield, Meade learned that recent reports placed most, if not all, of Lee's army in Pennsylvania. It appeared that the Rebels were advancing east toward Harrisburg and York. Based on this information, Meade wired Halleck that he would advance toward the Susquehanna River on a broad front that would cover both Washington and Baltimore. "My endeavor will be in my movements," he explained the next day, "to hold my force well together, with the hope of falling upon some portion of Lee's army in detail." In brief, Meade would keep his infantry corps in close support of each other, and send the cavalry ahead in search of the enemy. He issued orders for the march to begin on June 29.[39]

Before the army headed north from Frederick, the Cavalry Corps underwent organizational and command changes. With his assignment to command, Meade was granted the authority to promote and to remove "any officer." At the request of Alfred Pleasonton, Meade recommended the promotion of captains Elon Farnsworth, Wesley Merritt, and George A. Custer to brigadier generals. Meade's request surely must have surprised Halleck and Secretary of War Stanton. Farnsworth and Merritt had led regiments in the fighting at Brandy Station, but most of Custer's career had been as a staff officer. Pleasonton explained that he wanted subordinates whom he could trust. The War Department approved the promotions, and in time, Merritt and Custer had the opportunity to validate Pleasonton's judgment.[40]

In the reorganization, Pleasonton took Major General Julius Stahel's division, which had been assigned to the army from the defenses of Washington, and designated it as the Third Cavalry Division. Brigadier General Judson Kilpatrick replaced Stahel, who was transferred to another department. Farnsworth received command of one of the brigades, and Custer, whose adopted home was Michigan, was given four regiments from that state. The Reserve Brigade, with its fine record, became Merritt's.[41]

The final command change occurred in the Fifth Corps, where its senior officer, Major General George Sykes, succeeded Meade. Sykes had led the corps's division of Regulars. Duty and discipline guided this small, thin man as a soldier. Years in the old army had seemed to layer him with a hardened crust. A staff officer said of him that he had "a general air of one who is weary, and a little ill natured." Unlike other West Pointers and career soldiers, he retained contempt for the fighting qualities of volunteers. But Sykes was thorough and reliable.[42]

The search for Lee's army, then, began on the morning of June 29. Meade had planned to enter Pennsylvania with his advance units in a day's march, but it was an exhausted beast that started forth. Hundreds of stragglers stayed in Frederick, draining liquor shops and roaming the streets. On the roads, the columns plodded through rain. Many men had worn out their shoes and were barefoot. Maryland residents stood by the roadside, welcoming the long ranks of passing soldiers. One veteran wrote, "There is some fun in Soldiering in a country like this whare the citizens are about half humane."[43]

Tuesday, June 30, brought the advance elements of the army into Pennsylvania. By day's end, the First and Twelfth corps had crossed into the Keystone State, with the Second, Third, Fifth, and Eleventh corps just south of the Mason-Dixon line. Only the Sixth Corps lay to the rear at Manchester, Maryland, covering the army's right flank with David Gregg's cavalry division. To the front of the infantry, two of John Buford's brigades occupied Gettysburg, and Kilpatrick's troopers encamped at Hanover, where earlier they had been engaged in a spirited clash with Jeb Stuart's Rebel horsemen. During the day, Meade moved army headquarters to Taneytown, Maryland. There was a feeling of anxiety among Meade and staff members.[44]

Throughout June 30, reports indicated a Confederate concentration at Chambersburg, Gettysburg, or farther east. Gettysburg appeared to be the likely site, but Meade could not be certain. In response, he ordered Reynolds, with the First and Eleventh corps, to Gettysburg. If assailed by the enemy, Reynolds should retire to a defensive position, which had been laid out by army engineers, the so-called Pipe Creek Line in Maryland. Other corps commanders were assigned their places along the line. Meade put these instructions into a circular that was prepared overnight. Meade described it as a "contingent plan" that would be implemented if circumstances arose to make it "a necessity for falling back." Reynolds, however, evidently never received a copy of the circular. His orders did not preclude him from engaging the Rebels.[45]

For the officers and men in the ranks, this Tuesday passed with varied experiences. For some, it was restful, even leisurely; for others, it was physically demanding. Members of the Fifth Corps marched, and at day's end, one of them wrote, "Our brave boys are so wasted and worn . . . emaciated forms." The troops who entered Pennsylvania received a welcome warmer than in Maryland. Civilians in "holiday attire" waved flags, sang patriotic songs, and distributed food and water. A Wisconsin soldier remarked, "It seems almost like going home to go into some of these farmhouses." A New Yorker told his wife in a letter on this day, "If I ever felt I wanted to fight the enemy it was here where those ladies were calling us to drive the Rebels back into Virginia where they belonged." Wherever the units were located, the men mustered in for two months' pay.[46]

For weeks, they had believed, based on their experience, that somewhere up ahead, at the end of a road, they would meet their old nemeses again. In their thinking, it had to come. "But the Army of the Potomac was no band of school girls," wrote Lieutenant Frank Haskell of them at this time. "They were not the men likely to be crushed or utterly discouraged by any mere circumstances in which they might find themselves placed." They had known defeat and victory, had withstood "the hardest toils of the campaign, under unwelcome leadership, at all times, and under all circumstances, they were a reliable army still. The Army of the Potomac would do as it was told, always."[47]

At Gettysburg, meanwhile, John Buford had strung out his pickets to cover the roads into town. It was alleged later that when Buford met with his senior officers to discuss the prospects for July 1, brigade commander Colonel Thomas Devin assured him that his men could hold against the Rebels for twenty-four hours. "No, you won't," Buford shot back. "They will attack you in the morning and they will come booming—skirmishers three deep. You will have to fight like the devil to hold your own until supports arrive. The enemy must know the importance of this position and will strain every nerve to secure it, and if we are able to hold it, we will do well."[48]

ABOUT TEN O'CLOCK on the night of June 28—George Meade had been in command of the Union army less than a day—a "dirt-stained, travel-worn, and very much broken down" spy named Henry Harrison reached Chambersburg, Pennsylvania. An actor by trade, Harrison had been employed by Longstreet to secure information on the Federals. The news Harrison brought surprised Longstreet. The Yankees, said the spy, had crossed the Potomac into Maryland and were on the march toward Pennsylvania. Longstreet sent Harrison and a staff member to Robert E. Lee, who questioned the information until the aide vouchsafed for Longstreet's confidence in the spy.[49]

Harrison's report presented Lee with the first reliable intelligence on the whereabouts of the Army of the Potomac in days. In one of the campaign's unending controversies, Lee had granted Jeb Stuart permission to "pass around" the Union army. Lee expected his cavalry commander to advance on the Confederates' right flank, gather supplies and information, and contact Richard Ewell's corps in Pennsylvania. But the orders were vague and discretionary. When Stuart encountered a lengthy delay at the outset, his best course would have been to turn back and follow a route away from the Federals. Instead, he continued on, and for Lee's purposes, disappeared from the campaign for a week. At the least, Stuart committed a critical error in judgment.[50]

Based on Harrison's report, Lee ordered a concentration of his scattered units east of South Mountain at either Cashtown or Gettysburg. Toward these towns, then, the Southerners marched on June 29 and 30. By nightfall of the second day, two of Ewell's divisions bivouacked north and northeast of Gettysburg, while two of Hill's divisions encamped at Cashtown, eight miles west of the crossroads village. West of the mountain lay the army's other five divisions. If there were to be an engagement on the next day, seven of Lee's nine infantry divisions would have to use Chambersburg Pike, an almost certain prescription for delays.[51]

During June 30, Brigadier General J. Johnston Pettigrew's brigade of North Carolinians marched to Gettysburg's outskirts. When John Buford's Union horsemen appeared from the south, Pettigrew returned to near Cashtown. That evening he reported what he had seen to his division commander, Major General Henry Heth, and A. P. Hill. Pettigrew believed that the enemy cavalry belonged to the Army of the Potomac. Hill and Heth disagreed. "If there is no objection," interjected Heth, "I will take my division to-morrow and go to Gettysburg." "None in the world," replied Hill. The Third Corps commander then notified Lee that he was moving east the next morning to "discover what was in my front."[52]

Chapter 13

"An Army of Lions"

I T WAS GEOGRAPHY THAT CURSED Gettysburg. The town of about 2,400 inhabitants sat in the bottom of a shallow basin, framed by long, flat ridges and rounded hills. Fields of lush crops and pastures, edged by fences, colored the landscape. Ten roads radiated from Gettysburg like spokes of a wagon wheel. It was the roads that brought the armies and the contours of the ground that made it such a fine place for killing.[1]

The signs had been there for days, like billowing dark clouds from a summer storm on the horizon. When the fury blew in, it came from the west. About 7:30 A.M. on July 1, Union cavalry pickets posted along Chambersburg Pike three miles from town opened fire on the van of Henry Heth's Confederate infantry column. John Buford planned on "entertaining" the enemy until Union infantry reached the field. Armed with breechloading carbines and backed by a horse artillery battery, the Federals slowed Heth's men, forcing them to deploy skirmishers and unlimber cannon.[2]

Manning McPherson's Ridge, Buford's horse soldiers had to buy time, and time they bought. A combination of their gritty resistance and Heth's tentative leadership stalled the Confederate advance for two hours. Finally, about 9:30, Heth brought two brigades into line on each side of the pike and sent them forward from Herr Ridge, three-fourths of a mile west of the Federals' line. The breechloaders flashed with increasing rapidity.[3]

At this time or minutes before, John Reynolds rode up on a black horse. Where Reynolds found Buford remains a subject of historical debate. The cavalry commander described the tactical situation, remarking, "the devil's to pay." Reynolds decided to make a battle of it there on McPherson's Ridge. On his ride to Gettysburg, he had noticed the good defensive ground south of town. If the Union infantry could hang on west of Gettysburg until the rest of the army came up, that good ground would belong to them. He sent two aides to hurry forward the Eleventh and Third corps, and a third one to notify George Meade of the developing engagement. Reynolds had made a fateful decision, the finest in this noble soldier's career.[4]

Telling Buford to hold on until the infantry arrived, Reynolds rode away to speed up the march of the First Corps. He met Brigadier General James Wadsworth's leading division south of town on Emmitsburg Road. Wadsworth was a wealthy New Yorker who had interrupted his service in the war to run for and to lose his state's governorship the preceding fall. What the gray-haired general lacked in experience and skill, he compensated with a fighting spirit. Reynolds pointed Wadsworth's two brigades across the fields toward McPherson's Ridge. They moved at the double-quick. "I never saw the men more willing to fight than they were at Gettysburg," recalled a corps member.[5]

Wadsworth's troops neared McPherson's Ridge as time ran out for Buford's men. Heth's Rebels—"damned skunks of Hell," a Yankee called them—were ascending the slope. Brigadier General Lysander Cutler's five regiments led Wadsworth's command. Three of the units headed across the pike, while two turned west, replacing the cavalrymen on the ridge. Behind them, angling across the fields toward Herbst Woods, came the black-hatted Iron Brigade.[6]

Reynolds met the 2nd Wisconsin of the Iron Brigade on the eastern crest of McPherson's Ridge. Forty paces away, "howling like demons," Tennesseans and Alabamians leveled their rifles. Reynolds shouted to the Wisconsin veterans, "Forward men, forward, for God's sake, and drive those fellows out of the woods." The Southerners triggered a volley, and then a second one. Reynolds reeled in his saddle and tumbled to the ground. Aides rushed to him and discovered a bullet had hit him in the back of the head. John Reynolds was dead. They picked up the body of "The Old Man," as his staff members called him, and carried it into town.[7]

The volley had staggered the men of the 2nd Wisconsin, but they charged. On their left, fellow Westerners in three regiments entered the fight. Musketry exploded in the woods. "We discovered," professed an Alabamian, "that we had tackled a hard proposition." These Northerners were, arguably, the finest combat troops in the army, and they splintered the enemy ranks, driving the Confederates down the slope and across Willoughby Run at the base of the ridge. They seized two hundred prisoners, including Brigadier General James J. Archer, the first officer of that rank to be captured since Lee had assumed command of the army.[8]

North of Chambersburg Pike, meanwhile, Cutler's three regiments had suffered heavy losses and were forced to retreat against Brigadier General Joseph Davis's Confederate brigade. Swinging south, Davis's troops advanced to an unfinished railroad cut. Within minutes, the 6th Wisconsin of the Iron Brigade and the 95th New York and 14th Brooklyn of Cutler's charged the Rebels. At the edge of the cut, the opponents engaged in a hand-to-hand, frenzied melee. The Federals prevailed, trapping dozens of Confederates in the deepest section of the cut. The rest of Davis's men fled west to Herr Ridge. Wadsworth's infantrymen had secured McPherson's Ridge for the present as a lull in the combat ensued.[9]

Punctuated by occasional artillery exchanges, the interlude extended into mid-afternoon. During these hours, the gathering of warriors continued. The First Corps divisions of brigadiers Thomas A. Rowley and John C. Robinson arrived first. Acting corps commander Major General Abner Doubleday had come on the field only minutes before Reynolds's death. He had not spoken to Reynolds before the general was slain, but Doubleday believed that McPherson's Ridge must be held. To abandon it, he wrote later, "might have inflicted lasting disgrace upon the corps." A native New Yorker and academy graduate, Doubleday was an outspoken abolitionist, which endeared him to few of the army's socially conservative generals.[10]

Doubleday considered Herbst Woods the key to holding McPherson's Ridge and kept the Iron Brigade in the five-acre stand of trees, despite protests from its commander, Brigadier General Solomon Meredith. Doubleday placed Rowley's two brigades on McPherson's Ridge, one on each flank of Meredith's regiments. He then divided Robinson's two brigades, sending one north across Chambersburg Pike to Oak Ridge with Cutler's units, and keeping the other one south of the roadbed on Seminary Ridge. It would have been more prudent for Doubleday to place the entire corps on the wooded Oak Ridge–Seminary Ridge line. But Reynolds had lost his life in trying to secure McPherson's Ridge, and his successor meant to defend it.[11]

Before long, the Eleventh Corps reached Gettysburg. Corps commander Oliver Howard had preceded his troops and was in town when informed of Reynolds's death. As senior officer on the field, Howard assumed overall command. Unlike during his dismal performance at Chancellorsville on May 2, Howard acted decisively. When his corps arrived after noon, he ordered two divisions north of the town to cover Doubleday's right flank. He held the third division in reserve on Cemetery Hill, which dominated the surrounding terrain south of town. Like Reynolds, Howard recognized the ground's natural strength as a defensive position.[12]

Acting corps commander Carl Schurz deployed the two divisions about a mile north of Gettysburg's town square. Fortune had rarely favored these Federals—the "damned Dutch"—and it would not again on this day. Numbering barely 6,500 effectives, there were too few of them to cover the open, undulating ground. Brigadier General Francis Barlow stretched the ranks farther when, on his own, advanced his division to occupy Blocher's Knoll (today, Barlow's Knoll) on the right front. The men were, said an officer, "very tired." Morale had remained low since Chancellorsville, with few men willing to wear their corps badges that identified them as members.[13]

By now, Lee had ridden on to the battlefield. He had issued orders against bringing on a general engagement on this day, but subordinates had entangled him and part of the army in a billowing action. Even as Lee joined Hill and Heth along Chambersburg Pike, Robert Rodes's division of Ewell's corps was advancing against the enemy on Oak

Ridge. A staff officer had notified him that Jubal Early's division was approaching the field, coming in from the north toward the Eleventh Corps line. With William D. Pender's command of Hill's corps behind Heth's, the Confederates possessed a numerical superiority and a favorable tactical situation. Unable to reverse a powerful current, Lee reluctantly committed Heth's and Pender's troops to the offensive, which Rodes had begun.[14]

Rodes's assault against the north end of Oak Ridge signaled an end to the midday lull and a renewal of the bloodletting. Rodes went in initially with two brigades, one and then the other, piecemeal, and the blue-coated defenders wrecked the first one and repulsed the second. A third and fourth brigade—North Carolinians, all—came on against the Yankees of the First Corps. What they had secured in the morning, these Federals were not going to relinquish easily. "I remember, the still trees in the heat," wrote the 16th Maine's adjutant of the defense of Oak Ridge, "and the bullets whistling over us, and the stone wall bristling with muskets, and the line of our men, sweating and grimy, firing and loading and firing again, and here a man suddenly lying still, and there another rising all bloody and cursing and starting for the surgeon."[15]

Across the fields to the south, Heth's final two brigades stepped forth toward McPherson's Ridge and Herbst Woods, held by Colonel Roy Stone's three Pennsylvania regiments and the Iron Brigade. Doubleday had ordered these Federals to hold the position "at all hazards." Coming on were 2,500 Virginians and North Carolinians, ranks dressed "in perfect alignment." When the Rebels neared Willoughby Run, the Union ranks exploded in a gale of musketry. At the apex of the curved line of the Iron Brigade in the woods stood the 24th Michigan. Straight ahead, ascending the slope was the 26th North Carolina, a huge regiment of 850 officers and men. For the next twenty minutes, hell enveloped both regiments.[16]

For Michigander and North Carolinian alike, nothing in their experience compared to this head-to-head encounter. Volleys from both lines ravaged the other, fired from distances of forty yards or less. In each regiment the ranks almost seemed to disappear in a wholesale decimation as seven out of every ten men on each side fell killed or wounded. Any man who dared to hold the regimental colors was almost

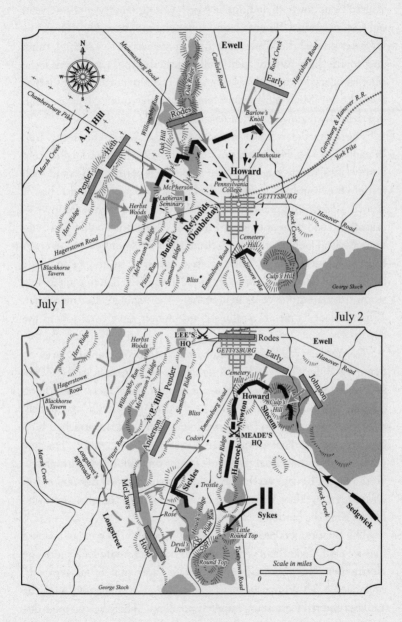

July 1

July 2

assuredly cut down, including the North Carolinians' twenty-one-year-old Colonel Henry Burgwyn, who suffered a mortal wound. The Confederates pressed the Westerners through the woods to a second, third, and fourth line. When additional Southern troops overlapped the Michiganders' left flank, they retreated to Seminary Ridge. At Gettysburg, the 24th Michigan and 26th North Carolina sustained more casualties than any regiment in their respective armies.[17]

The Confederates had wrenched Herbst Woods from the Iron Brigade. On the 24th Michigan's left, the 19th Indiana fought stubbornly until nearly engulfed. "No soldiers on earth could stand such terrible fire from both front and flank," declared a lieutenant. The 2nd and 7th Wisconsin joined in the withdrawal, as did Stone's Pennsylvanians, who had been also assailed in front and on the flank. From Seminary Ridge, Doubleday rushed forward the 151st Pennsylvania to cover their comrades' retreat. Caught in a crossfire in the open swale between the ridges—"Our poor boys fell around me like ripe apples in a storm," declared one of its lieutenants—the regiment lost more than 70 percent of its members, the second highest regimental loss in the battle.[18]

The Yankees rallied behind stone walls, fieldworks, and batteries on Seminary Ridge. They had not long to wait until three brigades of Pender's division crossed McPherson's Ridge on the attack. The Union gunners and infantrymen unleashed a withering fire. On the Rebels' right, Buford's horsemen lashed the enemy flank, but the attackers hit a gap between the First Corps defenders and the cavalrymen. The line unraveled, but individual regiments fought on until nearly surrounded. To the north, Rodes's veterans had finally overwhelmed the Yankees on Oak Ridge. A New Yorker described the fighting there as "an awful bloody time the hardest I ever saw."[19]

The Southerners pressed the fleeing Federals. They "were so close that we could hear them yelling at us to halt and surrender," wrote one Northerner. "It seems almost a miracle how any of us escaped," exclaimed a 7th Wisconsin man. Organization disintegrated once the Yankees entered Gettysburg's streets and alleys. "There was no more discipline or semblance of ranks," insisted a sergeant, "than would be found in a herd of cattle." The gray-coated pursuers shouted, "Halt, you

Yankee sons of bitches." The broken remnants of Eleventh Corps units added to the confusion and clogged streets.[20]

The hard-luck members of the Eleventh Corps had fought tenaciously and bravely until Jubal Early's Rebels overlapped their right flank and unhinged their entire line. Barlow's forward movement to Blocher's Knoll had left the Union ranks too thin and vulnerable. Hit on the front and flank, his division's line collapsed, and Barlow fell seriously wounded and was taken prisoner. Like First Corps troops, islands of these Federals resisted until nearly surrounded. A soldier in the 153rd Pennsylvania stated: "it seemed to me the rebels were bound to get to town. They shot a hole through the lines where we were."[21]

Earlier, Schurz had ordered forward Colonel Charles R. Coster's brigade of New Yorkers and Pennsylvanians from Cemetery Hill. Now, with the corps's ranks streaming toward town, Schurz placed the 1,150 Federals in a brickyard owned by a family named Kuhn to buy time for their comrades to escape. Assaulted by two enemy brigades, they never had a chance. "It seemed as though they had a battle flag every few rods," declared a New Yorker of the Rebels. The Confederate musketry decimated Coster's ranks, and the Southerners swarmed around both flanks, capturing hundreds of the Yankees. Those who escaped joined in the flight through the town.[22]

The Federal retreat ended on Cemetery Hill, where an Eleventh Corps brigade and artillery batteries were posted. As the officers and men arrived on the eminence, they encountered Winfield Scott Hancock and Oliver Howard. When Meade had been informed of Reynolds's fall—it was initially reported as a wound—he sent Hancock to assume command of the troops on the field. Hancock told Meade that Howard outranked him by the date of their commissions. Meade replied that he knew him better than Howard and trusted Hancock. In the written order assigning Hancock to command, Meade directed, "If you think the ground and position there a better one to fight a battle under existing circumstances, you will so advise the general, and he will order all the troops up."[23]

Although Howard would argue in the postwar years that he retained command, the evidence indicates that Howard acceded to Meade's order. The two generals divided responsibility, with Hancock deploying units on the west side of Baltimore Pike and Howard on the east. When they had restored order and positioned the commands, there were 43 cannon and perhaps 7,000 infantrymen on the hill. A 55th Ohio private, whose regiment lay in or near Evergreen Cemetery, thought it to be "one of the pleasantest burial places I ever saw." The Federals waited for an enemy assault that never came.[24]

Lee followed his victorious troops, halting on Seminary Ridge minutes after four o'clock to examine the Union position south of town. Shortly afterward, he sent an oral message by a staff officer to Ewell, instructing him "that it was only necessary to press 'those people' in order to secure possession of the heights, and that, if possible, he wished him to do this." Ewell studied the enemy lines on Cemetery Hill, received an erroneous report of an enemy force on his left flank, was told he would not get support from Hill's troops in an assault, and decided it was not possible, sparking one of the most strident Gettysburg controversies. Uncertain as to the size of the Federal force, Lee hesitated to issue a direct order for an assault. Unknown to Lee, the van of the Union Twelfth Corps approached the battlefield about five o'clock.[25]

In truth, the Twelfth Corps should have been at Gettysburg hours earlier. That it was not was directly attributable to its commander, Henry Slocum. Meade's Pipe Creek circular directed the corps to march to Two Taverns, five miles from Gettysburg on Baltimore Pike. Slocum had them there by noon and halted. Soldiers said later that they heard the sounds of the fighting at Gettysburg. At 1:30 P.M., a courier arrived from Howard, informing him that the left wing of the army was engaged with Hill's Confederate corps. But Slocum hesitated to act. Before long, a civilian arrived from Gettysburg and said, "a great battle [was] being fought" there. Slocum sent an aide up the pike to confirm the civilian's report. When he returned and said it was true, Slocum started the corps. It was after three o'clock.[26]

At the least, upon receipt of Howard's dispatch, Slocum or aides should have ridden to Gettysburg to ascertain the facts while the corps prepared to march. Had Slocum acted with dispatch, his men might have been on the field in time to support either the First or Eleventh corps or both of them. Finally, when Slocum reached the field, he refused twice to come to Cemetery Hill and assume command as the senior officer. He did so at last between six and seven o'clock. Less than a week after the battle, Charles Howard, a staff officer and brother of the general, derisively called him, "*Slow Come,*" adding, "*he would not assume the responsibility of that day's fighting* & of the two corps."[27]

Slocum's conduct contrasted with that of the generals on the battlefield. On this day, the rank and file received leadership worthy of their valor and sacrifice. There had not been a day like this in the army's past, when its senior officers acted decisively and aggressively. Buford and Reynolds had committed the army to a stand west of town, and Howard, Doubleday, Schurz, Wadsworth, Robinson, and numerous brigade and regimental commanders rendered capable, if not outstanding, service. Acting division commander Thomas Rowley, however, would be court-martialed for drunkenness. In the end, the Federals held an untenable position against a numerically superior foe. But as night fell, they had fallen back to the good ground that Reynolds had wanted.[28]

The price had been steep. A division commander, Francis Barlow, and brigade commanders Gabriel Paul, Solomon Meredith, and Roy Stone had been wounded. Paul, whom the men called "Apostle Paul," would be blinded for life when a bullet struck his right temple and exited through his left eye socket. Among the rank and file, casualties in the First and Eleventh corps amounted to nearly 9,000 killed, wounded, and captured, out of slightly more than 14,000 engaged. Between four and five thousand were prisoners. Lieutenant Colonel Rufus Dawes called it a "horrid butchery."[29]

GEORGE MEADE SPENT JULY 1 at army headquarters at Taneytown, Maryland. He had probably not slept nor changed clothes since he took command on June 28. His son, George, thought his father was "a little graver than he was in the Corps" but "seems to have confidence." He expected to have his Pipe Creek plan implemented on this day, but as happened to Lee, events shattered the plans. He learned of the engagement at Gettysburg at 1:00 P.M., when a courier arrived from the battlefield and reported John Reynolds's fall and the action. With five of his infantry corps spread across the region, Meade decided to direct their movements from a central location and await developments before committing them to Gettysburg. This was when he sent Winfield Scott Hancock to act in his stead.[30]

The afternoon hours must have seemed interminably long to Meade. He ordered Daniel Sickles to march one Third Corps division from Emmitsburg, Maryland, to Gettysburg, and alerted Sixth Corps commander John Sedgwick. A message from Hancock finally reached Taneytown before six o'clock. Minutes later, Meade wired General-in-Chief Halleck of the engagement and added: "At any rate, I see no other course than to hazard a general battle. Circumstances during the night may alter this decision, of which I will try to advise you." An hour later, a flurry of orders went out to corps commanders to move to Gettysburg.[31]

Before ten o'clock, Hancock rode up at army headquarters. With Henry Slocum in command at Gettysburg, Hancock returned to his Second Corps at Taneytown and personally described the situation to Meade. Before long, Meade and his staff headed for Gettysburg. Lieutenant William Paine guided the procession, riding "at a faster gait than I have ever gone since I have been in the army." The mood of the group might have been expressed by a staff member in a letter on this day: "I do hope this time the Army of the Potomac may meet with success. We cannot always be so unfortunate as we have been thus far."[32]

Meade's party rode on to Cemetery Hill before midnight. A coterie of generals met Meade, who inquired about the terrain. When told it was good ground, he replied that he was pleased to hear it, because "it was too late to leave it." About 2:00 A.M., Meade, Oliver Howard, and Henry Hunt examined the position, with an aide sketching a map for posting the corps as they arrived.[33]

The Army of the Potomac never had defended better ground. The terrain possessed natural strength and a convex character, which would expedite the movement of units from one section of the line to another. In time, it would be described as a fishhook. Rising sixty to eighty feet above its base, Cemetery Hill formed the hinge of the line. To the east, Culp's Hill, 140 feet high, anchored the Union right flank, the barb of the fishhook. Cemetery Ridge extended south from Cemetery Hill for nearly a mile and a half, its elevation diminishing into a bottomland at the base of Little Round Top. Although wooded Big Round Top towered more than a hundred feet above the lower hill, the western face of Little Round Top had been cleared of timber and dominated the ground on the left flank.[34]

By mid-morning of July 2, all the infantry corps except the Sixth had arrived on the battlefield. Meade assigned the units to their positions and conferred frequently with his senior generals. For a time, Meade considered undertaking an offensive from Culp's Hill but was dissuaded from it because of the difficult terrain on that part of the field. In the afternoon, Meade telegraphed Halleck, "I feel fully the responsibility resting upon me, but will endeavor to act with caution."[35]

Meade's decision "to act with caution" or to maintain a defensive position was prudent. July 2 marked his fifth day in command of the army. So far, he had fulfilled his orders to protect Washington and Baltimore and to locate the Confederate army. He had wisely delegated authority to officers he trusted, such as Reynolds and Hancock. It had not been his intention, nor Lee's, to become entangled in a general engagement on July 1. Although two of his corps had been defeated, their valiant stand had given Meade and the army a splendid position. For once events conspired to favor the Federals. In turn, the Southern victory on the previous day had given the tactical initiative at Gettysburg not to Meade, but to his opponent.

Lee had determined by the evening of July 1 to renew the offensive the next day. "A battle thus became, in a measure, unavoidable," he explained in his report. "Encouraged by the successful issue of the engagement of the first day, and in view of the valuable results that would ensue from the defeat of the army of General Meade, it was thought advisable to renew the attack" on July 2. The battle had been joined, and Lee wanted to settle it here. That singular fact shaped the final two days of fighting at Gettysburg.[36]

It took Lee most of the morning of July 2 to settle upon a strike against the Union left flank. His senior subordinate, James Longstreet, opposed a renewal of assaults, arguing for a broad turning movement around the Federals' flank, similar to Stonewall Jackson's march in the Second Bull Run Campaign. Longstreet voiced his objection twice, and twice Lee rejected it. Lee assigned the assault to Longstreet. The march of John Hood's and Lafayette McLaws's divisions of 14,000 troops into position consumed most of the afternoon. By four o'clock they had filed into line on Warfield Ridge and the southern end of Seminary Ridge.[37]

A belief in themselves as an army permeated the Confederate ranks. An artillery officer described it as "an overweening confidence." A staff officer argued that the Rebels "never seemed to me as invincible as on the 1st July 1863." A British observer with the army concluded that they possessed "a profound contempt for an enemy whom they have beaten so constantly, and under so many disadvantages." After talking with his captors, Union general Francis Barlow wrote of the Southerners, "They despised our army and meant to fight to the last."[38]

Across the fields, however, a resoluteness steeled the Rebels' foe. The Yankees understood the implications of a defeat on Northern soil. A sergeant in the 1st Minnesota recorded in his diary on the morning of July 2, "This AM say this is to be the Battle of the war and every man must stand." Another sergeant jotted in his diary, "Our troops were determined not be drove." "We are well prepared to meet the rascals," a Vermont soldier asserted in a letter on this day, "and I hope that none of them will escape." A captain, writing after noon, declared that the Confederates "are arrogant and think they can easily conquer us with anything like equal numbers. We hope that in this faith he will remain, and give us final and decisive battle here."[39]

John Gibbon issued an order to the troops in his Second Corps division, telling them as a man recorded it in his diary, "this is to be the great battle of the war & that any soldier leaving the ranks without leave will be instantly put to death." One of his brigade commanders, William Harrow, translated Gibbon's order into his own words. Drawing his pistol from its holster, Harrow said: "the first God damned man I see running or sneaking, I blow him to Hell in an instant. This God Damned running is played out, just stand to it and give them Hell." When the fighting began, Colonel Richard P. Roberts told the members of the 140th Pennsylvania: "Men of Pennsylvania, we are about to meet the enemy on our own soil. You are now to fight for your own homes and firesides, and if you ever did your duty I want you to do it now."[40]

Roberts spoke to his fellow Pennsylvanians as the sounds of combat rolled over Cemetery Ridge from the southwest. In a move that jeopardized Meade's entire line, Daniel Sickles had advanced his two Third

Corps divisions from the low ground at the southern end of Cemetery Ridge to higher ground along Emmitsburg Road, forming a salient with its apex at a peach orchard. The colorful general, whom his troops adored and whom Meade could barely abide, had done it of his own volition without informing army headquarters. When Meade confronted Sickles, the latter offered to withdraw. Confederate cannon then opened fire, and Meade allegedly said to him, "I only wish you could sir, but you see those people don't intend to let you."[41]

Sickles would spend the next five decades of his long life defending his decision. In his mind he had compelling reasons for securing the ground in his front—his skirmishers had clashed with enemy troops about noon; Alfred Pleasonton had allowed John Buford's cavalry division to withdraw from Sickles's left flank without replacing it; and perhaps he thought that if enemy batteries rolled onto the position they could blast his lines as they had done when his corps was ordered to abandon Hazel Grove at Chancellorsville two months previous. His 10,700 officers and men were, however, too few to man the line he chose, and "a salient angle" was vulnerable to assaults on front or flank. Time, then, ran out for the Third Corps.[42]

Hood's and McLaws's veterans moved to the attack about four o'clock. There were no finer soldiers in Lee's army than these Texans, Arkansans, Mississippians, Alabamians, Georgians, and South Carolinians. "Then was fairly commenced," Longstreet declared afterward, "what I do not hesitate to pronounce the best three hours' fighting ever done by any troops on any battle-field." Within minutes, new places entered American history—the Peach Orchard, the Wheatfield, Devil's Den, and Little Round Top—burned into the country's memory by the slaughter of good men by other good men.[43]

A Texan likened the combat to "a devil's carnival." Artillery shells and canister ripped into opposing lines; musketry flashed in fearful walls of flame. Watching from Cemetery Ridge, one of Gibbon's aides exclaimed, "What a hell is there down that valley!" A Confederate stated that when Union cannon opened on their ranks, "I could hear bones crash like glass in a hail storm." Another Southerner insisted, "It seemed to me that my life was not worth a straw." A Federal described death as "going to their long home," and many men made the journey on this day.[44]

The assault crushed Sickles's salient at the Peach Orchard, spreading across the ground into the Wheatfield, on to and over Houck's Ridge and Devil's Den and up the slopes of Little Round Top. "The Confederates," argued Colonel Regis de Trobriand, "appeared to have the devil in them." The Third Corps divisions of David Birney and Andrew Humphreys stood valiantly before the whirlwind until overwhelmed. A cannonball shattered the right leg of Sickles as he observed the fighting near the Abraham Trostle barn and farmhouse. He was carried to the rear.[45]

Amid the slaughter individual units displayed remarkable valor, exemplifying the spirit that belonged to the Army of the Potomac on this day—the 17th Maine, holding a stone wall along the southern edge of the Wheatfield, refusing to leave it despite three orders to withdraw because "the Rebel's were straining every nerve to get possession of it," and only retiring after all their ammunition had been expended; the 124th New York or "Orange Blossoms," supporting a battery above Devil's Den with barely two hundred men in the ranks against fierce attacks from Texans and Georgians; the Zouaves of the 114th Pennsylvania, defending John Sherfy's Peach Orchard and being savaged by Mississippians; the 9th Massachusetts Battery, in its first battle, pouring canister into the Southerners as they swarmed across the Trostle farm fields, losing dozens of horses and four guns by breasting the storm; and the 105th Pennsylvania, fighting, retiring, and re-forming ranks eight or ten times as they shouted, "Pennsylvania."[46]

This fighting spirit was a common commodity and desperately needed. It would have been difficult to find better shock troops than Hood's and McLaws's Southerners. The rugged terrain, Hood's wounding early in the battle, and disorganization inherent in an attack slowed their drive. But on this afternoon, the Army of the Potomac was as good as its opponents. Blue-uniformed officers reacted aggressively to the enemy assault, benefited from the favorable ground and their compact position, and exercised command and control over units. From Little Round Top through the Wheatfield to Cemetery Ridge, the Yankees began to exorcise ghosts.

Colonel Strong Vincent, acting with initiative and assuming responsibility, reacted to a request from chief engineer Gouverneur Warren by leading his Fifth Corps brigade onto unprotected Little Round Top. Vincent's troops arrived with only a few minutes to spare before the Alabamians and Texans ascended the hillside. At the far end of Vincent's line, Lieutenant Colonel Joshua Lawrence Chamberlain and the 20th Maine repulsed repeated charges, and then, out of ammunition, counterattacked with fixed bayonets. On their right, the 83rd Pennsylvania, 44th New York, and 16th Michigan clung to the hill. While he directed his command, Vincent fell with a mortal wound.[47]

The Confederates pressed their attack again up the southwestern face of the hill. The 16th Michigan's line began to waver when over the crest came the 140th New York. Warren had sent the regiment, assuming responsibility for detaching it without permission from its brigade. Leading the New Yorkers was Colonel Patrick O'Rorke, two years out of West Point, where he had ranked first in his class. As the Yankees topped the crest, the Rebels fired a volley. A bullet sliced through "Paddy" O'Rorke's neck, and he was gone.[48]

The New Yorkers' arrival and counterattack secured Little Round Top. Behind them, their comrades in Brigadier General Stephen Weed's brigade filed onto the hill, with a second battery joining the one already in place. Confederates from Devil's Den and Houck's Ridge still lashed the crest with rifle fire. One Southerner mortally wounded Weed, the second brigade commander to give his life in the defense of Little Round Top.[49]

To the west, beyond Houck's Ridge, the Wheatfield had become a seething cauldron. Two brigades of Brigadier General James Barnes's Fifth Corps division—Vincent's brigade belonged to it—were first to advance to the aid of the hard-pressed Third Corps ranks. These Northerners swept into the Wheatfield, added their blood to the ground, and were forced back into Trostle's Woods. As they retreated, Brigadier General John Caldwell's Second Corps division entered the fighting. This command had belonged to Hancock, and before him to Israel Richardson. Perhaps no division in the army matched these four brigades as a combat unit.[50]

Caldwell's brigades charged in succession and engaged George T. Anderson's Georgians and Joseph Kershaw's South Carolinians. The opposing lines ravaged each other. "How dark it was, so thick with battle-smoke," recalled a 140th Pennsylvania sergeant. "We would see the flash of every gun fired as if it were night." The struggle centered on the stone wall held earlier by the 17th Maine—possession of it changed six times altogether—and the so-called Stony Hill at the western edge of the Wheatfield. Brigade commander Samuel Zook was struck in the chest with a bullet as his men fought before Stony Hill. He reeled in the saddle and looked as "pale as death." Carried to a farmhouse, Zook died the next day.[51]

At the other end of the Wheatfield, Colonel Edward Cross, directing his brigade on foot, suffered a mortal wound. The former commander of the 5th New Hampshire, Cross had painted his face with gunpowder at Antietam and preferred to tie a black silk handkerchief around his head when in a battle. As his brigade prepared to march on this afternoon, Hancock rode up to him and said, "Colonel Cross, this day will bring you a star." Deserving of a brigadiership, Cross had had a premonition of his death and had spoken of it a number of times during the past week.

He replied, "No, General, this is my last battle."

The bullet struck him in the abdomen and exited near the spine. He lingered until minutes after midnight. "With Colonel Cross's death the glory of our regiment came to a halt," stated Captain Thomas Livermore of the 5th New Hampshire. Livermore believed, "If all the colonels in the army had been like him we should never have lost a battle."[52]

Caldwell's troops held on for nearly two hours. "The men were firing as fast as they could load," claimed a Union officer. "The din was almost deafening." Additional Confederate regiments joined in the desperate fight, driving the Federals out of the Wheatfield and Trostle's Woods. From the east, advancing over the shoulder of Little Round Top, five regiments of the Pennsylvania Reserve Division charged. The Rebels wheeled to meet them. "It was not a reassuring sight," declared Colonel Martin D. Hardin of the 12th Pennsylvania Reserves. A lieutenant in another regiment, however, told a friend in a letter, "I never felt better than I did when makeing that grand charge."[53]

Fifth Corps division commander Samuel Crawford shouted to his men "to make Pennsylvania their watchword." Seizing a flag, Crawford led the charge on foot. The Federals blunted the enemy thrust, and then retired. Cannon from Cemetery Ridge and Little Round Top pounded the enemy ranks, which withdrew beyond Houck's Ridge. Although the Confederates had gained the base of Big Round Top, Devil's Den, Houck's Ridge, the Wheatfield, and the Peach Orchard, they had not seized Little Round Top or the southern end of Cemetery Ridge. At last, the combat subsided into skirmish and sharpshooter firing.[54]

The struggle, meanwhile, shifted into the fields between Seminary Ridge and Cemetery Ridge. Here, Colonel George Willard's Second Corps brigade met William Barksdale's Mississippians, who had blown across the Peach Orchard and overrun the 9th Massachusetts Battery. Willard's New Yorkers had been part of the Harper's Ferry garrison, which had surrendered in September 1862. They had carried the stain of that with the nickname "Harper's Ferry Cowards." On this day, it became a rallying cry of "Remember Harper's Ferry!"[55]

Shouting it, they leaned into a Rebel volley and broke the Mississippians' assault, pushing them back and fatally wounding Barksdale. An artillery round, however, struck Willard in the head, killing the colonel. He was the fifth Union brigade commander to be either slain or mortally wounded on July 2. In his report, their division commander, Alexander Hays, declared: "The history of this brigade's operations is written in blood. . . . The acts of traitors at Harper's Ferry had not tainted their patriotism."[56]

In a final thrust, Cadmus M. Wilcox's Alabamians and Ambrose R. Wright's Georgians charged toward the center of the Union line on Cemetery Ridge. As the Confederates came on, Hancock rode up to the 1st Minnesota, which numbered fewer than three hundred officers and men, and ordered them to attack the Alabamians. "Every man realized in an instant what the order meant—death or wounds to us all," wrote a member. They double-quicked down the ridge into a shallow ravine along its base. Leveling their rifles, they triggered a volley into the stunned Rebels. But Wilcox's veterans returned the fire, raking the small regiment in front and on the flank. Fortunately for the Minnesotans, two Union regiments blasted the Alabamians, who retreated. The 1st Minnesota's sacrifice had cost it nearly four out of every five men in the ranks.[57]

On the Alabamians' left, Wright's Georgians drove through a gale of artillery fire and musketry to the crest of Cemetery Ridge near a small clump of trees before being hammered back by the Federals. Lee had expected additional units from A. P. Hill's corps to assail the Union position, but for reasons still uncertain, Wright's charge ended the Southern assaults. Lee's veterans had fought magnificently and nearly achieved a decisive breakthrough. Hood's and McLaws's 14,000 fighters had engaged upward of 20,000 Union infantrymen, wrecked the Third Corps, and mauled every other enemy command they encountered. Their casualties approached thirty percent of their numbers. They fell short because Union reserves plugged gaps, bought time, and fought valiantly. There was much truth in the words of a Rebel who was overheard exclaiming during the action: "Great God! Have we got the universe to whip?"[58]

The defenders incurred about 9,000 casualties, which testified to the combat prowess of their opponents. The losses also testified to the Union rank and file's stubborn resistance and willful sacrifices. Skillful, sometimes brilliant, leadership complemented the soldiers' valor. Many officers merited praise, but if one individual personified leadership on this day, it was Winfield Scott Hancock. In the judgment of Edwin Coddington: "Hancock loomed magnificently above the smoke of battle. . . . He seemed to be everywhere at once, and nothing escaped his notice." He had directed the counterattacks, ordered in his Second Corps units, and by his very physical presence inspired the troops. "Had General Hancock worn citizen's clothes," argued one of his men, "his orders would have been obeyed anywhere, for he had the appearance of a man born to command." No corps commander in the army had matched Hancock's performance on any previous battlefield.[59]

Like Hancock, George Meade provided active leadership. He issued instructions to corps commanders and remained close to the action. When he rode within range of enemy musketry, his favorite mount, Old Baldy, suffered a bullet wound. Meade made, however, a critical tactical mistake, which almost resulted in a disaster, when he ordered the Twelfth Corps to leave Culp's Hill and to move to the army's left flank. Whether Meade sent for the entire corps, stripping the hill's defenses, became an issue of disagreement between him and corps commander Henry Slocum. Slocum complied with the order but left behind Brigadier General George Greene's brigade of five New York regiments.[60]

Culp's Hill consisted of an upper and a lower section. During the morning, over objections from his division commander, John Geary, Greene had had his troops erect fieldworks, using felled trees and dirt. At sixty-two years of age, Greene was the oldest Union general in the army, popular with his young soldiers, who affectionately called him "Old Man Greene" or "Old Pop." He had 1,400 New Yorkers in his ranks, and when their comrades in the corps marched away, Greene extended his line to cover the several hundred yards of works. Within thirty minutes of the departure of the other units, three Confederate brigades, under Edward Johnson and numbering 5,000, advanced against the New Yorkers.[61]

"The rebels yelled like wild Indians," stated a member of the 60th New York, "and charged upon us on a double quick." Greene's men opened fire, and for the next three hours, musketry rolled up and down the hillside. The Confederates made four distinct charges, seizing the works on lower Culp's Hill. Protected by the logs and dirt on the upper section, the Yankees blistered the Rebels. "If ever men loaded and fired more rapidly . . . I never saw them do it," insisted a Federal. When regiments from Cemetery Hill arrived as reinforcements, the Northerners held the upper slope. The stand made by Greene's New Yorkers surely equaled that of Strong Vincent's brigade on Little Round Top. During the night, the other Twelfth Corps brigades returned to the area.[62]

While the combat engulfed Culp's Hill, two Confederate brigades launched an assault on East Cemetery Hill. Moving through shadowy evening light, the Rebels surged up the steep hillside, scattered Union infantrymen, and swarmed among cannon of two batteries. Yelling, "Surrender, you damned Yankees," the attackers clubbed and shot down the artillerists. As they had all afternoon, Federal reserves counterattacked, saving the guns and repulsing the enemy. With this furious struggle and the end of fighting on Culp's Hill, the pivotal day of battle at Gettysburg flickered into a welcome silence.[63]

ON THE NIGHT OF JULY 2, George Meade summoned his corps commanders to army headquarters for what he later described as a consultation, not a council of war. He had telegraphed Washington after the day's combat had ceased that he "shall remain in my present position to-morrow," but he wanted to know from his senior generals the morale of the troops and whether the army should stay on the defensive or assume the offensive. Intelligence reports had confirmed that Robert E. Lee had all of his infantry divisions on the field, except Major General George Pickett's Virginia brigades.[64]

The generals gathered about ten o'clock at headquarters, "a shabby little farm house," owned by a widow, Mrs. Lydia Leister, along Taneytown Road. The dozen officers, including Meade, crammed into a small, ten-foot-by-twelve-foot room in the Leister home. Those present included John Sedgwick and John Newton. Sedgwick's Sixth Corps had reached Gettysburg late in the afternoon after a grueling thirty-four-mile march. The ordeal was long remembered by Sedgwick's veterans, who as the miles piled up "reeled and staggered along as if they were drunken." With their arrival, Meade's entire army had been reunited.[65]

Newton attended the meeting as acting First Corps commander. On July 1, Oliver Howard had informed Meade that the First Corps "had given way at the first contact" with the enemy. Howard's statement was not accurate, and by implication, criticized Abner Doubleday's handling of the corps after John Reynolds's death. Meade did not like Doubleday personally nor the New Yorker's abolitionist views. James Wadsworth said Meade's "animosity" toward Doubleday rested in "past political difference." Without explanation, Meade replaced Doubleday with Newton, a West Pointer and one of Sedgwick's division commanders, who was regarded as a "pet" of Meade. One of the First Corps staff officers declared that Newton's replacement of Doubleday "was a gross outrage." After Gettysburg, Doubleday never again held a field command.[66]

At the meeting, Meade was told that the army had about 58,000 men still in the ranks, but rations were running low. Only Newton argued that "Gettysburg was no place in which to fight a battle." After further discussion and a vote, the generals decided that the army should remain on the defensive for at least another day. As the generals departed, Meade stopped John Gibbon, whose Second Corps division held the center of the Union line on Cemetery Ridge, and remarked, "If Lee attacks tomorrow, it will be *in your front*." When Gibbon inquired why he thought so, Meade replied, "Because he had made attacks on both our flanks and failed and if he concluded to try it again, it will be on our centre." Hours later, Meade approved Henry Slocum's request to retake the lost works on Culp's Hill at daylight on July 3.[67]

At Lee's headquarters, meanwhile, the Confederate commander had decided to renew the attacks on July 3. Unlike Meade, Lee did not confer with his senior generals but issued instructions for a renewal of the offensive at daylight. "With proper concert of attack," as he phrased it, Lee believed, "we should ultimately succeed." Richard Ewell's troops would try again to seize Culp's Hill, while James Longstreet, with George Pickett's division augmenting his force, would continue to assault the Union left flank. Contrary to what Meade predicted, Lee would strike the ends of the Federal position, not the center. As Lee stated it in his report, "The general plan was unchanged."[68]

The men of both armies, lying on the field, passed a long night. "A low, steady, indescribable moan" from the wounded haunted the darkness. Men searched for friends and comrades, as Union ambulances, with their "twinkling lanterns," filled up with broken bodies. In the rear of the Federals, bands played music in an effort to drown out the screams of soldiers in field hospitals. Meade had forbidden fires, and if the Yankees had any food, they ate hardtack.[69]

At daylight, on Culp's Hill, Gettysburg's final day began with a thunderclap of artillery fire. Union batteries along Baltimore Pike hammered the Rebels on the hillside for fifteen minutes, preparing the way for an assault by Federal infantry. Before the Yankees could advance, however, their foes charged up the slope. For the next seven hours, 9,000 Northerners battled 9,000 Southerners for possession of the key position. Their struggle became the longest sustained combat at Gettysburg.[70]

Veterans on both sides agreed that they had never been under such intense, unremitting musketry for so long. "The whole hillside seemed enveloped in a blaze," attested a Yankee, while a Rebel confessed, "I thought I had been in hot places before—I thought I had heard Minnie balls; but that day capped the climax." The Confederates launched three coordinated attacks and countless minor surges. But the terrain, the protection afforded by the fieldworks on upper Culp's Hill, and the rotation of fresh regiments into the line assured Union victory. In truth, the courageous Southerners never had a chance of taking the position, with the entire Twelfth Corps defending the hill.[71]

The casualties mounted. In the Union trenches, "the ground was saturated with Human blood," and the hillside, where the Rebels struggled, "was slippery with human blood." When an order came to some gray-coated soldiers to make the final assault, an officer asserted: "We knew at that time we were marching to almost certain death." With the bloody repulse of this last effort, the Confederates began withdrawing. Their losses amounted to approximately 2,400, with Union casualties fewer than 1,000. Federal division commander Alpheus Williams offered a fitting assessment, "The wonder is that the rebels persisted in an attempt that the first half hour must have told them it was useless."[72]

By the time the Confederates had little left to give on Culp's Hill, Lee had settled on an attack, which history knows commonly as Pickett's Charge. His original plan to assail Meade's left flank at daylight had been ruined when Longstreet failed to order Pickett's division to be on the field at that time. Pickett's Virginians had bivouacked three miles or so to the rear, and without instructions to move earlier, did not arrive until eight o'clock. Consequently, Lee was left with two choices— either refashion an offensive or let it end as it stood. But as Longstreet's chief of staff later argued, "Lee could not retreat without another effort."[73]

In targeting the Union center on Cemetery Ridge—as Meade had thought—Lee combined boldness with simplicity. The difficulty was for the assault force to cross fourteen hundred yards of open ground with minimal losses while maintaining unit cohesiveness. Throughout the advance, enemy batteries on Cemetery Hill and Cemetery Ridge could rake the ranks. The Union cannon would have to be silenced or seriously crippled by a sustained and unparalleled bombardment by Confederate gun crews. When the guns ceased, the infantry would go forward. Edwin Coddington has written of Lee's plan, "Apparently it never occurred to him that the position could not be taken."[74]

Lee committed Pickett's three brigades of Virginians and six brigades from A. P. Hill's Third Corps, in all about 13,500 officers and men. He assigned Longstreet to command of the attack force, despite his subordinate's protests against the assault. Longstreet had opposed Lee's offensive on July 2, but now his disagreement was more vehement, arguing to Lee, "It is my opinion that no fifteen thousand men ever arrayed for battle can take that position." Lee would not be swayed. He had brought the army to Pennsylvania for a settlement, and a possible victory lay across those fields. Lee's belief in his troops' valor and prowess was profound.[75]

Confederate preparations took hours, past noon to one o'clock. Except for skirmish fire and a heated fight for the William Bliss farmhouse and barn, which lay between the lines and was burned by the Federals, the Yankees on Cemetery Ridge passed a quiet morning, concerned mostly with acquiring food. Meade worried about the outcome on Culp's Hill, while issuing orders to several commands, amounting to 13,500 officers and men, to be ready to move forward if needed. He wrote a brief note to his wife, telling her, "Army in fine spirits & every one determined to do or die."[76]

The army's artillery chief, Henry Hunt, watched the massing of enemy batteries and concluded that the Confederates planned an infantry assault. He made sure that ammunition chests were filled, readied reserve batteries to be brought up, and sent instructions to battery commanders to reply to the Rebels' fire "slowly, deliberately and making target practice of it." For an artillery genius like Hunt, it had the look of a good day for his gun crews.[77]

The relative stillness ended a few minutes after one o'clock when 164 Southern artillery crews unleashed their fury. When Union crews responded, the cannonade surpassed anything in either army's experience. In both lines, infantrymen hugged the ground, and as a Yankee said, "we would have liked to go into it if we could." A Union officer professed, "It was the most fearfully magnificent scene imaginable." "The air seethed with old iron," stated a Maine soldier. "We hardly knew what it meant." A fellow New Englander contended, "it seemed as if all the Demons in Hell were let loose." Another soldier noticed that birds flew wildly, "all out of their wits with fright."[78]

The cannonade lasted approximately forty-five minutes as the Southerners depleted their long-range ammunition supplies. Although faulty fuses on rounds and numerous overshots hampered the effectiveness of their fire, they managed to disable or force to withdraw thirty-four Union guns. Between the time the Confederates ceased the bombardment and the infantry advanced, Hunt brought forward a total of forty-four pieces. Hunt's preparations had negated the impact of the Rebels' effort. Lee had expected too much from his artillery. Within minutes, the miscalculation would cost the army dearly.[79]

Then, the Confederate infantry appeared—ranks aligned as if on parade, flags unfurled, color guards, file closers, and officers at their posts. Here was the terrible pageantry of Civil War armies, arrayed lines of men, standing beneath colorful banners, possessing a magnificence that masked the reality into which they were about to enter. Tragedy had visited many soldiers in this awful conflict, but on this hot afternoon, it enfolded these men in its arms. The pageantry immediately gave way to carnage.[80]

If the Confederates ever had a chance—many of them sensed otherwise—it probably ended within a few hundred yards when Union artillery crews opened fire on their serried ranks. Solid shot gouged gaps in the lines, and shards of shells cut up men. A Confederate wrote of seeing arms and legs flying in the air "like feathers before wind." On Cemetery Ridge, unheard by the approaching Southerners, Yankees shouted: "Fredericksburg! Fredericksburg!" and "Come on, Come on; Come to Death." They, too, sensed the inevitable.[81]

When "the rising tide of armed men" reached Emmitsburg Road, Union infantry opened fire, and artillerists switched to canister. Waves of bullets and iron balls blew into the Southern lines, leveling the front rank "as if swept by a gigantic sickle swung by some powerful force of nature." Along a section of the road, the Rebels had to scale a sturdy post-and-rail fence, exposing them more to the enemy gunfire. Hundreds, perhaps more, of the attackers lay down in the roadbed unable or unwilling to go farther. Witnessing the scene along the road, a Yankee wrote later, "It looked like murder."[82]

The North Carolinians, Tennesseans, Mississippians, Alabamians, and Virginians who crossed the road entered hell itself. Clumps of men disappeared before canister blasts; the musketry sang along the slope, flattening remnants of companies. "I never saw such slaughter," exclaimed a Federal. But still the survivors came, up to the stone wall before the clump of trees and toward a stone wall farther back on the ridge. Vermonters who had been on garrison duty in Washington barely a week ago swung out into the fields and ripped into the Rebels' flank. At the opposite end, troops ran off the ridge, leveled rifles on fence rails, and tore apart the other flank.[83]

Led by Brigadier General Lewis Armistead, a few hundred Confederates crossed the lower stone wall, silencing cannon and pushing up the slope. A wild melee ensued, with Federal troops pouring down the ridge to meet the Rebels. "If ever men became devils that was one of times," recalled a 1st Minnesota lieutenant. "We were crazy with the excitement of the fight. We just rushed in like beasts. Men swore and cussed and struggled and fought, grappled in hand-to-hand fight, threw stones, clubbed their muskets, kicked, yelled, and hurrahed." Armistead collapsed with wounds, and would die two days later. He and Hancock had been close friends in the antebellum army.[84]

The Yankees overwhelmed the island of Southerners in the shadow of the copse of trees. On the slope of Cemetery Ridge and in the fields along Emmitsburg Road, hundreds of Rebels surrendered to swarms of Yankees, either throwing down their arms or waving white handkerchiefs. The survivors streamed toward Seminary Ridge. To the south, two Confederate brigades moved forward in support, met a wall of artillery fire and a blizzard of musketry, and retreated. Lee rode forward and met the men, telling them: "It was not your fault this time. It was all mine." He had asked too much of too few men.[85]

On Cemetery Ridge, "cheer upon cheer arose from our troops and spread right & left like wild fire," exclaimed a staff officer, "and even those a mile behind us echoed back the cry of victory." "Fredericksburg! Fredericksburg!" was heard again among the cheers. Alexander Hays and an aide rode along the ridge, dragging captured Confederate flags on the ground. New to Hancock's Third Division, the Pennsylvanian had distinguished himself, moving one of his men to declare, "he is the bravest division general I ever saw in the saddle." The celebration resulted in part from the feeling, as a lieutenant colonel expressed it, "the old army of the Potomac had at last redeemed itself."[86]

During the assault Gibbon and Hancock suffered wounds. A piece of a shell struck Gibbon in the shoulder, which required him to be taken to the rear. Hancock was with the Vermonters farther south on the ridge when a bullet hit the pommel of his saddle, driving a shard of a bent tenpenny nail into his thigh. After being assured that he would not bleed to death, Hancock refused to leave the field until the attack had been repulsed. Finally, he was carried to an ambulance. While en route to a hospital, Hancock dictated a message to Meade, which read in part: "I have never seen a more formidable attack, and if the Sixth and Fifth corps have pressed up, the enemy will be destroyed. The enemy must be short of ammunition, as I was shot with a tenpenny nail."[87]

Meade, meanwhile, had arrived on Cemetery Ridge as the final remnants of the Confederate assault force were being repulsed. The army commander had abandoned his headquarters at the Leister house at the pleadings of his staff during the cannonade. Enemy overshots had been raining down on the small farmhouse when Meade departed. Eventually, he rode to Cemetery Hill and then back to headquarters, where he remained until he came onto the ridge. He watched the retreat of the Southerners. At the time, Meade had eighteen brigades either close at hand or available to advance in a counterattack. But Meade never ordered one.[88]

Why Meade did not attempt a counterstrike, he did not address in his report. In truth, the prospects for success appeared slim. Lafayette McLaws's and John Hood's veterans still held the ground that they had taken in front of Little and Big Round Top on July 2. Meade could have used the Fifth Corps and brigades of the Sixth Corps, which had not been detached elsewhere, against these Confederates. If he had wanted to assault the enemy's center, he had the troops who had been brought forward from reserve. With Hancock down, however, he had no general who could match his aggressiveness or lead such an attack. Although grievously bloodied, the Army of Northern Virginia lay across the open fields, an army that had never been driven from a position it held. In the end, his army had won a decisive victory, and Meade wisely chose to settle for that.[89]

While Union infantrymen and artillerists gathered up prisoners and spoils on Cemetery Ridge, four miles to the east a cavalry engagement moved to a climax. Confederate cavalry commander Jeb Stuart and his three brigades had reunited with Lee's army on July 2. When Stuart met with Lee, the commanding general allegedly sharply rebuked his errant subordinate. For July 3, Lee instructed Stuart to operate beyond the army's left flank. What Lee specifically intended for the mounted units remains uncertain.[90]

Stuart and four brigades, numbering perhaps 5,000 troopers, rode on to Cress Ridge near the farm of John and Sarah Rummel (today's East Cavalry Battlefield) about ten o'clock on the morning of July 3. Lying about a mile to the south, guarding the Hanover Road–Low Dutch Road, was George Custer's Michigan cavalry brigade. With his appointment to brigadier on June 29, the twenty-three-year-old "Autie" Custer was the youngest general of that rank in Federal service at the time. Dressed in a black velveteen uniform, with golden braid on its coat sleeves, a broad-collared blue shirt with silver stars sewn on, and a red necktie, Custer was a striking, unmistakable figure. A staff officer thought he looked "like a circus rider gone mad!" To his Michiganders, he had much to prove.[91]

About noon, division commander David Gregg joined Custer, followed shortly by Colonel John McIntosh's mounted brigade. The fighting between the Michiganders and Rebels had been confined to dismounted skirmishing and would continue until about three o'clock. Finally, frustrated with the Yankee resistance, Stuart ordered a mounted charge. As the Southerners thundered across the farmers' fields, scattering the Federal skirmishers, Custer led the 7th Michigan in a counterattack, shouting to them, "Come on, you Wolverines." The opponents met head-on in a violent crash of men and horses, but the Yankees broke up the Confederate thrust.[92]

Stuart brought up more units and sent them forward. With drawn sabers "glistening like silver in the bright sunlight," the veteran Rebels spurred their mounts into a gallop. Once again, Custer met the enemy, this time with the 1st Michigan, summoning them also, "Come on, you Wolverines." When the foes collided, it sounded "like the falling of timber." It quickly became a wild, swirling melee. More Federals joined the Michiganders and swept Stuart's troopers back to Cress Ridge. The repulse ended the engagement.[93]

This cavalry fight marked the continuous emergence of the Union mounted arm. Custer's and McIntosh's troopers had prevented Stuart

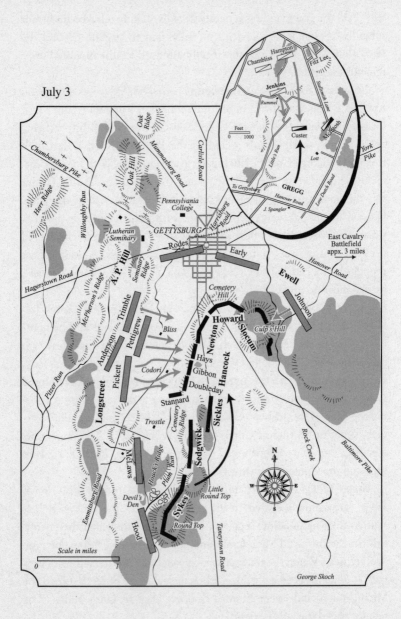

July 3

East Cavalry
Battlefield
appx. 3 miles

George Skoch

from possibly reaching Baltimore Pike, the Union army's supply line and main retreat route. Casualties on both sides amounted to slightly more than four hundred. The engagement also established Custer, with his long blond hair and a uniform the color of night, as one of the most promising cavalry officers in the army. A Michigan trooper wrote his mother the next day, "It is an honor to belong to Mich Cavalry." He could have added that it was becoming an honor to belong to the Cavalry Corps of the army.[94]

At the opposite end of the Union line, in the shadow of Big Round Top, the third day at Gettysburg produced one more brief spasm of fighting. Commander of the Third Cavalry Division Judson Kilpatrick, who would soon earn the nickname of "Kil-Cavalry" for his expenditure of horseflesh and of men, ordered a mounted charge against Southern infantrymen posted behind stone walls and among trees. It was an unwise, if not inexplicable, decision by Kilpatrick. The result was a debacle as Elon Farnsworth's troopers found themselves nearly encircled by Confederates. Farnsworth, who had been promoted to brigadier with Custer, died in the forlorn charge, and his troopers were forced to run a gauntlet of rifle fire to escape. A Texan crowed afterward, "It was simply a picnic to fight cavalry under such conditions."[95]

A UNION SOLDIER LIKENED July 4 at Gettysburg to "a funeral." Wherever men gazed, they saw dead bodies. A New Yorker thought they "lay as thick as the stones that is on fathers farm." A stench smothered the field, moving John Geary to tell his wife, "My very clothes smell of death." A Regular Army veteran exclaimed, "I have seen many a big battle, most of the big ones of the war, and I never saw the like."[96]

There had never been "the like" of it in this war, nor would there ever be again in a single battle. Union casualties totaled 23,049; Confederate, 28,063. Of those 51,000 killed, wounded, and missing, more than 9,600 had been slain or mortally wounded. When the Confederates retreated, an estimated 5,000 wounded men were left behind to be cared for by the Federal medical staffs. Both armies incurred grievous losses among regimental field officers, and brigade and division commanders. Only the Northerners suffered losses at the corps level—John

Reynolds, killed; Winfield Scott Hancock and Daniel Sickles, seriously wounded. It would be months before the last hospital at Gettysburg closed.[97]

Amid the carnage, a feeling of accomplishment pervaded the ranks of the Army of the Potomac. "Everybody was in the most exuberant spirits," wrote a newspaper correspondent on July 4. "For once this army had won a real victory." In a diary, a Third Corps staff officer declared: "The Fourth of July! A day made doubly dear by the Victory of Liberty over Slavery on the fields of Gettysburg." One soldier believed that Lee thought "he could walk right over the Army of Potomac." Instead the Yankees, as they said, had "redeemed" and "vindicated" themselves and the army's reputation.[98]

"History will do us full justice," asserted Dr. William W. Potter of the 57th New York shortly after the battle, "I have no doubt." In fact, history has focused more on the reasons for Confederate defeat than for Union victory. The causes of the Southern failure range from Jeb Stuart's absence to James Longstreet's recalcitrance; from Richard Ewell's and A. P. Hill's inadequacies to the breakdown of Lee's command system; and to Lee's decision to assail the Union position. Lee attributed it to the army's inability to achieve "a proper concert of action" on July 2. Ultimately, however, as a Union soldier put it, the Federals "gave the rebels one of the damdest lickens that they ever had."[99]

At Gettysburg, the Army of the Potomac confronted its past, a record of defeats unmatched by any American army since the American Revolution. On this battlefield, however, they benefited from fighting a defensive battle in a position of natural strength, along a compact line that expedited the movement of units from one sector to another. Unquestionably, it was the kind of engagement given to them by their opponents. "But at least Gettysburg showed," Paddy Griffith has written of the army, "that there were limits to its capacity for self-inflicted damage."[100]

Unlike in the past, the army's leadership did not fail the rank and file. From John Buford's and John Reynolds's actions on July 1 to the repulse of Pickett's Charge on July 3, aggressiveness characterized the army's operations. Meade and his subordinates handled their units skillfully, reacting with alacrity to the changing conditions on the field. It had not been a flawless performance, but it exceeded anything in the army's experience.[101]

Time would accord Gettysburg its significance; for the present, the campaign and battle marked a turning point for the Union army. The Federals would never possess their foes' élan on a battlefield, but with capable leadership, their steadiness—"the discipline of adversity," in Joshua Chamberlain's words—would tell for much. On the roads that led away from Gettysburg, the Army of the Potomac followed a different fork.[102]

RAIN BEGAN FALLING in the afternoon of July 4, swelling to a downpour by evening. After nightfall, in the drenching storm, the Army of Northern Virginia slipped away from Gettysburg, marching southwest toward Maryland and the Potomac River. Miles of wagons had preceded the infantry and artillery units. Jeb Stuart's cavalry escorted the trains and served as rear guards. Although the heavy rains turned roads into troughs of mud, the Southerners approached the swollen Potomac by July 7. Here the retreat stalled as the river's swift, rising current prevented a crossing and Lee's army dug in.[103]

George Meade had received reports from signal stations late on the afternoon of July 4 that indicated a Confederate withdrawal. He issued a proclamation to the army that read, in part, "Our task is not yet accomplished, and the commanding general looks to the army for greater efforts to drive from our soil every vestige of the presence of the invader." He then sent instructions for the army to prepare for a movement and ordered some cavalry units in pursuit. At night, he met with his corps commanders, who voted to await clear evidence of an enemy retreat and then to move cautiously. No general voiced a desire to attack the fleeing enemy.[104]

After midnight on July 5, Herman Haupt, the superintendent of railroads, arrived at Gettysburg. He and Meade had been classmates at West Point and had known each other for nearly three decades. Haupt had been at work all day insuring the flow of supplies to the army and had come to see Meade about the general's plans. Believing correctly that the Confederate retreat had begun, Haupt said to his old friend

that he presumed the Federals would follow at once. Meade replied that
the army required supplies and ammunition and the men needed rest.
Later that day, Haupt journeyed to Washington, where he told Abraham Lincoln that Meade seemed to be in no hurry to pursue the
enemy.[105]

Meade's concerns had legitimacy. Ammunition chests needed to be
replenished, and rations brought up and issued. Detachments were burdened with gathering up the wounded men, in both armies, still on the
field, burying the dead, and attending to the horde of prisoners. Thousands of men wanted for shoes and would have to march barefooted.
"All these things made our movements difficult," argued Henry Hunt.
"Then we couldn't move 'Straight' and movements depended more or
less on those of the enemy."[106]

The Union infantry corps did not begin the pursuit until July 7. As
Hunt noted, they did not march "Straight," but headed south toward
Frederick, Maryland, covering the roads to Baltimore and Washington
should Lee turn in that direction. The mud, "about the consistency of
lard," slowed the pace. Mail call brought a "joyous excitement" among
the troops. The rumor persisted, enlivening morale further, that George
McClellan had replaced either General-in-chief Henry Halleck or
Meade. "I cannot understand the intensity and vitality of the feeling,"
professed Hunt, "but it exists." By July 10, the army had crossed South
Mountain, west of Frederick, and closed on the extensive fieldworks
erected by its foes.[107]

During the march, Meade received a letter of praise from Halleck for
Gettysburg and notification of his promotion to brigadier general in the
Regular Army. Meade announced to the army that Andrew Humphreys
had succeeded Daniel Butterfield as its chief of staff. Butterfield had held
the post under Joseph Hooker, and he and Meade had had a strained personal relationship prior to the latter's appointment to command. Meade
had offered the position on June 28 to Gouverneur Warren, who
declined. He then approached Humphreys on July 5. Reluctantly,
Humphreys accepted, and with it, a promotion to major general. "I
regard it as temporary," he told his wife, "that is until I can get command
of a Corps; less than that I cannot stand." In time, Humphreys would
prove to be the finest chief of staff in the army's history.[108]

On the day Meade announced Humphreys's appointment, July 9, 9,000 troops from Harper's Ferry joined the army. If Meade contemplated using them as a blocking force to prevent a Confederate crossing of the Potomac, no evidence exists. Instead, he ordered them as reinforcements, assigning them to the Third Corps. Their commander, William French, assumed command of the corps, which had been Sickles's. French was a poor choice, a general with limited ability, a foul disposition, and a fondness for whiskey. In the Second Corps, Brigadier General William Hays had been brought in by Meade to assume temporary command with both Winfield Hancock and John Gibbon wounded. A better choice might have been Alexander Hays, who had distinguished himself on July 2 and 3.[109]

While the main body of the Union army marched in pursuit, Alfred Pleasonton's mounted units engaged daily in clashes with Stuart's horsemen. The Yankees continued to act with combativeness, but Stuart and his veterans countered the Federal probes. Once Meade's infantry arrived, skirmishes ignited between them and their Rebel counterparts.[110]

The Confederate works, which Meade's army encountered in Maryland, extended for nine miles from west of Hagerstown to below Falling Waters. They consisted of two parallel lines of entrenchments, with both flanks anchored on the Potomac, "a long, military bastion." In the judgment of historian Kent Masterson Brown, "No position ever held by Lee's army, save for Marye's Heights at Fredericksburg, was more formidable."[111]

On the night of July 12, Meade held another council of war with his corps commanders. He favored either a reconnaissance-in-force or an assault, but was uncertain as to the nature and extent of Lee's line. "I have to grope my way in the dark," he confided to his wife on this day. The sentiment of his senior generals, however, was against an attack. Five of the nine present argued that a defeat would risk what had been gained at Gettysburg. Meade's most trusted aides, Humphreys and Warren, advocated an advance the next day, believing it was worth the risk. Meade decided to conduct his own examination of the works the next day, and follow with a reconnaissance-in-force on July 14.[112]

The Yankees were, however, a day late. During the night of July

13–14, Lee's army crossed on pontoons into Virginia. A rear guard clash occurred on July 14 at Falling Waters, but the Rebels had escaped virtually unscathed. In the Union army's ranks, more men seemed to express dissatisfaction and disappointment over the Southerners' escape than thankfulness for not having to assail the works. "I do not think," wrote an artillery sergeant, "Lee will ever be catched up in as tight a place again." They knew that this meant an indefinite conclusion to this war. One of the most acerbic comments came from a surgeon who blamed Meade and the generals: "Our army is an anomaly—it is an army of lions commanded by jackasses!!"[113]

Lincoln learned of the Confederates' escape from Secretary of War Stanton as he was preparing to hold a Cabinet meeting. On hearing the news, Lincoln's "countenance indicated trouble and distress." He adjourned the meeting, and walked out with Secretary of the Navy Welles, telling the latter, "he had dreaded yet expected this." He spoke of "bad faith somewhere," asking, "What does it mean, Mr. Welles? Great God! what does it mean." Later, nineteen-year-old Robert Lincoln saw his father "in tears." The president told his son that if he could have gone up there, he could have whipped Lee.[114]

Lincoln's anguish and disappointment were profound. He believed wrongly that the Confederate army had been routed at Gettysburg. With Ulysses Grant's capture of Vicksburg, Mississippi, on July 4, the president saw the probability of a Union victory if Lee's forces were crushed. He had been troubled by Haupt's conversation with Meade and the general's proclamation about driving the Rebels "from our soil." When he read it, Lincoln complained to his secretary, John Hay: "Will our generals never get that idea out of their heads? The whole country is our soil."[115]

The president had Halleck telegraph Meade on July 14 about his feelings. The general-in-chief wrote, "I need hardly say to you that the escape of Lee's army without another battle has created great dissatisfaction in the mind of the President, and it will require an active and energetic pursuit on your part to remove the impression that it has not been sufficiently active heretofore."[116]

Within hours Meade shot back that the "censure of the President . . . is, in my judgment, so undeserved that I feel compelled most respectfully to ask to be relieved from command of the army." Halleck replied that it "was not intended as a censure" and "is not deemed as sufficient cause for your application to be relieved."[117]

The affair left both Lincoln and Meade bitter. To the president, it had been a simple matter: "We had them within our grasp. We had only to stretch forth our hands & they were ours." Lincoln's assessment of the situation before Meade was, however, deeply flawed and clouded by his intense desire for another victory. But it would have been better for Meade and for his relationship with Lincoln had he gone forward with his original plan to test Lee's strong entrenchments on July 13, when the Confederates were still north of the river.[118]

Lincoln wrote a letter to Meade afterward but filed it away and never sent it. "My dear General," stated Lincoln, "I do not believe you appreciate the magnitude of the misfortune involved in Lee's escape. He was within your easy grasp, and to have closed upon him would, in connection with our other late successes, have ended the war. As it is, the war will be prolonged indefinitely."[119]

Chapter 14

Virginia Interlude

THOMAS CARPENTER, AN ORDERLY at the headquarters of the Army of the Potomac, wrote home to Illinois on September 2, 1863: "I believe the reasons for inaction are good and sufficient and such being the case I am content to *wait* although it seems like a useless waste of time strength and treasure. The days wear slowly and wearily along it seems like a dead and useless existence but there is a time for all things and when the time for action comes this ·weather-beaten war-worn Army will shake off its lethargy and close in a death-grapple with the Rebellion."[1]

When Carpenter penned his letter, it had been more than seven weeks since the Confederate Army of Northern Virginia crossed the Potomac River, marking the end of the Gettysburg Campaign. In the interim, both armies had returned to central Virginia in the region drained by the Rappahannock and Rapidan rivers, upstream from their old works at Fredericksburg. As Carpenter noted, "there is a time for all things," and the time had come for an interlude before the opponents engaged in another "death-grapple." What the orderly and the tens of thousands of soldiers in both armies could not have known was that this relative quiet would last more than nine months.

Unlike George McClellan after Antietam, George Meade followed

Robert E. Lee's army into Virginia within days of the Confederates' recrossing. "The Government insists on my pursuing and destroying Lee," Meade told his wife. While the Rebels marched south through the Shenandoah Valley, the Federals moved east of the Blue Ridge. A clash occurred at Manassas Gap in the mountains before the Southerners entered Virginia's Piedmont and filed into position behind the Rappahannock River. By July 27, Meade's army had closed on its foe, establishing their lines along the river.[2]

The Gettysburg campaign and battle had worn each army to the bone. The long marches and staggering casualties had reduced regiments to the size of companies. Union soldiers complained of "footraces," and wrote of straggling and the breakdown of discipline upon their return to Virginia. "They had marched us most to death and poorly rationed us," grumbled one soldier. A New Yorker jotted in his diary after one day's march, "Never suffered so in my life." An officer expressed a common view, "A battle to veterans is an awful thing."[3]

The Union army's ranks were further reduced by the temporary detachment and permanent loss of dozens of regiments. When draft riots exploded in New York City in mid-July, the War Department ordered four regiments to the city to quell the burning, looting, and bloodshed. During the next few weeks, the Fifth Corps division of Regulars, a brigade of Vermonters, and nine more regiments followed. Most of them would not return to the army until September. Furthermore, nine two-year and nine-month regiments left for home with their terms of enlistment expired. In all, the depletion in numbers mounted to approximately 15,000.[4]

At the same time, thousands of recruits and drafted men joined the army. They arrived often under guard to prevent them from deserting. The veteran soldiers greeted them with contempt. One officer called them "cattle," and a New York sergeant described them as "a hard set look as if they had sent all the inmates of sing sing out hear." The veterans had to stand picket duty with them and watch them during drills to keep them from sneaking away. Most of them, however, proved to be good soldiers in time.[5]

Meade ordered officers to enforce discipline and instituted drills for the entire army. Trains on the Orange & Alexandria Railroad brought supplies, including soft bread, daily from Washington. Foraging was restricted, but there was not much to be found in what an officer termed "the impoverished valley of the Rappahannock." Most of the time, however, the troops passed the time "as we pleased." Morale improved. "The *Army* of the *Potomac*," wrote a soldier near the end of September, "is in tip top spirits and confident that it can whip the *Southern Army* on a fair field eny day."[6]

An increasing bitterness toward their enemy crept into their correspondence. "They have two rights," declared a Pennsylvania lieutenant of the Rebels. "A Constitutional right to be *hung* and a Divine right to be *Damned*." Their letters also reflected a more willing acceptance of abolition. A Vermonter argued that the country "is reaping the consequences" of "this institution of bondage," and it must be eradicated. A soldier in the 24th Michigan insisted: "There is no use, at this day, at attempting to deny, that a government that sanctions such a piece of injustice as human bondage, rests on a poor foundation and is liable to just such troubles as the present. If slavery is such an injustice, how can a government protecting or allowing it, hope for the favor of God."[7]

During these initial weeks along the Rappahannock and Rapidan rivers—"the two Raps" to soldiers—Meade kept his mounted units active in probing the Confederate lines and engaging Jeb Stuart's horsemen. Lee had withdrawn his army south of the Rapidan, leaving Stuart to prowl between the two rivers and to screen the Southern front. When the Yankee cavalrymen crossed the Rappahannock, the opponents clashed in a series of minor, spirited engagements. The fiercest encounter occurred around Culpeper Court House on September 13, a day-long affair in which the Federals pressed the Rebels for miles, holding the town at nightfall.[8]

On the night of September 14, Meade telegraphed General-in-Chief Henry Halleck, reporting that from information he had received James Longstreet's First Corps had been detached from Lee's army. (Two of Longstreet's infantry divisions and an artillery battalion had left for Tennessee on September 9.) "I should be glad to have your views as to what had better be done, if anything," stated Meade. In his view, "I see no object in advancing, unless it is with ulterior views, and I do not consider this army is sufficiently large to follow him [Lee] to Richmond." But Meade wanted Halleck's opinion, and by implication, Abraham Lincoln's.[9]

Until now, the administration had not pressed Meade to advance against Lee. According to Secretary of the Navy Gideon Welles, the president had complained to him about the inaction, saying: "It is . . . the same old story of this Army of the Potomac. Imbecility, inefficiency—don't want to *do*—is defending the capital. . . . it is terrible, terrible, this weakness, this indifference of our Potomac generals, with such armies of good and brave men." But neither Lincoln nor Halleck proposed any offensive movement.[10]

The replies from Halleck and Lincoln must have made Meade wonder. Halleck responded with two telegrams the next day, recommending "a sudden raid" that might "if possible, to cut off some portion" of Lee's army. The president addressed his suggestion to Halleck, writing: "My opinion is that he [Meade] should move upon Lee at once in manner of a general attack, leaving to developments whether he will make it a real attack." Lincoln added, "Of course, my opinion is not to control you and General Meade."[11]

The army marched within twenty-four hours, crossing the Rappahannock and moving toward the Rapidan into the area occupied by John Pope's Army of Virginia in the summer of 1862. Here the advance stalled, as Meade sent his cavalry forward on reconnaissances. Meade began fashioning plans for a turning movement around Lee's left flank. Then, news reached Washington of the defeat of Major General William Rosecrans's Union army at Chickamauga, Georgia, on September 19–20, and of its retreat into Chattanooga, Tennessee. Longstreet's troops from Lee's army had arrived in time to be the decisive edge in the battle.[12]

The administration summoned Meade to Washington for a conference on September 22. Three days earlier, Lincoln had written a lengthy letter to Halleck about operations of the Army of the Potomac. Based on reports he had read, the president calculated that Meade held a three-to-two manpower advantage over Lee. "Yet, it having been determined that choosing ground and standing on the defensive gives so great advantage that the three cannot safely attack the two, the three are left simply standing on the defensive also. If the enemy's 60,000 are sufficient to keep our 90,000 away from Richmond, why, by the same rule, may not 40,000 of ours keep their 60,000 away from Washington, leaving us 50,000 to put to some other use? Having practically come to the mere defensive, it seems to be no economy at all to employ twice as many men for that object as are needed. With no object, certainly, to mislead myself, I can perceive no fault in this statement, unless we admit we are not equal of the enemy, man for man."[13]

Continuing, Lincoln summarized the core of his strategic beliefs on the war in Virginia: "To avoid misunderstanding, let me say that to attempt to fight the enemy slowly back into his intrenchments at Richmond, and there to capture him, is an idea I have been trying to repudiate for quite a year. My judgment is so clear against it that I would scarcely allow the attempt to be made, if the general in command should desire to make it. My last attempt upon Richmond was to get McClellan, when he was nearer there than the enemy was, to run in ahead of him. Since then I have constantly desired the Army of the Potomac to make Lee's army, and not Richmond, its objective point. If our army cannot fall upon the enemy and hurt him where he is, it is plain to me it can gain nothing by attempting to follow him over a succession of intrenched lines into a fortified city."[14]

In the president's thinking, then, detaching units from Meade's army to meet the reversal in Tennessee made sense with the stalemate along the Rapidan. When Lincoln conferred with Halleck, Meade, and Secretary of War Edwin Stanton on the morning of September 23, they reached no decision. Meade returned to the army that afternoon, believing that he had convinced Lincoln not to detach troops. The next day, however, Halleck wired to send the Eleventh and Twelfth corps to Washington for transfer to the West. The 13,500 officers and men began boarding trains on September 25. To command these two corps, Lincoln appointed Joseph Hooker.[15]

The Eleventh and Twelfth corps had been with the army for slightly more than a year. They had served in Pope's army until they were incorporated into the Army of the Potomac before Antietam. The Twelfth Corps had fought in the battle at Chancellorsville, and had defended Culp's Hill at Gettysburg. Conversely, the Eleventh Corps, with its large contingent of immigrant Germans, had been stained irretrievably by its rout at Chancellorsville on May 2 and at Gettysburg on July 1. In the West, both units would render solid service.

With their departure, Meade retained an army that numbered 76,000 present for duty. Writing to his wife of the loss of two corps, he stated: "Of this I do not complain. The President is the best judge of where the armies can be best employed, and if he chooses to place this army strictly on the defensive, I have no right to object or murmur." In the estimation of a Pennsylvania cavalryman, "what is left is pure grit."[16]

When Meade met with Lincoln at the White House, the president discussed a matter of concern to him. Lincoln had heard that Meade and other generals had been soliciting funds for a testimonial and presentation to George McClellan, and he opposed the idea. Meade explained the effort, but Lincoln was unmoved. The next day, September 24, a Washington newspaper printed a story about the plan to honor McClellan, calling it political on the army's part. That afternoon, Meade informed Halleck that the officers involved with it had agreed to cease obtaining money. A few days later, Provost Marshal Marsena Patrick recorded a rumor in his diary, "The idea now seems to be that this army will be broken up, that it is so thoroughly McClellan as to be dangerous."[17]

ROBERT E. LEE HAD BEEN uncharacteristically passive since the conclusion of the Gettysburg campaign. Like the Yankees, his men required rest from the rigors of the movement into Pennsylvania. They sorely needed supplies, arms, and ammunition. Hundreds had deserted since their return to Virginia. Inactivity along the rivers came as a blessing to the army.[18]

Lee also showed the strains of the past two months. A recurrence of the illness that had struck him in the spring—believed to be angina—weakened him. When he learned of the public criticism of the army's defeat at Gettysburg, he tendered his resignation to President Jefferson Davis, citing his poor health and offering to relinquish command "that a younger & abler man than myself can readily be attained." Davis refused to accept it, calling Lee "my dear friend" and arguing, "To ask me to substitute you by some one in my judgment more fit to command, or who would possess more of the confidence of the army, or of the reflecting men in the country is to demand an impossibility."[19]

The Confederate commander had opposed initially the dispatch of Longstreet's troops to Tennessee, but acquiesced in Davis's decision. It left Lee with nearly 50,000 officers and men present for duty. But when he learned of the detachment of the two Union corps, Lee undertook an offensive with the purpose "of getting an opportunity to strike a blow at the enemy." In a movement reminiscent of operations against John Pope in August 1862, Lee swung his army around the right flank of the Federals, crossing the Rapidan River on October 9.[20]

The resultant Bristoe Campaign lasted for ten days and was aptly described by a Union surgeon as "a *great foot race*" to Centreville. Lee sought to catch the Yankees on the march and to strike the strung-out units. In turn, Meade retreated to protect his supply line, unwilling to risk an engagement, "without some opening to the rear in case of disaster." Consequently, Meade's army followed the tracks of the Orange & Alexandria Railroad, while Lee's units moved to the west and tried to overtake the Federals. A Union officer said it reminded him "of the old game of 'hide-and-go-seek.'"[21]

The bloodiest engagement of the campaign occurred on the afternoon of October 14, at Bristoe Station, between brigades of the Union Second Corps and the Confederate Third Corps. With Winfield Scott Hancock still recovering from his Gettysburg wound, Major General Gouverneur Warren, the army's former chief engineer, temporarily led Hancock's veterans. Meade had assigned Warren to the corps in August, removing William Hays from the post. In little more than a month, Hays had managed to alienate most of the corps's officers and men. They welcomed the appointment of Warren.[22]

The action at Bristoe Station resulted in a bloody repulse for the Confederates. Posted behind the railroad embankment, Warren's infantrymen and a pair of batteries tore apart the ranks of two Southern brigades. Rushed forward by Confederate commander A. P. Hill, the Rebels crossed open fields into a wall of Union musketry and canister from the numerically superior Federals. Division commander Alexander Hays described the fight as "one of the prettiest affairs I have ever seen." When Lee came onto the sad field, he censured Hill in "the most bitter terms."[23]

Meade's army won the race to the Manassas-Centreville area. With the Federals behind fieldworks, Lee turned his army south, back toward the Rappahannock. On October 19, Jeb Stuart's cavalrymen routed part of Judson Kilpatrick's mounted division in the so-called Buckland Races. Lee had garnered little, except about 2,400 prisoners, while incurring a similar number of casualties.[24]

Meade had been in a foul mood throughout the campaign. At such times when his temper boiled over, his staff called him the "Great Peppery." He had wanted to strike a blow against Lee, but his primary concern had been the security of his supply train. Only after operations had ended did he learn, as he put it, "Lee was *slow* and *ought* to have been farther ahead as I supposed he was, at the time." Meade had kept his army between Lee's and Washington, saved his wagon train, but inflicted only minor damage on his opponent.[25]

Within the army, the men questioned Meade's willingness to engage Lee in a battle. A lieutenant viewed Meade's actions as "useless marching and countermarching," adding, "everyone in the army from the highest to the lowest, have lost all confidence in Gen. Meade as a fighting man, but all have the greatest confidence in his ability to keep us out of the way of the Rebels." In his diary, Captain Francis Donaldson of the 118th Pennsylvania wrote, "We will never do much until some determined man gets command & then catching us by the neck, so to speak, holds us up and forces the fighting." Some soldiers blamed the "*wire pullers*" in Washington for preventing Meade from waging a battle. A sergeant took a longer view: "We look to history to give us our just due & to place all the blame where it belongs."[26]

With the army outside of the capital, Lincoln had Meade come to the White House for a talk. The meeting was cordial. Meade told his wife that Lincoln "was, as he always is, very considerate and kind." Although the President expressed no criticism of the recent operations, "he was disappointed that I had not got a battle out of Lee." Henry Halleck was present and urged an advance against the Confederates, but Lincoln did not press for one.[27]

Less than a week later, however, Meade told an aide that he wished "the Administration would get mad at me, and relieve me." He said that he had stated to them that if they were not satisfied with his performance to replace him. Shortly afterward, Meade confided to Hancock in a letter that he expected to be relieved "at any moment" and "accordingly keep my sabre packed." "I never desired the command," he continued. "I knew the result if I was placed in it, and shall feel no regret whenever the order relieving me arrives. While here I will do the best I can."[28]

The reasons for Meade's attitude at this time are unclear. His description of his meeting with Lincoln indicated no difficulty between them. He had heard rumors since the end of the Gettysburg campaign that the president was contemplating a successor for him, but at least to Meade, Lincoln had not voiced criticisms of the inactivity of the army. A few days before Meade wrote to Hancock, Lincoln and Halleck had rejected the general's plan to change his base of operations to Fredericksburg. Meade's letter may have simply reflected his feeling the burdens of command.[29]

Undoubtedly, the appearance of Daniel Sickles in the army's camps rankled Meade. When the army reached Centreville, the one-legged general, using a crutch to walk, visited his former Third Corps troops and allegedly sought reinstatement to command. His men crowded around his carriage—"I never before heard such hearty cheering," claimed one of them. Whatever his faults, they admired his personal courage and combative spirit. Meade, however, wanted nothing to do with Sickles, and if the subordinate asked for his command, Meade declined. In Sickles, Meade had an enemy who would do much to tarnish the army commander's reputation.[30]

AT SUNDOWN, IN THE DYING of an autumn day, they came—men from Maine, New York, Pennsylvania, and Wisconsin, moving at the double-quick, scrambling through a deep ditch, and emitting cheers. North Carolinians and Louisianans, the famed Louisiana Tigers, answered with volleys. Within minutes, however, the Northerners swarmed over the rifle pits and into a redoubt. The Southerners fled for a pontoon bridge across the Rappahannock River, but hundreds were trapped and taken prisoner. "It was *fun* for *us* to see the stew they were in," exclaimed a Union sergeant of the Confederates.[31]

It was November 7, at Rappahannock Station, and the Union suc-

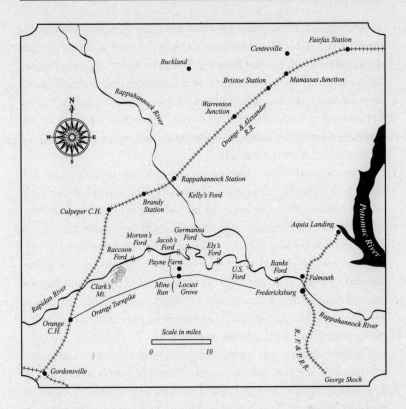

George Skoch

cess had come against an enemy defensive position on the north bank of the Rappahannock. The Yankees captured 1,600 prisoners, 2,000 stands of arms, eight battle flags, and four cannon. Although a minor affair, it buoyed the entire army. At George Meade's headquarters, "they were all feeling very jolly." When Meade appeared among the troops, they cheered him for the first time in months.[32]

The Rappahannock Station affair was a part of the Union army's push across the river against Robert E. Lee's lines. When the Southerners retreated to end the Bristoe Campaign, Meade pursued immediately. For the next fortnight, the stalemate resumed along the Rappahannock. With the administration opposing his plan to shift operations to Fredericksburg, Meade decided to move directly on Lee's position. The thrust compelled Lee to withdraw behind the Rapidan, and for another two weeks, the armies settled into a familiar pattern of watching each other.[33]

During this time, Meade learned from deserters and intelligence reports that Lee had begun erecting a line of entrenchments on his right flank, perpendicular to the Rapidan River. Acting on this information, Meade planned an offensive movement across the river. The Federals would either turn the enemy's right flank and attack the Rebels or force Lee to assail them. Rainy weather delayed the start of the advance, but on November 26, Meade's 80,000-man army headed for Jacob's and Germanna fords on the Rapidan.[34]

Once again, however, old habits cursed the army. The primary culprit was William French and the Third Corps. On the first day's march, one of French's divisions began to move hours behind schedule, stopping the trailing Sixth Corps in its tracks. On November 27, some of French's units became lost, and late in the afternoon became entangled in a fierce action, known as Payne's Farm, with Edward Johnson's Confederate veterans. The fighting's outcome ended in a draw, but the presence of Southerners indicated Lee was reacting quickly to the Federal movements. "Things did not go as Meade expected," wrote an officer close to members of the general's staff.[35]

William French was unquestionably the army's worst corps commander. His position was, in historian Stephen Sears's judgment, "far beyond his depth." Rumors, based upon apparently creditable evidence, had him drunk on both days. His Third Corps veterans despised him almost to a man. They called him "the old gin barrel," "a perfect ignoramious and bloat," and "an imbecile." During the Bristoe Campaign a bullet passed through French's hat. "It would have added much to our peace of mind," stated a private, "if said bullet had gone two inches lower."[36]

Rain fell on November 28, as the Yankees filed into a line east of Mine Run, about seven or eight miles southwest of the old Chancellorsville battlefield. The area was heavily wooded, and behind the stream, Lee's 50,000 troops were building an extensive series of fieldworks. Meade and his senior generals examined the Confederate position the next day. Second Corps commander Gouverneur Warren reported that he had "not the slightest doubt he could carry" the Rebels' entrenchments. Meade assigned 28,000 troops to Warren and ordered the assault for the following morning.[37]

When the sun rose on November 30 and brightened the woods along Mine Run, Union infantrymen saw that the enemy had strengthened and extended its works. A Massachusetts sergeant wrote that the Rebel position was "worse than Fredericksburg. I felt death in my very bones." While he and his comrades waited to advance, men prepared wills, gave personal items to chaplains, and attached pieces of paper with their names scribbled on to their blouses and coats. Speaking for thousands, a New Jersey soldier admitted: "I was so sure that my last day had come. . . . Time seemed to creep along. I wanted to get it over, have the worst happen and be done with."[38]

Before Warren sent the troops forward, he and an aide crawled on their hands and knees beyond their line to get a final view of the enemy's works. When Warren looked upon what his troops saw, he canceled the attack, sending his aide with a dispatch to army headquarters. Meade described Warren's message as "astounding intelligence." He rode at once to see Warren. Accounts vary as to Meade's demeanor when he met Warren, but it appears that if he controlled his explosive temper, it was a struggle for him. A member of Warren's staff said that Warren's worst failing was that he was "always ready to set up his own judgment against that of his superior officers." Marsena Patrick asserted in his diary that Warren "has been so puffed & elated & swelled up, that his arrogance and insolence are intolerable."[39]

Meade examined Lee's entrenchments and concurred with Warren's decision. Unwilling to sacrifice "my people," as he called the troops, Meade acted wisely and courageously. "It was my deliberate judgment," he professed to his wife, "that I ought not to attack; I acted on that judgment, and I am willing to stand or fall by it at all hazards." He believed, as he expressed it later, "the failure of the Army of the Potomac to do anything, at this moment, will be considered of vital consequence, and if I can be held responsible for this failure, I will be removed to prove that I am." If that occurred, it will be because of "political considerations."[40]

The Union army stayed in place throughout December 1. At headquarters, staff members avoided Meade, who "was like a Bear with a sore head." Along the lines, Rebels taunted their foes, "Yank, why the hell didn't you charge yesterday." Back came, "Go to hell, you Graybacks Sons of Bitches, you're damned glad we didn't." After dark, the Federals began the withdrawal. Temperatures had plummeted, and the men suffered much from the bitterly frigid weather and lack of food. By daylight of December 3, the last contingent of troops filed across the Rapidan. Work soon began on winter quarters.[41]

Meade informed Washington of the campaign's outcome and then awaited his expected removal from command. Weeks passed, but no order came from the War Department or letters from Lincoln and Halleck. The stalemate in Virginia had exasperated Lincoln, and he was probably convinced that Meade was unwilling to assail Lee. The Union cause had been given a boost in Tennessee, where Ulysses S. Grant had broken the siege of Chattanooga with a rout of the Confederate army, and Knoxville had been successfully defended. The president could wait to make any command changes.[42]

Had Lincoln talked with the army's officers and men he would have found steadfast support for Meade. When the general canceled the assault on November 30, he enhanced his standing with the troops. They appreciated deeply his unwillingness to sacrifice their lives needlessly just so it could be said that he had attacked the enemy. A lieutenant stated of Meade in a typical comment, "He saw that the fruits would be far less than the cost, and was BRAVE enough to withdraw, and save thousands of his army." A surgeon called it "a noble act" by Meade, adding, "Of all *hard looking* places, that of Mine Run was the hardest I ever beheld." A Massachusetts sergeant declared that Meade's "conduct in the last campaign has fastened his name firm in the hearts of those who compose his army."[43]

Captain Samuel Fiske of the 14th Connecticut offered his assessment of the past two months' operations: "The simple state of the case is this, that both the Virginia armies are now so well disciplined and experienced that they are very hard to beat. One side must make some serious blunder to meet any serious danger: and they don't make any great blunders. They have grown cautious over the experience of Fredericksburg and Gettysburg, and they have learned the value of even slight and hastily thrown-up breastworks."[44]

THE 1864 WINTER CAMPS of the Army of the Potomac sprawled from north of the Rappahannock near Warrenton to around Culpeper

Court House. Most of the infantry corps and a cavalry division lay between the Rappahannock and Rapidan. According to a Union soldier, the region "is a desolate looking place/war has swept over the fields of this state and left its marks here." Here, they would stay for five months, with their opponents, the Army of Northern Virginia, encamped just to the south, beyond the Rapidan.[45]

The winter months proved to be one of the quietest periods in the army's history. Cold weather, with howling winds and snow, arrived on New Year's Day and hung on tenaciously. Men had to serve on picket duty along the rivers and maintain roads. Officers enforced strict discipline, held drills as often as they could in the weather, and conducted weekly inspections on Sundays. Trains ran regularly on the Orange & Alexandria Railroad, with cars packed with foodstuffs. For other needs, sutlers were present in the camps.[46]

Most of the time, the men huddled in their huts, comforted themselves with their ubiquitous pipes—"Soldiers are great smokers," wrote a chaplain—wrote letters, and always thought of the war's end and home. A rumor, or a "pop" in their slang, had an eager audience. They played cards, listened to lectures and debates, joined temperance societies, and enjoyed "the *Negro Minstrels*" staged by the 14th New York. An artillerist, whose camp lay next to a heavy artillery unit of German immigrants, complained that they "made more noise in their camp than two brigades of Americans would or could have done." On Washington's Birthday, February 22, the army's ranking officers held a ball outside of Stevensburg, and on St. Patrick's Day, the Irish had "a great time."[47]

The major topic of conversation in the camps was the offer of a thirty-day furlough by the government and bounties by the states for veterans in three-year regiments to reenlist as Veteran Volunteers. Units held meetings, heard patriotic speeches, and debated the topic among themselves. Bounties ranged from three dollars for Vermonters to one thousand dollars for men from New Jersey. If such a vast discrepancy caused ill feeling among the men from different states, it went unrecorded. The temptation of a furlough—"an *Oasis* in the life of a Soldier," in the words of Sergeant Isaac Plumb—induced many.[48]

For a regiment to qualify for a furlough, the government required that three fourths of its members, present and absent, reenlist. Approximately 28,000 veterans extended their terms of enlistment, with the majority going home on leave during January and February. Lieutenant John Willoughby of the 5th Pennsylvania Reserves explained his decision to reenlist: "For myself I think I will return. Not that I hold a position or that I like soldiering but my country needs me and while the present rebellion exists. Then, with what honor could a man say I am an American, were the South allowed to secede. We *must* we *can* and we will whip her to submission." For those who refused to sign up, they would, if they survived, leave the army in the spring and summer.[49]

George Meade went on leave in mid-January and was away for a month. In his absence, John Sedgwick, the senior corps commander, held temporary command. He complained about the paperwork, "redtapism," and it seems that Chief of Staff Andrew Humphreys ran the army. When he initially assumed the position, Humphreys suffered daily with headaches, but they disappeared over time. Like Meade, he had a fearful temper, but associates and fellow staff members found him to be "an extremely gentlemanly man." No officer in the army enjoyed Meade's confidence more than Humphreys, who craved command of a corps.[50]

Winfield Scott Hancock returned to the army in January, not fully recovered from his Gettysburg wound. Before he came back, stories swirled that he was a possible successor to Meade. Hancock wrote to Meade, assuring him: "I am no aspirant, and I never could be a conspirator, had I other feelings toward you than I possess. I would sooner command a corps under you than have the supreme command. I have faith in you. . . . I have always served faithfully, so I intend to do."[51]

The news that shocked the army was the death of John Buford. He had taken a leave, suffering from fatigue and dysentery. While in Washington, he most likely contracted typhoid fever, and his condition deteriorated until his death on December 16, 1863. No one in the Cavalry Corps measured up to this excellent horse soldier. Whether dismounted or mounted, his men fought with a grittiness reflective of him. Although he appeared rough on the edges, he was a quiet and unassuming man, who, unlike Alfred Pleasonton, had little time for newspaper reporters and self-aggrandizement. Upon learning of his death, an officer stated, "He was decidedly the best cavalry general we had."[52]

Meade rejoined the army in mid-February, in time to become embroiled in a scheme concocted by another cavalry officer. Judson Kilpatrick had secured the approval of Abraham Lincoln to lead a cavalry raid into Richmond to free Union prisoners confined in Libby Prison and on Belle Isle in the James River. Pleasonton opposed the operation, but Meade acceded to Lincoln's desire. Kilpatrick's plan was myopic at the least, harebrained at the worst.[53]

Kilpatrick's 4,000-man raiding force never came close to the center of Richmond, or to liberating the captives. Repulsed by Confederate defenders, the Yankees lost more than three hundred men and five hundred horses. Among the Union dead was Colonel Ulric Dahlgren, son of Admiral John Dahlgren and one of Meade's former staff officers, who had had his right leg amputated below the knee from an earlier wound. The young officer had been killed in an ambush, and as Southerners examined his body, they discovered papers that allegedly outlined a plot to burn the city and to assassinate President Jefferson Davis and Confederate government officials.[54]

Richmond newspapers published the purported documents, igniting a storm of protest across the South about the perfidious Yankees. Robert E. Lee wrote to Meade, inquiring if they "were authorized, sanctioned or approved." Meade and the Federal administration denied their authenticity. In a letter to his wife, Meade described the affair as "a pretty ugly piece of business." Although Kilpatrick denied knowledge of Dahlgren's plan, the papers were genuine and the evidence indicates Kilpatrick's approval, if not initiation of the plot. Meade doubted the cavalry general's denial. Afterward, an officer called Kilpatrick "a frothy braggart without brains and not overstocked with desire to fall on the field." He predicted, "Kill has rather dished himself."[55]

Before the Dahlgren controversy broke, Meade traveled to Washington to testify before the Joint Committee on the Conduct of the War, whose members had undertaken investigations into the Chancellorsville and Gettysburg campaigns. The Radical Republicans in Congress believed that the army remained in the grip of "McClellanism" or in opposition to the government's policy of abolition and harsh prosecution of the war. In Meade, they saw a political conservative who seemed reluctant to engage the enemy. The Radicals' ulterior motive behind the hearings was to enhance the reputation of Joseph Hooker, a favorite of committee members, and to condemn Meade. In their minds, they wanted to ferret out generals with questionable patriotism, if not outright disloyalty.[56]

A host of generals followed Meade before the committee. Daniel Sickles and Abner Doubleday gave the most censorious testimony against Meade's actions at Gettysburg. For Sickles, it was a matter of deflecting criticism from his own conduct there and at Chancellorsville. Alfred Pleasonton and David Birney, a division commander under Sickles, supported the one-legged general. Humphreys, Hancock, and Warren endorsed Meade's performance and faulted Hooker at Chancellorsville. The hearings lasted into April, and in the end made John Sedgwick the scapegoat for Chancellorsville and stained Meade's reputation.[57]

No other Union army underwent such political scrutiny as did the Army of the Potomac. Self-serving politicians decried its failures, questioned the loyalty of its senior officers, and gave credence to the opinions of individuals who enjoyed the politicians' favor. Military operations were framed against the suspected political views of the army commanders, rather than against realities on battlefields or in movements. Weeks after Gettysburg, artillery chief Henry Hunt grumbled to his wife about the impact of such political interference and suspicions. "No army operating near Washington can be wholly successful, it is absolute impossibility."[58]

A SPECIAL TRAIN FROM Washington arrived at the camps of the Army of the Potomac on March 10, 1864. Rain fell as Lieutenant General Ulysses Grant stepped down from a car. "I was a stranger to most of the Army of the Potomac," wrote Grant in his memoirs, "I might say to all except the officers of the regular army who had served in the Mexican War." In fact, Grant was a stranger even to those who knew him well. His most trusted subordinate, William Sherman, confessed of his friend, "To me he is a mystery, and I believe he is a mystery to himself."[59]

On the day before he visited the army, Grant had received his commission of lieutenant general in a White House ceremony. Congress had authorized the rank, which was comparable to that held by George Washington, and Lincoln had appointed him general-in-chief of all Union forces. Earlier in the conflict, when criticism arose of Grant's generalship, Lincoln declared to a friend, *"I can't spare this man; he fights."* It was this attribute of Grant's and his string of unmatched victories in the West—forts Henry and Donelson, Shiloh, Vicksburg, and Chattanooga—that brought him the appointment. When Lincoln was assured that Grant had no political ambitions for the 1864 presidential election, he endorsed the creation of the rank.[60]

It would have been unfathomable, perhaps, to his former comrades in the antebellum army to have countenanced the idea in the spring of 1861 that Grant would eventually be the man at the pinnacle of the military hierarchy. A West Pointer, Grant had left the army in the 1850s with a reputation for alcoholic intemperance. Between then and the conflict's outbreak, he failed at various endeavors. But the war freed him, for he had an aptitude, if not genius, for the terrible trade of a soldier.[61]

When a member of Meade's staff met Grant, he remarked, "He habitually wears an expression as if he had determined to drive his head through a brick wall, and was about to do it." It was this inner core of "cold steel" that marked Grant. He saw warfare in unvarnished terms and was a relentless foe who understood and accepted that fighting meant killing. In even the worst of circumstances Grant seemed wrapped in an inner calmness, which braced men around him. Having watched Grant, a woman in the capital noted perceptively, "he walked through a crowd as though solitary."[62]

Grant lacked a commanding physical presence or magnetism. Of medium height, he eschewed glittering uniforms, walked stoop-shouldered as if he were downwind of a gale, constantly chewed on or smoked a cigar, and was reticent and unassuming. His friend Sherman explained to a fellow officer the difference between Grant and himself and many other generals: "I am a great deal smarter man than Grant; I see things more quickly than he does. I know more about law, and history, and war, and nearly everything else than he does; but I'll tell you where he beats me and where he beats the world. He don't care a damn for what he can't see the enemy doing, and it scares me like hell!"[63]

Months earlier, Margaret Meade had asked her husband about Grant. Meade responded that in Mexico Grant had been "considered a clever young officer, but nothing extraordinary." Meade thought, "his great characteristic is indomitable energy and great tenacity of purpose." Grant, however, had faced Confederates who "have never had in any of their Western armies either the generals or the troops they have had in Virginia, nor has the country been so favorable for them there as here." Meade admitted, "Grant has undoubtedly shown very superior abilities, and is I think justly entitled to all the honors they propose to bestow upon him."[64]

When Grant arrived, then, at Brandy Station, on March 10, the two former comrades in Mexico met for the first time in years. The private conversation between them was cordial and straightforward, befitting each man. Expecting that Grant might want "his own man in command," Meade offered to step aside and would be willing to "serve to the best of his ability wherever placed." "I assured him," Grant recounted, "that I had no thought of substituting any one for him." "This incident," stated Grant, "gave me even a more favorable opinion of Meade than did his great victory at Gettysburg the July before."[65]

During their meeting, Grant indicated that he would have his headquarters with the army. Originally, Grant had planned on remaining in the West, but changed his mind once he came to Washington. "It was plain," he explained later, "that here was the point for the commanding general to be. No one else could, probably, resist the pressure that would be brought to bear upon him to desist from his own plans and pursue others."[66]

Grant's presence with the army meant that he, not Meade, would direct its movements. Writing about the arrangement within days of their meeting, Meade told his wife, "So that you may look now for the Army of the Potomac putting laurels on the brows of another rather than your husband." In his memoirs, Grant admitted, "Meade's position afterwards proved embarrassing to me if not to him." For the present, however, their relationship could hardly have begun on a more favorable basis. "I intend to give him heartiest co-operation," stated Meade of Grant.[67]

Grant left the next day, returning to Tennessee to organize command arrangements for spring operations. While he was away, the army underwent its first major reorganization since September 1862, when John Pope's Army of Virginia had been incorporated into it. It had been contemplated and discussed for weeks.[68]

When Meade had returned from leave in mid-February, he had

stopped in Washington, where he met with Secretary of War Stanton. As Meade recounted their conversation, Stanton told him, "there were several officers in my army that did not have the confidence of the country, and that I was injuring myself by retaining them." Meade replied that he did not know who they were, but he would not object if Stanton wanted "to retire them."[69]

On March 23, the War Department announced the reorganization in General Orders No. 115. "By direction of the President of the United States," the army's five infantry corps were reduced to three. The units comprising the First and the Third corps were distributed among the Second, Fifth, and Sixth corps. In an order dated the next day, Meade assigned the First and Second divisions of the Third Corps to the Second Corps and the Third Division to the Sixth Corps. He consolidated the three divisions of the First Corps into two and transferred them to the Fifth Corps. Meade allowed the officers and men of each dissolved corps to retain "their badges and distinctive marks."[70]

The reaction of members of the First and Third corps to the changes ranged from sullen acceptance to open protest. In the Third Corps, officers held an "indignation meeting," and a group of soldiers erected a headstone in a "mock cemetery." They considered themselves the "Old Guard of the Potomac," attributing their dissolution to Meade's dislike of Daniel Sickles, their popular former commander. The veterans of the First Corps, which had been Joseph Hooker's and then John Reynolds's, evidently voiced less opposition. Chief of Staff Andrew Humphreys admitted, however, that when the two corps "were merged in other organizations their identity was lost and their pride and *esprit de corps* wounded."[71]

The disbandment of the two corps resulted in the removal of John Newton and William French, commanders of the First and Third, respectively. Almost assuredly, Stanton wanted to rid the army of both of these generals. A Virginian, Newton held political views that grated on Stanton and the Radical Republicans and had proven to be neither able nor popular as a corps commander. French merited removal as a despised and incompetent commander. One of his division commanders, David Birney, called him a "besotted, nervous, whimsical, irritable jealous old fossil."[72]

The command change that surprised the army occurred in the Fifth Corps, where Gouverneur Warren replaced George Sykes. Although a cautious, even plodding general, Sykes had been a dependable corps commander since his appointment before Gettysburg. A staff officer conjectured that he had been succeeded because the administration "disliked his rough manners." Sykes had been afflicted with health problems, but his performance had not warranted his dismissal. In the judgment of historian John Hennessy, Sykes "represented a significant and lamented loser in the reorganization."[73]

Meade resisted successfully Stanton's desire to transfer Sixth Corps commander John Sedgwick, a general who had been a McClellan loyalist. But Meade consented to Stanton's and Grant's decision to remove cavalry commander Alfred Pleasonton. According to Meade, the secretary of war had wanted Pleasonton gone from the army since June 1863. The general-in-chief had concluded that the army needed a more aggressive officer to lead the mounted units. The War Department relieved Pleasonton on March 25, and on April 4, announced the appointment of Philip H. Sheridan.[74]

Grant had come to know Sheridan during the Chattanooga Campaign, in which his infantry division stormed Missionary Ridge. The thirty-three-year-old Irish-American possessed the fiery temperament and energy Grant sought. He was preeminently a man of action. Standing barely five feet, three inches tall, Sheridan looked like the stump of a large oak tree set on sawed-off legs. A soldier described him as "the little man who rode so large a horse." But ambition burned within him, a relentless drive, much like Grant's, that he would bring to the cavalry corps.[75]

Except for Sheridan's appointment, the reorganization had been announced by the time Grant rejoined the army during the final week of March. For the next five weeks activity in the army quickened in preparation for the forthcoming spring campaign. Drills increased, and reviews were held. "We are stripping for work, and we anticipate plenty of it," wrote a colonel. In mid-April, Grant ordered sutlers out of the army and ceased the distribution of mail to the men, sure signs of an impending movement.[76]

On April 29, Major General Ambrose Burnside and the Ninth

Corps arrived, having been brought east from Tennessee. Since Burnside outranked Meade by seniority, Grant assigned the corps as an independent command, with Burnside reporting directly to him. The corps contained eighteen new regiments, and its Fourth Division consisted of 7,000 United States Colored Troops (USCT), the first unit of freedmen and former slaves to be associated with the Army of the Potomac. With Burnside's 19,000 officers and men, Grant had under him 119,000 "present for duty equipped."[77]

As general-in-chief, Grant had the responsibility for the entire Union war effort. He designated May 4 as the beginning of an offensive not only in Virginia but also in the Confederate heartland. In the West William Sherman would advance from Chattanooga against the Confederate Army of Tennessee, pushing toward Atlanta, Georgia, the region's railroad center. Grant expected Sherman to break up the Southern army and to destroy the enemy's logistical resources.[78]

In Virginia, meanwhile, the Federal offensive would consist of a three-prong thrust. One force, under Major General Franz Sigel, would advance up the Shenandoah Valley, while a second component, led by Major General Benjamin F. Butler, would move up the James River, and occupy Bermuda Hundred, a wedge of land between Richmond and Petersburg. If Sigel and Butler were successful, they would either damage or sever Lee's supply lines, forcing the Confederate general either to attack one of the Union columns or retreat to Richmond. For the Army of the Potomac, Grant put it bluntly to Meade: "Lee's army will be your objective point. Wherever Lee goes, there you will go also."[79]

"The art of war is simple enough," Grant stated later. "Find out where your enemy is. Get at him as soon as you can. Strike at him as hard as you can and as often as you can, and keep on moving." To Grant, it meant not a series of bloody engagements, but the application of implacable pressure upon one's opponent by maneuver. It also meant there would be no turning back regardless of the costs or reversals.[80]

Abraham Lincoln had been advocating such a strategy for a long time—the simultaneous convergence of the Union's superior reservoir of manpower upon various points of the Confederacy. When he and Grant met privately for the first time, he remarked to the general, as Grant recounted his words: "he had never professed to be a military man or to know how campaigns should be conducted, and never wanted to interfere in them: but that procrastination on the part of the commanders, and the pressure from the people at the North and Congress, *which was always* with him," had forced him to intervene. Lincoln had wanted only a commander who would "take the responsibility and act, and call on him for all the assistance needed."[81]

On April 30, before the operations began, Lincoln repeated these sentiments in a letter to Grant, writing: "The particulars of your plans I neither know, or seek to know. You are vigilant and self-reliant; and, pleased with this, I wish not to obtrude any constraints or restraints upon you." Both men knew, however, that the Northern people expected decisive action, particularly in Virginia against Lee. The president might espouse a willingness not to interfere, but his fate in the fall presidential election was inexorably linked to the outcome of Grant's campaigns. Lincoln ended his letter with these words: "If there is any thing wanting which is within my power to give, do not fail to let me know it. And now with a brave Army, and a just cause, may God sustain you."[82]

The heaviest burden—the central focus of Northerners' attention—rested upon the Army of the Potomac. Preparations for the campaign had been completed. A confidence in themselves and adherence to the cause infused the ranks. They liked what they had seen of Grant, but "we were inclined to wait and see," said a lieutenant. They knew that beyond the Rapidan River were "Bobby" Lee and his redoubtable legions. "Gen. Grant will have to remember," professed an Ohio officer, "that the best army of the Confederacy is in front of him commanded by one, if not the best, General on the Continent of America."[83]

They had no illusions about what lay ahead of them. "If Gen. Grant does as we expect him to that is Fight," asserted a New Yorker, "and I think he will give us enough of that article to suit most of us." A Pennsylvanian predicted, "we shall see this war ended this fall eather by the point of the Bayonet or the Election." A soldier in the 24th Michigan thought similarly, "you may be assured that there will be some big fighting here. . . . I now think it will crush the rebellion if we are victorious, and if we get whipped our government will be lost." Colonel Rufus Dawes of the 6th Wisconsin worried about something different. "I cannot deny that I never dreaded the battlefield as I do this spring."[84]

Chapter 15

"This War Is Horrid"

THE DAY REVELED IN LIFE, from the warmth of the air to the abundance of purple violets. In Virginia, May 4, 1864, was a "lovely spring day." For members of the Union Army of the Potomac and the Confederate Army of Northern Virginia, it was a time to be on the march along familiar roads. A shared destination lay ahead, a place beyond a divide, where the darkest of dreams became an unrelenting nightmare.[1]

May 4 marked the beginning of the forty-day Overland Campaign. When it ended, nothing that had come before compared to it—not Antietam, not Fredericksburg, not even Gettysburg. Death hung in the air, day and night, night and day, at the Wilderness, Spotsylvania Court House, North Anna and Cold Harbor. "We never knew what war was till this spring," professed a Union veteran. Fellow Yankees called it "a life struggle" and a "funeral procession."[2]

While they suffered through the ordeal, men's descriptions of it reveal the magnitude of the fighting and carnage. An officer thought it had begun "a half-year ago," when it had only been eleven days. "Many a man has gone crazy," claimed a captain, while a Massachusetts private asserted, "All of us see the frail threads that our lives hang on upon more vividly day by day." They began letters home with simple affirmations: "I just live, father, and this is about all"; "Still alive"; "Still in existence." After one of the worst days, the 7th Indiana's Captain Alexander B. Pattison recorded a prayer in his dairy: "Father spare us from more sorrows. For our griefs are more than we can bear."[3]

When it was over, the Overland Campaign "left a permanent imprint on the face of warfare and constituted a watershed in the accommodation of military doctrine to technology," in historian Gordon Rhea's judgment. Opposing lines of fieldworks scarred the land as never before, turning the ground into slaughterhouses. During this transformation, this refinement in killing, the two great armies that had met at Antietam, Fredericksburg, and Gettysburg died. Although his words applied to his army, they could have been for his foes' when Colonel Joshua Chamberlain asked at the campaign's end, "Is this identity a thing of substance, or spirit, or of name only?"[4]

But it began on a day brimming with life. The infantry and artillery units had begun the march after midnight, moving toward Ely's and Germanna fords on the Rapidan River. General-in-Chief Ulysses Grant and army commander George Meade's plan was to pass beyond Robert E. Lee's right flank, to clear the Wilderness, where Joseph Hooker had suffered defeat at Chancellorsville a year ago, and to meet the enemy on open ground with their numerically superior army. By moving along this flank, Grant could supply the army's gargantuan appetite for supplies by the Potomac River. The initial key for the Federals was to pass through the Wilderness before Lee's troops entangled them in another battle there.[5]

By the evening of May 4, the Second and Fifth corps had entered "the deeply hated Wilderness," with the Sixth and Ninth corps and the army's wagon train to the rear. A Fifth Corps captain recalled that upon their arrival: "All was quiet. An ominous silence was our only welcome." Convinced that Lee would keep his army behind its Mine Run works, Meade unwisely halted the march. But underestimating Lee was a dangerous proposition. At mid-afternoon reports came in that the Rebels were moving toward the Wilderness. That night at one campsite in the Wilderness, a Union soldier, using his bayonet, dug a skull of one of the Chancellorsville dead out of the ground and remarked to his comrades, "That is what you are all coming to, and some of you will start toward it tomorrow."[6]

The veteran's morbid prediction was approaching faster than he could have known. Before seven o'clock on the morning of May 5, Federal troops spotted enemy pickets to the west along Orange Turnpike. When Fifth Corps commander Gouverneur Warren received the unexpected news, he ordered Brigadier General Charles Griffin "to get ready to attack at once." Minutes later, a dispatch from Griffin reported the presence of Confederate infantry in line of battle and rising dust clouds behind them. Warren forwarded the information to Meade, suspended his divisions' planned marches, and directed Griffin to test the enemy's strength.[7]

The Confederates who were encountered belonged to the vanguard of Lieutenant General Richard Ewell's Second Corps. On Ewell's right, marching on Orange Plank Road, were the divisions of Lieutenant General A. P. Hill's Third Corps. Lee had decided to strike the Yankees in the Wilderness, thinking he could destroy a portion of Meade's army. At the least, an engagement in that forbidding terrain would negate the Federals' artillery superiority and lessen their numerical advantage. With the return of Lieutenant General James Longstreet's First Corps's two divisions from Tennessee, Lee had his entire army together, probably numbering more than 75,000 officers and men.[8]

When Meade received Warren's message about the enemy's appearance, he halted the advance of the Second and Sixth corps, just as Lee had hoped. Meade forwarded the information to Grant, who suggested, "If any opportunity presents itself of pitching into a part of Lee's army, do so without giving time for disposition." Then, a 10:15 A.M. dispatch came to army headquarters, announcing the approach of more Rebels— cavalry and Hill's infantry—on Orange Plank Road. Earlier, Meade had directed John Sedgwick's Sixth Corps to support Warren; now he ordered one of its divisions, George Getty's, to the intersection of the Plank Road and Brock Road, and redirected Winfield Hancock's Second Corps toward Getty's troops.[9]

Grant joined Meade about this time and, most likely, spurred his subordinate into taking decisive action. Meade sent orders for Warren to attack at once and for Sedgwick to hurry his advance. Getty's men won the race to the vital intersection by the narrowest of margins. It would be another two and a half hours, however, before Warren's divisions moved forward. As Grant was beginning to see, this army remained plagued with a cautious mind-set.[10]

Finally, at 1:00 P.M., Griffin's and Brigadier General James Wadsworth's Fifth Corps divisions advanced in an assault in the woods along Orange Turnpike. Both generals had resisted Warren's urgings to go forward until their flanks had been secured. Throughout the morning, their skirmishers had dueled with Ewell's veterans. During such exchanges, wrote a 27th Indiana private: "Muskets never seem to crack so loud and wicked as on the picket line when a great battle is expected. A few shots then sends the blood whirling to the fingertips of the whole army."[11]

On came the Yankees, and in the words of one of them, "suddenly these hitherto quiet woods seemed to be lifted up, shook, rent, and torn asunder." Within minutes, the reality of combat in this damnable region of stunted trees and thick underbrush gripped both armies. "It was," exclaimed a soldier, "a blind and bloody hunt to the death, in bewildering thickets, rather than a battle." Regiments and brigades stumbled into ambushes in the smoke-choked woods, as the musketry ignited fires in the matted leaves and brush. It rapidly became a place of "hell-like horrors . . . where desperate instinct replaced impossible tactics."[12]

For two hours, Getty's, Wadsworth's, and then Samuel Crawford's Fifth Corps veterans slugged it out with the battle-tested Southerners in major generals Edward Johnson's and Robert Rodes's divisions. A Fifth Corps officer described it as "a weird, uncanny contest—a battle of invisibles with invisibles." But they saw enough of each other for it to be, said a Confederate, "a butchery pure and simple." A Yankee likened the sound of the musketry to "one steady roar like Niagara." Ranks disappeared, knocked to the ground by point-blank volleys.[13]

Lieutenant Abner Small of the 16th Maine described the feelings of a man on a firing line. He was, Small wrote, "singularly" shocked by "the stiff disorder of the dead lying where they fell," but that shock soon gave way to indifference. "He resented it all, and at times his resentment grew into a hatred for those who forced the whirlpool of war—a whirlpool that had so soon engulfed him. He hated his surroundings and all that war implied." He knew it "was cruelty," but "always in front of him was the enemy, a something which, the more he thought of it, the more he hated; and as likely as not he never quite knew why."[14]

There was no better place to hate one's foe on this afternoon than at Saunders's Field, a four-hundred-yard by eight-hundred-yard opening in the Wilderness on both sides of Orange Turnpike. Here, some of the fiercest combat ebbed and flowed, until the Confederates pressed back Griffin's troops. When a Rebel counterattack splintered Wadsworth's ranks, the entire Federal line collapsed. For the first time in its history, the Union Iron Brigade broke and fled. The Yankees retreated two miles to the Lacy house, where they re-formed and began digging fieldworks. On their right, units of Sedgwick's Sixth Corps arrived and were pulled into the fury for more than an hour, incurring losses but gaining no ground.[15]

The combat shifted, meanwhile, to along Orange Plank Road, where George Getty's Sixth Corps brigades assailed Major General Henry Heth's Confederate division. Heth's 6,000 Rebels savaged Getty's ranks. On the Union left, the Vermont Brigade was forced to lie on the ground to survive the terrible musketry. "So many were at once shot down," recounted a Vermonter, "that it became plain that to advance was simply destruction." Brigadier General Gershom Mott's Second Corps division came up behind the Vermonters and plunged forward. Regiments became jammed, massing together Mott's two brigades. When the Rebels scorched them with volleys, the Federals broke and ran to the earthworks along Brock Road.[16]

By now, Hancock had arrived at the Brock Road–Orange Plank Road intersection. With the collapse of Mott's division, he ordered in David Birney's two brigades. The thin, pale, ascetic-looking Birney had been assigned to the Second Corps in the March reorganization. One of his brigade commanders was Alexander Hays, who had led the division at Gettysburg and until Birney came from the dissolved Third Corps. Minutes after Birney sent in his troops, Hays stopped to speak with his old regiment, the 63rd Pennsylvania, when a bullet struck him in the head. He lived for three hours. Hancock wrote later to his widow: "We never had a more fearless general and soldier than your husband, nor one whose power was more manifest among the troops on the field of battle."[17]

Heth's veterans, however, stopped Birney's thrust and drove toward Brock Road. Hancock committed John Gibbon's division, followed by Francis Barlow's advancing command. Gibbon's counterattack stopped Heth, whose men had reached their limits. With twelve brigades stacked in lines, Hancock ordered an assault. The Federals rolled ahead, shoving Heth's men rearward. To the west, A. P. Hill hurried forward Major General Cadmus Wilcox's division to bolster Heth's beleaguered ranks, who were clinging to a line of works, north and south of the Plank Road, against a succession of Union attacks.[18]

With the arrival of Wilcox's troops, the fighting escalated to an appalling intensity. "The roar of muskets became continuous," claimed a Southerner. On the Federal left, Barlow pressed hard against the enemy works. By now it was getting dark, which only added to the confusion and fearfulness of the combat. "The very trees seemed peopled by spirits that shrieked and groaned through those hours of combat," recalled a Second Corps staff officer. At points in the woods, the opposing lines were only "a biscuit's toss" away. Then, as if by common consent, the shooting ceased.[19]

Before Hancock's final assault went forward, Grant directed Meade to order Sedgwick and Warren to renew their attacks. Sedgwick managed to send forward two brigades, which ran into a blizzard of musketry, incurred casualties, and retired. Warren refused to undertake a frontal charge. He ordered two of Wadsworth's brigades toward Hill's left flank, but as they stumbled through the woods, a battalion of Alabamians, screaming their yell, surprised the Federals and scattered hundreds of them. Wadsworth's foray ended.[20]

Both armies endured a "hideous" night. Most troops slept where they had been when the fighting stopped, amid the dead and wounded. The fires kindled during the afternoon fed upon the evening breeze and spread through the underbrush, trapping wounded men within their flames. The horror of the unfortunate men's screams and of the smell of burning flesh could only have elicited images of hell. A New Jersey soldier recalled, however, that it seemed "as if every twig held a whip-poor-will, and as if each one vied with all the rest in the rapidity of the peculiar call."[21]

That night, Grant began to bend the army to his will. He had wit-

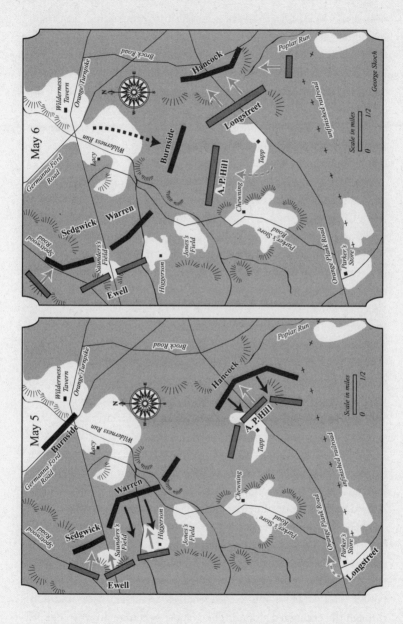

nessed the lack of aggressiveness among the army's senior leadership, including Meade. He would impose aggressiveness on them by taking the tactical initiative. While Sedgwick and Warren held Ewell's troops in place along the turnpike, Hancock would launch a frontal assault with the Second Corps on the Plank Road. Wadsworth's Fifth Corps division would advance south against Hill's left flank, supported by two divisions from Burnside's Ninth Corps, which had crossed the Rapidan. Meade conferred with the corps commanders, and he and Grant settled on a 5:00 A.M. advance.[22]

Minutes before 5:00 A.M., May 6, a signal gun broke the silence, and more than 30,000 Federals stepped forth. Hancock had his and Getty's Sixth Corps units stacked in four lines, while to their right, Wadsworth, with four brigades, came on at an angle. Up the Plank Road, Heth's and Wilcox's men were stirring, waiting for the promised arrival of Longstreet's First Corps troops. Suddenly, in front of them, musketry from thousands of rifles exploded. Caught unprepared, Heth's and Wilcox's veterans could not withstand such a powerful attack and began streaming to the rear. Some Confederate regiments resisted until nearly overrun on both flanks.[23]

Lee's entire right flank had disintegrated, except for a dozen cannon, whose crews were working the pieces as fast as they could. But the Union offensive stalled along the eastern edge of a large field on the Widow Tapp's farm. Then, in one of the war's dramatic scenes, there appeared the van of Longstreet's troops, coming down the Plank Road. Lee rode into their midst to hurry them forward. Longstreet deployed major generals Charles Field's and Joseph Kershaw's divisions into a heavy skirmish formation and sent them in. The famed Texas Brigade refused to advance until Lee went to the rear and safety.[24]

The Confederates unleashed a volley, which "seemed to shake the earth itself." The Yankees staggered, reeled, and then broke under the unexpected counterattack. A Maine veteran claimed that the musketry was "one of the most destructive fires I was ever under." The Federals rallied, and charges and countercharges stumbled back and forth through the entangled ground. The volume of gunfire drowned out officers' shouted commands. On the Union right, the Southerners hit Wadsworth's flank, shattering the enemy ranks, while on Hancock's left, the Vermont Brigade made a valiant stand as comrades from other units fled to the rear.[25]

Longstreet's counterattack had saved Lee's army from a looming defeat, but after two hours of fighting, its force was spent. During this interlude, a Confederate engineer officer scouted an unfinished railroad bed, which led past the Union left flank. Longstreet assigned four brigades to the assault force. At eleven o'clock, the Rebels barreled into the left flank of Hancock's frayed lines. North of the Plank Road, Longstreet resumed his attack.[26]

Hancock's flank collapsed in "a general skedaddle." What had begun so auspiciously for the Federals six hours earlier now became a struggle for the army's position along Brock Road, where the shattered units fled and began to re-form. James Wadsworth rode into ranks of his men, tried to rally them, and was mortally wounded by a bullet in the head. The wealthy New Yorker and popular general had had his finest day at Gettysburg on July 1, 1863. To the south, confused Confederate troops fired a volley into Longstreet's mounted party, seriously wounding Lee's senior general. Longstreet's fall—ironically, not far from Stonewall Jackson's fatal wounding a year ago—drained the impetus from the Southern attacks, and another pause in the fierce combat ensued.[27]

While the fighting raged along the Plank Road, the situation on Orange Turnpike remained stable. As on May 5, neither Warren nor Sedgwick was willing to assault Ewell's works. A Union soldier said any attack would have been "next to madness." Sedgwick tested the Rebel lines with a single brigade, which resulted in a bloody repulse. When informed of the outcome, Meade halted further attempts in this sector.[28]

Burnside's Ninth Corps, meanwhile, had come onto the battlefield, but hours behind schedule. "Burnside somehow is never up to the mark when the tug comes," grumbled an officer. A road clogged with wagons, batteries, and stragglers, however, had slowed their march. Nevertheless, Burnside acted without urgency to bring his units into position between Warren's left flank and Hancock's right flank. Had the Ninth Corps been in line on time, it would have supported Wadsworth's troops during Longstreet's assault. Instead, one of its brigades was mauled when the Rebels struck at eleven o'clock, and in mid-afternoon a division gained some ground before being stopped. A member of one of Burnside's new regiments confessed, "The glories of war were lost in its sickening sights."[29]

Like Grant, Lee was an unrelenting warrior when he believed he had an opponent on the edge. At four o'clock, emitting "a womanlike scream," the Rebels charged toward the Federal works at Brock Road. The Southerners came on, in the words of a Yankee, "seeming confident that they would carry everything before them." From behind the log breastworks, the Northerners triggered waves of volleys. Still, the enemy pressed to within thirty yards of the roadbed. Then, along a section of the works, the underbrush ignited, its flames hopping over the logs and driving away its defenders. Brigadier General J. H. Hobart Ward jumped on a limber chest, shouting to the driver "to drive like Hell" to the rear. A few days later, Ward was transferred from the army.[30]

South Carolinians poured into the gap, appearing like "so many devils through the flames." Directly to the rear, a line of Union cannon stood, and their crews blasted the Rebels with canister. Union infantry reserves rushed to seal the breach, clubbing the Southerners out of the works in a hand-to-hand melee. This repulse ended the Confederate assault. To the north, Burnside sent in two brigades, which scattered enemy units until Rebel reinforcements stopped the Federal advance. The fearful struggle for Brock Road brought an end to the fighting on this section of the battlefield.[31]

At the far end of the Union line beyond Orange Turnpike, the combat on this fiendish battlefield had one final spasm of killing and maiming. Three Confederate brigades struck the right flank of the Sixth Corps, shattering one Union brigade and shoving back a second. For several minutes, it appeared as if the Yankees' flank would be swept away, but Sedgwick personally rallied the fleeing troops and Brigadier General Thomas Neill's regiments stood firm and blunted the enemy attack. Trying to re-form their ranks, brigadiers Truman Seymour and Alexander Shaler were captured by the Rebels.[32]

"This war is horrid," a Union surgeon wrote in his diary on May 6. Two days of combat had resulted in 17,600 Federals killed, wounded, and captured, and nearly 11,000 Confederate casualties. Unknown numbers of wounded had been burned to death. The fighting had been a savage struggle in a landscape that fed men's natural fears. If war seemed like a passage through hell, this place was on the route. A Vermont private said that he and his comrades called it "a wilderness of woe."[33]

To Grant, the battle was the first in what he envisioned as a series of engagements with Lee, whose generalship and combative spirit impressed the Union commander. As Grant saw it, however, Meade's army had squandered opportunities to inflict serious damage on the enemy because of vacillating generalship. Neither Meade nor any of the corps commanders had measured up. A deeply ingrained attitude—a legacy of George McClellan—to avoid losing instead of seeking ways to win governed the actions of the army's leadership. Grant tried to create circumstances that resulted in outcomes. Meade and his generals, wanting control, allowed Lee to dictate actions.[34]

If Grant were to exorcise this debilitating method of command, he had to grab more direct control of operations. Grant and Meade could gaze down a similar road and see different destinations. Since 1862, the army's commanders, including Meade, had rarely looked beyond the immediate battlefield, but Grant measured the present against the future. According to historian Gordon Rhea, Grant's "ill-conceived" and "cumbersome" chain of command had been strained during the battle. He had placed Meade in a difficult position, but for Grant to put his imprint upon the army, he would have to diminish Meade's role.[35]

On the night of May 6, an unidentified general came to army headquarters to warn Grant and Meade that Lee would try to outflank the army and cut it off from the Rapidan. The habitually reserved Grant responded firmly to the general: "Oh, I am heartily tired of hearing about what Lee is going to do. Some of you always seem to think he is suddenly going to turn a double somersault, and land in our rear and on both of our flanks at the same time. Go back to your command, and try to think what we are going to do ourselves, instead of what Lee is going to do."[36]

By early on the morning of May 7, Grant had concluded that Lee would retreat south. At 6:30 A.M., he instructed Meade to "make all preparations during the day for a night march to take a position at Spotsylvania Court House." As Grant explained it later, "I wanted to get between his [Lee's] army and Richmond if possible; and, if not, to draw him into the open field." At 3:00 P.M., Meade issued the orders, specifying the routes for each corps. Grant was acting with an audacity that Lee understood.[37]

On the lines in the Wilderness, heated clashes between skirmishers characterized the action on May 7. Both armies probed the other's lines to get indications of a possible movement. Late in the day, Lee surmised that the Yankees were heading toward Spotsylvania. About seven o'clock, Lee directed Major General Richard Anderson, now commanding the First Corps in place of Longstreet, to march after nightfall. Lee wanted him to allow the men a few hours' sleep, but he had to resume the movement by 3:00 A.M., on May 8.[38]

A critical action occurred on this day south of the main armies at Todd's Tavern, between opposing mounted forces. Since the Federals had crossed the Rapidan, Philip Sheridan's horsemen had been guarding wagons and roaming along the army's left flank. Sheridan's and Meade's relationship had been adversarial from the time Sheridan assumed command of the cavalry. Both men had short fuses, and Sheridan had chafed under Meade's restrictive control. In turn, Meade regarded the cavalryman as an interloper from the West because of Grant.[39]

Meade unfettered Sheridan on May 7, instructing him to secure Brock Road as far south as possible. One day earlier George Custer's Michigan Brigade had fought a spirited engagement with Thomas Rosser's Confederates along the road. Now, Sheridan headed farther south to Todd's Tavern, where Catharpin Road intersected with Brock Road. Here, two Yankee divisions encountered Fitzhugh Lee's mounted division. From mid-morning until dark the foes battled. "Off and on we drove them and they us," wrote a Virginia trooper. At the end, although pressing Lee down Brock Road, Sheridan retired to Todd's Tavern, relinquishing control of a mile of the direct route to Spotsylvania. Meade was furious when he discovered Sheridan's troopers at Todd's Tavern.[40]

BURNING PINE KNOTS AND LEAVES tinted in amber the intense darkness of the night at the intersection of Orange Turnpike and Brock Road. Casting shadows against the fiery light, files of Union soldiers plodded to the crossroads and turned south on Brock Road. "The men seemed aged," thought a watching artillerist. "They were very tired and very hungry. They seemed to be greatly depressed." From the trailing column on Orange Turnpike arose a murmur of expectation as Grant and Meade and their staffs clattered past the marchers toward the crossroads. When Grant turned his mount into Brock Road, the troops shouted, "On to Richmond!" and threw their hats into the air.[41]

The generals and their aides tried to silence the demonstration lest it alert the enemy. But these men had been waiting too long for a general who would not turn back. George McClellan, Ambrose Burnside, Joseph Hooker, and, arguably, George Meade would not have led the army down a road to another battlefield. In the blackness of the night, amid the stench of carnage, accompanied by the clamor of voices, the army marched away from the past. They had no illusions about what lay ahead, but it was ahead, and that was what mattered. "I do not know that during the entire war," declared a soldier, "I had such a real feeling of delight and satisfaction as in the night when we came to the road leading to Spotsylvania Court House and turned to the right."[42]

Grant's plan for a rapid night march, however, unraveled from the troops' exhaustion, jammed roads, and inherent confusion in such a movement. When the van of Gouverneur Warren's Fifth Corps reached Todd's Tavern, Union cavalry barred the road. An irate Meade came up and started the troopers down Brock Road, where the resistance of Confederate troopers slowed the march. Finally, about 7:30 A.M., on May 8, Warren's infantry approached Laurel Hill, about a mile and a half northwest of Spotsylvania Court House. The Yankees, however, had lost the race.[43]

On Laurel Hill, Richard Anderson's Southerners were digging in when the Yankees appeared. Instead of allowing his men to sleep, Anderson had marched them all night because of the fires in the woods and the stench of death along the road. When Warren saw the enemy building fieldworks, he decided to attack them before they had completed the line. Warren ordered in Brigadier General John Robinson's division, followed by Charles Griffin's three brigades.[44]

Anderson's veterans and artillery batteries tore apart the attackers' ranks. Robinson suffered a leg wound, and his troops fled in a rout.

Behind them, Griffin's men charged, were blasted back, and fled precipitately. Warren then brought up Samuel Crawford's Pennsylvania Reserve Division and his fellow brigadier Lysander Cutler's brigades. These Federals advanced about 10:30 A.M., but they lacked spirit. The two days in the Wilderness had decimated their ranks and weakened morale. The Pennsylvanians' terms of enlistment were up within weeks, and survival meant more to them than needless sacrifice. To their right, the redoubtable Iron Brigade "got sort of panicky," noted a member, "(for the first time in our Brigade's history)." These fighters were reaching their limit.[45]

About 2:30 P.M., the Sixth Corps began arriving on the field and extended Warren's line eastward. Meade had ordered John Sedgwick to join Warren "in a prompt and vigorous attack on the enemy." By seniority, Sedgwick should have directed the two corps's assault, but Meade did not want to place Warren in a subordinate position. Instead, Meade told Warren to cooperate with Sedgwick. "General Meade," Warren shot back, "I'll be damned if I'll cooperate with Sedgwick or anybody else. You are the commander of this army and can give your orders and I will obey them; or you can put Sedgwick in command and he can give the orders and I will obey them; or you can put me in command and I will give the orders and Sedgwick will obey them; but I'll be God damned if I'll cooperate with General Sedgwick or anybody else."[46]

Grant joined Meade about 4:30 P.M., and together they surveyed the Confederate line on Laurel Hill. To one of Meade's aides, Grant appeared to be angry when neither Warren nor Sedgwick could specify a time for the attack. Earlier, Grant had sent a dispatch to Washington, writing in it, "the best of feeling prevails in this army, and I feel at present no apprehension for the result." He had expected to be beyond Spotsylvania Court House at day's end, moving to unite with Benjamin Butler's army below Richmond. Lee, however, had countered his move, and Meade's army seemed incapable of doing anything with alacrity and aggressiveness.[47]

Two hours later, under Meade's personal direction, units of the Fifth and Sixth corps moved to the attack. From Laurel Hill, "deafening musketry and a dense volume of smoke rolled up." Then as the Federals drove toward Anderson's right flank, Robert Rodes's Confederate division swung around the flank and charged the Yankees. The Northerners recoiled, and except for isolated fighting, the assault ended in retreat and confusion. Nightfall brought welcome sleep for most men in both armies.[48]

That night, Meade issued an order for the next day, "The army will remain quiet to-morrow, 9th instant, to give the men rest and to distribute ammunition and rations." He instructed corps commanders to "strengthen their positions by intrenchments." Hancock's Second Corps would close on the army's right, while Burnside's Ninth Corps extended its left farther to the east. Offensive operations had come to a halt from simple exhaustion.[49]

The killing and maiming did not cease on Monday, May 9—it never would in this campaign—but the day passed in relative quiet. It would have been an unremarkable day in the army's history except that at about 9:30 A.M., a Confederate sharpshooter killed John Sedgwick. Uncle John had been locating a battery. Minutes before, when a soldier had flinched from a bullet that whined past, Sedgwick remarked: "Why, what are you dodging for. They could not hit an elephant at that distance." Another bullet struck him under the left eye, and he crumpled into the arms of an aide, who fell to the ground with him.[50]

News of his death passed along the line of the Sixth Corps "like a flash," and "every person was stricken dumb." Colonel Charles Wainwright wrote, "'Uncle John' was loved by his men as no other corps commander ever was in this army." He had always put their welfare foremost, and it endeared them to him. He was equally popular among fellow generals. Sedgwick had been honest, loyal, and dutiful. He was not a great corps commander because he lacked fire. Caution marked his generalship, notably at Chancellorsville. But he was a man for whom the army deeply grieved, a fitting epitaph for a kind-spirited man.[51]

IN HIS DIARY, CORPORAL Arthur Wyman of the 59th New York recorded the name of the place as "Sponsey Crania burnt house." However Wyman or other men spelled it, they sensed that the nature of warfare had changed before them at Spotsylvania Court House. Frontal assaults in serried ranks against entrenchments of logs and dirt, manned by veteran troops, amounted to wholesale slaughter. Duty still impelled men to obey orders, but their acceptance of needless sacrifice was eroding amid the mounting carnage.[52]

Soldiers understood that death was never far away on a battlefield; it could come suddenly and randomly as it had to Uncle John Sedgwick. But it could come in a whirlwind of musketry and canister, engulfing entire units, sweeping away men's lives by the hundreds. Sending men across open ground against stout breastworks only invited the whirlwind. Writing of Spotsylvania, a veteran Union private declared in a letter, "I tell you that we old soldiers cant see *what good it will do us* for we are the ones to be killed off *first,* & it don't give us a fair chance for our lives."[53]

May 10 at Spotsylvania brought further proof that "a fair chance" for their lives was decreasing in such a landscape. Grant ordered additional attacks against the Confederate line, searching for weaknesses. By the morning of May 10, Lee had his entire army at hand in field-works that extended for more than four miles. At the center of Lee's line, engineers had laid out a salient, an inverted U that was three fourths of a mile deep and a half-mile wide, dubbed the "Mule Shoe." In front of the entrenchments, Lee's infantrymen and artillerists had open killing fields.[54]

The Union assaults went forth at Po River, on the Confederates' left flank, and at Laurel Hill. When the order was passed down to the men in the ranks for an attack, one of them recounted that they had "gloomy forebodings of disaster and death." The Yankees stepped out, and Southern rifles and cannon gouged holes in the lines. So intense was the fire that many attackers fell to the ground and began digging "glory holes." Many commands charged with valor, clung to the ground in the face of the brutal musketry and canister, and soaked the spring growth with their blood. "It seemed, indeed," stated Winfield Scott Hancock in his report, "that these gallant soldiers were devoted to destruction." That devotion, however, devoured men. A member of the Iron Brigade saw it differently from Hancock, asserting that it was "sure death to stand up there and a waste of powder to fire."[55]

Grant refused to abandon the costly attempts. In mid-afternoon, he approved an attack plan proposed by Colonel Emory Upton, a Sixth Corps brigade commander. The twenty-four-year-old Upton had been graduated from West Point in May 1861, had commanded the 121st New York, "Upton's Regulars," and had distinguished himself in combat. A fervent abolitionist, Upton was arrogant, ambitious, and intelligent. To him, the Federals could break through the enemy works only with a swift charge, with units stacked upon a narrow front. Once his lance of soldiers pierced the line, support troops could widen the breach and repulse counterattacks.[56]

George Meade assigned a dozen of the best regiments in the Sixth Corps to Upton and ordered Brigadier General Gershom Mott's Second Corps division to advance with Upton. The Union commanders targeted the western face of the salient for the assault. Through a misunderstanding and command failure, Mott advanced at five o'clock, his original appointed hour, suffered a quick repulse, and retired. No one informed Upton of Mott's abortive attack as he massed his twelve regiments—three regiments in each line, four lines deep—in woods. Scheduled to charge at six o'clock, Upton's force, roughly five thousand troops, did not go forward until twenty minutes later.[57]

"Not a word is spoken above a whisper in our ranks," wrote a Pennsylvanian as the men deployed. A New Yorker recalled the minutes before they charged: "I felt my gorge rise, and my stomach and intestines shrink together in a knot, and a thousand things rushed through my mind. I fully realized the terrible peril I was to encounter (gained from previous experience). I looked about in the faces of the boys around me, and they told the tale of expected death. Pulling my cap down over my eyes, I stepped out."[58]

When officers shouted, "Forward," the men cleared the trees on the run, yelling, with bayonets fixed. Less than two hundred yards away, their foes unleashed a volley, but orders were specific—do not stop to return fire. The first line of Yankees reached the works, blasted the Rebels, who "absolutely refused to yield," and hurled bayoneted rifles like spears. "Numbers prevailed," reported Upton, "and, like a resistless wave, the column poured over the works." The Northerners overran a second line of entrenchments and seized three cannon before Confederate reserves closed in on both flanks and in their front. Without support, Upton's troops could not withstand the counterattack of six enemy brigades. Grudgingly, they released their grip on the works and guns and retreated to the woods.[59]

Upton placed his losses at about 1,000, with Southern casualties exceeding 1,200, including nearly 1,000 prisoners. "Our officers and men accomplished all that could be expected of brave men," Upton stated in his report. Grant awarded him a battlefield commission of brigadier general for his performance. Upton's veterans reacted bitterly over the failure of support troops to come to their assistance. "When I got by myself where I would not be ashamed of it," confided Lieutenant Colonel Samuel E. Pingree of the 2nd Vermont in a letter, "I cried like a whipped spaniel—I saw many soldiers cry like girls, and many who took things less to heart, gave vent to their mortification at having lost all they had gained so nobly—by the fault of others, by letting off unnumbered salvos of profanity."[60]

Meade's army suffered an estimated 4,000 casualties on May 10, the worst single-day loss since the Wilderness. Brigadier General James C. Rice, a Fifth Corps brigade commander, had his leg shattered by a bullet and died after its amputation. A stray bullet killed Ninth Corps division commander Brigadier General Thomas G. Stevenson while he lay under a tree. A surgeon in Upton's former regiment professed to his wife: "I cannot even attempt to give you a *slight* idea of this field of death. All around you lie the unmistakable evidences that death is doing its most frightful work. The rebels fight like very devils! We have to fairly *club* them out of their rifle pits."[61]

Grant ceased offensive operations for May 11. In the morning, he sent a telegraph to Halleck, now chief of staff, stating, "The result to this time is much in our favor." Since the army had crossed the Rapidan, he calculated that it had sustained 20,000 casualties, but "I . . . propose to fight it out on this line if it takes all summer." The War Department made public Grant's declaration of resolve, which newspapers across the North printed.[62]

Grant surveyed Lee's lines during the day and then settled upon a grander version of Upton's attack scheme. He would crush the tip of the Mule Shoe salient with Hancock's entire Second Corps. Burnside's Ninth Corps would charge simultaneously against the salient's eastern face. Warren's Fifth Corps and the Sixth Corps, now commanded by Major General Horatio G. Wright, would be prepared either to advance or to shift units in support of the main assault. In his orders to Burnside, Grant made clear his intent: "You will move against the enemy with your entire force promptly and with all possible vigor." The general-in-chief scheduled the attack for 4:00 A.M., May 12.[63]

The assault required a redeployment of units and a night march by the Second Corps. A heavy rain slowed Hancock's men, who stumbled through the mud and darkness but started to file into position north of the salient by 12:30 A.M. Hancock arranged his four divisions in two lines, with one division behind another. A staff officer described it as a "solid rectangular mass of nearly 20,000 men." They remained the army's best combat troops, with three of its finest division commanders in John Gibbon, David Birney, and Francis Barlow. Ahead of them, through the rain and blackness, lay the 4,500-man Stonewall Division, whose proud record had begun on a July Sabbath at Bull Run in 1861.[64]

"A funeral like silence pervades the assembly," stated a Pennsylvanian, "and like specters the men in blue await the order to attack." Officers addressed their commands, telling them to "keep together as well as you can" and to carry the works at all hazards. Men shook hands and said their farewells. An aide remarked to his comrades: "Gentlemen, today may be for some of us the last on earth. Whilst we are waiting here would not be well to say a prayer?" They had a half-mile to cross before they reached the salient. Minutes past 4:30 A.M., the order, "Forward," passed down the ranks. Never before had the army launched such a powerful attack. And never before, nor again, would there be such a day in this war.[65]

Through the rain and fog the Yankees came, at common time and then in a headlong rush, shouting cheers. In the salient, the Southerners leveled their rifles, squeezed the triggers, but many of the weapons misfired because of wet powder. Within minutes, the Union avalanche flooded over the works "as if the devil had let loose." A frenzy of hand-to-hand combat ensued. "Men were so close their heads were at the end of gun muzzles as they shot each other," stated a defender. "When ammunition ran out or got wet they crushed each other's skulls with gun butts."

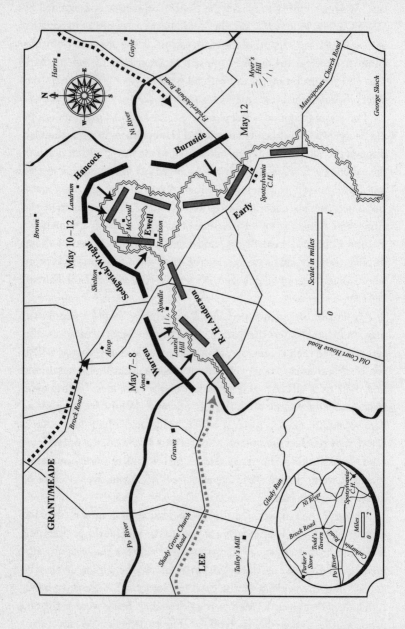

A Maine soldier declared: "For a time, every soldier was a fiend. The attack was fierce—the resistance fanatical." Overwhelmed by numbers, about 3,000 Confederates surrendered. Among the prisoners were their division commander, Edward Johnson, and two brigadiers.[66]

The attackers drove south up the salient in "a disorganized mass." The sounds of fighting and the stream of gray-coated survivors had alerted Major General John B. Gordon, who hurried one brigade forward to meet the oncoming Yankees, followed soon by two more brigades. During the night Lee had withdrawn thirty cannon from the Mule Shoe, believing that Grant was again moving south. Now Lee rode to the base of the salient—his army teetered on the edge of a crushing defeat. When Lee wanted to lead a counterattack, Gordon stopped him, insisting he not expose himself. Nearby troops yelled: "Lee, Lee, Lee to the rear. Lee to the rear."[67]

The counterattack by Gordon—"It'ud put fight into a whipped chicken just to look at him," one of his men said of the Georgian— slammed into the Federals. The momentum of the Union assault lurched to a halt. The Rebels "fought like demons," claimed a Northerner, and began pushing the Yankees back up the salient to its apex. Here, Hancock's troops filled the captured works and blasted the enemy ranks. Then, it began—hours of unremitting fighting, a madness of bloodletting and death. "All around that salient," the 17th Maine's Private John Haley professed, "was a seething, bubbling, roaring hell of hate and murder."[68]

Rain poured down, filling the trenches with water, mixed with gore and blood. Waves of rifle balls sang across the ground. The combat was, in the words of a Pennsylvania officer, "one of continual musketry such as has never been seen before in the war." Rifles fouled; ammunition ran out, requiring details to haul boxes through the fury. Grant and Lee shoved additional units into the "carnage infernal." "So continuous and heavy was our fire that the headlogs of the breastworks," remembered a Yankee, "were cut and torn until they resembled hickory brooms. . . . The mud was half-way to our knees, and by our constant movement the dead were almost buried at our feet." The intense gunfire sawed off a twenty-inch oak tree.[69]

At points along the works, foes were barely five feet from each other.

At such times, killing does not discriminate, or as Private Haley wrote, "War is a leveler like death; the best and the meanest blood here mingled." A fellow Mainer in Haley's regiment recounted, "the men were scattered in all directions fighting on their own hook, or not fighting at all, as suited them." Soldiers in the 19th Massachusetts began singing "The Battle Cry of Freedom." "I never heard it sung as then," wrote one of them.[70]

Through the morning and afternoon, into the evening, the "scene of horrid butchery" continued. At nightfall, it abated but did not cease for a few more hours. By then, Lee had constructed a new line of entrenchments at the base of the salient and his troops withdrew to it. The apex of the Mule Shoe with the staggering carnage became known as the "Bloody Angle."[71]

"Of all the battles I took part in," Lieutenant Thomas F. Galwey of the 8th Ohio wrote, "Bloody Angle at Spotsylvania exceeded all the rest in stubbornness, ferocity, and in carnage." Tens of thousands of fellow officers and men could echo Galwey's words. Combined casualties on this day amounted to 17,000. The vast majority of Union losses were sustained by troops of the Second and Sixth corps, who fought in the salient. It was not until mid-afternoon that Burnside attacked with Ninth Corps units, who were repulsed and swept back by a counter-assault. On the Union right, Warren's Fifth Corps tried the works again on Laurel Hill and failed for a third time. A 37th Massachusetts summarized May 12 as "nothing more than murder."[72]

PHILIP SHERIDAN ENCOUNTERED a furious George Meade on the morning of May 8. Meade's notorious foul temper had boiled over when he had found two of Sheridan's divisions at Todd's Tavern without orders and Brock Road to Spotsylvania still held by the enemy. By the time Sheridan appeared, according to one of Grant's aides, Meade "had worked himself into a towering passion" and lashed into Sheridan with "hammer and tongs." The diminutive cavalryman shot back with "expletives," accusing "Meade of mixing up infantry with cavalry." "If he could have matters his own way," snorted Sheridan, "he would concentrate all the cavalry, move out in force against Stuart's command, and whip it."[73]

Later, Meade recounted the confrontation to Grant, repeating Sheridan's words about whipping Jeb Stuart's Confederate horsemen. "Did Sheridan say that?" asked Grant. "Well, he generally knows what he is talking about. Let him start right out and do it." If Meade had expected Grant to support him over Sheridan's heated insubordination, he was disappointed. That night, army headquarters ordered Sheridan to concentrate his force and "proceed against the enemy's cavalry."[74]

Leaving only one regiment with the army, Sheridan led his three divisions, 10,000 troopers, south before daylight on May 9. The column of fours stretched for thirteen miles, an impressive array of horsemen. By day's end, the Yankees had crossed the North Anna River, after destroying tracks of the Virginia Central Railroad, capturing two locomotives, and releasing more than three hundred Union prisoners at Beaver Dam Station. The next day they angled southeast, covered eighteen miles, and bivouacked beyond the South Anna River. Jeb Stuart, meanwhile, with 3,000 troopers, had been hurrying south to interdict Sheridan's command.[75]

The collision came before noon on May 11, at Yellow Tavern, where Telegraph Road and Mountain Road intersected, two miles north of Richmond's outer line of defenses. Stuart deployed his brigades in an inverted L-shaped line on two ridges. Dismounted regiments dueled until late afternoon, when Custer led his Michigan Brigade and the 1st Vermont Cavalry in a mounted and dismounted charge on the base of the L. To the accompaniment of a band playing "Yankee Doodle," the Federals surged up the ridge, scattering a brigade of Virginians and overrunning two cannon.[76]

Leading a counterattack, Stuart plunged into the swirling action on the wooded ridge. A Michigander shot the dashing cavalry commander in the abdomen. Carried to the rear, Stuart was taken into the Confederate capital, where he died the next day. "The Michigan Brigade," Custer bragged to his wife, "has covered itself with undying glory." Sheridan pushed his troopers through the night, until the column collided with some of Richmond's defenders.[77]

Returning to the saddles at daylight on May 12, the Yankees rode east, scattered an enemy force at a bridge over the Chickahominy River, and camped at Mechanicsville. They then marched across the Peninsula to the James River, where Sheridan sent his wounded men down-river to Fort Monroe and rested the men until May 17. It would be another week until the hungry and exhausted cavalrymen rejoined the army. Sheridan had brought a cocksureness to the mounted corps.[78]

THE ARMY OF THE POTOMAC and the Army of Northern Virginia started to march away from Spotsylvania on May 20, moving south. More than a week had passed since the slaughter at the Bloody Angle. During those days, rain had fallen half the time, and the Confederates had repulsed two more Union assaults. From May 5 until now, the armies' combined losses approached 60,000, with the Federals incurring 50 percent more than their opponents.[79]

As replacements for the 36,000 Union casualties, the War Department sent 21,000 troops to the army. The reinforcements included recruits, reenlisted veterans, the Corcoran (Irish) Legion, comprised of four New York regiments, and Brigadier General Robert O. Tyler's division of five heavy artillery (H.A.) regiments converted to infantry units. Known as "Heavies," Tyler's troops had been serving in the Washington defenses and had never been in combat. Each of their regiments numbered at least 1,800 officers and men. When the veterans saw them, they taunted the Heavies, "The Johnnies will take the shine out of you" and "Haven't you brought your feather beds along?"[80]

The Heavies joined the army on May 18, and on the afternoon of the next day found themselves in an action against the veterans of the Confederate Second Corps at the Battle of Harris Farm. The inexperience of the Federals showed at once. A battalion of the 1st Massachusetts H.A. stumbled into a trap, and the 2nd New York H.A. triggered a volley into the ranks of the 7th New York H.A., which returned the fire. But when the Rebels broke their ranks, they rallied, and with the 1st Maine H.A., counterattacked. Additional Union regiments came up and pushed back the Southerners. "This baptism of fire was all that was needed to make us soldiers," insisted a New Yorker. It had been, however, "a most appalling initiation into the mysteries of war."[81]

The action at Harris Farm ended the combat at Spotsylvania. For both armies, it had been twelve days of constant toil, inadequate rations, filth, and bloody fighting. The Confederates clearly had the best of it, repulsing the assaults and incurring fewer casualties. The Army of the Potomac seemed like a clanging machine, incapable of coordinated efforts and tactical flexibility. At times, Grant had expected too much from an army that was losing its combat edge as bodies piled up before Lee's formidable works.[82]

The command relationship between Grant and Meade had undergone a critical change. It was to be expected, if not inevitable. In a letter to his wife, Meade attributed it to "the force of circumstances," but it went deeper than that. As Grant recognized that he needed to rid the army's senior leadership of its defensive thinking, he assumed greater control of operations. Grant appreciated Meade's ability to handle the workings of an army and recommended him for a major generalcy in the Regular Army. But it was the purpose of the army about which the two men differed. Much like Lee, Grant was a warrior; Meade was not. As the campaign progressed, Meade's role was reduced to that of an executive officer or chief of staff.[83]

In turn, the weaknesses of the corps commanders had become manifest. Winfield Scott Hancock had done the best, but his battlefield fire appeared to have been drained away by his Gettysburg wound, which required the daily attention of a surgeon as it continued to discharge pieces of bone. The army's former commander, Ambrose Burnside, seemed immovable and incapable of handling even a corps. Gouverneur Warren had quarreled with Meade and had balked at leading frontal assaults. He recoiled at Grant's method of warfare, unable to mask his feelings. John Sedgwick's successor, Horatio Wright, possessed "no special predilection for fighting," in the estimation of Assistant Secretary of War Charles Dana.[84]

Among the rank and file, Spotsylvania exposed a growing unwillingness to assail Confederate entrenchments. The strain of the campaign had left them physically exhausted from the night marches and the "constant state of excitement." A 7th Wisconsin lieutenant declared: "This campaign is trying our endurance as well as our courage. I never knew how much I could stand before." Like Grant, who remained popular with them, the men were determined to see it through to the end. But they had blanched before the sacrifice at Laurel Hill and the staggering carnage of the Bloody Angle. The veterans had reached limits in their acceptance of exposing themselves to senseless attacks.[85]

The Army of the Potomac, then, began leaving Spotsylvania after nightfall on May 20. Grant had concluded that Lee was planning to withdraw his army south, and he hoped to engage the Rebels while they were on the march. The movement accelerated the next day as both armies abandoned the scarred ground of Spotsylvania. During the march, the Yankees foraged widely. "Our men are robbing and burning fearfully in the country," wrote a staff officer, "and it is next to impossible to stop it." When Meade informed Grant of it, the general-in-chief replied that he was "strongly against protecting these people [civilians] at all."[86]

Both Lee and Grant either chose not to or missed opportunities to strike the other's strung-out columns. Grant's operations had been hampered by his decision to send most of his cavalry on Philip Sheridan's raid. By the end of May 22, Lee's army had crossed the North Anna River, winning the race for this natural barrier, roughly twenty miles north of Richmond. Meade urged Grant to sidestep the enemy behind the river, but Grant elected to follow Lee. Throughout May 23, the Federals closed on the North Anna, where Warren reported mistakenly that the enemy was not in strength.[87]

By late in the afternoon, Union engineers had laid a pontoon bridge across the North Anna at Jericho Mills, and Warren crossed his three divisions. The Fifth Corps troops probed the enemy works and were then hit with a counterattack. In the fighting, the Iron Brigade—"No brigade in the whole army had a higher reputation," insisted Colonel Charles Wainwright—broke, with half its members running across the river. Other Federals charged and repulsed the Rebels. Warren did not press the advantage. By nightfall, the Sixth Corps lay behind Warren's command on the north bank on the river, with the Ninth Corps two miles east at Ox Ford, and the Second Corps farther downstream at Chesterfield Bridge and beyond.[88]

"Every prominent officer" believed, according to one of Grant's aides, that Lee had retreated south during the night of May 23–24. Instead, Lee had formed his army in an inverted V with its apex at Ox Ford. Confederate engineers used the terrain's natural strengths, and the troops erected fieldworks. When Grant sent most of the army across the

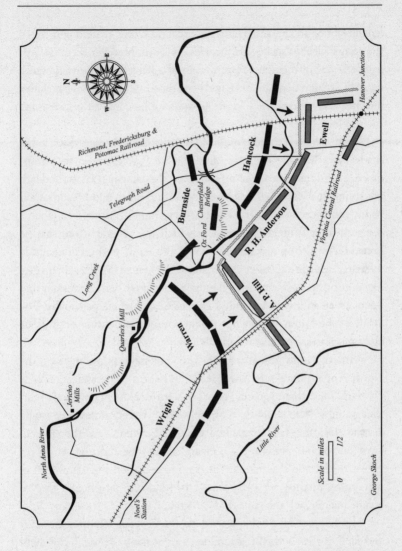

river on May 24, they ran into the formidable line. Colonel Theodore Lyman of Meade's staff described the situation for the Federals succinctly: "our army would be cut in two, if we attacked, and either wing subject to defeat." Lee had fashioned a brilliantly conceived trap.[89]

The Yankees were fortunate to escape without being severely punished. A drunken Brigadier General James H. Ledlie led his Ninth Corps brigade in a doomed charge against the western face of the Confederate line. To the east Hancock's Second Corps crossed and tested the works without success. Hancock's divisions, however, were isolated from the rest of the army. Here was an excellent opportunity to wreck an entire Union corps, but Lee had been prostrated with a severe case of diarrhea. Like Grant, he had no subordinate he could trust to execute such an assault.[90]

Grant admitted to aides on this day, "that this fighting throws in the shade everything he ever saw, and that he looked for no such resistance." Tensions at headquarters reflected the campaign's costs and failure to inflict a decisive blow on Lee's army. Grant's and Meade's staffs barely spoke to each other. When one of Grant's officers read aloud a dispatch from William Sherman in which the general wrote that he hoped Grant's "inspiration" could make the Army of the Potomac "do its share," Meade exploded. As recounted by Lyman, Meade, "in a voice like cutting an iron bar with a handsaw," declared: "Sir! I consider that despatch an insult to the army I command and to me personally. The Army of the Potomac does not require Grant's inspiration or anybody else's inspiration to make it fight."[91]

With the army stalemated and in vulnerable position along the North Anna, Grant met with Meade and corps commanders on May 25, with all of them agreeing that Lee's entrenchments precluded further assaults. "We could do nothing where we were unless Lee would assume the offensive," explained Grant. "I determined, therefore to draw out of our present position and make one more effort to get between him and Richmond. I had no expectation now, however, of succeeding in this; but I did expect to hold him far enough west to enable me to reach the James River high up."[92]

Rain fell on May 26, but after dark, the Federals recrossed the river and filed to the southeast around Lee's right flank. Through the night and the next day, the Yankees struggled on the roads. Heat felled many from the ranks. Few men had rations, and they scoured the countryside for something to eat. "We plundered without stint," bragged a Massachusetts veteran, "and completed our inroad only when everything had disappeared before the gun and knife." A sergeant lamented, "Grant must think the men are made of iron." Straggling, confusion, mud, and jammed roads slowed the march to a crawl at times.[93]

Grant's sidle to the left brought the army across the Pamunkey River by May 28. The troops had begun to use the word "flanking" to describe "everything from a night march to the capture of a sheep or a pig." The Federals lay a scant seven miles northeast of Mechanicsville, where the initial major engagement of the Seven Days Campaign had occurred nearly two years previous. Lee's army, meanwhile, had marched on a direct route and stood between the Yankees and Richmond, aligned behind Totopotomoy Creek. Along each army's front, cavalry roamed to secure intelligence on enemy locations and to screen their lines.[94]

With Sheridan's raiders back with the army, the Yankees searched for their Confederate foes. They collided at Haw's Shop, a large blacksmith shop three miles from Hanovertown. The cavalrymen fought dismounted, backed by artillery batteries. When Sheridan came up, he ordered George Custer's Michigan Brigade to charge. The Michiganders advanced on foot, breaking the Southern line and routing the enemy. "For all that this Brigade has accomplished all praise is due to Gen. Custer," a 6th Michigan Cavalry officer contended. "So brave a man I never saw and as competent as brave. Under him a man is ashamed to be cowardly. Under *him* our men can achieve wonders."[95]

Grant advanced the infantry corps toward Lee's line along Totopotomoy Creek during May 29 and 30. Skirmishes ignited along the front, but the Confederate lines were too strong to assault. Grant, meanwhile, had ordered Major General William Smith's Eighteenth Corps from Benjamin Butler's army at Bermuda Hundred to Meade's army, and it was en route. By June 1, the crossroads village of Old Cold Harbor had become a focal point for both armies as Grant continued his leftward sidle. Units of Sheridan's cavalry occupied Old Cold Harbor on May 31, with orders to hold it until Union infantry arrived.[96]

Throughout the morning of June 1, Sheridan's troopers, some of whom were armed with seven-shot repeating carbines, resisted Confederate infantry attacks. Before noon, the van of Horatio Wright's Sixth Corps arrived, replacing the horsemen. Smith's Eighteenth Corps, numbering about 17,000, joined Wright during the afternoon. With orders from Meade to attack, Wright and Smith aligned their units and were ready to advance at six o'clock. Once again, the Federals advanced against entrenched Rebels. "We went in on the run and with a yell," wrote a soldier in Smith's corps. The Southerners opened fire, and as a Vermonter described it, "Image how it looks on smooth water when it rains, and you have something of an idea how the ground looked around us, when the bullets struck."[97]

The Yankees recoiled before the musketry and cannon fire, incurring nearly 2,000 casualties before withdrawing. Among the regiments that charged was the 2nd Connecticut Heavy Artillery, which had arrived at the front less than two weeks earlier. "They dashed in like old veterans," said a Pennsylvanian. They paid dearly, however, for their valor and inexperience. When the Rebel fire hit the Heavies, killing their colonel, they "broke up in great confusion," and "staggered in every direction." Brigade commander Emory Upton rode into their midst, ordering them to lie down, where they stayed until after dark. "I did not know what war was before," exclaimed one of them. The next morning when the sun brightened the ground, the dead Heavies were distinctive in their "bright and fresh" uniforms.[98]

Grant ordered a concentration of the army and an assault at Cold Harbor for the morning of June 2. The attack was scheduled to begin when the Second Corps arrived. Hancock's men had begun their march after nightfall on June 1 from in front of Totopotomoy Creek. The movement became a physical ordeal for the exhausted troops. To make it to Cold Harbor by daylight was simply beyond the troops' capacity. In a letter home, Theodore Lyman stated: "It was badly managed, or rather it was difficult to manage, like all those infernal night marches, and so part of the troops went fifteen miles instead of nine and there was any amount of struggling and exhaustion. I consider fifteen miles by night equal to twenty-five miles by day, and you will remember our men have no longer the bodily strength they had a month before; indeed, why they are alive I don't see."[99]

Grant delayed the attack until five o'clock in the afternoon. Throughout the day, Lee extended his line southward along a ridge and hills. His troops dug rifle pits and built fieldworks, skillfully adapting the entrenchments to the terrain. When finished, the fortifications covered six miles and were the army's strongest position since the campaign began. Furthermore, Lee's ranks had been augmented with reinforcements from Bermuda Hundred, Shenandoah Valley, and other places.

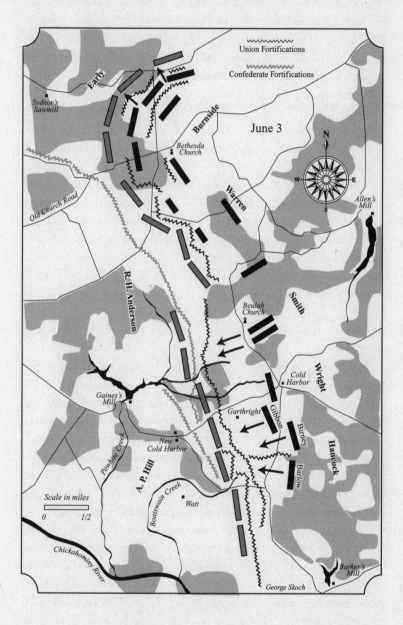

Union general Franz Sigel had been defeated at New Market in the Valley, and Butler had been effectively sealed up on Bermuda Hundred. The 25,000 reinforcements exceeded Lee's casualties since May 5.[100]

During the afternoon, Grant rescheduled the assault for 4:30 A.M., on June 3, "by reason of the exhausted state of the 2nd Corps." Late in the afternoon, the Rebels struck troops of the Fifth and Ninth corps at Bethesda Church on the right of the Union line. The Southerners inflicted an additional 1,500 Federal casualties before retiring. Rain began falling at night, snuffing out fires and puddling the trenches with muddy water.[101]

While at North Anna, Grant had informed Henry Halleck: "Lee's army is really whipped. . . . I may be mistaken, but I feel that our success over Lee's army is already assured." Lee's unwillingness to leave his works and to strike the Federals when opportunities arose had convinced Grant that his opponent was nearing a breaking point. One massive, final assault might be enough to crack the Confederate lines and to inflict an overwhelming defeat upon the enemy, opening the way into Richmond. So far, Grant's confrontation with Lee had brought no decisive result and had filled Northern newspapers with lengthy columns of casualties.[102]

In his memoirs, Grant admitted: "I have always regretted that the last assault at Cold Harbor was ever made. . . . At Cold Harbor no advantage whatever was gained to compensate for the heavy loss we sustained." Indeed he should have. Although he assigned the execution of the assault to Meade, neither he nor Meade had a grasp of Lee's position. Together, they were sending the army forward in a blind assault, with no contingency plans or reserves to exploit a breakthrough. Grant's assessment of the Confederates' morale and combat prowess was mistaken, and that miscalculation would be exposed early the next morning.[103]

Union officers had noticed that since Spotsylvania the enlisted men's "nerves had become so sensitive that the men would start at the slightest sound, and dodge at the flight of a bird or the sight of pebble tossed past them." They had begun to protest loudly to their officers about assailing enemy entrenchments, which they believed were manned by "fanatics." Their common opening in letters—"I am alive" and "I am still alive"—testified to the omnipresence of death and their belief that they had defied the odds. Each time, however, when they were ordered to assail entrenchments those odds of survival lessened.[104]

Duty compelled, however. At 4:30 A.M. on June 3, men of the Second, Sixth, and Eighteenth corps stepped forth. "Everyone knew it must be death to move," professed a New Yorker, "but not a man faltered." Then, it came—a searing blast of musketry and artillery fire from the Confederate works. The discharges ripped into ranks, knocked men down in clumps, and staggered the lines as if an unseen giant had clutched them in his hands and shaken them. A Yankee likened it to "a veritable tempest." Another one claimed, "The files of men went down like rows of blocks or bricks pushed over by striking against each other."[105]

Veteran regiments, even entire brigades, advanced so far and then went to ground, digging trenches with bayonets, plates, and cups. According to a member of the 7th Massachusetts, his Sixth Corps brigade did not charge, "as we expected the Rebs works to strong to make the attempt." Units floundered in the swampy bottomlands, exposing the men to the merciless fire. Some of the Heavies, trying to prove their worth, pushed ahead and paid dearly for it. The Second Corps had three brigade commanders killed or mortally wounded, including Colonel Frank Haskell, who as John Gibbon's aide had rallied troops on Cemetery Ridge at Gettysburg, on July 3, 1863. "We felt it was murder, not war," declared a New Yorker.[106]

The Confederates repulsed the assault within an hour. Union casualties amounted to nearly 3,500 within that time. But the combat did not abate as the Rebels pinned down the Yankees where they had halted. "The man who moved, even an arm, was remorsely shot," said a Federal soldier. A captain in the 12th New Hampshire accused the Southerners of deliberately shooting any wounded man who moved. Men lying among the fallen shielded themselves behind bodies and waited for darkness. Before the day ended, another 1,000 Northerners had been killed or wounded. Southern losses have been estimated at between 1,000 and 1,500.[107]

Grant rode to the front about eleven o'clock "to visit all the corps commanders to see for myself the different positions gained and to get their opinion of the practicability of doing anything more in their respective fronts." He heard what Meade had been listening to for hours, that nothing much, if anything, could be gained with additional assaults. At 12:30 P.M., Grant directed Meade to suspend a "farther advance for the present." Three days would pass before Grant and Lee worked out a truce arrangement for the Federals to collect the surviving wounded and to bury the dead on the evening of June 7. As the details went forth for the gruesome duty, Union bands played dirges.[108]

THE CAMPAIGN HAD BEGUN on a day vibrant with life and ended on a day sorrowful with music for the dead. The magnitude of the carnage surpassed that in all previous campaigns. Union casualties exceeded 55,000 in killed, wounded, and captured, or more than Antietam, Chancellorsville, and Gettysburg combined. Confederate losses amounted to nearly 32,000. With the reinforcements sent to both armies, the Northern casualty rate was 37 percent; Southern, 32 percent.[109]

"The country between the Rapidan and the James," wrote the historian of the Fifth Corps, "proved a mausoleum for over 7,000 Union men." When David Birney listed the casualties in his Second Corps division in a letter to a friend, he asked, "Is that not a large enough Butchers bill." A soldier in the 22nd Massachusetts admitted the men liked Grant, "although he is almost too much of a butcher, and has too little regard for human life." In many regiments it seemed that nearly everyone had been hit. When the 20th Indiana's Sergeant Thomas Stephens's messmate was killed, he confided in his diary: "Who will fall next? Oh God, prepare us for death and eternity."[110]

It was Stephens's question that echoed across the campaign. There had been no respite from death; it visited each army every day. The campaign transformed the nature of warfare, with entrenchments appearing as soon as men halted. Attacking them meant almost certain death or maiming. Joshua Chamberlain described the campaign as "where brightest valor was deepest loss." Filthy, exhausted men stumbled from one killing field to another, from one disfigured landscape to another. The passage changed the survivors.[111]

By the campaign's end, the Army of the Potomac—the army of Antietam, Fredericksburg, Chancellorsville, and Gettysburg—had virtually ceased to exist. It was not only the sheer number of casualties, but as John Gibbon asserted, "The quality of the loss was what made it almost disastrous, for the very best officers, and the very bravest men were those who fell."[112]

The expiration of enlistments of some of the army's most renowned units further depleted the army's ranks. During May and June, the Pennsylvania Reserves, original units of Philip Kearny's New Jersey Brigade, 4th and 8th Ohio, 14th Indiana, 1st and 9th Massachusetts, 26th and 71st Pennsylvania, and the Iron Brigade's 2nd Wisconsin left for home. Regiments and brigades required reorganization, and at the end of June, the Irish Brigade was broken up, with its units assigned to other commands.[113]

As they gathered up their own at Cold Harbor, the survivors knew it would not end until they or their foes ceased to exist as an army. "In all probability," Corporal John A. Miller of the 148th Pennsylvania told his wife in a letter of June 7, "Gen. Grant wont stop till he either gets licked or takes Richmond, which may [be] months yet." They had objected to Grant's methods of frontal attacks but not his iron determination to see it through.[114]

Grant had taken the initiative from Lee and had not relinquished it. The campaign had exposed the inherent weakness of his command structure, had seen him order assaults without proper reconnaissance and preparation, had found him and the army coming up short before Lee's skillful countermoves, and had him expecting too much from exhausted men. Despite the fearful losses and subordinates' failures, Grant persevered, with an unrelenting focus on the outcome. As entrenchments transformed warfare, Grant altered the nature of campaigns in the East.

Amid the ordeal of the Overland Campaign, there were moments when men could snatch time for thoughts of home and of the life around them. While the army headed for Cold Harbor, the 17th Vermont's Colonel Charles Cummings penned a letter to his wife: "I saw the scarlet trumpet honey suckle . . . in full bloom. . . . I also saw the sweet scented honey suckle in bloom, larger holly trees, bigger than our Scotch larch, and a hundred years old, in blossom, much as our hawthorn blossoms." It was a wonder that amid all the horror, a man could still appreciate life's beauty.[115]

Chapter 16

"A *Sit Down* Before the Wall of Petersburg"

A DELEGATION OF REPUBLICAN politicians came to the White House on June 9, officially to inform Abraham Lincoln that the party, which now used the banner of the National Union Party, had renominated him for the presidency. Meeting at Baltimore, the convention replaced Vice President Hannibal Hamlin with Andrew Johnson, military governor of Tennessee and War Democrat. Lincoln had remained rather aloof from the choice of a running mate, indicative of his opinion of the importance of the vice presidency. The convention had adopted a platform that called for the unconditional surrender of the Confederacy and a constitutional amendment abolishing slavery.[1]

Like other visitors to the Executive Mansion, these politicians probably noticed the dark rings beneath the president's eyes, the creases of sadness across his face, and the stoop of his shoulders, as if they bore an impossible weight. The past five weeks had been torture for Lincoln as the fighting raged in Virginia and the reports of the frightful bloodshed filtered back from the front. He walked the corridors of the White House, visited the War Department to read the latest dispatches, and scarcely slept. At one point, he exclaimed in anguish to a member of Congress: "Why do we suffer reverses after reverses! Could we have avoided this terrible, bloody war! . . . Is it ever to end!"[2]

That end appeared nowhere in sight. How long would the Northern populace sustain the war effort in the face of the appalling casualties without a foreseeable resolution? Lincoln confided to a newspaperman at this time that the people "expect too much at once" and "believe that the war is about to be substantially closed." If their expectations for an impending conclusion to the nightmare were not fulfilled by the autumn, the president's chances for a second term would be slim.[3]

Publicly, Lincoln made his views clear on the prospects for a conflict of unknown length. In an address at a Sanitary Commission fair in Philadelphia on June 16, he declared: "We accepted this war for an object, a worthy object, and the war will end when that object is attained. Under God, I hope it never will until that time. Speaking of the present campaign, General Grant is reported to have said, 'I am going through on this line if it takes all summer.' I say we are going through on this line if it takes three years more."[4]

This determination to see it through bound Lincoln and Grant together. The president did not interfere with the general's operations because he approved of the strategy. When Grant turned the army south after the Wilderness, Lincoln told John Hay, one of his personal secretaries, that only Grant would have done that. "The great thing about Grant," Lincoln remarked during the campaign, "is his perfect coolness and persistency of purpose. . . . He is not easily excited . . . and he has the *grit* of a bull-dog! Once let him get his 'teeth' *in,* and nothing can shake him off."[5]

Even as Lincoln welcomed his renomination, Grant was making preparations to shift the Army of the Potomac from the Cold Harbor lines to south of the James River. On June 5, Grant had wired Henry Halleck, "My idea from the start has been to beat Lee's army, if possible, north of Richmond, then, after destroying his lines of communication north of the James River, to transfer the army to the south side and besiege Lee in Richmond, or follow him south if he should retreat." The Confederates had been unwilling to come out of their entrenchments, and "without a greater sacrifice of human life than I am willing to make, all cannot be accomplished that I had designed outside of the city." While Philip Sheridan and two divisions of cavalry undertook a raid to destroy the Virginia Central Railroad, the army would march south to Petersburg.[6]

A week later, on June 12, after more than a week in the deadly trenches at Cold Harbor, the army abandoned the works after nightfall. William Smith's Eighteenth Corps marched down the Peninsula to White House, where the troops boarded transports for a trip down the Pamunkey and York rivers and then up the James. The other four infantry corps and their immense wagon train started a fifty-mile trek across the Peninsula. Although thick dust clouds choked the columns and they had to cross the Chickahominy, the vans of the corps arrived at the north bank of the James by the morning of June 14.[7]

Winfield Scott Hancock's Second Corps troops started the crossing, piling into a hodgepodge collection of boats at Wilcox's Landing to be ferried across. Downstream at Wyanoke Neck, engineers began construction of a 2,100-foot pontoon bridge. When finished at 11:00 P.M., the trains, artillery, and the Sixth and Ninth corps began their passage. "The approaches to the river were alive with troops marching here and there or waiting their turn to cross," remembered a Pennsylvanian. "Drums and brass bands filled the air with martial music." All through the night of June 14–15, on through the day and into the next night and beyond, the stream of men, cannon, wagons, and animals proceeded to the south bank of the James.[8]

An officer called the crossing "a miracle." Colonel Horace Porter of Grant's staff stated later, "This memorable operation, when examined in all its details, will furnish one of the most valuable and instructive studies in logistics." For a while on June 15, Grant stood on a bluff and watched the passage. "It was a matchless pageant," wrote Porter, "that could not fail to inspire all beholders with the grandeur of achievement and the majesty of military power." When he had finished, Grant rode to City Point, where he established his headquarters on a bluff above the confluence of the Appomattox and James rivers. By the morning of June 17, when Gouverneur Warren's Fifth Corps and Brigadier General James H. Wilson's cavalry division, which had been protecting the army's flank and rear, crossed, the movement had been completed.[9]

Grant and the army had not only executed a brilliant maneuver but had stolen a march on Lee and the Army of Northern Virginia. Lee had learned of the Yankees' disappearance from their Cold Harbor works on the morning of June 13. He hesitated to act until he had better intelligence on the Federals' destination. He had been forced to send cavalry to interdict Sheridan and had started Lieutenant General Jubal Early's Second Corps for Lynchburg, Virginia, where a Union army, under Major General David Hunter, threatened the vital railroad center. Lee had told Early a week earlier: "We must destroy this Army of Grant's before he gets to the James River. If he gets there it will become a siege, and then it will be a mere question of time."[10]

It was not until June 15 that Lee dispatched an infantry division to Petersburg. General P. G. T. Beauregard, the hero of Fort Sumter and First Bull Run, commanded the Confederate forces south of the James River. Beauregard had only 5,400 troops to keep Benjamin Butler's Union Army of the James stalled at Bermuda Hundred and to defend Petersburg. Coming toward him were Smith's Eighteenth Corps and the Army of the Potomac, in all more than 100,000 officers and men.[11]

Petersburg was a prize of inestimable value, the city where railroad lines from the south and west joined before running north to Richmond. If this "guardian of Richmond's lifeline to the Southern heartland" fell to the Yankees, Lee's army would have to either defend Richmond with its supply links severed or abandon the capital. For a few critical days, Petersburg was a vulnerable prize, weakly defended against a powerful foe. But misunderstandings, timid generalship, and the exhaustion of the troops denied it to the Federals.[12]

From June 15 to 18, the Yankees launched a series of attacks against Petersburg's defenses. On the first day, Smith's troops took the outer works, the so-called Dimmock Line, and then halted. Grant had wanted Hancock's Second Corps to join Smith, but that order was never relayed to Hancock. The next day, Hancock's troops attacked, met a severe fire "before which our first line disappeared," said a soldier, and retired. Two days later, Hancock, who seemed to be but a shell of a man, temporarily relinquished command of the corps, "completely disabled" by his Gettysburg wound.[13]

It was Ambrose Burnside's Ninth Corps troops' turn on June 17. They managed to secure a section of the works only to be driven back by a Confederate counterattack. One of the Union brigades mistakenly advanced at a right angle to the Rebel lines, had their flank riddled, and lost about eight hundred men in minutes. Afterward, Burnside came to army headquarters, storming about his "worthless" Heavy Artillery troops, because he "couldn't find thirty of them" during the attack.[14]

On June 18, the Confederates manned their final line of defenses, but veterans from Lee's army now held sections of the entrenchments. When soldiers of the Union Second and Fifth corps charged late in the afternoon, they advanced piecemeal and into "a withering fire." A Pennsylvanian stated: "The instant we emerged from that low ground into view we met an avalanche of balls. They seemed as thick as insects in the air on a summer eve." A regimental commander protested the order to attack, calling it "a deathtrap." When they went forward, the Rebels "cut our men down like hail cuts the grain and grass."[15]

A corporal in the 12th United States Infantry claimed that the enemy artillery fire was the worst "I ever was in." "Men were cut in two & hurled a disfigured mass of flesh & rags to the ground." The 1st Maine Heavy Artillery braved the searing discharges, advancing farther than any unit, and lost 632 men killed and wounded, the greatest loss sustained by any regiment in a single battle during the war. Colonel Joshua Chamberlain, the hero of Little Round Top at Gettysburg, suffered a severe wound, but Grant later promoted him to brigadier general to date from June 18. Colonel Rufus Dawes of the 6th Wisconsin expressed many men's views of the bloody assaults in a letter to his wife: "Yesterday afternoon another horrid massacre of our corps was enacted. . . . It is awfully disheartening to think we have Generals who will send their men to such sure destruction."[16]

The four days of attacks had cost the Federals nearly 10,000 casualties. Grant and Meade were "very much dissatisfied" with the army's failure to take Petersburg. Chief of Staff Andrew Humphreys blamed it on the loss of so many officers during the Overland Campaign and on the men's exhaustion. Hancock agreed with Humphreys's assessment, noting that he had "scarcely any good brigade & regimental commanders left in whom his men had confidence." Fifth Corps artillery chief Colonel Charles Wainwright saw it differently: "even the stupidest private now knows that it cannot succeed, and the natural consequence: the men will not try it. The very sight of a bank of fresh earth now brings them to a dead halt." Wainwright thought, "never has the Army of the Potomac been so demoralized as at this time."[17]

The rank and file's words convey the level of discouragement. A 1st Delaware corporal told his mother that he and his comrades "are A Playing out very fast." A Massachusetts private professed: "These times are getting almost too hard. They draw upon the body tremendously." Since May 5, more than 75,000 of them had been killed, wounded, or captured. "The feeling here in the army," wrote an officer, "is that we have been absolutely butchered, that our lives have been periled to no purpose, and wasted. In the Second Corps the feeling is so strong that the men say they will not charge any more works."[18]

Major Washington Roebling of Warren's staff wrote on June 23: "They must put fresh steam on the man factories up North; the demand down here for killing purposes is far ahead of the supply. Thank God, however, for the consolation that when the last man is killed the war will be over.

"The biggest heroes in this war are the privates in the line—the man with the musket. When I think sometimes what those men all do and endure day after day, with their lives constantly in danger, I can't but wonder that there should be men who are such fools. I can't call them anything else. And that is just the trouble we are laboring under now—the fools have all been killed and the rest think it is about played out to stand up and get shot."[19]

The discontent with the costly assaults extended to the army's senior officers, whose attitudes had darkened, resulting in heated exchanges between them. The army's leadership was in turmoil. For the past few weeks, Meade's foul temper had flared with increasing rapidity. Fellow officers described Meade as "wrathy" and "perfectly beside himself" at times. When Edward Cropsey of the Philadelphia *Inquirer* wrote a false story that claimed Meade had urged Grant to retreat after the Wilderness, Meade had Cropsey paraded through the army wearing a placard with "Libeler of the Press" printed on it, and then banished from the field.[20]

To his wife, Meade complained more and more about his reduced role and criticized Grant's tactics. "I think Grant has had his eyes opened," he wrote in early June, "and is willing to admit now Virginia and Lee's army is not Tennessee and Bragg's army." He then followed with, "Now, to tell you the truth, the latter [Grant] has greatly disappointed me, and since the campaign I really begin to think I am something of a general." After they had reached Petersburg, Meade indicated, however, that he shared Grant's steadfastness to stay the course: "it is a question of tenacity and nerve, and it won't do to look behind, or to calculate the cost in blood and treasure; if we do we are lost and our enemies succeed."[21]

In turn, Meade's relationships with his corps commanders had deteriorated. He spared only Hancock of harsh criticism, writing of him, "I have for him the most friendly feeling and highest appreciation of his talents." Burnside's performance in the recent operations had not enhanced his standing with Meade or with the army. Grant had assigned the Ninth Corps to the army, making Burnside answerable to Meade. One of Burnside's aides confessed that he thought army headquarters found the corps "wanting in many of those qualities that go to make a brave & efficient army."[22]

Difficulties and personal clashes between Warren and Meade mounted until the army commander spoke to Grant about relieving the Fifth Corps general. Of all of the army's senior officers, Warren felt himself trapped in a recurring nightmare. Since Spotsylvania, he had balked about ordering assaults and openly voiced his opposition to the tactics. To others, he appeared stubborn and insubordinate to the point where Wainwright called him "a very loathsome, profane ungentlemanly & disgusting puppy in power," and attributed his actions to "a sort of insanity." After the bloody June 3 attack at Cold Harbor, Warren unleashed a torrent of oaths, which an aide said, "fairly made my hair stand on end with their profaneness."[23]

On June 20, Warren submitted a letter to Meade, offering his opinion on assailing the Confederate lines. Warren was arrogant and self-righteous, and his letter apparently led to some confrontation with Meade. Warren informed his wife late that day that he and Meade "had a square understanding today, to the effect that I was no creature of his. I am so satisfied with my efforts and integrity—that I would not fear to run against General Grant if necessary." The dispute between the two generals abated for some time after this. At one time Grant regarded Warren as a likely successor to Meade if something befell the latter, but Warren no longer enjoyed the general-in-chief's confidence.[24]

Meade's harshest critic was, however, William "Baldy" Smith, Eighteenth Corps commander. Since he had joined the army at Cold Harbor, Smith had disparaged Meade's generalship and allegedly had tried to have him removed from command. He and Grant were old friends, and Grant complied with Smith's request not to serve directly under Benjamin Butler by giving him field command of the Army of the James. But when Smith complained about the campaign's "useless slaughter," a direct criticism of Grant, the quarrelsome general was removed from command and sent packing to New York. Few members of the army regretted Smith's departure.[25]

Although Smith would maintain until the end of his days that Butler had conspired against him, his constant carping and inability to work with his superiors had doomed him. His removal left Butler again in full command of the Army of the James and its two corps, the Tenth and Eighteenth. The former Democratic congressman, whom Lincoln had made the first major general of volunteers in April 1861, had few attributes of a general, and his campaign at Bermuda Hundred had been a miserable failure. A member of Grant's staff described him "to be more dangerous, sharper, & more disagreeable than any man I have ever seen." But Grant would be saddled with him for months as Butler's troops operated with the Army of the Potomac.[26]

"THUS BEGAN THE SIEGE of Petersburg," wrote Grant in his memoirs. He dated it as of June 19, 1864, a day after the final Union assaults failed to capture the city. From the campaign's outset, Grant knew that it could come to a siege of either Petersburg or Richmond. He now adopted the strategy of attrition, the strangling of enemy supply lines and the eroding away of Lee's army. It was "a process for defeating the foe and winning the war." There would be no more frontal assaults against heavily defended entrenchments.[27]

Before long, dozens of miles of earthworks, forts, bombproofs, and traverses disfigured the ground from Richmond to the east and south of Petersburg. The 64,000 Confederate defenders had to hold the lines and to protect the Petersburg & Weldon Railroad and the Southside Railroad, which connected the Rebels to the harvests of the lower South. "If this

cannot be done," declared Lee, "I see no way of averting the terrible disaster that will ensue." The 110,000 Yankees had to push their lines westward, envelop Petersburg, and seize and destroy the railroads. Thrusts
north of the James River against Richmond's defenses and forays against
the rail links would characterize the pattern of operations for months.[28]

Grant moved quickly against both railroads. He sent James Wilson's
and Brigadier General August Kautz's cavalry divisions on a raid against
the Southside Railroad and committed the Second, Fifth and Sixth
corps to an effort to seize the Weldon Railroad. The horsemen started
forth on the morning of June 22 as the infantry corps pushed west
toward Jerusalem Plank Road and the railroad beyond.[29]

Disaster, however, struck the infantry units during the afternoon. As
they pushed beyond the Plank Road, a gap developed between the
Sixth Corps and the Second Corps, under the temporary command of
David Birney. Veterans of Lee's army struck the front and exposed flank
of Birney's troops. The attack shattered Francis Barlow's division.
"Death filled the air like snowflakes in a winter storm," declared a 17th
Maine private. Barlow's men panicked and ran, exposing the flank and
rear of Gershom Mott's and John Gibbon's divisions, whose members
joined in the flight. Earlier, Barlow had sent a brigade to close the gap,
and upon its line, the Yankees rallied, repulsing the enemy. A Fifth
Corps officer scoffed, "The line of the Second Corps was just eaten up
like a flame travels up a slip of paper."[30]

When the fighting began, Hancock wanted to go to the front, but a
surgeon would not allow it. He wrote later: "Birney has had command in
my absence. He has not been very fortunate—for which I am sorry for he
deserved to be." Birney blamed veteran regiments with their terms of
enlistment soon to expire as unwilling to fight. Since May 5, the proud
Second Corps had lost twenty brigade commanders, dozens of regimental field officers, and thousands of its best troops. Like their commander,
Hancock, they were a shadow of their former selves. The action on June
22, which troops dubbed "Barlow's skedaddle," had cost them another
2,400 officers and men, including more than 1,700 captured.[31]

Wilson's and Kautz's horsemen, meanwhile, raided west along the
Southside Railroad, destroying sections of the tracks. They encountered
minor opposition until their return march reached Ream's Station on

the Weldon Railroad. Here Confederate infantry and cavalry nearly surrounded Wilson's division. The Union general had to burn his wagons and abandon 13 cannon to escape the trap, but still lost 1,000 of his men as prisoners. Meade described it as "a serious disaster," noting that he had opposed the operation but "was overruled." The raiders rejoined the army on July 1.[32]

With the return of Wilson's and Kautz's commands, Grant had the army's entire cavalry corps reunited. On June 26, Sheridan and the divisions of David Gregg and Wesley Merritt had arrived at Petersburg, having been away from the army for more than a fortnight. Sheridan's assignment had been to destroy miles of the Virginia Central Railroad and to march to Charlottesville, where David Hunter's Union army might be marching to from the Shenandoah Valley. Instead, Hunter moved toward Lynchburg, while Sheridan's troopers turned back miles from Charlottesville after fighting a two-day engagement, June 11–12, at Trevilian Station.[33]

Major General Wade Hampton and 5,000 Confederate horsemen intercepted Sheridan's 6,000-man column west of Louisa Court House along the Virginia Central Railroad on June 10. The next morning, Sheridan and Hampton advanced to the attack north of Trevilian Station. The most desperate action of the day, however, occurred at the station, where George Custer's Michigan Brigade charged into Hampton's wagon train, stirring up attacks by three Southern brigades. The Michiganders fought on foot "on the inside of a living triangle," as an eyewitness described their position. At one point in the three-hour fight, an officer asked Custer if he should move their horses to the rear. "Where in hell is the rear?" replied Custer.[34]

"It is the most mixed up fight I ever saw," insisted a Michigander. Late in the afternoon, their comrades in the other units punched a hole in Hampton's line north of the station and relieved Custer's men. On June 12, the Yankees launched seven dismounted charges against their foes, but were repulsed each time. During the night, Sheridan withdrew, crossing the North Anna River and beginning his return march to the army. The engagement had cost him 1,000 casualties, with Hampton losing about 1,100. The Southerners had won a clear victory, stopping Sheridan's raid.[35]

While Sheridan's cavalrymen marched toward Petersburg, Abraham Lincoln visited the army. Arriving on June 21, the president spent a day with Grant and Meade before joining Butler's Army of the James at Bermuda Hundred. He and Grant rode along the army's lines, with Lincoln receiving a warm welcome from the troops. In particular, African-American soldiers crowded around his horse and kissed his hands. In a conversation with Grant, he told the general, "I cannot pretend to advise, but I do sincerely hope that all may be accomplished with as little bloodshed as possible."[36]

A 22ND MASSACHUSETTS SOLDIER wrote at the end of June that the Federals "seem to be preparing for a *sit down* before the wall of Petersburg." In the initial days of their arrival at Petersburg, they had built entrenchments, and when Grant ordered siege operations, work on fortifications became the primary duty of the army. As a result, miles of trenches mirrored similar scars built by the Confederates. A captain described the labor simply as "we are *diging diging diging*."[37]

The works consisted of trenches dug deep enough so men could be protected while standing in them. Logs and dirt topped the trenches, and in front of them, abatis, laced with iron wire on stakes, were built to impede attackers. Every twenty feet, traverses, running at right angles, divided the works into sections. Bombproofs, with roofs of logs and dirt, dotted the trenches. They reminded a soldier of "the underground saloons" of New York City. Earthen redans, or fortifications with a salient front and open rear, anchored points along the works and were designated as forts. One of these redans, Fort Sedgwick, soon received the nickname "Fort Hell" because soldiers serving in it said they were "going to hell."[38]

Life in the trenches, thought the 6th Wisconsin's Colonel Rufus Dawes, had to be worse than "the Calcutta black hole." Regiments rotated in and out of the works every two days. When the men were in the rear, those at the front called them "Sugar Eaters." While in the trenches, the duty required, said a newspaperman, "eternal vigilance which is the price of their lives." They slept "with their accouterments on and their guns by them." The summer's sweltering heat—"Purgatory is at least a week back, and hell itself is not far ahead," was one description of it—sapped men's strength and worsened conditions in the works.[39]

A Yankee claimed that while at the front the men were "frightened half to death all the time." Most likely, he exaggerated their fears, but duty in the trenches was dangerous work. Sharpshooters in both armies killed or wounded careless men daily. Dawes called one unfortunate victim "a *fool*." The troops learned quickly "to *dodge*" when firing began. An officer claimed, however, "Our men give nobody the privilege of dodging but the cook, and the reason they give for that is they are afraid the 'Johnnies' might put a hole through their coffee kettle and no tin shop here to get it mended." They described a miss by a sharpshooter "as good as a *mile of old women*."[40]

A Berdan Sharpshooter recounted that he and his comrades practiced "squibbling" while in the trenches. A "squib" was a moistened cartridge rammed down on top of a dry round. "This prank was played after it was dark," he wrote, "by pointing the rifle into the air about forty-five degrees, muzzle up, and then let her go. The damp powder would leave a trail all along from the muzzle of the rifle until it struck the ground, which looked like a fuse of a bombshell with its fuse burning all the way over."[41]

The Yankees fired squibs to unnerve the Rebels as men in the trenches dreaded rounds arced into the air by mortars. Federals used the slang term "gopher" to describe efforts by men to burrow holes into the ground as protection from artillery rounds. The Northerners enjoyed an advantage in the number of and caliber of their ordnance. The troops called the field cannon and mortars "*Grant's Minstrels.*" Seven thirty-pound Rodman Cannon, heavy and powerful weapons, were initially dubbed the "Petersburg Express" until the soldiers named them the "Seven Sisters." Whether death came from the barrel of a rifle or the tube of an artillery piece, it struck even careful men with a chilling randomness.[42]

While a Federal soldier described the war as a "Hell-bound rebellion," fellow Americans occupied the opposite trenches, and the Northerners and Southerners conducted "a brisk trade" between them. Yankees coveted tobacco; Rebels, real coffee. The parties met halfway between the works to do business. When officers were not present, the foes agreed to truces, which were "sacred and . . . honorably observed." At one time, a Confederate accidentally fired a shot during a truce, bringing a shout from their line, "we'll fix him." One Yankee stated that watching the opposing pickets, "you would think that they were both in the same army."[43]

During these early weeks at Petersburg, recruits and conscripts continued to stream into the Union army. Veterans scorned them as "worthless creatures." As soon as these men joined a regiment, desertions in that unit increased. "The trouble is *this:* we have not the machinery to work up *poor material,*" contended Colonel Theodore Lyman of Meade's staff. "They won't let us shoot the rascals, and few regiments have the discipline to mould them into decent troops; the consequence is, they are the stragglers, pillagers, skulkers and run-aways of the army." Despite the old soldiers' low opinion of them, the majority evidently served honorably.[44]

At the same time, more veteran units headed for home, with the expirations of their enlistments. Through the summer and into the fall, more than twenty regiments left the service. These volunteers had answered the call in the weeks and months after First Bull Run and had fought in nearly all of the army's battles. For the reenlisted members of units, their comrades' departure meant consolidation into other commands. The Iron Brigade lost its identity, its members assigned elsewhere. No longer did troops carry the proud identification of a singular brigade—Iron, Excelsior, Irish, New Jersey.[45]

LIEUTENANT COLONEL HENRY Pleasants examined the lay of ground with a professional's eye. A Ninth Corps brigade commander, Pleasants had been a civil and mining engineer before the war. While at the front, "I noticed a little cup of a ravine near to the enemy's works," stated Pleasants afterward, and "it occurred to me that a mine could be excavated there." He proposed the idea to his superior officer, who passed it on to Ninth Corps headquarters. Ambrose Burnside approved the plan, without seeking permission from either Grant or Meade. Once work commenced, Burnside discussed it with Meade, who sanctioned it.

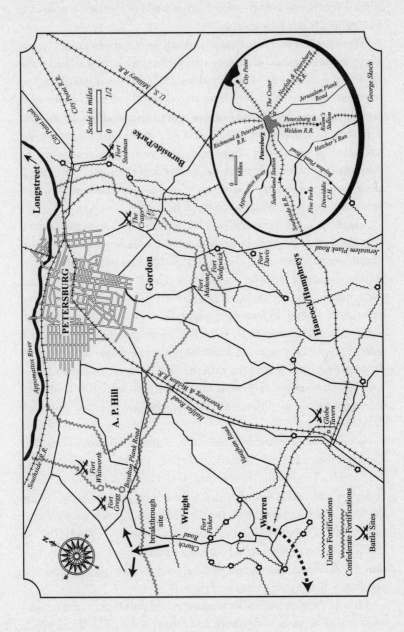

When officers and men in other corps learned of Pleasants's project, it was "generally much laughed at."[46]

Pleasants had been the former commander of the 48th Pennsylvania, whose ranks contained anthracite coal miners. With these skilled workers, Pleasants began the digging on June 25. "I found it impossible to get any assistance from anybody," he testified later. "I had to do all the work myself." He and his Pennsylvanians solved the ventilation problem, fashioned tools from army picks, and hauled the dirt out in cracker boxes lashed to hickory sticks. Pleasants required a theodolite, an instrument used to determine the proper length of the mine. Army headquarters had a theodolite, but Burnside had to secure "an old-fashioned" one from Washington for Pleasants.[47]

Once the mine was completed, Pleasants's idea was to pack it with kegs of gunpowder and to blow a gap in the Confederate works through which Union troops could charge. The Rebels had learned of the project but could not discover its location. The Pennsylvanians finished the mine on July 23, having dug it forward 525 feet, with two lateral galleries of 37 and 38 feet. Four days later they began filling the galleries with 320 twenty-five-pound kegs of gunpowder. Pleasants had wanted six tons but received only four. They completed the project by running a fuse and sealing the galleries with sandbags and logs to force the explosion upward. The mine lay beneath the section of Confederate works known as Elliott's Salient, located east of Jerusalem Plank Road.[48]

While work progressed on the mine, Burnside designated Brigadier General Edward Ferrero's United States Colored Troops division to lead the assault. This would be the first real chance for these African-American volunteers to demonstrate their willingness to fight. During the Overland Campaign, Ferrero's men had guarded the army's wagon train and "marched and sang." Brigadier General Edward Hincks's USCT division of the Eighteenth Corps participated in the attack of June 15. A Union sergeant admitted afterward, "The Niggers fight well and that is all the praise I can give them."[49]

Lincoln's Emancipation Proclamation had provided for the recruitment and enlistment of freedmen and former slaves. The War Department established the Bureau of Colored Troops to administer the process and to examine and approve officers for each regiment. The War Department, however, opposed the appointment of African-American commissioned officers, so white officers held the field- and company-level posts in the units. The department also refused to grant USCT volunteers the same monthly pay of white privates—thirteen dollars a month—setting it at eleven dollars. Eventually, nearly 180,000 black soldiers joined Federal service, augmenting Union forces, particularly during the conflict's final eighteen months.[50]

Ferrero's division consisted of nine USCT regiments in two brigades, in all slightly more than 3,000 officers and men. When Burnside assigned the main role to them, the division began daily drills and maneuvers in preparation for the attack. Burnside wanted some of Ferrero's units to sweep the works north and south of the anticipated crater that would be caused by the explosion, while the main body of the division drove west for Cemetery Hill along the Plank Road. By the time the mine had been filled with gunpowder, Ferrero and his officers had readied their troops. As a white corporal in the army noted earlier, "These blacks have something tangible to fight for."[51]

On July 28, concerned about the reliability of Ferrero's troops, Meade directed Burnside to replace them with one of the white divisions. Grant had been willing to use the African-Americans. He later offered an explanation for Meade's action, saying that if the assault failed, he and Meade would have been accused of "shoving these people ahead to get killed because we did not care anything about them." Burnside had his three division commanders draw lots to see which command would lead the attack. Brigadier James H. Ledlie, the incompetent drunk, selected the lot.[52]

Grant, meanwhile, had ordered a feint across the James River to draw Confederate units away from Petersburg. He assigned the operation to Winfield Scott Hancock, who had returned to command of the Second Corps, and Philip Sheridan's cavalry units. Hancock still showed the effects of his physical ailments, acted cautiously, and missed an opportunity to strike the undermanned works at Deep Bottom. But as Grant had hoped, Lee dispatched an infantry division to the scene.[53]

At 4:44 A.M., on July 30, after a lieutenant and a sergeant had respliced the broken fuse, the kegs of gunpowder in the Pennsylvanians' mine exploded. "It gave forth a low, rumbling sound," stated an eyewitness, "that shook the earth for a considerable distance, and sent up into the air a cloud of red sand and earth that resembled a water spout at sea." The three hundred South Carolinians and thirty gunners of a battery above the mine were hurled into the air like rag dolls. Two hundred seventy-eight were killed or wounded by the explosion. The crater created by the stunning blast measured more than 170 feet in length, 60 feet wide, and 30 feet deep. The ground outside the massive hole had been churned into "a labyrinth."[54]

Minutes later, 110 Union cannon and 54 mortars under Henry Hunt's direction opened fire, targeting Confederate batteries. Ledlie's troops rose from the ground and advanced. Less than two weeks before, an army inspector found an "indifferent" attitude in the Ninth Corps to discipline, drill, appearance of the men, and performance of duties. Ledlie's orders to his brigade commanders were to bypass the crater and to push ahead toward Cemetery Hill. Instead, the division's ranks became quickly disorganized, and the men plunged into the crater. "Some jumped in," said a lieutenant, "some tumbled in, others rolled in." Behind them, lay "a winnow of dead and dying" from enemy fire.[55]

Confusion stalled the Federal attack as troops tried to claw their way out of the "loose, light sand" of the large pit. Confederate reinforcements rushed in. The Yankees lurched ahead and were raked by musketry and artillery fire. Union division commander Orlando Willcox sent in one brigade to bolster the attackers. The combat raged for more than two hours in and around the crater. Finally, Burnside ordered in Ledlie's USCT regiments.[56]

The fighting escalated into a frenzy, which lasted into the afternoon. Watching from the Fifth Corps lines, Colonel Rufus Dawes asserted later: "I never saw more desperate, sanguinary fighting. Thank God we were not in the assaulting column." Three Confederate divisions joined the fury, hitting the Federal ranks with counterattacks. The sight of the black soldiers incensed the Southerners. "This day was the jubilee of fiends in human shape, and without souls," declared a Rebel. "Most of the fighting was done with bayonets and the butts of muskets." They shoved the Yankees into the crater and along its edges.[57]

"What a butchery it was" in the crater, insisted a USCT officer. The black troops fought with desperation, uncertain of their fate if captured. "Whites and blacks were squeezed so tightly together that there was hardly standing room," related a Massachusetts officer. "Even many of those killed were held in a standing position until jostled to the ground. . . . It was one seething cauldron of struggling, dying men." "Torn fragments of men" littered the bottom and sides of the crater.[58]

At mid-morning Grant had joined Burnside and told him: "The entire opportunity has been lost. There is now no chance for success. These troops must be immediately withdrawn. It is a slaughter to leave them here." But Burnside hoped "that something could be accomplished." Consequently, they were left there for hours and slaughtered. Finally, the survivors extricated themselves from the horrid pit and retired. Accounts make it clear that a number of black troops were shot down after they had been captured until Confederate officers halted the bloody work. The Battle of the Crater cost the Federals 3,800 in killed, wounded, and captured, while Southern losses amounted to approximately 1,500.[59]

The debacle of the Crater cost Burnside his command. He and Meade had been feuding for weeks, and as Meade put it, "The affair was very badly managed by Burnside." Chief of Staff Andrew Humphreys averred, "I have never been so completely disappointed in any military operation." Grant believed "the effort was a stupendous failure," blaming Burnside and Ledlie. He concluded that it "greatly impaired" Burnside's "usefulness" and granted him a personal leave. Ledlie was accorded a leave for health reasons, and neither man held field command again. Eventually a court of inquiry assigned blame for the failure to Burnside and his subordinate officers. Burnside's chief of staff, Major General John G. Parke, assumed command of the Ninth Corps.[60]

In December, Burnside met with the president and Grant to discuss future assignments. He had been contemplating resigning from the service but agreed to their request to remain in the army. Lincoln had appreciated his honesty, frankness, unselfishness, and his willingness to accept command of the army in place of George McClellan. But the Overland Campaign and Petersburg operations revealed his shortcomings as a general, even in corps command. When the interview ended, as he wrote, "I was not informed of any duty upon which I am to be placed." Word of a new post never came, and Burnside resigned his commission on April 15, 1865.[61]

On July 31, a day after the Crater fiasco, Grant met with Lincoln at Fort Monroe. The president had requested a meeting because of the past six weeks' events in the Shenandoah Valley. Lee's gamble in mid-June of sending Jubal Early's Second Corps to the region had resulted in the saving of Lynchburg, the chasing of David Hunter's Union army into the mountains of West Virginia, and a daring raid across the Potomac River. Early's veterans had defeated a Union force at the Battle of Monocacy on July 9, followed by a march to the edges of Washington. Even Lincoln, while visiting one of the forts, came under enemy fire.[62]

As the crisis had mounted over Early's raid, Grant had sent Horatio Wright's Sixth Corps to the capital. One of its divisions had arrived in time to fight at Monocacy. Wright led the pursuit of the Rebels, but Early's units returned safely to Virginia. On July 24, the Southerners had routed a Union command in the Second Battle of Kernstown. Six days later, Confederate cavalrymen rode into Chambersburg, Pennsylvania. When they were refused a tribute, they ignited a conflagration that destroyed more than four hundred homes, stores, and other buildings. "The thing seemed so much out of keeping with the position of affairs elsewhere," the New York *Times* editorialized. It was "the old story over again. The back door, by way of Shenandoah Valley, has been left invitingly open."[63]

Lincoln had sought this conference with Grant to find a commander who could shut "the back door" finally to enemy excursions. In truth, Grant had paid scant attention to Union operations in the region, but it had become for Lincoln not only a military, but also a political, matter. (Later in August, Lincoln had each Cabinet member sign, unread, a letter in which all of them agreed to support the next administration, which Lincoln thought would be Democratic.) With Sherman's army still outside Atlanta, the administration could not politically withstand further military embarrassments, such as Early's raid and the burning of Chambersburg.[64]

Lincoln and Grant agreed that the four departments embracing the region outside Washington should be consolidated into one, and a sufficient force assigned to it to defeat the enemy. Grant proposed George Meade for commander, who he knew would accept the post. Lincoln demurred, arguing that for months he had been resisting efforts to have Meade removed as army commander, and if he agreed now, it would appear as though he had bowed to the pressure. When Grant offered William Franklin, Lincoln dismissed the former Sixth Corps commander as too closely associated with McClellan. The two men parted without a decision.[65]

On August 3, Grant telegraphed that he wanted his cavalry commander, Philip Sheridan, appointed. Meade was not only disappointed by Grant's choice, he was galled that it was Sheridan. Within four days, Sheridan joined his new command at Harper's Ferry. While he passed through Washington, administration officials warned him to act cautiously because a defeat would have grave consequences for the president's reelection. Later in the month, Grant sent Wesley Merritt's and James Wilson's cavalry divisions to Sheridan, believing that they would be of more value in the open Shenandoah Valley.[66]

The campaign between Early and Sheridan in the Valley affected operations at Petersburg. When Lee learned of the buildup of Union forces in the region, he dispatched an infantry and a cavalry division to Early. Locked in the life-draining siege at Petersburg, Lee looked to the Valley for a possible decisive victory and recovery of the strategic initiative in Virginia. In turn, Grant undertook a series of offensive strikes on both sides of the James River. During these weeks, Lee enjoyed the closest parity in numbers to Grant since the campaign had commenced.[67]

Grant's offensives began in mid-August. Troops from the Union Second Corps and Tenth Corps from the Army of the James struck first at Deep Bottom, north of the James, on August 14. The Southern defenders repulsed the disjointed assaults, and the operation ended three days later. On August 18, Gouverneur Warren's Fifth Corps moved to seize the Weldon Railroad at Globe Tavern or "Yellow Tavern." A member of Meade's staff said at the time: "It is touching a tiger's cubs to get on that road! They [the Rebels] will not stand it."[68]

Meade's aide had it right, as Henry Heth's Confederate division came howling against the Yankees, plowing through a gap in the Federal line. Major General Romeyn B. Ayres's division broke in a panic-stricken flight. Warren's other infantry units and artillery batteries stopped Heth's troops. The next day, with John Parke's Ninth Corps moving up to support Warren, the Yankees repulsed an assault by Heth's and William Mahone's divisions. The Southerners tried again on August 21 to release the Federals' hold on the railroad. A Northern gunner exclaimed, "our canister layed them out." An officer noted, "For once it was all on our side." With this enemy failure, the Yankees had severed the Weldon Railroad permanently, forcing the Confederates to haul supplies by wagons in a thirty-mile detour.[69]

A staff officer at headquarters argued during the Globe Tavern fighting, "our men [are] not worth half what they were when we started on this campaign." Further evidence of the decline in the troops' fighting spirit came on August 25, at Ream's Station on the Weldon Railroad. Sent to wreck the tracks, Hancock's Second Corps was in a U-shaped line when Confederate infantry assailed its western face. The Yankees there belonged to the division of Francis Barlow, who had been forced a week earlier to relinquish command because of his health and depression over his wife's recent death. "He had been more like a dead man than a living man," thought an officer.[70]

Brigadier General Nelson Miles had succeeded Barlow, who left the army on leave. Twice Miles's troops repulsed Southern attacks. When the Confederates advanced for a third time, three of Miles's regiments on the right flank panicked suddenly and fled. Miles hurried to a brigade he had held in reserve, but its members either refused to advance or ran. Hancock rode into the shattered ranks, looking "more like a wild man, or a soldier possessed with a restless and demoniac spirit." He rallied some troops and had his horse killed under him. At points along his collapsing line, Miles's men and artillery crews resisted fiercely.[71]

Hancock ordered John Gibbon to send in two brigades, but as Gibbon admitted in a letter, "My men, I am sorry to say, did not behave well." He believed they "were 'fought out.'" Enough units, however, either rallied or held firm, saving the corps from a rout. Brigade commander James A. Beaver suffered a wound that led to the amputation of his right leg just below the hip. For his conduct on this day, he was promoted to brigadier general. Miles had shown the promise of an excellent division commander as he valiantly re-formed units and led them in minor counterattacks.[72]

Hancock retreated east after nightfall. The Battle of Ream's Station had cost him 550 killed and wounded and nearly 2,100 captured. Provost Marshal Marsena Patrick wrote a few days later that Hancock was "very low" in spirit and that "he now has no confidence in the Corps." When Gibbon offered to have his division broken up and assigned to other commands, Hancock replied that it might be for the best if Gibbon relinquished command of it. Incensed at his friend's words, Gibbon asked to be relieved. Hancock, however, relented and withdrew his letter. Much had transpired since they had stood together on Cemetery Ridge on July 3, 1863.[73]

Chief of Staff Humphreys offered his assessment of how far the combat efficiency of the army had fallen in a September 6 letter: "At the beginning of this campaign the command of the Second, Fifth, or Sixth Corps was something to desire; each was a splendid corps. It is not so any longer; their losses have stripped them of their best officers and best men and the additions made to them are of very, very inferior quality. The effect of such continuous fighting and such excessive fatigue is everywhere visible in depressing the spirit of men." He thought, however, with the coming of fall's cooler weather and the return of recovered wounded veterans, "we may expect a restoration of the former spirit."[74]

Three weeks after Humphreys penned his letter, Grant undertook a fifth offensive, with assaults north and south of the James River. The five-day operation achieved limited results and cost another 6,200 casualties. Union losses for the months of August and September exceeded 18,000, with Southern casualties half that number. A Maine private grumbled at this time, "It is my humble opinion that he [Grant] thinks no more for wounded men than the angler does the worm wriggling on his hook." After the most recent offensive, Grant told his wife, "I think it cannot be long now before the tug will come which, if it does not secure the prize, will put us where the end will be in sight."[75]

While Lee thwarted Grant's offensives, operations elsewhere resulted, at last, in stunning victories. On September 2, Sherman's Yankees entered Atlanta. "Atlanta is ours, and fairly won," wired Sherman. In the Shenandoah Valley, after a personal visit from Grant, Sheridan's Federals won decisive victories at Third Winchester on September 19, and at Fisher's Hill on September 22. Sheridan's cavalry then implemented a systematic destruction of the region's crops, livestock, barns, and mills, which residents called "The Burning." Finally, on October 19, following a stunning morning's defeat, Sheridan rallied his army and routed Jubal Early's Rebels in an afternoon counterattack in the Battle of Cedar Creek. Prospects for Lincoln's reelection had been enhanced. [76]

At Petersburg, autumn's cool weather was most welcome. Old regiments continued to leave the army, recruits arrived, coming in at a rate of 1,000 a day at times, and commands underwent further reorganizations. As always, death stalked the trenches, and men noticed the increasing flocks of buzzards. They took in more Rebel deserters and witnessed the execution of men who had been paid a bounty to enlist, then deserted and enlisted under another name to collect additional money. One of the condemned men had jumped bounty seventeen times before being caught. [77]

A member of the 11th Massachusetts wrote home in October that the news from Petersburg was the same as it had been for months, "nothing but war! war! war! all the time." But at about the same time, Sergeant Walter Carter of the 22nd Massachusetts declared: "*I would rather be as poor as Lazarus was, and die as he did, than have remained at home during these historical times. I glory in the word soldier, as applicable to myself even, and I'll never regret my army life.*" [78]

OFFICERS AND MEN TALKED about it for weeks, around campfires, in the trenches, and on picket duty. When the Democratic Party nominated the army's former commander, George McClellan, for president at the end of August, the presidential election assumed a special meaning for the remaining veterans in the army. No other general had enjoyed the popularity of Little Mac. His return to command had been in their dreams for months. In the hearts of his old soldiers, no general had ever replaced him. [79]

The Democratic convention adopted a platform that called for "a cessation of hostilities," an armistice. Although McClellan disavowed the plank, as the party's candidate he became identified with it. The men in the army, though, felt that he had abandoned them. A Pennsylvania sergeant asserted that there was "considerable indignation" over the call for an armistice. "For my part," he wrote, "I wish to see no kind of an armistice but a subjugation of the South." When the Confederates made clear that McClellan was their choice, an officer stated, "How have the mighty fallen!" Another soldier, in writing about the Southerners desiring McClellan's election, affirmed, "I think that is enough to make any loyal man try to defeat him."[80]

Like the folks at home, the officers and men believed that the victories of Sherman and Sheridan had made it only a matter of time before the Union prevailed. The War Department provided furloughs for troops who lived in states that did not allow absentee ballots. The Army of the Potomac voted on election day, November 8. By George Meade's figures, Lincoln received 13,500 ballots; McClellan, 5,500. In other Union armies, the soldiers overwhelmingly supported the president. Lincoln received 55 percent of the popular vote and 212 electoral votes to McClellan's 21.[81]

Private Theodore Gerrish declared later, "That grand old army performed many heroic acts . . . but never in its history did it do a more devoted service" than in casting its vote for Lincoln. A Michigander explained his regiment's vote, "We proposed to fight for peace, not to crawl and beg for it." Corporal Alexander Chisholm explained his reasons to his father, "Old Abe is the man that fears no noise so far away from home his head is level and his clothes fit him."[82]

Chapter 17

"I Never Seen a Crazier Set of Fellows"

W INFIELD SCOTT HANCOCK left the Army of the Potomac for a final time on November 26, 1864. At one time, he had been Hancock the Superb, the personification of the warrior's spirit. His tenure as a corps commander had been nearly eighteen months, the longest for any general in the army. His finest day and greatest service to the cause had come at Gettysburg on July 2, 1863. But the recurring effects of that battle's wound had sapped his physical strength and fiery presence on a battlefield. Like the Second Corps he led, Hancock was now but a vestige.[1]

The war ground away at men, even those, such as Hancock, who had survived their wounds. Earlier, Second Corps division commander Francis Barlow had had to relinquish his post because of wounds. Another of Hancock's subordinates, David Birney, had died from an intestinal hemorrhage on October 18 in Philadelphia. Birney had commanded the Tenth Corps when stricken ill and forced to take a leave. His death, said George Meade, "shocked every one here." Theodore Lyman of Meade's staff wrote of him: "Birney was one who had many enemies, but, in my belief, we had few officers who could command 10,000 men as well as he. He was a pale, Puritanical figure, with a demeanor of unmovable coldness," but, added Lyman, "I always felt safe when he had the division; it was always well put in and safely handled."[2]

The War Department had selected Hancock to recruit and organize a new Veteran Volunteer Corps. The department believed that the prestige of Hancock's name would induce former soldiers to reenlist and to serve under the renowned soldier. Unfortunately, the effort fell far short of the needed volunteers. Hancock finished the conflict as commander of the Middle Military Division. Before he departed from the army, Hancock had told Meade, "I am not ambitious to command Armies or Corps other than the Second (2d) Corps unless the public service is thought to be in question." The bond between him and the Second Corps had been forged at too many bloody places to be readily severed.[3]

Meade and Grant left Hancock's beloved corps in excellent hands when they assigned the army's chief of staff, Andrew Humphreys, to the command. War Department observer Charles Dana, who accompanied the army, called Humphreys "the great soldier of the Army of the Potomac," describing him as "a fighter" and as "a strategist, a tactician." Although Humphreys had proven to be the army's finest chief of staff, he had desired a corps command for more than a year. In July, he had rejected command of the Tenth Corps, which consisted of a white and a USCT division, stating that he would only command "my own race and my own people."[4]

Humphreys was, reported Lyman, "in high glee" at the appointment. As a division commander in the former Third Corps, Humphreys had shown "a perfect coolness under fire." He had been a strict disciplinarian, and in Dana's opinion, "was one of the loudest swearers that I ever knew." Physically small and lean, he wore a "bright red necktie" and a large black felt hat, which made him look "like a Quaker." Before long, men of the Second Corps nicknamed him "Humpy."[5]

Humphreys's appointment brought a request from John Gibbon to be relieved of command. As the Second Corps's senior division commander, Gibbon felt he deserved the position. "This," he wrote, "I regard as a slight which I am not willing to submit to." His relationship with Hancock had been strained since Ream's Station in August. Whether Hancock recommended Humphreys, a close friend and Gibbon's senior in rank, is uncertain. But Grant disapproved Gibbon's request and evidently mollified him.[6]

Two months later, the Army of the James underwent command and organizational changes. Major General E. O. C. Ord assumed command, succeeding Benjamin Butler, who had been on leave for months. The Tenth and Eighteenth corps were restructured and redesignated. The two divisions of white troops formed the Twenty-fourth Corps, while the pair of USCT divisions became the Twenty-fifth Corps, the only all-African-American army corps in American military history. Gibbon received command of the Twenty-fourth Corps; Major General Godfrey Weitzel, the Twenty-fifth.[7]

During these weeks, the armies at Petersburg settled into winter quarters. The Federals conducted another raid against the Weldon Railroad from December 7 to 12. The Yankees destroyed fifteen miles of track, culverts, and bridges about thirty miles south of Petersburg. The destruction inflicted a serious blow on the Confederates' supply links. On the Northerners' retreat, Rebel guerrillas killed blue-coated stragglers, enraging the Yankees, who torched nearby homes, barns, and outbuildings. A Union officer thought, however, that it "was carried . . . beyond all bounds."[8]

The season's first storm of sleet and snow blew in as the Weldon Railroad raid proceeded. It heralded what would become a bitter winter. A Maine veteran wrote in February 1865, "The weather has been very cold for a long time, much more so than I ever knew it to be before [or] since I've been a soldier." The inclement weather and the stalemate of trench warfare reduced operations to daily exchanges of picket and artillery fire. Whether in cold or hot weather, the reality in the works had not changed. The 2nd Vermont's Private Wilbur Fisk complained, "It is regular cold blooded dueling, day after day, with no decisive result on either side, and fellows no braver than I am, get tired of it after a while."[9]

Fisk belonged to the Vermont Brigade of the Sixth Corps, which had returned to the army in mid-December. These veterans had been the backbone of Philip Sheridan's army in the Shenandoah Valley during the fall campaign. With the Federals' victory at Cedar Creek and the approach of winter, active operations ceased in the region, and Sheridan willingly sent the infantry corps back to Petersburg. Sheridan kept two cavalry divisions with him for the winter in the Winchester area. When the Sixth Corps passed through Washington on its return march, the members were, according to one of them, "treated more as a band of convicts than as victorious troops."[10]

The arrival of the Sixth Corps and the ongoing flow of recruits, conscripts, and men who had recovered from their wounds brought the Union strength at Petersburg and at Bermuda Hundred to more than 120,000 by the end of 1864. Approximately 72,000 Confederates manned the Richmond and Petersburg defenses, including the troops who had served with Jubal Early in the Shenandoah Valley. "I admire the Southern people for one thing," wrote a Union surgeon, "and that is for their love of their own sunny homes. Would to God that all this blood was expended in a better cause."[11]

That cause was teetering across the Confederacy. In Georgia, Sherman's troops undertook the "March to the Sea," from Atlanta to Savannah, burning a scar of destruction across thousands of square miles of the state. When Savannah surrendered in December, Sherman presented the city to Abraham Lincoln as a Christmas present. In Tennessee, Major General George H. Thomas's Federals defeated John Hood's Confederate Army of Tennessee at the Battle of Franklin, and then routed the Southerners at Nashville on December 15 and 16. The Confederacy remained little more than a hollow shell.[12]

During the final week of January 1865, Confederate vice president Alexander H. Stephens and two commissioners entered Union lines at Petersburg. The delegation had come to discuss terms of peace. Grant informed Washington of their presence and then transported them to Hampton Roads to meet with Lincoln and Secretary of State William Seward. They held the conference on the president's steamer, the *River Queen*.[13]

Lincoln and Stephens had served together in Congress and had enjoyed a warm personal relationship. Negotiations on the status of the rebellious states, said Lincoln, could not be discussed until there was a cessation of hostilities and an acceptance of the Emancipation Proclamation. Seward informed the Confederate commissioners that Congress had submitted the Thirteenth Amendment, which outlawed involuntary servitude, to the Northern states for ratification. When one of the delegates described Lincoln's terms as nothing but "uncondi-

tional surrender on the part of the Confederate States and their people," the conference ended.[14]

The Hampton Roads Conference had scant, if any, chance of reaching a peaceful settlement. Lincoln would not compromise on the
restoration of the Union and the abolition of slavery, and Confederate
president Jefferson Davis would not accept such an admission of defeat.
All that remained was further bloodletting until Southern resistance
was crushed. A day after the conference ended, on February 4, Grant
ordered another offensive against Lee's lines at Petersburg.[15]

Grant committed most of his infantry and a cavalry division to the
movement, whose purpose was to extend Federal lines westward to
Boydton Plank Road. Meade had misgivings about the operation and
accompanied the columns. After months of personal frustration, Meade
had had his promotion to major general in the Regular Army confirmed
recently by the Senate. But his presence with the strike force could not
avert an embarrassing rout.[16]

The Confederates reacted swiftly and fiercely to the Union thrust,
shattering the ranks of two of Gouverneur Warren's Fifth Corps divisions at Hatcher's Run on February 6. A Pennsylvania officer called it
"the greatest skedaddle that has taken place yet." Federal reserves
repulsed the Rebels, but a brigade commander admitted that most of his
troops refused to advance. The next day, the Yankees regained some of
the lost ground. At a cost of 1,500 casualties, they had extended their
lines west three miles. Warren grumbled privately, "We are getting to
have an array of such poor soldiers that we have to lead them everywhere, and even then they run away from us."[17]

Several days before Hatcher's Run, Sergeant George Englis of the
89th New York wrote home: "We in the Army are watching the notion
of things with the greatest of anxiety, yet we want nothing but honorable terms. We want a peace that will be a suitable reward for what we
have endured to gain it & no other. Let us have no patch work about
it." The 17th Maine's Private John Haley professed, "the confounded
Rebels are as defiant as ever."[18]

"ONE OF THE MOST ANXIOUS periods of my experience during the
rebellion was the last few weeks before Petersburg," professed Grant in his

memoirs. "I felt that the situation of the Confederate army was such that they would try to make an escape at the earliest practicable moment, and I was afraid, every morning, that I would awake from my sleep to hear that Lee had gone, and that nothing was left but a picket line."[19]

Continuing, Grant wrote, "I was led to this fear by the fact that I could not see how it was possible for the Confederates to hold out much longer where they were." Nightly, Rebel deserters entered Union lines at Bermuda Hundred and Petersburg. Sherman's army had now marched into South Carolina, burning and wrecking the birthplace of secession. By the final week of March, Sherman was deep into North Carolina. His veterans had defeated a Confederate army under General Joseph Johnston at Bentonville, and were encamped at Goldsboro. Only Richmond and Petersburg stood as the final bastions of the Confederacy.[20]

In Petersburg, meanwhile, Lee, who had been appointed general-in-chief of the Confederate armies, wrestled with the grim reality that Grant saw as inevitable. He had roughly 55,000 officers and men in the miles of Richmond's and Petersburg's works. He had contemplated a union of his and Johnston's forces, but that possibility was remote at best. Lee settled finally on a desperate plan proposed by Major General John Gordon.[21]

An aggressive fighter, Gordon thought he could break the Union lines at Fort Stedman, a Federal redoubt due east of Petersburg. Once he had overrun the fort, Gordon planned to sweep down the enemy trenches and force the Yankees to abandon a major section of their line. Lee gave Gordon his entire Second Corps and brigades from other divisions, in all about 11,500 men in the main assault force, with an additional 8,000 troops available to exploit a decisive breakthrough.[22]

The Confederates came in the predawn darkness of March 25. Accomplishing a complete surprise, they seized Fort Stedman and batteries X, XI, and XII. Some of the unprepared Federals resisted but were overwhelmed by an enemy floodtide. Southern units wheeled north to seize Battery IX and south toward Fort Haskell. Blue-jacketed gunners in these works and from batteries in the rear pounded the attackers. The works in this section were held by Ninth Corps troops. To the rear of Fort Stedman, Brigadier General John Hartranft led three of his raw Pennsylvania regiments in a counterattack.[23]

Hartranft's 200th, 208th, and 209th Pennsylvania, and the 57th Massachusetts and 100th Pennsylvania of Orlando Willcox's division spearheaded the Federal counterassault. Members of the band of the 208th Pennsylvania discarded their instruments, picked up rifles, and joined their comrades. "The Johnnys rifles [were] crackling like corn in A hot skillet," wrote a Yankee. The 200th Pennsylvania lost more than one hundred men in less than twenty minutes. The Northerners had limited the enemy penetration, and now it became a matter of numbers and the fearful fire of Union cannon.[24]

Gordon's Confederates clung to Fort Stedman and nearby works for four hours. But minutes before eight o'clock, the Yankees charged from the north, south, and east. Hartranft's Pennsylvanians were in the forefront of the assault, retaking Fort Stedman. Late in the afternoon, troops from the Fifth and Sixth corps probed the enemy lines and suffered repulses. Total Union casualties for the day amounted to more than 2,000. Estimates of Southern losses range from 2,600 to more than 4,000. Only desperation could explain Lee's willingness to approve an attack that cost him nearly one tenth of his army.[25]

For the once magnificent Army of Northern Virginia, it had come down to a forlorn hope to break the enemy death grip at Petersburg and Richmond. Since the armies had arrived at Petersburg eight months ago, Lee's army had witnessed its life seep away by inches. Like the Federals, the Confederates had lost many of their finest officers and best troops during the Overland Campaign. Grant's offensives at Petersburg and the stream of deserters had further eroded the ranks. Too few men now stood beneath their star-crossed, red battle flags. But still they stood, manning the trenches and awaiting the enveloping darkness.[26]

A few days before Fort Stedman, Lincoln, his wife, Mary, and son Tad arrived at City Point, at the invitation of Grant. The general-in-chief and Julia Grant welcomed the Lincolns with lunches, parties, and dinners. The president surveyed the works, talked with officers and men, and visited hospitals. On March 28, on the *River Queen*, Lincoln met with Grant, Admiral David D. Porter, and William Sherman, who had traveled from North Carolina. The president brought them together to discuss future operations and terms of a peace settlement.[27]

Grant and Sherman tried to allay Lincoln's fears that Lee's army would elude Grant's grasp and unite with Johnston's. Lincoln stressed that neither general could accept terms other than the "capitulation" of their opponent's army. He desired, however, that generous terms of surrender be offered to the Southerners. "Let them all go, officers and all," said Lincoln, "I want submission, and no more bloodshed. . . . I want no one punished; treat them liberally all around. We want those people to return to their allegiance to the Union and submit to the laws."[28]

As Lincoln and his senior military officers conferred on the *River Queen*, Grant had set in motion an offensive that he hoped would break Lee's lines at Petersburg and end the war. A Pennsylvania sergeant described the activity on March 28: "Great excitement along the line, something big will happen soon sure. The sick is all ordered to the rear and all extra clothing. The Johnnies will get the devil soon or we will for the Army of the Potomac is getting in great earnest, and something will be done soon or I am no judge of faces or facts."[29]

Philip Sheridan and the cavalry divisions of Wesley Merritt and George Custer had rejoined the army. After spending the winter in the lower Shenandoah Valley, Sheridan had marched south at the end of February. On March 2, the Federals routed a remnant of Jubal Early's Confederate army at Waynesborough, and then headed east. When the horse soldiers reached White House on the Pamunkey River, Sheridan rested them and their mounts for a week. They started across the Peninsula on March 25, arriving at Petersburg two days later.[30]

Grant welcomed the return of the feisty Sheridan and his cavalrymen. Merritt's and Custer's troopers were, arguably, the finest combat units in the army. They were well equipped, well armed, and well led. They had been Sheridan's cutting edge in the Shenandoah Valley, and Grant planned for them a major role in the forthcoming offensive. The general-in-chief assigned Sheridan to overall command of the force, which consisted of the three reunited cavalry divisions of the Army of the Potomac, Gouverneur Warren's Fifth Corps, and Andrew Humphreys's Second Corps.[31]

The western flank of the Confederate defenses terminated at Five Forks, located six miles north of Dinwiddie Court House. If the Federals could seize the road intersection at Five Forks, Lee's lines at Petersburg would be unhinged. On the night of March 27–28, three infantry divisions and a cavalry division of E. O. C. Ord's Army of the James began crossing the Appomattox River to man the works held by Humphreys's troops. Ord's units arrived on the morning of March 29 as Sheridan's command started the movement. A soldier in the Sixth Corps, which remained in its Petersburg works with the Ninth Corps, predicted: "No doubt a few days more will settle the fate of Petersburg."[32]

Union cavalry reached Dinwiddie Court House on March 29, while Warren's infantry clashed with the Rebels along Boydton Plank Road, repulsing enemy charges. During the evening, a steady spring rain began to fall, continued the next day, and turned the roads into sloughs of mud. Colonel Horace Porter wrote, "The roads had become sheets of water; and it looked as if saving of the army would require the services, not of a Grant, but of a Noah." On March 30, Sheridan pushed some mounted units north toward Five Forks on a reconnaissance. They encountered Confederate horsemen and skirmished with the enemy before retiring. Lee had shifted infantry commands to Five Forks, bringing the force to 10,600 men. Major General George Pickett commanded the Southerners.[33]

The rain resumed on March 31, but Lee had ordered counterstrikes against the Union forces. Confederate infantry brigades slammed into the flank of one of Warren's divisions north of Boydton Plank Road, routing the Yankee troops. Warren's reserves and batteries blunted the enemy drive and drove the Southerners back into their works along White Oak Road. At Dinwiddie Court House, Sheridan's troopers repulsed assaults from Confederate infantrymen and cavalrymen. Darkness ended the combat, with opposing lines only a few hundred yards apart. Lee's orders to Pickett were clear: "Hold Five Forks at all hazards."[34]

Sheridan believed that his hold on Dinwiddie Court House was tenuous. He reported the situation to Meade, who informed Grant that Sheridan "will either have to come in or support must be sent to him." Grant directed that a Fifth Corps division be sent to Sheridan, but Meade suggested, "Would it not be well for Warren to go down with his whole corps and smash up the force in front of Sheridan?" Grant approved, and orders went out to Warren, "not to stop for anything."[35]

The critical confrontation at Five Forks developed slowly on April 1. During the night, Pickett had withdrawn from in front of Dinwiddie Court House to his works along White Oak Road when his cavalry picked up stragglers from the Union Fifth Corps. The van of Warren's corps arrived during the morning. Sheridan possessed a notoriously short fuse and had expected Warren hours earlier. He had already received permission from Grant to relieve Warren of command if the corps commander evidenced his characteristic stubbornness.[36]

Sheridan met with Warren at 1:00 P.M. and explained the Fifth Corps's role. While the Union cavalry demonstrated against the Confederate right flank, Warren's three divisions should press down Gravelly Run Church Road and roll up the enemy's left flank. Once the infantry became engaged, the horse soldiers would charge dismounted. According to reconnaissance reports and a map Warren had, the Rebels' line bent north at the intersection of White Oak and Gravelly Run Church roads. Instead, it lay seven hundred yards to the west.[37]

Consequently, when Warren reached the intersection and met only scattered resistance, he pushed two of his divisions north through the wooded ground. His left division, under Romeyn Ayres, however, located the Southern works about 4:30 P.M. Pickett and fellow generals had been enjoying a shad bake in the rear when the blue-coated storm broke. Warren rectified his error and sent Samuel Crawford's division into the Rebel rear. Pickett's position dissolved under the onslaught. Sheridan was at the front, shouting to the Federal infantrymen: "See the Sons of Bitches run! Give them Hell, boys!" The Yankees bagged about 2,400 prisoners, six cannon, and thirteen battle flags, at a loss of roughly eight hundred.[38]

"Everybody was riotous over the victory," contended Colonel Horace Porter, who had been sent by Grant to keep headquarters posted on the fighting. The victory had been complete and decisive. Porter rode east to inform Grant of the triumph. When Porter finished his report, Grant issued orders for "a general assault" along the Petersburg lines for 4:00 A.M. on April 2.[39]

At Five Forks, meanwhile, Warren received a message from Sheridan: "Major-General Warren, commanding Fifth Army Corps, is relieved from duty, and will report at once for orders to Lieutenant-General, commanding Armies of the United States." Sheridan's anger with Warren's perceived slowness had flared when Sheridan had been unable to locate Warren with the corps during the fighting. At the time Sheridan rode to his lines, Warren was redirecting Crawford's advance in the woods to the north. A staff officer with the corps had written only weeks before that the general "is never in the rear during an engagement with his corps." After he had corrected the movement of his units, Warren had acted gallantly at Five Forks.[40]

When he received the message, Warren rode to Sheridan. In a tone described as "very insubordinate," Warren said, "General, I trust you will reconsider your determination." Sheridan shot back: "Reconsider? Hell! I don't reconsider my decisions! Obey the order!" Sheridan had already assigned Brevet Major General Charles Griffin to temporary command of the corps, and Warren headed east to report to Grant's headquarters.[41]

Warren met with Grant that night and learned from the general-in-chief that he had given Sheridan the authorization to remove him. In Warren's account, Grant told him, "he thought well of my judgment but that I was too much inclined to use it in questioning orders before executing them; that I did not cooperate well with others, doubted too much the sense of my superiors, and interfered with my subordinates." Warren denied Grant's accusations. When Meade voiced similar words to Warren, the subordinate replied that he had been unwilling to have men slaughtered when "there was a hope of modifying even at a risk of a sacrifice of position, my sense of duty compelled me to act as I ever had done in these matters."[42]

To Grant and Meade, Warren's reluctance to obey orders for frontal assaults and his outspoken criticism of them had been his damning flaws as a corps commander. He demonstrated them initially at Spotsylvania and continued to act with stubborn caution as the campaign progressed. Warren possessed the attributes of a capable, if not excellent, corps commander—intelligence, executive ability, training, and personal bravery. But he was undoubtedly a difficult subordinate, whose arrogance and bouts with depression fueled his temper. He was ultimately, it would seem, a misfit at a time when an unblinking warrior directed the army. Eventually, a court of inquiry exonerated him of Sheridan's charges and his dismissal from command.[43]

THE STORM GATHERED BEHIND a veil of darkness. It had been swelling for nearly ten months, a looming presence on the horizon, waiting to be unleashed in a thunderclap of voices from thousands of men. During the night of April 1–2, 1865, Federal troops filed into position behind their works at Petersburg. They knew what was coming at the sound of signal guns. It was "the unknown in battle" that they dreaded, remembered a veteran, more "than the fear of death or combat." He thought of it as "the feeling which possesses one when in a dream he is falling from a great height."[44]

As they waited for "the *dead* work to come," 150 Union cannon hammered the Confederate works for three hours. When the bombardment ended, Southern pickets began firing into the blackness. With orders not to respond, the Yankees hugged the ground, keeping as quiet as possible. There were more than 40,000 of them, men from the Sixth, Ninth, and Twenty-fourth corps. At 4:40 A.M., the signal guns fired, and the storm burst upon the gray-coated defenders of Petersburg.[45]

Cheering men of the Sixth Corps—they had been Uncle John Sedgwick's boys—broke through enemy works south of Boydton Plank Road within an hour. The Southerners had fought stoutly until Union numbers prevailed. The Rebels belonged to Lieutenant General A. P. Hill's Third Corps, and he rode toward their shattered ranks. The Yankees pushed north across the Plank Road. In one of those fateful encounters in war, two Pennsylvanians stumbled upon Hill and an orderly. At a range of ten yards or so, the Federals fired their rifles, killing Hill instantly with a bullet in the heart.[46]

The Southerners, said a Federal, "fought like Tigers and we like Lions." It could hardly have been otherwise, as this was the Army of Northern Virginia. Once the Rebels' outer lines were overrun, they had to stop the Federals if they expected to escape from Petersburg. Along the city's eastern defenses, John Gordon's Second Corps troops limited the gains of the Union Ninth Corps. To the southwest, a small band of Mississippians made a valiant stand, which characterized the very best of Lee's army.[47]

Forts Gregg and Whitworth lay outside the western face of the Dimmock Line, the Confederates' inner works at Petersburg. Three hundred fifty members of the 12th and 16th Mississippi manned Fort Gregg; two hundred men of the 19th and 48th Mississippi, Fort Whitworth to the north. Their brigade commander, Nathaniel Harris, admonished Fort

Gregg's defenders, "Stand like iron, my brave boys!" The Mississippians gathered as many rifles as they could find and loaded them.[48]

Federals of the Twenty-fourth Corps attacked Fort Gregg about 1:00 P.M. The Mississippians triggered a withering fire, and in the words of a Yankee, "mowed down our men unmercifully." The attackers recoiled, rallied, and advanced again, enduring the blistering gunfire and reaching the ditch around the fort. Corps commander John Gibbon ordered in reinforcements, and this wave of Northerners was overwhelming. The Union soldiers poured over the parapets, "yelling, cursing and shooting with all the frenzy and rage of a horde of merciless barbarians."[49]

The defense of forts Gregg and Whitworth had cost the Mississippians two thirds of their numbers, but the two-hour stand allowed Lee to move troops into the Dimmock Line. When the Federals charged the inner works, they were blasted back. As the afternoon lengthened, Nelson Miles's Second Corps division shattered a Confederate line at Sutherland Station on the Southside Railroad west of Petersburg. For miles along the Appomattox River, Rebel units were fleeing north and west. Earlier, Lee had alerted President Davis that his line had been broken and "all preparation be made for leaving Richmond to-night." All the works around the capital were abandoned, and its defenders began the march away from the symbol of the Confederacy.[50]

Through the night of April 2–3, the Army of Northern Virginia abandoned Petersburg, crossing the Appomattox River and turning west. To the north, a red glow tinged the night sky as tobacco and cotton warehouses set on fire by the retreating troops burned. Mobs of residents soon roamed the streets, pillaging stores and torching buildings. A night of hell had descended upon the capital, where hours earlier, Davis, his Cabinet, and members of the president's staff had boarded a special train and steamed away toward Danville, Virginia.[51]

Richmond had served as capital of the Confederacy for thirty-one months. On the morning of April 3, blocks of the city lay in charred ruins as fires still raged. About 8:15 A.M., Godfrey Weitzel and troops of his Twenty-fifth Corps marched into the city. Details of Yankees hurried to raise United States flags over public buildings and herded remaining Confederate soldiers into Libby Prison, where Federals had been held. Later in the day, USCT regiments entered the city, eliciting stares and comments from the residents. By nightfall, Weitzel's troops had extinguished the fires and restored order.[52]

The next morning, Abraham Lincoln visited Richmond. He had spent the previous day in Petersburg, and had ignored warnings about his personal safety. When African-Americans recognized the president, they flocked to him, exclaiming, "Bless the Lord, Father Abraham Come." Lincoln stopped at the Confederate White House and the Virginia statehouse. He met with one of the Hampton Roads commissioners to discuss the impending peace. Whether Southerners understood it or not, Lincoln had been their greatest foe, but now he thought of the future. When an officer advised the president to be more careful about his safety, Lincoln said, "I cannot bring myself to believe that any human being lives who would do me harm."[53]

"THE ROAD WAS STREWN with equipments," stated Captain Clifford Stickney of the Union Second Corps staff, "dead and dying horses and mules, wagons, guns, caissons and in some cases we got cannon they had buried." Stickney's words described the leavings of a dying Army of Northern Virginia as it fled west from Petersburg. When Robert E. Lee abandoned Petersburg and Richmond on the night of April 2–3, it became a race for survival, a race that the remnants of his once magnificent army could no longer win.[54]

Lee's goal was to reach Danville, Virginia, and then turn south and unite with Joseph Johnston's army in North Carolina. At best, it was a remote possibility, at worst a forlorn hope. With each successive mile, more of Lee's men left the ranks, draining away not only numbers but also the army's weakening vitality. A South Carolinian remembered: "The Confederacy was considered as 'gone up,' and every man felt it his duty, as well as his privilege, to save himself. . . . The army was so crushed by the defeats of the last few days, that it straggled along without strength, and almost without thought. So we moved on in disorder, keeping no regular column, no regular pace . . . there were not many words spoken. An indescribable sadness weighed upon us."[55]

The end came swiftly. Philip Sheridan's cavalry units spearheaded the Union pursuit, gnawing at the edges of the Confederate columns, and racing ahead to cut off the retreat. The blue-jacketed Yankees rode south of the Appomattox River, trailed by the Second, Fifth, and Sixth corps of the Army of the Potomac. Farther south, troops from the Army of the James and the Ninth Corps plodded west. Forced to halt at Amelia Court House to secure food from local citizens on April 4 and 5, Lee's army lost two critical days.[56]

The Southerners marched through the night of April 5–6. Late on the afternoon of April 6, Sheridan's horsemen and Horatio Wright's Sixth Corps troops struck the rear of the Confederate column in the bottomlands along Sayler's Creek. The Southerners resisted stubbornly but were caught in a vise of Union cavalry and infantry. "Yelling like Indians," the Yankees surged into the enemy ranks, seizing thousands of prisoners, including eight generals, cannon, and wagons. When Lee saw the shards of two of his corps, he exclaimed: "My God! Has the army dissolved?" That night, Sheridan told Grant, "If the thing is pressed I think Lee will surrender."[57]

The Federals pressed the pursuit on April 7. The Southerners crossed the Appomattox River during the day at Farmville and High Bridge. The day before, a band of Rebels defended this latter site, which consisted of an imposing railroad span and a wagon bridge. The Confederates mauled a Union cavalry and infantry force, routing their foes and capturing eight hundred Federals. In the fighting, Brigadier General James Dearing fell mortally wounded, the last general in Lee's army to lose his life.[58]

On the morning of April 7, John Gordon's Confederate Second Corps crossed at High Bridge and destroyed the railroad span. Before his men could burn the smaller bridge, however, Andrew Humphreys's Second Corps arrived. The 19th Maine hurried to the wooden wagon bridge and doused the fires, saving the structure. Humphreys pushed ahead, and at Cumberland Church, his troops attacked Gordon's rear guard. Gordon's men still had grit and repulsed the assaults. Union Brigadier General Thomas A. Smyth suffered a mortal wound, dying two days later and becoming the last Federal general to die in the war.[59]

Lee gave his exhausted troops a few hours rest before resuming the march through the night of April 7–8. Before Lee left a residence near Cumberland Church, a courier delivered him a letter from Grant. "The

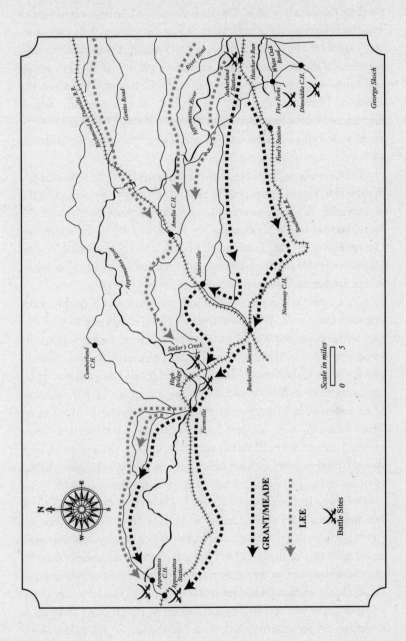

result of the last week must convince you of the hopelessness of further resistance on the part of the Army of Northern Virginia in this struggle," wrote Grant. "I feel that it is so, and regard it as my duty to shift from myself the responsibility of any further effusion of blood by asking of you the surrender of that portion of the C. S. Army known as the Army of Northern Virginia." Lee replied, disagreeing with Grant's assessment of "the hopelessness of further resistance." But desiring "to avoid useless effusion of blood," Lee asked what "the terms you will offer on condition of its surrender."[60]

The Confederates followed Lynchburg Stage Road throughout April 8, their rear dogged by the Federal Second and Sixth corps. South of the Appomattox River, Union cavalry and infantry from the Army of the James and Fifth and Ninth corps angled west. Late in the afternoon, George Custer's Third Cavalry Division reached Appomattox Station on the Southside Railroad. Engines and railroad cars stood at the depot, and the mounted Yankees galloped in and seized them.[61]

On a ridge to the east, Lee's surplus artillery and a small cavalry brigade were posted. When the Federals charged at the station, Rebel gun crews opened fire. Custer gathered his regiments and attacked, only to be repulsed. The dashing general added more troopers to the assault, and in the dark, the Yankees surged up the ridge and into the gun crews, capturing more than 20 cannon, five battle flags, and 1,000 prisoners. More importantly, Custer's division had cut off the retreat of Lee's army, which bivouacked to the east in the valley near Appomattox Court House. Joining Custer, Sheridan sent a dispatch to Grant, writing in it that if Union infantry "can get up tonight we will perhaps finish the job in the morning. I do not think Lee means to surrender to do so."[62]

Defiant to the end, the proud Army of Northern Virginia undertook one final attack on the morning of April 9. John Gordon's Second Corps—what was left of Stonewall Jackson's foot cavalry—tried to open an escape route for the rest of the army. But as they advanced, infantrymen from the Army of the James manned the ridge west of Appomattox Court House. Fighting flared for an hour or so, and then it was finished. Lee and Grant had exchanged more letters, which centered on terms of surrender. At about ten o'clock on the morning of April 9, Lee sent a final message, "I therefore request an interview, at such time and place as you may designate, to discuss the terms of the surrender of this army in accordance with your offer to have such an interview."[63]

Officers worked out a truce between the armies. At 1:30 P.M., Grant and Lee met in the parlor of the Wilmer McLean home in Appomattox Court House. A cluster of Union generals watched the proceedings, while Lee, dressed in a full uniform, with a sash and sword, had with him only his military secretary, Lieutenant Colonel Charles Marshall. George Meade, who had been ill most of the week, was not present, miles to the rear with his infantry corps.[64]

Grant was generous in his terms as Abraham Lincoln had wanted. The Confederates would be paroled and allowed to return to their homes, officers could keep their sidearms and personal property, and cavalrymen and artillerymen could retain the horses that belonged to them. Grant insisted, however, that Lee's troops must formally surrender their rifles, cannon, and battle flags. Both men designated three officers to work out the details of the surrender. When Lee mentioned his men's lack of food, Grant promised to furnish them with 25,000 rations.[65]

When Grant left the McLean house, he sent a telegram to Washington: "General Lee surrendered the Army of Northern Virginia this afternoon upon terms proposed by myself." In his memoirs Grant stated, "I felt anything rather than rejoicing at the downfall of a foe who had fought so long and valiantly, and had suffered so much for a cause, though that cause was, I believe, one of the worst for which a people ever fought, and one for which there was the least excuse."[66]

The news of Lee's surrender swept through the Union ranks like a volley of musketry. Men threw hats, knapsacks, canteens, and "everything else" into the air. They shouted, rolled in the mud, danced, and laughed. "In fact I never seen a crazier set of fellows anywhere before or since," averred a Pennsylvania sergeant. "We never saw a happier day in my life," insisted another soldier. When Meade passed along the ranks, "His name was yelled and screamed in a way I dreamt any man's could be," declared army chief of staff Alexander Webb.[67]

The 2nd Rhode Island's Captain Charles Perkins felt that the surrender of Lee's army "cansels all of the hardships that I have seen and goin through." A fellow New Englander, Private John Haley of the 17th Maine, wrote: "It was not easy to adjust to the new order of things. All that we have suffered and fought for and almost died for, at last consummated. Three years of suspense and horror were broken." Artillery commander Charles Wainwright thought that it would have been "more in accordance with what poetical justice would seem to owe to the Army of the Potomac" if it had ended in a climactic battle, such as Gettysburg. On this day of celebration, few survivors would have agreed with Wainwright.[68]

On the morning of Wednesday, April 12, the Army of Northern Virginia marched down its final road. As Grant had prescribed, its members were required to lay down their arms and cherished battle flags in a formal ceremony. Waiting to receive them, aligned in ranks on both sides of Lynchburg Stage Road, were members of the Union Fifth Corps, under the command of Brigadier General Joshua Chamberlain. It took hours for these redoubtable warriors to march past, stack their rifles, and yield their flags. When it was finished, the Southerners headed toward their homes and toward a society that had been shattered. "Setting aside the cause in which it was engaged," concluded Wainwright, "the history of the Army of Northern Virginia has been a glorious one."[69]

Stillness returned to Appomattox Court House during the next few days as the various Union corps marched away. Ultimately, this journey would end at their homes, and the mood in the ranks reflected that promise. Then on April 15 came the news that President Abraham Lincoln had been struck down by an assassin on April 14, and had died at 7:22 A.M. that morning. In time they would learn that an actor and Southern sympathizer, John Wilkes Booth, had shot Lincoln while the president attended a play at Ford's Theatre in Washington.[70]

The officers and men were given the news at evening dress parade. "A silent gloom fell upon us like a pall," wrote Sergeant Samuel Clare of the 116th Pennsylvania. "No one spoke or moved, our sorrow was so great that we could scarcely realize what had happened." It was as "if we each had lost a near and dear friend at home." Another soldier recalled, "What a death like stillness came over the army that night not a stir in all the camp nor a sound save the whipperwill in the tree tops. Seamed as if all our hardship and Sufering had been for nothing."[71]

"What a hold Old Honest Abe Lincoln had on the hearts of the soldiers of the army," continued Sergeant Clare, "could only be told by the way they showed their mourning for him." Perhaps in their quietude they recalled his awkwardness on a horse as he reviewed them, the sadness in his eyes, and his tenderness as he walked through hospitals. They belonged to him as no other army in American history belonged to a president. They had not always agreed with his decisions, but in their hearts, they knew that their welfare was always on his mind. The depth of their sadness could not be measured.[72]

"THE WEATHER WAS ABSOLUTELY perfect," a newspaperman wrote of May 23, 1865. Two days of rain had given away to bright sunshine and warmth. President Andrew Johnson had appointed this day and the next for grand reviews of the Army of the Potomac and William Sherman's army. A reviewing stand had been erected on Pennsylvania Avenue, filled with dignitaries—the president, Cabinet members, governors, Grant, Sherman, and Meade. Thousands of residents, visitors, and schoolchildren, who had been given a holiday, lined the streets. "Talk about big Things," attested a soldier, "this takes The cap sheaf off of all big times."[73]

The Grand Review of the Army of the Potomac began about nine o'clock. At the head of the columns rode the cavalry regiments, at their post in the forefront, leading the army toward a destination. It had taken Joseph Hooker to appreciate their potential and to organize them into a corps. In turn, they fulfilled the promise at Brandy Station, Gettysburg, Yellow Tavern, Haw's Shop, Trevilian Station, the Shenandoah Valley, and Appomattox. They had been led by such men as Philip Sheridan, John Buford, Benjamin "Grimes" Davis, David Gregg, Wesley Merritt, and George Custer, whose horse bolted in front of the grandstand. By war's end, there were few, if any, better fighters in the Union armies.[74]

Behind the horsemen marched members of the provost marshal and engineer brigades. Then came the infantry, striding forth in files of twenty men across. In the lead was the Ninth Corps, originally commanded by Ambrose Burnside. They had fought at South Mountain and Antietam and had watched Fredericksburg's horrors before being transferred to Tennessee. Returning to the east in the spring of 1864, they saw the worst of the war in the Overland Campaign and at Petersburg. During those final months, the Ninth Corps included USCT regiments, men who carried, by their presence, the promise of a better future for their own people.[75]

Next came the Fifth Corps, wearers of the Maltese cross, who had followed Fitz John Porter, George Sykes, and Gouverneur Warren. In its column were former members of the First Corps, veterans who had stood with John Reynolds on McPherson's Ridge on July 1, 1863. Gone from their ranks were the Pennsylvania Reserves, the Iron Brigade, the "Red Devils" of the 5th New York, 4th Michigan, 22nd Massachusetts, and the Regulars. Beneath torn flags the 20th Maine, 140th New York, 83rd Pennsylvania, 118th Pennsylvania, and 16th Michigan passed in review. These Yankees had held the lines at Mechanicsville, Malvern Hill, and on Little Round Top. They were tough and steady soldiers.[76]

Finally, bringing up the rear, tramped the Second Corps. Terrible places had always seemed to find them—West Woods, Bloody Lane, Marye's Heights, Wheatfield, Cemetery Ridge, and Bloody Angle. Edwin Sumner, Winfield Scott Hancock, and Andrew Humphreys had led them. They had stood with John Gibbon, Francis Barlow, David Birney, Edward Cross, Israel Richardson, and Alexander Hays. Some of them had learned soldiering in the old Third Corps, wearing the "red patch" of Philip Kearny. They could tell all who would listen that their record needed no embellishment.[77]

Absent this day was the Sixth Corps, which had been delayed with assignments after Appomattox. They would pass in review on June 8. In the beginning they belonged to William Franklin and at the end to Horatio Wright, but always to Uncle John Sedgwick. They had been the army's fortunate corps, spared from some of the worst combat until the spring of 1864. Their forced march to Gettysburg had been one of their most memorable achievements. Unlike the other corps, their flags carried the names of Third Winchester, Fisher's Hill, and Cedar Creek in the Shenandoah Valley.[78]

Sherman's tough Westerners followed the next day, May 24. The conflict had not ended for them until April 24, when Sherman accepted the surrender of Joseph Johnston's army outside Durham Station, North Carolina. Artillery officer Charles Wainwright claimed after watching Sherman's veterans pass, "It was generally thought that they marched somewhat better than the Army of the Potomac." For Sherman's men and their comrades in other Western armies, the campaigns had covered hundreds of miles, from Tennessee and Mississippi, through Georgia, to the Carolinas. Operations in this theater contrasted sharply in geographic size to the narrow confines of carnage in the East.[79]

The disbandment of the armies took weeks. On June 28, General Order No. 35 consolidated the few units still at Washington into a Provisional Division, and the Army of the Potomac ceased to exist. By then, most of its members had arrived at their homes. As one of them wrote when he returned to his family, "Hardtack a thing of the past." "Citizen Clothes" had replaced "the old Army Blue," and he had begun making a living.[80]

Hundreds of thousands of his comrades stored away their uniforms and set to work as he had done. In time, they renewed old associations as members of the Grand Army of the Republic and the Military Order of the Loyal Legion of the United States. They marched in Decoration Day or Memorial Day parades, met on former battlefields, wrote memoirs, guarded their regiments' reputations, and tried to mold history. For veterans of the Army of the Potomac, history would rub hard.

The first study of the army appeared within a year of the conflict's end, written by William Swinton, a wartime correspondent for the New York *Times*. Swinton's purpose for the book was "to speak the truth with candor, and to challenge for that army the recognition which is justly its due, but which has not yet been accorded it—the work it did and the circumstances under which it was done being both little understood." Describing the army as "that mighty creation of the patriotism of a free people," Swinton argued that it "never gave up, but made a good fight, and finally reached the goal. For that, it should be accorded history's due."[81]

More than 135 years have passed since Swinton presented his case for "the recognition" due the army. Historians and scholars have written biographies of its leaders, histories of some of its units, and detailed studies of various battles and campaigns. Still, its record remains, or as a modern military historian, Williamson Murray, has concluded, "the Army of the Potomac had a record of unambiguous failure matched by no other unit of equivalent size in the history of the United States Army." By his count, it tallied twelve defeats, one draw (Antietam), and two victories (Gettysburg and Five Forks).[82]

It can be argued that the army won tactical victories at Glendale and Malvern Hill, but the crux of the historian's argument remains valid. Several critical factors contributed to that record. From its creation, its primary duty was the defense of Washington. From the White House and from the War Department came constant reminders to its commanders that the security of the capital could not be risked. Because of its proximity to Washington and its primacy in the eyes of the Northern populace, it was the army most identified with the administration's war aims. This burden brought politics into the army's campaigns and into its selection of commanders.[83]

No commander of the army reflected these tensions and fostered them more than George B. McClellan. His imprint on the army was indelible. When McClellan told his generals during the Seven Days Campaign, "If we were defeated, the Army and the country would be lost," he defined his generalship. He waged his campaigns not to lose, rather than to win. To be sure, he was a cautious man by nature and inordinately sensitive about his reputation. In his estimation, his crowning achievement was the Battle of Antietam, an engagement he neither won nor lost.[84]

At the root of his difficulties with Abraham Lincoln was McClellan's willful disregard of the political pressures on the administration. The general possessed both political astuteness and blindness to the fundamental tie between the military and civilians in a democratic society. He opposed viscerally the direction of the government's policies as the conflict deepened and lengthened during 1862. To his discredit, he allowed his personal disagreements with the administration to poison the army's senior leadership, which led to internal bickering and eventual crisis. Ironically, had McClellan attained a decisive victory on the Peninsula he might have stayed the currents he so feared.[85]

McClellan's cautious generalship sank deep into the marrow of the army's leadership. Ambrose Burnside, Joseph Hooker, and George

Meade proved to be men who saw the war in a narrow framework. Each had to assure the protection of the capital before he could conduct a campaign, but none of them saw beyond the next battlefield. Of the four of them, only McClellan demonstrated a strategic vision with his movement to the Peninsula. Meade, for example, was an excellent administrator, prudent, competent, and a capable tactician. In the words of historian Richard J. Sommers, "He made limited efforts for limited gains." Meade, Sommers has argued, "would never have lost the war in Virginia, but, unaided, he would never have won it, either." None of the army's four commanders would have turned the army south as Ulysses Grant did on the night of May 7, 1864, after two bloody days of battle in the Wilderness.[86]

From its earliest days, the Regular Army's seniority system cursed it with generals such as Irvin McDowell, Samuel Heintzelman, Edwin Sumner, and Erasmus Keyes. It took time to move them aside and bring younger, less hidebound officers to leadership positions. Philip Kearny stood out in 1862 because he had the temperament of a warrior, in contrast to so many of the other generals. With Hooker's replacement of Burnside and the removal of other generals, the senior leadership of the army began to change. It never rid itself entirely of cautiousness, but excellent, more aggressive officers emerged to lead divisions and brigades.

Any evaluation of the army's record has to take into account its opponent. "War is a nasty business," historian Murray has contended, "and the Confederate generals in the East were extremely good at it." From the summer of 1862 through the spring of 1864, the Army of Northern Virginia forged its own record of achievement, which ranks it among the finest armies in American history. To be sure, Robert E. Lee matched skills with McClellan, Burnside, Hooker, and Meade, but his army fought with a spirit and fierceness. Lee, Stonewall Jackson, James Longstreet, and other generals infused it with an aggressiveness that overcame Union numerical advantages. Against long odds, it carried the Confederacy nearly to independence.[87]

The Army of Northern Virginia's battlefield prowess and victories came against an opponent that at its core—its rank and file—was a great army. No other Union army opposed such a formidable foe, fought more battles, incurred more casualties, and withstood more command turmoil than the Army of the Potomac. At times, its soldiers despaired of the outcome and cursed their leaders. But they remained devoted to the cause, despite the fearful losses and inept generalship. Resiliency became one of their defining characteristics. They wanted a fair fight with their enemy, convinced that they could whip them every time on such a field.

If the greatness of men can be found in specific places, there was no better place to measure the rank and file of the Army of the Potomac than before the stone wall at Fredericksburg. It was an insane place, but time and again men went forth—because of orders, because of duty, because of something beyond themselves. It was a place of greatness.

One of their own gave them a fitting epitaph. Writing in October 1863, Sergeant Charles Bowen of the 12th United States Infantry told his wife: "It is actually wonderful how the Army of the Potomac stand the deprivations, trials, & reverses that have been heaped on them without stint or mercy to meet the foe with undaunted spirits. I do not believe there ever was an army in any country that would endure the same treatment this army has & yet be ready to fight as good a battle, & perhaps a better one than they could when they first came out. Although we have been deprived of the privilege of winning any lasting victories, it has not been our fault, as history in future days will show. I look forward to the time when a man can say with pride, 'I belonged to the *Army of the Potomac.*' We look to history to give us our just due & to place all the blame where it belongs."[88]

⊰ ABBREVIATIONS ⊱

Works cited by the author and short titles will be found in full in the
Bibliography. The following abbreviations are used in the notes:

AAS	American Antiquarian Society
ACHS	Augusta County Historical Society
ADAH	Alabama Department of Archives and History
AFHS	Asa Fitch Historical Society
ANB	Antietam National Battlefield
BC	Bowdoin College
B&G	*Blue & Gray Magazine*
B&L	*Battles and Leaders*
BP	*Bachelder Papers*
BPL	Bancroft Public Library
BU	Brown University
BUL	Boston University Library
CHS	Chicago Historical Society
CMU	Central Michigan University
CR	Compiled Records
CSL	Connecticut State Library
CSR	Compiled Service Records
CTHS	Connecticut Historical Society
CU	Cornell University
CV	*Confederate Veteran*
CWTI	*Civil War Times Illustrated*
DCHS	Dutchess County Historical Society
DHSTC	DeWitt Historical Society of Tompkins County
DPA	Delaware Public Archives
DPL	Detroit Public Library
DU	Duke University
ECHS	Erie County Historical Society
ECU	East Carolina University

EU	Emory University
FM	Franklin and Marshall College
FSA	Florida State Archives
FSNMP	Fredericksburg-Spotsylvania National Military Park
GC	Gettysburg College
GHS	Georgia Historical Society
GM	*Gettysburg Magazine*
GNMP	Gettysburg National Military Park
HFNHP	Harpers Ferry National Historical Park
HL	Huntington Library
HSP	Historical Society of Pennsylvania
HU	Harvard University
IHS	Indiana Historical Society
ISL	Indiana State Library
IU	Indiana University
LC	Library of Congress
LSU	Louisiana State University
LVA	Library of Virginia
MAHS	Massachusetts Historical Society
MC	Museum of the Confederacy
MCHM	Monroe County Historical Museum
MDAH	Mississippi Department of Archives and History
MDHS	Maryland Historical Society
MESA	Maine State Archives
MGA	Middle Georgia Archives
MNBP	Manassas National Battlefield Park
MNHS	Minnesota Historical Society
MOHS	Missouri Historical Society
MOLLUS	Military Order of the Loyal Legion of the United States
MSA	Mississippi State Archives
MSU	Michigan State University
NA	National Archives
NC	Navarro College
NCSA	North Carolina State Archives
NHHS	New Hampshire Historical Society
N&S	*North & South Magazine*
NYHS	New-York Historical Society
NYSA	New York State Archives
NYSL	New York State Library
OHS	Ohio Historical Society
OR	*War of the Rebellion: Official Records of Union and Confederate Armies*
OSU	Ohio State University
PHMC	Pennsylvania Historical and Museum Commission

PMHB	*Pennsylvania Magazine of History and Biography*
PSU	Penn State University
PU	Princeton University
QU	Queen's University
RHSP	*Rockbridge Historical Society Proceedings*
RPL	Rochester Public Library
SAM	State Archives of Michigan
SHSP	*Southern Historical Society Papers*
SHSW	State Historical Society of Wisconsin
SOR	*Supplement to the Official Records of the Union and Confederate Armies*
TSLA	Tennessee State Library and Archives
TU	Tulane University
UC	University of Chicago
UCGS	Ulster County Genealogical Society
UGA	University of Georgia
UM	University of Michigan
UME	University of Maine
UNC	University of North Carolina
UPA	University of Pennsylvania
UR	University of Rochester
USAMHI	United States Army Military History Institute
USC	University of South Carolina
USMA	United States Military Academy
UT	University of Texas
UVA	University of Virginia
UVT	University of Vermont
UWLC	University of Wisconsin–La Crosse
VATU	Virginia Tech University
VHS	Virginia Historical Society
VMHB	*Virginia Magazine of History and Biography*
VMI	Virginia Military Institute
VSL	Virginia State Library
VTHS	Vermont Historical Society
WL	Washington and Lee University
WLM	War Library and Museum
WM	The College of William and Mary
WMH	*Wisconsin Magazine of History*
WMU	Western Michigan University
WRHS	Western Reserve Historical Society
YU	Yale University

⊰ NOTES ⊱

Chapter 1: "Things Look Very Mutch Like War"

1. Henry L. Martin, pseudonym "D. L. Dalton"–Jefferson Davis, June 29, 1861, Martin Letter, USAMHI.
2. Davis, *Battle at Bull Run*, pp. 52–53.
3. Wiley, *Life of Billy Yank*, pp. 296, 307–9, 324; Cowley, ed., *With My Face to the Enemy*, p. 60; Paludan, *Presidency*, p. 9.
4. Wiley, *Life of Billy Yank*, p. 296; Starr, *Union Cavalry*, v. 1, p. 54; Small, ed., *Road*, p. 1; Niven, *Connecticut*, p. 47; Livermore, *Days and Events*, p. 7.
5. Weigley, *Great Civil War*, pp. xxvi; Wiley, *Life of Billy Yank*, pp. 37–38; McPherson, *For Cause and Comrades*, passim.
6. William G. Davis–Parents, July 10, 1862, Davis Letters, MNBP; James B. Flynn–most affectionate Parents, May 5, June 4, 1861, Flynn Papers, NC; Horace Emerson–Brother, April 24, 1861, Emerson Letters, UM; Weigley, *Great Civil War*, p. xxvi.
7. Miers, ed., *Wash Roebling's War*, p. 22; James B. Flynn–affectionate parents, June 10, 1861, Flynn Papers, NC; Weigley, *Great Civil War*, p. xxviii.
8. Nevins, ed., *Diary of the Civil War*, p. 123.
9. Donald, *Lincoln*, p. 296; Starr, *Union Cavalry*, v. 1, p. 47; Reese, *Sykes' Regular Infantry Division*, pp. 8–10; Cowley, ed., *With My Face to the Enemy*, p. 33.
10. Jones, *Civil War Command*, p. 3; Davis, *Lincoln's Men*, p. 35; Small, ed., *Road*, pp. 1–2; Niven, *Connecticut*, p. 47.
11. Starr, *Union Cavalry*, v. 1, p. 63; Copeland, *Logan Guards*, p. 19; Miller, *Training of an Army*, pp. 3, 5.
12. Cooling, *Symbol*, pp. 34, 47.
13. Ibid., pp. 34, 37, 38, 40; Davis, *Lincoln's Men*, pp. 28–30; Copeland, *Logan Guards*, pp. 23, 27.
14. Nevins, ed., *Diary of the Civil War*, pp. 120, 124, 127; Lash, *"Duty Well Done,"* p. 1; Herdegen, *Men Stood*, p. 20; Love, *Wisconsin*, pp. 140–43.
15. Jones, *Civil War Command*, p. 4; Davenport, *Camp and Field Life*, pp. 20–21; Sauers, *Advance the Colors!*, v. 1, p. 247; Weigley, *Great Civil War*, p. 56; Geary, *We Need Men*, p. 81; Pearson, *James S. Wadsworth*, p. 61.
16. Conyngham, *Irish Brigade*, p. 23; Edward Hollister–Brother, June 25, 1861, Hollister Letters, MNBP; Styple, ed., *Writing*, p. 16; Mead, "Journal," SHSW.

17. James B. Flynn–affectionate Parents, May 18, 22, 1861, Flynn Papers, NC; Caleb H. Beal–Father, May 31, 1861, Beal Papers, MAHS; Jordan, ed., *Civil War Journals*, p. 31; Styple, ed., *Writing*, p. 19; Curtis C. Pollock–Ma, April 28, 1861, Pollock Letters, USAMHI.

18. James B. Flynn–affectionate Parents, May 7, 1861, Flynn Papers, NC; Robert A. Browne–Dearest Mary, May 18, 1861, Browne Letters, PSU; C. E. Davison–Friend Hollister, July 1, 1861, Hollister Letters, MNBP; Jordan, ed., *Civil War Journals*, p. 24.

19. Hill, *Our Boys*, p. 59; Samito, ed., *Commanding Boston's Irish Ninth*, p. 16; John H. Burrill–Parents, July 5, 1861, Burrill Letters and Diary, USAMHI.

20. Livermore, *Days and Events*, p. 7; Styple, ed., *Writing*, pp. 13, 18; Lord, *Civil War*, v. 1, pp. 311–14; Gallagher, ed., *Wilderness Campaign*, p. 202; Wright, *No More Gallant a Deed*, p. 42; Gambone, *Major-General John Frederick Hartranft*, pp. 10–11.

21. Bacarella, *Lincoln's Foreign Legion*, pp. 26–27; Styple, ed., *Writing*, p. 26; Conyngham, *Irish Brigade*, pp. 19, 20, 40; Samito, ed., *Commanding Boston's Irish Ninth*, pp. xxiii–xxiv, 7; Wiley, *Life of Billy Yank*, pp. 307–9.

22. Hennessy, ed., *Fighting*, p. 7; Styple, ed., *Writing*, p. 26; Jordan, ed., *Civil War Journals*, pp. 26, 28.

23. Davis, *Battle at Bull Run*, p. 5; Williams, *Lincoln and His Generals*, p. 3; Wert, *Custer*, p. 41.

24. Davis, *Battle at Bull Run*, p. 5; Adams, *Our Masters*, p. 79; Beale, ed., *Diary*, v. 1, p. 172.

25. Small, ed., *Road*, p. 17; Perret, "Anaconda," *N&S*, 6, 4, pp. 38–39.

26. Perret, "Anaconda," *N&S*, 6, 4, pp. 38–39; Donald, *Lincoln*, pp. 305–6; Warner, *Generals in Blue*, pp. 297–98, 309; Hassler, *Commanders*, p. xviii; Davis, *Battle at Bull Run*, pp. 11, 35; Stine, *History*, p. 6.

27. Warner, *Generals in Blue*, p. 298; Miller, ed., *Peninsula Campaign*, v. 2, p. 82n; Hassler, *Commanders*, p. xviii; Davis, *Battle at Bull Run*, p. 9.

28. John C. Tidball, Memoir, pp. 226, 226a, Tidball Papers, USMA; Williams, *Lincoln and His Generals*, p. 19; Hassler, *Commanders*, p. 4; Beatie, *Army*, p. 165; Cozzens and Girardi, eds., *Military Memoirs*, p. 214; Miller, ed., *Peninsula Campaign*, v. 2, p. 82n.

29. John C. Tidball, Memoir, pp. 224, 229, Tidball Papers, USMA; Williams, *Lincoln and His Generals*, p. 19; Hassler, *Commanders*, p. 3; Cozzens and Girardi, eds., *Military Memoirs*, p. 214; Miller, ed., *Peninsula Campaign*, v. 2, p. 82n.

30. Welcher, *Union Army*, p. 27; Scott, ed., *Forgotten Valor*, pp. 260–64; Comings, *Personal Reminiscences*, pp. 4, 7; Donald, *Lincoln*, p. 306.

31. Welcher, *Union Army*, p. 71; Davis, *Battle at Bull Run*, pp. 12, 13; Beattie, *Army*, p. 166.

32. Welcher, *Union Army*, p. 72; Hennessey, *First Battle of Manassas*, pp. 130–32; Williams, *Lincoln and His Generals*, p. 19.

33. Welcher, *Union Army*, p. 72; Snell, *From First to Last*, p. 58; Cowley, ed., *With My Face to the Enemy*, p. 35; Davis, *Battle at Bull Run*, p. 14.

34. Warner, *Generals in Blue*, pp. 244, 514; Davis, *Battle at Bull Run*, p. 39, Welcher, *Union Army*, p. 72.

35. Warner, *Generals in Blue*, pp. 227–28; Davis, *Battle at Bull Run*, pp. 39–40; Beattie, *Army*, p. 190; Eby, ed., *Virginia Yankee*, p. 89; Catton, *Mr. Lincoln's Army*, p. 113; Nevins, ed., *Diary*, p. 38.

36. Welcher, *Union Army*, p. 72; Warner, *Generals in Blue*, pp. 37, 57, 159, 237, 402–3, 558–59; Snell, *From First to Last*, pp. xii, 1–4, 18–32, 50, 55, 59; Marvel, *Burnside*, pp. 5, 11, 14, 15; Scott, ed., *Forgotten Valor*, pp. 240–49; Small, ed., *Road*, p. 8.

37. Davis, *Battle at Bull Run*, pp. 29, 34, 60–63, 66.

38. Ibid., pp. 5, 6, 46; Hennessey, *First Battle of Manassas*, p. 5; Thomas and Sauers, eds., *Civil War Letters*, p. 9n; Cooling, *Symbol*, p. 58.

39. Davis, *Battle at Bull Run*, pp. 69–75; Hassler, *Commanders*, p. 6; Hennessy, *First Battle of Manassas*, p. 5; *B&L*, 1, pp. 174–75.

40. Perret, "Anaconda," *N&S*, 6, 4, pp. 39–41; Davis, *Battle at Bull Run*, pp. 74, 75.

41. Jones, *Civil War Command*, p. 21; Davis, *Battle at Bull Run*, pp. 74, 75; Perret, "Anaconda," *N&S*, 6, 4, pp. 39, 40, 41.

42. Jones, *Civil War Command*, p. 21; Perret, "Anaconda," *N&S*, 6, 4, pp. 40–41.

43. Davis, *Battle at Bull Run*, pp. 35, 76, 78; Perret, "Anaconda," *N&S*, 6, 4, pp. 41–42.

44. Horace Emerson–Brother, June 27, 1861, Emerson Letters, UM; Moe, *Last Full Measure*, p. 41.

45. SOR, 1, p. 146; Frank L. Lemont–My Dear Mother, July 8, 1861, Lemont Letters, UME.

46. Andrew McClintock–Sister, July 6, 1861, Chesson Collection, USAMHI.

47. Cooling, *Symbol*, p. 58; Baquet, *History*, p. 413; Styple, ed., *Writing*, p. 27; Davis, *Lincoln's Men*, p. 45; William F. Bacon–Mother, June 2, 1861, 2nd Maine Letters File, MNMP.

48. McClure, *Abraham Lincoln*, p. 64; Duncan, ed., *Blue-Eyed Child*, pp. 82, 91.

49. Samito, ed., *Commanding Boston's Irish Ninth*, p. 13; Duncan, ed., *Blue-Eyed Child*, p. 91.

50. Davis, *Battle at Bull Run*, p. 91.

51. Joseph B. Laughton–Father & Mother, July 10, 1861, Laughton Papers, DU.

52. Frank L. Lemont–My Dear mother, July 8, 1861, Lemont Letters, UME.

Chapter 2: Bloody Sabbath at Bull Run

1. Davis, *Battle at Bull Run*, pp. 91–93; Scott, ed., *Forgotten Valor*, p. 287; Eckert and Amato, eds., *Ten Years*, p. 289.

2. Davis, *Battle at Bull Run*, pp. 94–99; Otis, *Second Wisconsin*, p. 135.

3. Davis, *Battle at Bull Run*, pp. 102, 112–19; *B&L*, v. 1, p. 179; Wert, *General James Longstreet*, pp. 64–67; OR, 2, pp. 310–11.

4. Warner, *Generals in Blue*, pp. 402–3; Scott, ed., *Forgotten Valor*, p. 250.

5. Hitchcock, *War*, p. 39; Cole, *Under Five Commanders*, p. 86; Davis, *Battle at Bull Run*, p. 36.

6. OR, 2, pp. 311–14; Davis, *Battle at Bull Run*, pp. 119–24; Mead, "Journal," SHSW.

7. OR, 2, p. 318; Davis, *Battle at Bull Run*, pp. 123–24; Eckert and Amato, eds., *Ten Years*, p. 291; Fishel, *Secret War*, pp. 36, 37.

8. OR, 2, pp. 317–18; Fishel, *Secret War*, pp. 33, 37; Davis, *Battle at Bull Run*, pp. 154–55; Beatie, *Army*, p. 372.

9. OR, 2, p. 318; Journal, September [?] 1861, Heintzelman Papers, LC; Eckert and Amato, eds., *Ten Years*, p. 293; Davis, *Battle at Bull Run*, pp. 154–56; *B&L*, v. 1, p. 184; Beatie, *Army*, pp. 372, 373.

10. Journal, September [?] 1861, Heintzelman Papers, LC; Davis, *Battle at Bull Run*, pp. 155–57, 181; Eckert and Amato, eds., *Ten Years*, p. 293.

11. Wert, *General James Longstreet*, pp. 62–63, 71; Hennessy, *First Battle of Manassas*, pp. 4, 5, 32, 33.

12. Sauers, ed., *Civil War Journal*, p. 23; Gambone, *Major-General John Frederick Hartranft*, pp. 23–25; Snell, *From First to Last*, p. 62.

13. Eckert and Amato, eds., *Ten Years*, p. 292; Frank L. Lemont–My Dear Father, August 24, 1861, Lemont Letters, UME; Sears, ed., *For Country*, p. 55; William G. Davis–Parents, July 20, 1861, Davis Letters, MNBP; George Rollins–Father, July 26, 1861, Rollins Correspondence, USAMHI.

14. *B&L*, v. 1, p. 184; Davis, *Battle at Bull Run*, pp. 159, 162; Moe, *Last Full Measure*, p. 47; Clark S. Edwards–Wife, July 28, 1861, Edwards Papers, NC; Favill, *Diary*, p. 31.

15. *B&L*, v. 1, p. 185; Davis, *Battle at Bull Run*, pp. 167–74; Rhodes, ed., *All for the Union*, pp. 26, 33; Marvel, *Burnside*, pp. 22–24; Albert G. Bates–My Dear Beloved Wife Edith, July 23, 1861, Bates Letters and Diary, USAMHI.

16. Davis, *Battle at Bull Run*, pp. 173–82; Hennessy, *First Battle of Manassas*, Chapter V; *B&L*, v. 1, p. 185; Marvel, *Burnside*, pp. 24–25; Westervelt, Memoir and Diary, p. 4, USAMHI; Journal, September [?] 1861, Heintzelman Papers, LC; Henry F. Ritter–Uncle, July 23, 1861, Ritter Letter, MNBP.

17. Ai Baker Thompson–Father, July 24, 1861, Thompson Letters, MNBP; *SOR*, 1, p. 152.

18. *B&L*, v. 1, p. 187; Snell, *From First to Last*, pp. 59, 64.

19. Hennessy, *First Battle of Manassas*, pp. 60–62; Mead, "Journal," SHSW; *OR*, 2, p. 369; Wert, *Brotherhood*, p. 40.

20. Hennessy, *First Battle of Manassas*, pp. 63, 72–73; Eckert and Amato, eds., *Ten Years*, p. 301; Wert, *Brotherhood*, p. 40; *OR*, 2, p. 324.

21. James M. Nihiser–Wife, July 24, 1861, Nihiser Letter, FSNMP.

22. Hennessy, *First Battle of Manassas*, pp. 65–76; Slocum, *Life*, pp. 10, 11, 12, 14, 15; Journal, July 21, September [?] 1861, Heintzelman Papers, LC; *OR*, 2, p. 353; Wert, *Brotherhood*, p. 41; B. F. Smart–Father, July 23, 1861, 2nd Maine Letters File, MNBP; Pullen, *Twentieth Maine*, p. 78.

23. Hennessy, *First Battle of Manassas*, pp. 77–79; Adelbert Ames–John C. Ropes, May 14, 1894, Ropes Papers, BUL; Charles Griffin–Alexander Webb, February 18, 1862, Webb Papers, YU; Wert, *Brotherhood*, p. 41; Naisawald, *Grape and Canister*, pp. 17, 18.

24. Snell, *From First to Last*, p. 62; Caleb H. Beal–Folks, July 23, 1861, Beal Papers, MAHS; New York *Leader*, August 3, 1861; [?]–Friend Willie, July 24, 1861, 2nd New Hampshire File, MNBP; Moe, *Last Full Measure*, pp. 48–50.

25. Moe, *Last Full Measure*, pp. 50–52, 63; Edward Hollister–My Dear Brother, July 23, 25, 1861, Hollister Letters, MNBP; Wright, *No More Gallant a Deed*, p. 60; Hennessy, *First Battle of Manassas*, pp. 80–82; Scott, ed., *Forgotten Valor*, p. 292.

26. Wert, *Brotherhood*, pp. 43–44; Wells Account, MNBP; Hennessy, *First Battle of Manassas*, pp. 83–86, 97.

27. Wert, *Brotherhood*, pp. 44–45; *B&L*, v. 1, p. 188; Hennessy, *First Battle of Manassas*, pp. 98–100; Scott, ed., *Forgotten Valor*, pp. 292–94.

28. Scott, ed., *Forgotten Valor*, pp. 290–95; John H. H. Ward–W. P. Franklin, July 29, 1861, Ward Papers, USAMHI; Wert, *Brotherhood*, pp. 45–46; Hennessy, *First Battle of Manassas*, pp. 99–102; Black, "A Wife's Devotion," *B&G*, 11, 5, p. 22.

29. *OR*, 2, p. 369; Alured Larke–Tom & Ethel, August 13, 1861, Larke Letters, SHSW; Ross, *Empty Sleeve*, p. 35; Gaff, *If This Is War*, pp. 197–201; Quiner, *Correspondence*, v. I, p. 105, SHSW.

30. *OR*, 2, pp. 369–70; Gaff, *If This Is War*, pp. 204, 205, 223, 224; Wert, *Brotherhood*, pp. 46–47.

31. *OR*, 2, p. 369; Gaff, *If This Is War*, pp. 229, 231; Nolan, *Iron Brigade*, pp. 7–8; Cavanagh, *Memoirs*, p. 400; William G. Davis–Father, August 4, 1861, Davis Letters, MNBP; Hennessy, *First Battle of Manassas*, pp. 104, 106.

32. *OR*, 2, pp. 418–19; Gould, *Major-General Hiram G. Berry*, pp. 65, 67; Frank L. Lemont–My Dear Father, August 24, 1861, Lemont Letters, UME; George W. Dyer–Governor, July 23, 1861, Dyer Papers, MESA; Small, ed., *Road*, pp. 22–23; Hennessy, *First Battle of Manassas*, pp. 109–15.

33. Davis, *Battle at Bull Run*, pp. 229–31, 238; Hennessy, *First Battle of Manassas*, pp. 107, 115–16; *B&L*, v. 1, p. 191.

34. *OR*, 2, pp. 320, 370; Frank L. Lemont–My Dear Father, August 24, 1861, Lemont Letters, UME; Sedgwick, ed., *Correspondence*, v. 2, p. 32; Davis, *Battle at Bull Run*, pp. 236–38.

35. *OR*, 2, p. 320; Davis, *Battle at Bull Run*, pp. 238–39; John Fales–Sister, July 23, 1861, Fales Papers, NC; Rhodes, ed., *All for the Union*, p. 34; Robertson, ed., *Civil War Letters*, p. 50; Favill, *Diary*, p. 37.

36. *OR*, 2, pp. 321, 322, 747; Memoir, Tidball Papers, USMA; Sears, ed., *For Country*, pp. 56, 57; Daniel McCook–My Dear Son, July 26, 1861, McCook File, MNBP; Frank L. Lemont–My Dear Father, August 24, 1861, Lemont Letters, UME; Davis, *Battle at Bull Run*, pp. 242, 251; *B&L*, v. 1, p. 192.

37. Davis, *Battle at Bull Run*, pp. 251–52; Henry McCormick–W. N. Jennings, July 22, 1861, McCormick Letter, MNBP.

38. *OR*, 2, p. 322; Davis, *Battle at Bull Run*, p. 352; Eckert and Amato, eds., *Ten Years*, pp. 303–4.

39. Davis, *Battle at Bull Run*, p. 252.

40. Ibid., p. 252; Snell, *From First to Last*, p. 66; Jacob A. Camp–My Dear Wife, July 27, 1861, Camp Letters, CU; Eckert and Amato, eds., *Ten Years*, p. 290; Hennessy, *First Battle of Manassas*, pp. 130–32; *SOR*, 1, p. 152.

41. Casualty numbers based on Hennessy, *First Battle of Manassas*, pp. 130–35; official returns in *OR*, 2, p. 327; Clark S. Edwards–Wife, August [?] 1861, Clark Papers, NC; W. B. Rice–Sister, July 31, 1861, Rice Letter, UME.

42. Davis, *Battle at Bull Run*, p. 219.

43. Beatie, *Army*, p. 379.

44. *OR*, 2, pp. 753, 763; Sears, ed., *Civil War Papers*, p. 67; Sears, *George B. McClellan*, p. 95.

45. Sears, *George B. McClellan*, pp. 2–3; Scott, ed., *Forgotten Valor*, pp. 55, 509; Waugh, *Class of 1846*, p. 341.

46. Sears, *George B. McClellan*, pp. 15, 33, 44, 46, 47, 50, 58, 61–63.

47. Ibid., pp. 25, 69, 72.

48. Ibid., pp. 70, 89–93.

49. Ibid., p. 74; McClellan, *McClellan's Own Story*, pp. 66, 67; Welcher, *Union Army*, p. 8.

50. Sears, ed., *Civil War Papers*, p. 70.

51. Ibid., p. 71.

Chapter 3: An Army Born

1. Sears, ed., *Civil War Papers*, p. 163.

2. Eckert and Amato, eds., *Ten Years*, p. 305; Peter Tissot–George B. McClellan, August 5, 1861, N. Kee–George B. McClellan, August 5, 1861, RG 393, NA; Sears, ed., *For Country*, p. 126; Higginson, *Harvard Memorial Biographies*, v. 1, p. 59; Alexander Webb–Dearest Annie, July 29, 1861, Webb Papers, YU.

3. Eckert and Amato, eds., *Ten Years*, pp. 305, 306; Carter, *Four Brothers*, pp. 31, 46; Brady, ed., *Hurrah*, p. 38; John C. Babcock–Mrs. Horace Clarke, December 26, 1861, Babcock Papers, LC; Michie, *General McClellan*, p. 100.

4. Michie, *General McClellan*, pp. 100, 101; *B&L*, v. 2, pp. 161, 162; Richard B. Smart–Friends, July 26, 27, 1861, Smart Papers, DU.

5. Swinton, *Campaigns*, p. 62; Sears, *George B. McClellan*, p. 97; E. E. Camp–Seth Williams, August 23, 24, 29, September 2, 10, 16, 17, 18, 27, 30, October 2, 22, 1861; Silas Casey–Seth Williams October 12, 25, 31, November 1, 2, 1861, RG 393, NA.

6. Sears, *To the Gates*, p. 125; Newton, *Battle of Seven Pines*, p. 8; Warner, *Generals in Blue*, pp. 74–75; Nelson Chapin–Elizabeth, December 14, 1861, Chapin Correspondence, USAMHI.

7. E. A. Brown–Wife, August 13, 1861, Brown Letters, SHSW; George W. Dyer–Governor, July 27, 1861, Dyer Papers, MESA; Sneden, *Eye of the Storm*, p. 5; Amos Downing–P. Downing, October 20, 1861, Downing Letters, USAMHI; Hill, *Our Boys*, p. 31.

8. Favil, *Diary*, pp. 51, 59; Gould, *Major-General Hiram G. Berry*, p. 87; Nolan and Vipond, eds., *Giants*, p. 67.

9. Frank L. Lemont–Father, September 13, 1861, Lemont Letters, UME; Blake, *Three Years*, p. 33; Bruen and Fitzgibbons, eds., *Through Ordinary Eyes*, p. 62; Duncan, ed., *Blue-Eyed Child*, pp. 144–45; Orson Parker–Father, November 12, 1861, Parker Letters, SHSW.

10. Samito, ed., *Commanding Boston's Irish Ninth*, pp. 34, 39; Scott, ed., *Fallen Leaves*, p. 44; David Samson–Friend, October 3, 1861, Samson Letters, USAMHI; Sears, ed., *For Country*, p. 99; Orson Parker–Father, November 30, 1861, Parker Letters, SHSW; Timothy Emerton–Sister, August 6, 1861, Emerton Letter, 11th Massachusetts File, MNBP; de Trobriand, *Four Years*, p. 81.

11. Mitchell, *Civil War Soldiers*, pp. 57, 59; Meade, *Life and Letters*, v. 1, p. 223; Gerrish, *Army Life*, p. 45.

12. Moore, "Reminiscence," IHS; Cook, "Memoir," p. 1, SHSW; Dunn, *Iron Men*, p. 2; Trask, *Fire Within*, p. 45; Mitchell, *Vacant Chair*, p. 21.

13. Mitchell, *Vacant Chair*, pp. xiii, 4, 12, 16, 154, 158; Hess, *Union Soldier*, p. 198; William G. Davis–Mother, August 9, 1861, Davis Letters, MNBP; Rood, *Memoir*, p. 4, SHSW; Cassedy, ed., *Dear Friends*, p. 13.

14. Mitchell, *Vacant Chair*, pp. 22, 23, 25, 45, 46, 48; Simpson and Simpson, "Dear Daul," USAMHI; Small, ed., *Road*, p. 199; William H. Myers–My dear Parents, February 15, 1863, Myers Letters, USAMHI.

15. Meade, *Life and Letters*, v. 1, p. 223.

16. Michie, *General McClellan*, pp. 100, 101; *B&L*, v. 2, pp. 112–13; Eckert and Amato, eds., *Ten Years*, pp. 315, 316; Sears, *George B. McClellan*, p. 100.

17. *B&L*, v. 2, p. 112; Swinton, *Campaigns*, p. 63n; Sears, ed., *Civil War Papers*, p. 93; E. A. Brown–Father, September 1, 1861, Brown Letters, SHSW; William T.

Sherman–Seth Williams, August 14, 1861, RG393, NA; Brennan, "Army Commander," N&S, 5, 5, pp. 16–17; Sears, ed., For Country, pp. 71–72; Sears, George B. McClellan, p. 98.

18. Davis, Lincoln's Men, p. 53; Thomas Paxton–Cousin Ellie, September 18, 1861, Paxton Papers, NC; de Trobriand, Four Years, p. 91; Sears, ed., For Country, p. 77; Eckert and Amato, eds., Ten Years, p. 320; Styple, ed., Writing, p. 44; Leo Faller–Mother, August 23, 1861, Faller Correspondence, USAMHI; Caleb H. Beal–Parents, December 17, 1861, Beal Papers, MAHS; Diary, Thaxter Papers, USAMHI.

19. Frank L. Lemont–Parents, September 1, 1861, Lemont Letters, UME; Robert A. Browne–Dearest Mary, September 13, 1861, Browne Letters, PSU; Alexander Webb–Father, October 2, 1861, Webb Papers, YU; Scott, ed., Fallen Leaves, p. 45; de Trobriand, Four Years, pp. 76, 77; Horace Currier–[?], September 29, 1861, Currier Papers, SHSW; Sears, ed., Civil War Papers, p. 103.

20. Sears, George B. McClellan, p. 111; Hennessy, ed., Fighting, pp. 38, 43; J. H. Bacon–Mother, November 11, 1861, 2nd Maine Letters File, MNBP.

21. Tucker, Hancock, p. 135; Williams, Lincoln and His Generals, p. 29; Sears, Controversies, p. 13; B&L, v. 2, p. 112; Michie, General McClellan, p. 103; Sears, George B. McClellan, p. 110; Swinton, Campaigns, p. 67n.

22. Welcher, Union Army, pp. 8, 79; Davis, Lincoln's Men, p. 60; Sears, George B. McClellan, p. 100.

23. Welcher, Union Army, pp. 245–48; McClellan, McClellan's Own Story, pp. 70, 71.

24. Welcher, Union Army, pp. 246–48; Warner, Generals in Blue, pp. 17–18, 37, 233–34, 378–79, 462–63, 480–81; Hebert, Fighting Joe Hooker, pp. 21, 38.

25. Sypher, History, pp. 60, 67–90, 95, 101, 103, 109, 118; Sauers, Advance the Colors!, v. 1, pp. 80, 247; Minnigh, History, pp. 29, 30, 36.

26. Welcher, Union Army, pp. 246–48; Warner, Generals in Blue, pp. 17–18, 37, 233–34, 378–79, 462–63, 480–81; Snell, From First to Last, p. xiii.

27. Welcher, Union Army, pp. 245–48; Warner, Generals in Blue, pp. 47, 95, 161, 178, 203, 259, 316, 318, 344, 396, 430, 446, 451, 475, 532; Slocum, Life, p. 16; Marvel, Burnside, p. 32.

28. Benedict, Vermont, v. 1, p. 236; Wickman, ed., Letters to Vermont, v. 1, p. 70; Baquet, History, p. 418; Toombs, New Jersey Troops, p. 3; Swanberg, Sickles, pp. 115–17, 124; Mead, "Journal," SHSW; George Mitchell–Friend Maria, September 30, 1861, Mitchell Papers, UWLC; Conyngham, Irish Brigade, pp. 47–53, 55, 56, 68, 93.

29. Boyle, Party, pp. 14, 15, 391, 392, 394; Cavanagh, ed., Memoirs, p. 425; Conyngham, Irish Brigade, p. 5; Kohl and Richard, eds., Irish Green, p. 102; Corby, Memoirs, p. 21; Wesson Diary, p. 2, USAMHI.

30. Naisawald, Grape and Canister, pp. 21, 24.

31. Ibid., pp. 21, 26–28; Longacre, Man Behind the Guns, p. 97; Catton, Stillness, p. 32.

32. Longacre, Man Behind the Guns, pp. 97, 98; Naisawald, Grape and Canister, p. 24.

33. Alexander Webb–Father, October 2, 1861, Webb Papers, YU; OR, 5, p. 7; Longacre, Man Behind the Guns, pp. 30, 33, 44–46, 69, 88, 91; Naisawald, Grape and Canister, p. 23; Schaff, Battle, p. 45; Henry J. Hunt–My dear Bragg, April 23, 1861, Hunt File, GNMP.

34. Longacre, *Man Behind the Guns*, pp. 35, 36, 103, 186; Nevins, ed., *Diary*, p. 473.

35. Starr, *Union Cavalry*, v. 1, pp. 48, 58, 59, 65, 235, 236.

36. Ibid., pp. 235–37; Welcher, *Union Army*, p. 509; Schiller, "Taste of Northern Steel," *N&S*, 2, 2, pp. 34, 36, 39; Longacre, *Lincoln's Cavalrymen*, pp. 53–60.

37. John F. Reynolds–My dear Sisters, October 14, 1861, Reynolds Family Papers, FM.

38. Wert, *General James Longstreet*, pp. 78–80.

39. Catton, *Mr. Lincoln's Army*, p. 81.

40. McClellan, *McClellan's Own Story*, p. 69; OR, 5, pp. 6–8.

41. OR, 5, pp. 6–8.

42. Sears, *George B. McClellan*, p. 104; Michie, *General McClellan*, p. 152.

43. OR, 11, pt. 3, p. 4; Sears, ed., *Civil War Papers*, p. 100; Fishel, *Secret War*, pp. 53, 54, 84.

44. Fishel, *Secret War*, pp. 102, 103, 106; Sears, "Little Mac," *N&S*, 2, 3, p. 67.

45. Adams, *Our Masters the Rebels*, pp. 94, 95; Sears, "Little Mac," *N&S*, 2, 3, pp. 67, 68; Burton, *Extraordinary Circumstances*, p. 17; Sears, *George B. McClellan*, p. 104.

46. Sears, "Little Mac," *N&S*, 2, 3, p. 66; Sears, ed., *Civil War Papers*, pp. 75, 81, 85–86, 103–4.

47. Sears, ed., *Civil War Papers*, pp. 75, 81, 103–4; OR, 12, pt. 3, p. 4.

48. Sears, ed., *Civil War Papers*, pp. 85–86, 106–7, 135; Boritt, ed., *Lincoln's Generals*, p. 12.

49. Meade, *Life and Letters*, v. 1, p. 152; McClellan, *McClellan's Own Story*, pp. 32, 33, 35; Sears, ed., *Civil War Papers*, pp. 113, 132; Donald, ed., *Inside Lincoln's Cabinet*, p. 101; Sears, *George B. McClellan*, pp. 106, 128; Alexander Webb–Father, December 11, 1861, Webb Papers, YU; Goss, *War*, p. 110.

50. Jones, *Civil War Command*, pp. x, 2; Weigley, *Great Civil War*, p. xv; Goss, *War*, p. 116.

51. Jones, *Civil War Command*, p. 2; Paludan, *Presidency*, p. 101.

52. Michie, *General McClellan*, p. 116; Sears, *George B. McClellan*, p. 133; Davis, *Lincoln's Men*, pp. 9, 49–51.

53. Paludan, *Presidency*, p. 107; Adams, *Our Masters the Rebels*, p. 107; McClure, *Abraham Lincoln*, p. 70.

54. Adams, *Our Masters the Rebels*, p. 107; Wert, *Gettysburg*, pp. 43–44; an insightful analysis of the importance of the war in the West and its impact on Confederate defeat is McMurry, *Fourth Battle of Winchester, passim*.

55. OR, 5, p. 32; Cooling, *Symbol*, p. 77; Map of the Encampment of Hooker's Division, RG393, NA.

56. OR, 5, p. 32; Wert, *General James Longstreet*, pp. 87–88; Hardman P. Petrikin–Hugh McAllister, September 30, 1861, Beaver Collection, PSU.

57. OR, 5, p. 32; Holien, *Battle*, pp. 23–28; Lash, "Duty Well Done," pp. 107, 108.

58. Holien, *Battle*, pp. 27, 28, 31; Scott, ed., *Fallen Leaves*, p. 60; Coco, ed., *From Ball's Bluff to Gettysburg*, pp. 42, 43.

59. Holien, *Battle*, pp. 42–50; Sears, *Controversies*, p. 34; Burns Diary, p. 3, USAMHI; Lash, "Duty Well Done," pp. 114–18; Rhodes, *History*, p. 34.

60. Scott, ed., *Fallen Leaves*, p. 61; Michael Donlan–Brother, October 23, 1861, Donlan Letters, USAMHI; Coco, ed., *From Ball's Bluff to Gettysburg*, pp. 48, 49; Holien, *Battle*, p. 62, 66, 69, 70, 71; Norman Vance–Sister, October 28, 1861, Vance Papers, NC.

61. Burns Diary, pp. 3–4; Michael Donlan–Brother, October 23, 1861, Donlan Letters, USAMHI; Holien, *Battle*, p. 88; Lash, *"Duty Well Done,"* pp. 126, 135.
62. Holien, *Battle*, pp. 88, 95; *OR*, 5, p. 626; Sears, ed., *Civil War Papers*, p. 111; Meade, *Life and Letters*, v. 1, p. 225; Sears, *Controversies*, p. 36.
63. *OR*, 5, pp. 9–11; Sears, ed., *Civil War Papers*, p. 118n.
64. *OR*, 5, p. 9.
65. Ibid., p. 11; *B&L*, v. 2, p. 13; Meade, *Life and Letters*, p. 239; Michie, *General McClellan*, pp. 137, 152.
66. Sears, *George B. McClellan*, pp. 122–25; Nevins, ed., *Diary of the Civil War*, p. 188; Laas, ed., *Wartime Washington*, p. 89; *OR*, 5, p. 639.
67. Sears, ed., *Civil War Papers*, p. 123; Lash, *"Duty Well Done,"* p. 74.
68. Sears, *George B. McClellan*, pp. 132–33.
69. Ibid.
70. Meade, *Life and Letters*, v. 1, p. 228; Edward S. Bragg–My dear Wife, November 21, 1861, Bragg Papers, SHSW; Davis, *Lincoln's Men*, p. 56; Sneden, *Eye of the Storm*, p. 6.
71. Robertson, ed., *Civil War Letters*, p. 96; Heffelfinger Diary, p. 24, USAMHI; Meade, *Life and Letters*, v. 1, p. 228; Alanson Wiles–Mother, November 21, 1861, Wiles Papers, NC; Davis, *Lincoln's Men*, p. 56; Sears, ed., *For Country*, pp. 129, 130.
72. Sneden, *Eye of the Storm*, p. 6; Edward S. Bragg–My dear Wife, November 21, 1861, Bragg Papers, SHSW; Robertson, ed., *Civil War Letters*, p. 96; Reuben Huntley–Wife, November 21, 1861, Huntley Papers, SHSW; Westbrook, *History*, p. 93.
73. Davis, *Lincoln's Men*, p. 56; Meade, *Life and Letters*, v. 1, p. 229; Heffelfinger Diary, p. 24, USAMHI.
74. Sears, ed., *Civil War Papers*, p. 137; Davis, *Lincoln's Men*, p. 56; Eckert and Amato, eds., *Ten Years*, p. 372.

Chapter 4: To the Peninsula

1. Trask, *Fire Within*, p. 78; J. H. Bacon–Mother, December 22, 1861, 2nd Maine Letters File, MNBP; Conyngham, *Irish Brigade*, p. 73.
2. Isaac C. Dowling–Friend Osgood, September 9, 1861, Jim Burlingame Wildes–Friend Osgood, Osgood Papers, November 23, 1861, DU; Arnold P. Dains–Friend Marg, February 6, 1862, Dains Letters, USAMHI; James Wadsworth–Irvin McDowell, November 1, 1861, RG393, NA; Blake, *Three Years*, p. 311; Stewart, *Camp*, p. 50.
3. Miles Peabody–Brother George, December 24, 1861, Peabody Letters, USAMHI; Otis, *Second Wisconsin*, p. 136.
4. Plumb, "Record," p. 6; Mesnard, "Reminiscence," p. 24, USAMHI.
5. Benedict, *Vermont*, v. 1, pp. 237, 238; Pride and Travis, *My Brave Boys*, pp. 54, 55; J. Loyal Brown–Sisters, January 1, 1863, Brown Letters, UME; John F. Reynolds–My dear Sister, January 12, 1862, Reynolds Family Papers, FM.
6. Sneden, *Eye of the Storm*, p. 9; Holford Diary, LC; Longhenry, "Yankee Piper," pp. 1–19, ANB.
7. Charles Osgood–Brother, February 23, 1862, Osgood Papers, DU; Snell, *From First to Last*, pp. 82–83; Rhodes, ed., *All for the Union*, p. 54; William T. H.

Brooks–Father, February 18, 1862, Brooks Papers, USAMHI; Osborne, ed., *Civil War Diaries*, pp. 8–9; Carter, *Four Brothers*, p. 46.

8. Coco, ed., *From Ball's Bluff to Gettysburg*, p. 57; Alanson Wiles–Emily, January 21, 1862, Wiles Papers, NC; E. A. Brown–Father & Mother, November 24, 1861, Brown Letters, SHSW; Woodward, "Civil War," *PMHB*, 88, p. 45; Mannis and Wilson, eds., *Bound to Be a Soldier*, pp. 3, 6; Horace Emerson–Mother, February 12, 1862, Emerson Letters, UM; David Samson–Friend, January 9, 1862, Samson Letters, USAMHI.

9. James Converse–Affectionate Companion, January 15, 1862, Converse Letters, CHS; Alanson Wiles–Emily, January 21, 1862, Wiles Papers, NC; Horace Emerson–Mother, February 12, 1862, Emerson Letters, UM.

10. William C. Wiley–Brother, December 31, 1861, January 22, 1862, Wiley Papers, PSU.

11. *B&L*, v. 2, pp. 120, 161; Rhodes, ed., *All for the Union*, p. 47; Snell, *From First to Last*, p. 77.

12. Hattaway and Jones, *How the North Won*, p. 86; Snell, *From First to Last*, p. 77; Swinton, *Campaigns*, p. 74.

13. Miller, ed., *Peninsula Campaign*, v. 2, p. 82; Swinton, *Campaigns*, pp. 78–80; Snell, *From First to Last*, pp. 77–78.

14. Snell, *From First to Last*, pp. 79–81; Sears, *George B. McClellan*, pp. 140–41.

15. Boritt, ed., *Lincoln's Generals*, p. 23; Swinton, *Campaigns*, pp. 81–85; Donald, *Lincoln*, p. 331; Snell, *From First to Last*, p. 81.

16. Boritt, ed., *Lincoln's Generals*, pp. 20, 23; Swinton, *Campaigns*, p. 74; Hattaway and Jones, *How the North Won*, p. 95; Donald, *Lincoln*, p. 331.

17. Donald, *Lincoln*, pp. 325–26.

18. Ibid., pp. 333–34; Welcher, *Union Army*, p. 1; Thomas and Hyman, *Stanton*, pp. 23, 91, 112, 127–31, 135–37; Fishel, *Secret War*, p. 107; Beale, ed., *Diary*, v. 1, p. 58.

19. Donald, *Lincoln*, p. 333; Thomas and Hyman, *Stanton*, pp. 161–64; McClure, *Abraham Lincoln*, pp. 155, 156, 159; Staudenraus, ed., *Mr. Lincoln's Washington*, p. 176; Cozzens and Girardi, eds., *Military Memoirs*, pp. 115, 267n; Nevins, ed., *Diary of the Civil War*, p. 203.

20. Donald, *Lincoln*, p. 334; Dana, *Recollections*, p. 157, 159; McClure, *Abraham Lincoln*, pp. 160, 171; "Lincoln and Stanton," p. 6, Chandler Papers, USAMHI.

21. Meade, *Life and Letters*, v. 1, p. 243; Alexander Webb–My Dear Father, January 20, 1862, Webb Papers, YU; Sears, ed., *Civil War Papers*, p. 154.

22. *B&L*, v. 2, pp. 163, 164; Thomas and Hyman, *Stanton*, pp. 133, 134, 148, 170.

23. Weigley, *Great Civil War*, p. 92; Meade, *Life and Letters*, v. 1, p. 247; Nevins, ed., *Diary*, p. 9; Gallagher, ed., *Richmond Campaign of 1862*, p. 156; Jones, *Civil War Command*, p. 24; Rafuse, "McClellan," *Columbiad*, 1, 3, p. 25.

24. Meade, *Life and Letters*, v. 1, pp. 243–44.

25. Weigley, *Great Civil War*, pp. 92, 93; Rafuse, "McClellan," *Columbiad*, 1, 3, pp. 25, 26, 30, 31; Gallagher, ed., *Richmond Campaign of 1862*, p. 156.

26. Weigley, *Great Civil War*, p. 92; Tap, *Over Lincoln's Shoulder*, pp. 2, 101; Donald, *Lincoln*, pp. 313–17, 326–27.

27. Tap, *Over Lincoln's Shoulder*, pp. 2, 21, 24; Snell, *From First to Last*, p. 73.

28. Tap, *Over Lincoln's Shoulder*, pp. 2, 5, 45, 101–4; Adams, *Our Masters the Rebels*, pp. 109, 110; Donald, *Lincoln*, p. 318; Weigley, *Great Civil War*, p. 83; Michie, *General McClellan*, p. 165.

29. Tap, *Over Lincoln's Shoulder*, pp. 56, 58, 62, 65; Sears, *Controversies*, pp. 34, 35, 44; Sears, ed., *Civil War Papers*, pp. 526–27.

30. Sears, *George B. McClellan*, pp. 144–46; Tap, *Over Lincoln's Shoulder*, p. 69; Sears, ed., *Civil War Papers*, pp. 526–27; *OR*, 5, pp. 342–46.

31. Meade, *Life and Letters*, v. 1, p. 245; Philip Kearny–Oliver S. Halsted, Jr., May 15, 1862, Lincoln Papers, LC.

32. Tap, *Over Lincoln's Shoulder*, pp. 105, 106, 107; Paludan, *Presidency*, p. 104; Donald, *Lincoln*, pp. 319, 327.

33. *OR*, 5, p. 41; Donald, *Lincoln*, p. 334.

34. Sears, *George B. McClellan*, pp. 147–49; Rafuse, "McClellan," *Columbiad*, 1, 3, pp. 25, 26; Weigley, *Great Civil War*, p. 93; Sears, *To the Gates*, p. 4; *B&L*, v. 2, p. 121.

35. Mitchell, *Vacant Chair*, p. 155; Weigley, *Great Civil War*, p. 93; Sears, *George B. McClellan*, pp. 149–50; Rafuse, "McClellan," *Columbiad*, 1, 3, p. 25; *OR*, 5, pp. 42–45; Sears, ed., *Civil War Papers*, pp. 170n–171n.

36. Sears, *George B. McClellan*, pp. 148, 153, 154.

37. Donald, *Lincoln*, pp. 153, 154, 336, 337.

38. Sparks, ed., *Inside Lincoln's Army*, pp. 45, 48; Sears, *To the Gates*, p. 5; Meade, *Life and Letters*, v. 1, p. 248.

39. Snell, *From First to Last*, pp. 85, 86; Sears, *To the Gates*, pp. 5–7; Michie, *General McClellan*, p. 204; John G. Barnard–Edward D. Townsend, October 3, 1864, Lincoln Papers, LC.

40. Snell, *From First to Last*, pp. 86, 87; Sears, *To the Gates*, pp. 6–8; *B&L*, v. 2, p. 166; Welcher, *Union Army*, pp. 300, 313, 343, 359, 363; *OR*, 5, pp. 18, 50.

41. *B&L*, v. 2, p. 166; Walker, *History*, pp. 9, 10; Meade, *Life and Letters*, v. 1, p. 250.

42. Schiller, ed., *Autobiography*, p. 32; Meade, *Life and Letters*, v. 1, pp. 251, 253.

43. Sears, *George B. McClellan*, p. 162.

44. Ibid., p. 163; Wert, *General James Longstreet*, pp. 96–97.

45. Trask, *Fire Within*, pp. 93–94; Horace Currier–[?], March 12, 1862, Currier Papers, SHSW; Favill, *Diary*, p. 71; Frank L. Lemont–Father, March 12, 1862, Lemont Letters, UME; Wesley H. Shaw–father & mother & sister, March 20, 1862, Shaw Papers, NYSL; Sears, ed., *For Country*, p. 202.

46. *SOR*, 1, p. 361; Thomas and Sauers, eds., *Civil War Letters*, pp. 39, 40; Elkanah M. Gibson–Sylvester Jessup, March 25, 1862, Jessup Letters, IHS; Charles Osgood–Brother, March 16, 1862, Osgood Papers, DU.

47. James McDonald Smith–My Darling Little Wife, March 18, 1862, Smith Papers, NC; Favill, *Diary*, p. 68; Nevins, ed., *Diary of the Civil War*, p. 213; *SOR*, 1, p. 362; Frank L. Lemont–Father, March 15, 1862, Lemont Letters, UME.

48. *B&L*, v. 2, p. 121; Sears, *George B. McClellan*, p. 163; *OR*, 5, pp. 57–58.

49. *OR*, 5, p. 54; *B&L*, v. 2, p. 122; Nevins, ed., *Diary*, p. 26; Sparks, ed., *Inside Lincoln's Army*, p. 51.

50. *OR*, 5, p. 54; Sears, *George B. McClellan*, pp. 164–65; Donald, *Lincoln*, p. 341; Sears, ed., *Civil War Papers*, p. 213.

51. Miller, ed., *Peninsula Campaign*, v. 2, p. 85; Sears, *George B. McClellan*, p. 169.

52. Miller, ed., *Peninsula Campaign*, v. 2, p. 86; Swinton, *Campaigns*, pp. 94, 95, 97; Michie, *General McClellan*, p. 211; *OR*, 5, pp. 57–58.

53. Sears, ed., *Civil War Papers*, p. 211.

54. Furst Diary, p. 17, USAMHI; Sears, *To the Gates*, p. 23; *OR*, 11, pt. 1, p. 158; Charles A. Wheeler–My dear C, April 1, 1862, Wheeler Papers, NC.

55. OR, 11, pt. 1, p. 158; B&L, v. 2, p. 168; SOR, 2, p. 24; Sneden, *Eye of the Storm*, p. 25.

56. Adams, *Reminiscences*, p. 25; John W. Ames–Father and Mother, March 30, 1862, Ames Papers, USAMHI; Livermore, *Days and Events*, p. 52.

57. John W. Ames–Father and Mother, March 30, 1862, Ames Papers, USAMHI; Davis, *Duel*, pp. 70, 71; Dubbs, *Defend This Old Town*, p. 36; Lash, "*Duty Well Done*," p. 180; SOR, 2, pp. 24, 26, 27; Dennis Tuttle–My Dear Wife, March 26, 1862, Tuttle Papers, NC.

58. OR, 11, pt. 1, pp. 158, 160; SOR, 2, pp. 25, 28, 30, 32, 37; Sears, *To the Gates*, p. 24; Stewart Van Vliet–Montgomery Meigs, April 28, 1862, Webb Papers, YU.

59. SOR, 2, pp. 28, 29, 30; Sneden, *Eye of the Storm*, pp. 36, 37; Sears, *George B. McClellan*, pp. 173–74; Webb, *Peninsula*, pp. 33, 42, 43.

60. OR, 11, pt. 1, pp. 10–11; Joseph B. Laughton–Mother and Father & Brothers, April 14, [1862], Laughton Papers, DU; Sears, *George B. McClellan*, pp. 174, 175.

61. OR, 11, pt. 1, p. 11; Michie, *General McClellan*, pp. 238–40; Sears, *George B. McClellan*, p. 175; Dubbs, *Defend This Old Town*, pp. 70, 71.

62. OR, 11, pt. 1, pp. 10–11; Joinville, *Army*, pp. 38, 53; Sears, *George B. McClellan*, p. 175; Webb, *Peninsula*, pp. 53–57; Fleming, ed., *Life*, p. 208; Michie, *General McClellan*, p. 245.

63. OR, 11, pt. 1, pp. 10, 11; Joinville, *Army*, p. 41; Sears, ed., *Civil War Papers*, pp. 219, 230; Welcher, *Union Army*, pp. 300, 364.

64. OR, 11, pt. 1, p. 15; Cooling, *Symbol*, p. 70; Sears, *George B. McClellan*, pp. 170–71; B&L, v. 2, pp. 168, 170; McClellan, *Letter*, p. 66.

65. OR, 11, pt. 1, p. 15; Sears, *George B. McClellan*, p. 171.

66. OR, 11, pt. 3, p. 121; Sears, ed., *Civil War Papers*, pp. 231n, 235, 250–51; McClellan, *Letter, passim*.

67. Jones, *Civil War Command*, pp. 61–62.

68. Ibid., p. 61; Donald, *Lincoln*, pp. 350, 352.

69. Donald, *Lincoln*, p. 352; Wert, *General James Longstreet*, p. 100; Mead, "Journal," SHSW; Snell, *From First to Last*, pp. 93, 96; Meade, *Life and Letters*, v. 1, pp. 259, 260, 262.

70. OR, 11, pt. 1, p. 15; Sears, ed., *Civil War Papers*, p. 234n; Gallagher, ed., *Richmond Campaign of 1862*, pp. 9–10.

71. Sears, ed., *Civil War Papers*, p. 234.

72. Wright, *No More Gallant a Deed*, p. 113; John F. Hallack–Cousins, all, April 26, 1862, Hallack Papers, NYSL; John W. Ames–My dear Mother, April 3, 1862, Ames Papers, USAMHI; Stevens, *Three Years*, p. 45; Miller, ed., *Peninsula Campaign*, v. 1, pp. 184–86; Favill, *Diary*, pp. 77, 78; Weld, *War Diary*, p. 96; Spear, ed., *Civil War Recollections*, p. 56.

73. Hennessy, ed., *Fighting*, pp. 52, 53; Lash, "*Duty Well Done*," pp. 187, 189.

74. Wert, *General James Longstreet*, p. 102; Sears, ed., *On Campaign*, p. 29; Styple, ed., *Writing*, p. 95; Samuel J. Alexander–My Dear Wife, May 1, 1862, Alexander Correspondence, USAMHI; Hennessy, ed., *Fighting*, p. 57.

75. Lash, "*Duty Well Done*," p. 184; Sears, ed., *Civil War Papers*, p. 249; Weld, *War Diary*, pp. 99, 100.

76. Warner, *Generals in Blue*, pp. 378–79; Weld, *War Diary*, pp. 54, 59, 99.

77. SOR, 2, p. 40; Sneden, *Eye of the Storm*, p. 57; Styple, ed., *Letters from the Peninsula*, pp. 45, 55.

78. SOR, 2, p. 43; Dubbs, *Defend This Old Town*, pp. 75–76; Wert, *General James Longstreet*, pp. 102–3.

79. Lash, "*Duty Well Done*," p. 192; Cassedy, ed., *Dear Friends*, p. 82; Samito, ed., *Commanding Boston's Irish Ninth*, pp. 98, 99; Sears, ed., *Civil War Papers*, p. 252; Dubbs, *Defend This Old Town*, p. 77.

Chapter 5: Along the Chickahominy

1. Hebert, *Fighting Joe Hooker*, p. 114; Schiller, ed., *Autobiography*, p. 32; Boritt, ed., *Lincoln's Generals*, p. 71; Joseph Hooker–George W. Mindil, April 5, 1874, January 12, 1875, Mindil Papers, USAMHI; Styple, ed., *Letters from the Peninsula*, pp. 10, 36, 37.

2. Hebert, *Fighting Joe Hooker*, pp. 17, 21, 28–33, 38, 39, 40, 41, 46, 48, 50; Nevins, ed., *Diary*, p. 17.

3. Hassler, *Commanders*, pp. 129, 130; Nevins, ed., *Diary*, p. 12; Eby, ed., *Virginia Yankee*, p. 89; Schiller, ed., *Autobiography*, p. 32; Gibbon, *Personal Recollections*, p. 107; Hebert, *Fighting Joe Hooker*, p. 114; Boritt, ed., *Lincoln's Generals*, p. 71.

4. Werstein, *Kearny*, pp. 22–24, 34, 45, 46, 54, 60, 69, 85–89, 96, 111, 162–63; Warner, *Generals in Blue*, pp. 258–59; Catton, *Mr. Lincoln's Army*, p. 31; Styple, ed., *Letters from the Peninsula*, pp. 14, 19.

5. Werstein, *Kearny*, pp. 163, 165, 166; Styple, ed., *Letters from the Peninsula*, pp. 20, 21; Baquet, *History*, pp. 9, 10; Robertson, ed., *Civil War Letters*, pp. 74, 76, 77.

6. Baquet, *History*, p. 421; Cudworth, *History*, p. 278; Meade, *Life and Letters*, v. 1, p. 255; Werstein, *Kearny*, p. 167.

7. Beach, *First New York (Lincoln) Cavalry*, pp. 78, 79; Styple, ed., *Letters from the Peninsula*, pp. 10, 34, 36, 37, 44, 45; Werstein, *Kearny*, p. 195; SOR, 1, pp. 357–58; Butterfield, *Biographical Memorial*, p. 31.

8. Styple, ed., *Letters from the Peninsula*, p. 21; Baquet, *History*, pp. 16, 17; McClellan, *McClellan's Own Story*, p. 138; Fleming, ed., *Life*, p. 214; SOR, 2, pp. 41, 42; John F. Hallack–My Dear Cousins, May 11, 1862, Hallack Papers, NYSL.

9. Dubbs, *Defend This Old Town*, pp. 90–94; William L. Candler–My dear Uncle, May 10, 1862, Candler Papers, VATU; Nevins, ed., *Diary*, p. 56; Wert, *General James Longstreet*, pp. 103–4.

10. Jeremiah Downes–Mother, May 6, 1862, Downes Letters, USAMHI; Dubbs, *Defend This Old Town*, pp. 92, 96, 102, 108–20, 124; Nevins, ed., *Diary*, pp. 48, 50, 51–54; Crumb and Dhalle, eds., *No Middle Ground*, pp. 24–27; Wert, *General James Longstreet*, pp. 104–5.

11. Dubbs, *Defend This Old Town*, pp. 101, 130, 142, 145; Nevins, ed., *Diary*, p. 57; SOR, 2, p. 53; William T. H. Brooks–Father, May 7, 1862, Brooks Papers, USAMHI; Sears, ed., *Civil War Papers*, p. 257.

12. Dubbs, *Defend This Old Town*, pp. 104, 131–32; William C. Wiley–Dear Ones at Home, May 15, 1862, Wiley Papers, PSU; David B. Birney–Gross, May 6, 1862, Birney Papers, USAMHI; Styple, ed., *Letters from the Peninsula*, p. 63; Joseph B. Laughton–Brothers, John & William, Mother and Father, May 11, 1862, Laughton Papers, DU.

13. John F. Hallack–My Dear Cousins, May 7, 1862, Hallack Papers, NYSL; Styple, ed., *Writing*, p. 93; Sears, ed., *For Country*, pp. 231, 232, 237–38, 303; Baquet,

History, p. 429; Dubbs, *Defend This Old Town*, pp. 131–41; Newhall, *Memoir*, p. 60; Wert, *General James Longstreet*, p. 104.

14. Dubbs, *Defend This Old Town*, pp. 142–48; McClellan, *McClellan's Own Story*, p. 140; Catton, *Mr. Lincoln's Army*, p. 9; Smith, *History*, p. 77; Westbrook, *History*, p. 108; John W. Geary–Henry J. Hunt, July 17, 1879, Hunt Papers, LC; O'Brien, ed., *My Life*, p. 87; Trask, *Fire Within*, p. 109; Walker, *General Hancock*, p. 55.

15. Dubbs, *Defend This Old Town*, pp. 143–44, 149–51, 159–70; Wert, *General James Longstreet*, pp. 104–5; Tucker, *Hancock*, p. 89; Walker, *General Hancock*, p. 32; Bingham, "Anecdotes," WRHS; *OR*, 11, pt. 1, p. 448; Sears, ed., *Civil War Papers*, p. 256.

16. *OR*, 11, pt. 1, p. 450, Union reports on the battle are pp. 447–564; *SOR*, 2, p. 52; *B&L*, 2, p. 200; Dubbs, *Defend This Old Town*, pp. 187, 188; Fox, *Regimental Losses*, p. 428.

17. *SOR*, 4, p. 466; Gould, *Major-General Hiram G. Berry*, pp. 129, 133, 189; Warner, *Generals in Blue*, p. 31.

18. Warner, *Generals in Blue*, p. 34; Agassiz, ed., *Meade's Headquarters*, p. 188; Silliker, ed., *Rebel Yell*, p. 39; Davis, *Life*, pp. 25, 26, 40, 41.

19. *SOR*, 2, p. 52; Philip Kearny–Oliver S. Halsted, Jr., May 15, 1862, Lincoln Papers, LC; de Trobriand, *Four Years*, p. 214; Styple, ed., *Letters from the Peninsula*, p. 102.

20. Philip Kearny–Oliver S. Halsted, Jr., May 15, 1862, Lincoln Papers, LC; Joseph Hooker–George W. Mindil, April 5, 1874, Mindil Papers, USAMHI; Werstein, *Kearny*, p. 207; Styple, ed., *Letters from the Peninsula*, pp. 74–76; Gibbon, *Personal Recollections*, p. 107; Hebert, *Fighting Joe Hooker*, p. 91.

21. Samuel Heintzelman–Alexander Webb, April 30, 1863; Alexander Webb–My Dear James, May 6, 1862; Extracts from the Diary of Brig. Gen. D. N. Couch, Webb Papers, YU; Dubbs, *Defend This Old Town*, pp. 153–54; Nevins, ed., *Diary*, p. 68; *OR*, 11, pt. 3, pp. 153–54.

22. Sears, ed., *Civil War Papers*, p. 259n.

23. Welcher, *Union Army*, pp. 360, 364–66, 394–96; *SOR*, 2, p. 56; Powell, *Fifth Army Corps*, p. 29; Nevins, ed., *Diary*, p. 65; Favill, *Diary*, pp. 90–91; Snell, *From First to Last*, pp. 106, 109.

24. Carter, *Four Brothers*, pp. 57–60; Miller, ed., *Peninsula Campaign*, v. 1, pp. 186–88; *SOR*, 2, pp. 55, 346, 347; Joinville, *Army*, p. 61; McClellan, *McClellan's Own Story*, p. 320; *OR*, 11, pt. 1, p. 26.

25. Sedgwick, ed., *Correspondence*, v. 2, p. 46; Styple, ed., *Writing*, p. 105; Stevens, *Three Years*, p. 74; O'Brien, ed., *My Life*, p. 47; Nevins, ed., *Diary*, p. 69; Stanfield, Diary, USAMHI; Charles A. Wheeler–My dear C, May 9, 1862, Wheeler Papers, NC.

26. Nevins, ed., *Diary*, p. 62; Grimsley, *Hard Hand*, pp. 2, 3; Rhodes, ed., *All for the Union*, p. 66; David C. Ashley–Folks, May 17, 1862, Ashley Family Papers, USAMHI; Billings, *Hardtack*, p. 234; Furst, Diary, p. 20, USAMHI; Bruen and Fitzgibbons, ed., *Through Ordinary Eyes*, p. 134; John F. Hallack–Cousins one and all, May 28, 1862, Hallack Papers, NYSL; Hyde, *Civil War Letters*, p. 12; Sears, ed., *For Country*, p. 234.

27. Webb, *Peninsula*, pp. 82–84; McClellan, *Letter*, p. 93; Extracts from the Diary of Brigadier General D. N. Couch, Webb Papers, YU; Sears, *George B. McClellan*, p. 184; Wert, *General James Longstreet*, pp. 106–7.

28. Gallagher, ed., *Richmond Campaign of 1862*, pp. 47, 48, 49–60; Katcher, ed., *Building the Victory*, p. 9; Ira Spaulding–My Dear Dunkle, May 31, 1862, Spaulding Papers, NYSL; Livermore, *Days and Events*, p. 63; Pride and Travis, *My Brave Boys*, pp. 75, 76.

29. A. H. Davis, Report of Inspection of Hospitals, Depot & Captives at White House, May 26, 1862, RG393, NA; Nevins, ed., *Diary*, pp. 65, 66, 70; Miller, ed., *Peninsula Campaign*, v. 2, pp. 130–76.

30. Sears, ed., *Civil War Papers*, pp. 264–65, 269, 270, 275.

31. OR, 11, pt. 1, pp. 27, 28; Sears, *George B. McClellan*, p. 188.

32. Wert, *Brotherhood*, pp. 105–18.

33. Ibid., pp. 111–18; Sears, ed., *Civil War Papers*, pp. 275n, 276n.

34. OR, 11, pt. 1, pp. 28–32; Extracts from the Diary of Brigadier General D. H. Couch, Webb Papers, YU; Wert, *General James Longstreet*, p. 106.

35. OR, 11, pt. 1, p. 53; Sears, ed., *Civil War Papers*, p. 277.

36. OR, 11, pt. 1, pp. 32, 46, 47, 51; Sears, *George B. McClellan*, pp. 186–87, 191–92.

37. Sears, ed., *Civil War Papers*, pp. 273, 275, 277, 279; Gallagher, ed., *Richmond Campaign of 1862*, p. 33; Miller, ed., *Peninsula Campaign*, v. 2, pp. 1–37; Parker, *Henry Wilson's Regiment*, p. 105; OR, 11, pt. 1, p. 35.

38. Joseph D. Baker–Mother, May 20, 1862, Baker Letters; George Williams–Parents, May 25, 1862, Williams Family Letters; David B. Birney–Gross, May 28, 1862, Birney Papers, William T. H. Brooks–Father, May 24, 1862, Brooks Papers, USAMHI; Samito, ed., *Commanding Boston's Irish Ninth*, p. 102.

39. Wert, *General James Longstreet*, pp. 106–11.

40. Ibid., pp. 108–10.

41. Ibid., pp. 114–15; Miller, "Disaster," *Columbiad*, 3, 4, pp. 22, 23; A. H. Davis, R. B. Marcy, May 29, 1862, RG393, NA; Newton, *Battle of Seven Pines*, p. 9.

42. Sears, ed., *Civil War Papers*, p. 285; Newton, *Battle of Seven Pines*, pp. 39–46; Miller, "Disaster," *Columbiad*, 3, 4, pp. 31–36; Wert, *General James Longstreet*, p. 115; William E. Dunn–Sister, June 8, 1862, "Dear Sister," p. 13, USAMHI.

43. Newton, *Battle of Seven Pines*, pp. 43–49, 53, 57; Extracts from the Diary of Brigadier General D. N. Couch, Webb Papers, YU; Nevins, ed., *Diary*, p. 79.

44. Walker, *History*, p. 129; Catton, *Glory Road*, p. 169; Newton, *Battle of Seven Pines*, pp. 56, 57; Wert, *General James Longstreet*, pp. 115–17; J. Pyewell–Mother, June 10, 1862, Pyewell Papers, NC.

45. Styple, ed., *Letters from the Peninsula*, p. 91; Alanson Barnard–Anna, June 2, 1862, Barnard Letters, USAMHI; Styple, ed., *Writing*, p. 105; Hays, ed., *Under the Red Patch*, pp. 96, 97; Scott, *History*, p. 45; Davis, *Life*, p. 74.

46. Extracts from the Diary of Brigadier General D. N. Couch, Webb Papers, YU; Styple, *Letters from the Peninsula*, p. 89; Newton, *Battle of Seven Pines*, pp. 64–69, 75–76; Wert, *General James Longstreet*, pp. 116–17.

47. OR, 11, pt. 1, p. 763; Wert, *General James Longstreet*, p. 118; Schiller, ed., *Autobiography*, p. 36.

48. Woodworth, *Leadership*, p. 69; Walker, *History*, p. 130; Sears, *Landscape*, p. 216; Favill, *Diary*, p. 59; Sears, ed., *For Country*, p. 292; Carter, *Four Brothers*, p. 68.

49. OR, 11, pt. 1, pp. 763, 798, 799; Carter, *Four Brothers*, p. 62; Newton, *Battle of Seven Pines*, pp. 73–76.

50. Newton, *Battle of Seven Pines*, pp. 79–82; Brown, *Cushing*, p. 87; Charles

Osgood–Bro. Steven, June 8, 1862, Osgood Papers, DU; Wert, *General James Longstreet*, pp. 118–19.

51. *OR*, 11, pt. 1, pp. 763, 764; pt. 3, p. 203; Newton, *Battle of Seven Pines*, pp. 85, 88; Extracts from the Diary of Brigadier General D. N. Couch, Webb Papers, YU; Wert, *General James Longstreet*, p. 119.

52. *OR*, 11, pt. 1, pp. 764–79; Child, *History*, pp. 82, 83; Favill, *Diary*, p. 110; Chester F. Hunt–Mother, June 9, 1862, Hunt Papers, NC; Pride and Travis, *My Brave Boys*, p. 84.

53. *OR*, 11, pt. 1, pp. 765, 769, 771, 776, 782; Catton, *Mr. Lincoln's Army*, p. 205; Styple, ed., *Writing*, p. 99; Livermore, *Days and Events*, pp. 73, 84; Sears, ed., *For Country*, p. 151; Fuller, *Personal Recollections*, p. 14.

54. *OR*, 11, pt. 1, p. 769; Child, *History*, p. 82; Favill, *Diary*, p. 112; Vanderslice, ed., *Civil War Letters*, p. 88.

55. Lash, *"Duty Well Done,"* p. 259; Abner Doubleday–Samuel P. Bates, October 19, 1875, Bates Papers, LC.

56. *OR*, 11, pt. 1, pp. 769, 771–72, 773; Pride and Travis, *My Brave Boys*, pp. 5, 6, 83; Child, *History*, pp. 83, 85; Warner, *Generals in Blue*, p. 18; Catton, *Stillness*, pp. 119, 120; Fuller, *Personal Recollections*, pp. 9, 10.

57. Conyngham, *Irish Brigade*, pp. 47–70; Styple, ed., *Writing*, p. 100; Cavanagh, *Memoirs*, p. 445; *OR*, 11, pt. 1, pp. 776–77.

58. Cavanagh, *Memoirs*, pp. 13–17, 289, 295, 300, 309, 310, 314, 346; Garrish, *Memoirs*, p. 17, USAMHI; O'Brien, ed., *My Life*, pp. 15, 16.

59. Newton, *Battle of Seven Pines*, pp. 92–93; *OR*, 11, pt. 1, p. 762; Wert, *General James Longstreet*, p. 120; Rhodes, ed., *All for the Union*, p. 71; Conyngham, *Irish Brigade*, p. 158; *SOR*, 2, p. 68.

60. Newton, *Battle of Seven Pines*, p. 98; Miller, "Disaster," *Columbiad*, 3, 4, p. 37; Wert, *General James Longstreet*, pp. 120–21; Sears, ed., *Civil War Papers*, p. 302; William E. Dunn–Sister, June 8, 1862, "Dear Sister," p. 14, USAMHI; *OR*, 11, pt. 1, p. 916.

61. Newton, *Battle of Seven Pines*, p. 85; Miller, "Disaster," *Columbiad*, 3, 4, pp. 38, 40; *OR*, 11, pt. 1, p. 816; Welcher, *Union Army*, p. 360; Crumb and Dhalle, eds., *No Middle Ground*, p. 55.

62. *OR*, 11, pt. 3, p. 210.

63. Charles E. Perkins–Sister, June 2, 1862, Perkins Civil War Letters, USAMHI.

64. Billings, *Hardtack*, p. 135; John W. Ames–My dear Fisher, April 20, 1862, Ames Papers; James De Clark–Parents, May 18, 1862, De Clark Papers, USAMHI; Miers, ed., *Wash Roebling's War*, p. 9; Rosenblatt and Rosenblatt, eds., *Hard Marching*, p. 32; Sears, *To the Gates*, p. 163.

65. Wright, *No More Gallant a Deed*, p. 137; Snell, *From First to Last*, pp. 120, 121; Hiram S. Wilson–Mrs. Elizabeth Wilson, June 21, 1862, Wilson Papers, NYSL; Hyde, *Civil War Letters*, p. 18; Daniel Sickles–Captain Chauncey McKeever, June 18, 1862, RG393, NA; George Bronson–[Mary Bronson], n.d., Pavlik Collection; John F. Hallack–My Dear Cousins, June 21, 1862, Hallack Papers, NYSL.

66. Thompson, "This Hell," *CWTI*, 12, 6, p. 20; Cassedy, ed., *Dear Friends*, p. 100; Favill, *Diary*, p. 125; Cudworth, *History*, p. 198.

67. Hastings, ed., *Letters*, pp. 4, 5; Styple, ed., *Writing*, p. 86; Racine, *"Unspoiled Heart,"* pp. 117, 136; Hiram Berdan–Hugh Harbison, May 8, 1862, Berdan Letter, USAMHI; White, ed., *Civil War Diary*, p. 18.

68. Gibbs, *Three Years*, pp. 126–27; Dunn, *Harvestfields*, pp. 65, 67, 74.
69. Sears, ed., *For Country*, p. 251.
70. Reed, ed., *Historical Family Letters*, p. 18; Squire Tuttle–[?], June [?] 1862, Tuttle Papers, USAMHI.
71. Priest, ed., *One Surgeon's Private War*, p. 31; Conyngham, *Irish Brigade*, p. 166; Alexander Webb–My Dear Father, June 9, 1862, Webb Papers, YU; Sears, ed., *Civil War Papers*, pp. 301, 302.
72. Eby, ed., *Virginia Yankee*, p. 129; de Trobriand, *Four Years*, p. 216.
73. OR, 11, pt. 1, pp. 106–32, 152–61, 164–77.
74. Warner, *Generals in Blue*, p. 311; McClellan, *McClellan's Own Story*, p. 122; Smart, ed., *Radical View*, v. 2, p. 4; Fleming, ed., *Life*, p. 140; Young, *Battle of Gettysburg*, p. 347; Schaff, *Battle*, pp. 44, 45; Hitchcock, *War*, p. 32; Agassiz, ed., *Meade's Headquarters*, p. 28.
75. OR, 11, pt. 1, p. 48; Minnigh, *History*, p. 38; Miller, ed., *Peninsula Campaign*, v. 1, p. 21; Sears, *To the Gates*, pp. 156, 157; Burton, *Extraordinary Circumstances*, pp. 15, 16, 402–3.
76. Michie, *General McClellan*, pp. 320, 321; Swinton, *Campaigns*, pp. 140, 141.
77. B&L, v. 2, p. 176; Sears, ed., *Civil War Papers*, p. 305; SOR, 2, p. 77; Weld, *War Diary*, pp. 111, 112; Meade, *Life and Letters*, v. 1, pp. 277–78.
78. Sears, ed., *Civil War Papers*, pp. 305, 306–7.
79. Burton, *Extraordinary Circumstances*, pp. 18–23; Welcher, *Union Army*, pp. 511–12; Starr, *Union Cavalry*, v. 1, pp. 262, 263; Miller, ed., *Peninsula Campaign*, v. 1, pp. 140, 141.
80. Wert, *General James Longstreet*, pp. 124–25; Isaac C. Dowling–Friend Osgood, August 30, 1862, Osgood Papers, DU.
81. Sears, ed., *Civil War Papers*, pp. 244–45.
82. Wert, *Gettysburg*, pp. 42–43; Harsh, *Confederate Tide Rising*, pp. 57, 58, 59; Gallagher, *Confederate War*, p. 116.
83. Wert, *Gettysburg*, p. 43; Harsh, *Confederate Tide Rising*, pp. 59–62; Gallagher, *Confederate War*, p. 127.
84. Harsh, *Confederate Tide Rising*, pp. 66–67; Wert, *Gettysburg*, pp. 42–44.
85. Wert, *General James Longstreet*, pp. 130–31; Styple, ed., *Letters from the Peninsula*, p. 109.

Chapter 6: "If We Were Defeated, the Army and the Country Would Be Lost"

1. Thomas C. Devin–My dear John, April 22, 1865, Devin Letter, USAMHI.
2. OR, 11, pt. 1, pp. 49–50; Burton, *Extraordinary Circumstances*, pp. 41, 42.
3. OR, 11, pt. 1, p. 50; Sears, ed., *On Campaign*, p. 31; Burton, *Extraordinary Circumstances*, pp. 44–51.
4. OR, 11, pt. 1, p. 51.
5. Ibid., pt. 3, p. 259.
6. Ibid., p. 254; B&L, v. 2, p. 180; Burton, *Extraordinary Circumstances*, p. 57; Sears, ed., *Civil War Papers*, p. 311.
7. Wert, *General James Longstreet*, pp. 130–36; Burton, *Extraordinary Circumstances*, p. 403.
8. OR, 11, pt. 2, pp. 221–22; B&L, v. 2, pp. 321, 325, 326; Wert, *General James Longstreet*, p. 133; Powell, *Fifth Army Corps*, pp. 78, 79.

9. OR, 11, pt. 2, p. 222; Powell, *Fifth Army Corps*, p. 78; Warner, *Generals in Blue*, pp. 315, 396, 432.

10. Nichols, *Toward Gettysburg*, pp. 4, 11, 20, 75, 76; McClellan, *McClellan's Own Story*, p. 140; Rosengarten, *Reynolds Memorial Address*, p. 33; Meade, *Life and Letters*, v. 1, p. 346; Hitchcock, *War*, pp. 101, 102; Hill, *Our Boys*, p. 139; John F. Reynolds–My dear Sister, June 4, 10, 1862, Reynolds Family Papers, FM.

11. Wert, *General James Longstreet*, pp. 132–33.

12. Ibid., pp. 133–34; OR, 11, pt. 2, pp. 222–23; B&L, v. 2, pp. 325–27; SOR, 2, p. 424; John M. Fullerton–Honored Parents, Brother, Sister, July 4, 1862, Miller Family Letters, USAMHI.

13. OR, 11, pt. 3, p. 223; Sears, *George B. McClellan*, p. 209; Miller, ed., *Peninsula Campaign*, v. 1, pp. 163–64; Priest, ed., *One Surgeon's Private War*, p. 33.

14. Burton, *Extraordinary Circumstances*, pp. 62, 63; Sears, *To the Gates*, pp. 210, 211; Swinton, *Campaigns*, pp. 146, 147.

15. OR, 11, pt. 2, p. 223; Sears, *To the Gates*, p. 211; Swinton, *Campaigns*, pp. 146, 147; Burton, *Extraordinary Circumstances*, p. 63; Livermore, *Days and Events*, p. 78.

16. OR, 11, pt. 2, pp. 223–24; F. J. Porter–J. G. Barnard, April 3, 1863, Webb Papers, YU; Powell, *Fifth Army Corps*, pp. 84–85; Hennessy, ed., *Fighting*, pp. 23n, 24n; Reese, *Sykes' Regular Infantry Division*, pp. 17, 73, 74, 131; John W. Ames–My dear Fisher, May 24, 1862, Ames Papers, USAMHI; Michie, *General McClellan*, p. 347.

17. Wert, *General James Longstreet*, pp. 132, 134.

18. Ibid., pp. 134–35; Burton, *Extraordinary Circumstances*, pp. 91–93; Davenport, *Campaign*, p. 208; M. Warrenton–Parents, July 4, 1862, Warrenton Papers, NC.

19. Burton, *Extraordinary Circumstances*, pp. 93, 96, 98; William C. Kent–Father, July 28, 1862, Kent Memoirs, USAMHI; Wert, *General James Longstreet*, pp. 134–35.

20. Davenport, *Campaign*, pp. 10, 22–38; Nevins, ed., *Diary*, p. 36; Fowler, "Making of a Zouave," p. 20, USAMHI.

21. Jordan, "Happiness," pp. x, 1, 3, 6, 8, 33–34, 41; Nevins, ed., *Diary*, pp. 338–39; Agassiz, ed., *Meade's Headquarters*, p. 26.

22. Jordan, "Happiness," p. 46; Reese, *Sykes' Regular Infantry Division*, pp. 83, 95; Davenport, *Campaign*, p. 212; John W. Ames–My dear Father and Mother, July 5, 1862, Ames Papers, USAMHI.

23. Wert, *General James Longstreet*, p. 135; OR, 11, pt. 2, pp. 224–25, 432; Sears, ed., *Civil War Papers*, p. 321n; Baquet, *History*, pp. 25, 312, 313.

24. Edmund Hawley–Brother, July 14, 1862, Hawley Letter, USAMHI; Slocum, *Life*, pp. 27–31; Baquet, *History*, pp. 25, 314; Gibbs, *Three Years*, pp. 114–16; Wert, *General James Longstreet*, pp. 135–36; OR, 11, pt. 2, pp. 225–26; Parker, *Henry Wilson's Regiment*, pp. 119–21; Slocum, *Life*, p. 29; Robertson, ed., *Civil War Letters*, p. 185; Cassedy, ed., *Dear Friends*, pp. 112, 113.

25. Jackson, *History*, pp. 58, 59, 60–70; Parker, *Henry Wilson's Regiment*, pp. 119–21, 122–26; Butterfield, *Biographical Memorial*, p. 76; Sauers, *Advance the Colors!*, v. 1, p. 226; Warner, *Generals in Blue*, p. 62; OR, 11, pt. 2, pp. 290–91, 301–2, 316–18, 344–45.

26. OR, 11, pt. 2, p. 438; Powell, *Fifth Army Corps*, pp. 106, 107; Thomson and Rauch, *History*, p. 119; Baquet, *History*, pp. 316–19, 362, 394; Gibbs, *Three Years*, pp. 114–21; Cassedy, ed., *Dear Friends*, pp. 112, 113; Walker, *History*, pp.

62, 63; Herberger, ed., *Yankee at Arms*, p. 45; Burton, *Extraordinary Circumstances*, pp. 132–35.

27. Burton, *Extraordinary Circumstances*, pp. 149–50; John F. Reynolds–My dear sisters, July 3, 1862, Reynolds Family Papers, FM; Nichols, *Toward Gettysburg*, pp. 97, 100.

28. Robertson, ed., *Civil War Letters*, p. 185; Fox, *Regimental Losses*, p. 430; SOR, 2, p. 418; Burton, *Extraordinary Circumstances*, pp. 135–37.

29. Robertson, ed., *Civil War Letters*, p. 185; Michie, *General McClellan*, p. 344; Burton, *Extraordinary Circumstances*, pp. 140–41; Sears, *George B. McClellan*, p. 211; Wert, *General James Longstreet*, p. 134.

30. Diary and Copies of Notes, Heintzelman Papers, LC; Swinton, *Campaigns*, pp. 153, 154; SOR, 2, p. 84.

31. SOR, 2, p. 84; Swinton, *Campaigns*, p. 154; Gallagher, ed., *Richmond Campaign of 1862*, p. 35; Jones, *Civil War Command*, p. 69.

32. OR, 11, pt. 1, p. 61; Sears, ed., *Civil War Papers*, pp. 322–23.

33. Sears, ed., *Civil War Papers*, p. 323n, 367; Weigley, *Great Civil War*, p. 132.

34. SOR, 2, p. 84; B&L, v. 2, p. 182; Sears, *George B. McClellan*, p. 256; Burton, *Extraordinary Circumstances*, pp. 159, 165.

35. Extracts from the Diary of Brigadier General D. N. Couch, Webb Papers, YU; Sears, *To the Gates*, pp. 250, 256; Page, *Letters*, p. 17; Seth Gilbert Evans–My Dear Mother & Sisters, July 20, 1862, Evans Papers, NC.

36. Westbrook, *History*, pp. 114, 115; Walker, *History*, pp. 64–65; Burton, *Extraordinary Circumstances*, pp. 172, 174, 176, 177; Schiller, ed., *Autobiography*, p. 42; Martin et al., eds., *History*, pp. 35, 36; Dunn, *Harvestfields*, p. 86.

37. Seth Gilbert Evans–My Dear Mother & Sisters, July 20, 1862, Evans Papers, NC; Favill, *Diary*, p. 135; Burton, *Extraordinary Circumstances*, p. 175; Lash, "*Duty Well Done*," p. 227; Young Diary; Stephens, "Civil War Diary," p. 24, USAMHI.

38. Wert, *General James Longstreet*, p. 137.

39. Ibid., pp. 137–38.

40. Elliott Diary, USAMHI; Davenport, *Campaign*, p. 240; Moe, *Last Full Measure*, p. 151; Hard, *History*, p. 151; Coco, ed., *From Ball's Bluff to Gettysburg*, p. 108; Newhall, *Memoir*, p. 67.

41. OR, 11, pt. 2, pp. 193, 227–28, 389, 435; Extracts from the Diary of Brigadier General D. N. Couch, Webb Papers, YU; Miller, ed., *Peninsula Campaign*, v. 1, pp. 34, 35; Burton, *Extraordinary Circumstances*, pp. 194–98.

42. Burton, *Extraordinary Circumstances*, pp. 203–4; Herberger, ed., *Yankee at Arms*, p. 49.

43. Rhodes, *History*, p. 97; Livermore, *Days and Events*, p. 79; Westbrook, *History*, p. 112; Trask, *Fire Within*, p. 119; Coco, ed., *From Ball's Bluff to Gettysburg*, p. 106; Favill, *Diary*, p. 136.

44. SOR, 2, p. 415; Page, *Letters*, p. 19; Burton, *Extraordinary Circumstances*, p. 204; Herberger, ed., *Yankee at Arms*, p. 49.

45. SOR, 2, p. 405; Miller, ed., *Peninsula Campaign*, v. 3, p. 151; Charles A. Wheeler–My dear C, July 6, 1862, Wheeler Papers, NC; Sneden, *Eye of the Storm*, pp. 70–72; Burton, *Extraordinary Circumstances*, p. 205.

46. OR, 11, pt. 2, p. 50; G. W. Goulding–Mother, July 6, 1862, Goulding Papers, NC; Walker, *History*, p. 67; Burton, *Extraordinary Circumstances*, pp. 212–14.

47. *OR*, 11, pt. 2, p. 50; Burton, *Extraordinary Circumstances*, pp. 212–14; Walker, *History*, p. 67; Plumb, "Record," p. 6; Jonathan P. Stowe–Kind friends at home, July 11, 1862, Stowe Letters, USAMHI; *B&L*, v. 2, p. 371.

48. *OR*, 11, pt. 2, pp. 91–92; Walker, *History*, p. 67; Wright, *No More Gallant a Deed*, p. 128.

49. Burton, *Extraordinary Circumstances*, pp. 214–22; *OR*, 11, pt. 2, pp. 477, 479; Benedict, *Vermont*, v. 1, pp. 291, 297, 300.

50. *OR*, 11, pt. 2, p. 479; *B&L*, v. 2, p. 373; Fox, *Regimental Losses*, p. 430; Walker, *History*, p. 67; Burton, *Extraordinary Circumstances*, pp. 214–22.

51. Michie, *General McClellan*, p. 352; Joinville, *Army*, p. 93; Gallagher, ed., *Richmond Campaign of 1862*, p. 36.

52. Eckert and Amato, eds., *Ten Years*, p. 361; Sears, *George B. McClellan*, pp. 217–18; *OR*, 11, pt. 2, p. 51.

53. Extracts from the Diary of Brigadier General D. N. Couch, Webb Papers, YU; Schiller, ed., *Autobiography*, pp. 44–45; Snell, *From First to Last*, p. 130.

54. Rhodes, ed., *All for the Union*, p. 72; Westbrook, *History*, p. 116; Lash, "Duty Well Done," p. 234; Sears, ed., *On Campaign*, p. 33.

55. Sears, "Lee's Lost Opportunity," *N&S*, 5, 1, p. 13; Burton, *Extraordinary Circumstances*, pp. 235, 239; Snell, *From First to Last*, p. 134.

56. *B&L*, v. 2, p. 377; Sneden, *Eye of the Storm*, p. 84; Sears, *To the Gates*, p. 281; Gallagher, ed., *Richmond Campaign of 1862*, p. 37.

57. *SOR*, 2, p. 86; Schiller, ed., *Autobiography*, p. 46; Burton, *Extraordinary Circumstances*, pp. 239, 252, 277.

58. Wert, *General James Longstreet*, pp. 138–39; Burton, *Extraordinary Circumstances*, p. 239.

59. Wert, *General James Longstreet*, p. 139; Sears, "Lee's Lost Opportunity," *N&S*, 5, 1, p. 21; Burton, *Extraordinary Circumstances*, pp. 249, 264–66.

60. Woodward, *On Campaign*, p. 104; Wert, *General James Longstreet*, p. 140; Sears, "Lee's Lost Opportunity," *N&S*, 5, 1, p. 22; Hall, *History*, p. 90.

61. Sypher, *History*, pp. 275, 277; Meade, *Life and Letters*, v. 1, pp. 299, 299n, 300, 301; Cleaves, *Meade*, pp. 68–69, 72; Powell, *Fifth Army Corps*, p. 142.

62. *OR*, 11, pt. 2, pp. 390–92; Sears, "Lee's Lost Opportunity," *N&S*, 5, 1, p. 22; Sypher, *History*, p. 288; William L. Candler–My dear Brother, July 7, 1862, Candler Papers, VATU; Wert, *General James Longstreet*, p. 141.

63. Robertson, ed., *Civil War Letters*, p. 158; Sears, ed., *On Campaign*, p. 34; Davenport, *Camp and Field Life*, pp. 240–41; Fuller, *Personal Recollections*, p. 52; David B. Birney–Gross, June 28, October 26, 1862, Birney Papers; Ellis C. Strouss–Mother, June 8, 1862, Strouss Letters, USAMHI.

64. Agassiz, ed., *Meade's Headquarters*, p. 139; Sears, ed., *On Campaign*, p. 37; Baquet, *History*, pp. 30–32; *OR*, 11, pt. 2, pp. 162–63, 182, 186; Sears, "Lee's Lost Opportunity," *N&S*, 5, 1, p. 23; Wert, *General James Longstreet*, p. 141.

65. Fleming, ed., *Life*, pp. 1, 9, 14, 50, 99, 113, 135, 138, 139, 240, 241, 243; Hays, ed., *Under the Red Patch*, p. 105; *OR*, 11, pt. 2, p. 167.

66. *OR*, 11, pt. 2, pp. 81, 111–12; Walker, *History*, p. 76; Burton, *Extraordinary Circumstances*, pp. 285–86, 292, 296–98; Sedgwick, ed., *Correspondence*, v. 2, p. 70; William L. Candler–My dear Brother, July 7, 1862, Candler Papers, VATU; William C. Wiley–Dear Ones at Home, June 28, 1862, Wiley Papers, PSU; Charles R. Johnson–Nellie, June 26, 1862, Johnson Letters, USAMHI; Hess, *Union Soldier*, p. 1.

67. Burton, *Extraordinary Circumstances*, p. 298; Sears, "Lee's Lost Opportunity," *N&S*, 5, 1, p. 24; Miller, ed., *Peninsula Campaign*, v. 1, p. 43; Fox, *Regimental Losses*, p. 430.

68. Wert, *General James Longstreet*, pp. 141–43; Sears, "Lee's Lost Opportunity," *N&S*, 5, 1, p. 24.

69. *OR*, 11, pt. 3, pp. 280, 281.

70. Sears, ed., *Civil War Papers*, pp. 326n, 327n.

71. Burton, *Extraordinary Circumstances*, p. 304; *OR*, 11, pt. 2, p. 112.

72. Wert, *General James Longstreet*, p. 144; *B&L*, v. 2, p. 409; Powell, *Fifth Army Corps*, pp. 153, 165; Gallagher, ed., *Richmond Campaign of 1862*, pp. 217, 220; Sneden, *Eye of the Storm*, p. 95.

73. *B&L*, v. 2, p. 414; Powell, *Fifth Army Corps*, p. 153; Cowley, ed., *With My Face to the Enemy*, p. 124; Carter, *Four Brothers*, p. 69; Tap, *Over Lincoln's Shoulder*, p. 121; Sears, *George B. McClellan*, p. 221.

74. Wormeley, *Other Side*, p. 177; Sears, *George B. McClellan*, p. 221; David B. Birney–Gross, February 25, 1863, Birney Papers, USAMHI; Fuller, *Personal Recollections*, pp. 43, 46.

75. Longacre, *Man Behind the Guns*, pp. 104, 108; Naisawald, *Grape and Canister*, p. 97; Burton, *Extraordinary Circumstances*, pp. 307–8; McClellan, *McClellan's Own Story*, p. 117.

76. M. Edgar Richards–Col., July 5, 1862, Richards Letters, USAMHI; Longacre, *Man Behind the Guns*, p. 112.

77. Sears, ed., *For Country*, pp. 265, 266.

78. *OR*, 11, pt. 2, pp. 229, 431; Burton, *Extraordinary Circumstances*, pp. 306, 308–10, 312.

79. *OR*, 11, pt. 2, pp. 495, 496; Wert, *General James Longstreet*, pp. 143, 144.

80. Wert, *General James Longstreet*, p. 145; Burton, *Extraordinary Circumstances*, pp. 324, 325; Kent, Memoirs, USAMHI.

81. *OR*, 11, pt. 2, p. 496; Wert, *General James Longstreet*, p. 145.

82. Wert, *General James Longstreet*, p. 146.

83. Bruen and Fitzgibbons, ed., *Through Ordinary Eyes*, p. 150; Ames, *History*, pp. 35, 36; Cassedy, ed., *Dear Friends*, p. 116; William C. Wiley–Dear Ones at Home, July 6, 1862, Wiley Papers, PSU.

84. Wert, *General James Longstreet*, p. 146.

85. Ibid.

86. Judson, *History*, p. 78; Parker, *Henry Wilson's Regiment*, p. 128; Powell, *Fifth Army Corps*, pp. 167–68; Walker, *History*, pp. 82–84; F. J. Porter–Samuel Heintzelman, July 10, 1862, Webb Papers, YU; detailed description of Malvern Hill is in Burton, *Extraordinary Circumstances*, Chapters 17–19.

87. A. A. Humphreys–My dear General, March 31, 1863, Webb Papers, YU; Sears, *George B. McClellan*, pp. 221–22.

88. Extracts from the Diary of Brigadier General D. N. Couch, Webb Papers, YU; Burton, *Extraordinary Circumstances*, pp. 362, 366–67; Sneden, *Eye of the Storm*, p. 98; LeDuc, *Recollections*, p. 89; Woodward, "Memories," p. 22, USAMHI.

89. Diary, Heintzelman Papers, LC; Favill, *Diary*, pp. 149, 161; LeDuc, *Recollections*, p. 91; Herberger, ed., *Yankee at Arms*, p. 53; Sears, ed., *On Campaign*, p. 39; Westbrook, *History*, p. 116; de Trobriand, *Four Years*, pp. 282, 283.

90. *OR*, 11, pt. 2, pp. 497–98; Wert, *General James Longstreet*, pp. 148–49; Sears, *To the Gates*, p. 343; Burton, *Extraordinary Circumstances*, p. 386.

91. A. S. Daggart–Samuel R. Lemont, July 6, 1862, Lemont Letters, UME; Sears, ed., *For Country*, p. 263; Pride and Travis, *My Brave Boys*, p. 106; John F. Hallack–Cousins, July 4, 1862, Hallack Papers, NYSL; Sears, ed., *For Country*, p. 263.

92. Thomas Paxton–Ellie, July 29, 1862, Paxton Papers; G. W. Goulding–Mother, July 6, 1862, Goulding Papers; Seth Gilbert Evans–My Dear Mother & Sisters, July 20, 1862, Evans Papers, NC; John F. Hallack–Cousin, July 4, 1862, Hallack Papers, NYSL; Dunn, *Harvestfields*, pp. 98–99.

93. Burton, *Extraordinary Circumstances*, p. 386; OR, 11, pt. 3, p. 299; Michie, *General McClellan*, p. 365; Sears, *To the Gates*, p. 257.

94. Crumb and Dhalle, eds., *No Middle Ground*, p. 66; Rhea et al., "What Was Wrong," *N&S*, 4, 3, p. 17.

95. Favill, *Diary*, p. 158; William L. Candler–My dear Brother, July 7, 1862, Candler Papers, VATU; Crumb and Dhalle, eds., *No Middle Ground*, p. 57; Young Diary, USAMHI; G. W. Goulding–Mother, July 6, 1862, Goulding Papers, NC; Catton, *Mr. Lincoln's Army*, p. 14.

96. Crumb and Dhalle, eds., *No Middle Ground*, pp. 57, 62, 64; William L. Candler–My dear Brother, July 7, 1862, Candler Papers, VATU; Favill, *Diary*, p. 158; de Trobriand, *Four Years*, p. 282; Sears, *To the Gates*, p. 257; Sneden, *Eye of the Storm*, p. 97; William C. Wiley–Dear Ones at Home, July 6, 1862, Wiley Papers, PSU.

97. Sypher, *History*, p. 309; Sears, *To the Gates*, pp. 257, 265; order of battle and casualty returns are in OR, 11, pt. 2, pp. 24–41.

98. Winslow, *General John Sedgwick*, p. 29; Favill, *Diary*, pp. 158, 159; Sneden, *Eye of the Storm*, pp. 97–98; de Trobriand, *Four Years*, pp. 272, 275, 282; Schiller, ed., *Autobiography*, pp. 33, 47; Sears, *George B. McClellan*, p. 231; David B. Birney–Gross, October 26, 1862, Birney Papers, USAMHI; Snell, *From First to Last*, p. 144.

99. Burton, *Extraordinary Circumstances*, pp. 148–49; Styple, ed., *Letters from the Peninsula*, pp. 128, 129; Joseph Hooker–George W. Mindil, January 12, 1875, Mindil Papers, USAMHI.

100. B&L, v. 2, pp. 173, 187; Sears, ed., *Civil War Papers*, p. 338; Sears, "Little Mac," *N&S*, 2, 3, p. 68.

101. Sears, *George B. McClellan*, pp. 225, 226; Jones, *Civil War Command*, p. 74; Sears, *Controversies*, pp. 13, 14, 15, 17, 19.

102. Jones, *Civil War Command*, pp. 74, 136; Joinville, *Army*, p. 97; Sears, ed., *On Campaign*, p. 44.

103. Wright, *No More Gallant a Deed*, p. 171.

Chapter 7: "McClellan Has the Army with Him"

1. Wormeley, *Other Side*, pp. 189, 190; Abraham Lincoln, Memorandum on Interviews with Officers of the Army of the Potomac, July 8–9, 1862, Lincoln Papers, LC.

2. Wormeley, *Other Side*, p. 190; Abraham Lincoln, Memorandum on Interviews with Officers of the Army of the Potomac, July 8–9, 1862, Lincoln Papers, LC.

3. Wormeley, *Other Side*, pp. 189, 191; Walker and Walker, eds., *Diary*, p. 42; Wray, *Birney's Zouaves*, p. 75; Davenport, *Campaign*, p. 256; Davis, *Lincoln's Men*, pp. 68, 69; Ritchie, ed., *Four Years*, p. 74; Becker Diary, USAMHI.

4. Abraham Lincoln, Memorandum on Interviews with Officers of the Army of the Potomac, July 8–9, 1862, Lincoln Papers, LC; Sears, ed., *Civil War Papers*, p. 348.

5. OR, 11, pt. 1, pp. 73–74; Sears, *George B. McClellan*, p. 227; Sears, ed., *Civil War Papers*, p. 346; McClellan, *McClellan's Own Story*, pp. 487–89.

6. OR, 11, pt. 1, pp. 73–74.

7. Ibid., p. 73; Williams, *Lincoln and His Generals*, p. 133; Adams, *Our Masters the Rebels*, p. 113.

8. Gallagher, ed., *Richmond Campaign of 1862*, p. 177; Sutherland, *Fredericksburg*, pp. 7, 9; Tap, *Over Lincoln's Shoulder*, p. 126; Grimsley, *Hard Hand*, p. 95; Nevins, ed., *Diary of the Civil War*, pp. 239, 241, 244, 246; Styple, ed., *Letters from the Peninsula*, pp. 148–49.

9. Sutherland, *Fredericksburg*, p. 7; Gallagher, ed., *Richmond Campaign of 1862*, p. 177; Sears, "Little Mac," *N&S*, 2, 3, p. 67; Donald, *Lincoln*, pp. 363–65.

10. Donald, *Lincoln*, pp. 365–66.

11. Ibid., p. 366; Weigley, *Great Civil War*, p. xvii.

12. Geary, *We Need Men*, pp. 3, 8, 28, 29, 32, 34, 35, 81; McClellan, *McClellan's Own Story*, p. 259; Pullen, *Shower of Stars*, p. 35; Marvel, *Race*, pp. 1–3; Sauers, *Advance the Colors!*, v. 1, p. 247; Baquet, *History*, p. 222.

13. Welcher, *Union Army*, pp. 297–98; Warner, *Generals in Blue*, p. 376; Cozzens, *General John Pope*, pp. 3, 9, 26; Cozzens and Girardi, eds., *Military Memoirs*, pp. 129, 132.

14. Hennessy, *Return to Bull Run*, pp. 12, 14; Cozzens and Girardi, eds., *Military Memoirs*, p. 121.

15. Welcher, *Union Army*, p. 420; Parker, *History*, pp. 191, 200; Marvel, *Burnside*, pp. 100–103.

16. Laas, ed., *Wartime Washington*, p. 166; Warner, *Generals in Blue*, p. 196; Simon, "Lincoln and 'Old Brains,'" *N&S*, 2, 1, p. 41.

17. Warner, *Generals in Blue*, p. 196; Hattaway and Jones, "'Old Brains,'" *Columbiad*, 1, 1, pp. 72, 73, 75, 76, 78; Simon, "Lincoln and 'Old Brains,'" *N&S*, 2, 1, pp. 40, 44.

18. Warner, *Generals in Blue*, p. 196; Hattaway and Jones, "'Old Brains,'" *Columbiad*, 1, 1, pp. 76–81; Simon, "Lincoln and 'Old Brains,'" *N&S*, 2, 1, pp. 39, 41.

19. Sears, *George B. McClellan*, pp. 241, 241; Miller, ed., *Peninsula Campaign*, v. 2, p. 107; Donald, *Lincoln*, p. 369.

20. OR, 11, pt. 1, pp. 74, 75; SOR, 2, pp. 96, 98, 99, 100; Sears, ed., *Civil War Papers*, pp. 354, 361, 362, 363, 365; George B. McClellan–My Dear Bishop, July 7, 1862, McClellan Papers, NC; Meade, *Life and Letters*, v. 1, p. 304; Styple, ed., *Letters from the Peninsula*, p. 146; Miller, ed., *Peninsula Campaign*, v. 2, pp. 102, 103.

21. Miller, ed., *Peninsula Campaign*, v. 2, pp. 104, 105, 106, 107–8; Sears, *George B. McClellan*, p. 241.

22. Scores of letters attest to the bond between McClellan and the rank and file. Those referred to or quoted are Styple, ed., *Our Noble Blood*, p. 68; Trask, *Fire Within*, p. 124; Cowles, ed., *History*, p. 392; Sears, ed., *For Country*, p. 267; Cassedy, ed., *Dear Friends*, pp. 123, 124; Styple, ed., *Writing*, pp. 108–9; Ellis C. Strouss–Father, July 6, 1862, Strouss Letters; Thomas T. Tanfield–My Dear Sister,

July 7, 1862, Tanfield Family Papers; William Henry Walling–My Dear Sister, July 12, 1862, Walling Letters; John Faller–Folks at Home, July 12, 1862, Faller Correspondence, USAMHI; Hammond, ed., "Dear Mollie," *PHMB*, v. 89, p. 37; Charles A. Wheeler–My Dear C, July 14, 1862, Wheeler Papers, NC: Alexander Webb–Father, July 10, 1862, Webb Papers, YU; Fleming, ed., *Life*, pp. 252, 264.

23. Stevens, *Three Years*, p. 114; Adams, *Reminiscences*, p. 38; Lash, "Duty Well Done," pp. 242, 245, 246; Martin et al., eds., *History*, p. 46; Westbrook, *History*, p. 117; Thomas Paxton–Ellie, July 29, 1862, Paxton Papers, NC: Cowles, ed., *History*, p. 403; Baxter, ed., *Hoosier Farm Boy*, p. 36; Snell, *From First to Last*, p. 146; de Trobriand, *Four Years*, pp. 287, 288; Charles E. Perkins–Brother, July 17, 1862, Perkins Civil War Letters; Theodore Smith–Father, July 20, 1862, Smith Letter; Fowler, "Making of a Zouave," p. 37, USAMHI.

24. Sears, *George B. McClellan*, pp. 241, 242; *SOR*, 2, p. 99.

25. Donald, ed., *Inside Lincoln's Cabinet*, pp. 106, 107; *OR*, 11, pt. 1, pp. 80–81; Paludan, *Presidency*, p. 208; Henry W. Halleck–Francis Lieber, August 4, 1863, Lieber Papers, HL.

26. Donald, ed., *Inside Lincoln's Cabinet*, p. 107; McClure, *Abraham Lincoln*, p. 167; Donald, *Lincoln*, p. 370.

27. *OR*, 11, pt. 1, pp. 87–88; pt. 3, pp. 372–73, 378; A. A. Humphreys–George B. McClellan, July 17, 1862, RG 393, NA; *SOR*, 2, pp. 102, 103; Sears, ed., *Civil War Papers*, pp. 368, 388; Stine, *History*, p. 151; Sears, *Controversies*, pp. 54, 55; Adams, *Our Masters the Rebels*, p. 114; Weigley, *Great Civil War*, p. 142; Donald, *Lincoln*, pp. 370–71.

28. Moe, *Last Full Measure*, p. 165; Edward A. Walker–Friend Knight, October 5, 1862, Walker Papers, NC; Miller, ed., *Peninsula Campaign*, v. 1, p. 205; Powell, *Fifth Army Corps*, pp. 193, 194; William B. Franklin–John C. Ropes, October 16, 1897, Franklin Letter File, MNBP; Scott, ed., *Fallen Leaves*, p. 139.

29. Wert, *General James Longstreet*, pp. 154–55.

30. The finest study of Second Bull Run or Second Manassas is Hennessy, *Return to Bull Run*, see Chapters 4–7.

31. Ibid., Chapters 8–11.

32. Michie, *General McClellan*, p. 383; Sears, ed., *Civil War Papers*, pp. 406, 424; Winslow, *General John Sedgwick*, p. 38; Ford, ed., *Cycle*, v. 1, pp. 177–78, 181.

33. Sears, *Controversies*, pp. 79–81; Michie, *General McClellan*, pp. 390, 391.

34. *OR*, 11, pt. 1, pp. 94–98; 12, pt. 3, pp. 689–91, 708–10, 722, 723, 744, 747; William B. Franklin–John C. Ropes, October 20, 1897, Franklin Letter File, MNBP.

35. *OR*, 11, pt. 1, pp. 95, 98, 99; Sears, ed., *Civil War Papers*, pp. 416n, 417; William B. Franklin–John C. Ropes, October 20, 1897, Franklin Letter File, MNBP.

36. Sears, *Controversies*, pp. 78–81; Cozzens, *General John Pope*, p. 160.

37. *OR*, 11, pt. 1, pp. 98, 99; 12, pt. 3, pp. 708, 709, 710, 744–45; Cozzens, *General John Pope*, p. 108; William B. Franklin–John C. Ropes, October 20, 1897, Franklin Letter File, MNBP; Snell, *From First to Last*, pp. 165, 168; accounts of the condition of Second and Sixth corps troops can be found in Carter, *Four Brothers*, p. 89; Dayton E. Flint–Father, September [?] 1862, Flint Civil War Letters, USAMHI; Edward A. Walker–Friend Knight, October 5, 1862, Walker Papers, NC; W. H. Medill–Sister, August 21, 1862, Hanna–McCormick Family Papers, LC.

38. *OR*, 12, pt. 2, p. 79; pt. 3, pp. 771–72; Hennessy, *Return to Bull Run*, p. 437.

39. Hennessy, *Return to Bull Run*, Chapters 12–15, 19–30; Wert, *General James Longstreet*, pp. 165–75.

40. Hennessy, *Return to Bull Run*, pp. 437–39; Wert, *General James Longstreet*, p. 175.

41. Hennessy, *Return to Bull Run*, pp. 446–50; Styple, ed., *Writing*, p. 132; Gambone, *Major-General John Frederick Hartranft*, p. 57.

42. William C. Wiley–Dear Ones at Home, September 4, 1862, Wiley Papers, PSU; Sears, ed., *For Country*, p. 282; Styple, ed., *Our Noble Blood*, p. 70.

43. Joseph D. Baker–Affectionate Mother, September 30, 1862, Baker Papers; Edgar Williams–Parents, September 18, 1862, Williams Letters, USAMHI; Martin et al., eds., *History*, p. 57; Sneden, *Eye of the Storm*, p. 112; de Trobriand, *Four Years*, p. 298.

44. Beale, ed., *Diary*, v. 1, p. 104; Sears, *Controversies*, pp. 82, 85–87; Sears, ed., *Civil War Papers*, p. 428.

45. OR, 12, pt. 2, p. 83.

46. Donald, *Lincoln*, p. 371; Sears, *Controversies*, p. 91.

47. Beale, ed., *Diary*, v. 1, p. 229; Donald, *Lincoln*, p. 371; Nevins, ed., *Diary of the Civil War*, p. 246.

48. Donald, *Lincoln*, p. 371; Sears, *Controversies*, pp. 87–88.

49. Davis, *Lincoln's Men*, p. 76; Sears, *Controversies*, pp. 88, 91.

50. Sears, *Controversies*, p. 88; Donald, *Lincoln*, pp. 371–72; Sears, ed., *Civil War Papers*, p. 428.

51. Beale, ed., *Diary*, v. 1, pp. 104–5, 120; Donald, ed., *Inside Lincoln's Cabinet*, pp. 118, 119; Sears, *Controversies*, pp. 89–90; Donald, *Lincoln*, p. 372.

52. Sears, *Controversies*, p. 91; Beale, ed., *Diary*, v. 1, pp. 112–13.

53. Andrew Knox–My dear Wife, September 4, 1862, Knox Letters; Benjamin F. Ashenfelter–Father Churchman, September 26, 1862, Ashenfelter Letters, USAMHI; Henry F. Young–Father, September 9, 1862, Young Papers, SHSW; Stevens, *Three Years*, p. 131; Adams, *Our Masters the Rebels*, p. 102; Raab, ed., *With the 3rd Wisconsin*, p. 81; Scott, ed., *Fallen Leaves*, p. 140; Weld, *War Diary*, pp. 81, 132; Livermore, *Days and Events*, p. 110.

54. Eby, ed., *Virginia Yankee*, p. 100; McClellan, *McClellan's Own Story*, p. 537; Cozzens, *General John Pope*, p. 195; David B. Birney–Gross, February 25, 1863, Birney Papers, USAMHI; Sears, *George B. McClellan*, pp. 261–62.

55. Cozzens, *General John Pope*, p. 195; John Gibbon–My darling Mama, September 3, 1862, Gibbon Papers, HSP; Weld, *War Diary*, pp. 82, 136; Miller, *Drum Taps in Dixie*, p. 38.

56. Wert, *Brotherhood*, p. 165; Nevins, ed., *Diary of the Civil War*, p. 252; Cassedy, ed., *Dear Friends*, p. 144; Hiram S. Wilson–Mrs. Elizabeth Wilson, August 29, 1862, Wilson Papers, NYSL.

Chapter 8: "Behold, a Pale Horse"

1. Sparks, ed., *Inside Lincoln's Army*, p. 140.

2. Wert, *General James Longstreet*, p. 176; Wert, *Brotherhood*, p. 163.

3. OR, 19, pt. 1, p. 144; pt. 2, pp. 590, 591; Harsh, *Taken at the Flood*, pp. 25, 492; Griffith, *Battle Tactics*, p. 35.

4. Harsh, *Taken at the Flood*, pp. 37–45.

5. Ibid., pp. 108–9; Fishel, *Secret War*, p. 211; Favill, *Diary*, p. 182.

6. Sears, ed., *Civil War Papers*, p. 435; *B&L*, v. 2, pp. 160, 161; Sears, *George B. McClellan*, pp. 265, 267; Schildt, *Roads to Antietam*, p. 35; Gould, *Major-General Hiram G. Berry*, p. 207; Walker and Walker, eds., *Diary*, p. 52; Beale, ed., *Diary*, v. 1, p. 124.

7. Sears, *George B. McClellan*, p. 267; Sears, ed., *Civil War Papers*, p. 441.

8. Welcher, *Union Army*, pp. 457–58, 464–65; Winslow, *General John Sedgwick*, p. 43; OR, 19, pt. 1, p. 157; Warner, *Generals in Blue*, p. 309.

9. Welcher, *Union Army*, pp. 301–2; Sears, ed., *Civil War Papers*, pp. 436, 449; Sears, *George B. McClellan*, pp. 266–67; Joseph Hooker–George W. Mindil, January 12, 1875, Mindil Papers, USAMHI; Nevins, ed., *Diary*, pp. 90, 93.

10. Joseph Hooker–George W. Mindil, January 12, 1875, Mindil Papers, USAMHI; Nevins, ed., *Diary*, p. 93.

11. Gallagher, ed., *Antietam Campaign*, pp. 143–45; Silas Casey–Seth Williams, September 5, 6, 8, 1862; E. E. Camp–Seth Williams, September 14, 1862, RG 393, NA; Sauers, *Advance the Colors!*, v. 2, pp. 395, 396, 398, 400, 402, 404, 405, 458; Mancha Diary, pp. 2, 3, 10–12, USAMHI; Swinfen, *Ruggles' Regiment*, pp. 1–3; Marvel, *Race*, pp. 5–18, 27; Page, *History*, p. 23; Sauers, ed., *Civil War Journal*, p. 79; Niven, *Connecticut*, pp. 213, 218; Jordan, *Civil War Journals*, p. 186.

12. Gallagher, ed., *Antietam Campaign*, pp. 146, 147; Sauers, *Advance the Colors!*, v. 2, p. 313; Humphreys, *Andrew A. Humphreys*, pp. 30, 156, 168, 170; Gallagher, ed., *Fredericksburg Campaign*, p. 81.

13. Welcher, *Union Army*, p. 315; Walker, *History*, p. 97; Meade, *Life and Letters*, v. 1, p. 310; Nichols, *Toward Gettysburg*, pp. 102, 126, 127.

14. OR, 19, pt. 2, pp. 282–83; Longacre, *Man Behind the Guns*, p. 119; Nevins, ed., *Diary*, p. 94.

15. Nevins, ed., *Diary*, pp. 94–95; Henry J. Hunt–Artillery Commanders, September 12, 1862, Army of the Potomac, RG 393, NA.

16. OR, 19, pt. 1, p. 180; SOR, 2, pp. 132, 135; Welcher, *Union Army*, p. 513; Warner, *Generals in Blue*, p. 373.

17. Welcher, *Union Army*, p. 345; a complete order of battle for the Army of the Potomac is in OR, 19, pt. 1, pp. 169–80.

18. OR, 12, pt. 2, pp. 12–17; 19, pt. 2, p. 188; Sears, ed., *Civil War Papers*, pp. 436–37; Nevins, ed., *Diary of the Civil War*, p. 255.

19. Quaife, ed., *From the Cannon's Mouth*, p. 121; Harsh, *Taken at the Flood*, pp. 108–9, 166–67; OR, 19, pt. 2, p. 219; Fishel, *Secret War*, p. 217.

20. Gallagher, ed., *Antietam Campaign*, pp. 147, 148; Harsh, *Taken at the Flood*, pp. 108–9, 166–67, 189; Sears, *Landscape*, p. 108; Murfin, *Gleam*, p. 131; Carter, *Four Brothers*, p. 126; Sears, ed., *Mr. Dunn Browne's Experiences*, pp. 1, 3, 5; James R. Simpson–Sister, September 13, 1862, Simpson and Simpson, "Dear Daul"; Leib Diary, USAMHI.

21. Harsh, *Taken at the Flood*, Chapters 3 and 4; OR, 19, pt. 2, p. 232; *B&L*, v. 2, p. 551.

22. Harsh, *Taken at the Flood*, Chapter 3, quotation on p. 167.

23. Ibid., pp. 177, 181–82, 189–90; 198–211; Edward A. Walker–Friend Knight, October 5, 1862, Walker Papers, NC: Pride and Travis, *My Brave Boys*, p. 122; Walker, *History*, p. 93.

24. Furst Diary, p. 26, USAMHI; Jones, *Giants*, pp. 229, 230, 231; Sears, *George B. McClellan*, pp. 280–81.

25. Harsh, *Taken at the Flood*, p. 242; Fishel, *Secret War*, pp. 225–26; OR, 19, pt. 2, p. 281; Sears, *George B. McClellan*, pp. 281, 282.

26. Harsh, *Taken at the Flood*, pp. 237–41; Fishel, *Secret War*, pp. 225, 226; Sears, *George B. McClellan*, pp. 282, 285.

27. Criticisms of McClellan's reaction to the Lost Order can be found in Catton, *Mr. Lincoln's Army*, pp. 213–16; Swinton, *Campaigns*, p. 202; Murfin, *Gleam*, pp. 129, 133–34, 160–64; Sears, *George B. McClellan*, pp. 283–86; a more balanced and accurate view of it is in Harsh, *Taken at the Flood*, pp. 239–41; Bryce, "Battle of South Mountain," p. 32, ANB.

28. Harsh, *Taken at the Flood*, pp. 239–41.

29. Ibid., pp. 239–41, 252; Sears, *George B. McClellan*, pp. 283–87; Fishel, *Secret War*, pp. 225, 226.

30. A careful analysis of this in Harsh, *Taken at the Flood*, pp. 239–41, quotation on p. 241.

31. Ibid., pp. 244, 245.

32. Ibid., pp. 244–49.

33. Wert, *General James Longstreet*, p. 185.

34. Ibid., pp. 185–86; Harsh, *Taken at the Flood*, pp. 256–59; the fullest treatment of the Battle of South Mountain is in Priest, *Before Antietam*, passim; Wert, *Brotherhood*, p. 171.

35. Wert, *General James Longstreet*, pp. 185–86; Harsh, *Taken at the Flood*, pp. 263–67.

36. Priest, *Before Antietam*, Chapters 10–12; Gallagher, ed., *Antietam Campaign*, p. 155; George Bronson–[Mary Bronson], September 14, 1862, Pavlik Collection; Parker, *History*, pp. 225, 226; Harsh, *Taken at the Flood*, pp. 263, 267; Wert, *General James Longstreet*, p. 186; Murfin, *Gleam*, p. 181; Gibbs, *Three Years*, p. 176.

37. Wert, *Brotherhood*, pp. 100–101, 168; Herdegen and Beaudot, *In the Bloody Railroad Cut*, p. 337.

38. Wert, *Brotherhood*, pp. 98–101; Gaff, *On Many a Bloody Field*, p. 95; Herdegen and Murphy, eds., *Four Years*, p. 99; Herdegen and Beaudot, *In the Bloody Railroad Cut*, pp. 331–33.

39. Wert, *Brotherhood*, pp. 148–53; Herdegen, *Men Stood*, p. 93; Smith, *Twenty-fourth Michigan*, p. 237.

40. Wert, *Brotherhood*, pp. 169–72, 188–89; Record of the 6th Wisconsin, Dawes Papers; Frank A. Haskell–Brothers and Sisters, September 22, 1862, Haskell Papers, SHSW; John Gibbon–My darling Mama, September 15, 1862, Gibbon Papers, HSP.

41. Wert, *General James Longstreet*, p. 186; Priest, *Before Antietam*, pp. 324–26; James S. Brisbin–My Dear Wife, September 16, 1862, Brisbin Letters, USAMHI; Harsh, *Taken at the Flood*, pp. 291, 299.

42. OR, 19, pt. 1, pp. 45–46, Harsh, *Taken at the Flood*, p. 240.

43. OR, 19, pt. 1, p. 45; Harsh, *Taken at the Flood*, pp. 279, 280; A. K. Nichols–My Dear Wife, September 16, 1862, Nichols Papers, NC.

44. Harsh, *Taken at the Flood*, pp. 275–84; Snell, *From First to Last*, pp. 175, 181, 182, 185.

45. Harsh, *Taken at the Flood*, p. 309; Thomas and Sauers, eds., *Civil War Letters*, p. 93; Hartwig, "It Looked Like a Task," *N&S*, 5, 7, p. 48.

46. Harsh, *Taken at the Flood*, pp. 309–10; George H. Nye–Charlie, September 16, 1862, Nye Papers, Picerno Collection.

47. Harsh, *Taken at the Flood*, p. 311; Thomas and Sauers, eds., *Civil War Letters*, p. 93; George H. Nye–Charlie, September 16, 1862, Nye Papers, Picerno Collec-

tion; Hitchcock, *War*, p. 40; Sparks, ed., *Inside Lincoln's Army*, p. 146; Carman, "Maryland Campaign," Chapter 9, pp. 31, 33, Carman Papers, LC.

48. Wert, *Brotherhood*, pp. 173, 175–76; Snell, *From First to Last*, pp. 187, 189; Harsh, *Taken at the Flood*, pp. 311–14.

49. Sears, ed., *Civil War Papers*, p. 449.

50. Wert, *General James Longstreet*, pp. 186–88; Harsh, *Taken at the Flood*, pp. 324, 367; Wert, *Brotherhood*, p. 175; Carman, "Maryland Campaign," Chapter 23, pp. 23, 27, Carman Papers, LC.

51. Wert, *General James Longstreet*, p. 187; Snell, ed., *Civil War Regiments*, 6, 2, p. 144.

52. Harsh, *Taken at the Flood*, pp. 318–19, 320–21, 334, 356–60.

53. Ibid., pp. 344–46; Alexander, "Antietam," *N&S*, 5, 7, p. 78.

54. Harsh, *Taken at the Flood*, pp. 345–49; OR, 19, pt. 1, p. 54; Maycock Diary, p. 13, USAMHI; McClellan, *George B. McClellan*, pp. 297–98; *B&L*, v. 2, p. 631; Alexander, "Antietam," *N&S*, 5, 7, p. 78.

55. Harsh, *Taken at the Flood*, pp. 350–54.

56. Hitchcock, *War*, p. 55; Saunders Diary, MESA; Child, *History*, p. 119; New York *Times*, September 23, 1862; Diary, Vautier Papers; Maycock Diary, p. 13, USAMHI; Rood, Memoir, p. 20, SHSW.

57. Wert, *Brotherhood*, p. 177.

58. Sawyer et al., eds., *Letters*, pp. 45–46.

59. Frank A. Haskell–Brother, September 19, 1862, to Brothers and Sisters, September 22, 1862, Haskell Letters, SHSW; Raab, ed., *With the 3rd Wisconsin*, p. 89.

60. Wert, *Brotherhood*, p. 177; Sears, *Landscape*, pp. 180, 181, 196; Snell, ed., *Civil War Regiments*, 6, 2, p. 145.

61. Stevens, *Three Years*, p. 179; Harsh, *Taken at the Flood*, pp. 372, 373; Nolan and Vipond, eds. *Giants*, p. 85.

62. OR, 19, pt. 1, p. 218; Chiles, "Artillery Hell!," *B&G*, 16, 2, p. 15; Sears, *Landscape*, p. 188; Whitehouse, ed., *Letters*, p. 58; Harsh, *Taken at the Flood*, p. 372; Hugh C. Perkins–Friend, September 21, 1862, Perkins Letters, USAMHI.

63. Small, ed., *Road*, p. 185; OR, 19, pt. 1, p. 218; Horace Emerson–Mother and Sister, September 28, 1862, Emerson Letters, UM; Robbie–My dear, dear, wife, [December 1862], Robbie Letter, ANB; Hall, *History*, p. 92; Taggart Diary, USAMHI.

64. Wert, *Brotherhood*, pp. 182–83; OR, 19, pt. 1, pp. 149, 923; Harsh, *Taken at the Flood*, pp. 373–74; Holsworth, "Uncommon Valor," *B&G*, 13, 6, pp. 16, 18, 20; *Sketches of War History*, v. 3, p. 258; Edward S. Bragg–E. A. Carman, December 26, 1894, Bragg Letter, ANB; Julius A. Murray–Daughters, September 27, 1862, Murray Family Papers, SHSW; Quaife, ed., *From the Cannon's Mouth*, pp. 3, 6–8, 123, 125, 126, 133; Duncan, ed., *Blue-Eyed Child*, p. 238; Gallagher, ed., *Antietam Campaign*, pp. 156, 164; Hess, *Union Soldier*, p. 86.

65. George H. Nye–My Own Darling Charlie, November 13, 1862, Nye Papers, Picerno Collection.

66. Jordan, ed., *Civil War Journals*, pp. 194, 195; George H. Nye–Darling Charlie, October 1, 1862, Nye Papers, Picerno Collection; Catton, *Mr. Lincoln's Army*, p. 279; Sears, *Landscape*, p. 206; Glover, *Bucktailed Wildcats*, p. 195; Quaife, ed., *From the Cannon's Mouth*, p. 255; Boston *Journal*, September 25, 1862; Free-

man, *Lee's Lieutenants*, v. 2, p. 209; Harsh, *Taken at the Flood*, pp. 373, 376; Brady, ed., *Hurrah*, p. 161.

67. George H. Nye–Darling Charlie, October 1, 1862, Nye Papers, Picerno Collection.

68. Stinson, "Operations," pp. 2, 8, 9, ANB; Murfin, *Gleam*, p. 227; Woodworth, *Leadership*, p. 76; Harsh, *Taken at the Flood*, p. 377.

69. Stinson, "Operations," pp. 8, 9, 24, 29, 31, 32, 44, 45, ANB; Quaife, ed., *From the Cannon's Mouth*, p. 135; Hebert, *Fighting Joe Hooker*, p. 142; Harsh, *Taken at the Flood*, p. 377.

70. *OR*, 19, pt. 1, pp. 275, 305; Woodworth, *Leadership*, pp. 77, 120, 121, 123; Stinson, "Operations," pp. 44, 45, ANB; Murfin, *Gleam*, p. 227

71. Lash, "*Duty Well Done*," p. 262; Scott, ed., *Fallen Leaves*, pp. 80, 106n; Small, ed., *Road*, p. 31; Coffin, *Battered Stars*, p. 12; Byrne and Weaver, eds., *Haskell*, p. 132; Agassiz, ed., *Meade's Headquarters*, pp. 37, 108; Schaff, *Battle*, p. 43; McClellan, *McClellan's Own Story*, p. 140; Sedgwick, ed., *Correspondence*, v. 2, p. 31.

72. Walker, *History*, pp. 101, 105; Stinson, "Operations," pp. 3, 11, ANB; Philadelphia *Times*, April 8, 1882; Edward A. Walker–Friend Knight, October 5, 1862, Walker Papers, NC; Murfin, *Gleam*, pp. 227, 229; Sears, *Landscape*, p. 218; *OR*, 10, pt. 1, pp. 276, 305, 311, 317, 865, 874, 878, 883, 915, 956; Snell, ed., *Civil War Regiments*, 6, 2, pp. 37, 39; Philadelphia *Inquirer*, October 1, 1862; Coco, ed., *From Ball's Bluff to Gettysburg*, p. 124; Gallagher, ed., *Antietam Campaign*, pp. 208–10.

73. *OR*, 19, pt. 1, pp. 276, 306–7, 311–13; Rosentreter, "Samuel Hodgman's Civil War," *Michigan History*, v. 64, p. 36; Coco, ed., *From Ball's Bluff to Gettysburg*, pp. 124, 127; Philadelphia *Times*, April 8, 1882; Higginson, *Harvard Memorial Biographies*, v. 1, p. 199; Winslow, *General John Sedgwick*, p. 47; Walker, *History*, pp. 106, 107; Burns Diary, p. 37, USAMHI; Milano, "Letters, Part 3," *Civil War*, v. 13, p. 51; Woodworth, *Leadership*, pp. 95, 97; Bruce, *Twentieth Regiment*, p. 169.

74. Sears, *Landscape*, p. 225; *OR*, 19, pt. 1, pp. 192, 193, 308; Stinson, "Operations," p. 39, ANB; Boston *Journal*, September 25, 1862.

75. Harsh, *Taken at the Flood*, p. 395; Sears, *Landscape*, pp. 236–37.

76. Harsh, *Taken at the Flood*, p. 395; Warner, *Generals in Blue*, pp. 161–62; Hitchcock, *War*, p. 39; Page, *History*, p. 70; Plumb, "Record," p. 6, USAMHI; Seth Gilbert Evans–[?], March 31, 1864, Evans Papers, NC; Welcher, *Union Army*, p. 315; Gallagher, ed., *Antietam Campaign*, p. 164.

77. *OR*, 19, pt. 1, pp. 323–24; Sears, *Landscape*, pp. 237–40; Galwey, *Valiant Hours*, p. 40.

78. Galwey, *Valiant Hours*, pp. 40, 42; Hays, "His Account," pp. 11–13, USAMHI; Hitchcock, *War*, p. 77; Sears, ed., *Mr. Dunn Browne's Experiences*, pp. 8, 9; Cassedy, ed., *Dear Friends*, p. 151; Baxter, *Gallant Fourteenth*, pp. 99, 100; John S. Weiser–Mother, October 13, 1862, Weiser Letters, USAMHI; *OR*, 19, pt. 1, p. 324; Hitchcock, *War*, pp. 20, 60, 61, 63.

79. O'Brien, "Follow That Green Flag!," *N&S*, 2, 5, pp. 62–63; Cavanaugh, *Memoirs*, pp. 461, 462; Sears, *Landscape*, pp. 243–44.

80. O'Brien, "Follow That Green Flag!," *N&S*, 2, 5, pp. 63–64; Plumb, "Record," p. 14, USAMHI; Fuller, *Personal Recollections*, p. 58; Pride and Travis, *My Brave*

Boys, p. 133; Kohl and Richard, eds., *Irish Green*, p. 81; Sears, *Landscape*, p. 243; Hale, "Story," p. III, USAMHI; Livermore, *Days and Events*, p. 133; a different version of Cross's speech is in Child, *History*, p. 121.

81. Sears, *Landscape*, pp. 244–47; Fuller, *Personal Recollections*, pp. 58, 59; Hemmingen Diary; Oliver H. Palmer–My Dear Wife, September 19, 1862, Palmer Letter, USAMHI; Pride and Travis, *My Brave Boys*, pp. 133–35; Quaife, ed., *From the Cannon's Mouth*, p. 130; Wert, *General James Longstreet*, p. 193.

82. Wert, *General James Longstreet*, pp. 193–94; Pride and Travis, *My Brave Boys*, pp. 137–39; Fuller, *Personal Recollections*, p. 60; Plumb, "Record," p. 7, USAMHI; Sears, *Landscape*, pp. 248, 251–53.

83. Sears, *Landscape*, pp. 254–55; Pride and Travis, *My Brave Boys*, p. 139; Sears, ed., *Mr. Dunn Browne's Experiences*, p. 9; Snell, ed., *Civil War Regiments*, 6, 2, p. 156; Seth Gilbert Evans–My Dear Mother, November 13, 1862, Evans Papers, NC.

84. Harsh, *Taken at the Flood*, pp. 413–14; calculations of Union numbers based on original strengths, reduced by a 50 percent casualty and absentee rate.

85. Ibid., pp. 413–14; Snell, *From First to Last*, pp. 194, 195.

86. OR, 19, pt. 1, p. 279; Tucker, *Hancock*, p. 93; Walker, *General Hancock*, p. 48; Trask, *Fire Within*, p. 128; Westbrook, *History*, pp. 124, 125.

87. OR, 19, pt. 1, p. 420; Harsh, *Taken at the Flood*, p. 413.

88. OR, 19, pt. 1, pp. 418–19; Harsh, *Taken at the Flood*, pp. 400–401; Marvel, *Burnside*, pp. 129, 131.

89. OR, 19, pt. 1, pp. 419, 425; George Bronson–[Mary Bronson], September 19, 1862, Pavlik Collection; Marvel, *Race*, p. 55; Gambone, *Major-General John Frederick Hartranft*, pp. 63, 64; Parker, *History*, pp. 231, 235.

90. OR, 19, pt. 1, p. 427; Harsh, *Taken at the Flood*, pp. 400–401.

91. OR, 19, pt. 1, p. 427; Sears, *Landscape*, pp. 277–86; Harsh, *Taken at the Flood*, pp. 415, 418.

92. OR, 19, pt. 1, pp. 427–29; Harsh, *Taken at the Flood*, pp. 421–23; Niven, *Connecticut*, p. 222; Gallagher, ed., *Antietam Campaign*, pp. 173, 176, 177; Hines, *Civil War*, p. 183; Jacob C. Bauer–My Sweet Wife, September 20, 1862, 16th Connecticut File, ANB.

93. Priest, *Antietam*, pp. 331, 343; Sears, *Landscape*, pp. 295–96; Harsh, *Taken at the Flood*, p. 423; OR, 19, pt. 1, pp. 200, 813; Trask, *Fire Within*, p. 130; Henry H. Young–Mother, September 27, 1862, Young Letters; John O. Moore–Home, September 18, 1862, Moore Letters, USAMHI; Thomas and Sauers, ed., *Civil War Letters*, p. 97; Charles A. Wheeler–My dear C, September 20, 1862, Wheeler Papers; Thomas Paxton–Cousin Ellie, September 27, 1862, Paxton Papers, NC; Moe, *Last Full Measure*, p. 190.

94. Duncan, ed., *Blue-Eyed Child*, p. 241; Harsh, *Taken at the Flood*, pp. 437–38.

95. Harsh, *Taken at the Flood*, pp. 430–33; OR, 19, pt. 1, p. 151; Wert, *General James Longstreet*, pp. 196–97.

96. OR, 19, pt. 1, pp. 65, 330; Harsh, *Taken at the Flood*, pp. 452–56; Alexander Webb–My Dear Father, September 24, 1862, Webb Papers, YU; McGrath, "Corn Exchange Regiment's Baptism," *B&G*, 16, 1, p. 23.

97. OR, 19, pt. 1, p. 330; Harsh, *Taken at the Flood*, pp. 452–56.

98. Smith, *History of the 118th Pennsylvania*, pp. 3, 25, 57–71, 94; Sauers, *Advance the Colors!*, v. 2, p. 386; McGrath, "Corn Exchange Regiment's Baptism," *B&G*,

16, 1, pp. 23–26; Acken, ed., *Inside*, pp. 116, 129–41; Snell, ed., *Civil War Regiments*, 6, 2, pp. 120, 134, 135.

99. Sears, ed., *Civil War Papers*, pp. 469, 473.

100. Weigley, *Great Civil War*, p. 153; Michie, *General McClellan*, p. 429, Sears, *George B. McClellan*, pp. 310, 323.

101. McPherson, *Crossroads*, pp. 116, 117, 119, 125; Harsh, *Taken at the Flood*, pp. 372–73, 376, 382–83; Quaife, ed., *From the Cannon's Mouth*, p. 135.

102. Sears, *Landscape*, pp. 303, 314; Smart, ed., *Radical View*, v. 1, pp. 232, 233; Nevins, ed., *Diary*, pp. 103–4; Cozzens, ed., *B&L*, v. 5, pp. 197–98; McPherson, *Crossroads*, pp. 129–31; Michie, *General McClellan*, p. 429.

103. McPherson, *Crossroads*, pp. 154–55.

104. OR, 19, pt. 2, p. 330; Donald, *Lincoln*, pp. 374–76.

105. Sparks, ed., *Inside Lincoln's Army*, p. 151; John Gibbon–My darling Mama, September 21, 1862, Gibbon Papers, HSP; Best, *History*, p. 24; Thomas Paxton–Cousin Ellie, September 17, 1862, Paxton Papers, NC.

Chapter 9: The Army's "Saddest Hour"

1. Marvel, *Burnside*, p. 159; Hezekiah Long–Wife, November 9, 1862, Long Civil War Letters, MESA; O'Reilly, *Fredericksburg Campaign*, pp. 1, 2; OR, 19, pt. 2, p. 545.

2. O'Reilly, *Fredericksburg Campaign*, p. 2; Marvel, *Burnside*, pp. 159, 160; Stine, *History*, pp. 241–42; Scott, ed., *Forgotten Valor*, pp. 282–83.

3. Marvel, *Burnside*, p. 160; O'Reilly, *Fredericksburg Campaign*, p. 2; Carter, *Four Brothers*, p. 174.

4. Jordan, ed., *Civil War Journals*, p. 205; Quaife, ed., *From the Cannon's Mouth*, p. 135; Glover, *Bucktailed Wildcats*, p. 162; Tyler, *Recollections*, p. 39; George G. Meade Report, September 23, 1862, RG 393, NA; Nevins, ed., *Diary*, p. 108; OR, 19, pt. 2, pp. 336, 454, 674.

5. B&L, v. 3, p. 102; William T. H. Brooks–Father, October 2, 1862, Brooks Papers, USAMHI; Nevins, ed., *Diary*, pp. 114, 115, 117; Henry C. Marsh–Father, October 10, 11, 1862, Marsh Letters, ISL; OR, 19, pt. 1, pp. 12, 13; Sears, ed., *Civil War Papers*, p. 488.

6. Sears, *George B. McClellan*, p. 330; E. J.–Friend Ellen, October 4, 1862, "Battle of Antietam" File, PSU; Anson B. Shuey–My Dear Wife, October 5, 1862, Shuey War Letters, USAMHI; Hard, *History*, p. 196; Marshall, *Company "K,"* p. 67; Davis, *Lincoln's Men*, p. 81; Holford Diary, LC; Clark S. Edwards–My Dear Wife, October 5, 1862, Edwards Papers, NC; Thurner, ed., "Young Soldier," PMHB, v. 87, p. 143; Nevins, ed., *Diary*, pp. 109–10; John F. Reynolds–My dear Sisters, October 5, 1862, Reynolds Family Papers, FM; Jackson Diary, IHS; Vanderslice, ed., *Civil War Letters*, p. 114; Stephen O. McCurdy–Hon. Revs. Friend, October 6, 1862, McCurdy Letter, ANB.

7. Davis, *Lincoln's Men*, pp. 83, 94; Vanderslice, ed., *Civil War Letters*, pp. 114, 116; Greiner et al., eds., *Surgeon's Civil War*, p. 47; Dunn, *Harvestfields*, p. 122; Duncan, ed., *Blue-Eyed Child*, p. 245; Walker and Walker, eds., *Diary*, p. 58n.

8. Sears, *Controversies*, pp. 133–36.

9. Sears, ed., *Civil War Papers*, p. 488; Meade, *Life and Letters*, v. 1, p. 317; Davis, *Lincoln's Men*, p. 81; Snell, *From First to Last*, p. 199; William T. H.

Brooks–Father, October 2, 1862, Brooks Papers, USAMHI; Gallagher, ed., *Wilderness Campaign*, p. 71; Brady, ed., *Hurrah*, p. 169; Nevins, ed., *Diary*, p. 109; John Gibbon–My darling Mama, November 21, 1862, Gibbon Papers, HSP.

10. John Gibbon–My darling Mama, November 21, 1862, Gibbon Papers, HSP; *OR*, 19, pt. 2, p. 395.

11. Sears, ed., *Civil War Papers*, pp. 490, 500n; *OR*, 19, pt. 1, pp. 11–12, 16; pt. 2, pp. 387, 390; Sears, *George B. McClellan*, p. 330; Donald, *Lincoln*, p. 387; Gallagher, ed., *Antietam Campaign*, pp. 56, 58.

12. *OR*, 19, pt. 1, p. 81; pt. 2, pp. 387, 484, 485.

13. Tap, *Over Lincoln's Shoulder*, p. 139; Rable, *Fredericksburg!*, pp. 29, 30, 33, 35; McPherson, *Crossroads*, pp. 149–50.

14. Hebert, *Fighting Joe Hooker*, p. 57; William L. Candler–My dear Brother, November 6, 1862, Candler Papers, VATU; *SOR*, 3, p. 447; Sears, *Controversies*, pp. 137–38; Donald, ed., *Inside Lincoln's Cabinet*, pp. 154, 158, 159; Snell, *From First to Last*, pp. 199, 200; Meade, *Life and Letters*, v. 1, pp. 318, 319; *OR*, 19, pt. 1, p. 182.

15. McPherson, *Crossroads*, p. 150; *OR*, 19, pt. 2, p. 417; Starr, *Union Cavalry*, v. 1, pp. 313, 315; Crowninshield, *History*, p. 89; Meade, *Life and Letters*, v. 1, p. 320.

16. Brennan, "Little Mac's Last Stand," *B&G*, 17, 2, pp. 8–14; Hiram S. Wilson–My own Sweet Darling, November 6, 1862, Wilson Papers, NYSL; Lassen, ed., *Dear Sarah*, p. 38; Hennessy, ed., *Fighting*, p. 142; William Henry Walling–My dear Sisters, November 6, 1862, Walling Letters, USAMHI; Walker, *History*, p. 134; Robert A. Browne–Wife, November 3, 1862, Browne Letters, PSU; Hitchcock, *War*, p. 103; Grimsley, *Hard Hand*, pp. 105–7; Gavin, ed., *Infantryman Pettit*, p. 35.

17. Brennan, "Little Mac's Last Stand," *B&G*, 17, 2, p. 54; Rable, *Fredericksburg!*, pp. 30, 32, 37; McPherson, *Crossroads*, pp. 153–54; Tap, *Over Lincoln's Shoulder*, p. 139.

18. Tap, *Over Lincoln's Shoulder*, p. 135; Sears, *George B. McClellan*, pp. 338, 339; McPherson, *Crossroads*, p. 152; Donald, *Lincoln*, pp. 388–89; Davis, *Lincoln's Men*, p. 83; Paludan, *Presidency*, p. 159.

19. Rable, *Fredericksburg!*, p. 42.

20. Acken, ed., *Inside*, p. 162; Parker, *Henry Wilson's Regiment*, p. 269; Mitchell, *Vacant Chair*, p. 43; Rhodes, ed., *All for the Union* , p. 88; C. C. Starbuck–Cousin, November 13, 1862, Starbuck Civil War Letters, IHS; Townsend, "History," p. 57, UME; Nevins, ed., *Diary*, p. 124; Elliott Diary, USAMHI; Duncan, ed., *Blue-Eyed Child*, p. 259; Mannis and Wilson, eds., *Bound to Be a Soldier*, p. 42; Brown, *Cushing*, p. 139; Davis, *Lincoln's Men*, p. 85; Hiram S. Wilson–My own Sweet Darling, November 6, 1862, Wilson Papers, NYSL; Carter, *Four Brothers*, p. 159.

21. Wright, *No More Gallant A Deed*, p. 225; Crumb and Dhalle, eds., *No Middle Ground*, p. 88; George H. Nye–Darling Charlie, November 10, 1862, Nye Papers, Picerno Collection; Gavin, ed., *Infantryman Pettit*, p. 36; Samito, ed., *Commanding Boston's Irish Ninth*, p. 151; Ford, ed., *Cycle*, v. 1, p. 194; Otis, *Second Wisconsin*, p. 65n; Dawes, *Service*, p. 107; Spear, *Civil War Recollections*, pp. 16–17; Fuller, *Personal Recollections*, p. 75; Davis, *Lincoln's Men*, p. 84; Rable, *Fredericksburg!*, p. 45.

22. Meade, *Life and Letters*, v. 1, p. 325; John Gibbon–My darling Mama, November

9, 1862, Gibbon Papers, HSP; David B. Birney–Gross, October 26, 1862, March 23, 1864, Birney Papers; Henry J. Hunt–My dear Eunice, July 28, 1863, Ford Papers, USAMHI; Scott, ed., *Forgotten Valor*, p. 394; Snell, *From First to Last*, p. 203; Tucker, *Hancock*, pp. 96, 97; Nichols, *Toward Gettysburg*, p. 146.

23. Sears, ed., *Civil War Papers*, p. 520.

24. Ibid., pp. 520–21, 521n; *OR*, 19, pt. 2, p. 551; the version in the text is that of the broadside read by the army. McClellan later crossed out "Farewell!," and added, "We shall also ever be comrades in supporting the Constitution of our country & the nationality of our people."

25. Sears, *George B. McClellan*, p. 341; Carter, *Four Brothers*, p. 161; Sparks, ed., *Inside Lincoln's Army*, p. 173; John C. Babcock–Aunt, December 7, 1862, Babcock Papers, LC; Rable, *Fredericksburg!*, pp. 44, 47–48.

26. Thomas and Sauers, ed., *Civil War Letters*, p. 115; Duram and Duram, eds., *Soldier*, p. 25; Osborne, *Civil War Diaries*, p. 49; Vanderslice, ed., *Civil War Letters*, pp. 143, 144; Cassedy, ed., *Dear Friends*, pp. 186, 187; Clark S. Edwards–My Dear Wife, November 10, 1862, Edwards Papers, NC; Walker and Walker, eds., *Diary*, pp. 67, 68n; Smith, *History*, p. 19; *B&L*, v. 3, pp. 106–7; Sears, ed., *Civil War Papers*, p. 522; Scott, ed., *Fallen Leaves*, p. 142; Nevins, ed., *Diary*, p. 125; Furst Diary; Heffelfinger Diary, p. 91; Berry Diary; Liston Gray–My Dear Sister, November 14, 1862, Gray Letter; Diary, Halsey Papers, USAMHI; Carter, *Four Brothers*, p. 176; Child, *History*, p. 145; Rable, *Fredericksburg!*, p. 48.

27. Sears, *George B. McClellan*, p. 343.

28. Ibid., pp. xi, xii; Sears, "Little Mac," *N&S*, 2, 3, p. 69; McClure, *Abraham Lincoln*, p. 196; Meade, *Life and Letters*, v. 1, p. 345; Swinton, *Campaigns*, p. 228; Jones, *Civil War Command*, p. 126.

29. Chamberlain, *Passing of the Armies*, p. 27.

30. Sears, ed., *Civil War Papers*, p. 520; *B&L*, v. 3, p. 106.

31. Oliver S. Halsted, Jr.–John G. Nicolay, November 7, 1862, Lincoln Papers; Daniel R. Larned–Henry, October 16, 1862, Larned Correspondence, LC; William L. Candler–My dear Brother, November 6, December 21, 1862, Candler Papers, VATU; Walker, *History*, p. 137; Schiller, ed., *Autobiography*, p. 59; Meade, *Life and Letters*, v. 1, p. 304; de Trobriand, *Four Years*, p. 351; Snell, *From First to Last*, p. 202; Quaife, ed., *From the Cannon's Mouth*, p. 151.

32. Charles E. Perkins–Brother, November [?] 1862, Perkins Civil War Letters; Keiser Diary, p. 44, USAMHI; Silliker, ed., *Rebel Yell*, p. 50; Favill, *Diary*, p. 199; Mannis and Wilson, eds., *Bound to Be a Soldier*, p. 42; Livermore, *Days and Events*, p. 159; Duncan, ed., *Blue-Eyed Child*, p. 255; Robertson, ed., *Civil War Letters*, p. 219.

33. Thomas Carpenter–Phil, November 9, 1862, Carpenter Letters, MOHS; Sears, ed., *Mr. Dunn Browne's Experiences*, pp. 32–33; Coco, ed., *From Ball's Bluff to Gettysburg*, p. 141; Eby, ed., *Virginia Yankee*, p. 120.

34. Sears, ed., *For Country*, p. 288; Timothy O. Webster–My dear Wife and Children, December 2, 1862, Webster Papers, NC; Howe, ed., *Touched with Fire*, p. 73; Rable, *Fredericksburg!*, p. 61; Wallace, *Soul*, p. 49; Miles Peabody–Parents, December 1, 1862, Peabody Letters, USAMHI.

35. *OR*, 19, pt. 2, pp. 546, 552–54.

36. Rable, *Fredericksburg!*, p. 58; O'Reilly, *Fredericksburg Campaign*, p. 7; Wert, *General James Longstreet*, p. 210.

37. Marvel, *Burnside*, pp. 163, 164; Meade, *Life and Letters*, v. 1, pp. 326, 327; Rable, *Fredericksburg!*, pp. 58–59; O'Reilly, *Fredericksburg Campaign*, p. 21.

38. *OR*, 19, pt. 2, pp. 583–84; O'Reilly, *Fredericksburg Campaign*, p. 24.

39. *OR*, 19, pt. 2, p. 545; Powell, *Fifth Army Corps*, p. 322; Cowles, ed., *History*, p. 486; John W. Ames–My dear Mother, November 16, 1862, Ames Papers, USAMHI.

40. A transcript of the proceedings against Porter is in *OR*, 12, pt. 2, Supplement, *passim*; Warner, *Generals in Blue*, pp. 379–80.

41. *OR*, 19, pt. 2, p. 579; O'Reilly, *Fredericksburg Campaign*, p. 25.

42. Dwight Peck–Sister, November 30, 1862, Peck Letter; Benjamin F. Appleby–My Dear Wife, December 10, 1862, Appleby Correspondence, USAMHI; Lucius Shattuck–Gile and Mary, November 16, 1862, Shattuck Letters, UM; Acken, ed., *Inside*, p. 167; Duram and Duram, eds., *Soldier*, p. 29; Nevins, ed., *Diary*, p. 131; Wert, *Brotherhood*, pp. 203–4.

43. Marvel, *Burnside*, p. 166; Ira Spaulding–My Dear Dunkle, December 16, 1862, Spaulding Papers, NYSL; O'Reilly, *Fredericksburg Campaign*, pp. 27, 37; Thomas Carpenter–Mary, November 26, 1862, Carpenter Letters, MOHS.

44. Marvel, *Burnside*, p. 166; Catton, *Glory Road*, p. 30; Snell, *From First to Last*, p. 208; O'Reilly, *Fredericksburg Campaign*, pp. 49–50.

45. Marvel, *Burnside*, pp. 168–70; Rable, *Fredericksburg!*, pp. 116–17; O'Reilly, *Fredericksburg Campaign*, pp. 50–51; Sparks, ed., *Inside Lincoln's Army*, pp. 182, 183.

46. Smith, *History*, p. 26; Turino, ed., *Civil War Diary*, p. 14; Edmund Hawley–Brother, July 14, 1862, Hawley Letter; Frederick Ranger–My Darling Wife, November 21, 1862, Ranger Letters, USAMHI; Timothy O. Webster–My Dear Wife and Children, November 9, 1862, Webster Papers, NC: Rable, *Fredericksburg!*, p. 64; Barber and Swinson, eds., *Civil War Letters*, p. 151.

47. Wright, *No More Gallant a Deed*, p. 115; Patch, ed., *This from George*, p. 45; Cheek and Pointon, *History*, pp. 24, 25; Pride and Travis, *My Brave Boys*, p. 163; Caleb H. Beal–Uncle Elijah, August 27, 1861, Beal Papers, MAHS; Southwick, *Duryee Zouave*, p. 56; Smith, *History*, p. 25; Walker, *History*, pp. 143–44; Favill, *Diary*, p. 206.

48. Carter, *Four Brothers*, p. 169; Bennett, *Sons of Old Monroe*, pp. 111, 112; William C. Wiley–Brother, December 4, 1862, Wiley Papers, PSU; Favill, *Diary*, p. 207; Seth Gilbert Evans–My Dear Mother & Sisters, November 25, 1862, Evans Papers, NC.

49. O'Reilly, *Fredericksburg Campaign*, pp. 42, 50–52.

50. Ibid., p. 53; *B&L*, v. 3, p. 107; Rable, *Fredericksburg!*, p. 150; Snell, *From First to Last*, p. 208.

51. *B&L*, v. 3, pp. 107–8.

52. Ibid., pp. 108, 126; Rable, *Fredericksburg!*, p. 150; O'Reilly, *Fredericksburg Campaign*, p. 53.

53. O'Reilly, *Fredericksburg Campaign*, pp. 54, 59, 61; Brainerd, *Bridge Building*, p. 107; Ira Spaulding–My Dear Dunkle, December 16, 1862, Spaulding Papers, NYSL; Katcher, ed., *Building the Victory*, p. 12.

54. O'Reilly, *Fredericksburg Campaign*, pp. 61–77; Ira Spaulding–My Dear Dunkle, December 16, 1862, Spaulding Papers, NYSL; Crary, ed., *Dear Belle*, p. 173; Favill, *Diary*, pp. 208, 209.

55. O'Reilly, *Fredericksburg Campaign*, pp. 77–78; John S. Weiser–Parents, January 1, 1863, Weiser Letters, USAMHI; Seth Gilbert Evans–Mother, December 12, 1862, Evans Papers, NC.

56. O'Reilly, *Fredericksburg Campaign*, pp. 78–80; Rable, *Fredericksburg!*, p. 168; Walker, *History*, p. 149; Smith, *History*, pp. 27, 28; Patch, ed., *This from George*, p. 59.

57. The most detailed description of the action in the town is in O'Reilly, *Fredericksburg Campaign*, Chapter 4.

58. O'Reilly, *Fredericksburg Campaign*, p. 100; Thomas Carpenter–Phil, December 11, 1862, Carpenter Letters, MOHS; Norman Williams–Parents, December 12, 1862, Williams Family Letters, USAMHI.

59. OR, 21, pp. 89, 90; O'Reilly, *Fredericksburg Campaign*, pp. 107–13; Rable, *Fredericksburg!*, p. 175; Herberger, ed., *Yankee at Arms*, p. 85.

60. O'Reilly, *Fredericksburg Campaign*, pp. 118–21; Aaron H. Blake–Sister, December 19, 1862, Blake Letters, USAMHI; Baxter, *Gallant Fourteenth*, pp. 114, 115; Gallagher, ed., *Fredericksburg Campaign*, p. 155; Sears, ed., *For Country*, p. 297; Galwey, *Valiant Hours*, pp. 58, 59; William C. Brown–Mother, December 17, 1862, Brown Letter, UME.

61. Coco, ed., *From Ball's Bluff to Gettysburg*, p. 142; Oliver H. Palmer–My dear wife, December 16, 1862, Palmer Papers, NC; O'Reilly, *Fredericksburg Campaign*, pp. 118–24.

62. OR, 21, pp. 66, 89–90.

63. Ibid., p. 90; Wert, *General James Longstreet*, p. 213; O'Reilly, *Fredericksburg Campaign*, p. 121.

64. Wert, *General James Longstreet*, p. 213; O'Reilly, *Fredericksburg Campaign*, p. 116; Darius Couch claimed that Burnside denied the existence of the millrace, but that seems dubious as troops attacked the paper mill and shut off the water, Walker, *History*, pp. 155, 156.

65. Wert, *General James Longstreet*, pp. 213–14.

66. OR, 21, pp. 71, 89, 90; Marvel, *Burnside*, p. 180; *B&L*, v. 3, pp. 132–33; Rable, *Fredericksburg!*, p. 184; O'Reilly, *Fredericksburg Campaign*, pp. 117–18.

67. Gibbon, *Personal Recollections*, p. 252.

68. Hess, *Union Soldier*, pp. 95, 96.

69. Reminiscence, p. 12, Rollins Papers, SHSW; Small, ed., *Road*, p. 186.

70. OR, 21, p. 71; Marvel, *Burnside*, pp. 182–83; O'Reilly, *Fredericksburg Campaign*, pp. 135–36; Rable, *Fredericksburg!*, p. 191; *B&L*, v. 3, pp. 133, 134.

71. OR, 21, pp. 71, 90, 94; Marvel, *Burnside*, pp. 182–85, 192; O'Reilly, *Fredericksburg Campaign*, pp. 136–38; Rable, *Fredericksburg!*, pp. 191, 193; Meade, *Life and Letters*, v. 1, pp. 361–62; Nevins, ed., *Diary*, pp. 147, 148; SOR, 3, p. 688.

72. OR, 21, pp. 91, 94.

73. Nevins, ed., *Diary*, p. 143; Snell, *From First to Last*, pp. 225, 277; Meade, *Life and Letters*, v. 1, p. 338; O'Reilly, *Fredericksburg Campaign*, p. 138.

74. Marvel, *Burnside*, p. 183; OR, 21, pp. 453, 454, 510, 511; O'Reilly, *Fredericksburg Campaign*, pp. 113, 139–44, 147–65; Heffelfinger Diary, p. 97; Taggart Diary, USAMHI; Meade, *Life and Letters*, v. 1, p. 337.

75. O'Reilly, *Fredericksburg Campaign*, pp. 166–73; Sypher, *History*, p. 416; Meade, *Life and Letters*, v. 1, p. 337; Cleaves, *Meade*, p. 97.

76. OR, 21, pp. 480, 511–12; O'Reilly, *Fredericksburg Campaign*, pp. 179–85,

194–97, 212–21; John Gibbon–My darling Mama, November 4, 1862, Gibbon Papers, HSP; Thomas and Sauers, eds., *Civil War Letters*, p. 127; Meade, *Life and Letters*, v. 1, p. 340; Smith, *History*, p. 77.

77. Cleaves, *Meade*, p. 92; Taggart Diary, USAMHI; Gibbs, *Three Years*, p. 206; Alanson Wiles–Mother, January 1, 1863, Wiles Papers, NC; *OR*, 21, pp. 139, 140.

78. John F. Reynolds–My dear Sisters, December 17, 1862, Reynolds Family Papers, FM; *SOR*, 3, pp. 688, 690; Campbell, ed., "*Grand Terrible Dramma,*" p. 81; Cleaves, *Meade*, p. 92.

79. *B&L*, v. 3, p. 111; O'Reilly, *Fredericksburg Campaign*, pp. 88, 254.

80. *OR*, 21, pp. 90, 94; Rable, *Fredericksburg!*, p. 221; *B&L*, v. 3, p. 111; O'Reilly, *Fredericksburg Campaign*, pp. 250–51.

81. *OR*, 21, p. 290; Galwey, *Valiant Hours*, pp. 59, 60; O'Reilly, *Fredericksburg Campaign*, pp. 250–53; Wert, *General James Longstreet*, p. 216.

82. *OR*, 21, pp. 290, 297, 298; O'Reilly, *Fredericksburg Campaign*, pp. 253–55.

83. *OR*, 21, p. 287; Oliver H. Palmer–My dear Wife, December 16, 1862, Palmer Papers, NC; Walker, *History*, p. 158; Rable, *Fredericksburg!*, p. 222.

84. Oliver H. Palmer–My dear Wife, December 16, 1862, Palmer Papers, NC; *OR*, 21, p. 287; Gibbon, *Personal Recollections*, p. 106; Hagerty, *Collis' Zouaves*, p. 180; George Hopper–Brother, December 21, 1862, Hopper Papers, USAMHI; Hitchcock, *War*, pp. 117, 122; John Pellet–Father and Mother, December 21, 1862, Pellet Papers; Benjamin F. Appleby–Wife, December 18, 1862, Appleby Correspondence, USAMHI; Gallagher, ed., *Fredericksburg Campaign*, p. 53; Hess, *Union Soldier*, pp. 11, 114, 115; Sutherland, *Fredericksburg*, p. 61.

85. O'Reilly, *Fredericksburg Campaign*, p. 297; Pride and Travis, *My Brave Boys*, p. 170; Bandy and Freeland, eds., *Gettysburg Papers*, v. 2, pp. 1021, 1025; Oliver, *Ancestry*, p. 37; Byrne and Weaver, eds., *Haskell*, p. 133; Hagemann, ed., *Fighting Rebels*, pp. 191–92; Agassiz, ed., *Meade's Headquarters*, pp. 82, 134, 189.

86. Tucker, *Hancock*, p. 108; Wert, *General James Longstreet*, pp. 216–17; O'Reilly, *Fredericksburg Campaign*, pp. 293–310; Gambone, *Life*, pp. 116, 117; Favill, *Diary*, pp. 211, 212.

87. O'Brien, ed., *My Life*, pp. vi, 167, 228; Conyngham, *Irish Brigade*, pp. 324, 325, 342, 343, 466; Mulholland, *Story*, pp. 11, 12, 44; Cassedy, ed., *Dear Friends*, p. 169; Gallagher, ed., *Fredericksburg Campaign*, p. 53; Kohl and Richard, eds., *Irish Green*, pp. 40, 43, 46.

88. Conyngham, *Irish Brigade*, pp. 343, 344, 356; O'Brien, ed., *My Life*, pp. viii, 178, 229; Kohl and Richard, eds., *Irish Green*, pp. 43, 46; Galwey, *Valiant Hours*, p. 62; Corby, *Memoirs*, p. 132; Herberger, ed., *Yankee at Arms*, p. 95; Gavin A. Lambie–Friend, January 18, 1863, Lambie Papers, USAMHI; Mulholland, *Story*, pp. 49, 54, 69.

89. Child, *History*, pp. 150, 152–56; Tucker, *Hancock*, p. 110; Pride and Travis, *My Brave Boys*, p. 172; Livermore, *Days and Events*, p. 173; Fuller, *Personal Recollections*, pp. 79, 80; O'Reilly, *Fredericksburg Campaign*, pp. 317–23.

90. Rable, *Fredericksburg!*, p. 339; Bingham, Memoirs, WRHS; Sheldon, "*Twenty-seventh,*" p. 25; Cowley, ed., *With My Face to the Enemy*, p. 174; *B&L*, v. 3, p. 113; *OR*, 21, pp. 94, 95, 303; O'Reilly, *Fredericksburg Campaign*, p. 363.

91. O'Reilly, *Fredericksburg Campaign*, Chapter 11, quotations p. 339; Scott, ed., *Fallen Leaves*, pp. 148–49, 160n; Turino, ed., *Civil War Diary*, pp. xv, 17, 18; Pope Diary, pp. 33, 34, USAMHI; Patrick Walker–My Friend, January 27, 1863,

Walker Papers, NYSL; Parker, *History*, pp. 270–73; Wert, *General James Longstreet*, p. 217.

92. Rable, *Fredericksburg!*, pp. 255, 256; Gallagher, ed., *Fredericksburg Campaign*, p. 87; Styple, ed., *Writing*, pp. 145, 151; Cozzens, ed., *B&L*, v. 5, p. 204; Carter, *Four Brothers*, pp. 196, 207, 208, 213; William C. Brown–Mother, December 17, 1862, Brown Letter, UME; Acken, ed., *Inside*, p. 179–86; Pullen, *Twentieth Maine*, p. 53; Hennessy, ed., *Fighting*, p. 121.

93. Gallagher, ed., *Fredericksburg Campaign*, pp. 53, 55, 91, 93; Powell, *Fifth Army Corps*, p. 386; Conyngham, *Irish Brigade*, p. 343.

94. O'Reilly, *Fredericksburg Campaign*, pp. 254, 305, 329, 366, 395, 416; *OR*, 21, pp. 90, 129–42, 1121; Fox, *Regimental Losses*, pp. 36, 37, 434; Winkler, *Letters*, p. 23.

95. Gibbon, *Personal Recollections*, p. 105; Rable, *Fredericksburg!*, p. 269; Snell, *From First to Last*, p. 224; Daniel R. Larned–My dear Henry, December 15, 1862, Larned Correspondence, LC; O'Reilly, *Fredericksburg Campaign*, pp. 251–52.

96. Rable, *Fredericksburg!*, pp. 270, 272, 281; Marvel, *Burnside*, p. 198; *B&L*, v. 3, pp. 117–18, 127; Daniel R. Larned–My dear Henry, December 16, 1862, Larned Correspondence, LC.

97. Cozzens, ed., *B&L*, v. 5, pp. 205, 206; Haggerty Diary, p. 4, UCGS; Daniel R. Larned–My dear Henry, December 16, 1862, Larned Correspondence, LC; Gallagher, ed., *Fredericksburg Campaign*, p. 54; Charles R. Johnson–Nellie, December 15, 1862, Johnson Letters, USAMHI; Cassedy, ed., *Dear Friends*, p. 205; Rable, *Fredericksburg!*, p. 276; de Trobriand, *Four Years*, p. 378.

98. O'Reilly, *Fredericksburg Campaign*, p. 441.

99. Sears, ed., *Mr. Dunn Browne's Experiences*, p. 50; Hemmenau, "Reminiscence," p. 2, USAMHI; Rable, *Fredericksburg!*, pp. 282–83; Oliver H. Palmer–My dear Wife, December 16, 1862, Palmer Papers, NC; Rhodes, ed., *All for the Union*, p. 91; White, ed., *Civil War Diary*, p. 117; Gallagher, ed., *Fredericksburg Campaign*, p. 80; Acken, ed., *Inside*, p. 192.

100. *OR*, 21, p. 142; Rable, *Fredericksburg!*, p. 288; Fox, *Regimental Losses*, p. 41.

101. Meade, *Life and Letters*, v. 1, p. 338; Crary, ed., *Dear Belle*, p. 176; *B&L*, v. 3, p. 136; Snell, *From First to Last*, p. 227; Finnell, "Without Fear," *B&G*, 4, 1, p. 40.

Chapter 10: Winter of Transition

1. Nevins, ed., *Diary of the Civil War*, p. 281; Gallagher, ed., *Fredericksburg Campaign*, p. 51; Rable, *Fredericksburg!*, pp. 326–28.

2. Staudenraus, ed., *Mr. Lincoln's Washington*, pp. 42, 44; Fleming, ed., *Life*, p. 285; Tap, *Over Lincoln's Shoulder*, pp. 142, 143, 144.

3. Cozzens, ed., *B&L*, v. 5, p. 112; Staudenraus, ed., *Mr. Lincoln's Washington*, p. 29; Duncan, ed., *Blue-Eyed Child*, p. 271; *SOR*, 3, p. 672; Rable, *Fredericksburg!*, p. 325.

4. Sutherland, *Fredericksburg*, p. 70; Smart, ed., *Radical View*, v. 1, pp. 242, 243, 244, 253; Rable, *Fredericksburg!*, pp. 330–32, 350; Tap, *Over Lincoln's Shoulder*, pp. 145, 146; Snell, *From First to Last*, p. 228; Sparks, ed., *Inside Lincoln's Army*, pp. 193, 194.

5. *OR*, 21, pp. 868–70.

6. Ibid., p. 95; Snell, *From First to Last*, pp. 237–38, 240–41; Sears, *Controversies*, pp. 142–44; *SOR*, 3, p. 679.

7. OR, 21, p. 96; Sears, *Controversies*, pp. 144, 145; Rable, *Fredericksburg!*, pp. 390, 391; Snell, *From First to Last*, p. 241.

8. Sears, *Controversies*, pp. 146, 147; Rable, *Fredericksburg!*, p. 392; OR, 21, pp. 96, 941–42, 1006–12; Meade, *Life and Letters*, v. 1, p. 344.

9. Donald, *Lincoln*, p. 410; Rable, *Fredericksburg!*, pp. 392–93; OR, 21, p. 940.

10. OR, 21, pp. 940, 941; Donald, *Lincoln*, p. 410; Simon, "Lincoln and 'Old Brains,'" *N&S*, 2, 1, pp. 42, 44.

11. Sutherland, *Fredericksburg*, p. 70; Smart, ed., *Radical View*, v. 1, p. 253; Rable, *Fredericksburg!*, pp. 330–31, 350; Snell, *From First to Last*, pp. 224, 228, 230, 234–35; Tap, *Over Lincoln's Shoulder*, p. 146.

12. Rable, *Fredericksburg!*, pp. 392–93; Sears, *Controversies*, p. 145; Donald, *Lincoln*, pp. 410–11.

13. Sears, *Chancellorsville*, p. 14.

14. Donald, *Lincoln*, pp. 407–8.

15. Oliver H. Palmer–My dear wife, December 16, 1862, Palmer Papers, NC.

16. Ibid.; Pula, *Sigel Regiment*, p. 74; Norman Vance–Sister, December 27, 1862, Vance Papers, NC; Scott, ed., *Fallen Leaves*, p. 152; William L. Candler–My dear Brother, December 21, 1862, Candler Papers, VATU; Carter, *Four Brothers*, p. 202; Crumb and Dhalle, eds., *No Middle Ground*, p. 95.

17. P. Larry Meshach–Sister, January 12, 1863, Meshach Letters; Emory Upton–My dear sister Louise, December 23, 1862, Upton Letter, USAMHI; Frank M. Rood–Father and Mother, December 20, 1862, Rood Papers; William B. Durie–Father, December 22, 1862, Durie Papers, NC; Hamilton R. Dunlap–Sister, January 1, 1863, Dunlap Letters, PSU; Priest, ed., *One Surgeon's Private War*, p. 54; Longacre, *To Gettysburg*, pp. 62–63; Thomas Carpenter–Phil, December 21, 1862, Carpenter Letters, MOHS; Weld, *War Diary*, p. 153; Scott, ed., *Fallen Leaves*, p. 152; Acken, ed., *Inside*, pp. 177, 344.

18. Sears, ed., *On Campaign*, p. 120; Clark S. Edwards–My Dear Wife, December 22, 1862, Edwards Papers, NC; William Bacon–Mother, December 26, 1862, 2nd Maine Letters File, MNBP; John S. Willey–My Dear Wife, December 17, 1862, Willey Correspondence, USAMHI; Leehan, *Pale Horse*, p. 8; Bird, ed., *Quill*, pp. 54–55; Ford, ed., *War Letters*, p. 61; Henry Beecham–Mother, December 19, 1862, Beecham Letters, SHSW; Jordan, "Happiness," p. 63; Woodward, ed., "Civil War," *PMHB* v. 87, p. 51; Davis, *Lincoln's Men*, p. 98.

19. Sutherland, *Fredericksburg*, p. 87; Mannis and Wilson, eds., *Bound to Be a Soldier*, p. 47; Johnston, *Dear Pa*, p. 231; William C. Wiley–Brother, December 26, 1862, Wiley Papers, PSU.

20. Haines, *History*, p. 37; William Orr–Mother, December 24, 1862, Orr Papers, IU; Alanson Wiles–My Dear Mother, January 18, 1863, Wiles Papers, NC; Hezekiah Long–Wife, January 18, 1863, Long Civil War Letters, MESA; Robertson, ed., *Civil War Letters*, p. 258; Best, *History*, p. 53; Craft, *History*, p. 46; Patrick Walker–My Friend, January 27, 1863, Walker Papers, NYSL; Townsend, "History," p. 76, UME; Lucius Shattuck–Gill, January 12, 1863, Shattuck Letters, UM; William C. Wiley–Brother, December 26, 1862, Wiley Papers, PSU.

21. Trask, *Fire Within*, p. 160; Haines, *History*, p. 37; Styple, ed., *Writing*, pp. 156, 157; Bird, ed., *Quill*, p. 154; Thomas Carpenter–Phil, January 4, 1863, Carpenter Letters, MOHS; Sears, ed., *On Campaign*, p. 127; Herberger, ed., *Yankee at*

Arms, p. 88; Freland N. Holman–Sister, December 25, 1862, Holman Letters, USAMHI.

22. Sears, *Chancellorsville*, pp. 17, 18; Rosenblatt and Rosenblatt, eds., *Hard Marching*, p. 69; Lassen, ed., *Dear Sarah*, p. 53; Sears, ed., *For Country*, p. 308; Sparks, ed., *Inside Lincoln's Army*, p. 204; Cassedy, ed., *Dear Friends*, p. 206.

23. William L. Candler–my dear Brother, December 21, 1862, Candler Papers, VATU; Sawyer et al., eds., *Letters*, pp. 73, 79; George H. Legate–Sister, December 27, 1862, Legate Letter; Abel G. Peck–Lina, January 16, 1863, Peck Letter, FSNMP; Reid–Green, ed., *Letters Home*, p. 39; Hagerty, *Collis' Zouaves*, p. 132; Rhodes, ed., *All for the Union*, p. 92; Higginson, *Harvard Memorial Biographies*, v. 1, p. 50; Timothy O. Webster–My Dear Wife and Children, December 19, 1862, Webster Papers, NC.

24. John W. St. Clair–Father, December 30, 1862, St. Clair Papers, SHSW; Baxter, ed., *Hoosier Farm Boy*, p. 42; Pride and Travis, *My Brave Boys*, p. 163; Merton S. Tanner–Mother, December 27, 1862; S. B. Tarleton–Amy, January 12, 1863, Tarleton Letter; Harry W. Roose–Cousin, January 16, 1863, Delp Civil War Letters, USAMHI; Muffly, ed., *Story*, p. 613; Dunkelman, "Reflection," *N&S*, 3, 2, pp. 76, 77; Sears, ed., *On Campaign*, p. 110.

25. Davis, *Lincoln's Men*, p. 100; Rable, *Fredericksburg!*, pp. 377, 378; Miles Peabody–Brother & Sister, February 19, 1863, Peabody Letters, USAMHI.

26. Sears, ed., *On Campaign*, p. 138, Davis, *Lincoln's Men*, p. 100; Samito, ed., *Commanding Boston's Irish Ninth*, p. xxv; Kohl and Richard, eds., *Irish Green*, p. 62; Reed, ed., *Historical Family Letters*, p. 25; Charles R. Johnson–Nellie, February [?] 1863, Johnson Letters; Anson B. Shuey–My Dear Wife, January 11, February 14, 1863, Shuey War Letters, USAMHI; John M. Kyle–James Kelley, February 15, 1863, Kelley Civil War Letter Collection, PSU; Elisha B. Odle–Friend, March 7, 1863, Odle Papers, ANB; Rable, *Fredericksburg!*, pp. 377, 378; Timothy O. Webster–My Dear Wife and Children, March 8, 1863, Webster Papers; Seth Gilbert Evans–My Dear Mother, January 22, 1863, Evans Papers, NC.

27. Davis, *Lincoln's Men*, p. 102; Rable, *Fredericksburg!*, p. 378; A. Caldwell–Brother, January 11, 1863, Caldwell Family Correspondence, USAMHI; Thomas Carpenter–Phil, December 11, 1862, January 4, 1863, Carpenter Letters, MOHS; Crumb and Dhalle, eds., *No Middle Ground*, p. 105.

28. Parker, *History*, p. 282; Rable, *Fredericksburg!*, p. 378; Thomas Carpenter–Mary, December 30, 1862, Carpenter Letters, MOHS; Marshall, *Company "K,"* p. 200; Frank M. Rood–Father and Mother, December 20, 1862, Rood Papers, NC; Greiner et al., eds., *Surgeon's Civil War*, p. 91; Mannis and Wilson, eds., *Bound to Be a Soldier*, p. 52; William Orr–Father and Mother, January 7, 1863, Orr Papers, IU; Osborne, ed., *Civil War Diaries*, p. 60.

29. Noble, "Diary," UM; J. B. Tarleton–Amy, January 12, 1863, Tarleton Letter, USAMHI.

30. Snell, *From First to Last*, p. 243; Stewart, *History*, p. 30; Diary, Evans Papers, NC; Sears, *Chancellorsville*, p. 19; OR, 21, p. 944.

31. OR, 21, pp. 953–54; Sears, *Chancellorsville*, p. 19; Rable, *Fredericksburg!*, p. 409; Meade, *Life and Letters*, v. 1, p. 346.

32. OR, 21, pp. 976, 977; Meade, *Life and Letters*, v. 1, p. 348; Nevins, ed., *Diary*, pp. 157–58.

33. Cassedy, ed., *Dear Friends*, p. 216; Scott, ed., *Fallen Leaves*, p. 164; Meade, *Life and Letters*, v. 1, p. 348; Dunkelman and Winey, *Hardtack Regiment*, p. 43.

34. Cassedy, ed., *Dear Friends*, p. 216; Siegel, *For the Glory*, p. 121; Bennett, *Sons of Old Monroe*, p. 140; Sears, ed., *On Campaign*, p. 153; Nevins, ed., *Diary*, p. 159; Greiner et al., eds., *Surgeon's Civil War*, p. 71; Acken, ed., *Inside*, p. 206.

35. Bird, ed., *Quill*, p. 66; Acken, ed., *Inside*, p. 207; Albert Morton Hayward–Dear Brother, January 27, 1863, Hayward Papers, NC; Mannis and Wilson, eds., *Bound to Be a Soldier*, pp. 50, 51; Parker, *Henry Wilson's Regiment*, pp. 244, 245; Carter, *Four Brothers*, p. 226; Rable, *Fredericksburg!*, pp. 415, 418.

36. Rood, Memoir, pp. 38, 39, SHSW; Carter, *Four Brothers*, pp. 227, 228, 230; Mannis and Wilson, eds., *Bound to Be a Soldier*, p. 51; Sears, *Controversies*, p. 151; Thomas Carpenter–Phil, January 26, 1863, Carpenter Letters, MOHS; Duram and Duram, eds., *Soldier*, p. 52; Dayton E. Flint–Father, January 27, 1863, Flint Civil War Letters, USAMHI.

37. Timothy O. Webster–My Dear Wife and Children, January 27, 1863, Webster Papers, NC; John C. Babcock–Aunt, January 25, 1863, Babcock Papers, LC; Frank W. Dickerson–Father, January 23, 1863, Dickerson Letters, USAMHI; Thomas and Sauers, eds., *Civil War Letters*, p. 143; Quaife, ed., *From the Cannon's Mouth*, pp. 159–60; Nichols, *Toward Gettysburg*, pp. 158–59; Cassedy, ed., *Dear Friends*, pp. 218, 223; Gallagher, ed., *Fredericksburg Campaign*, p. 205; Carter, *Four Brothers*, pp. 227, 228; Meade, *Life and Letters*, v. 1, p. 348.

38. Meade, *Life and Letters*, v. 1, p. 349; Sears, *Chancellorsville*, pp. 20–21; Rable, *Fredericksburg!*, pp. 421–22; OR, 21, pp. 998–99.

39. OR, 21, pp. 998–99; Sears, *Controversies*, pp. 150, 151; O'Reilly, *Fredericksburg Campaign*, p. 489; Sparks, ed., *Inside Lincoln's Army*, pp. 199, 199n.

40. Sears, *Chancellorsville*, pp. 22, 23; Rable, *Fredericksburg!*, p. 422; Snell, *From First to Last*, p. 248.

41. Sears, *Controversies*, pp. 151, 155; Donald, *Lincoln*, p. 411; Rable, *Fredericksburg!*, p. 422.

42. O'Reilly, *Fredericksburg Campaign*, pp. 490–91; Sears, *Controversies*, p. 155; Donald, *Lincoln*, p. 411; OR, 21, pp. 1004–5.

43. OR, 21, pp. 1004–5; Meade, *Life and Letters*, v. 1, p. 353; Snell, *From First to Last*, pp. 250, 251, 252; Schiller, ed., *Autobiography*, p. 66; Warner, *Generals in Blue*, pp. 160, 374, 463.

44. Rhea et al., "What Was Wrong," *N&S*, 4, 3, pp. 12–15.

45. OR, 21, p. 1005; Warner, *Generals in Blue*, pp. 489–90; Furst, Diary, p. 34, USAMHI; Nevins, ed., *Diary*, p. 174.

46. OR, 21, p. 1005; Scott, ed., *Fallen Leaves*, p. 163; Meade, *Life and Letters*, v. 1, p. 351.

47. OR, 21, p. 96; Gallagher, ed., *Fredericksburg Campaign*, p. 20; Scott, ed., *Fallen Leaves*, p. 164; Winkler, *Letters*, p. 31.

48. Meade, *Life and Letters*, v. 1, p. 351.

49. Donald, *Lincoln*, p. 411; Sears, *Controversies*, p. 151; Staudenraus, ed., *Mr. Lincoln's Washington*, p. 84; Meade, *Life and Letters*, v. 1, pp. 318, 319, 346, 351, 352; Daniel Leasure–My Dearest Best Wife, July 4, 1863, Leasure, Daniel Letters, PSU; de Trobriand, *Four Years*, pp. 413, 414; Henry W. Halleck–Francis Lieber, August 4, 1863, Lieber Papers, HL; Scott, ed., *Fallen Leaves*, p. 165; Nevins, ed., *Diary*, pp. 153, 162.

50. Staudenraus, ed., *Mr. Lincoln's Washington*, p. 84; William L. Candler–My dear Brother, December 21, 1862, Candler Papers, VATU; Meade, *Life and Letters*, v. 1, pp. 319, 351, 352; Sears, *Controversies*, pp. 182, 183; de Trobriand, *Four Years*, p. 413; Nevins, ed., *Diary*, pp. 161, 162.

51. Sears, *Chancellorsville*, pp. 57–58; Donald, *Lincoln*, pp. 411–12.

52. Sears, *Controversies*, p. 181; Donald, *Lincoln*, p. 426.

53. Donald, *Lincoln*, pp. 408–9.

54. Meade, *Life and Letters*, v. 1, p. 352; Cassedy, ed., *Dear Friends*, p. 229; Anson B. Shuey–My Dear Wife, January 27, 1863, Shuey War Letters, USAMHI; Samito, ed., *Commanding Boston's Irish Ninth*, p. 163; Fleming, ed., *Life*, p. 306.

55. *OR*, 25, pt. 2, p. 51.

56. Ibid.

57. Meade, *Life and Letters*, v. 1, pp. 341, 343; Nevins, ed., *Diary*, pp. 149, 183.

58. Welcher, *Union Army*, p. 459; Styple, ed., *Writing*, p. 136; Henry Van Aernum–My dear Dora, October 15, 1862, Van Aernum Papers, USAMHI; Sears, ed., *On Campaign*, p. 98; Winkler, *Letters*, pp. 27, 36, 38.

59. Welcher, *Union Army*, p. 459; Winkler, *Letters*, pp. 40, 41, 86; Sears, *Gettysburg*, p. 189; Abner Doubleday–Samuel P. Bates, October 19, 1875, Bates Papers, LC; Carl Schurz–Abraham Lincoln, February 4, 1863, Lincoln Papers, LC; Pula, *Sigel Regiment*, p. 102; Robert Hubbard–Darling Nellie, April 7, 1863, Hubbard Letters, USAMHI; Le Duc, *Recollections*, p. 98; Warner, *Generals in Blue*, pp. 426–27.

60. Warner, *Generals in Blue*, pp. 451–52; Quaife, ed., *From the Cannon's Mouth*, p. 141; Wert, *Gettysburg*, p. 54.

61. Warner, *Generals in Blue*, p. 431; Byrne and Weaver, eds., *Haskell*, pp. 132, 133; H. Blanchard–Dearest Mother, July 11, 1863, Blanchard Letter, USAMHI.

62. Swanberg, *Sickles*, pp. 77–83, 88, 89, 105; de Trobriand, *Four Years*, p. 426; Sears, *Controversies*, p. 198; Laas, ed., *Wartime Washington*, p. 182.

63. Swanberg, *Sickles*, p. 86; Gallagher, ed., *Second Day at Gettysburg*, p. 36; Sears, *Controversies*, p. 200.

64. Swanberg, *Sickles*, pp. 139, 145, 146, 147, 153; Sears, *Controversies*, pp. 201, 203; William C. Wiley–Dear Ones at Home, March 24, May 25, 1862, Wiley Papers, PSU; Styple, ed., *Writing*, p. 111.

65. Swanberg, *Sickles*, pp. 145, 146, 158–63; Warner, *Generals in Blue*, p. 446; *OR*, 25, pt. 2, p. 51; Nevins, ed., *Diary*, pp. 30, 33, 183; Sears, *Controversies*, pp. 202, 203; Jordan, "*Happiness*," p. 68.

66. Welcher, *Union Army*, p. 515; *OR*, 25, pt. 2, p. 51; Starr, *Union Cavalry*, v. 1, pp. 339, 365; Wittenberg, *Union Cavalry*, pp. 8–9.

67. Warner, *Generals in Blue*, p. 481; Frank W. Dickerson–Father, February 12, 1863, Dickerson Letters, USAMHI; Wittenberg, *Union Cavalry*, pp. 14, 15.

68. Starr, *Union Cavalry*, v. 1, p. 339; Welcher, *Union Army*, p. 515; Sparks, ed., *Inside Lincoln's Army*, p. 213; Wittenberg, *Union Cavalry*, pp. 15–16, 18–19, 22–23.

69. Longacre, *General John Buford*, pp. 12, 13, 16, 31, 85, 87, 88, 115; Frank W. Dickerson–Father, February 17, 1863, Dickerson Letters, USAMHI; Hagemann, ed., *Fighting Rebels*, p. 214; Wittenberg, *Union Cavalry*, p. 26.

70. Wittenberg, *Union Cavalry*, pp. 26, 27, 31, 32, 42–45, quotation on p. 31.

71. Gallagher, ed., *Chancellorsville*, p. 1; Bennett, *Sons of Old Monroe*, p. 143; Cassedy, ed., *Dear Friends*, p. 233; Seth Gilbert Evans–My Dear Mother, Febru-

ary 1, 1863, Evans Papers, NC; Dunn, *Harvestfields*, p. 149; William R. Holmes–Cousin Maggie, Holmes Letter; Harry W. Roose–Cousin, February 5, 1863, Delp Civil War Letters, USAMHI; Horace Emerson–Brother Irvey, January 31, 1863, Emerson Letters, UM; Ford, ed., *Cycle*, v. 1, p. 250; Crary, ed., *Dear Belle*, p. 183; Blair, ed., *Politician*, p. 88; Thomas Carpenter–Phil, January 25, 1863, Carpenter Letters, MOHS; Osborne, ed., *Civil War Diaries*, p. 63; Mannis and Wilson, eds., *Bound to Be a Soldier*, p. 65.

72. Bates, *Battle of Chancellorsville*, p. 21; Gallagher, ed., *Chancellorsville*, p. 2; Thomas Carpenter–Phil, November 22, 1862, Carpenter Letters, MOHS; Wesley H. Shaw–Father & Mother, February 10, 1863, Shaw Papers, NYSL; Pula, *Sigel Regiment*, p. 100; Sears, ed., *On Campaign*, p. 175; Gibbon, *Personal Recollections*, p. 111; Favill, *Diary*, p. 222.

73. Coddington, *Gettysburg Campaign*, pp. 27, 28; Gallagher, ed., *Chancellorsville*, p. 10; Stewart, *History*, p. 36; Haggerty Diary, p. 5, UCGS; G. W. Goulding–Mother, March 4, 1863, Goulding Papers, NC; Jothan D. Williams–Mother, March 10, 1863, Williams Letters, UME; Hezekiah Long–Sarah, April 11, 17, 1863, Long Civil War Letters, MESA; Sears, ed., *On Campaign*, p. 176; Horace Emerson–Irvey, February 23, 1863, Emerson Letters, UM.

74. Gallagher, ed., *Chancellorsville*, pp. 9, 10, 11; Coddington, *Gettysburg Campaign*, pp. 28, 29; Stevens, *Three Years*, pp. 180, 182; Duram and Duram, eds., *Soldier*, p. 62; Parker, *Henry Wilson's Regiment*, p. 272; Keiser Diary, p. 56; Henry Crofoot–Cousin, May 10, 1863, Smith Correspondence, USAMHI.

75. *OR*, 25, pt. 2, p. 152; Gallagher, ed., *Chancellorsville*, p. 10.

76. Gallagher, ed., *Chancellorsville*, p. 10; Coddington, *Gettysburg Campaign*, p. 28; Diary, Boudwin Papers, NC; Thomas and Sauers, eds., *Civil War Letters*, p. 160; Townsend, "History," p. 74, UME; Longhenry, "Yankee Piper," pp. 3–15, ANB; Stephens, "Civil War Diary," pp. 54, 55, USAMHI.

77. Weld, *War Diary*, pp. 169, 170, 171; Nevins, ed., *Diary*, pp. 177, 178; Thomas and Sauers, eds., *Civil War Letters*, p. 157; David B. Birney–Gross, April 7, 1863, Birney Papers, USAMHI; Carter, *Four Brothers*, pp. 235, 236; Styple, ed., *Writing*, p. 180; Haggerty Diary, p. 6, UCGS; Bauer, ed., *Soldiering*, p. 33; Gallagher, ed., *Chancellorsville*, p. 68; Kohl and Richard, eds., *Irish Green*, p. 84; Diary, Boudwin Papers, NC; William C. Wiley–Brother, April 10, 1863, Wiley Papers, PSU.

78. Styple, ed., *Writing*, p. 180; Staudenraus, ed., *Mr. Lincoln's Washington*, pp. 148, 158; Wesson Diary, p. 9, USAMHI; *B&L*, v. 3, pp. 119, 120.

79. Robert Hubbard–Darling Nellie, April 11, 1863, Hubbard Letters; Benjamin C. Pennell–Cousin, March 26, 1863, Pennell Letters, USAMHI; Blair, ed., *Politician*, p. 89; Stevens, ed., *As if It Were Glory*, p. 40; Kohl and Richard, eds., *Irish Green*, p. 93; Townsend, "History," pp. 82–83, UME; Weld, *War Diary*, p. 158; Mannis and Wilson, eds., *Bound to Be a Soldier*, p. 67; Sears, *Controversies*, p. 191.

80. Robert B. Goodyear–Sarah, February 14, 1863, Goodyear Letters; David Acheson–Father, March 25, 1863, Acheson, "Family Letters," p. 373; A. Caldwell–Brother, March 7, 1863, Caldwell Family Correspondence; David Seibert–Father and All, April 12, 1863, Seibert Family Papers, USAMHI; Dawes, *Service*, p. 123; Small, ed., *Road*, p. 186; Carter, *Four Brothers*, pp. 230–31, 238; Noble, "Diary," UM; Reed, ed., *Historical Family Letters*, p. 29; Mannis and Wilson, ed., *Bound to Be a Soldier*, pp. 56, 64, 65, 69–70; Byrne and Weaver, ed., *Haskell*, p. 55.

81. Kohl and Richard, eds., *Irish Green*, p. 65.
82. Ibid., pp. 79, 80; Duram and Duram, eds., *Soldier*, pp. 77, 78; Stewart, *History*, pp. 43, 44.
83. Wittenberg, *Union Cavalry*, pp. 48–60, quotation on p. 61.
84. The best account of Kelly's Ford is in ibid., Chapter 3.
85. Ibid., pp. 98–101.
86. Sears, *Chancellorsville*, pp. 102, 104; John E. Ryder–Sister, March 29, 1863, Ryder Letters, UM; Weld, *War Diary*, pp. 163, 175, 176; Ira Spaulding–My Dear Mrs. Dunkle, April 15, 1863, Spaulding Papers, NYSL.
87. Fishel, *Secret War*, pp. 287–89, 294, 298; Sears, *Chancellorsville*, pp. 68, 69, 101, 102, 130.
88. Sears, *Chancellorsville*, pp. 103–4; de Trobriand, *Four Years*, p. 429; Staudenraus, ed., *Mr. Lincoln's Washington*, pp. 170, 171; Thomas Vincent–Joseph Hooker, April 22, 25, 1863, RG 393, NA.
89. Geary, *We Need Men*, pp. 49, 50, 66, 67; Davenport, *Campaign*, p. 378; Racine, "Unspoiled Heart," p. 6; Bird, ed., *Quill*, pp. 90, 93; Gibbon, *Personal Recollections*, pp. 112–14.
90. Sears, *Chancellorsville*, pp. 102, 103, 119–23; OR, 25, pt. 2, pp. 199–200, 262, 263, 266–67, 268, 269; Gallagher, ed., *Chancellorsville*, pp. 68, 69; Wittenberg, *Union Cavalry*, pp. 119–28; Osborne, *Civil War Diaries*, p. 77; Sedgwick, ed., *Correspondence*, v. 2, pp. 90–91
91. Gallagher, ed., *Chancellorsville*, pp. 15, 16, 17; OR, 25, pt. 2, p. 320; Meade, *Life and Letters*, v. 1, p. 369; *B&L*, v. 3, p. 257; John E. Ryder–Mother, March 7, 1863, Ryder Letters, UM; Byrne and Weaver, eds., *Haskell*, pp. 58, 60; Timothy O. Webster–My Dear Wife & Children, March 18, 1863, Webster Papers, NC.

Chapter 11: "God Almighty Could Not Prevent Me from Winning a Victory"

1. Wert, *Brotherhood*, p. 225.
2. Sears, *Chancellorsville*, pp. 97, 100, 178, 193–94.
3. Ibid., p. 131; Fishel, *Secret War*, pp. 360, 362; Weigley, *Great Civil War*, p. 227.
4. OR, 25, pt. 2, pp. 255, 256, 262, 264, 266–67, 268, 320; Sears, *Chancellorsville*, pp. 131–32, 136–39; Gallagher, ed., *Chancellorsville*, p. 70; Weigley, *Great Civil War*, p. 226.
5. Sears, *Chancellorsville*, pp. 141–47; Cassedy, ed., *Dear Friends*, pp. 254, 255; OR, 25, pt. 1, p. 213; Robert Cruikshank–Wife, May 8, 1863, Cruikshank Civil War Letters, AFHS.
6. Quaife, ed., *From the Cannon's Mouth*, pp. 180, 183; Pula, *Sigel Regiment*, p. 115; James E. Crane–My Darling Gussie, May 8, 1863, Crane Papers, NC; Cassedy, ed., *Dear Friends*, p. 255; Bennett, *Sons of Old Monroe*, p. 175; Sears, ed., *On Campaign*, p. 245.
7. Sears, *Chancellorsville*, pp. 156–59; Wert, *Brotherhood*, pp. 223–25; Weld, *War Diary*, p. 189; Westbrook, *History*, p. 144; Mancha Diary, p. 42, USAMHI.
8. OR, 25, pt. 2, p. 320; Sears, *Chancellorsville*, pp. 175–81; Quaife, ed., *From the Cannon's Mouth*, pp. 183–85; James Biddle–Alexander Webb, May 7, 1863; Alexander Webb–My Dear Father, May 12, 1863, Webb Papers, YU; Meade, *Life and Letters*, v. 1, p. 370.

9. Meade, *Life and Letters*, v. 1, p. 379; Sears, *Chancellorsville*, p. 171; *B&L*, v. 3, p. 157.

10. Sears, *Chancellorsville*, p. 191; Quaife, ed., *From the Cannon's Mouth*, p. 186; OR, 25, pt. 1, p. 171.

11. OR, 25, pt. 2, pp. 306–7, 320; Fishel, *Secret War*, p. 375; Sears, *Chancellorsville*, p. 151.

12. Sparks, ed., *Inside Lincoln's Army*, p. 239.

13. Sears, *Chancellorsville*, pp. 167, 187, 188; Wert, *General James Longstreet*, pp. 225–28, 233–34.

14. OR, 25, pt. 1, pp. 796–97; pt. 2, p. 765; Sears, *Chancellorsville*, pp. 174, 188.

15. OR, 25, pt. 1, p. 797; Sears, *Chancellorsville*, pp. 188–90.

16. Quaife, ed., *From the Cannon's Mouth*, p. 186; Cassedy, ed., *Dear Friends*, p. 256; Sears, *Chancellorsville*, p. 202; Lucius Shattuck–Gil and Mary, May 17, 1863, Shattuck Letters, UM.

17. OR, 25, pt. 1, pp. 198, 507, 525, 670; pt. 2, p. 324; Quaife, ed., *From the Cannon's Mouth*, p. 186; Sears, *Chancellorsville*, pp. 199–200, 202.

18. OR, 25, pt. 1, pp. 525, 670, 850–51, 825; Cassedy, ed., *Dear Friends*, p. 256; James Biddle–Alexander Webb, May 7, 1863, Webb Papers, YU; Sears, *Chancellorsville*, pp. 197, 204–8.

19. OR, 25, pt. 1, pp. 198–99, 670; pt. 2, pp. 325, 326; Quaife, ed., *From the Cannon's Mouth*, p. 187; Sears, *Chancellorsville*, pp. 197, 210, 211.

20. OR, 25, pt. 1, pp. 311, 525–26; James Biddle–Alexander Webb, May 7, 1863, Webb Papers, YU; Sears, *Chancellorsville*, pp. 213, 219–24; Jordan, "Happiness," p. 73.

21. Slocum, *Life*, pp. 76, 77.

22. Jordan, "Happiness," pp. 73, 74; James Biddle–Alexander Webb, May 7, 9, 1863, Webb Papers, YU; Meade, *Life and Letters*, v. 1, p. 379.

23. Sears, *Chancellorsville*, pp. 210, 211; Fishel, *Secret War*, p. 391; Meade, *Life and Letters*, v. 1, p. 372.

24. James Biddle–Alexander Webb, May 9, 1863, Webb Papers, YU; Meade, *Life and Letters*, v. 1, p. 372.

25. Sears, *Chancellorsville*, p. 201; Fishel, *Secret War*, p. 391.

26. Sears, *Chancellorsville*, pp. 230–34.

27. Ibid., pp. 234–35.

28. OR, 25, pt. 1, pp. 199, 385, 507, 633, 650, 678, 729; Sears, *Chancellorsville*, pp. 235–36; *B&L*, v. 3, pp. 192, 220.

29. OR, 25, pt. 1, pp. 254–55; Sparks, ed., *Inside Lincoln's Army*, pp. 240–41; Joseph Hooker–George W. Mindil, January 12, 1875, Mindil Papers, USAMHI; Sears, *Chancellorsville*, pp. 228, 229, 235, 237; *B&L*, v. 3, p. 219.

30. OR, 25, pt. 1, pp. 386, 408, 678; Fishel, *Secret War*, pp. 395, 396, 397, 401; *B&L*, v. 3, p. 163; White, ed., *Civil War Diary*, p. 142; Sears, *Chancellorsville*, pp. 245, 254–56, 266, 271; Quaife, ed., *From the Cannon's Mouth*, p. 189.

31. Sears, *Chancellorsville*, pp. 247, 263, 266, 267, 269; Winkler, *Letters*, p. 53; Raphelson, "Alexander Schimmelfennig," *PMHB*, v. 87, pp. 167, 168; Keifer, *History*, p. 22.

32. Baumgartner, *Buckeye Blood*, p. 18; Francis Barlow–My dear Bob, August 12, 1863, Barlow Papers, MAHS; Henry Van Aernum–My dearest Lis, May 15, 1863, Van Aernum Papers, USAMHI; Sears, *Chancellorsville*, pp. 263, 276;

Bates, *Battle of Chancellorsville*, p. 175; Raphelson, "Alexander Schimmelfennig," *PMHB*, v. 87, pp. 157, 167, 168.

33. Sears, *Chancellorsville*, pp. 272, 274; Mannis and Wilson, eds., *Bound to Be a Soldier*, p. 73; Mesnard, "Reminiscence," p. 28, USAMHI; Sears, ed., *On Campaign*, p. 250; Keifer, *History*, p. 249.

34. Mannis and Wilson, eds., *Bound to Be a Soldier*, p. 73; Isaac W. Gardner–[Parents], [no date], Gardner Letters and Diaries; Henry Van Aernum–My dearest Lis, May 15, 1863, Van Aernum Papers, USAMHI; Sears, ed., *On Campaign*, p. 263; Francis Barlow–My dearest Mother & brothers, May 8, 1863, Barlow Papers, MAHS; Baumgartner, *Buckeye Blood*, pp. 15–16; Dunkelman and Winey, *Hardtack Regiment*, pp. 57, 58, 60; Pula, *Sigel Regiment*, pp. 123, 126, 129; Winkler, *Letters*, p. 53; Sears, *Chancellorsville*, p. 277; James E. Crane–My Darling Gussie, May 8, 1863, Crane Papers, NC; Sutherland, *Fredericksburg*, p. 155.

35. OR, 25, pt. 1, pp. 200, 388; Sears, *Chancellorsville*, pp. 285, 286; Sutherland, *Fredericksburg*, p. 156; de Trobriand, *Four Years*, p. 444; Marbaker, *History*, p. 62.

36. OR, 25, pt. 1, pp. 678–79; Quaife, ed., *From the Cannon's Mouth*, p. 191; Sears, *Chancellorsville*, pp. 286, 287.

37. OR, 25, pt. 1, pp. 678–79; James E. Crane–My Darling Gussie, May 8, 1863, Crane Papers, NC; Robert Hubbard–My dear Nellie, May 9, 1863, Hubbard Letters, USAMHI; Quaife, ed., *From the Cannon's Mouth*, pp. 192, 193; a detailed description of Stonewall Jackson's ride and wounding is in Krick, *Smoothbore Volley*, Chapter 1.

38. OR, 25, pt. 1, pp. 390, 409; Silliker, ed., *Rebel Yell*, pp. 80, 81; Racine, ed., *"Unspoiled Heart,"* pp. 13, 15; Townsend, "History," p. 94, UME; Collins, *Memoirs*, p. 107.

39. OR, 25, pt. 1, p. 255; pt. 2, p. 320; Sutherland, *Fredericksburg*, p. 161; Sears, *Chancellorsville*, pp. 227, 228, 303; *B&L*, v. 3, p. 164.

40. OR, 25, pt. 1, p. 201.

41. *Ibid.*, pp. 201, 255, 508; Sears, *Chancellorsville*, pp. 228, 303, 315; *B&L*, v. 3, p. 164; Sutherland, *Fredericksburg*, p. 161.

42. Sears, *Chancellorsville*, pp. 322, 326, 329, 333; Cowles, ed., *History*, p. 580; Robert Cruikshank–Wife, May 8, 1863, Cruikshank Civil War Letters, AFHS; Silliker, ed., *Rebel Yell*, p. 81; Luther A. Granger–Wife, May 7, 1863, Granger Letters, USAMHI; Quaife, ed., *From the Cannon's Mouth*, p. 195.

43. Sears, *Chancellorsville*, pp. 314, 316.

44. *Ibid.*, pp. 312–14; OR, 25, pt. 1, p. 823; Sutherland, *Fredericksburg*, p. 161; Hagerty, *Collis' Zouaves*, p. 186, 187; Walker, *History*, p. 246.

45. Sutherland, *Fredericksburg*, p. 164; Sears, *Controversies*, pp. 187, 188, 189; James Biddle–Alexander Webb, May 9, 1863, Webb Papers, YU; Weld, *War Diary*, p. 203; *B&L*, v. 3, pp. 167, 169.

46. OR, 25, pt. 1, pp. 250, 306; Quaife, ed., *From the Cannon's Mouth*, pp. 198, 199; Sears, *Chancellorsville*, pp. 358, 360, 361, 363; Nevins, ed., *Diary*, pp. 193, 194, 195, 198.

47. OR, 25, pt. 1, pp. 313–14; Stewart, *History*, p. 53; Favill, *Diary*, pp. 234–35; Bingham, Memoirs, WRHS; Joseph H. Law–Mary, May 7, 1863, Law Family Papers, USAMHI; Muffly, ed., *Story*, p. 531.

48. OR, 25, pt. 1, p. 314; Gallagher, ed., *Chancellorsville*, pp. 143, 165, 169; Cava-

naugh, *Memoirs*, p. 484; "Military Record of General Nelson Miles, U.S.A.," p. 5, Miles Papers, USAMHI; Sears, *Chancellorsville*, p. 380.

49. Sears, *Chancellorsville*, pp. 323, 366; Gould, *Major-General Hiram G. Berry*, p. 267; Silliker, ed., *Rebel Yell*, p. 82; Crumb and Dhalle, eds., *No Middle Ground*, p. 137; James E. Crane–My Darling Gussie, May 8, 1863, Crane Papers, NC.

50. *OR*, 25, pt. 2, p. 268; Sparks, ed., *Inside Lincoln's Army*, p. 238; Sears, *Chancellorsville*, p. 249.

51. *OR*, 25, pt. 1, p. 558; Sears, *Chancellorsville*, pp. 250, 304.

52. *OR*, 25, pt. 1, p. 558; pt. 2, pp. 338, 339, 340, 342, 343, 353, 355, 357, 359, 361, 363, 365; Sears, *Chancellorsville*, pp. 196, 228, 229, 304, 309.

53. *OR*, 25, pt. 1, p. 559; *B&L*, v. 3, pp. 227–28; Stevens, *Three Years*, p. 198; Hiram S. Wilson–My own Sweet Darling, May 4, 1863, Wilson Papers, NYSL; Sears, *Chancellorsville*, p. 356.

54. *OR*, 25, pt. 1, pp. 559, 567; *B&L*, v. 3, p. 229; Rhodes, ed., *All for the Union*, p. 106; Fox, *Regimental Losses*, pp. 36, 436; Sears, *Chancellorsville*, pp. 374, 377–78.

55. *OR*, 25, pt. 1, pp. 559, 826, 827, 857; Sears, *Chancellorsville*, p. 381, 385.

56. *OR*, 25, pt. 1, pp. 568, 827; Greiner et al., eds., *Surgeon's Civil War*, p. 145; Baquet, *History*, pp. 79–82; *B&L*, v. 3, pp. 230, 231; Sears, *Chancellorsville*, pp. 378–84.

57. Sutherland, *Fredericksburg*, p. 170; Fox, *Regimental Losses*, p. 436; Rhodes, ed., *All for the Union*, pp. 106–7; Baquet, *History*, p. 249; *OR*, 25, pt. 1, p. 560.

58. *OR*, 25, pt. 1, p. 560; pt. 2, p. 396; Sears, *Chancellorsville*, p. 386.

59. *OR*, 25, pt. 1, pp. 560, 827–28, 852; Sutherland, *Fredericksburg*, p. 174; Sears, *Chancellorsville*, pp. 390, 393–94, 410.

60. Sears, *Chancellorsville*, pp. 390–94; Gibbon, *Personal Recollections*, p. 117.

61. Sutherland, *Fredericksburg*, p. 174; Warner, *Generals in Blue*, p. 239; de Trobriand, *Four Years*, p. 312; Westbrook, *History*, p. 146; Sears, *Chancellorsville*, pp. 410–17.

62. *OR*, 25, pt. 2, pp. 405–12; Sutherland, *Fredericksburg*, p. 174.

63. *OR*, 25, pt. 2, pp. 418, 419.

64. Sedgwick, ed., *Correspondence*, v. 2, p. 92.

65. Ibid., p. 109; Cowley, ed., *With My Face to the Enemy*, p. 62; Rhea et al., "What Was Wrong," *N&S*, 4, 3, pp. 14, 15; Sears, *Chancellorsville*, p. 249.

66. *OR*, 25, pt. 1, pp. 801, 802, 888; Sears, *Chancellorsville*, pp. 390, 391, 403.

67. Mulholland, *Story*, p. 102; Acken, ed., *Inside*, pp. 249–50; Silliker, ed., *Rebel Yell*, pp. 66, 83.

68. Sears, *Chancellorsville*, pp. 388, 406; Badeau, "Battle of Chancellorsville," NC; Nevins, ed., *Diary*, p. 197.

69. *B&L*, v. 3, p. 171; Jordan, "Happiness," pp. 77, 78; Powell, *Fifth Army Corps*, p. 475.

70. Meade, *Life and Letters*, v. 1, pp. 372, 374; James Biddle–Alexander Webb, May 7, 1863; Alexander Webb–Robert, May [?] 1863, Webb Papers, YU; Powell, *Fifth Army Corps*, pp. 474, 475; Jordan, "Happiness," p. 78; *B&L*, v. 3, p. 171; Sears, *Chancellorsville*, pp. 421, 422.

71. *B&L*, v. 3, p. 171; Jordan, "Happiness," p. 78; Powell, *Fifth Army Corps*, p. 475; Alexander Webb–Robert, May [?] 1863, Webb Papers, YU; Nevins, ed., *Diary*, p. 199; Meade, *Life and Letters*, v. 1, p. 373.

72. Nevins, ed., *Diary*, pp. 199, 200; *OR*, 25, pt. 1, p. 251; Sears, *Chancellorsville*, pp. 426–28.

73. Nevins, ed., *Diary*, p. 200; Sparks, ed., *Inside Lincoln's Army*, p. 242; Hiram S. Wilson–My own Sweet wife, May 6, 1863, Wilson Papers, NYSL; Cassedy, ed., *Dear Friends*, p. 257; Fribley Diaries; Hart, "1863 Civil War Diary," p. 5, USAMHI; Johnston, *Dear Pa*, p. 245; Bennett, *Sons of Old Monroe*, p. 195; Dreese, *Imperishable Fame*, p. 100; Brainerd, *Bridge Building*, p. 145.

74. Alexander Webb–My Dear Father, May 12, 1863; James Biddle–Alexander Webb, May 9, 1863, Webb Papers, YU; Sparks, ed., *Inside Lincoln's Army*, p. 242.

75. Walker and Walker, ed., *Diary*, p. 97; Quaife, ed., *From the Cannon's Mouth*, p. 201; James Biddle–Alexander Webb, May 7, 8, 1863, Webb Papers, YU; Gallagher, ed., *First Day at Gettysburg*, p. 57.

76. John F. Reynolds–My dear Sisters, May 9, 1863, Reynolds Family Papers, FM; William M. Sayre–Father, May 9, 1863, Sayre Letters, USAMHI; modern casualty figures from Sears, *Chancellorsville*, pp. 389, 440, 442; official figures in OR, 25, pt. 1, pp. 172–92, 806–9; Fox, *Regimental Losses*, p. 541.

77. Donald, *Lincoln*, pp. 435, 436; Beale, ed., *Diary*, v. 1, p. 291; OR, 25, pt. 2, pp. 379, 401, 434.

78. Staudenraus, ed., *Mr. Lincoln's Washington*, pp. 179, 180; Donald, *Lincoln*, p. 436; OR, 25, pt. 2, p. 435.

79. Donald, *Lincoln*, p. 438; Meade, *Life and Letters*, v. 1, p. 372.

80. Abraham Lincoln–Joseph Hooker, May 14, 1863; George G. Meade–Andrew G. Curtin, May 15, 1863; George H. Baker–John W. Forney, May 20, 1863, Lincoln Papers, LC; SOR, 4, p. 472; Sears, *Controversies*, pp. 158–60.

81. Brown, *Cushing*, p. 183; William T. H. Brooks–Father, May 11, 1863, Brooks Papers, USAMHI; Silliker, ed., *Rebel Yell*, p. 146; Rufus R. Dawes–My dear Mary, May 18, 1863, Dawes Papers, SHSW; Weld, *War Diary*, pp. 194, 198; Frank L. Lemont–Dearest Mother, May 9, 1863, Lemont Letters, UME; James Biddle–Alexander Webb, May 7, 1863, Webb Papers, YU.

82. Alexander Webb–My Dear Father, May 12, 1863, Webb Papers, YU; Gibbon, *Personal Recollections*, p. 119; Swinton, *Campaigns*, p. 280; Child, *History*, p. 187; Meade, *Life and Letters*, v. 1, pp. 372, 379.

83. Meade, *Life and Letters*, v. 1, pp. 373, 379.

84. Sears, *Controversies*, p. 158.

85. Francis Barlow–My dearest mother & brothers, May 8, 1863, Barlow Letters, MAHS; Samito, ed., *Commanding Boston's Irish Ninth*, p. 188; Mannis and Wilson, eds., *Bound to Be a Soldier*, p. 75; Scott, ed., *Fallen Leaves*, p. 176; Winkler, *Letters*, p. 51.

86. Nevins, ed., *Diary*, pp. 212, 213; Gibbon, *Personal Recollections*, pp. 121, 122; Sedgwick, ed., *Correspondence*, v. 2, p. 127.

87. Gallagher, ed., *Chancellorsville*, Chapter 3; Wittenberg, *Union Cavalry*, Chapter 7.

88. OR, 25, pt. 1, p. 1063; pt. 2, p. 463; Wittenberg, *Union Cavalry*, pp. 236, 237, 330.

89. Wittenberg, *Union Cavalry*, p. 237; Frank W. Dickerson–Father, May 23, 1863, Dickerson Letters, USAMHI; Coddington, *Gettysburg Campaign*, p. 44; Sears, *Gettysburg*, p. 33.

90. Sears, *Controversies*, p. 159; Sparks, ed., *Inside Lincoln's Army*, p. 248; Meade, *Life and Letters*, v. 1, pp. 373, 379; Walker, *History*, pp. 253, 254; Coddington,

Gettysburg Campaign, pp. 36, 37; Darius Couch–Seth Williams, June 5, 1863, RG 393, NA.

91. Winslow, *General John Sedgwick*, p. 88; Tucker, *Hancock*, p. 124; Coddington, *Gettysburg Campaign*, pp. 36, 37.

92. Meade, *Life and Letters*, v. 1, p. 385; Trudeau, *Gettysburg*, p. 14; Coddington, *Gettysburg Campaign*, pp. 37–38; Sears, *Gettysburg*, pp. 40, 41.

93. James Biddle–Alexander Webb, May 7, 1863; Alexander Webb–Robert, May [?] 1863; Alexander Webb–Annie, May 18, 1863, Webb Papers, YU; Nevins, ed., *Diary*, p. 202; Gibbon, *Personal Recollections*, p. 120; John Gibbon–My dearest Mama, June 1, 1863, Gibbon Papers, HSP; Swanberg, *Sickles*, pp. 196–97; Coddington, *Gettysburg Campaign*, p. 36; Meade, *Life and Letters*, v. 1, p. 373.

94. Alexander Webb–My Dear Father, May 12, 1863, Webb Papers, YU; Weigley, *Great Civil War*, p. 229.

95. Swinton, *Campaigns*, p. 267; Weld, *War Diary*, p. 213.

96. Dreese, *151st Pennsylvania Volunteers*, p. 8; Rufus R. Dawes–My dear Mary, May 18, 1863, Dawes Papers, SHSW.

97. OR, 25, pt. 1, p. 802; Sears, *Chancellorsville*, p. 430.

98. Wert, *General James Longstreet*, pp. 238, 239.

Chapter 12: *"Big Fight Some Wears Ahead"*

1. Wert, *Gettysburg*, p. 19.

2. Ibid., pp. 18, 43–44; Gallagher, *Confederate War*, pp. 8, 10; Harsh, *Confederate Tide Rising*, pp. 57, 58, 59–62, 66.

3. Wert, *General James Longstreet*, p. 247.

4. OR, 27, pt. 1, pp. 29, 30; Coddington, *Gettysburg Campaign*, pp. 38, 52.

5. OR, 27, pt. 1, pp. 31, 32.

6. Ibid., p. 32, pt. 3, pp. 27–28; Gallagher, "Brandy Station," *B&G*, 8, 1, pp. 11, 12.

7. Wittenberg, *Union Cavalry*, pp. 259–60.

8. Ibid., pp. 16, 260–61; Hagemann, ed., *Fighting Rebels*, pp. 147, 148; Sparks, ed., *Inside Lincoln's Army*, p. 256; Gibbon, *Personal Recollections*, p. 123.

9. Wittenberg, *Union Cavalry*, pp. 265–72, 278–90, quote p. 284; Gallagher, "Brandy Station," *B&G*, 8, 1, pp. 17–20, 22, 44–46.

10. Wittenberg, *Union Cavalry*, pp. 296–307; Gallagher, "Brandy Station," *B&G*, 8, 1, pp. 47–48, 50–51.

11. Stuart's report is in OR, 27, pt. 2, pp. 679–85; pt. 1, pp. 903, 904, 905; Wittenberg, *Union Cavalry*, p. 308.

12. Wittenberg, *Union Cavalry*, pp. 308–11; Coddington, *Gettysburg Campaign*, pp. 63–64.

13. Wert, *Gettysburg*, p. 22.

14. OR, 27, pt. 1, pp. 34–35.

15. Ibid., p. 438; Fishel, *Secret War*, pp. 439, 440.

16. Hiram S. Wilson–Sweet one, June 18, 1863, Wilson Papers; Archibald McDougall–Edward Dodd, June 21, 1863, McDougall Papers, NYSL; Moe, *Last Full Measure*, pp. 248–49; Racine, *"Unspoiled Heart,"* pp. 38, 39; Chamberlin, *History*, p. 109; Cavada Diary, HSP; Robert Hubbard–My Darling Nellie, June 15, 1863, Hubbard Letters; Diary, Burrill Letters and Diary, USAMHI.

17. William Speed–Charlotte Speed, June 21, 1863, Speed Papers, UM; Cassedy, ed., *Dear Friends*, pp. 284, 285; Archibald McDougall–Phil, June 23, 1863, McDougall Papers, NYSL; Robert Cruikshank–Wife, June 17, 1863, Cruikshank Civil War Letters, AFHS; Townsend, "History," pp, 115–18, UME; John D. Hill–Sir, June 16, 1863, Hill Civil War Letters, USAMHI; Marshall, *Company "K,"* p. 105; Campbell, ed., *"Grand Terrible Dramma,"* p. 108.

18. Diary, Paine Papers, NYHS; Fishel, *Secret War*, p. 457; Coddington, *Gettysburg Campaign*, pp. 80, 82; Sparks, ed., *Inside Lincoln's Army*, p. 260.

19. OR, 27, pt. 1, p. 48; pt. 3, pp. 171, 172, 244; the best description of the cavalry engagements at Aldie, Middleburg, and Upperville is O'Neill, *Cavalry Battles*, Chapters 3–12.

20. Schildt, *Roads to Gettysburg*, pp. 173–74, 180–93, 223–39; Wert, *Gettysburg*, pp. 22–23.

21. Coddington, *Gettysburg Campaign*, pp. 122, 126; Marvin Diary, MNHS; Cavada Diary, HSP; Ira Spaulding–My Dear Dunkle, June 24, 1863, Spaulding Papers, NYSL; "General Benham's Report of Services," pp. 83–84, Benham Papers; Coburn Diary; Howard, Memoranda; Henry Van Aernum–My Dearest Lis, June 27, 1863, Van Aernum Papers, USAMHI.

22. Coddington, *Gettysburg Campaign*, pp. 98–99, 134–36; OR, 27, pt. 3, pp. 136–37; McLean, *Cutler's Brigade*, p. 4.

23. Coddington, *Gettysburg Campaign*, pp. 98, 99; Walker, *History*, pp. 259, 260; Woodward, *Our Campaigns*, pp. 205, 207; Record of Movements in 1863, Crawford Papers, LC; Clarence H. Bell–Sister, June 28, 1863, Bell Letters; John A. Willoughby–Daul Simpson, June [?] 1863, Simpson and Simpson, "Dear Daul," USAMHI.

24. OR, 27, pt. 1, p. 60; Coddington, *Gettysburg Campaign*, pp. 128–29; Sears, "Meade Takes Command," *N&S*, 5, 6, pp. 18, 19.

25. Coddington, *Gettysburg Campaign*, pp. 43, 131, 132, 133; Henry W. Halleck–Francis Lieber, August 4, 1863, Lieber Papers, HL; OR, 27, pt. 1, p. 60.

26. OR, 27, pt. 1, p. 61; Nevins, *Diary*, p. 227; de Trobriand, *Four Years*, p. 483; Powell, *Fifth Army Corps*, p. 501; Trudeau, *Gettysburg*, pp. 94, 98, 99.

27. Beale, ed., *Diary*, v. 1, p. 348.

28. OR, 27, pt. 1, p. 61; pt. 3, p. 369; Powell, *Fifth Army Corps*, p. 500n; Wert, *Gettysburg*, p. 25; Coddington, *Gettysburg Campaign*, p. 209; George Meade–Mama, July 1, 1863, Meade Collection, HSP.

29. *Annals*, p. 207; OR, 27, pt. 1, p. 61; Beale, ed., *Diary*, p. 349.

30. Wert, *Gettysburg*, p. 48; Cleaves, *Meade*, p. 127.

31. Wert, *Gettysburg*, p. 49; Coddington, *Gettysburg Campaign*, pp. 210, 211; Young, *Battle of Gettysburg*, p. 339; Gallagher, ed., *Wilderness Campaign*, p. 68; John W. Ames–Mother, June 28, 1863, Ames Papers, USAMHI; Agassiz, ed., *Meade's Headquarters*, p. 25.

32. Scott, ed., *Fallen Leaves*, p. 189; Gibbs, *Three Years*, p. 48; Gallagher, ed., *Wilderness Campaign*, pp. 69–70; John W. Ames–My dear Mother, July 19, 1863, Ames Papers, USAMHI; Wert, *Gettysburg*, p. 48.

33. Scott, ed., *Fallen Leaves*, p. 189; Smith, *History*, p. 77; John W. Ames–My dear Mother, July 19, 1863, Ames Papers, USAMHI; Wert, *Gettysburg*, p. 48.

34. Agassiz, ed., *Meade's Headquarters*, pp. 25, 57; George Meade–Mama, July 1, 1863, Meade Collection; James C. Biddle–My own darling little Wife, July 1,

1863, Biddle Civil War Letters; John Gibbon–My darling Mama, June 29, 1863, Gibbon Papers, HSP; Quaife, ed., *From the Cannon's Mouth*, p. 221; Sparks, ed., *Inside Lincoln's Army*, p. 265; *B&L*, v. 3, p. 270; Jordan, "*Happiness*," p. 87.

35. Walker and Walker, eds., *Diary*, p. 109; Favill, *Diary*, p. 242; Hiram S. Wilson–My Dear Wife, June 28, 1863, Wilson Papers, NYSL; Acken, ed., *Inside*, p. 293; Henry Clare–My dear William, June 30, 1863, Clare Letters, GC; Moe, *Last Full Measure*, p. 253; Collins, *Memoirs*, p. 129; David Acheson–Mother, June 28, 1863, Acheson, "*Family Letters*," p. 382; Henry J. Hunt–My dear Eunice, July 28, 1863, Ford Papers; James Gillette–Parents, July 2, 1863, Gillette Papers; Joshua G. Wilbur–My dear Wife, June 28, 1863, Wilbur Letters, USAMHI; Stevens, *Three Years*, p. 238.

36. Coddington, *Gettysburg Campaign*, p. 217; Powell, *Fifth Army Corps*, p. 500n; *Diary*, Paine Papers, NYHS; *OR*, 27, pt. 3, pp. 373–74.

37. *OR*, 27, pt. 1, p. 61.

38. Quaife, ed., *From the Cannon's Mouth*, p. 221.

39. *OR*, 27, 1, pt. 1, pp. 61–62, 64–65, 66–67; pt. 3, pp. 329, 334, 336, 344, 352, 360, 363, 375; analysis of Meade's plans in Coddington, *Gettysburg Campaign*, pp. 224–25.

40. *OR*, 27, pt. 3, p. 373, Wert, *Custer*, pp. 81, 82.

41. *OR*, 27, pt. 3, pp. 376, 806.

42. *OR*, 27, pt. 1, p. 61; Agassiz, ed., *Meade's Headquarters*, pp. 9, 80; Gibbon, *Personal Recollections*, p. 131; Byrne and Weaver, eds., *Haskell*, p. 133; Acken, ed., *Inside*, p. 343.

43. Coddington, *Gettysburg Campaign*, p. 227; Smart, ed., *Radical View*, v. 2, p. 12; Howard, Memoranda, USAMHI; Flanigan Diary, DPL; Smith, *History*, p. 62; Cassedy, ed., *Dear Friends*, p. 288; Favill, *Diary*, p. 241; Marvin Diary, MNHS; Schildt, *Roads to Gettysburg*, pp. 357–58.

44. Schildt, *Roads to Gettysburg*, pp. 400–401; Howard, Memoranda, USAMHI; Pfanz, *Gettysburg—The First Day*, p. 45; Cavada Diary, HSP; Gouverneur K. Warren–Emily, June 29, 1863, Warren Papers, NYSA.

45. *OR*, 27, pt. 1, pp. 458–59; pt. 3, pp. 416, 417, 419, 420, 421, 422, 423, 701; Pfanz, *Gettysburg—The First Day*, p. 45; Coddington, *Gettysburg Campaign*, pp. 237–41; Trudeau, *Gettysburg*, pp. 150–51; Sears, *Gettysburg*, pp. 186–87.

46. Racine, "*Unspoiled Heart*," p. 46; Cassedy, ed., *Dear Friends*, p. 288; Bee, *Boys*, p. 143; Bennett, *Sons of Old Monroe*, pp. 220, 223; *Snyder County Historical Society Bulletins*, v. 1, p. 357; Holford Diary, LC; Robert Cruikshank–Wife, June 30, 1863, Cruikshank Civil War Letters, USAMHI.

47. Hiram S. Wilson–My Darling Love, June 13, 20, 1863, Wilson Papers, NYSL; Lassen, ed., *Dear Sarah*, p. 132; Bryne and Weaver, eds., *Haskell*, p. 92.

48. Longacre, *General John Buford*, p. 188; Pfanz, *Gettysburg—The First Day*, p. 42; Sears, *Gettysburg*, p. 153.

49. Wert, *General James Longstreet*, p. 251.

50. Wert, *Gettysburg*, p. 24.

51. Wert, *General James Longstreet*, pp. 251–52.

52. Coddington, *Gettysburg Campaign*, pp. 263–64; Trudeau, *Gettysburg*, pp. 140–41; *OR*, 27, pt. 2, p. 607.

Chapter 13: "An Army of Lions"

1. Coddington, *Gettysburg Campaign*, pp. 264–65; Sears, *Gettysburg*, pp. 154–55.
2. Pfanz, *Gettysburg—The First Day*, pp. 53, 58, 59; Trudeau, *Gettysburg*, pp. 164–67.
3. Wert, *Brotherhood*, p. 250; Pfanz, *Gettysburg—The First Day*, pp. 60–65.
4. Coddington, *Gettysburg Campaign*, p. 277, 278; Pfanz, *Gettysburg—The First Day*, pp. 73–74; Sears, *Gettysburg*, p. 166; Account of Gettysburg, Wadsworth Papers, LC.
5. Wert, *Gettysburg*, pp. 250–51; William Riddle–Sir, August 4, 1863, Reynolds Family Papers, FM; Pfanz, *Gettysburg—The First Day*, p. 81; Higginson, *Harvard Memorial Biographies*, v. 1, p. 7; Jacob F. Slagle–Brother, September 13, 1863, Slagle Letter; Jennings, "Reminiscences," p. 3, USAMHI.
6. Wert, *Brotherhood*, p. 251; Pfanz, *Gettysburg—The First Day*, pp. 84–86; McLean, *Cutler's Brigade*, pp. 66–69; Coco, ed., *From Ball's Bluff to Gettysburg*, p. 158; Abel G. Peck–Child [Alice], November 2, 1862, Peck Letters, MSU.
7. Wert, *Brotherhood*, pp. 251–52; Trudeau, *Gettysburg*, p. 184; William Riddle–Sir, August 4, 1863, Reynolds Family Papers, FM; Rosengarten, *Reynolds Memorial Address*, p. 31; Nichols, *Toward Gettysburg*, p. 189.
8. Wert, *Brotherhood*, pp. 252, 254; William Orr–Maggie, July 27, 1863, Orr Papers, IU.
9. Pfanz, *Gettysburg—The First Day*, pp. 86, 87; McLean, *Cutler's Brigade*, Chapters 5–7; Wert, *Brotherhood*, pp. 255–58.
10. Pfanz, *Gettysburg—The First Day*, pp. 120–22, 124–29; Trudeau, *Gettysburg*, p. 206; Account of Gettysburg, Wadsworth Papers, LC.
11. Pfanz, *Gettysburg—The First Day*, pp. 120, 127–30; Wert, *Brotherhood*, p. 259; Coddington, *Gettysburg Campaign*, pp. 282, 300.
12. Gallagher, ed., *First Day at Gettysburg*, pp. 70–74; Howard, Memoranda, USAMHI; Keifer, *History*, p. 121; Pfanz, *Gettysburg—The First Day*, pp. 136–37.
13. Coddington, *Gettysburg Campaign*, p. 301; Winkler, *Letters*, p. 69; Keifer, *History*, p. 209; Pfanz, *Gettysburg—The First Day*, pp. 236, 351; Gallagher, ed., *First Day at Gettysburg*, pp. 77, 78; Hartwig, "11th Army Corps," GM, v. 2, pp. 33, 34, 35, 39.
14. Wert, *General James Longstreet*, p. 253; Pfanz, *Gettysburg—The First Day*, pp. 275–76; Trudeau, *Gettysburg*, pp. 218–20.
15. Pfanz, *Gettysburg—The First Day*, pp. 157–93; Hall, *History*, p. 138; Small, ed., *Road*, p. 100.
16. Pfanz, *Gettysburg—The First Day*, pp. 194–96; Wert, *Brotherhood*, pp. 259–60.
17. Wert, *Brotherhood*, pp. 260, 262, 265.
18. Ibid., pp. 261–62; William Orr–Maggie, July 27, 1863, Orr Papers, IU; Charles W. Fuller–Brother, July 20, 1863, Fuller Papers, SHSW; Chamberlin, *History*, pp. 122, 128, 130, 133; Pfanz, *Gettysburg—The First Day*, pp. 194, 198, 291–92; Trudeau, *Gettysburg*, p. 232; Dreese, *151st Pennsylvania Volunteers*, p. 3.
19. Wert, *Brotherhood*, p. 263; Pfanz, *Gettysburg—The First Day*, pp. 305–20; Stevens, "Account," MESA; Hubler, "Narrative," p. 6, USAMHI; Barber and Swinson, eds., *Civil War Letters*, p. 136.
20. Wert, *Brotherhood*, pp. 263–64; William Orr–Maggie, July 27, 1863, Orr Papers, IU; Charles W. Fuller–Brother, July 20, 1863, Fuller Papers, SHSW.

21. Hartwig, "11th Army Corps," *GM*, v. 2, p. 49; Pfanz, *Gettysburg—The First Day*, pp. 236, 248; Charles H. Howard–My Dear [?], July 9, 1863, Howard Papers, BC; Winkler, *Letters*, pp. 68–71; Pula, *Sigel Regiment*, pp. 163, 166, 168; Francis Barlow–My dear Mother, July 7, 1863, Barlow Papers, MAHS; Keifer, *History*, pp. 173, 180, 210, 213.

22. Pfanz, *Gettysburg—The First Day*, pp. 258–68; Gallagher, ed., *First Day at Gettysburg*, pp. 81, 82; Dunkelman and Winey, *Hardtack Regiment*, pp. 73, 75, 76.

23. Pfanz, *Gettysburg—The First Day*, pp. 337, 338; Cozzens, ed., *B&L*, v. 5, p. 353; Walker, *History*, p. 265; *OR*, 27, pt. 3, p. 461.

24. Pfanz, *Gettysburg—The First Day*, pp. 338–39; Abner Doubleday–S. O. Donnell, February 26, 1891, Doubleday Letter; Henney, *Diary and Letters*, p. 108, USAMHI.

25. Trudeau, *Gettysburg*, pp. 247, 256–57; Pfanz, *Gettysburg—The First Day*, pp. 344–49; Sears, *Gettysburg*, pp. 233–34, 241.

26. Gallagher, ed., *Second Day at Gettysburg*, pp. 94–96, 98; Coddington, *Gettysburg Campaign*, pp. 311, 312; Pfanz, *Gettysburg—The First Day*, pp. 142, 143; *OR*, 27, pt. 3, p. 463; Henry W. Slocum–Messrs. T. H. Davis & Co., September 8, 1875, Bates Collection, PHMC.

27. Coddington, *Gettysburg Campaign*, pp. 312, 313; Sears, *Gettysburg*, p. 241; Gallagher, ed., *Second Day at Gettysburg*, pp. 100, 101; Trudeau, *Gettysburg*, p. 222; Henry W. Slocum–Messrs. T. H. Davis & Co., September 8, 1875, Bates Collection, PHMC; Charles H. Howard–My Dear [?], July 9, 1863, Howard Papers, BC.

28. Coddington, *Gettysburg Campaign*, p. 307; Rowley, Testimony, pp. 1–23, USAMHI.

29. Pfanz, *Gettysburg—The First Day*, p. 333; *OR*, 27, pt. 1, pp. 173–74, 182–83; Coddington, *Gettysburg Campaign*, p. 307; Rufus R. Dawes–My dear Mary, July 9, 1863, Dawes Papers, SHSW; Schildt, *Roads to Gettysburg*, p. 98.

30. Smart, ed., *Radical View*, v. 2, p. 17; James C. Biddle–My own darling Wife, July 6, 1863, Biddle Civil War Letters; George Meade–Mama, July 1, 8, 1863, Meade Collection, HSP; *OR*, 27, pt. 1, pp. 70, 71; pt. 3, pp. 462, 463.

31. *OR*, 27, pt. 1, pp. 71–72; pt. 3, pp. 465–68; Trudeau, *Gettysburg*, pp. 264–66.

32. Trudeau, *Gettysburg*, p. 266; Clement Hoffman–Mother, July 5, 1863, Hoffman Papers, USAMHI; Diary, Paine Papers, NYHS; James Biddle–My own darling little Wife, July 1, 1863, Biddle Civil War Letters, HSP.

33. Pfanz, *Gettysburg—The Second Day*, pp. 42, 58; Wert, *Gettysburg*, p. 28.

34. Wert, *Gettysburg*, pp. 28–29.

35. Ibid., p. 29; Trudeau, *Gettysburg*, p. 291; *OR*, 27, pt. 1, p. 72.

36. *OR*, 27, pt. 2, p. 308; Wert, *General James Longstreet*, pp. 254–55.

37. Wert, *General James Longstreet*, pp. 254–55, 258, 265–70.

38. Wert, *General James Longstreet*, p. 255; Francis Barlow–My dear Mother, July 7, 1863, Barlow Papers, MAHS.

39. James C. Biddle–My own darling little Wife, July 1, 1863, Biddle Civil War Letters, HSP; Marvin Diary, MNHS; Diary, Garcelon Papers, USAMHI; Byrne and Weaver, eds., *Haskell*, p. 122; Francis Long–Wife, July 2, 1863, Picerno Collection; Sears, *Gettysburg*, p. xiii.

40. Moe, *Last Full Measure*, p. 261; Coco, ed., *From Ball's Bluff to Gettysburg*, pp. 196–97; Gambone, *Life*, p. 7.

41. Trudeau, *Gettysburg*, pp. 119, 421; John H. Burrill–Ella, July 1, 1863, Burrill

Letters and Diary, USAMHI; Styple, ed., *Writing*, p. 218; Gallagher, ed., *Second Day at Gettysburg*, p. 41; Ford, ed., *War Letters*, p. 318; Cavada Diary, HSP; Cleaves, *Meade*, p. 149n.

42. Pfanz, *Gettysburg—The Second Day*, pp. 87–88, 91, 124, 425; Byrne and Weaver, eds., *Haskell*, p. 177; Gallagher, ed., *Second Day at Gettysburg*, pp. 46–48, 50, 54–56; Trudeau, *Gettysburg*, p. 421; Coddington, *Gettysburg Campaign*, pp. 347, 348, 351, 352; *B&L*, v. 3, pp. 301–2.

43. Wert, *General James Longstreet*, pp. 270–72, 274.

44. Wert, *Gettysburg*, p. 29; Byrne and Weaver, eds., *Haskell*, p. 120; John E. Ryder–Father, February 10, 1863, Ryder Letters, UM.

45. De Trobriand, *Four Years*, p. 497; Pfanz, *Gettysburg—The Second Day*, Chapters 8–13 are the most detailed account of the action.

46. Pfanz, *Gettysburg—The Second Day*, pp. 185–87, 343–45; Silliker, ed., *Rebel Yell*, pp. 101–2; Townsend, "History," pp. 17, 18, UME; Campbell, ed., "*Grand Terrible Dramma*," pp. 114–15; Scott, *History*, p. 83.

47. Pfanz, *Gettysburg—The Second Day*, pp. 208–24; Jordan, "*Happiness*," pp. 92–93, 125, 126, 127, 128; Joshua L. Chamberlain–Fanny, July 4, 11, 1863; Gettysburg report, July 6, 1863, Chamberlain Papers, LC; Oliver Norton–Henry S. Burrage, May 6, 1910, Norton Papers, CMU.

48. Pfanz, *Gettysburg—The Second Day*, pp. 77, 236–37; Bennett, *Sons of Old Monroe*, pp. 229, 230, 231, 233–35.

49. Bennett, *Sons of Old Monroe*, pp. 235, 237, 241, 243, 244; Pfanz, *Gettysburg—The Second Day*, pp. 237–40.

50. Pfanz, *Gettysburg—The Second Day*, pp. 256–66; Joshua G. Wilbur–My dear Wife, July 2, 3, 1863, Wilbur Letters, USAMHI; P. R. Guiney–My dear General, October 26, 1865, Chamberlain Papers, LC; Sears, *Gettysburg*, p. 35; Campbell, "Caldwell," GM, v. 3, pp. 26, 31, 33, 35; Gallagher, ed., *Second Day at Gettysburg*, pp. 136–37, 141, 146.

51. Campbell, "Caldwell," GM, v. 3, pp. 34–35, 37, 39, 41, 49; Gallagher, ed., *Second Day at Gettysburg*, pp. 147, 156, 170; Gambone, *Life*, pp. 12, 32, 33; Favill, *Diary*, pp. 245–48; Linn, "Journal," pp. 11, 12, USAMHI.

52. Pride and Travis, *My Brave Boys*, pp. 234, 235, 238, 239, 243; Child, *History*, pp. 206, 213; Bingham, "Anecdotes," WRHS; Charles Hale, "With Colonel Cross in the Gettysburg Campaign," pp. 1–4, 6, 7, 10, 12, Brooke Papers, HSP; Livermore, *Days and Events*, pp. 255, 256.

53. The best description of the Wheatfield fight by Caldwell's division is in Pfanz, *Gettysburg—The Second Day*, Chapter 12; Pride and Travis, *My Brave Boys*, p. 241; Trudeau, *Gettysburg*, p. 365; Gibbs, *Three Years*, p. 222; Hardin, *History*, p. 153; Benjamin F. Ashenfelter–Father Churchman, July 29, 1863, Ashenfelter Letters, USAMHI.

54. Gibbs, *Three Years*, pp. 222, 224; J. R. Dobson–Samuel Crawford, January 16, 1882, Crawford Papers, LC; E. M. Woodward–Samuel P. Bates, February 7, 1876, Pennsylvania–31ˢᵗ Infantry Reserves, USAMHI; Pfanz, *Gettysburg—The Second Day*, pp. 394–401.

55. Pfanz, *Gettysburg—The Second Day*, pp. 404–7; Willson, *Disaster*, pp. 170, 171, 177.

56. Lewis H. Crandell–Eunice, July 6, 1863, Crandell Account, USAMHI; Coddington, *Gettysburg Campaign*, p. 418; *OR*, 27, pt. 1, p. 453.

57. Leehan, *Pale Horse*, pp. 56–59, 62–67, 69, 74, 75, 173, 179; Marvin Diary;

Alfred Carpenter–[?], July 30, 1863, Carpenter Papers, MNHS; Smith, *History*, p. 71; Moe, *Last Full Measure*, pp. 265–73.

58. Pfanz, *Gettysburg—The Second Day*, pp. 414–15; Coddington, *Gettysburg Campaign*, pp. 424–26; Busey and Martin, *Regimental Strengths*, pp. 16, 32, 44, 61, 64, 65, 66; Wert, *General James Longstreet*, pp. 274–75.

59. Coddington, *Gettysburg Campaign*, p. 426; Pfanz, *Gettysburg—The First Day*, p. 355; Young, *Battle of Gettysburg*, p. 343; Smith, *History*, p. 77.

60. Sears, *Gettysburg*, pp. 305–6; Trudeau, *Gettysburg*, pp. 292, 420, 421; George G. Meade–Margaret, July 8, 1863, Meade Collection, HSP; Magner, *Traveller*, p. 6; OR, 27, pt. 1, p. 826; Gallagher, ed., *Second Day at Gettysburg*, pp. 113–17; Henry W. Slocum–Messrs. T. H. Davis & Co., September 8, 1875, Bates Collection, PHMC.

61. OR, 27, pt. 1, p. 856; Motts, "To Gain a Second Star," GM, v. 3, pp. 65, 67, 68; Tagg, *Generals*, p. 162; Washington *Post*, July 9, 1899; Steuben W. Coon–Father, August 14, 1863, Coon Papers, USAMHI; Robert Cruikshank–Wife, July 2, 1863, Cruikshank Civil War Letters, AFHS; Collins, *Memoirs*, p. 137; Ladd and Ladd, eds., *Bachelder Papers*, v. 2, pp. 290, 293; Busey and Martin, *Regimental Strengths*, pp. 96, 151.

62. Steuben W. Coon–My Dear Father, August 14, 1863, Coon Papers, USAMHI; OR, 27, pt. 1, pp. 856, 857; Ladd and Ladd, eds., *Bachelder Papers*, v. 1, pp. 293, 295, 296; Baumgartner, *Buckeye Blood*, pp. 112, 113; Powell, Memoirs, OHS; Sauers, ed., *Fighting Them Over*, pp. 357–58.

63. Coddington, *Gettysburg Campaign*, pp. 435–37; Keifer, *History*, p. 142; Wert, *General James Longstreet*, p. 276.

64. Wert, *Gettysburg*, pp. 15, 16; Rollins, "George Gordon Meade," GM, v. 19, p. 77; OR, 27, 1, p. 72; McLean and McLean, eds., *Gettysburg Sources*, v. 2, p. 83; Trudeau, *Gettysburg*, p. 413; Fishel, *Secret War*, pp. 527, 528.

65. Wert, *Gettysburg*, pp. 16, 17; Byrne and Weaver, eds., *Haskell*, pp. 110, 134; Cleaves, *Meade*, p. 155; Gibbon, *Personal Recollections*, p. 140; Westbrook, *History*, pp. 153, 154; Keiser Diary, p. 70, USAMHI; Rhodes, ed., *All for the Union*, pp. 115, 116; Maier, *Rough and Regular*, p. 82.

66. OR, 27, pt. 3, p. 465; Hyde, *Civil War Letters*, p. 97; SOR, 5, pp. 93, 120; John C. Robinson–Sir, June 3, 1888, Participant Accounts, WRHS; Account of Gettysburg, Wadsworth Papers, LC; Jacob Slagle–Brother, September 13, 1863, Slagle Letters, NYHS; David B. Birney–Gross, October 28, 1863, Birney Papers, USAMHI; Pfanz, *Gettysburg—The First Day*, p. 355.

67. Wert, *Gettysburg*, pp. 16–17; Gallagher, ed., *Three Days*, pp. 233, 234; Sickles et al., "Further Recollections," *North American Review*, March 1891, p. 276; John Gibbon–Henry J. Hunt, May 31, 1879, Hunt Papers, LC; OR, 27, pt. 1, pp. 73–74; Gibbon, *Personal Recollections*, pp. 140–45.

68. OR, 27, pt. 2, p. 320; Wert, *General James Longstreet*, pp. 278–80.

69. Benedict, *Army Life*, p. 169; Byrne and Weaver, eds. *Haskell*, p. 128; Excerpt of a letter of Felix Brannigan, 73rd New York, Brake Collection; Philo H. Conklin–Friend Mary, July 31, 1863, Johnson Family Papers, USAMHI; Maust, "Union Second Corps Hospital," GM, v. 10, p. 59; Henry Clare–My dear William, July 5, 1863, Clare Letters, GC.

70. Wert, *Gettysburg*, Chapters 3–4.

71. Ibid., pp. 61–70, 75–88.

72. Ibid., pp. 75–91; 137th New York Soldier–Father & Mother, July 7, 1863, 137th New York Infantry File, GNMP; William Sayre–Father and Mother Brother and Sisters, July 5, 1863, Sayre Letters, USAMHI; OR, 27, pt. 3, p. 500.

73. Wert, Gettysburg, pp. 98–101; Sorrel, Recollections, p. 162.

74. Wert, Gettysburg, pp. 101–2; Coddington, Gettysburg Campaign, pp. 459, 463.

75. Wert, Gettysburg, pp. 102–4.

76. Ibid., pp. 120–26, 156–57, 159–63; Silliker, ed., Rebel Yell, p. 103; Byrne and Weaver, eds., Haskell, p. 139; David M. Smith–[Family], July 10, 1863, Smith Letters, NYHS; George H. Woods–David B. Birney, July 3, 1863, Woods Papers, USAMHI; George G. Meade–Dearest Love, July 3, 1863, Meade Collection, HSP.

77. OR, 27, pt. 1, p. 238; Griffith, Battle Tactics, pp. 167, 168; Ladd and Ladd, eds., Bachelder Papers, v. 1, pp. 228, 229.

78. Wert, Gettysburg, Chapter 9; George Cramer–Wife, July 11, 1863, 11th Pennsylvania Infantry File, GNMP; Hartwig, "It Struck Horror," GM, v. 4, p. 95; Alexander Webb–Father, July 17, 1863, Webb Papers, YU; Diary, Paine Papers, NYHS; Gallagher, ed., Third Day, pp. 140, 141; Archer, "Remembering," GM, v. 9, p. 74.

79. Wert, Gettysburg, pp. 182–85.

80. Ibid., p. 192.

81. Ibid., Chapter 10; Moe, Last Full Measure, p. 289; Alfred P. Carpenter–[?], July 30, 1863, Carpenter Papers, MNHS; Ladd and Ladd, eds., Bachelder Papers, v. 3, p. 1409; Scott, ed., Fallen Leaves, p. 188; Tully McCrae, "Reminiscence About Gettysburg," 1st U.S. Artillery, Battery I File, GNMP; "Weather Conditions During the Battle of Gettysburg," Kauffman Collection, USAMHI; Mahood, "Written in Blood," p. 126.

82. Haines, History, p. 41; Bee, Boys, p. 150; Archer, "Remembering," GM, v. 9, p. 77; undated newspaper clipping, Robbins Papers, UNC; Wright, "Story," p. 610, GNMP; Longacre, To Gettysburg and Beyond, p. 135; Gallagher, ed., Third Day, p. 142.

83. Wert, Gettysburg, Chapters 11–12; Stevens and Knowlton, Address, p. 22; Belknap Diary, USAMHI; Cyril Tyler–Father, July 7, 1863, 7th Michigan Infantry File, GNMP; Nathan Hayward–Father, July 8, 1863, Hayward Papers, MAHS.

84. Wert, Gettysburg, pp. 231–32; Meinhard, "First Minnesota," GM, v. 5, p. 87; Wright, "Story," p. 612, GNMP; Alexander Webb–Father, July 17, 1863, Webb Papers, YU.

85. Minneapolis State Atlas, August 26, 1863; Loren H. Goodrich–Friends, July 17, 1863, Goodrich Papers, CTHS; Belknap Diary; Frank Whittemore–Parents, July 5, 1863, Whittemore Letter, USAMHI; Wert, Gettysburg, pp. 231–36, 240–42, quote on p. 251.

86. Cavada Diary, HSP; Alexander Webb–Dearest Annie, July 27, 1863, Webb Papers, YU; Francis Long–Wife, July 5, 1863, Picerno Collection; Fleming, Life, p. 442; Belknap Diary; Alexander McNeil–Friend Porter, August 16, 1863, Chesson Collection; John D. Musser–[?], September 15, 1863, Musser Correspondence, USAMHI.

87. "Sketches from . . . Gettysburg—The Third Day," p. 6, Gibbon Papers, HSP; Gibbon, Personal Recollections, p. 170; Winfield S. Hancock–P. F. Rothermel, December 31, 1868, Rothermel Papers, PHMC; Wert, Gettysburg, p. 219; OR, 27, pt. 1, p. 366.

88. George G. Meade–John R. Bachelder, December 4, 1869, Rothermel Papers, PHMC; Ladd and Ladd, eds., *Bachelder Papers*, v. 2, pp. 854–55; George Meade–Alexander S. Webb, November 11, 1883, Webb Papers, YU; Wert, *Gettysburg*, pp. 175, 253.

89. Wert, *Gettysburg*, pp. 253–54; Coddington, *Gettysburg Campaign*, p. 534; Trudeau, *Gettysburg*, pp. 527–28.

90. Wert, *Gettysburg*, pp. 259–60.

91. Ibid., pp. 255–58, 260–61; Crowninshield, *History*, p. 300; Meyer, *Civil War*, pp. 48, 49; Agassiz, ed., *Meade's Headquarters*, p. 17.

92. Wert, *Gettysburg*, pp. 266–68.

93. Ibid., pp. 268–71; William Brooke-Rawle–William E. Miller, June 12, 1878, Rawle Papers, HSP; Andrew Newton Buck–Brother & Sisters, July 9, 1863, Buck Family Papers; James Kidd–Father & Mother, July 9, 1863, Kidd Papers; J. A. Clark–Friend, July 30, 1863, UM; OR, 27, pt. 1, pp. 956–57.

94. Wert, *Gettysburg*, pp. 271, 272; OR, 27, pt. 1, pp. 957, 958; Edward Corselius–Mother, July 4, 1863, Corselius Papers, UM.

95. Wert, *Gettysburg*, pp. 272–80.

96. Rufus R. Dawes–My dear Mary, July 6, 1863, Dawes Papers, SHSW; John L. Harding–Sister, July 18, 1863, Harding Papers, IU; John H. Burrill–Parents, July 13, 1863, Burrill Letters; Norman Williams–Brother, July 10, 1863, Williams Family Letters, USAMHI; Whitmore Diary, MAHS; Fleming, ed., *Life*, p. 421; Cassedy, ed., *Dear Friends*, p. 291; Washburn, *Complete Military History*, p. 124; Blair, ed., *Politician*, p. 100; Albert Stokes Emmell, " 'Now Is the Time for Buck & Ball': The Life and Civil War Experience of Albert Stokes Emmell," 12th New Jersey Infantry File; Extract of a letter of E. Corbin, July 5, 1863, Pettit's Battery Letters; Homer Baldwin–Father, July 7, 1863, 5th United States Artillery, Battery C File, GNMP.

97. Wert, *Gettysburg*, p. 290; Fox, *Regimental Losses*, pp. 41, 42, 439–40; Sears, *Gettysburg*, pp. 496, 516–43.

98. Smart, ed., *Radical View*, v. 2, p. 63; Silliker, ed., *Rebel Yell*, p. 111; Bennett, *Sons of Old Monroe*, p. 255; Toledo *Blade*, July 11, 1863; Cavada Diary, HSP; Walton, ed., *Civil War Courtship*, p. 51; William A. Allison–Stock, July 18, 1863, Allison Letters, NYHS; Baxter, *Gallant Fourteenth*, p. 152; "Civil War Union Soldier's 1863 Diary," USAMHI; David E. Beem–My dear Wife, July 5, 1863, Beem Papers, IHS.

99. Priest, ed., *One Surgeon's Private War*, p. 77; Wert, *Gettysburg*, p. 294; Samuel B. Carter–Vincent B. Brewer, July 9, 1863, Carter Letter, USAMHI.

100. Wert, *Gettysburg*, p. 298; Griffith, *Battle Tactics*, p. 38.

101. Sears, *Gettysburg*, pp. 506, 507; Griffith, *Battle Tactics*, p. 38; Wert, *Gettysburg*, p. 298; Nevins, ed., *Diary of the Civil War*, p. 330; George G. Meade–Margaret, July 5, 1863; George Meade–My Dear Mama, July 6, 1863, Meade Collection, HSP; Crumb and Dhalle, eds., *No Middle Ground*, p. 149; Byrne and Weaver, eds., *Haskell*, pp. 112, 187; Israel Thickstun–Brother Comp, July 6, 1863, Thickstun Family Papers, USAMHI; Powell, *Fifth Army Corps*, p. 559.

102. Chamberlain, *Passing of the Armies*, p. 30.

103. Alexander, "Ten Days in July," *N&S*, 2, 6, pp. 13–14, 16–18, 22–24; Wert, *Gettysburg*, p. 300.

104. OR, 27, pt. 1, p. 78; pt. 3, p. 519; Coddington, Gettysburg Campaign, pp. 539–41, 544.

105. Coddington, Gettysburg Campaign, pp. 545, 546; Williams, "'We Had Only,'" N&S, 2, 2, p. 69; Alexander, "Ten Days in July," N&S, 2, 6, p. 12.

106. Alexander, "Ten Days in July," N&S, 2, 6, p. 12; Rufus R. Dawes–My dear Mary, July 14, 1863, Dawes Papers, SHSW; Marshall, Company "K," p. 114; A. H. Davis–Seth Williams, July 9, 1863, RG 393, NA; Oliver O. Howard–Wife, July 18, 1863, Howard Papers, BC; William J. Evans–Father & Mother, July 9, 1863, Evans Letters; Howard, Memoranda; Henry J. Hunt–My dear Eunice, July 28, 1863, Ford Papers, USAMHI.

107. Saunders Diary, MESA; Silliker, ed., Rebel Yell, p. 109; Rhodes, History, p. 222; Gulian V. Weir–Dearest Father, July 5, 1863, 5th United States Artillery, Battery C File, GNMP; Henry J. Hunt–My dear Eunice, July 28, 1863, Ford Papers, USAMHI; Coddington, Gettysburg Campaign, pp. 552, 555, 556, 564.

108. OR, 27, pt. 1, p. 82; Pfanz, Gettysburg—The Second Day, p. 426; Cleaves, Meade, p. 130; Jordan, "Happiness," p. 87; Gouverneur K. Warren–Emily, July [?] 1863, Warren Papers, NYSA; Marbaker, History, p. 112; Cavada Diary, HSP; Humphreys, Andrew A. Humphreys, pp. 200, 201.

109. Welcher, Union Army, p. 30; de Trobriand, Four Years, p. 517; Leivelsberger Diary, USAMHI; Townsend, "History," p. 141, UME; Poulter, "Errors," N&S, 2, 6, pp. 86, 87; Warner, Generals in Blue, p. 225; Sears, Gettysburg, p. 495.

110. Alexander, "Ten Days in July," N&S, 2, 6, pp. 13–14, 16–18, 22–24, 26–29.

111. Brown, "Golden Bridge," N&S, 2, 6, pp. 56, 58.

112. Cleaves, Meade, p. 179; de Trobriand, Four Years, pp. 521, 522; Page, Letters, p. 35; Henry J. Hunt–My dear Eunice, July 28, 1863, Ford Papers, USAMHI; Coddington, Gettysburg Campaign, pp. 567–69; Sears, Gettysburg, p. 489.

113. Coddington, Gettysburg Campaign, pp. 570–72; Brady, ed., Hurrah, p. 263; Joseph J. Bartlett–W. W. Winthrop, August 12, 1863, Bartlett Papers, LC; Cavada Diary, HSP; Byrne and Weaver, eds., Haskell, p. 183; Walker and Walker, eds., Diary, p. 116; Cortland (N.Y.) Gazette and Banner, August 13, 1863; Noble, "Diary," UM; Cassedy, ed., Dear Friends, p. 296; Furst Diary; David Nichol–Father, July 16, 1863, Nichol Papers; Henry Van Aernum–My dearest Lis, July 15, 1863, Van Aernum Papers, USAMHI.

114. Beale, ed., Diary, v. 1, p. 370; Boritt, ed., Lincoln's Generals, p. 83.

115. Boritt, ed., Lincoln's Generals, pp. 89, 91.

116. OR, 27, pt. 1, p. 92.

117. Ibid., pp. 93, 94.

118. Boritt, ed., Lincoln's Generals, p. 105.

119. Ibid., pp. 110, 111.

Chapter 14: Virginia Interlude

1. Thomas Carpenter–Phil, September 2, 1863, Carpenter Letters, MOHS.

2. Meade, Life and Letters, v. 2, p. 136; Cassedy, ed., Dear Friends, pp. 297–98, 301, 303, 304, 306; Silliker, ed., Rebel Yell, p. 115.

3. Muffly, ed., Story, p. 96; Sparks, ed., Inside Lincoln's Army, pp. 274, 275; Andrew A. Humphreys–Wife, August 4, 1863, Humphreys Papers, HSP; Henry F. Prindle–Mother, July 30, 1863, Prindle Letters; Henry Blanchard–Parents, July

26, 1863, Blanchard Letters, USAMHI; Silliker, ed., *Rebel Yell*, p. 113; Cassedy, ed., *Dear Friends*, p. 314; Herdegen, *Men Stood*, p. 17; Dunn, *Iron Men*, p. 217; William Glossinger–Friend Thomas, July 28, 1863, Glossinger Papers; Diary, Stacy Papers, NC; Rufus R. Dawes–My dear Mary, August 6, 1863, Dawes Papers, SHSW.

4. Welcher, *Union Army*, p. 14; Dunn, *Harvestfields*, p. 199; Rosenblatt and Rosenblatt, eds., *Hard Marching*, pp. 140, 147, 150; Galwey, *Valiant Hours*, pp. 132, 139; Keifer, *Slavery*, v. 2, pp. 45, 47; Reese, *Sykes' Regular Infantry Division*, p. 289; Walker, *History*, p. 311; Meade, *Life and Letters*, v. 2, p. 143.

5. Geary, *We Need Men*, pp. 70, 81, 85; Meade, *Life and Letters*, v. 2, pp. 143, 146; Nevins, ed., *Diary*, p. 270; Willis M. Porter–Esther, October 9, 1863, Porter Civil War Diary and Letters, MESA; Small, ed., *Road*, p. 116; Charles A. Wheeler–My dear C, September 8, 29, 1863, Wheeler Papers, NC; William H. Peacock–Sarah, September 13, 1863, Peacock Letters, USAMHI; Dawes, *Service*, p. 202; Seth Gilbert Evans–Home, September 1, 1863, Evans Papers, NC; Smith, *History*, p. 134.

6. Muffly, ed., *Story*, p. 479; Hezekiah Long–Loved ones at home, August 19, 1863, Long Civil War Letters; Townsend, "History," pp. 151, 152, UME; Agassiz, ed., *Meade's Headquarters*, p. 13; Blair, ed., *Politician*, p. 106; William Orr–Father, September 28, 1863, Orr Papers, IU; Timothy O. Webster–My dear Wife and Children, September 4, 1863, Webster Papers; Alanson Wiles–My Dear Mother, September 22, 1863, Wiles Papers, NC.

7. W. H. Diffenbaugh–Friend, September 27, 1863, Simpson and Simpson, "Dear Daul," USAMHI; Rosenblatt and Rosenblatt, eds., *Hard Marching*, p. 135; Thomas Carpenter–Phil, August 15, 1863, Carpenter Letters, MOHS; Elmer Wallace–Parents, August 23, 1863, Wallace Papers, UM.

8. Cowles, ed., *History*, p. 724; OR, 29, pt. 1, pp. 111–35; Henderson, *Road*, pp. 27–28, 33–41.

9. OR, 29, pt. 2, pp. 179–80; Wert, *General James Longstreet*, pp. 300–301.

10. OR, 29, pt. 2, pp. 3–178; Meade, *Life and Letters*, v. 2, pp. 141, 142; Boritt, ed., *Lincoln's Generals*, p. 114.

11. OR, 29, pt. 2, p. 186, 187.

12. Ibid., pp. 191–92; Henderson, *Road*, pp. 42–63; Wert, *General James Longstreet*, pp. 306–17.

13. OR, 29, pt. 2, pp. 207, 220.

14. Ibid., pp. 207–8.

15. Ibid., pt. 1, pp. 147, 151; pt. 2, 118; Meade, *Life and Letters*, v. 2, p. 150.

16. OR, 29, pt. 1, p. 226; Meade, *Life and Letters*, v. 2, p. 150; William S. Keller–Sister, September 27, 1863, Keller Letters, USAMHI.

17. Nevins, ed., *Diary*, p. 284; Walker and Walker, eds., *Diary*, pp. 128, 129; OR, 29, pt. 2, p. 227; Sparks, ed., *Inside Lincoln's Army*, p. 291.

18. OR, 29, pt. 2, pp. 625, 628, 631, 647, 649.

19. Wert, *General James Longstreet*, pp. 297–98; Henderson, *Road*, p. 6; Sears, *Gettysburg*, p. 500; OR, 29, pt. 2, pp. 639–40.

20. Wert, *General James Longstreet*, pp. 300–301; OR, 29, pt. 1, pp. 405, 410; pt. 2, p. 811.

21. Charles A. Wheeler–My Dear C, October 20, 1863, Wheeler Papers, NC; OR, 29, pt. 1, p. 410; Sparks, ed., *Inside Lincoln's Army*, p. 298; Sedgwick, ed., *Corre-*

spondence, v. 2, p. 160; George G. Meade–Winfield S. Hancock, November 6, 1863, Hancock Papers, DU; Samito, ed., *Commanding Boston's Irish Ninth,* p. 228.

22. Henderson, *Road,* pp. 163–70; Walker, *History,* p. 313; Scott, ed., *Fallen Leaves,* p. 191; Jordan, *"Happiness,"* pp. 100, 101; Fleming, ed., *Life,* p. 512; Livermore, *Days and Events,* pp. 272, 285; David B. Birney–Gross, October 28, 1863, Birney Papers, USAMHI.

23. Henderson, *Road,* Chapter 12; reports of Bristoe Station in OR, 29, pt. 1, pp. 235–310, 426–38; Willis M. Porter–Etta, October 25, 1863, Porter Civil War Diary and Letters, USAMHI; Rhodes, *History,* p. 248; Fleming, ed., *Life,* p. 496.

24. OR, 29, pt. 1, p. 411; Wert, *Custer,* pp. 118–22; Henderson, *Road,* pp. 201–8.

25. Sparks, ed., *Inside Lincoln's Army,* p. 296; Agassiz, ed., *Meade's Headquarters,* pp. 128–29, 176; George G. Meade–Winfield S. Hancock, November 6, 1863, Hancock Papers, DU.

26. Walker and Walker, eds., *Diary,* pp. 137, 137n; Rhodes, ed., *All for the Union,* p. 128; Acken, ed., *Inside,* pp. 377–78; Cassedy, ed., *Dear Friends,* pp. 344, 347.

27. Meade, *Life and Letters,* v. 2, p. 154.

28. Agassiz, ed., *Meade's Headquarters,* pp. 38–39; George G. Meade–Winfield S. Hancock, November 6, 1863, Hancock Papers, DU.

29. Meade, *Life and Letters,* v. 2, p. 137; OR, 29, pt. 2, pp. 409–10, 412.

30. Bird, ed., *Quill,* p. 135; Marbaker, *History,* p. 125; Robertson, ed., *Civil War Letters,* p. 345, OR, 29, pt. 1, p. 316; de Trobriand, *Four Years,* pp. 545, 546.

31. Reports on Rappahannock Station are in OR, 29, pt. 1, pp. 575–636; Trask, *Fire Within,* p. 209; Westbrook, *History,* p. 168; John D. Fish–My Dear Brother, November 12, 1863, Fish Letters, USAMHI; Greiner et al., eds., *Surgeon's Civil War,* p. 155; Cassedy, ed., *Dear Friends,* p. 352.

32. OR, 29, pt. 1, p. 575; pt. 2, p. 435; Clark S. Edwards–Wife, November 8, 1863, Edwards Papers, NC; Hyde, *Civil War Letters,* p. 113; Nevins, ed., *Diary,* p. 299; Meade, *Life and Letters,* v. 2, p. 155; Thomas Carpenter–Phil, November 13, 1863, Carpenter Letters, MOHS.

33. Meade, *Life and Letters,* v. 2, pp. 155–56; OR, 29, pt. 2, pp. 409–10, 412.

34. Meade, *Life and Letters,* v. 2, p. 157; OR, 29, pt. 2, pp. 480–81, 488.

35. OR, 29, pt. 1, pp. 736–38, 761–64, 847; Freeman, *Lee's Lieutenants,* v. 3, pp. 272–73; Robertson, ed., *Civil War Letters,* p. 364; Wert, *Brotherhood,* pp. 277–78; Nevins, ed., *Diary,* p. 304.

36. Sears, *Gettysburg,* p. 495; Winslow, *General John Sedgwick,* p. 135; Silliker, ed., *Rebel Yell,* p. 112; David B. Birney–Gross, October 28, 1863, Birney Papers, USAMHI; Arner, *Mutiny,* p. 24; Townsend, "History," pp. 152, 158, UME.

37. Sparks, ed., *Inside Lincoln's Army,* pp. 315, 316; Freeman, *Lee's Lieutenants,* v. 3, p. 275; Jordan, *"Happiness,"* p. 113; Meade, *Life and Letters,* v. 2, p. 157.

38. Carter, *Four Brothers,* p. 375; Freeman, *Lee's Lieutenants,* v. 3, p. 275; Acken, ed., *Inside,* p. 406; Wright, *No More Gallant a Deed,* pp. 386, 387; Page, *History,* p. 202; Fleming, ed., *Life,* p. 524; Robertson, ed., *Civil War Letters,* p. 368; Longacre, *To Gettysburg,* p. 167.

39. Jordan, *"Happiness,"* pp. 113, 114; Agassiz, ed., *Meade's Headquarters,* pp. 56, 57; Meade, *Life and Letters,* v. 2, p. 157; Livermore, *Days and Events,* p. 304; Sparks, ed., *Inside Lincoln's Army,* p. 317.

40. Porter, *Campaigning with Grant*, p. 29; Agassiz, ed., *Meade's Headquarters*, p. 272; Gallagher, ed., *Wilderness Campaign*, p. 67; Meade, *Life and Letters*, v. 2, pp. 157, 158.

41. Sparks, ed., *Inside Lincoln's Army*, p. 318; Galwey, *Valiant Hours*, p. 177; Furst Diary, p. 53, USAMHI; Parker, *Henry Wilson's Regiment*, p. 386; Willis M. Porter–Esther, December 13, 1863, Civil War Diary and Letters, MESA; James Converse–Wife & Children, December 7, 1863, Converse Letters, CHS; Cassedy, ed., *Dear Friends*, pp. 359, 360; Baxter, ed., *Hoosier Farm Boy*, p. 55.

42. Meade, *Life and Letters*, v. 2, pp. 159, 160; Donald, *Lincoln*, p. 490.

43. Wickman, ed., *Letters to Vermont*, v. 1, p. 183; Parker, *Henry Wilson's Regiment*, p. 387; Sears, ed., *Mr. Dunn Browne's Experiences*, p. 216; Gallagher, ed., *Wilderness Campaign*, pp. 67, 96n; Burr, *Life*, p. 78; Thomas Paxton–Cousin Ellie, December 13, 1863, Paxton Papers; Francis McLean–Friend McFarland, April 2, 1864, McFarland Papers, NC; Styple, ed., *With a Flash of His Sword*, pp. 154–55; Greiner et al., eds., *Surgeon's Civil War*, p. 160; Carter, *Four Brothers*, p. 378.

44. Sears, ed., *Mr. Dunn Browne's Experiences*, p. 205.

45. Hall, "Season of Change," *B&G*, 8, 4, pp. 11–13, 15, 16, 18, 19; A. Spafford–Wife, February 14, 1864, Spafford Papers, NC.

46. Katcher, ed., *Building the Victory*, p. 22; William J. Ketner–[?], March 6, 1864, Ketner Papers, SHSW; Reid-Green, ed., *Letters Home*, p. 75; Wilkeson, *Recollections*, p. 30; J. F. Salley–Mother, March 17, 1864, Salley Letter, UME; Nolan and Vipond, eds., *Giants*, p. 114; Baxter, ed., *Hoosier Farm Boy*, p. 57; Bennett, *Sons of Old Monroe*, p. 367; Seth Gilbert Evans–My Dear Sister Ada & M. L. And our Mother, February 24, 1864, Evans Papers, NC.

47. Robertson, ed., *Civil War Letters*, p. 389; *B&L*, v. 2, p. 154; Caleb H. Beal–Parents, December 23, 1862, Beal Papers, MAHS; Charles A. Wheeler–My dear C, February 14, 1864, Wheeler Papers, NC; Wilkeson, *Recollections*, p. 25; Duram and Duram, eds., *Soldier*, p. 23; J. Lloyd Brown–Sister, March 25, 1864, Brown Letters, UME; Walker and Walker, eds., *Diary*, p. 153; Priest, ed., *One Surgeon's Private War*, p. 93; Hezekiah Long–Sallie, March 17, 1864, Long Civil War Letters, MESA.

48. Jackson Diary, IHS; Rosenblatt and Rosenblatt, eds., *Hard Marching*, pp. 179, 186, 187; Plumb, "Record," p. 23, USAMHI; Longhenry, "Yankee Piper," pp. 3–34, ANB; Noble, "Diary," UM; Rood, Memoir, SHSW.

49. Jackson Diary, IHS; Hall, "Season of Change," *B&G*, 8, 4, p. 52; Cheek and Pointon, *History*, p. 84; Wickman, ed., *Letters to Vermont*, v. 1, p. 186; Sauers, *Advance the Colors!*, v. 2, p. 247; *OR*, 29, pt. 2, pp. 558, 560; Cassedy, ed., *Dear Friends*, p. 374; John A. Willoughby–Daul Simpson, October 29, 1863, Simpson and Simpson, "Dear Daul," USAMHI.

50. Sparks, ed., *Inside Lincoln's Army*, pp. 330, 331; Sedgwick, ed., *Correspondence*, v. 2, p. 175; Agassiz, ed., *Meade's Headquarters*, pp. 6, 7, 8, 73, 307; Andrew A. Humphreys–Wife, August 4, 1863, Humphreys Papers, HSP; David B. Birney–Gross, October 28, 1863, Birney Papers, USAMHI; Humphreys, *Andrew A. Humphreys*, p. 207.

51. Walker, *History*, p. 392; Meade, *Life and Letters*, v. 2, pp. 163, 164; Tucker, *Hancock*, pp. 172, 173.

52. Longacre, *General John Buford*, pp. 241, 243, 244, 245, 246; Agassiz, ed., *Meade's Headquarters*, p. 21; Nevins, ed., *Diary*, p. 309.

53. Wert, *Custer*, p. 139.
54. Ibid., p. 142; Meade, *Life and Letters*, v. 2, p. 190.
55. Meade, *Life and Letters*, v. 2, pp. 190, 191; Wert, *Custer*, p. 142; Schultz, *Dahlgren Affair*, Chapter 22; Sears, *Controversies*, pp. 233, 241–45.
56. Agassiz, ed., *Meade's Headquarters*, p. 78; Meade, *Life and Letters*, v. 2, pp. 173–76; Stowe, "Certain Grave Charges," *Columbiad*, 3, 1, p. 23; Tap, "'Bad Faith Somewhere,'" *N&S*, 2, 6, pp. 77, 78, 80.
57. Tap, "Bad Faith Somewhere," *N&S*, 2, 6, p. 80; Stowe, "Certain Grave Charges," *Columbiad*, 3, 1, pp. 24–28, 29, 30, 32, 33, 35, 36.
58. Gibbon, *Personal Recollections*, pp. 206–7; Henry J. Hunt–My dear Eunice, July 28, 1863, Ford Papers, USAMHI.
59. Meade, *Life and Letters*, v. 2, p. 177; Grant, *Personal Memoirs*, v. 2, p. 117; Catton, *Grant Takes Command*, p. 160.
60. Staudenraus, ed., *Mr. Lincoln's Washington*, pp. 289, 290; McClure, *Abraham Lincoln*, p. 180; Donald, *Lincoln*, pp. 490, 491.
61. Warner, *Generals in Blue*, pp. 183–84; Wert, *General James Longstreet*, p. 50.
62. Agassiz, ed., *Meade's Headquarters*, p. 81; Winik, *April 1865*, pp. 179–80; Schaff, *Battle*, p. 47; Beale, ed., *Diary*, v. 1, p. 539; Cozzens, ed., *B&L*, v. 5, p. 116; Fry, *Military Miscellanies*, pp. 294, 295; Catton, *Grant Takes Command*, p. 160.
63. Agassiz, ed., *Meade's Headquarters*, pp. 83, 84; Ritchie, ed., *Four Years*, p. 153; Ford, ed., *War Letters*, p. 316; Wert, *Custer*, pp. 145, 146; Meade, *Life and Letters*, v. 2, p. 191; Cozzens, ed., *B&L*, v. 5, pp. 113, 114.
64. Meade, *Life and Letters*, v. 2, pp. 162–63.
65. Smith, *Grant*, p. 292; Sumner, ed., *Diary*, p. 260; Meade, *Life and Letters*, v. 2, pp. 176, 177, 178; Grant, *Personal Memoirs*, v. 2, p. 117.
66. Meade, *Life and Letters*, v. 2, p. 178; Grant, *Personal Memoirs*, v. 2, p. 116.
67. Meade, *Life and Letters*, v. 2, pp. 178, 181, 182; Grant, *Personal Memoirs*, v. 2, pp. 117, 118.
68. Grant, *Personal Memoirs*, v. 2, pp. 118, 119; Meade, *Life and Letters*, v. 2, p. 165; Winslow, *General John Sedgwick*, p. 138; Sumner, ed., *Diary*, p. 261.
69. Meade, *Life and Letters*, v. 2, pp. 164, 165; Sumner, ed., *Diary*, p. 261.
70. OR, 33, pp. 717–18, 722–23.
71. Arner, *Mutiny*, pp. 41, 45, 46; Robertson, ed., *Civil War Letters*, pp. 399, 401, 402, 404; Blake, *Three Years*, p. 274; Marbaker, *History*, p. 158; David B. Birney–My dear Gross, March 16, 1864, Birney Papers, USAMHI; Humphreys, *Virginia Campaign*, p. 3.
72. Sumner, ed., *Diary*, p. 261; Gallagher, ed., *Wilderness Campaign*, pp. 82, 83, 84; David B. Birney–My dear Gross, April 4, 1864, Birney Papers, USAMHI.
73. Meade, *Life and Letters*, v. 2, p. 185; OR, 33, pp. 717, 718; Agassiz, ed., *Meade's Headquarters*, p. 80; Gallagher, ed., *Wilderness Campaign*, p. 84.
74. Meade, *Life and Letters*, v. 2, pp. 182, 183, 185; Gibbon, *Personal Recollections*, p. 209; Gallagher, ed., *Wilderness Campaign*, p. 85; OR, 33, pp. 732, 798.
75. Warner, *Generals in Blue*, pp. 437–38; Agassiz, *Meade's Headquarters*, p. 82; Walker and Walker, eds., *Diary*, p. 197; Sparks, ed., *Inside Lincoln's Army*, p. 355; Nevins, ed., *Diary*, p. 517; Wert, *From Winchester*, p. 517.
76. Porter, *Campaigning with Grant*, p. 24; Winslow, *General John Sedgwick*, p. 149; Howe, ed., *Touched with Fire*, p. 101; Fleming, ed., *Life*, p. 583; Plumb, "Record," p. 28; William H. Peacock–Sarah, April 11, 1864, Peacock Letters, USAMHI;

Edward A. Johnson–Brother Albert, April 17, 1864, Johnson Letters, MNBP; Charles A. Wheeler–My dear C, April 22, 1864, Wheeler Papers, NC.

77. Weld, *War Diary*, p. 282; Gould, *Story*, p. 174; Staudenraus, ed., *Mr. Lincoln's Washington*, p. 314; Marvel, *Burnside*, pp. 345, 346, 347; Rhea, *Battle of the Wilderness*, p. 34; *OR*, 33, pp. 1036, 1045.

78. Wert, "All-Out War," *CWTI*, 43, 1, pp. 34, 35.

79. Ibid., pp. 39, 40; Gallagher, ed., *Wilderness Campaign*, pp. 6, 7; Porter, *Campaigning with Grant*, p. 37.

80. Grimsley, *And Keep Moving On*, p. xiii; Sommers, *Richmond Redeemed*, p. 423; Wert, "All-Out War," *CWTI*, 43, 1, pp. 38, 40; Weigley, *Great Civil War*, p. 328.

81. Donald, *Lincoln*, pp. 498, 499; Grant, *Personal Memoirs*, v. 2, p. 122.

82. Abraham Lincoln–Ulysses S. Grant, April 30, 1864, Lincoln Papers, LC; Oates, *Abraham Lincoln*, p. 126; Gallagher, ed., *Wilderness Campaign*, pp. 1, 5; Paludan, *Presidency*, p. 260; Catton, *Grant Takes Command*, p. 175.

83. Gallagher, ed., *Spotsylvania Campaign*, p. 176; George W. Shingle–Sir, April 2, 1864, Shingle Letter; John L. Barnes–father & mother, March 25, 1864, Barnes Letter, USAMHI; Cassedy, ed., *Dear Friends*, p. 409; Carter, *Four Brothers*, p. 383; Wilkeson, *Recollections*, p. 37; Nevins, ed., *Diary*, p. 347; Small, ed., *Road*, p. 125; Rufus Ricksecker–Folks at Home, April 3, 1864, Ricksecker Letters, OSU.

84. Frasier Rosenkranz–Cousin Fronie, April 28, 1864, Rosenkranz Letters, USAMHI; J. B. Ewing–James Kelley, April 16, 1864, Kelley Civil War Letter Collection, PSU; Timothy O. Webster–My Dear Wife and Children, May 1, 1864, Webster Papers, NC; Rufus R. Dawes–My dear Wife, May 1, 1864, Dawes Papers, SHSW.

Chapter 15: "This War Is Horrid"

1. Agassiz, ed., *Meade's Headquarters*, p. 87; Bennett, *Sons of Old Monroe*, p. 386.

2. Gallagher, ed., *Spotsylvania Campaign*, p. 170; Adams, *Memorial*, p. 148; Agassiz, ed., *Meade's Headquarters*, p. 147.

3. Agassiz, ed., *Meade's Headquarters*, p. 85; Carter, *Four Brothers*, pp. 397, 439; Reese, *Sykes' Regular Infantry Division*, p. 312; Hess, *Union Soldier*, pp. 67, 118, 119.

4. Rhea, *Battles for Spotsylvania*, p. 5; Craft, *History*, p. 200; Weld, *War Diary*, p. 307; Elmer Wallace–Parents, June 7, 1864, Wallace Papers, UM; Grimsley, *And Keep Moving On*, p. xv; Chamberlain, *Passing of the Armies*, p. 5.

5. Rhea, *Battle of the Wilderness*, pp. 51, 52, 60–69; Grimsley, *And Keep Moving On*, p. 27.

6. Rhea, *Battle of the Wilderness*, pp. 57, 73–77, 78; Memoirs, George Papers, LC; Trudeau, *Bloody Roads*, p. 35; Seth Gilbert Evans–Friends, May 18, 1864, Evans Papers, NC; Bennett, *Sons of Old Monroe*, pp. 387–88; Agassiz, ed., *Meade's Headquarters*, p. 87; Carmichael, "Lee's Search," *N&S*, 3, 5, p. 57; Grimsley, *And Keep Moving On*, p. 27.

7. Rhea, *Battle of the Wilderness*, pp. 100–102, 104.

8. Ibid., p. 34, places Lee's strength at 65,000; Newton, *Lost for the Cause*, pp. 45–46, gives Lee a force of 79,860, as of April 20, 1864; Carmichael, "Lee's Search," *N&S*, 3, 5, p. 57.

9. Rhea, *Battle of the Wilderness*, pp. 103, 106, 108, 119; OR, 36, pt. 2, p. 403.

10. Rhea, *Battle of the Wilderness*, pp. 132, 133, 135, 139–44.

11. Ibid., pp. 139, 141, 144; Jones, *Giants*, p. 3.

12. Trudeau, *Bloody Roads*, pp. 68, 73; Winik, *April 1865*, p. 91; Chamberlain, *Passing of the Armies*, p. 3; Schaff, *Battle*, pp. 58, 59.

13. Powell, *Fifth Army Corps*, p. 610; Rhea, *Battle of the Wilderness*, Chapter IV; Wallar Diary, USAMHI; Trudeau, *Bloody Roads*, p. 68; Scott, ed., *Forgotten Valor*, p. 516; Wilkinson, *Mother, May You Never See*, p. 64; Page, *Letters*, p. 50; Bennett, *Sons of Old Monroe*, p. 402; Seth Gilbert Evans–Friends, May 18, 1864, Evans Papers; Frank M. Rood–Father and Mother, May 6, 1864, Rood Papers, NC.

14. Small, ed., *Road*, p. 194.

15. Rhea, *Battle of the Wilderness*, pp. 149–84; Cassedy, ed., *Dear Friends*, p. 458; Wert, *Brotherhood*, pp. 291–92.

16. Rhea, *Battle of the Wilderness*, pp. 193–200; Gallagher, ed., *Wilderness Campaign*, pp. 205–9, 212–15; Agassiz, ed., *Meade's Headquarters*, p. 93; Rosenblatt and Rosenblatt, eds., *Hard Marching*, pp. 215–17.

17. Rhea, *Battle of the Wilderness*, pp. 197, 199, 202, 203; Hays, ed., *Under the Red Patch*, p. 232; Silliker, ed., *Rebel Yell*, p. 143; Schaff, *Battle*, p. 186; Agassiz, ed., *Meade's Headquarters*, pp. 92–93; Fleming, ed., *Life*, pp. 598, 656.

18. Rhea, *Battle of the Wilderness*, pp. 206, 222, 223–25.

19. Ibid., pp. 226–39; Rosenblatt and Rosenblatt, eds., *Hard Marching*, p. 221; Walker, *History*, p. 415.

20. Rhea, *Battle of the Wilderness*, pp. 237–38, 242–46.

21. Ibid., p. 251; Diary, Halsey Papers, USAMHI; Baquet, *History*, p. 116.

22. Grant, *Personal Memoirs*, v. 2, pp. 193, 196; Trudeau, *Bloody Roads*, pp. 78, 79; Rhea, *Battle of the Wilderness*, pp. 264–67; Sumner, ed., *Diary*, p. 264.

23. Rhea, *Battle of the Wilderness*, pp. 283–89; W. F. M. Coy–Father, May 19, 1864, Coy Family Papers, NC; Walker, *History*, pp. 421–22.

24. Wert, *General James Longstreet*, pp. 379–80.

25. Ibid., pp. 380–81; Rhea, *Battle of the Wilderness*, pp. 302–13; Smith, *History*, p. 136; Walker, *History*, pp. 422–26.

26. Wert, *General James Longstreet*, pp. 381–82.

27. Ibid., pp. 382–85; Rhea, *Battle of the Wilderness*, pp. 352–66; Rood, "Memoir," pp. 101, 102, SHSW; Nolan and Vipond, eds., *Giants*, pp. 136, 137; Wade Hampton–George G. Meade, May 16, 1864, Wadsworth Papers, LC.

28. Rhea, *Battle of the Wilderness*, pp. 320–23.

29. Ibid., pp. 324–26, 330–32, 337–39, 380–87; Nevins, ed., *Diary*, p. 352; Weld, *War Diary*, pp. 285–86; Wilkinson, *Mother, May You Never See*, pp. 71–74, 87.

30. Rhea, *Battle of the Wilderness*, pp. 390–94; Menge and Shimrak, eds., *Civil War Notebook*, p. 13; White, ed., *Civil War Diary*, pp. 231, 232; Papers Relative to the Mustering Out of Brig. Gen. J. H. Hobart Ward, U.S.V., Ward File, FSNMP.

31. Rhea, *Battle of the Wilderness*, pp. 392–402; Walker, *History*, pp. 432–33.

32. Rhea, *Battle of the Wilderness*, pp. 406–22; Baquet, *History*, p. 117; John Brooker–Friend Eva, July 30, 1864, Brooker Papers, NC; Coffin, *Battered Stars*, p. 141.

33. Soule Diary, USAMHI; Rhea, *Battle of the Wilderness*, pp. 435, 436, 440; New-

ton, *Lost for the Cause*, p. 69; Walker, *History*, p. 438; Fox, *Regimental Losses*, p. 445; Rosenblatt and Rosenblatt, eds., *Hard Marching*, p. 215.

34. Grimsley, *And Keep Moving On*, pp. 229, 230; Rhea, *Battle of the Wilderness*, pp. 431, 432, 433; Gallagher, ed., *Wilderness Campaign*, p. 14.

35. Rhea, *Battles for Spotsylvania*, pp. 5, 8; Gallagher, ed., *Spotsylvania Campaign*, p. 30; Grimsley, *And Keep Moving On*, p. 230; Weigley, *Great Civil War*, p. xxiv.

36. Porter, *Campaigning with Grant*, pp. 69, 70.

37. OR, 36, pt. 2, pp. 481, 483–84; Agassiz, ed., *Meade's Headquarters*, p. 102; Grant, *Personal Memoirs*, v. 2, p. 211; Rhea, *Battles for Spotsylvania*, p. 16.

38. Rhea, *Battles for Spotsylvania*, pp. 17–28; OR, 36, pt. 1, p. 1056; Turino, ed., *Civil War Diary*, p. 83; Corbin Diary, USAMHI.

39. Rhea, *Battles for Spotsylvania*, pp. 30, 37; Wert, *Custer*, p. 154.

40. Rhea, *Battles for Spotsylvania*, pp. 32–37, 40; Wert, *Custer*, pp. 152–54; Grimsley, *And Keep Moving On*, p. 64.

41. Nevins, ed., *Diary*, p. 355; Wilkeson, *Recollections*, p. 77; Small, ed., *Road*, p. 134; Schaff, *Battle*, pp. 344, 345.

42. Grimsley, *And Keep Moving On*, pp. 59, 229; Gallagher, ed., *Spotsylvania Campaign*, p. 176; Sommers, *Richmond Redeemed*, p. 437; Rhea, *Battles for Spotsylvania*, p. 39; Dana, *Recollections*, p. 194.

43. Rhea, *Battles for Spotsylvania*, pp. 45–50; Miers, ed., *Wash Roebling's War*, p. 32.

44. Rhea, *Battles for Spotsylvania*, pp. 28–29, 50–53; Wert, *Brotherhood*, p. 298.

45. Rhea, *Battles for Spotsylvania*, pp. 54–59, 62–64; Small, ed., *Road*, pp. 136, 139; Charles McKnight, Diary, Vautier Papers, USAMHI; Cowley, ed., *With My Face to the Enemy*, p. 413; McPherson, *For Cause and Comrades*, pp. 44, 45; Rood, Memoir, p. 104, SHSW; Wert, *Brotherhood*, p. 298.

46. OR, 36, pt. 2, pp. 540, 545; Rhea, *Battles for Spotsylvania*, pp. 72, 73.

47. Grant, *Personal Memoirs*, v. 2, p. 214; OR, 36, pt. 2, p. 526; Rhea, *Battles for Spotsylvania*, pp. 73, 74.

48. Rhea, *Battles for Spotsylvania*, pp. 74–85.

49. OR, 36, pt. 2, pp. 529, 566, 568, 581; Swinfen, *Ruggles' Regiment*, p. 38.

50. Ritchie, ed., *Four Years*, p. 160; Agassiz, ed., *Meade's Headquarters*, pp. 107–8; Howe, ed., *Touched with Fire*, pp. 109, 110; Durham, "The Man Who Shot John Sedgwick," *B&G*, 13, 2, p. 26.

51. Westbrook, *History*, p. 189; Greiner et al., eds., *Surgeon's Civil War*, p. 185; Nevins, ed., *Diary*, p. 360; Beal, ed., *Diary*, v. 2, pp. 27–28; Grant, *Personal Memoirs*, v. 2, pp. 214, 220.

52. Diary, Wyman Papers, USAMHI.

53. Dunn, *Harvestfields*, p. 241; Greiner et al., eds., *Surgeon's Civil War*, pp. 187, 188; Coffin, *Battered Stars*, p. 226; Miers, ed., *Wash Roebling's War*, p. 26; Cassedy, ed., *Dear Friends*, p. 469.

54. Rhea, *Battles for Spotsylvania*, pp. 123, 124.

55. Ibid., pp. 132–50; Diary, Vautier Papers, USAMHI; Rood, Memoir, pp. 106, 107; Rufus R. Dawes–My Dear Wife, May 11, 1864, Dawes Papers, SHSW; OR, 36, pt. 1, p. 332.

56. Warner, *Generals in Blue*, pp. 519–20; Rhea, *Battles for Spotsylvania*, p. 163; John D. Fish–My Dear Brother, November 12, 1863, Fish Letters, USAMHI; OR, 36, pt. 1, p. 667; Best, *History*, p. vii.

57. OR, 36, pt. 1, pp. 204, 490, 667; pt. 2, pp. 602, 603, 609; Best, *History*, p. 135,

136; Mertz, "Upton's Attack," *B&G*, 18, 6, pp. 16, 17, 19; Westbrook, *History*, p. 189; Rhea, *Battles for Spotsylvania*, pp. 164, 165–68.

58. Westbrook, *History*, p. 191; Best, *History*, p. 129.

59. *OR*, 36, pt. 1, pp. 667–68, 1072, 1078; Best, *History*, p. 130; Westbrook, *History*, p. 191; Mertz, "Upton's Attack," *B&G*, 18, 6, pp. 23–25, 46, 50, 59; Rhea, *Battles for Spotsylvania*, pp. 168–75; Stevens, *Three Years*, p. 334.

60. *OR*, 36, pt. 1, p. 668; Rhea, *Battles for Spotsylvania*, p. 176; Humphreys, *Virginia Campaign*, p. 87; Porter, *Campaigning with Grant*, p. 96; Smith, *Grant*, p. 358; Coffin, *Battered Stars*, pp. 167–68.

61. Rhea, *Battles for Spotsylvania*, p. 185; Fox, *Regimental Losses*, p. 41; Agassiz, ed., *Meade's Headquarters*, p. 109; Schaff, *Battle*, p. 90; Diary, Wyman Papers, USAMHI; Weld, *War Diary*, p. 290; Greiner et al., eds., *Surgeon's Civil War*, p. 188.

62. *OR*, 36, pt. 2, p. 627.

63. Ibid., pp. 629, 634, 635, 638, 643; George G. Meade–Horatio G. Wright, May 11, 1864, Meade Papers, NC.

64. Rhea, *Battles for Spotsylvania*, pp. 223–25; Smith, *History*, p. 154; Gibbon, *Personal Recollections*, p. 220; Wert, *Brotherhood*, p. 299.

65. Lash, "*Duty Well Done*," p. 392; Turino, ed., *Civil War Diary*, p. 85; Rhea, *Battles for Spotsylvania*, pp. 231–33.

66. Menge and Shimrak, eds., *Civil War Notebook*, p. 15; Wert, *Brotherhood*, p. 300; Walker and Walker, eds., *Diary*, p. 182; Silliker, ed., *Rebel Yell*, p. 155; Macneal, "Centre County Regiment," *Centre County Heritage*, 36, 1, p. 118; Osborne, ed., *Civil War Diaries*, p. 138.

67. Walker and Walker, eds., *Diary*, p. 183; Wert, *Brotherhood*, pp. 300, 301; Rhea, *Battles for Spotsylvania*, pp. 246–50.

68. Wert, *From Winchester*, p. 58; Rhea, *Battles for Spotsylvania*, p. 251; Walker and Walker, eds., *Diary*, p. 183; Silliker, ed., *Rebel Yell*, p. 157.

69. Robertson, ed., *Civil War Letters*, p. 419; *B&L*, v. 4, p. 173; Swinfen, *Ruggles' Regiment*, p. 41; John R. Brooke–Frank H. Burr, May 31, 1882, Beaver Collection, PSU; Craft, *History*, pp. 195, 196; Silliker, ed., *Rebel Yell*, p. 153; Hess, *Union Soldier*, p. 69; Rhea, *Battles for Spotsylvania*, p. 292.

70. Rood, *Memoir*, pp. 108, 109; Rufus R. Dawes–My dear Wife, May 14, [1864], Dawes Papers, SHSW; Silliker, *Rebel Yell*, p. 157; Townsend, "History," p. 194, UME; Diary, Halsey Papers, USAMHI; Turino, ed., *Civil War Diary*, p. 86.

71. Rufus R. Dawes–My dear Wife, May 16, [1864], Dawes Papers, SHSW; Muffly, ed., *Story*, p. 122; the best description of the struggle for the Bloody Angle is Rhea, *Battles for Spotsylvania*, Chapters 7–8.

72. Galwey, *Valiant Hours*, p. 210; Grimsley, *And Keep Moving On*, p. 18; Rhea, *Battles for Spotsylvania*, pp. 282–88, 294–301, 311; *OR*, 36, pt. 2, p. 661; Cassedy, ed., *Dear Friends*, p. 463; Stephen Rich–Brother, May 17, 1864, Rich Letters, USAMHI.

73. Porter, *Campaigning with Grant*, pp. 83–84.

74. Ibid., p. 84; *OR*, 36, pt. 2, p. 552.

75. Gallagher, ed., *Spotsylvania Campaign*, p. 33; Trudeau, *Bloody Roads South*, p. 143; Wert, *Custer*, pp. 154–55.

76. Wert, *Custer*, pp. 155–56.

77. Ibid., pp. 156–57.

78. Ibid., pp. 156–58; Wittenberg, *Little Phil*, pp. 33, 52, 53.

79. Rhea, *To the North Anna*, Chapters 1–6; Grant, *Personal Memoirs*, v. 2, pp. 235–42; Newton, *Lost for the Cause*, p. 69.

80. *OR*, 36, pt. 2, p. 696; Miller, *Drum Taps in Dixie*, pp. 80, 87; Wesley H. Shaw–Cousin Mary, September 10, 1864, Shaw Papers, NYSL; Benedict, *Vermont*, v. 2, p. 352; Walker, *History*, p. 483; Keating, *Carnival of Blood*, pp. 30, 32, 34.

81. John M. Steward–Abby, May 16, 1864, Steward Letters, USAMHI; Rich Diary, pp. 22, 23, UME; Keating, *Carnival of Blood*, pp. 41–49, 53, 57, 61; Rhea, *To the North Anna*, pp. 168, 171–88.

82. Rhea, *Battles for Spotsylvania*, pp. 313, 314; Gallagher, ed., *Spotsylvania Campaign*, pp. 171, 177, 179, 182.

83. Rhea, *Cold Harbor*, pp. 6, 7, 9, 10; Meade, *Life and Letters*, v. 2, pp. 195, 197.

84. Rhea, *Battles for Spotsylvania*, pp. 314, 315, 316, 317, 318; Bingham, "Anecdotes," WRHS; Gallagher, ed., *Spotsylvania Campaign*, p. 77; Miers, ed., *Wash Roebling's War*, p. 24; Dana, *Recollections*, p. 191.

85. Gallagher, ed., *Spotsylvania Campaign*, pp. 177, 183–92; Humphreys, *Virginia Campaign*, pp. 117–18; Grimsley, *And Keep Moving On*, p. 185; Rhodes, ed., *All for the Union*, p. 153; Henry F. Young–Delia, May 24, 1864, Young Papers, SHSW; Townsend, "History," p. 197, UME; Wilkinson, *Mother, May You Never See*, p. 121; Marshall, *Company "K,"* p. 160; Benjamin Thaxter–Eleanor, May 15, 1864, Thaxter Papers; Bateman Diary; Plumb, "Record," pp. 33, 36, 39; Charles E. Perkins–Sister, June 10, 1864, Perkins Civil War Letters, USAMHI; McPherson, *For Cause and Comrades*, pp. 44, 45.

86. Rhea, *To the North Anna*, pp. 212–19, 223–47; Cassedy, ed., *Dear Friends*, p. 474; Walker and Walker, eds., *Diary*, p. 193; Hyde, *Civil War Letters*, p. 134; Menge and Shimrak, eds., *Civil War Notebook*, p. 18; Sparks, ed., *Inside Lincoln's Army*, p. 376.

87. Rhea, *To the North Anna*, Chapter 8; Sumner, ed., *Diary*, p. 269; Cassedy, ed., *Dear Friends*, pp. 474, 475.

88. Katcher, ed., *Building the Victory*, p. 61; Coffin, *Battered Stars*, p. 260; Nevins, ed., *Diary*, p. 386; Rhea, *To the North Anna*, pp. 293–319.

89. Dana, *Recollections*, p. 203; Agassiz, ed., *Meade's Headquarters*, p. 127; Rhea, *To the North Anna*, p. 335; Grant, *Personal Memoirs*, v. 2, pp. 249–50.

90. Weld, *War Diary*, pp. 296, 297, 311; Wilkinson, *Mother, May You Never See*, pp. 135–39, 141; Rhea, *To the North Anna*, pp. 342–46.

91. Agassiz, ed., *Meade's Headquarters*, p. 126.

92. Rhea, *To the North Anna*, p. 361; Grant, *Personal Memoirs*, v. 2, p. 252.

93. Sumner, ed., *Diary*, p. 270; Cassedy, ed., *Dear Friends*, p. 478; Jones Diary, p. 6, USAMHI; Gibbon, *Personal Recollections*, p. 225; Smith, *History*, p. 182; Westbrook, *History*, p. 203; Elmer Wallace–Parents, May 30, 1864, Wallace Papers, UM; Carter, *Four Brothers*, p. 410; Seth Gilbert Evans–Friends, June 5, 1864, Evans Papers, NC.

94. Rhea, *Cold Harbor*, pp. 61–64, 81; Page, *Letters*, p. 82; Morrill Diary, MESA.

95. Wert, *Custer*, pp. 158, 159.

96. Rhea, *Cold Harbor*, Chapters 4–6; Grant, *Personal Memoirs*, v. 2, pp. 264–66.

97. Rhea, *Cold Harbor*, pp. 225–27, 234, 239; *OR*, 36, pt. 3, p. 427; Orlando P. Sawtelle–Parent, June 5, 1864, Sawtelle Family Papers, USAMHI; Coffin, *Battered Stars*, p. 293.

98. Rhea, *Cold Harbor*, p. 268; Keiser Diary, p. 116; Henry Hoyt–Dear Ones at Home, June 2, 1864, Hoyt Papers, USAMHI; Swinfen, *Ruggles' Regiment*, p. 43; Vaill, *History*, pp. 63, 64; Niven, *Connecticut*, pp. 249, 251.

99. Rhea, *Cold Harbor*, pp. 279–80; OR, 36, pt. 3, pp. 440, 452; Agassiz, ed., *Meade's Headquarters*, p. 139.

100. Rhea, *Cold Harbor*, pp. 291, 307–12; Agassiz, ed., *Meade's Headquarters*, p. 140; Newton, *Lost for the Cause*, pp. 51, 69, 71.

101. Rhea, *Cold Harbor*, pp. 295–307, 311.

102. OR, 36, pt. 3, p. 206; Grant, *Personal Memoirs*, v. 2, pp. 276, 277; Gallagher, ed., *Wilderness Campaign*, pp. 30, 31.

103. Grant, *Personal Memoirs*, v. 2, p. 276; Rhea, *Cold Harbor*, pp. 313–17; OR, 36, pt. 3, p. 206; Grimsley, *And Keep Moving On*, p. 92.

104. Porter, *Campaigning with Grant*, p. 140; Wilkeson, *Recollections*, p. 121; Hyde, *Civil War Letters*, p. 136; Valentine Barney–Maria, May 30, 1864, Barney Letters, VTHS; Trask, *Fire Within*, p. 227; Silliker, ed., *Rebel Yell*, p. 165; Thomas Hamilton–My dear Wife, June 1, 1864, Hamilton Letters, PSU; Rufus R. Dawes–My dear Wife, June 1, [1864], Dawes Papers, SHSW; Swinfen, *Ruggles' Regiment*, p. 43.

105. Detailed description of June 3 attack in Rhea, *Cold Harbor*, Chapter 10, quotations on pp. 320, 353; O'Beirne, "Into the Shadow," *N&S*, 3, 4, p. 72.

106. Rhea, *Cold Harbor*, pp. 333–37, 342, 347, 357, 358; Albert Martin-Hayward–Dear Brother, June 6, 1864, Hayward Papers, NC; Gibbon, *Personal Recollections*, pp. 229, 232, 233; Westbrook, *History*, p. 205; O'Beirne, "Into the Shadow," *N&S*, 3, 4, pp. 75, 76, 77; Smith, *History*, p. 190; Fox, *Regimental Losses*, pp. 42, 449, 450.

107. Trudeau, *Bloody Roads South*, p. 296; Henry R. Swan–Abbie, June 4, 7, 1864, Swan Letters, USAMHI; Rufus R. Dawes–Wife, June 4, [1864], Dawes Papers, SHSW; Rhea, *Cold Harbor*, pp. 354, 358, 361, 362, 382.

108. Grant, *Personal Memoirs*, v. 2, pp. 272, 273–76; Agassiz, ed., *Meade's Headquarters*, p. 154; Trudeau, *Bloody Roads South*, pp. 307, 308.

109. Newton, *Lost for the Cause*, pp. 69, 84; Fox, *Regimental Losses*, p. 561; Grimsley, *And Keep Moving On*, p. 161; OR, 36, pt. 1, pp. 119–88; Rhea, *Battles for Spotsylvania*, p. 319; Winfield S. Hancock–Daniel Butterfield, June 20, 1864, Hancock Papers, NC.

110. Powell, *Fifth Army Corps*, p. 677; Edward Heller–Sisters, June 9, 1864, Heller Letters; David B. Birney–My dear Gross, June 2, 1864, Birney Papers; William T. Haynes–Grandmother, June 7, 1864, Haynes Letters, USAMHI; Carter, *Four Brothers*, p. 428; Albert, ed., *History*, p. 259; Henry F. Young–Father, June 8, 1864, Young Papers, SHSW; Dunn, *Harvestfields*, p. 258.

111. Chamberlain, *Passing of the Armies*, p. 3; Ritchie, ed., *Four Years*, p. 169; Seth Gilbert Evans–My Friend Mr. Banks, June 9, 1864, Evans Papers, NC; Coffin, *Battered Stars*, p. 339; Cassedy, ed., *Dear Friends*, p. 489.

112. Gibbon, *Personal Recollections*, p. 227.

113. Hardin, *History*, p. 191; Glover, *Bucktailed Wildcats*, p. 265; Woodward, *Our Campaigns*, p. 254; Gibbs, *Three Years*, p. 281; Walker, *History*, pp. 552, 553; Carter, *Four Brothers*, p. 428; Baquet, *History*, pp. 129, 130, 134; Otis, *Second Wisconsin*, p. 99; Menge and Shimrak, eds., *Civil War Notebook*, p. 26.

114. Macneal, "Centre County Regiment," *Centre County Heritage*, 36, 1, p. 122; E. T. Peters–Friend Sidney, June 27, 1864, Peters Letter, USAMHI; Rhea, *Cold Harbor*, p. 387; Agassiz, ed., *Meade's Headquarters*, p. 148n.

115. Coffin, *Battered Stars*, p. 280.

Chapter 16: "A Sit Down Before the Wall of Petersbury"

1. Donald, *Lincoln*, pp. 504–7.

2. Ibid., p. 500; Winik, *April 1865*, pp. 246, 247, 251; Gallagher, ed., *Wilderness Campaign*, pp. 30, 31.

3. Gallagher, ed., *Wilderness Campaign*, p. 31; Staudenraus, ed., *Mr. Lincoln's Washington*, pp. 342–43.

4. Catton, *Grant Takes Command*, p. 295.

5. Boritt, ed., *Lincoln's Generals*, p. 168; Rhea, *To the North Anna*, pp. 1, 260–61; Donald, *Lincoln*, p. 501.

6. *OR*, 36, pt. 3, pp. 598–99.

7. Ibid., pp. 747–49; Sumner, ed., *Diary*, p. 272; Trudeau, *Last Citadel*, pp. 17–19, 20–22.

8. Katcher, ed., *Building the Victory*, pp. 89, 90; Agassiz, ed., *Meade's Headquarters*, p. 161; Samuel B. Salsburg–Sister, June 18, 1864, Salsburg Letter, USAMHI; Wilkinson, *Mother, May You Never See*, pp. 167, 169; Trudeau, *Last Citadel*, pp. 22, 23.

9. Trudeau, *Last Citadel*, pp. 21–22, 25; Porter, *Campaigning with Grant*, pp. 199, 200, 201.

10. Freeman, *Lee's Lieutenants*, v. 3, pp. 528–30; Wert, *From Winchester*, p. 7; Trudeau, *Last Citadel*, pp. 19, 24.

11. Freeman, *Lee's Lieutenants*, v. 3, p. 529; Grant, *Personal Memoirs*, v. 2, p. 295; Trudeau, *Last Citadel*, p. 31.

12. Trudeau, *Last Citadel*, p. xiii.

13. Meade, *Life and Letters*, v. 2, pp. 204, 205; Grant, *Personal Memoirs*, v. 2, pp. 293–96; Greene, *Breaking the Backbone*, pp. 7, 8; Trudeau, *Last Citadel*, pp. 41, 42, 47, 49; Agassiz, ed., *Meade's Headquarters*, p. 162; Silliker, ed., *Rebel Yell*, pp. 171, 172; Marbaker, *History*, p. 193; Walker, *General Hancock*, pp. 236, 241; Winfield S. Hancock–Daniel Butterfield, June 24, 1864, Hancock Papers, NC.

14. Wilkinson, *Mother, May You Never See*, pp. 177, 178; Thomas J. Kessler–My Dear Sister, June 20, 1864, Kessler Papers, NC; Gambone, *Major-General John Frederick Hartranft*, p. 100; Agassiz, ed., *Meade's Headquarters*, p. 168n.

15. Agassiz, ed., *Meade's Headquarters*, pp. 169, 170; Marshall, *Company "K,"* p. 173; Wilkeson, *Recollections*, p. 181; Robertson, ed., *Civil War Letters*, pp. 443, 444.

16. Cassedy, ed., *Dear Friends*, p. 499; Rich Diary, p. 27, UME; Marbaker, *History*, pp. 196, 197; Robertson, ed., *Civil War Letters*, pp. 444n, 446; Trudeau, *Last Citadel*, p. 54; Joshua L. Chamberlain–My darling wife, June 19, 1864, Chamberlain Papers, BC; Pullen, *Twentieth Maine*, pp. 211, 212; Gaff, *On Many a Bloody Field*, p. 363; Silliker, ed., *Rebel Yell*, p. 173; Loring Winslow–Parents, June 19, 23, 1864, Winslow Letters; Rufus R. Dawes–My dear Wife, June 19, 1864, Dawes Papers, SHSW.

17. Meade, *Life and Letters*, v. 2, pp. 204, 205; Dana, *Recollections*, p. 220; Trudeau, *Last Citadel*, p. 55; Agassiz, ed., *Meade's Headquarters*, pp. 170, 224; Humphreys, *Virginia Campaign*, p. 225; Sumner, ed., *Diary*, p. 274; Nevins, ed., *Diary*, pp. 425, 426.

18. Thomas D. G. Smith–Mother, June 26, 1864, Smith Letters; Arthur B. Wyman–My dear Sister, June 19, 1864, Wyman Papers, USAMHI; Carter, *Four Brothers*, p. 446; Sparks, ed., *Inside Lincoln's Army*, p. 388; Austin Fenn–Distant

Wife, June 17, 1864, Fenn Papers, NC; Gibbon, *Personal Recollections*, p. 229; Newton, *Lost for the Cause*, p. 69; Weld, *War Diary*, p. 318.

19. Miers, ed., *Wash Roebling's War*, p. 27.

20. Sparks, ed., *Inside Lincoln's Army*, pp. 393, 394; Agassiz, ed., *Meade's Headquarters*, p. 188; Gibbon, *Personal Recollections*, p. 239; Meade, *Life and Letters*, v. 2, pp. 202, 203.

21. Meade, *Life and Letters*, v. 2, pp. 201, 202, 207, 208.

22. Ibid., p. 215; Miers, ed., *Wash Roebling's War*, p. 26; Porter, *Campaigning with Grant*, p. 144; Daniel R. Larned–My dear Sister, June 20, 1864, Larned Correspondence, LC.

23. Jordan, "*Happiness*," pp. 152, 170; Nevins, ed., *Diary*, p. 409; Chamberlain, *Passing of the Armies*, p. 154; Sparks, ed., *Inside Lincoln's Army*, p. 381; Nevins, ed., *Diary*, p. 405.

24. Jordan, "*Happiness*," pp. 167, 168, 171; Grant, *Personal Memoirs*, v. 2, p. 214.

25. Sparks, ed., *Inside Lincoln's Army*, pp. 401, 402; Miers, ed., *Wash Roebling's War*, p. 26; Meade, *Life and Letters*, v. 2, pp. 214, 215; Sumner, ed., *Diary*, p. 282; Trudeau, *Last Citadel*, p. 55.

26. Trudeau, *Last Citadel*, p. 55; Warner, *Generals in Blue*, pp. 60–61; Grimsley, *And Keep Moving On*, p. 11; Sumner, ed., *Diary*, p. 277.

27. Grant, *Personal Memoirs*, v. 2, p. 299; Humphreys, *Virginia Campaign*, p. 198; Weigley, *Great Civil War*, pp. 328, 329; Sommers, *Richmond Redeemed*, pp. 423, 424.

28. Grant, *Personal Memoirs*, v. 2, p. 326; Sommers, *Richmond Redeemed*, pp. 2–3; Freeman, *Lee's Lieutenants*, v. 3, p. 538; Newton, *Lost for the Cause*, p. 74.

29. Trudeau, *Last Citadel*, pp. 62, 64, 68, 69, 70; *SOR*, 7, p. 239; Nevins, ed., *Diary*, p. 427.

30. Keating, *Carnival of Blood*, pp. 216, 218; Smith, *History*, pp. 206–9; Rich Diary, p. 27, UME; Silliker, ed., *Rebel Yell*, p. 175; David B. Birney–My dear Gross, July 4, 1864, Birney Papers, USAMHI; Page, *Letters*, p. 138; Winfield S. Hancock–Daniel Butterfield, June 24, 1864, Hancock Papers, NC; Trudeau, *Last Citadel*, pp. 58, 75, 78; Nevins, ed., *Diary*, p. 427.

31. Trudeau, *Last Citadel*, pp. 76, 78; Winfield S. Hancock–Daniel Butterfield, June 24, 1864, Hancock Papers, NC; Gibbon, *Personal Recollections*, p. 228; David B. Birney–My dear Gross, July 4, 1864, Birney Papers, USAMHI; Smith, *History*, p. 206; Keating, *Carnival of Blood*, p. 216.

32. *SOR*, 7, pp. 239–41; Ide, *History*, pp. 185–92; Freeman, *Lee's Lieutenants*, v. 3, p. 540; Meade, *Life and Letters*, v. 2, pp. 209, 210.

33. Grant, *Personal Memoirs*, v. 2, pp. 300–302; Wert, *Custer*, pp. 161–62.

34. Wert, *Custer*, pp. 163–64; Freeman, *Lee's Lieutenants*, v. 3, pp. 519–21.

35. Wert, *Custer*, pp. 163, 164, 165; Freeman, *Lee's Lieutenants*, v. 3, pp. 521, 522, 522n.

36. Trudeau, *Last Citadel*, p. 66; Sauers, ed., *Civil War Journal*, p. 220; Porter, *Campaigning with Grant*, pp. 216–19, 223.

37. Carter, *Four Brothers*, p. 449; Henry F. Young–Father, July 26, 1864, Young Papers, SHSW.

38. Nevins, ed., *Diary*, p. 435; Elmer Wallace–Mother & Father, July 17, 1864, Wallace Papers, UM; Weld, *War Diary*, pp. 372, 373; Cowles, ed., *History*, p. 920; Carter, *Four Brothers*, p. 464; Parker, *Henry Wilson's Regiment*, p. 477; de Trobriand, *Four Years*, p. 639; Maier, *Rough and Regular*, p. 275.

39. Rufus R. Dawes–My dear Wife, June 23, [1864], Dawes Papers; Henry F. Young–Father, June 27, 1864, Young Papers, SHSW; Albert S. Garland–Sister Mother & all, September 2, 1864, Garland Letter; William H. Walling–My Dear Sisters, July 20, 1864, Walling Letters, USAMHI; J. Loyal Brown–Sister, September 4, 1864, Brown Letters, UME; Child, *History*, p. 263; Page, *Letters*, pp. 143, 151.

40. Soule Diary; George Hopper–Brother & Sister, July 2, 1864, Hopper Papers, USAMHI; Weld, *War Diary*, p. 328; Townsend, "History," p. 216, UME; Rufus R. Dawes–My dear Wife, June 23, [1864], Dawes Papers, SHSW; Thomas Hamilton–My dear Wife, July 1, 1864, Hamilton Letters; George Leasure–Papa, July 2, 1864, Leasure, George Papers, PSU; Wilkinson, *Mother, May You Never See*, p. 223.

41. White, ed., *Civil War Diary*, p. 291.

42. Agassiz, ed., *Meade's Headquarters*, p. 135; McBride, *In the Ranks*, p. 103; Townsend, "History," p. 259, UME; Parker, *Henry Wilson's Regiment*, p. 480; Carter, *Four Brothers*, pp. 463, 468; Weld, *War Diary*, pp. 325, 326; Orlando P. Sawtelle–Mother, July 5, 1864, Sawtelle Family Papers, USAMHI; George W. Ross–Mrs. Harriet Webster, August 25, September 10, 1864, Webster Papers, NC.

43. Hamilton R. Dunlap–Sister Dollie, July 26, August 10, 1864, Dunlap Letters, PSU; Townsend, "History," p. 224, UME; Styple, ed., *Writing*, p. 288; Page, *Letters*, p. 211; Silliker, ed., *Rebel Yell*, p. 179; Agassiz, ed., *Meade's Headquarters*, pp. 181, 182; Carter, *Four Brothers*, p. 457.

44. Marshall, *Company "K,"* p. 195; Marbaker, *History*, p. 224; Sauers, *Advance the Colors!*, v. 2, p. 247; Wilkeson, *Recollections*, pp. 185, 189; Sawyer et al., eds., *Letters*, p. 273; Agassiz, ed., *Meade's Headquarters*, p. 209.

45. Walker, *History*, pp. 609, 610, 643, 644; Rhodes, ed., *All for the Union*, p. 164; Herdegen and Murphy, eds., *Four Years*, p. 317; Judson, *History*, pp. 229, 231; Trask, *Fire Within*, pp. 228, 229; Marshall, *Company "K,"* p. 184; Parker, *Henry Wilson's Regiment*, p. 488, 527; Chamberlin, *History*, pp. 278, 279; Dunn, *Harvestfields*, p. 266.

46. Gould, *Story*, p. 208; Trudeau, *Last Citadel*, pp. 100, 102, 103, 104; Nevins, ed., *Diary*, p. 439.

47. Gould, *Story*, p. 212; Trudeau, *Last Citadel*, pp. 103, 104.

48. Cuffel, *History*, p. 195; Gould, *Story*, pp. 212, 213, 215; Trudeau, *Last Citadel*, pp. 106, 107.

49. Trudeau, *Last Citadel*, pp. 105, 106; Stevens, ed., *As if It Were Glory*, pp. 169, 170; Wilkinson, *Mother, May You Never See*, p. 172; Fred C. Ployer–Friend Israel, August 3, 1864, Ployer Letters, USAMHI; Woodward, ed., "Civil War," *PMHB*, v. 88, p. 55.

50. Cornish, *Sable Arm*, pp. ix, 209, 214; Hunt and Brown, *Brevet Brigadier Generals in Blue*, pp. 18, 39, 57, 296, 329, 521, 526, 556, 618, 648, 671, 694.

51. Wilkinson, *Mother, May You Never See*, p. 234; *OR*, 36, pt. 1, p. 915; Stevens, ed., *As if It Were Glory*, p. 167; Austin Fenn–Wife, May 14, 1864, Fenn Papers, NC; Cassedy, ed., *Dear Friends*, p. 509.

52. Trudeau, *Last Citadel*, pp. 107, 108; Smith, *Grant*, p. 381; *B&L*, v. 4, p. 548; George Leasure–Papa, July 6, 1864, Leasure, George Letters, PSU.

53. Grant, *Personal Memoirs*, v. 2, pp. 310, 312; Suderow, "Glory Denied," *N&S*, 3, 7, pp. 18–19, 21–23, 26, 27, 31, 32.

54. Gould, *Story*, p. 216; Priest, ed., *One Surgeon's Private War*, p. 117; Trudeau, *Last Citadel*, p. 109; Wilkinson, *Mother, May You Never See*, p. 248.
55. Trudeau, *Last Citadel*, pp. 109, 110; Nevins, ed., *Diary*, p. 443; Report of Inspector-General E. Shriver, August 20, 1864, RG 393, NA; Stevens, ed., pp. 178, 179; Wilkinson, *Mother, May You Never See*, pp. 237, 238; Chase, *Charge*, pp. 16, 19.
56. Trudeau, *Last Citadel*, pp. 113–15; Scott, ed., *Forgotten Valor*, p. 557; Arthur B. Wyman–My dear Sister, July 19, 1864, Wyman Papers, USAMHI; Weld, *War Diary*, p. 353.
57. Trudeau, *Last Citadel*, pp. 116–19, quotations pp. 122–23; Rufus R. Dawes–My dear Wife, July 30, 1864, Dawes Papers, SHSW; Weld, *War Diary*, p. 353.
58. Stevens, ed., *As if It Were Glory*, p. 181; Weld, *War Diary*, pp. 353, 354; Trudeau, *Last Citadel*, p. 123.
59. Porter, *Campaigning with Grant*, pp. 264, 265, 266, 267; Weld, *War Diary*, p. 354; Trudeau, *Last Citadel*, pp. 123, 124, 127; Fox, *Regimental Losses*, p. 454.
60. Meade, *Life and Letters*, v. 2, pp. 217, 218, 219, 221; Humphreys, *Andrew A. Humphreys*, pp. 243, 244; Sumner, ed., *Diary*, pp. 284, 285; Nevins, ed., *Diary*, p. 443; Scott, ed., *Forgotten Valor*, p. 562; Grant, *Personal Memoirs*, v. 2, p. 315; Porter, *Campaigning with Grant*, p. 269; Marvel, *Burnside*, pp. 410–12.
61. Scott, ed., *Forgotten Valor*, p. 593; Warner, *Generals in Blue*, p. 58.
62. Wert, *From Winchester*, pp. 7–11.
63. Ibid., p. 8; New York *Times*, July 11, 1864.
64. Wert, *From Winchester*, p. 8; Grant, *Personal Memoirs*, v. 2, pp. 316, 317.
65. Wert, *From Winchester*, pp. 8, 9; Sparks, ed., *Inside Lincoln's Army*, p. 410; Meade, *Life and Letters*, v. 2, pp. 216, 218.
66. Wert, *From Winchester*, pp. 12, 13, 36, 37; Meade, *Life and Letters*, v. 2, pp. 218, 219, 220, 221.
67. Wert, *From Winchester*, pp. 33, 34; Swinton, *Campaigns*, p. 551; Newton, *Lost for the Cause*, p. 74; Porter, *Campaigning with Grant*, p. 276.
68. Trudeau, *Last Citadel*, pp. 151–52, 158, 161; Suderow, "'Nothing but a Miracle,'" *N&S*, 4, 2, pp. 12, 13, 17, 23, 31; Agassiz, ed., *Meade's Headquarters*, p. 217; William H. Peacock–Sarah, September 18, 1864, Peacock Letters, USAMHI.
69. Dawes, *Service*, pp. 307–10; Agassiz, ed., *Meade's Headquarters*, pp. 219, 220; Reese, *Sykes' Regular Infantry Division*, p. 332; Gibbs, ed., *History*, pp. 124, 125; Trudeau, *Last Citadel*, pp. 167, 169, 173; Campbell, ed., *"Grand Terrible Dramma,"* p. 261; Nevins, ed., *Diary*, p. 453; Grant, *Personal Memoirs*, v. 2, p. 324.
70. Sumner, ed., *Diary*, p. 286; Trudeau, *Last Citadel*, pp. 181, 183, 184; de Trobriand, *Four Years*, p. 637; Nevins, ed., *Diary of the Civil War*, p. 467; Walker, *History*, p. 578.
71. Trudeau, *Last Citadel*, pp. 187, 188; Charles E. Field–Hattie, August 27, 1864, Burleigh Papers, USAMHI; Smith, *History*, p. 238; Bingham, "Memoirs," WRHS.
72. Gibbon, *Personal Recollections*, pp. 258, 259; Billings, *History*, pp. 308–39; Humphreys, *Andrew A. Humphreys*, pp. 247, 248; Trudeau, *Last Citadel*, p. 188; Burr, *Life*, pp. 12, 164, 173; Muffly, ed., *Story*, pp. 137, 138; Statement of Dr. G. B. Mitchell, November 13, 1864, Beaver Collection, PSU.
73. Trudeau, *Last Citadel*, pp. 188, 189; Sparks, ed., *Inside Lincoln's Army*, p. 417;

Priest, ed., *One Surgeon's Civil War*, p. 120; Gibbon, *Personal Recollections*, pp. 260, 261, 263.

74. Humphreys, *Andrew A. Humphreys*, pp. 249–50.

75. A thorough and excellent study of the Fifth Offensive at Petersburg is Sommers, *Richmond Redeemed, passim;* Swinton, *Campaigns*, p. 551; Newton, *Lost for the Cause*, p. 80; Silliker, ed., *Rebel Yell*, p. 188; Trudeau, *Last Citadel*, p. 221.

76. Wert, *From Winchester*, p. 39, Chapters 4–13.

77. Newton, *Lost for the Cause*, p. 74; Robertson, ed., *Civil War Letters*, pp. 505, 512; Thomas and Sauers, ed., *Civil War Letters*, pp. 245, 245n; Townsend, "History," p. 253, UME; Miers, ed., *Wash Roebling's War*, p. 29; Thomas J. Kessler–My dear friends, October 14, 1864, Kessler Papers, NC.

78. Oscar Cram–Ellen, October 1, 1864, Cram Letters, USAMHI; Carter, *Four Brothers*, p. 484.

79. Donald, *Lincoln*, p. 530.

80. Robertson, ed., *Civil War Letters*, p. 518; Woodward, ed., "Civil War," *PMHB*, v. 87, p. 56; Dunn, *Harvestfields*, pp. 263–64; Nevins, ed., *Diary*, p. 461; Elmer Wallace–Mother, September 27, October 16, 1864, Wallace Papers, UM; Hamilton R. Dunlap–Father, September 29, 1864, Dunlap Letters, PSU.

81. Donald, *Lincoln*, p. 544; McClure, *Abraham Lincoln*, p. 187; William S. Keller–Sister, November 8, 1864, Keller Letters; Hugh C. Perkins–Friends, October 16, 1864, Perkins Letters, USAMHI; Meade, *Life and Letters*, v. 2, p. 239.

82. Pullen, *Twentieth Maine*, p. 231; Charles E. Field–Hattie, October 10, 1864, Burleigh Papers, USAMHI; Husby and Wittenberg, eds., *Under Custer's Command*, p. 121; Menge and Shimrak, eds., *Civil War Notebook*, p. 138.

Chapter 17: "I Never Seen a Crazier Set of Fellows"

1. Walker, *History*, p. 641; Meade, *Life and Letters*, v. 2, p. 248.

2. Walker, *History*, p. 557; Davis, *Life*, pp. 275, 278, 279; Meade, *Life and Letters*, v. 2, p. 235; Agassiz, ed., *Meade's Headquarters*, p. 266.

3. Welcher, *Union Army*, p. 336; Menge and Shimrak, eds., *Civil War Notebook*, p. 51; Tucker, *Hancock*, pp. 264, 265.

4. Dana, *Recollections*, p. 192; Humphreys, *Andrew A. Humphreys*, pp. 239, 240, 241, 256, 258.

5. Agassiz, ed., *Meade's Headquarters*, p. 279; Dana, *Recollections*, p. 192; de Trobriand, *Four Years*, pp. 687, 688; Smith, *History*, p. 257; Menge and Shimrak, eds., *Civil War Notebook*, p. 57.

6. Gibbon, *Personal Recollections*, pp. 273, 274, 275; Smith, *History*, p. 258; Cleaves, *Meade*, p. 302; Warner, *Generals in Blue*, pp. 172, 241.

7. Meade, *Life and Letters*, v. 2, p. 256; Sparks, ed., *Inside Lincoln's Army*, p. 448; Gibbon, *Personal Recollections*, pp. 277, 278; Cornish, *Sable Arm*, p. 281.

8. Trudeau, *Last Citadel*, pp. 264–69, 271–74, 276–78, 280, 283, 285; Smith, *History of the 118th Pennsylvania*, p. 543; Townsend, "History," pp. 319–24, UME; William F. Winkleman–Parents, December 24, 1864; Diary, Morrow Papers, USAMHI.

9. Bird, ed., *Quill*, p. 254; Humphreys, *Virginia Campaign*, p. 311; Greene, *Breaking the Backbone*, pp. 60, 61; Rosenblatt and Rosenblatt, eds., *Hard Marching*, p. 287.

10. Rosenblatt and Rosenblatt, eds., *Hard Marching*, p. 288; Westbrook, *History*, p. 227; Wert, *From Winchester*, p. 250; Haines, *History*, p. 289.

11. Sauers, *Advance the Colors!*, v. 1, p. 247; v. 2, pp. 501–17; Embick, *Military History*, p. 4; Pascal P. Gilmore–My Dear Father, November 15, 1864, Gilmore Letters, USAMHI; Wert, *From Winchester*, p. 250; Sawyer et al., eds., *Letters*, p. 227.

12. Grant, *Personal Memoirs*, v. 2, Chapters 59–60.

13. Ibid., pp. 420–22; Donald, *Lincoln*, pp. 557, 558.

14. Donald, *Lincoln*, pp. 557–59; Cleaves, *Meade*, p. 304; Meade, *Life and Letters*, v. 2, pp. 249, 261.

15. Trudeau, *Last Citadel*, pp. 305, 306.

16. Ibid., pp. 312, 313; Cleaves, *Meade*, p. 304; Meade, *Life and Letters*, v. 2, pp. 249, 261.

17. Trudeau, *Last Citadel*, pp. 317, 318, 320, 322; Townsend, "History," pp. 346–50, UME; Erwin H. Flagg–Sister, February 14, 1865, Flagg Letters, SHSW; Reid–Green, ed., *Letters Home*, pp. 107–8; Pullen, *Twentieth Maine*, p. 238; Morrow Diary, USAMHI.

18. Patch, ed., *This from George*, p. 183; Silliker, ed., *Rebel Yell*, p. 233.

19. Grant, *Personal Memoirs*, v. 2, p. 424.

20. Ibid., pp. 416–19, 425.

21. Freeman, *Lee's Lieutenants*, v. 3, pp. 644, 645, 651, 652.

22. Ibid., pp. 646, 647; Trudeau, *Last Citadel*, p. 337.

23. Trudeau, *Last Citadel*, pp. 337–45; Gambone, *Major-General John Frederick Hartranft*, pp. 128, 130, 131, 133; Embick, *Military History*, p. 14.

24. Embick, *Military History*, p. 15; Gambone, *Major-General John Frederick Hartranft*, pp. 137, 139, 140; *Snyder County Historical Society Bulletins*, v. 1, p. 210; Austin Fenn–Wife, March 26, 1865, Fenn Papers, NC.

25. Trudeau, *Last Citadel*, pp. 349–54; Gambone, *Major-General John Frederick Hartranft*, pp. 140, 141, 147; Scott, ed., *Forgotten Valor*, pp. 615, 618; Fox, *Regimental Losses*, p. 460; Freeman, *Lee's Lieutenants*, v. 3, pp. 645, 651, 654.

26. Greene, *Breaking the Backbone*, pp. 12–24; Freeman, *Lee's Lieutenants*, v. 3, Chapter 31.

27. Donald, *Lincoln*, pp. 571–73

28. Ibid., pp. 573, 574.

29. Grant, *Personal Memoirs*, v. 2, pp. 436–37; Menge and Shimrak, eds., *Civil War Notebook*, p. 71.

30. Wert, *Custer*, pp. 205–13.

31. Ibid., p. 219; Grant, *Personal Memoirs*, v. 2, pp. 436, 437; Greene, *Breaking the Backbone*, pp. 206, 207.

32. Greene, *Breaking the Backbone*, pp. 207–11; Rhodes, ed., *All for the Union*, p. 222.

33. Greene, *Breaking the Backbone*, pp. 215–17, 219, 220; Wert, *Custer*, pp. 214–15.

34. Greene, *Breaking the Backbone*, pp. 225–33; Wert, *Custer*, pp. 215–16; Freeman, *Lee's Lieutenants*, p. 661.

35. OR, 46, pt. 3, pp. 339, 340, 341, 342.

36. Greene, *Breaking the Backbone*, pp. 236–38; Trudeau, *Out of the Storm*, pp. 30, 32; *B&L*, v. 4, p. 711.

37. Greene, *Breaking the Backbone*, p. 239; Chamberlain, *Passing of the Armies*, p. 158.

38. Greene, *Breaking the Backbone*, pp. 239–41; Chamberlain, *Passing of the Armies*, p. 158; Wert, *Custer*, pp. 218, 219.

39. Porter, *Campaigning with Grant*, pp. 441, 442, 443; OR, 46, pt. 3, pp. 394, 397; Grant, *Personal Memoirs*, v. 2, p. 446.

40. *OR*, 46, pt. 1, p. 836; Nevins, ed., *Diary*, p. 514; Campbell, ed., "*Grand Terrible Dramma*," p. 304.

41. Jordan, "*Happiness*," p. 232.

42. Ibid., pp. 232–33, 234.

43. A detailed account of the court of inquiry's hearings and report are in ibid., Chapters 26–30.

44. Embick, *Military History*, p. 19; Clifford Stickney–My dear brother, April 13, 1865, Stickney Papers, NC; W. H. Medill–Sister Kate, March 15, 1863, Hanna–McCormick Family Papers, LC; Livermore, *Days and Events*, p. 190.

45. Greene, *Breaking the Backbone*, pp. 270, 271, 293; *OR*, 36, pt. 3, pp. 389, 390; Clifford Stickney–My dear brother, April 13, 1865, Stickney Papers, NC.

46. The fullest description of the Sixth Corps's assault is in Greene, *Breaking the Backbone*, Chapters 7–8; account of Hill's death, pp. 346–49.

47. Ibid., pp. 386, 442–51; William F. Winkleman–Parents, April 19, 1865, Winkleman Papers, USAMHI.

48. Greene, *Breaking the Backbone*, pp. 384, 386; Trudeau, *Out of the Storm*, p. 62.

49. Trudeau, *Out of the Storm*, pp. 62, 63, 64; Greene, *Breaking the Backbone*, pp. 396–406; Freeman, *Lee Lieutenants*, v. 3, p. 682.

50. Greene, *Breaking the Backbone*, pp. 419–29, 433–42; *OR*, 46, pt. 3, p. 1378; Freeman, *Lee's Lieutenants*, v. 3, p. 680.

51. Trudeau, *Out of the Storm*, pp. 68, 74, 75, 76; Freeman, *Lee's Lieutenants*, v. 3, pp. 684, 685.

52. Trudeau, *Out of the Storm*, pp. 80–84; George Bronson–Wife, April 7, 1865, Pavlik Collection; D. T. Chandler–My dear Wife, April 6, 1865, Chandler Papers, NC.

53. Trudeau, *Out of the Storm*, p. 85; Donald, *Lincoln*, pp. 576, 577, 578.

54. Clifford Stickney–My dear brother, April 13, 1865, Stickney Papers, NC.

55. Freeman, *Lee's Lieutenants*, v. 3, pp. 687, 688–89.

56. Ibid., pp. 689–92; Wert, *Custer*, pp. 219–20; Trudeau, *Out of the Storm*, pp. 90–102.

57. Wert, *Custer*, p. 220; Wittenburg, *Little Phil*, p. 153; Freeman, *Lee's Lieutenants*, v. 3, pp. 698–707; Trudeau, *Out of the Storm*, pp. 108–16; *OR*, 46, pt. 3, p. 610.

58. Freeman, *Lee's Lieutenants*, v. 3, pp. 708–9, 712–14; Trudeau, *Out of the Storm*, pp. 102–6; H. B. Scott–Colonel, April 7, 1865, Scott Letter, USAMHI; Menge and Shimrak, eds., *Civil War Notebook*, p. 76.

59. Freeman, *Lee's Lieutenants*, pp. 716–17; Trudeau, *Out of the Storm*, pp. 120, 121; Charles E. Field–Hattie, April 16, 1865, Burleigh Papers, USAMHI; Maull, *Life*, pp. 43, 44.

60. Trudeau, *Out of the Storm*, pp. 121, 125; *OR*, 46, pt. 3, p. 619.

61. Trudeau, *Out of the Storm*, pp. 126–30; Wert, *Custer*, pp. 222–23.

62. Wert, *Custer*, p. 223; *OR*, 46, pt. 3, p. 653.

63. Trudeau, *Out of the Storm*, pp. 133–36; Wert, *Custer*, p. 224; *OR*, 46, pt. 3, pp. 619, 641, 664, 665, 666.

64. Freeman, *Lee's Lieutenants*, v. 3, pp. 738–39; Trudeau, *Out of the Storm*, pp. 142, 143; Agassiz, ed., *Meade's Headquarters*, p. 345; Meade, *Life and Letters*, v. 2, p. 270; Cleaves, *Meade*, pp. 330, 331.

65. *OR*, 46, pt. 3, pp. 666, 667; Trudeau, *Out of the Storm*, pp. 143, 144; Grant, *Personal Memoirs*, v. 2, pp. 491–92.

66. *OR*, 46, pt. 3, p. 663; Grant, *Personal Memoirs*, v. 2, p. 489.

67. Keiser Diary, p. 169; Moorhead, "Civil War Diary," p. 5, USAMHI; K. E. Newell–[?], [no date], Newell Papers; Clifford Stickney–My dear brother, April 13, 1865, Stickney Papers, NC; Menge and Shimrak, eds., *Civil War Notebook*, p. 78; Cleaves, *Meade*, p. 332.

68. Charles E. Perkins–Sister, April 10, 1865, Perkins Civil War Letters; Henry Rinker–My Dear Mary, April 9, 1865, Rinker Letters; Thomas C. Devin–My dear John, April 22, 1865, Devin Letter, USAMHI; Rich Diary, p. 58, UME; Silliker, ed., *Rebel Yell*, p. 265; Nevins, ed., *Diary*, pp. 520–21.

69. Freeman, *Lee's Lieutenants*, v. 3, pp. 745–51; Chamberlain, *Passing of the Armies*, p. 56; Marshall, *Company "K,"* p. 245; Nevins, ed., *Diary*, p. 520.

70. Meade, *Life and Letters*, v. 2, pp. 272, 273; Menge and Shimrak, eds., *Civil War Notebook*, p. 81; Beale, ed., *Diary*, v. 2, p. 288; Donald, *Lincoln*, pp. 594–96.

71. Menge and Shimrak, eds., *Civil War Notebook*, pp. 81–82; Campbell, Memoir, p. 22, USAMHI.

72. Menge and Shimrak, eds., *Civil War Notebook*, p. 82.

73. Staudenraus, ed., *Mr. Lincoln's Washington*, pp. 471–74; Grant, *Personal Memoirs*, v. 2, p. 534; Townsend, "History," p. 419, UME; Menge and Shimrak, eds., *Civil War Notebook*, p. 91.

74. Nevins, ed., *Diary*, pp. 525, 526; Chamberlain, *Passing of the Armies*, p. 329; Wert, *Custer*, p. 228.

75. Nevins, ed., *Diary*, p. 527; Chamberlain, *Passing of the Armies*, p. 329; Carter, *Four Brothers*, p. 506.

76. Nevins, ed., *Diary*, p. 527; Chamberlain, *Passing of the Armies*, p. 329.

77. Nevins, ed., *Diary*, p. 527; Chamberlain, *Passing of the Armies*, p. 359.

78. Chamberlain, *Passing of the Armies*, p. 359.

79. Nevins, ed., *Diary*, pp. 529, 530.

80. Welcher, *Union Army*, p. 292; Menge and Shimrak, eds., *Civil War Notebook*, p. 100.

81. Swinton, *Campaigns*, pp. 16, 622, 623.

82. Cowley, ed., *With My Face to the Enemy*, p. 61.

83. Rhea et al., "What Was Wrong," *N&S*, 4, 3, pp. 12, 14, 15; Weigley, *Great Civil War*, p. xxiv; Grimsley, *And Keep Moving On*, p. 229.

84. Grimsley, *And Keep Moving On*, p. 229; Weigley, *Great Civil War*, p. xxiv.

85. Rhea et al., "What Was Wrong," *N&S*, 4, 3, pp. 12, 14.

86. Weigley, *Great Civil War*, p. xxiv; Sommers, *Richmond Redeemed*, p. 437.

87. Cowley, ed., *With the Face to the Enemy*, p. 62.

88. Cassedy, ed., *Dear Friends*, p. 344.

⊰ BIBLIOGRAPHY ⊱

Unpublished Sources

ANTIETAM NATIONAL BATTLEFIELD, LIBRARY, SHARPSBURG, MD

Bragg, Edward S. Letter. Sixth Wisconsin Infantry File
Bryce, John W. "The Battle of South Mountain"
"The Civil War Letters of William C. White 69th PA Vols."
Longhenry, Ludolph, "A Yankee Piper in Dixie." 7th Wisconsin Infantry File
McCurdy, Stephen O. Letter
Odle, Elisha B. Papers. Typescript. 19th Indiana Infantry File
Peebles, Dudley Thomas. Memoir
Robbie, Member of the Stonewall Brigade. Letter. 33rd Virginia Infantry File
16th Connecticut Volunteer Infantry Regiment File
Stinson, Dwight E., Jr. "Operations of Sedgwick's Division in the West Woods." March
    1862

ASA FITCH HISTORICAL SOCIETY, SALEM, NY

Cruikshank, Robert. Civil War Letters. Typescript

BOSTON UNIVERSITY, LIBRARY, BOSTON, MA

Ropes, John C. Papers

BOWDOIN COLLEGE, HAWTHORNE-LONGFELLOW LIBRARY, BRUNSWICK, ME

Chamberlain, Joshua L. Papers
Howard, Oliver O. Papers

CENTRAL MICHIGAN UNIVERSITY, CLARKE HISTORICAL LIBRARY,
MOUNT PLEASANT, MI

Norton, Oliver W. Papers

CHICAGO HISTORICAL SOCIETY, CHICAGO, IL

Benedict, Edwin D. Diary
Converse, James L. Letters

CONNECTICUT HISTORICAL SOCIETY, HARTFORD, CT

Goodrich, Loren H. Papers

CORNELL UNIVERSITY, COLLECTION OF REGIONAL HISTORY,
UNIVERSITY ARCHIVES, ITHACA, NY
Camp, Jacob A. Letters

DETROIT PUBLIC LIBRARY, DETROIT, MI

Burton Historical Collection
Flanigan, Mark. Diary

Ward, E. B. Papers

DUKE UNIVERSITY, WILLIAM R. PERKINS LIBRARY, DURHAM, NC
Hancock, Winfield S. Papers
Smart, Richard B. Papers

Special Collections
Laughton, Joseph B. Papers
Osgood, Stephen. Papers

FRANKLIN AND MARSHALL COLLEGE, LANCASTER, PA
Reynolds Family. Papers

FREDERICKSBURG-SPOTSYLVANIA NATIONAL MILITARY PARK,
LIBRARY, FREDERICKSBURG, VA
Legate, George H. Letter. Typescript
Nihiser, James M. Letter. Typescript
Peck, Abel G. Letter. Typescript
Ward, J. H. Hobart. File

GETTYSBURG COLLEGE, SPECIAL COLLECTIONS, LIBRARY,
GETTYSBURG, PA
Clare, Henry Pentland. Letters

GETTYSBURG NATIONAL MILITARY PARK, LIBRARY, GETTYSBURG, PA
1st South Carolina Infantry File
1st U.S. Artillery, Battery I File
5th U.S. Artillery, Battery C File
7th Michigan Infantry File
11th Pennsylvania Infantry File
12th New Jersey Infantry File
137th New York Infantry File

Gregory A. Coco Collection
Pettit's Battery Letters
Wright, James A. "The Story of Co. F, 1st Minn. Inf." Typescript

Doubleday, Abner. File
Hunt, Henry J. File
Williams, Seth. File

HARPERS FERRY NATIONAL HISTORICAL PARK, HARPERS FERRY, WV
Doubleday, Abner. Journal

THE HISTORICAL SOCIETY OF PENNSYLVANIA, PHILADELPHIA, PA
Biddle, James Cornell. Civil War Letters
Brooke, John R. Papers
Cavada, Adolphus F. Diary
Gibbon, John. Papers
Gregg, David McMurtrie. Papers
Humphreys, Andrew A. Papers
Lynch, John Wheat. Letters
Meade, George G. Collection
Rawle, William Brooke. Papers

HUNTINGTON LIBRARY, SAN MARINO, CA
Lieber, Francis. Papers

INDIANA HISTORICAL SOCIETY, INDIANAPOLIS, IN
Beem, David E. Collection
Jackson, William N. Diary. Typescript
Jessup, John C. Letters
Meredith, Soloman. Papers
Moore, William Roby. Civil War Letters and Reminiscences
Starbuck, Julietta. Civil War Letters

INDIANA STATE LIBRARY, INDIANAPOLIS, IN
Henry C. Marsh Collection
Marsh, Henry C. Letters and Diary

19th Indiana Regimental Correspondence

INDIANA UNIVERSITY, LILLY LIBRARY, BLOOMINGTON, IN
Manuscripts Department
Harding, John L. Papers

Orr, William. Papers

LIBRARY OF CONGRESS, WASHINGTON, D.C.
Babcock, John C. Papers
Bartlett, Joseph J. Papers
Bates, Samuel P. Papers
Carman, Ezra. Papers
Chamberlain, Joshua L. Papers
Crawford, Samuel. Papers
George, Harold C. Papers
Hanna-McCormick Family. Papers
Heintzelman, Samuel P. Papers

Holford, Lyman C. Diary
Hunt, Henry J. Papers
Larned, Daniel Reed. Correspondence
Lincoln, Abraham. Papers
Love, John J. H. Papers
Porter, Fitz John. Papers
Wadsworth, James W., Jr. Papers

MAINE STATE ARCHIVES, AUGUSTA, ME

Dow, Edwin B. "Account of the 6th Maine Battery at Gettysburg." Typescript
Dyer, George W. Papers
Howe, William. "The Battle of Aldie"
Long, Hezekiah. Civil War Letters
Morrill, DeWitt Clinton. Diary
Porter, Willis M. Civil War Diary and Letters
Saunders, George C. Diary. Typescript
Stevens, Greenleaf T. "Account of the 5th Maine Battery at Gettysburg"

MANASSAS NATIONAL MILITARY PARK, LIBRARY, MANASSAS, VA

2nd Maine Letters File
2nd New Hampshire Anonymous Account of, 1st Manassas File
2nd Wisconsin Infantry File. Davis, William G. Letters
3rd Maine Letters File

11th Massachusetts
Emerton, Timothy O. Letter. 8/6/61 File

Bryant, Walter C. Memoir
Buford, John. File
Caskin, J. H. "Report of Armaments and Forts on Potomac, July 3, 1862."
Franklin, William B. Letter File
Hollister, Edward. Letters. Typescript
Johnston, Edward A. Letters
McCook, Daniel. File
McCormick, Henry. Letter
Paulus, Margaret B., ed. "Papers of General Robert Huston Milroy: Volume 1, Milroy
    Family Letters, 1862–1863." Copy
Ritter, Henry F. Letter
Taylor, George W. "Account of Excelsior Brigade"
Thompson, Al Baker. Letters. Typescript
Wells, John A. Account, 14th Brooklyn, 1st Manassas File

MASSACHUSETTS HISTORICAL SOCIETY, BOSTON, MA

Barlow, Francis. Papers
Beal, Caleb Hadley. Papers
Hayward, Nathan. Papers
Morse, Charles F. Papers
Whitmore, George A. Diary

MICHIGAN STATE UNIVERSITY, UNIVERSITY ARCHIVES AND HISTORICAL COLLECTIONS, MAIN LIBRARY, LANSING, MI

Peck, Abel G. Letters

MINNESOTA HISTORICAL SOCIETY, ST. PAUL, MN

Carpenter, Alfred P. Papers
Marvin, Matthew. Diary

MISSOURI HISTORICAL SOCIETY, ST. LOUIS, MO

Bulkley Family. Papers
Carpenter, Thomas. Letters

NATIONAL ARCHIVES, WASHINGTON, D.C.

John B. Bachelder Papers
Silbey, Franklin R. Collection

Compiled Service Records, Records Group 94
Records Group 94
Records Group 393. U.S. Army Continental Commands. 1821–1920. Army of the Potomac
Records Group 729

NAVARRO COLLEGE, PEARCE CIVIL WAR COLLECTION, CORSICANA, TX

"The Battle of Chancellorsville"
Blandin, A. A. Papers, 1863
Boudwin, John A. Papers
Brooker, John. Papers
Buchanan, S. T. Papers
Burpee, Edgar. Papers
Chamberlain, Joshua Lawrence. Papers
Chandler, D. T. Papers, 1865
Coy Family. Papers
Crandall, Lewis H. Papers, 1863
Crane, James E. Papers
Crawford, Lewis. Papers, 1864
Dadswell, Thomas. Papers
Devin, Thomas Casimer. Papers
Dibble, Oliver. Papers
Doubleday, Abner. Papers, c. 1861–1879
Durie, William B. Papers
Ebling, Jonathan S. Papers
Edwards, Clark S. Papers
Evans, Seth Gilbert. Papers, 1861–1864
Fales, John. Papers
Fenn, Austin. Papers
Flynn, James B. Papers
Fonda, Ten Eyck. Papers

Glossinger, William. Papers
Goulding, G. W. Papers
Hancock, Winfield Scott. Papers
Hayward, Albert Morton. Papers
Hoitt, William P. Papers
Hubbard, H. D. Papers
Hunt, Chester F. Papers
Kessler, Thomas J. Papers
McClellan, George B. Papers
McLean, Francis. Papers
Meade, George G. Papers
Newell, K. E. Papers
Nichols, A. K. Papers
Palmer, Oliver H. Papers
Paxton, Thomas, and Paxton, Wilson. Papers
Pyewell, J. Papers
Rood, Frank M. Papers
Slocum, Henry Warner. Papers
Smith, James McDonald. Papers, 1861–1862
Spafford, A. Papers
Stacy, Manly T. Papers, 1863
Stickney, Clifford. Papers
Taggart, Charles A. Papers
Tuttle, Dennis. Papers
Vance, Norman. Papers
Walker, Edward A. Papers
Warrenton, M. Papers
Webster, Timothy O. Papers
Wheeler, Charles A. Papers, 1861–1864. Typescript
Wiles, Alanson. Papers

NEW-YORK HISTORICAL SOCIETY, NEW YORK, NY
Barnes, James. Papers

Gilder Lehrman Collection
Allison, William A. Letters
Slagle, Jacob. Letters
Smith, David M. Letters

Paine, William Henry. Papers
Paine, William H. Diary

NEW YORK STATE ARCHIVES, ALBANY, NY
Warren, Gouverneur K. Papers

NEW YORK STATE LIBRARY, ALBANY, NY
Carpenter, Henry B. Papers
Hallack, John F. Papers

McDougall, Archibald. Papers
Shaw, Wesley H. Papers
Sickles, Daniel Edgar. Papers
Spaulding, Ira. Papers
Walker, Patrick. Papers
Wilson, Hiram Sickles. Papers

OHIO HISTORICAL SOCIETY, COLUMBUS, OH
Powell, Eugene. Memoirs

OHIO STATE UNIVERSITY, RARE BOOKS LIBRARY, COLUMBUS, OH
Ricksecken, Rufus. Letters

Oliver, James. "Civil War Diary of Dr. James Oliver, 1862–1864." Typescript copy in
     possession of author
Pavlik, Mary Lou. Collection, Torrington, CT

PENNSYLVANIA HISTORICAL AND MUSEUM COMMISSION,
HARRISBURG, PA
Bates, Samuel P. Collection
Rothermel, Peter F. Papers

PENNSYLVANIA STATE UNIVERSITY, PATTEE-PATERNO LIBRARY,
SPECIAL COLLECTIONS, UNIVERSITY PARK, PA
Beaver, James A. Collection

Civil War Letter Collection
Kelley, James

Mary Dyla McDowell Collection
"Battle of Antietam." File
Browne, Robert A. Letters
Dunlap, Hamilton R. Letters
Hamilton, Thomas. Letters. Typescript
Leasure, Daniel. Letters
Leasure, George. Letters
Miscellaneous Letters Home (1861–1887)
Stevenson, Silas. "A History of the Roundheads"

Wiley, William Campbell. Papers

NICHOLAS P. PICERNO, SR., COLLECTION, BRIDGEWATER, VA
Nye, George H. Papers

STATE HISTORICAL SOCIETY OF WISCONSIN, MADISON, WI
Adjutant General Reports, Series 1200, Iron Brigade
Beecham, Henry W. Letters
Bragg, Edward S. Papers
Brown, Edwin A. Letters. Typescript

Carter, [Dick] Letter
Cook, John H. "Memoir"
Currier, Horace. Papers. Typescript
Dawes, Rufus R. Papers
Flagg, Erwin H. Letters
Fuller, Caleb F. Papers
Haskell, Frank A. Letters. Typescript
Huntley, Reuben. Papers
Ketner, William J. Papers
Larke, Alured. Letters
Mead, Sydney B. "A Journal of the Marches, Reconnaissances, Skirmishes and Battles
    of the Second Regiment of Wisconsin Volunteer Infantry, June 11, 1861–March
    29, 1864"
Murray, Julius A. Family Papers
Noble, William. Diary
Parker, Orson. Letters
Perry, James M. Papers
Quiner, E. B. Correspondence of the Wisconsin volunteers, 1861–1865
Rollins, Nathaniel. Papers
Rood, Amos D. Memoir. Typescript
St. Clair, John Weslie. Papers
Watrous, Jerome. Papers
Winslow, Loring B. F. Letters
Young, Henry F. Papers

ULSTER COUNTY GENEALOGICAL SOCIETY, KINGSTON, NY
Haggerty, James C. Diary. Typescript

UNITED STATES ARMY MILITARY HISTORY INSTITUTE, ARCHIVES,
CARLISLE BARRACKS, PA
Ames, John W. Papers. Typescript
Benham, Henry W. Papers
Birney, David B. Papers

Boyer, Ronald D. Collection
Musser, John D. Correspondence. Typescript

Brake, Robert L. Collection
Pennsylvania–31st Infantry Regiment

Brooks, William T. H. Papers
Burleigh, Hattie. Papers
Chandler, Albert B. Papers

Civil War Miscellaneous Collection
Alexander, Samuel J. Correspondence
Ashley Family. Papers
Baker, Joseph D. Letters
Barnes, John L. Letter

Bateman, Timothy. Diary. Typescript

Bean, Thomas. Letter

Belknap, Charles Wesley. Diary

Bell, Clarence H. Letters

Berdan, Hiram. Letter

Bevan, John H. Letters

Bingham, Origen G. Letter

Blake, Aaron K. Letters

Boring, John F. Letter

Brown, Orrel. Diary and Letters

Campbell, Henry C. Memoir

Chandler, George C. Letters

"Civil War Union Soldier's 1863 Diary." Typescript

Corbin, Elbert. Diary

Cram, Oscar. Letters

Crandell, Lewis H. Account of Gettysburg

Dains, Arnold P. Letters

Davis, Leander E. "The Artillery Man, Parts I and II." Edited by W. C. Niesen

DeClark, James. Papers

Delp, Hannah E. Civil War Letters

Dickerson, Frank Wilberforce. Letters. Typescript

Donlon, Michael. Letters

Downes, Jeremiah. Letters

Downing, Amos. Letters

Elliott, Joseph P. Diary

Fish, John D. Letters

Flint, Dayton E. Civil War Letters. Typescript

Fowler, Frederick K. "The Making of a Zouave"

Fribley, Charles W. Diaries

Garcelon, Charles A. Diary

Gilmore, Pascal P. Letters

Gourlie, John. Letters

Granger, Luther A. Letters

Gray, Liston. Letter

Hatton, Thomas. Diary. Typescript

Hawkins, Benjamin S. Letters

Hawley, Edmund. Letter

Haynes, William T. Letter

Hays, John. "His Account of the Battle of Antietam Read at the Court House, Carlisle, PA on September 17, 1890"

Heller, Calvin S. Diary. Typescript

Henry, Edward. Letters

Herzog, Charles. Papers

Hill, John D. Civil War Letters. Typescript

Holloway, John B. Letter

Holman, Freland N. Letters

Holmes, William R. Letter

Homan, William. Diary. Typescript

Hoyt, Henry. Papers

Hubler, Simon. "Narrative of Simon Hubler, First Sergeant, Late of Co 'I' 143 Reg. Pa. Vol. Inf."

Law Family. Papers. Typescript

Leivelsberger, Jacob C. Diary

Linn, John B. "Journal of My Trip to the Battlefield at Gettysburg." Typescript

Mancha, J. Franklin. Diary. Typescript

Martin, Henry L. Letter

McCreight, Robert. Letters

Meshach, P. Larry. Letters

Mesnard, Luther B. "Reminiscence." Typescript

Miller Family Letters

Moorhead, Robert Scott. "Civil War Diary of Private Robert Scott Moorhead of Erie County, Pennsylvania"

Myers, William H. Letters

Norton, Oliver. Letter

Palmer, Oliver H. Letter

Peabody, Miles. Letters

Peacock, William H. Letters

Peck, Dwight. Letter

Pennell, Benjamin C. Letters

Plumb, Isaac. "Record of Life & Service Compiled from Letters"

Pollock, Curtis C. Letters. Typescript

Post, James B. Letters

Ranger, Frederick. Letters

Rich, Stephen. Letters

Richards, M. Edgar. Letters

Root, Samuel H. Letters

Rosenkranz, Frasier. Letters. Typescript

Salsburg, Samuel B. Letter

Samson, David. Letters

Sawtelle Family. Papers

Sayre, William Moore. Letters. Typescript

Shingle, George W. Letter

Shuey, Anson B. War Letters. Typescript

Simpson, James Randolph and George. "Dear Daul": Civil War Letters. Typescript

Slagle, Jacob F. Letter

Soule, Horatio S. Diary

Stanfield, Joseph. Diary

Steward, John M. Letters

Tanner, Merton S. Letter

Tarbell, Doctor. Diary

Tarleton, S. B. Letter

Wallar, Francis Asbury. Diary

Walling, William Henry. Letters. Typescript

Walthall, Howard Malcolm. "Reminiscences." Typescript

Weiser, John S. Letters

Westervelt, William B. Memoir and Diary

Whittemore, Franklin. Letter, July 5, 1863
Wilbur, Joshua G. Letters
Williams Family Letters
Wilson, Hiram S. Papers
Wyman, Arthur B. Papers
Young, Frank R. Diary
Young, Henry H. Letters

Civil War Times Illustrated *Collection*

Appleby, Benjamin F. Correspondence
Berry, John. Diary
Brisbin, James S. Letters. Typescript
Brown, Charles L. Letter
Brown, Elon F. Daily Journal
Burrill, John H. Letters. Typescript
Caldwell Family Correspondence
Cartwright Family Correspondence
Chapin, Nelson. Correspondence
Chesson, Frederick W. Collection
Coburn, Robert S. Diary
Coon, Steuben H. Papers
Coriette, Frederick. Letter
Croop, William. Letters
"'Dear Sister': The Civil War Letters of William E. Dunn." Edited by Edward K. Eckert and Boyd Litzinger
Devin, Thomas C. Letter. Typescript
Fisk, Wilbur. Letters
Gerrish, Henry. Memoirs. Typescript
Gillette, James. Papers
Hale, Charles A. "Story of My Personal Experience at the Battle of Antietam"
Hart, James M. "1863 Civil War Diary James M. Hart 7th Indiana Volunteer Infantry." Edited by Jerry M. Easley
Heffelfinger, Jacob. Diary. Typescript
Hemmeniva, William. "Reminiscence of Battle of Fredericksburg." Typescript
Henney, Henry. Diary and Letters. Typescript
Hodgkins, Thomas. Letters. Typescript
Jennings, Frank. "Reminiscences." Typescript
Jones, J. N. Diary. Typescript
Keller, William S. Letters
Kent, William C. Memoirs
McQuaide, John M. Letters
Perkins, Charles E. Civil War Letters. Typescript
Peters, E. T. Letter. Typescript
Pope, Albert A. Diary. Typescript
Rollins, George. Correspondence
Smith, Perry R. Correspondence
Stowe, Jonathan P. Letters
Strouss, Ellis C. Letters

Swan, Henry Richard. Letters
Wesson, Silas W. Diary. Typescript
Woodward, John H. "Memories of the Civil War." Typescript

Ford, Stanley H. Papers
Fuller, Charles W. Letter
Hancock, Winfield Scott. Papers
Halsey, Edmund D. Papers

Harrisburg Civil War Round Table Collection
Ashenfelter, Benjamin F. Letters
Coco, Gregory A. Collection
Evans, William J. Letters
Fullerton, John M. Letters
Gardner, Isaac W. Letters and Diaries
Johnson, Charles R. Letters
Knox, Andrew. Letters
Scott, H. B. Letter
Shaw, Walter B. Letter
Daniels, Norman Collection of Civil War Papers
Willey, John S. Correspondence

Faller, John and Leo. Correspondence. Typescript
Flinchbaugh, Dawson Collection
Treziyulny, J. Frank P. Diary

Furst, Luther. Diary. Typescript
Hoffman, Clement. Papers
Jones, A. Stokes. Letters
Kauffman, George. Collection
Keiser, Henry. Diary. Typescript
Leib, Henry. Diary
Martin, William H. Papers
Maycock, James John. Diary. Typescript
Nichol, David. Papers
Ployer, Fred K. Letters
Rinker, Henry. Letters
Rowley, Thomas A. "Testimony at his Court Martial for Gettysburg." Typescript
Seibert Family Papers
Steljes Collection
Blanchard, Henry. Letters
Garland, Albert S. Letter

Upton, Emory. Letter
Williams, Edgar. Letter

Henry Family Papers

Hess, Earl M. Collection
Hunt, Chester F. Letter

Hopper, George. Papers
Hubbard, Robert. Letters. Typescript
Johnson Family. Papers

Keller, Keith R. Collection
Smith, Thomas D. G. Letters

Lambie, Gavin Allen. Papers. Typescript

Leigh, Lewis Collection
Carter, Samuel B. Letter, July 9, 1863
Gardner, Thomas W. Letter, June 23, 1863
Howard, Oliver D. Memoranda, July 25, 1863

Luvaas, Jay Collection
Smith, Theodore. Letter
Taggart, Robert. Diary. Typescript .

Massachusetts MOLLUS Collection
Hancock, Winfield Scott. Papers

Miles, Nelson A. Papers
Mindil, George W. Papers

Morrow-Boniface Family Papers
Morrow, Henry A. Diary, November 11, 1864–March 3, 1865

Northwest Corner Civil War Round Table Collection
Adams, Alexander. Civil War Letters. Typescript
Barnard, Alanson. Letters. Typescript
Doubleday, Abner. Letter
Prindle, Henry F. Letters

Palm, Ronn Collection
McJunkin, Milton E. Letters

Pellett, John. Papers

Pennsylvania "Save the Flags" Collection
Acheson, Alexander W., and Acheson, David. "Family Letters in a Civil War Century." Edited by Jane M. Fulcher, 1986
Becker, Charles. Diary
Burns, William J. Diary. Typescript
Moore, John D. Letters

Poriss, Ralph G. Collection
Blanchard, H. Letter. July 11, 1863

Stephens, Thomas W. "The Civil War Diary of Thomas White Stephens Sergeant, Company K 20th Indiana Regiment of Volunteers." Edited by Paul E. Wilson and Harriet Stephens Wilson, 1985

Stone, Thomas R. Collection
Perkins, Hugh C. Letters. Typescript

Sword, Wiley Collection
Bates, Albert G. Letters and Diary
Edwards, Clark S. Letters
Goodyear, Robert B. Letters

Tanfield Family Papers
Thaxter, Benjamin. Papers
Thickstun Family Papers
Tuttle, Squire and Chester. Papers
Van Aernum, Henry. Papers
Vautier, John D. Papers
Vreeland-Warden Papers
Ward, John Henry Hobart, Papers

Winey, Michael Collection
Hemmingen, John D. Diary. Typescript

Winkleman, William F. Papers
Woods, George H. Papers

UNITED STATES MILITARY ACADEMY, WEST POINT, NY
Tidball, John C. Papers

UNIVERSITY OF MAINE, RAYMOND H. FOGLER LIBRARY, SPECIAL COLLECTIONS DEPARTMENT, ORONO, ME

Bean, Paul W. Collection
Brown, J. Loyal. Letters, 1862–1864
Brown, William C. Letter, December 17, 1862
Lemont, Frank L. Letters, 1861–1864
Rice, W. B. Letter, July 31, 1861. Typescript
Rich, James M. Diary. Typescript
Salley, J. F. Letter, March 17, 1864
Townsend, Fred E. "History and Reminiscences of the 17th Maine Volunteer Infantry."
Williams, Jothan D. Letters, 1862–1864

UNIVERSITY OF MICHIGAN, ANN ARBOR, MI

Bentley Historical Library
Buck Family Papers
Corselius, George. Papers
Kidd, James Harvey. Papers

Noble, Alfred. "A 'G.I.' View of the Civil War: The Diary of Alfred Noble." Alfred
    Noble Papers
O'Brien Family Papers
Ryder, John E. Letters
Shattuck, Lucius L. Letters. Typescript
Wallace, Elmer D. Papers

William L. Clements Library

Alger, Russell A. Papers
Emerson, Horace. Letters
Schoff Civil War Collection: Soldiers' Letters
Speed, William, and Speed, Frederick. Papers, 1857–1874

UNIVERSITY OF NORTH CAROLINA, WILSON LIBRARY, SOUTHERN
HISTORICAL COLLECTION, CHAPEL HILL, NC

Baker, William B. Papers
Robbins, William M. Papers

UNIVERSITY OF VERMONT, BURLINGTON, VT

Clinn, Charles H. Civil War Diary

UNIVERSITY OF WISCONSIN–LA CROSSE, MURPHY LIBRARY,
LA CROSSE, WI

Mitchell, George. Papers

VERMONT HISTORICAL SOCIETY, BARRE, VT

Barney, Valentine. Letters
Benedict, G. G. Papers

VIRGINIA TECH UNIVERSITY, SPECIAL COLLECTIONS DEPARTMENT,
UNIVERSITY LIBRARIES, BLACKSBURG, VA

Candler, William Latham. Papers, 1861–63

WESTERN RESERVE HISTORICAL SOCIETY, WILLIAM P. PALMER
COLLECTION, CLEVELAND, OH

Bingham, Henry H.
"Anecdotes Concerning Gen. Hancock and Other Officers at Gettysburg and Else-
    where," 1874
"Memoirs of Hancock," 1872

Participant Accounts

YALE UNIVERSITY, BEINECKE RARE BOOK AND MANUSCRIPT
LIBRARY, HISTORICAL MANUSCRIPTS DIVISION, NEW HAVEN, CT

Webb, Alexander S. Papers

Newspapers

Boston *Journal*
Cortland (N.Y.) *Gazette and Banner*
Detroit *Advertiser and Tribune*
Maine Farmer
Minneapolis State Atlas
New York *Leader*
Philadelphia *Inquirer*
Philadelphia *North American*
Springfield [Mass.] *Daily Republican*
Toledo *Blade*
Washington *Post*

Published Books and Articles

Acken, J. Gregory, ed. *Inside the Army of the Potomac: The Civil War Experience of Captain Francis Adams Donaldson*. Mechanicsburg, PA: Stackpole, 1998.

Adams, John G. B. *Reminiscences of the Nineteenth Massachusetts Regiment*. Boston: Wright & Potter, 1899.

Adams, John R. *Memorial and Letters of Rev. John R. Adams, D.D.* Cambridge: University Press, John Wilson and Son, 1890.

Adams, Michael C. C. *Our Masters the Rebels: A Speculation on Union Military Failure in the East, 1861–1865*. Cambridge: Harvard University Press, 1978.

Agassiz, George R., ed. *Meade's Headquarters, 1863–1865: Letters of Colonel Theodore Lyman from the Wilderness to Appomattox*. Boston: Atlantic Monthly Press, 1922.

Albert, Allen D., ed. *History of the Forty-fifth Regiment Pennsylvania Veteran Volunteer Infantry, 1861–1865*. Williamsport, PA: Grit Publishing Company, 1912.

Alexander, Ted. "Antietam: The Bloodiest Day." *North & South*, vol. 5, no. 7 (October 2002).

———. "Ten Days in July: The Pursuit to the Potomac." *North & South*, vol. 2, no. 6 (August 1999).

Ames, Nelson. *History of Battery G First Regiment New York Light Battery*. Reprint, Wolcott, NY: Benedum, 2000.

The Annals of the War Written by Leading Participants North and South. Reprint, Dayton, OH: Morningside House, 1988.

Archer, John M. "Remembering the 14th Connecticut Volunteers." *Gettysburg Magazine*, no. 9 (July 1993).

Arner, Frederick B. *The Mutiny at Brandy Station—The Last Battle of the Hooker Brigade: A Controversial Army Reorganization, Courts Martial, and the Bloody Days That Followed*. Kensington, MD: Bates and Blood Press, 1993.

Bacarella, Michael. *Lincoln's Foreign Legion: The 39th New York Infantry, the Garibaldi Guard*. Shippensburg, PA: White Mane, 1996.

Bandy, Ken, and Freeland, Florence, eds. *The Gettysburg Papers*. Two volumes. Dayton, OH: Press of Morningside Bookshop, 1978.

Banes, Charles H. *History of the Philadelphia Brigade*. Philadelphia: J. B. Lippincott, 1876.

Baquet, Camille. *History of the First Brigade, New Jersey Volunteers from 1861 to 1865*. Reprint, Gettysburg, PA: Stan Clark Military Books, 1991.

Barber, Raymond G., and Swinson, Gary E., eds. *The Civil War Letters of Charles Barber, Private, 104th New York Volunteer Infantry.* Torrance, CA: Gary E. Swinson, 1991.

Bates, Samuel P. *The Battle of Chancellorsville.* Reprint, Gaithersburg, MD: Ron R. Van Sickle Military Books, 1987.

Bauer, K. Jack. *Soldiering: The Civil War Diary of Rice C. Bull, 123rd New York Volunteer Infantry.* San Rafael, CA: Presidio, 1977.

Baumgartner, Richard A. *Buckeye Blood: Ohio at Gettysburg.* Huntington, WV: Blue Acorn, 2003.

Baxter, Nancy Niblack. *Gallant Fourteenth: The Story of an Indiana Civil War Regiment.* Indianapolis: Guild Press of Indiana, 1991.

———, ed. *Hoosier Farm Boy in Lincoln's Army: The Civil War Letters of Pvt. John R. McClure.* Privately printed, 1971.

Beach, William H. *The First New York (Lincoln) Cavalry, From April 19, 1861 to July 7, 1865.* Reprint, Annandale, VA: Bacon Race, 1988.

Beale, Howard K., ed. *Diary of Gideon Welles.* Three volumes. New York: W. W. Norton, 1960.

Bearss, Ed, and Calkins, Chris. *Battle of Five Forks.* Lynchburg, VA: H. E. Howard, Inc., 1985.

Beatie, Russel H. *The Army of the Potomac: Birth of Command, November 1860–September 1861, Volume I.* New York: Da Capo, 2002.

Beaudot, William J. K., and Herdegen, Lance J., eds. *An Irishman in the Iron Brigade: The Civil War Memoirs of James P. Sullivan, Sergt., Company K, 6th Wisconsin Volunteers.* New York: Fordham University Press, 1993.

Bee, Robert L. *The Boys from Rockville: Civil War Narratives of Sgt. Benjamin Hirst, Company D, 14th Connecticut Volunteers.* Knoxville: University of Tennessee Press, 1998.

Benedict, George Grenville. *Army Life in Virginia: Letters from the Twelfth Vermont Regiment and Personal Experiences of Volunteer Service in the War for the Union, 1862–63.* Reprint, Newport, VT: Tony O'Connor Civil War Enterprises, n.d.

———. *Vermont in the Civil War: A History of the Part Taken by the Vermont Soldiers and Sailors in the War for the Union, 1861–5.* Two volumes. Burlington, VT: Free Press Association, 1886–1888.

Bennett, Brian A. *Sons of Old Monroe: A Regimental History of Patrick O'Rorke's 140th New York Volunteer Infantry.* Dayton, OH: Morningside House, 1999.

Benton, Charles E. *As Seen from the Ranks: A Boy in the Civil War.* New York: G. P. Putnam's Sons, 1902.

Best, Isaac O. *History of the 121st New York State Infantry.* Reprint, Baltimore, MD: Butternut & Blue, 1996.

Bicknell, George W. *History of the Fifth Regiment Maine Volunteers.* Portland, ME: Hall L. Davis, 1871.

Billings, John D. *Hardtack and Coffee or the Unwritten Story of Army Life.* Boston: George M. Smith, 1888.

———. *The History of the Tenth Massachusetts Battery of Light Artillery in the War of the Rebellion.* Reprint, Baltimore, MD: Butternut & Blue, n.d.

Bird, Kermit Molyneux, ed. *Quill of the Wild Goose: Civil War Letters and Diaries of Private Joel Molyneux, 141st P.V.* Shippensburg, PA: Burd Street Press, 1996.

Black, Linda G. "A Wife's Devotion: The Story of James and Fanny Rickets." *Blue & Gray Magazine,* vol. 11, no. 5 (June 1994).

Blair, William Alan, ed. *A Politician Goes to War: The Civil War Letters of John White Geary*. University Park: Pennsylvania State University Press, 1995.

Blake, Henry N. *Three Years in the Army of the Potomac*. Boston: Lee & Shepard, 1865.

Boritt, Gabor S., ed. *Lincoln's Generals*. New York: Oxford University Press, 1994.

Boyle, Frank A. *A Party of Mad Fellows: The Story of the Irish Regiments in the Army of the Potomac*. Dayton, OH: Morningside House, 1996.

Boyle, John Richards. *Soldiers True: The Story of the One Hundred and Eleventh Regiment Pennsylvania Veteran Volunteers, and of Its Campaigns in the War for the Union, 1861–1865*. New York: Eaton & Mains, 1903.

Brady, James P., ed. *Hurrah for the Artillery!: Knap's Independent Battery "E," Pennsylvania Light Artillery*. Gettysburg, PA: Thomas, 1992.

Brainard, Mary Genevie Green, ed. *Campaigns of the 146th Regiment New York State Volunteers Also Known as Halleck's Infantry, the Fifth Oneida, and Garrad's Tigers*. Preface and New Material by Patrick A. Schroeder. Daleville, VA: Schroeder, 2000.

Brainerd, Wesley. *Bridge Building in Wartime: Colonel Wesley Brainerd's Memoir of the 50th New York Volunteer Engineers*. Edited by Ed Malles. Knoxville: University of Tennessee Press, 1997.

Brennan, Patrick. "The Army Commander Who Never Was." *North & South*, vol. 5, no. 5 (July 2002).

Brennan, Patrick J. "Little Mac's Last Stand." *Blue & Gray Magazine*, vol. 17, no. 2 (December 1999).

Brown, Kent Masterson. *Cushing of Gettysburg: The Story of a Union Artillery Commander*. Lexington: University Press of Kentucky, 1993.

———. "A Golden Bridge: Lee's Williamsport Defense Lines and His Escape Across the Potomac." *North & South*, vol. 2, no. 6 (August 1999).

Bruce, George A. *The Twentieth Regiment of Massachusetts Volunteer Infantry, 1861–1865*. Reprint, Baltimore: Butternut & Blue, 1988.

Bruen, Ella Jane, and Fitzgibbons, Brian M., eds. *Through Ordinary Eyes: The Civil War Correspondence of Rufus Robbins, Private, 7th Regiment, Massachusetts Volunteers*. Westport, CT: Praeger, 2000.

Buell, Augustus. *The Cannoneer: Recollections of Service in the Army of the Potomac*. Washington, D.C.: National Tribune, 1897.

Burr, Frank A. *Life and Achievements of James Addams Beaver. Early Life, Military Services and Public Career*. Philadelphia: Ferguson Bros., 1882.

Burton, Brian K. *Extraordinary Circumstances: The Seven Days Battles*. Bloomington and Indianapolis: Indiana University Press, 2001.

Busey, John W. *These Honored Dead: The Union Casualties at Gettysburg*. Hightstown, NJ: Longstreet House, 1988.

———, and Martin, David G. *Regimental Strengths at Gettysburg*. Baltimore: Gateway, 1982.

Butterfield, Julia Lorrilard, ed. *A Biographical Memorial of General Daniel Butterfield Including Many Addresses and Military Writings*. New York: Grafton, 1904.

Byrne, Frank L., and Weaver, Andrew T., eds. *Haskell of Gettysburg: His Life and Civil War Papers*. Madison: State Historical Society of Wisconsin, 1970.

Campbell, Eric A. "Caldwell Clears the Wheatfield." *Gettysburg Magazine*, no. 3 (July 1990).

———, ed. "A Grand Terrible Dramma" from Gettysburg to Petersburg: The Civil War Letters of Charles Wellington Reed*. New York: Fordham University Press, 2000.

Carmichael, Peter. "Lee's Search for the Battle of Annihilation." *North & South*, vol. 3, no. 5 (June 2000).

Carter, Robert Goldthwaite. *Four Brothers in Blue; Or, Sunshine and Shadows of the War of the Rebellion: A Story of the Great Civil War from Bull Run to Appomattox.* Reprint, Austin: University of Texas Press, 1979.

Cassedy, Edward K., ed. *Dear Friends at Home: The Civil War Letters and Diaries of Sergeant Charles T. Bowen Twelfth United States Infantry First Battalion, 1861–1864.* Baltimore: Butternut & Blue, 2001.

Catton, Bruce. *Glory Road.* Garden City, NY: Doubleday, 1952.

———. *Grant Takes Command.* Boston: Little, Brown, 1969.

———. *Mr. Lincoln's Army.* Garden City, NY: Doubleday, 1962.

———. *A Stillness at Appomattox.* Garden City, NY: Doubleday, 1953.

Cavanagh, Michael, ed. *Memoirs of Gen. Thomas Francis Meagher, Comprising the Leading Events of His Career.* Reprint, Gaithersburg, MD: Olde Soldier Books, n.d.

Chamberlain, Joshua Lawrence. *The Passing of the Armies: An Account of the Final Campaign of the Army of the Potomac Based upon Personal Reminiscences of the Fifth Army Corps.* Reprint, Gettysburg, PA: Stan Clark Military Books, 1994.

Chamberlin, Thomas. *History of the One Hundred and Fiftieth Regiment Pennsylvania Volunteers, Second Regiment, Bucktail Brigade.* Reprint, Baltimore: Butternut & Blue, 1986.

Chase, J. J. *The Charge at Day-Break: Scenes and Incidents at the Battle of the Mine Explosion, Near Petersburg, Va., July 30, 1864.* Lewiston, ME: Journal Office, 1875.

Cheek, Philip, and Pointon, Mair. *History of the Sauk County Riflemen.* Reprint, Gaithersburg, MD: Butternut Press, 1984.

Child, William. *A History of the Fifth Regiment New Hampshire Volunteers in the American Civil War, 1861–1865.* Reprint, Gaithersburg, MD: Ron R. Van Sickle Military Books, 1988.

Chiles, Paul. "Artillery Hell!: The Guns of Antietam." *Blue & Gray Magazine*, vol. 16, no. 2 (December 1998).

Cleaves, Freeman. *Meade of Gettysburg.* Norman: University of Oklahoma Press, 1960.

Clemens, Tom. "'Black Hats' Off to the Original 'Iron Brigade.'" *Columbiad*, vol. 1 no. 1 (Spring 1997).

Coco, Gregory A., ed. *From Ball's Bluff to Gettysburg . . . and Beyond: The Civil War Letters of Private Roland E. Bowen, 15th Massachusetts Infantry, 1861–1864.* Gettysburg, PA: Thomas, 1994.

Coddington, Edwin B. *The Gettysburg Campaign: A Study in Command.* New York: Charles Scribner's Sons, 1968.

Coffin, Howard. *The Battered Stars: One State's Civil War Ordeal During Grant's Overland Campaign.* Woodstock, VT: Countryman, 2002.

———. *Nine Months to Gettysburg: Stannard's Vermonters and the Repulse of Pickett's Charge.* Woodstock, VT: Countryman, 1997.

Cole, Jacob H. *Under Five Commanders; Or, a Boy's Experience with the Army of the Potomac.* Paterson, NJ: News Printing Company, 1906.

Collins, George K. *Memoirs of the 149th Regt. N.Y. Vol. Inft. 3d Brig., 2d Div., 12th and 20th A.C.* Reprint, Hamilton, NY: Edmonston Publishing, Inc., 1995.

Comings, H. H. *Personal Reminiscences of Co. E, N.Y. Fire Zouaves Better Known as Ellsworth's Fire Zouaves.* Malden, MA: J. Gould Tilden, 1886.

Conyngham, D. P. *The Irish Brigade and Its Campaigns: With Some Account of the Corcoran Legion, and Sketches of the Principal Officers.* Reprint, Gaithersburg, MD: Olde Soldier Books, n.d.

Cooling, Benjamin Franklin. *Symbol, Sword, and Shield: Defending Washington During the Civil War.* Hamden, CT: Archon, 1975.

Copeland, Willis R. *The Logan Guards of Lewistown, Pennsylvania: Our First Defenders of 1861.* Lewistown, PA: Mifflin County Historical Society, 1962.

Corby, William. *Memoirs of Chaplain Life.* Notre Dame, IN: "Scholastic" Press, 1894.

Cornish, Dudley Taylor. *The Sable Arm: Black Troops in the Union Army, 1861–1865.* Lawrence: University Press of Kansas, 1987.

Cowles, Luther E., ed. *History of the Fifth Massachusetts Battery.* Reprint, Baltimore: Butternut & Blue, 1996.

Cowley, Robert, ed. *With My Face to the Enemy: Perspectives On the Civil War.* New York: G. P. Putnam's Sons, 2001.

Cozzens, Peter, ed. *Battles and Leaders of the Civil War, Volume 5.* Urbana and Chicago: University of Illinois Press, 2002.

———. *General John Pope: A Life for the Nation.* Urbana and Chicago: University of Illinois Press, 2000.

———, and Girardi, Robert I., eds. *The Military Memoirs of General John Pope.* Chapel Hill: University of North Carolina Press, 1998.

Craft, David. *History of the One Hundred Forty-first Regiment, Pennsylvania Volunteers, 1862–1865.* Reprint, Baltimore: Butternut & Blue, 1991.

Crary, Catherine S., ed. *Dear Belle: Letters from a Cadet and Officer to His Sweetheart, 1858–1865.* Middletown, CT: Wesleyan University Press, 1965.

Crowninshield, Benjamin W. *A History of the First Regiment of Massachusetts Cavalry Volunteers.* Reprint, Baltimore: Butternut & Blue, 1995.

Crumb, Herb S., and Dhalle, Katherine, eds. *No Middle Ground: Thomas Ward Osborn's Letters from the Field (1862–1864).* Hamilton, NY: Edmonston, 1993.

Cudworth, Warren H. *History of the First Regiment (Massachusetts Infantry), from the 25th of May, 1861, to the 25th of May, 1864: Including Brief References to the Operations of the Army of the Potomac.* Boston: Walker, Fuller, 1866

Cuffel, Charles A. *History of Durell's Battery in the Civil War (Independent Battery D, Pennsylvania Volunteer Artillery).* Philadelphia: Craig Finley, 1903.

Curtis, O. B. *History of the Twenty-fourth Michigan of the Iron Brigade.* Reprint, Gaithersburg, MD: Butternut Press, 1984.

Dana, Charles A. *Recollections of the Civil War with the Leaders at Washington and in the Field in the Sixties.* New York: D. Appleton, 1899.

Davenport, Alfred. *Camp and Field Life of the Fifth New York Volunteer Infantry. (Duryee Zouaves).* Reprint, Gaithersburg, MD: Olde Soldier Books, 1995.

Davis, Oliver Wilson. *Life of David Bell Birney, Major-General United States Volunteers.* Reprint, Gaithersburg, MD: Ron R. Van Sickle Military Books, 1987.

Davis, William C. *Battle at Bull Run: A History of the First Major Campaign of the Civil War.* Garden City, NY: Doubleday, 1977.

———. *Duel Between the First Ironclads.* Garden City, NY: Doubleday, 1975.

———. *Lincoln's Men: How President Lincoln Became Father to an Army and a Nation.* New York: The Free Press, 1999.

Dawes, Rufus R. *Service with the Sixth Wisconsin Volunteers.* Reprint, Dayton, OH: Press of Morningside Bookshop, 1991.

de Trobriand, Regis. *Four Years with the Army of the Potomac.* Reprint, Gaithersburg, MD: Ron R. Van Sickle Military Books, 1988.

Dickert, D. Augustus. *History of Kershaw's Brigade.* Reprint, Dayton, OH: Press of Morningside Bookshop, 1973.

Dickey, Luther S. *History of the Eighty-fifth Regiment Pennsylvania Volunteer Infantry, 1861–1865.* New York: J. C. & W. E. Powers, 1915.

Donald, David Herbert, ed. *Gone for a Soldier: The Civil War Memoirs of Private Alfred Bellard.* Boston: Little, Brown, 1975.

———, ed. *Inside Lincoln's Cabinet: The Civil War Diaries of Salmon P. Chase.* New York: Longmans, Green, 1954.

———. *Lincoln.* New York: Simon & Schuster, 1995.

Dreese, Michael A. *An Imperishable Fame: The Civil War Experience of George Fisher McFarland.* Mifflintown, PA: Juniata County Historical Society, 1997.

———. *The 151st Pennsylvania Volunteers at Gettysburg: Like Ripe Apples in a Storm.* Jefferson, NC: McFarland, 2000.

Dubbs, Carol Kettenburg. *Defend This Old Town: Williamsburg During the Civil War.* Baton Rouge: Louisiana State University Press, 2002.

Duncan, Russell, ed. *Blue-Eyed Child of Fortune: The Civil War Letters of Colonel Robert Gould Shaw.* Athens: University of Georgia Press, 1992.

Dunkelman, Mark H. "A Reflection of Their Own Image." *North & South,* vol. 3, no. 2 (January 2000).

———, and Winey, Michael J. *The Hardtack Regiment: An Illustrated History of the 154th Regiment, New York State Infantry Volunteers.* London and Toronto: Associated University Presses, 1981.

Dunn, Craig L. *Harvestfields of Death: The Twentieth Indiana Volunteers of Gettysburg.* Carmel, IN: Guild Press of Indiana, 1999.

———. *Iron Men, Iron Will: The Nineteenth Indiana Regiment of the Iron Brigade.* Indianapolis: Guild Press of Indiana, 1995.

Duram, James C., and Eleanor A., eds. *Soldier of the Cross: The Civil War Diary and Correspondence of Rev. Andrew Jackson Hartsock.* Manhattan, KS: MA/AH Publishing, 1979.

Durham, Roger S. "The Man Who Shot John Sedgwick." *Blue & Gray Magazine,* vol. 13, no. 2 (December 1995).

Eby, Cecil D., Jr., ed. *A Virginia Yankee in the Civil War: The Diaries of David Hunter Strother.* Chapel Hill: University of North Carolina Press, 1961.

Echoes from the Marches of the Famous Iron Brigade. Reprint, Gaithersburg, MD: Ron R. Van Sickle Military Books, 1988.

Eckert, Edward K., and Amato, Nicholas J., eds. *Ten Years in the Saddle: The Memoir of William Woods Averell.* San Rafael, CA: Presidio, 1978.

Ellis, Thomas T. *Leaves from the Diary of an Army Surgeon; Or, Incidents of Field Camp, and Hospital Life.* New York: John Bradburn, 1863.

Embick, Milton A. *Military History of the Third Division, Ninth Corps Army of the Potomac.* Harrisburg, PA: C. E. Aughinbaugh, 1913.

Favill, Josiah Marshall. *The Diary of a Young Officer.* Reprint, Baltimore: Butternut & Blue, 2000.

Finnell, David V. "Without Fear Without Reproach: The Life of General George D. Bayard." *Blue & Gray Magazine,* vol. 4, no. 1 (September 1986).

Fishel, Edwin C. *The Secret War for the Union: The Untold Story of Military Intelligence in the Civil War.* Boston: Houghton Mifflin, 1996.

Fleming, George Thornton, ed. *Life and Letters of Alexander Hays*. Pittsburgh: Gilbert Adams Hays, 1919.

Ford, Worthington Chauncey, ed. *A Cycle of Adams Letters, 1861–1865*. Two volumes. Boston: Houghton Mifflin, 1920.

———. *War Letters 1862–1865 of John Chipman Gray and John Codman Ropes*. Boston: Houghton Mifflin, 1927.

Forman, Stephen M. "A Glimpse of Wartime Washington." *Blue & Gray Magazine*, vol. 13, no. 4 (April 1996).

Fox, William F. *Regimental Losses in the American Civil War, 1861–1865*. Reprint, Dayton, OH: Press of Morningside Bookshop, 1985.

Freeman, Douglas Southall. *Lee's Lieutenants: A Study in Command*. Three volumes. New York: Charles Scribner's Sons, 1942–1944.

Fry, James B. *Military Miscellanies*. New York: Brentano's, 1889.

Fuller, Charles A. *Personal Recollections of the War of 1861*. Reprint, Hamilton, NY: Edmonston Publishing, 1990.

Gaff, Alan D. *Brave Men's Tears: The Iron Brigade at Brawner Farm*. Dayton, OH: Morningside House, 1988.

———. *If This Is War: A History of the Campaign of Bull's Run by the Wisconsin Regiment Thereafter Known as the Ragged Ass Second*. Dayton, OH: Morningside House, 1991.

———. *On Many a Bloody Field: Four Years in the Iron Brigade*. Bloomington and Indianapolis: Indiana University Press, 1996.

Gallagher, Gary W., ed. *The Antietam Campaign*. Chapel Hill: University of North Carolina Press, 1999.

———. "Brandy Station: The Civil War's Bloodiest Arena of Mounted Combat." *Blue & Gray Magazine*, vol. 8, no. 1 (October 1990).

———, ed. *Chancellorsville: The Battle and Its Aftermath*. Chapel Hill: University of North Carolina Press, 1996.

———. *The Confederate War*. Cambridge: Harvard University Press, 1997.

———, ed. *The First Day at Gettysburg: Essays on Confederate and Union Leadership*. Kent, OH: Kent State University Press, 1992.

———, ed. *The Fredericksburg Campaign: Decision on the Rappahannock*. Chapel Hill: University of North Carolina Press, 1995.

———, ed. *Lee: The Soldier*. Lincoln: University of Nebraska Press, 1996.

———, ed. *The Richmond Campaign of 1862: The Peninsula and the Seven Days*. Chapel Hill: University of North Carolina Press, 2000.

———, ed. *The Second Day at Gettysburg: Essays on Confederate and Union Leadership*. Kent, OH: Kent State University Press, 1993.

———, ed. *The Spotsylvania Campaign*. Chapel Hill: University of North Carolina Press, 1998.

———, ed. *The Third Day at Gettysburg and Beyond*. Chapel Hill: University of North Carolina Press, 1994.

———, ed. *Three Days at Gettysburg: Essays on Confederate and Union Leadership*. Kent, OH: Kent State University Press, 1999.

———, ed. *The Wilderness Campaign*. Chapel Hill: University of North Carolina Press, 1997.

Galwey, Thomas Francis. *The Valiant Hours*. Edited by W. S. Nye. Harrisburg, PA: Stackpole, 1961.

Gambone, A. M. *The Life of General Samuel K. Zook: Another Forgotten Union Hero*. Baltimore: Butternut & Blue, 1996.

———. *Major-General John Frederick Hartranft: Citizen Soldier and Pennsylvania Statesman*. Baltimore: Butternut & Blue, 1995.

Gavin, William Gilfillan, ed. *Infantryman Pettit: The Civil War Letters of Corporal Frederick Pettit Late of Company C 100th Pennsylvania Veteran Volunteer Infantry Regiment "The Roundheads."* Shippensburg, PA: White Mane Publishing, 1990.

Geary, James W. *We Need Men: The Union Draft in the Civil War*. DeKalb: Northern Illinois University Press, 1991.

Gerrish, Theodore. *Army Life: A Private's Reminiscences of the Civil War*. Portland, ME: Hoyt, Fogg & Donham, 1882.

Gibbon, John. *Personal Recollections of the Civil War*. Reprint, Dayton, OH: Press of Morningside Bookshop, 1978.

Gibbs, James M., ed. *History of the First Battalion Pennsylvania Six Months Volunteers and 187th Regiment Pennsylvania Volunteer Infantry*. Harrisburg, PA: Central Printing and Publishing House, 1905.

Gibbs, Joseph. *Three Years in the Bloody Eleventh: The Campaigns of a Pennsylvania Reserves Regiment*. University Park: Pennsylvania State University Press, 2002.

Glover, Edwin A. *Bucktailed Wildcats: A Regiment of Civil War Volunteers*. New York: Thomas Yoseloff, 1960.

Goss, Thomas J. *The War Within the Union High Command: Politics and Generalship During the Civil War*. Lawrence: University Press of Kansas, 2003.

Gould, Edward K. *Major-General Hiram G. Berry: His Career as a Contractor, Bank President, Politician and Major-General of Volunteers in the Civil War*. Rockland, ME: Press of the Courier-Gazette, 1899.

Gould, Joseph. *The Story of the Forty-Eighth: A Record of the Campaigns of the Forty-eighth Regiment Pennsylvania Veteran Volunteer Infantry*. Philadelphia: Alfred M. Slocum, 1908.

Grant, Ulysses S. *Personal Memoirs of U. S. Grant*. Two volumes. New York: Charles L. Webster, 1885–1886.

Greene, A. Wilson. *Breaking the Backbone of the Rebellion: The Final Battles of the Petersburg Campaign*. Mason City, IA: Savas, 2000.

Greiner, James M., Coryell, Janet L., and Smither, James R., eds. *A Surgeon's Civil War: The Letters and Diary of Daniel M. Holt, M.D.* Kent, OH: Kent State University Press, 1994.

Griffith, Paddy. *Battle Tactics of the Civil War*. New Haven: Yale University Press, 1989.

Grimsley, Mark. *And Keep Moving On: The Virginia Campaign, May–June 1864*. Lincoln: University of Nebraska Press, 2002.

———. *The Hard Hand of War: Union Military Policy Toward Southern Civilians, 1861–1865*. Cambridge: Cambridge University Press, 1995.

Hagemann, E. R., ed. *Fighting Rebels and Redskins: Experiences in Army Life of Colonel George B. Sanford, 1861–1892*. Norman: University of Oklahoma Press, 1969.

Hagerty, Edward J. *Collis' Zouaves: The 114th Pennsylvania Volunteers in the Civil War*. Baton Rouge: Louisiana State University Press, 1997.

Haines, Alanson A. *History of the Fifteenth Regiment New Jersey Volunteers*. Reprint, Gaithersburg, MD: Butternut Press, 1987.

Haines, William P. *History of the Men of Co. F, with Description of the Marches and Battles of the 12th New Jersey Vols*. Camden, NJ: C. S. Magrath, 1897.

Hall, Clark B. "Season of Change: The Winter Encampment of the Army of the Potomac, December 1, 1863–May 4, 1864." *Blue & Gray Magazine*, vol. 8, no. 4 (April 1991).

Hall, Isaac. *History of the Ninety-Seventh Regiment New York Volunteers, ("Conkling Rifles,") in the War for the Union.* Reprint, Baltimore: Butternut & Blue, 1991.

Hamblen, Charles P. *Connecticut Yankees at Gettysburg.* Edited by Walter L. Powell. Kent, OH: Kent State University Press, 1993.

Hammond, Mary Acton, ed. "'Dear Mollie': Letters of Captain Edward A. Acton to His Wife, 1862." *Pennsylvania Magazine of History and Biography*, vol. 89 (1989).

Hancock, Almira Russell. *Reminiscences of Winfield Scott Hancock.* New York: Charles L. Webster, 1887.

Hard, Abner. *History of the Eighth Cavalry Regiment Illinois Volunteers, During the Great Rebellion.* Reprint, Dayton, OH: Press of Morningside Bookshop, 1984.

Hardin, M. D. *History of the Twelfth Regiment Pennsylvania Reserve Volunteer Corps (41st Regiment of the Line), from Its Muster into the United States Service, August 10th, 1861, to Its Muster out, June 11th, 1864.* New York: M. D. Hardin, 1890.

Harsh, Joseph L. *Confederate Tide Rising: Robert E. Lee and the Making of Southern Strategy, 1861–1862.* Kent, OH: Kent State University Press, 1998.

———. *Taken at the Flood: Robert E. Lee and Confederate Strategy in the Maryland Campaign of 1862.* Kent, OH: Kent State University Press, 1999.

Hartwig, H. Scott. "The 11th Army Corps on July 1, 1863." *Gettysburg Magazine*, no. 2 (January 1990).

———. "'It Looked Like a Task to Storm': The Pennsylvania Reserves Assault South Mountain, September 14, 1862." *North & South*, vol. 5, no. 7 (October 2002).

———. "It Struck Horror to Us All." *Gettysburg Magazine*, no. 4 (January 1991).

Hassler, Warren W., Jr. *Commanders of the Army of the Potomac.* Baton Rouge: Louisiana State University Press, 1962.

Hastings, William H., ed. *Letters from a Sharpshooter: The Civil War Letters of Private William B. Greene, Co. G 2nd United States Sharpshooters (Berdan's) Army of the Potomac.* Belleville, WI: Historic Publications, 1993.

Hattaway, Herman, and Jones, Archer. *How the North Won: A Military History of the Civil War.* Urbana: University of Illinois Press, 1983.

———. "'Old Brains' Was Brainy After All." *Columbiad*, vol. 1, no. 1 (Spring 1997).

Hays, Gilbert Adams, ed. *Under the Red Patch: Story of the Sixty-third Regiment Pennsylvania Volunteers, 1861–1864.* Pittsburgh: Sixty-third Pennsylvania Volunteers Regimental Association, 1908.

Hebert, Walter H. *Fighting Joe Hooker.* Indianapolis: Bobbs-Merrill, 1944.

Henderson, William D. *The Road to Bristoe Station: Campaigning with Lee and Meade, August 1–October 20, 1863.* Lynchburg, VA: H. E. Howard, 1987.

Hennessy, John J. *The First Battle of Manassas: An End to Innocence, July 18–21, 1861.* Lynchburg, VA: H. E. Howard, 1989.

———, ed. *Fighting with the Eighteenth Massachusetts: The Civil War Memoir of Thomas H. Mann.* Baton Rouge: Louisiana State University Press, 2000.

———. *Return to Bull Run: The Campaign and Battle of Second Manassas.* New York: Simon & Schuster, 1993.

———. "Thunder at Chantilly." *North & South*, vol. 3, no. 3 (March 2000).

Herberger, Charles F., ed. *A Yankee at Arms: The Diary of Lieutenant Augustus D. Ayling, 29th Massachusetts Volunteers.* Knoxville: University of Tennessee Press, 1999.

Herdegen, Lance J. *The Men Stood Like Iron: How the Iron Brigade Won Its Name*. Bloomington and Indianapolis: Indiana University Press, 1997.

———, and Beaudot, William J. K. *In the Bloody Railroad Cut at Gettysburg*. Dayton, OH: Morningside House, 1990.

———, and Murphy, Sherry, eds. *Four Years with the Iron Brigade: The Civil War Journals of William R. Ray, Co. F, Seventh Wisconsin Infantry*. New York: Da Capo, 2002.

Hess, Earl J. *The Union Soldier in Battle: Enduring the Ordeal of Combat*. Lawrence: University Press of Kansas, 1997.

Higginson, Thomas Wentworth. *Harvard Memorial Biographies*. Two volumes. Cambridge: Sever & Francis, 1866.

Hill, A. F. *Our Boys: The Personal Experiences of a Soldier in the Army of the Potomac*. Philadelphia: John E. Potter, 1864.

Hines, Blaikie. *Civil War Volunteer Sons of Connecticut*. Thomaston, ME: American Patriot Press, 2002.

Hitchcock, Frederick L. *War from the Inside; Or, Personal Experiences, Impressions, and Reminiscences of One of the "Boys" in the War of the Rebellion*. Philadelphia: J. B. Lippincott, 1904.

Holien, Kim Bernard. *Battle at Ball's Bluff*. Orange, VA: Rapidan Press, 1989.

Holsworth, Jerry W. "Uncommon Valor: Hood's Texas Brigade in the Maryland Campaign." *Blue & Gray Magazine*, vol. 13, no. 6 (August 1996).

Howe, Mark De Wolfe, ed. *Touched with Fire: Civil War Letters and Diary of Oliver Wendell Holmes, Jr., 1861–1864*. Cambridge: Harvard University Press, 1947.

Humphreys, Andrew A. *The Virginia Campaign of '64 and '65: The Army of the Potomac and the Army of the James*. New York: Charles Scribner's Sons, 1903.

Humphreys, Henry H. *Andrew Atkinson Humphreys: A Biography*. Reprint, Gaithersburg, MD: Ron R. Van Sickle Military Books, 1988.

Hunt, Gaillard, ed. *Israel, Elihu and Cadwallader Washburn: A Chapter in American Biography*. New York: Da Capo, 1969.

Hunt, Roger D., and Brown, Jack R. *Brevet Brigadier Generals in Blue*. Gaithersburg, MD: Olde Soldier Books, 1997.

Husby, Karla Jean, comp., and Wittenberg, Eric J., ed. *Under Custer's Command: The Civil War Journal of James Henry Avery*. Washington, D.C.: Brassey's, 2000.

Hyde, Thomas W. *Civil War Letters*. [No city]: John H. Hyde, 1933.

Ide, Horace K. *History of the First Vermont Cavalry Volunteers in the War of the Great Rebellion*. Edited by Elliott W. Hoffman. Baltimore: Butternut & Blue, 2000.

Johnson, Curt, and Anderson, Richard D., Jr. *Artillery Hell: The Employment of Artillery at Antietam*. College Station: Texas A & M University Press, 1995.

Johnson, Robert Underwood, and Buel, Clarence Clough, eds. *Battles and Leaders of the Civil War*. Four volumes. Reprint, New York: Thomas Yoseloff, 1956.

Johnston, Gertrude K. *Dear Pa—And So It Goes*. Harrisburg, PA: Business Service Company, 1971.

Joinville, Prince de. *The Army of the Potomac: Its Organization, Its Commander, and Its Campaign*. New York: Anson D. F. Randolph, 1862.

Jones, Archer. *Civil War Command and Strategy: The Process of Victory and Defeat*. New York: The Free Press, 1992.

Jones, Wilbur D., Jr. *Giants in the Cornfield: The 27th Indiana Infantry*. Shippensburg, PA: White Mane, 1997.

Jordan, David M. *"Happiness Is Not My Companion": The Life of General G. K. Warren*. Bloomington and Indianapolis: Indiana University Press, 2001.

Jordan, William G., Jr., ed. *The Civil War Journals of John Mead Gould, 1861–1866*. Baltimore: Butternut & Blue, 1997.

Judson, Amos M. *History of the Eighty-third Regiment Pennsylvania Volunteers*. With Foreword and Notes by John J. Pullen. Reprint, Dayton, OH: Morningside, 1986.

Katcher, Philip, ed. *Building the Victory: The Order Book of the Volunteer Engineer Brigade, Army of the Potomac, October 1863–May 1865*. Shippensburg, PA: White Mane, 1998.

Keating, Robert. *Carnival of Blood: The Civil War Ordeal of the Seventh New York Heavy Artillery*. Baltimore: Butternut & Blue, 1998.

Keifer, Joseph Warren. *Slavery and Four Years of War: A Political History of Slavery in the United States*. Two volumes. New York: G. P. Putnam's Sons, 1900.

Keifer, W. R. *History of the One Hundred and Fifty-third Regiment Pennsylvania Volunteers Infantry*. Reprint, Baltimore: Butternut & Blue, 1996.

Kohl, Lawrence Frederick, and Richard, Margaret Cosse, eds. *Irish Green and Union Blue: The Civil War Letters of Peter Welsh Color Sergeant 28th Regiment Massachusetts Volunteers*. New York: Fordham University Press, 1986.

Krick, Robert K. *The Smoothbore Volley That Doomed the Confederacy: The Death of Stonewall Jackson and Other Chapters on the Army of Northern Virginia*. Baton Rouge: Louisiana State University Press, 2002.

Laas, Virginia Jeans, ed. *Wartime Washington: The Civil War Letters of Elizabeth Blair Lee*. Urbana and Chicago: University of Illinois Press, 1991.

Ladd, David L., and Audrey J., eds. *The Bachelder Papers: Gettysburg in Their Own Words*. Three volumes. Dayton, OH: Morningside House, 1994–95.

Lash, Gary G. *"Duty Well Done": The History of Edward Baker's California Regiment (71st Pennsylvania Infantry)*. Baltimore: Butternut & Blue, 2001.

———. "The Philadelphia Brigade at Gettysburg." *Gettysburg Magazine*, no. 7 (July 1992).

Lassen, Coralou Peel, ed. *Dear Sarah: Letters Home from a Soldier of the Iron Brigade*. Bloomington and Indianapolis: Indiana University Press, 1999.

Lavery, Dennis S., and Jordan, Mark H. *Iron Brigade General: John Gibbon, a Rebel in Blue*. Westport, CT: Greenwood, 1993.

LeDuc, William G. *Recollections of a Civil War Quartermaster: The Autobiography of William G. LeDuc*. St. Paul, MN: North Central, 1963.

Leehan, Brian. *Pale Horse at Plum Run*. St. Paul: Minnesota Historical Society Press, 2002.

Livermore, Thomas L. *Days and Events, 1860–1866*. Boston: Houghton Mifflin, 1920.

Livingston, E. A. "Bud." "New York City and the Civil War." *Blue & Gray Magazine*, vol. 14, no. 2 (December 1996).

Longacre, Edward G. *General John Buford*. Consohocken, PA: Combined Books, 1995.

———. *Lincoln's Cavalrymen: A History of the Mounted Forces of the Army of the Potomac*. Mechanicsburg, PA: Stackpole, 2000.

———. *The Man Behind the Guns: A Biography of General Henry Jackson Hunt, Chief of Artillery, Army of the Potomac*. South Brunswick, NJ: A. S. Barnes, 1977.

———. *To Gettysburg and Beyond: The Twelfth New Jersey Volunteer Infantry, II Corps, Army of the Potomac, 1862–1865*. Hightstown, NJ: Longstreet House, 1988.

Longstreet, James. *From Manassas to Appomattox: Memoirs of the Civil War in America.* Philadelphia: J. B. Lippincott, 1896.

Lord, Francis A. *Civil War Collector's Encyclopedia: Arms, Uniforms, and Equipment of the Union and Confederacy.* Vol. 1. Harrisburg, PA: Stackpole, 1963.

Lord, Walter, ed. *The Fremantle Diary: Being the Journal of Lieutenant Colonel James Arthur Lyon Fremantle, Coldstream Guards, on His Three Months in the Southern States.* Boston: Little, Brown, 1954.

Love, William DeLoss. *Wisconsin in the War of the Rebellion: A History of All Regiments and Batteries.* Chicago: Church & Goodman, 1866.

Luvaas, Jay. "Lee and the Operational Art: The Right Place, the Right Time." *Parameters, U.S. Army War College Quarterly,* vol. 22, no. 3 (Autumn 1992).

Macnamara, Daniel George. *The History of the Ninth Regiment Massachusetts Volunteer Infantry Second Brigade, First Division, Fifth Army Corps, Army of the Potomac, June, 1861–June, 1864.* Boston: E. B. Stillings, 1899.

Macneal, Douglas. "'The Centre County Regiment': Story of the 148th Regiment, Pennsylvania Volunteers," *Centre County Heritage,* vol. 36, no. 1 (2000).

Madaus, Howard Michael. "Into the Fray: The Flags of the Iron Brigade, 1861–1865." *Wisconsin Magazine of History,* vol. 69, no. 1 (Autumn, 1985).

Magner, Blake A. *Traveller and Company: The Horses of Gettysburg.* Gettysburg, PA: Farnsworth House Military Impressions, 1995.

Mahood, Wayne. *"Written in Blood": A History of the 126th New York Infantry in the Civil War.* Hightstown, NJ: Longstreet House, 1997.

Maier, Larry B. *Rough and Regular: A History of Philadelphia's 119th Regiment of Pennsylvania Volunteer Infantry, the Gray Reserves.* Shippensburg, PA: Burd Street, 1997.

Mannis, Jedediah, and Wilson, Galen R., eds. *Bound to Be a Soldier: The Letters of Private James T. Miller, 111th Pennsylvania Infantry, 1861–1864.* Knoxville: University of Tennessee Press, 2001.

Marbaker, Thomas D. *History of the Eleventh New Jersey Volunteers from Its Organization to Appomattox.* Trenton, NJ: MacCrellish & Quigley, 1898.

Marshall, D. P. *Company "K," 155th Pa. Volunteer Zouaves.* Reprint, Butler, PA: Mechling Associates, 1998.

Martin, James M., et al., eds. *History of the Fifty-seventh Regiment, Pennsylvania Veteran Volunteer Infantry.* Reprint, Kearny, NJ: Belle Grove, 1995.

Marvel, William. *Burnside.* Chapel Hill: University of North Carolina Press, 1991.

———. *Race of the Soil: The Ninth New Hampshire Regiment in the Civil War.* Wilmington, NC: Broadfoot, 1988.

Matter, William D. *If It Takes All Summer: The Battle of Spotsylvania.* Chapel Hill: University of North Carolina Press, 1988.

Maull, D. W. *The Life and Military Services of the Late Brigadier General Thomas A. Smyth.* Wilmington, DE: H. & E. F. James, 1870.

Maust, Roland R. "The Union Second Corps Hospital at Gettysburg, July 2 to August 8, 1863." *Gettysburg Magazine,* no. 10 (January 1994).

McBride, Robert E. *In the Ranks: From the Wilderness to Appomattox Court House.* Cincinnati: Walden & Stowe, 1881.

McBride, Robert W. *Lincoln's Body Guard: The Union Light Guard of Ohio with Some Personal Recollections of Abraham Lincoln.* Indianapolis: Edward J. Hecker, 1911.

McClellan, George B. *Letter of the Secretary of War, Transmitting Report on the Organization of the Army of the Potomac, and of Its Campaigns in Virginia and Maryland,*

Under the Command of Maj. Gen. George B. McClellan, from July 26, 1861 to November 7, 1862. Washington, D.C.: Government Printing Office, 1864.

———. *McClellan's Own Story: The War for the Union, the Soldiers Who Fought It, the Civilians Who Directed It and His Relations to It and to Them.* New York: Charles L. Webster, 1887.

McClure, A. K. *Abraham Lincoln and Men of War-Times: Some Personal Recollections of War and Politics During the Lincoln Administration.* Philadelphia: Times Publishing Company, 1892.

McGrath, Thomas. "The Corn Exchange Regiment's Baptism of Fire." *Blue & Gray Magazine,* vol. 16, no. 1 (October 1998).

McLean, James L., Jr. *Cutler's Brigade at Gettysburg.* Baltimore, MD: Butternut & Blue, 1994.

———, and Judy W., eds. *Gettysburg Sources.* Three volumes. Baltimore, MD: Butternut & Blue, 1986–1990.

McMurry, Richard M. *The Fourth Battle of Winchester: Toward a New Civil War Paradigm.* Kent: Kent State University Press, 2002.

McPherson, James M. *Crossroads of Freedom: Antietam.* New York: Oxford University Press, 2002.

———. *For Cause and Comrades: Why Men Fought in the Civil War.* New York: Oxford University Press, 1997.

Meade, George. *The Life and Letters of George Gordon Meade.* Two volumes. Reprint, Baltimore: Butternut & Blue, 1994.

Meinhard, Robert W. "The First Minnesota at Gettysburg." *Gettysburg Magazine,* no. 5 (July 1991).

Menge, W. Springer, and Shimrak, J. August, eds. *The Civil War Notebook of Daniel Chisholm: A Chronicle of Daily Life in the Union Army, 1864–1865.* New York: Orion, 1989.

Mertz, Gregory A. "Upton's Attack and the Defense of Doles' Salient Spotsylvania Court House, Va., May 10, 1864." *Blue & Gray Magazine,* vol. 18, no. 6 (August 2001).

Meyer, Henry C. *Civil War Experiences Under Bayard, Gregg, Kilpatrick, Custer, Raulston, and Newberry 1862, 1863, 1864.* New York: Knickerbocker Press, 1911.

Michie, Peter S. *General McClellan.* New York: D. Appleton, 1915.

Miers, Earl Schenck, ed. *Wash Roebling's War: Being a Selection from the Unpublished Civil War Letters of Washington Augustus Roebling.* Newark, DE: Curtis Paper Company, 1961.

Milano, Anthony J. "Letters from the Harvard Regiments, Part Three." *Civil War,* vol. 13 (1988).

Miller, Delavan S., ed. *Drum Taps in Dixie: Memories of a Drummer Boy, 1861–1865.* Reprint, Baltimore: Butternut & Blue, 2000.

Miller, J. Michael. *The North Anna Campaign: "Even to Hell Itself," May 21–26, 1864.* Lynchburg, VA: H. E. Howard, 1989.

Miller, William J. "The Disaster of Casey." *Columbiad,* vol. 3, no. 4 (Winter 2000).

———, ed. *The Peninsula Campaign of 1862: Yorktown to the Seven Days.* Three volumes. Campbell, CA: Savas Woodbury, 1997.

———. *The Training of an Army: Camp Curtin and the North's Civil War.* Shippensburg, PA: White Mane, 1990.

Minnigh, H. N. *History of Company K. 1st (Inft.) Penn'a Reserves.* Reprint, Gettysburg, PA: Thomas, 1998.

Mitchell, Reid. *Civil War Soldiers.* New York: Viking, 1988.

———. *The Vacant Chair: The Northern Soldier Leaves Home.* New York: Oxford University Press, 1993.

Moe, Richard. *The Last Full Measure: The Life and Death of the First Minnesota Volunteers.* New York: Henry Holt, 1993.

Motts, Wayne E. "To Gain A Second Star: The Forgotten George S. Greene." *Gettysburg Magazine,* no. 3 (July 1990).

Muffly, J. W., ed. *The Story of Our Regiment: A History of the 148th Pennsylvania Vols.* Des Moines, IA: Kenyon Printing & Mfg. Co., 1904.

Mulholland, St. Clair A. *The Story of the 116th Regiment, Pennsylvania Volunteers in the War of the Rebellion.* Edited by Lawrence Frederick Kohl. Reprint, New York: Fordham University Press, 1996.

Murfin, James V. *The Gleam of Bayonets: The Battle of Antietam and the Maryland Campaign of 1862.* New York: Thomas Yoseloff, 1968.

Naisawald, L. VanLoan. *Grape and Canister: The Story of the Field Artillery of the Army of the Potomac, 1861–1865.* Mechanicsburg, PA: Stackpole, 1999.

Nevins, Allan, ed. *A Diary of Battle: The Personal Journals of Colonel Charles S. Wainwright, 1861–1865.* Reprint, Gettysburg, PA: Stan Clark Military Books, 1993.

———, ed. *Diary of the Civil War, 1860–1865: George Templeton Strong.* New York: Macmillan, 1962.

Newhall, Walter S. *A Memoir.* Philadelphia: Caxton Press of C. Sherman, Son & Co., 1864.

Newton, Steven H. *The Battle of Seven Pines, May 31–June 1, 1862.* Lynchburg, VA: H. E. Howard, 1993.

———. *Lost for the Cause: The Confederate Army in 1864.* Mason City, IA: Savas, 2000.

New York at Gettysburg: Final Report on the Battlefield of Gettysburg. Three volumes. Albany: J. B. Lyon, 1900.

Nichols, Edward J. *Toward Gettysburg: A Biography of General John F. Reynolds.* University Park: Pennsylvania State University Press, 1958.

Niven, John. *Connecticut for the Union: The Role of the State in the Civil War.* New Haven: Yale University Press, 1965.

Nolan, Alan T. *The Iron Brigade: A Military History.* New York: Macmillan, 1961.

———, and Vipond, Sharon Eggleston, eds. *Giants in Their Tall Black Hats: Essays on the Iron Brigade.* Bloomington and Indianapolis: Indiana University Press, 1998.

Oates, Stephen B. *Abraham Lincoln: The Man Behind the Myths.* New York: Harper & Row, 1984.

O'Beirne, Kevin M. "Into the Shadow of the Shadow of Death: The Corcoran Legion at Cold Harbor." *North & South,* vol. 3, no. 4 (April 2000).

O'Brien, Kevin E. "Follow That Green Flag!: John Dillon, Irish Brigade Color Bearer." *North & South,* vol. 2, no. 5 (June 1999).

———, ed. *My Life in the Irish Brigade: The Civil War Memoirs of Private William McCarter, 116th Pennsylvania Infantry.* Campbell, CA: Savas, 1996.

Oliver, James. *Ancestry, Early Life and War Record of James Oliver, M.D.* Athol, MA: Athol Transcript Company, 1961.

O'Neill, Robert F., Jr. *The Cavalry Battles of Aldie, Middleburg and Upperville: Small but Important Riots, June 10–27, 1863.* Lynchburg, VA: H. E. Howard, 1993.

O'Reilly, Francis Augustin. *The Fredericksburg Campaign: Winter War on the Rappahannock*. Baton Rouge: Louisiana State University Press, 2003.

Orwig, Joseph R. *History of the 131st Penna. Volunteers, War of 1861–5*. Williamsport, PA: Sun Book and Job Printing House, 1902.

Osborne, Seward R., ed. *The Civil War Diaries of Col. Theodore B. Gates, 20th New York State Militia*. Hightstown, NJ: Longstreet House, 1991.

———. "Kingston in the Civil War." *Bicentennial Magazine of Kingston, New York*, 1976.

Otis, George H. *The Second Wisconsin Infantry*. Reprint, Dayton, OH: Press of Morningside Bookshop, 1984.

Page, Charles A. *Letters of a War Correspondent*. Boston: L. C. Page, 1899.

Page, Charles D. *History of the Fourteenth Regiment, Connecticut Vol. Infantry*. Reprint, Gaithersburg, MD: Ron R. Van Sickle Military Books, 1987.

Palmer, E. F. *The Second Brigade; Or, Camp Life*. Montpelier, VT: E. I. Walton, 1864.

Paludan, Phillip Shaw. *The Presidency of Abraham Lincoln*. Lawrence: University Press of Kansas, 1994.

Parker, John L. *Henry Wilson's Regiment: History of the Twenty-second Massachusetts Infantry, the Second Company Sharpshooters, and the Third Light Battery, in the War of the Rebellion*. Reprint, Baltimore: Butternut & Blue, 1997.

Parker, Thomas H. *History of the 51st Regiment of P.V. and V.V.* Reprint, Baltimore: Butternut & Blue, 1998.

Patch, Eileen Mae Knapp, ed. *This from George: The Civil War Letters of Sergeant George Magusta Englis, 1861–1865, Company K, 89th New York Regiment of Volunteer Infantry Known as the Dickinson Guard*. Binghamton, NY: Broome County Historical Society, 2001.

Pearson, Henry Greenleaf. *James S. Wadsworth of Geneseo Brevet Major-General of United States Volunteers*. New York: Charles Scribner's Sons, 1913.

Perret, Geoffrey. "Anaconda: The Plan That Never Was." *North & South*, vol. 6, no. 4 (May 2003).

Pfanz, Harry W. *Gettysburg—The First Day*. Chapel Hill: University of North Carolina Press, 2001.

———. *Gettysburg—The Second Day*. Chapel Hill: University of North Carolina Press, 1987.

Porter, Horace. *Campaigning with Grant*. Reprint, New York: Bonanza, 1961.

Poulter, Keith. "Errors That Doomed a Campaign." *North & South*, vol. 2, no. 6 (August 1999).

Powell, William H. *The Fifth Army Corps (Army of the Potomac): A Record of Operations During the Civil War in the United States of America, 1861–1865*. Reprint, Dayton, OH: Press of Morningside Bookshop, 1984.

Pride, Mike, and Travis, Mark. *My Brave Boys: To War with Colonel Cross and the Fighting Fifth*. Hanover: University Press of New England, 2001.

Priest, John M. *Antietam: The Soldiers' Battle*. Shippensburg, PA: White Mane, 1989.

———. *Before Antietam: The Battle for South Mountain*. Shippensburg, PA: White Mane, 1992.

———, ed. *One Surgeon's Private War: Doctor William W. Potter of the 57th New York*. Shippensburg, PA: White Mane, 1996.

Prowell, George R. *History of the Eighty-seventh Regiment, Pennsylvania Volunteers, Prepared From Official Records, Diaries, and Other Authentic Sources of Information*. York, PA: Press of the York Daily, 1903.

Pula, James S. *The Sigel Regiment: A History of the Twenty-sixth Wisconsin Volunteer Infantry, 1862–1865*. Campbell, CA: Savas, 1998.

Pullen, John J. *A Shower of Stars: The Medal of Honor and the 27th Maine*. Philadelphia: J. B. Lippincott, 1966.

———. *The Twentieth Maine: A Volunteer Regiment in the Civil War*. Philadelphia: J. B. Lippincott, 1957.

Pyne, Henry R. *Ride to War: The History of the First New Jersey Cavalry*. Edited by Earl Schenck Miers. New Brunswick, NJ: Rutgers University Press, 1961.

Quaife, Milo M., ed. *From the Cannon's Mouth: The Civil War Letters of General Alpheus S. Williams*. Detroit: Wayne State University Press and Detroit Historical Society, 1959.

Raab, Steven S., ed. *With the 3rd Wisconsin Badgers: The Living Experience of the Civil War Through the Journals of Van R. Willard*. Mechanicsburg, PA: Stackpole, 1999.

Rable, George C. *Fredericksburg! Fredericksburg!* Chapel Hill: University of North Carolina Press, 2002.

Racine, Philip N. *"Unspoiled Heart": The Journal of Charles Mattocks of the 17th Maine*. Knoxville: University of Tennessee Press, 1994.

Rafuse, Ethan S. "McClellan, von Clausewitz, and the Politics of War." *Columbiad*, vol. 1, no. 3 (Fall, 1997).

Raphelson, Alfred C. "Alexander Schimmelfennig: A German-American Campaigner in the Civil War." *Pennsylvania Magazine of History and Biography*, vol. 87 (1987).

Reed, John A. *History of the 101st Regiment Pennsylvania Veteran Volunteer Infantry, 1861–1865*. Chicago: L. S. Dickey, 1910.

Reed, Lois M. McNitt, ed. *Historical Family Letters: James C. McNitt Civil War et al.* [No city]: Lois M. McNitt Reed, 1986.

Reese, Timothy J. *Sykes' Regular Infantry Division, 1861–1864: A History of Regular United States Infantry Operations in the Civil War's Eastern Theater*. Jefferson, NC: McFarland, 1990.

Reid-Green, Marcia, ed. *Letters Home: Henry Matrau of the Iron Brigade*. Lincoln: University of Nebraska Press, 1993.

Rhea, Gordon C. *The Battle of the Wilderness, May 5–6, 1864*. Baton Rouge and London: Louisiana State University Press, 1994.

———. *The Battles for Spotsylvania Court House and the Road to Yellow Tavern, May 7–12, 1864*. Baton Rouge: Louisiana State University Press, 1997.

———. *Cold Harbor: Grant and Lee, May 26–June 3, 1864*. Baton Rouge: Louisiana State University Press, 2002.

———. *To the North Anna River: Grant and Lee, May 13–25, 1864*. Baton Rouge: Louisiana State University Press, 2000.

———, Rollins, Richard, Sears, Stephen, and Simon, John Y. "What Was Wrong with the Army of the Potomac." *North & South*, vol. 4, no. 3 (March 2001).

Rhodes, John H., ed. *The History of Battery B First Regiment Rhode Island Light Artillery in the War to Preserve the Union, 1861–1865*. Reprint, Baltimore: Butternut & Blue, 1997.

———, ed. *All for the Union: The Civil War Diary and Letters of Elisha Hunt Rhodes*. New York: Orion, 1991.

Ritchie, Norman L., ed. *Four Years in the First New York Light Artillery: The Papers of David F. Ritchie*. Hamilton, NY: Edmonston, 1997.

Robertson, James I., Jr., ed. *The Civil War Letters of General Robert McAllister*. New Brunswick, NJ: Rutgers University Press, 1965.

Rollins, Richard. "George Gordon Meade and the Defense of Cemetery Ridge." *Gettysburg Magazine*, no. 19.

———, and Schultz, David L. "A Combined and Concentrated Fire: The Federal Artillery at Gettysburg, July 3, 1863." *North & South*, vol. 2, no. 3 (March 1999).

Rosenblatt, Emil, and Rosenblatt, Ruth, eds. *Hard Marching Every Day: The Civil War Letters of Private Wilbur Fisk, 1861–1865*. Lawrence: University Press of Kansas, 1992.

Rosengarten, J. G. *Reynolds Memorial Address, March 8th, 1880*. [No publishing information].

Rosentreter, Roger L. "Samuel Hodgman's Civil War." *Michigan History*, vol. 64 (November–December 1980).

———. "Those Damned Black Hats: The Twenty-fourth Michigan at Gettysburg." *Michigan History Magazine*. July–August 1991.

Ross, Sam. *The Empty Sleeve: A Biography of Lucius Fairchild*. Madison: State Historical Society of Wisconsin, 1964.

Ryan, James G. "'Say It Ain't So': Debunking the Myth of Butterfield's Twins." *Blue & Gray Magazine*, vol. 13, no. 6 (June 1996).

Samito, Christian G., ed. *Commanding Boston's Irish Ninth: The Civil War Letters of Colonel Patrick R. Guiney, Ninth Massachusetts Volunteer Infantry*. New York: Fordham University Press, 1998.

Sauers, Richard A. *Advance the Colors!: Pennsylvania Civil War Battle Flags*. Two volumes. Harrisburg, PA: Capital Preservation Committee, 1987 and 1991.

———, ed. *The Civil War Journal of Colonel William J. Bolton, 51st Pennsylvania, August 20, 1861–August 2, 1865*. Conshohocken, PA: Combined Publishing, 2000.

———, ed. *Fighting Them Over: How the Veterans Remembered Gettysburg in the Pages of the National Tribune*. Baltimore, MD: Butternut & Blue, 1998.

Sawyer, Merrill C., Sawyer, Betty, and Sawyer, Timothy C., eds. *Letters from a Civil War Surgeon: The Letters of Dr. William Child of the Fifth New Hampshire Volunteers*. Solon, ME: Polar Bear, 2001.

Saxton, William. *A Regiment Remembered: The 157th New York Volunteers from the Diary of Capt. William Saxton*. Cortland, NY: Cortland County Historical Society, 1996.

Schaff, Morris. *The Battle of the Wilderness*. Reprint, Gaithersburg, MD: Butternut Press, 1986.

Schildt, John W. *Roads to Antietam*. Shippensburg, PA: Burd Street Press, 1997.

———. *Roads to Gettysburg*. Parsons, WV: McClain, 1982.

Schiller, Herbert M., ed. *Autobiography of Major General William F. Smith, 1861–1864*. Dayton, OH: Morningside House, 1990.

Schiller, Laurence D. "A Taste of Northern Steel: The Evolution of Federal Cavalry Tactics, 1861–1865." *North & South*, vol. 2, no. 2 (January 1999).

Schultz, Duane. *The Dahlgren Affair: Terror and Conspiracy in the Civil War*. New York: W. W. Norton, 1998.

Scott, Kate M. *History of the One Hundred and Fifth Regiment of Pennsylvania Volunteers*. Reprint, Baltimore: Butternut & Blue, 1993.

Scott, Robert Garth, ed. *Fallen Leaves: The Civil War Letters of Major Henry Livermore Abbott*. Kent, OH: Kent State University Press, 1991.

———, ed. *Forgotten Valor: The Memoirs, Journals, and Civil War Letters of Orlando B. Willcox*. Kent, OH: Kent State University Press, 1999.

Sears, Stephen W. *Chancellorsville*. Boston: Houghton Mifflin, 1996.

———, ed. *The Civil War Papers of George B. McClellan: Selected Correspondence, 1860–1865*. New York: Ticknor & Fields, 1989.

———. *Controversies and Commanders: Dispatches from the Army of the Potomac*. Boston: Houghton Mifflin, 1999.

———, ed. *For Country, Cause and Leader: The Civil War Journal of Charles B. Haydon*. New York: Ticknor & Fields, 1993.

———. *George B. McClellan: The Young Napoleon*. New York: Ticknor & Fields, 1988.

———. *Gettysburg*. Boston: Houghton Mifflin, 2003.

———. *Landscape Turned Red: The Battle of Antietam*. New Haven: Ticknor & Fields, 1983.

———. "Lee's Lost Opportunity: The Battle of Glendale." *North & South*, vol. 5, no. 1 (December 2001).

———. "Little Mac and the Historians." *North & South*, vol. 2, no. 3 (March 1999).

———. "Meade Takes Command." *North & South*, vol. 5, no. 6 (September 2002).

———, ed. *Mr. Dunn Browne's Experiences in the Army: The Civil War Letters of Samuel W. Fiske*. New York: Fordham University Press, 1998.

———, ed. *On Campaign with the Army of the Potomac*. New York: Cooper Square Press, 2001.

———. *To the Gates of Richmond: The Peninsula Campaign*. New York: Ticknor & Fields, 1992.

Sedgwick, Henry D., ed. *Correspondence of John Sedgwick Major General*. Two volumes in one. Reprint, Baltimore: Butternut & Blue, 1999.

Seville, William P. *History of the First Regiment, Delaware Volunteers, from the Commencement of the "Three Months' Service" to the Final Muster-Out at the Close of the Rebellion*. Reprint, Hightstown, NJ: Longstreet House, 1998.

Sheldon, Winthrop D. *The "Twenty-seventh": A Regimental History*. New Haven, CT: Morris & Benham, 1866.

Shultz, David. *"Double Canister at Ten Yards": The Federal Artillery and the Repulse of Pickett's Charge*. Redondo Beach, CA: Rank and File, 1995.

Sickles, Daniel E., Gregg, D. McM., Newton, John, and Butterfield, Daniel. "Further Recollections of Gettysburg." *North American Review*, vol. 152, no. 412 (March 1891).

Siegel, Alan A. *For the Glory of the Union: Myth, Reality, and the Media in Civil War New Jersey*. Rutherford, NJ: Fairleigh Dickinson University Press, 1984.

Silliker, Ruth L., ed. *The Rebel Yell and the Yankee Hurrah: The Civil War Journal of a Maine Volunteer*. Camden, ME: Down East Books, 1985.

Simon, John Y. "Lincoln and 'Old Brains.'" *North & South*, vol. 2, no. 1 (November 1998).

Sketches of War History, 1861–1865: Papers Prepared for the Ohio Commandery of the Military Order of the Loyal Legion of the United States. Nine volumes. Reprint, Wilmington, NC: Broadfoot, 1991–93.

Slocum, Charles Elihu. *The Life and Services of Major-General Henry Warner Slocum*. Toledo, OH: Slocum Publishing Company, 1913.

Small, Harold A., ed. *The Road to Richmond: The Civil War Memoirs of Major Abner R. Small of the Sixteenth Maine Volunteers. Together with the Diary Which He Kept When He Was a Prisoner of War*. New York: Fordham University Press, 2000.

Smart, James G., ed. *A Radical View: The "Agate" Dispatches of Whitelaw Reid, 1861–1865*. Two volumes. Memphis: Memphis State University Press, 1976.

Smith, Donald L. *The Twenty-fourth Michigan of the Iron Brigade*. Harrisburg, PA: Stackpole, 1962.

Smith, Jean Edward. *Grant*. New York: Simon & Schuster, 2001.

Smith, John Day. *The History of the Nineteenth Regiment of Maine Volunteer Infantry, 1862–1865*. Reprint, Gaithersburg, MD: Ron R. Van Sickle Military Books, 1988.

Smith, John L. *History of the 118th Pennsylvania Volunteers: Corn Exchange Regiment from Their First Engagement at Antietam to Appomattox*. Philadelphia: J. L. Smith, 1905.

Sneden, Robert Knox. *Eye of the Storm: A Civil War Odyssey*. Edited by Charles F. Bryan, Jr. and Nelson D. Lankford. New York: The Free Press, 2000.

Snell, Mark A., ed. *Civil War Regiments: A Journal of the American Civil War*, vol. 6, no. 2. Campbell, CA: Regimental Studies, 1998.

———. *From First to Last: The Life of Major General William B. Franklin*. New York: Fordham University Press, 2002.

The Snyder County Historical Society Bulletins from Volume 1, Number 1 to 1972 in Three Volumes (Volume 1). Selinsgrove, PA: Penn Valley Printing Company, n.d.

Sommers, Richard J. *Richmond Redeemed: The Siege at Petersburg*. Garden City, NY: Doubleday, 1981.

Sorrel, G. Moxley. *Recollections of a Confederate Staff Officer*. Edited by Bell Irvin Wiley. Reprint, Jackson, TN: McCowat-Mercer Press, 1958.

Southwick, Thomas P. *A Duryee Zouave*. Reprint, Brookneal, VA: Patrick A. Schroeder, 1995.

Sparks, David S., ed. *Inside Lincoln's Army: The Diary of Marsena Rudolph Patrick, Provost Marshal General, Army of the Potomac*. New York: Thomas Yoseloff, 1964.

Spear, Abbott, et al., eds. *The Civil War Recollections of General Ellis Spear*. Orono: University of Maine Press, 1997.

Starr, Stephen Z. *The Union Cavalry in the Civil War*. Three volumes. Baton Rouge: Louisiana State University Press, 1979–1985.

Staudenraus, P. J., ed. *Mr. Lincoln's Washington: Selections from the Writings of Noah Brooks, Civil War Correspondent*. New York: Thomas Yoseloff, 1967.

Stevens, George T. *Three Years in the Sixth Corps*. Reprint, Alexandria, VA: Time-Life, 1984.

Stevens, H. S., and Knowlton, J. W. *Address Delivered at the Dedication of Monument of the 14th Connecticut Volunteers at Gettysburg, PA., July 3rd 1884*. Middletown, CT: n.p., 1884.

Stevens, Michael E., ed. *As if It Were Glory: Robert Beecham's Civil War from the Iron Brigade to the Black Regiments*. Madison, WI: Madison House, 1998.

Stevenson, David. *Indiana's Roll of Honor*. Indianapolis: David Stevenson, 1864.

Stewart, A. M. *Camp, March and Battlefield; Or, Three Years and a Half with the Army of the Potomac*. Philadelphia: James B. Rodgers, 1865.

Stewart, Robert Laird. *History of the One Hundred and Fortieth Regiment Pennsylvania Volunteers*. [No city]: Regimental Association, 1912.

Stine, J. H. *History of the Army of the Potomac*. Washington, D.C.: Gibson Bros., 1893.

Stone, James Madison. *Personal Recollections of the Civil War*. Boston: James Madison Stone, 1918.

Stowe, Christopher S. "Certain Grave Charges." *Columbiad*, vol. 3, no. 1 (Spring 1999).

Sturtevant, Ralph Orson. *Pictorial History Thirteenth Regiment Vermont Volunteers War of, 1861–1865*. Reprint, Newport, VT: Tony O'Connor Civil War Enterprises, n.d.

Styple, William B., ed. *Letters from the Peninsula: The Civil War Letters of General Philip Kearny*. Kearny, NJ: Belle Grove, 1988.

———, ed. *Our Noble Blood: The Civil War Letters of Regis de Trobriand Major-General U.S.V.* Translated by Natahlie Chartrain. Kearny, NJ: Belle Grove, 1997.

———, ed. *With a Flash of His Sword: The Writings of Major Holman S. Melcher 20th Maine Infantry*. Kearny, NJ: Belle Grove, 1994.

———, ed. *Writing and Fighting the Civil War: Soldier Correspondence to the New York Sunday Mercury*. Kearny, NJ: Belle Grove Publishing Company, 2000.

Suderow, Bryce A. "Glory Denied: The First Battle of Deep Bottom July 27th–29th, 1864." *North & South*, vol. 3, no. 7 (September 2000).

———. "'Nothing but a Miracle Could Save Us': Second Battle of Deep Bottom, Virginia, August 14–20, 1864." *North & South*, vol. 4, no. 2 (January 2001).

Sumner, Merlin E., ed. *The Diary of Cyrus B. Comstock*. Dayton, OH: Morningside House, 1987.

Supplement to the Official Records of the Union and Confederate Armies. One hundred volumes. Wilmington, NC: Broadfoot, 1994–2001.

Sutherland, Daniel E. *Fredericksburg and Chancellorsville: The Dare Mark Campaign*. Lincoln: University of Nebraska Press, 1998.

Swanberg, W. V. *Sickles the Incredible*. New York: Charles Scribner's Sons, 1956.

Swinfen, David B. *Ruggles' Regiment: The 122nd New York Volunteers in the American Civil War*. Hanover: University Press of New England, 1982.

Swinton, William. *Campaigns of the Army of the Potomac: A Critical History of Operations in Virginia, Maryland and Pennsylvania from the Commencement to the Close of the War, 1861–5*. Reprint, Secaucus, NJ: Blue & Grey, 1988.

Sypher, J. R. *History of the Pennsylvania Reserve Corps*. Lancaster, PA: Elias Barr, 1865.

Tagg, Larry. *The Generals of Gettysburg: The Leaders of America's Greatest Battle*. Campbell, CA: Savas, 1998.

Tap, Bruce. "'Bad Faith Somewhere': George Gordon Meade and the Committee on the Conduct of the War." *North & South*, vol. 2, no. 6 (August 1999).

———. *Over Lincoln's Shoulder: The Committee on the Conduct of the War*. Lawrence: University Press of Kansas, 1998.

Thomas, Benjamin P., and Hyman, Harold M. *Stanton: The Life and Times of Lincoln's Secretary of War*. New York: Alfred A. Knopf, 1962.

Thomas, Mary Warner, and Sauers, Richard A., eds. *The Civil War Letters of First Lieutenant James B. Thomas Adjutant, 107th Pennsylvania Volunteers*. Baltimore: Butternut & Blue, 1995.

Thompson, Benjamin W. "'This Hell of Destruction': The Benjamin W. Thompson Memoir, Part II." *Civil War Times Illustrated*, vol. 12, no. 6 (October 1973).

Thomson, O. R. Howard, and Rauch, William H. *History of the "Bucktails": Kane Rifle Regiment of the Pennsylvania Reserve Corps.* Reprint, Dayton, OH: Morningside House, 1988.

Thurner, Arthur W., ed. "A Young Soldier in the Army of the Potomac: Diary of Howard Helman, 1862." *Pennsylvania Magazine of History and Biography,* vol. 87 (1963).

Tilney, Robert. *My Life in the Army: Three Years and a Half with the Fifth Army Corps Army of the Potomac, 1862–1865.* Philadelphia: Ferris & Leach, 1912.

Toombs, Samuel. *New Jersey Troops in the Gettysburg Campaign From June 5 to July 31, 1863.* Orange, NJ: Evening Mail Publishing House, 1888.

Trask, Kerry A. *Fire Within: A Civil War Narrative from Wisconsin.* Kent, OH: Kent State University Press, 1995.

Trudeau, Noah Andre. *Bloody Roads South: The Wilderness to Cold Harbor, May–June 1864.* Boston: Little, Brown, 1989.

———. *Gettysburg: A Testing of Courage.* New York: HarperCollins, 2002.

———. *The Last Citadel: Petersburg, Virginia, June 1864–April 1865.* Boston: Little, Brown, 1991.

———. *Out of the Storm: The End of the Civil War, April–June 1865.* Boston: Little, Brown, 1994.

Trulock, Alice Rains. *In the Hands of Providence: Joshua L. Chamberlain and the American Civil War.* Chapel Hill: University of North Carolina Press, 1992.

Tucker, Glenn. *Hancock the Superb.* Indianapolis: Bobbs-Merrill, 1960.

Turino, Kenneth C., ed. *The Civil War Diary of Lieut. J. E. Hodgkins 19th Massachusetts Volunteers from August 11, 1862 to June 3, 1865.* Camden, ME: Picton, 1994.

Turner, Ann, ed. *A Chronology of Indiana in the Civil War.* Indianapolis: Indiana Civil War Centennial Commission, 1965.

Tyler, Mason Whiting. *Recollections of the Civil War: With Many Original Diary Entries and Letters Written from the Seat of War, and with Annotated References.* New York: G. P. Putnam's Sons, 1912.

Vaill, Theodore F. *History of the Second Connecticut Volunteer Heavy Artillery.* Winsted, CT: Winsted Printing Company, 1868.

Vanderslice, Catherine H., ed. *The Civil War Letters of George Washington Beidelman.* New York: Vantage, 1978.

Viola, Herman J., ed. *The Memoirs of Charles Henry Veil: A Soldier's Recollections of the Civil War and the Arizona Territory.* New York: Orion, 1993.

Walker, Charles N., and Walker, Rosemary, eds. *Diary of the War by Robt S. Robertson.* Fort Wayne, IN: Allen County–Fort Wayne Historical Society, 1965.

Walker, Francis A. *General Hancock.* New York: D. Appleton, 1894.

———. *History of the Second Army Corps in the Army of the Potomac.* Reprint, Gaithersburg, MD: Olde Soldier Books, n.d.

Wallace, Willard M. *Soul of the Lion: A Biography of General Joshua L. Chamberlain.* Edinburgh: Thomas Nelson & Sons, 1960.

Walton, William, ed. *A Civil War Courtship: The Letters of Edwin Weller from Antietam to Atlanta.* Garden City, NY: Doubleday, 1980.

The War of the Rebellion: A Compilation of the Official Records of the Union and Confederate Armies. 128 volumes. Washington, D.C.: Government Printing Office, 1880–1902.

Warner, Ezra J. *Generals in Blue: Lives of the Union Commanders*. Baton Rouge: Louisiana State University Press, 1981.

Washburn, George H. *A Complete Military History and Record of the 108th Regiment N.Y. Vols. from 1862 to 1864*. Rochester, NY: E. R. Andrews, 1894.

Waugh, John C. *The Class of 1846: From West Point to Appomattox: Stonewall Jackson, George McClellan and Their Brothers*. New York: Warner, 1994.

Webb, Alexander S. *The Peninsula: McClellan's Campaign of 1862*. New York: Charles Scribner's Sons, 1881.

Webb and His Brigade at the Angle Gettysburg. Albany, NY: J. B. Lyon, 1916.

Weigley, Russell F. *A Great Civil War: A Military and Political History, 1861–1865*. Bloomington and Indianapolis: Indiana University Press, 2000.

Welcher, Frank J. *The Union Army, 1861–1865: Organization and Operations, Volume I: The Eastern Theater*. Bloomington and Indianapolis: Indiana University Press, 1989.

Weld, Stephen Minot. *War Diary and Letters of Stephen Minot Weld*. Boston: Massachusetts Historical Society, 1979.

Werstein, Irving. *Kearny the Magnificent: The Story of General Philip Kearny, 1815–1862*. New York: John Day, 1962.

Wert, Jeffry D. "All-Out War," *Civil War Times Illustrated*, Volume 43, no. 1 (April 2004).

———. *A Brotherhood of Valor: The Common Soldiers of the Stonewall Brigade, C.S.A., and the Iron Brigade, U.S.A.* New York: Simon & Schuster, 1999.

———. *Custer: The Controversial Life of George Armstrong Custer*. New York: Simon & Schuster, 1996.

———. *From Winchester to Cedar Creek: The Shenandoah Valley Campaign of 1864*. Carlisle, PA: South Mountain Press, 1987.

———. *General James Longstreet: The Confederacy's Most Controversial Soldier*. New York: Simon & Schuster, 1993.

———. *Gettysburg: Day Three*. New York: Simon & Schuster, 2001.

Westbrook, Robert S. *History of the 49th Pennsylvania Volunteers*. Reprint, Baltimore: Butternut & Blue, 1999.

Weygant, Charles H. *History of the One Hundred Twenty-fourth Regiment, N.Y.S.V.* Reprint, Celina, OH: Ironclad, 2002.

White, Russell, C., ed. *The Civil War Diary of Wyman S. White, First Sergeant of Company F, 2nd United States Sharpshooter Regiment, 1861–1865*. Baltimore: Butternut & Blue, 1997.

Whitehouse, Hugh L., ed. *Letters from the Iron Brigade: George Washington Partridge, Jr., 1839–1863, Civil War Letters to His Sister*. Indianapolis: Guild Press of Indiana, 1994.

Wickman, Donald H., ed. *Letters to Vermont: From Her Civil War Soldier Correspondents to the Home Press, Volume I*. Bennington, VT: Images from the Past, 1998.

Wiley, Bell Irvin. *The Life of Billy Yank: The Common Soldier of the Union*. Indianapolis: Bobbs-Merrill, 1952.

Wilkeson, Frank. *Recollections of a Private Soldier in the Army of the Potomac*. Reprint, Freeport, NY: Books for Libraries Press, 1972.

Wilkinson, Warren. *Mother, May You Never See the Sights I Have Seen: The Fifty-seventh Massachusetts Veteran Volunteers in the Army of the Potomac, 1864–1865*. New York: Harper & Row, 1990.

Williams, Frank J. "'We Had Only to Stretch Forth Our Hands': Abraham Lincoln and George Gordon Meade." *North & South*, vol. 2, no. 6 (August 1999).

Williams, T. Harry. *Lincoln and His Generals*. New York: Alfred A. Knopf, 1952.

Willson, Arabella M. *Disaster, Struggle, Triumph: The Adventures of 1000 "Boys in Blue," from August, 1862, to June, 1865*. Albany: Argus, 1870.

Winey, Michael J. *Union Army Uniforms at Gettysburg*. Gettysburg, PA: Thomas, 1998.

Winik, Jay. *April 1865: The Month That Saved America*. New York: HarperCollins, 2001.

Winkler, Frederick C. *Letters of Frederick C. Winkler, 1862 to 1865*. Milwaukee: Privately printed, 1963.

Winslow, Richard Elliott III. *General John Sedgwick: The Story of a Union Corps Commander*. Novato, CA: Presidio, 1982.

Wittenberg, Eric J. *Little Phil: A Reassessment of the Civil War Leadership of Gen. Philip H. Sheridan*. Washington, D.C.: Brassey's, 2002.

———, ed. *One of Custer's Wolverines: The Civil War Letters of Brevet Brigadier General James H. Kidd, 6th Michigan Cavalry*. Kent, OH: Kent State University Press, 2000.

———. *The Union Cavalry Comes of Age: Hartwood Church to Brandy Station*. Washington, D.C.: Brassey's, 2003.

Woodward, Daniel H. "The Civil War of a Pennsylvania Trooper." *Pennsylvania Magazine of History and Biography*, vol. 88 (1987).

Woodward, Evan Morrison. *Our Campaigns: The Second Regiment Pennsylvania Reserve Volunteers*. Edited by Stanley W. Zamonski. Reprint, Shippensburg, PA: Burd Street Press, 1995.

Woodworth, Steven E., ed. *Leadership and Command in the American Civil War*. New York: Da Capo, 1996.

Wormeley, Katherine Prescott. *The Other Side of War with the Army of the Potomac*. Boston: Ticknor, 1889.

Wray, William J. *Birney's Zouaves: Life of the 23rd Pennsylvania Volunteers*. Reprint, Springville, PA: Lisa Wray, 1999.

Wright, James A. *No More Gallant a Deed: A Civil War Memoir of the First Minnesota Volunteers*. Edited by Steven J. Keillor. St. Paul: Minnesota Historical Society Press, 2001.

Young, Jesse Bowman. *The Battle of Gettysburg: A Comprehensive Narrative*. New York: Harper & Brothers, 1913.

INDEX

Page numbers in *italics* refer to maps.

Abbott, Henry L., 214, 255

Adams, Charles Francis, 223

African-Americans, *see* slaves, slavery;
    United States Colored Troops

Aldie, engagement at, 264

Alexander, E. Porter, 116, 193, 199, 200,
    233, 236, 244

Allen, Ethan, 6

Ames, John W., 104–5

Anderson, George T., 289

Anderson, Richard H., 235, 238, 243,
    344, 345–46

Andrew, John A., 4

Antietam (Sharpsburg), Battle of,
    155–71, 266, 310, 333, 334, 366,
    411, 414

    Burnside Bridge sector of, 167–69

    campaign leading to, *see* Maryland
        Campaign

    carnage of, 159–60, 169–70

    casualties in, 160, 163, 166, 169

    Confederate deployment in, 155–56

    Confederate withdrawal from, 170–71

    Cornfield fight in, 158–60, 167

    East Woods fight in, 158–59, 160,
        162, 163, 167

    Emancipation Proclamation and, 173

    Hill's arrival in, 169

    Irish Brigade in, 164–65

    McClellan's failure in, 167, 172–73

    Sumner's tactical error in, 161–63

    Sunken Road (Bloody Lane) fight in,
        163–66, 167, 168, 412

    terrain of, 158–59

    West Woods fight in, 158–59,
        162–63, 166, 167, 172, 217, 222,
        512, 414

Appomattox Campaign, 405–10, 407,
    411

Archer, David, 91–92

Archer, James J., 276

Ariel, 126, 127

Armistead, Lewis A., 119, 299

Army of Northern Virginia, C.S.A., x,
    96, 119, 134, 136, 139, 142, 175,
    184, 232, 258, 259, 260, 315, 323,
    397, 398

    assessment of, 415–16

    corps organization of, 260

    surrender of, 406–9

Army of Tennessee, C.S.A., 40, 331,
    395

Army of the James, U.S., 371, 375, 378,
    387, 400, 406, 408

    reorganization of, 394

Army of the Potomac, U.S.:

    African-American troops in, *see*
        United States Colored Troops

    artillery arm of, 39–41, 146

    assessment of, 414–15

    Burnside's reorganization of, 185

    camp life of, 52–54

    cautious mindset of, 336, 339–40,
        343, 357, 414–15

    cavalry arm of, 41, 146, 178, 220,
        223–24, 228–29

    commanders of, 7–8, 37–39, 220–24,
        329–30, 357

Army of the Potomac, U.S. (*continued*)
  corps badges of, 226
  corps reorganized in, 80, 185, 220
  defense of Washington and, 45–46
  democratization of, 209–12, 214–17, 227
  desertions from, 211, 214, 218, 225, 227, 380
  disbandment of, 413
  disease in, 53, 91
  draft riots and, 311
  1864 election and, 391
  ethnic diversity of, 39
  expiring enlistments in, 311, 346, 367, 380
  Fredericksburg aftermath and, 209–15
  Grand Review of, 411–12
  Hooker named commander of, 216–19
  Hooker's reorganization of, 220–26
  Lincoln's 1863 visit to, 226–27
  McClellan named commander of, 28–29
  McClellan's bond with soldiers of, 36–37, 92–93, 122–23, 140–41, 143–44, 181–82
  McClellan's farewell address to, 181
  McClellan's grand review of, 49–51
  McClellan's reorganizations of, 32–37, 39–41, 143–47
  McClellan's restoration to command and, 138–41
  McDowell's organization of, 11–12
  Meade's reorganization of, 328–30
  morale in, 53–54, 372–73
  official naming of, 37
  post-Gettysburg morale of, 311–12
  in reaction to Emancipation Proclamation, 176–77, 211–12
  record of, 414
  reenlistments in, 323–24
  resiliency of, 28, 227, 257–58, 416
  Reynolds's assessment of, 41–42
  shortages in, 175, 227
  studies and histories of, 413–14

Army of Virginia, U.S., 129–30, 134, 144, 152, 185, 220, 313, 328
Averell, William W., 26, 32, 112, 223–24, 228–29
Ayling, Augustus D., 191
Ayres, Romeyn B., 388, 401

Baker, Edward, 47–48, 59
Ballou, Sullivan, 15
Ball's Bluff, Battle of, 46–48, 87
  JCCW investigation of, 58–59
Banks, Nathaniel P., 37, 46, 61, 62, 69, 82, 83, 144
Barksdale, William, 189, 190, 291
Barlow, Francis, 88, 286, 338, 351, 376, 412
  at Antietam, 165–66
  command relinquished by, 388, 392
  at Gettysburg, 277, 281, 283
  McClellan assessed by, 124
  wounded, 166, 283
Barnard, John, 61, 93
Barnes, James, 289
Barry, Camp, 40
Barry, William F., 23, 39–40, 146
"Battle Cry of Freedom, The" (song), 354
Bayard, George D., 204
Beauregard, P. G. T., 12, 13, 16, 18, 19, 371
Beaver, James A., 388–89
Bee, Barnard B., 21
Bentonville, Battle of, 397
Berdan, Hiram, 91
Berdan's Sharpshooters (1st United States Sharpshooters), 91, 119
Bermuda Hundred, 331, 361, 371, 375, 378, 395, 397
Berry, Hiram G., 78, 116, 241, 245
Bethesda Church, engagement at, 364
Biddle, James, 254
Birney, David B., 140, 196, 288, 326, 351, 366, 376, 392, 412
  at Chancellorsville, 239, 243
  French assessed by, 329
  Kearny's assessment of, 78

McClellan criticized by, 180
    at Wilderness, 337–38
Birney, James G., 78
Blair, Austin, 17
Blair, Francis P., Jr., 222
Blenker, Louis, 37–38, 68, 145
Bliss, George N., 229
Bliss, William, 297
Blodgett, William, 258
Booth, John Wilkes, 410
Bowen, Charles T., 141, 236, 416
Bowen, Roland E., 192
Bragg, Braxton, 40, 373
Brandy Station, Battle of, 260–62, 267,
    270, 411
Brawner's Farm (Groveton), Battle of,
    134, 153
Bristoe Campaign, 316–17, 319, 320
Bristoe Station, Battle of, 316
Brooke, John R., 165
Brooks, Noah, 252–53
Brooks, William, 111
Brooks, William T. H., 38, 215, 247
Brown, Kent Masterson, 307
Buchanan, James, 56
Buckingham, Catharinus P., 174–75,
    179, 180
Buckland Races, 317
Buford, John, 224, 256, 260–61, 271,
    272, 273, 287, 411
    death of, 324
    at Gettysburg, 274–75, 280, 283, 304
Bull Run (Manassas), First Battle of,
    16–26, 54, 88, 89
    Blackburn's Ford fight in, 17–18
    casualties in, 27
    Confederate reinforcements in, 19
    Henry House Hill fight in, 21–25
    McDowell's battle plan for, 18–19, 20
    Matthews Hill fight in, 20–21, 22, 27
    Union advance to, 16–17
    Union rout in, 25–26, 27
Bull Run (Manassas), Second Battle of,
    135–38, 142, 145–46, 183, 185,
    221, 232
Bureau of Colored Troops, 382–83

Bureau of Military Intelligence, 229, 234
Burgwyn, Henry, 280
"Burning, the," 390
Burnside, Ambrose E., x, 11, 39, 82,
    131, 132, 146–47, 148, 149, 172,
    205, 221, 223, 229, 330–31, 345,
    347, 357, 411, 414–15
    at Antietam, 157, 167–70
    appointed wing commander, 146–47
    Army of the Potomac reorganized by,
        185
    assessment of, 217–18
    at Bull Run, 20, 21
    Crater debacle and, 380–82, 383, 385
    Fredericksburg Campaign and,
        184–88, 190, 192, 193, 194–97,
        199, 201–4
    General Orders No. 8, of, 215–16
    Gibbon on, 193
    Hooker's replacement of, 216–19,
        224–25
    McClellan replaced by, 174–75,
        179–81, 183
    Mud March and, 214–15
    named Ninth Corps commander, 130
    in N.C. operations, 60
    at Petersburg, 371–72, 374, 380–82,
        383, 385
    resignations of, 215–16, 385–86
    at South Mountain, 151
    at Spotsylvania, 350–51, 354
    subordinates' opposition to, 206–8,
        213, 215–16
    at Wilderness, 340, 341–42
Butler, Benjamin F., 331, 346, 361, 364,
    371, 375, 378, 394
Butterfield, Daniel, 105, 248–49, 250,
    251, 253, 264, 268, 269, 306
Byron, George Gordon, Lord, 191

Caldwell, John, 165, 289, 290
Cameron, James, 25
Cameron, Simon, 5, 8, 25, 48, 57
    resignation of, 56
Camp Barry, 40
Camp Curtin, 4

Carpenter, Thomas, 310
Carter, Walter, 187–88, 390
Casey, Silas, 33, 85, 89–90
Cavalry Corps, U.S.:
    at Brandy Station, 260–62
    organizational changes in, 270
Cedar Creek, Battle of, 390, 394, 412
Cedar Mountain, Battle of, 133–34
Center Grand Division, Army of the
        Potomac, U.S., 185
Chamberlain, Lawrence Joshua, 289,
        305, 334, 366, 372, 410
Chambersburg, burning of, 386
Chancellor, George, 231
Chancellorsville, Battle of, 231–58, 242,
        259, 266, 287, 314–15, 325–26,
        337, 366
    aftermath of, 253–54, 257
    assessment of, 254–55, 258
    casualties in, 237, 240, 241, 245, 247,
        252, 258
    Hooker's lack of fighting spirit in,
        236–38
    initial Union movements in, 232–36
    intelligence on Confederate numbers
        in, 234
    Jackson's flank movement and attack
        in, 238–41
    McGee's Hill fight in, 236–37
    Sedgwick's failed operation in,
        246–49
    Stoneman's raids and, 232, 238,
        255–56
    Union council of war in, 250–51
    Union retreat in, 250–52
    Wilderness terrain of, 231, 236,
        237–38
Chandler, Zachariah, 58, 59
Chantilly, Battle of, 137
Chase, Salmon P., 8, 9, 30, 55, 133, 140,
        178
Chattanooga, siege of, 322, 327, 330
Chickamauga, Battle of, 313
Chickasaw Bluffs, Battle of, 220
Child, William, 158
"Childe Harold's Pilgrimage" (Byron),
        191

Chisholm, Alexander, 391
Clare, Samuel, 410–11
Clark, Henry F., 93
Cobb, Thomas R. R., 199
Cochrane, John, 206, 215
Coddington, Edwin, 292, 296
Cold Harbor, Battle of, 333, 361–65,
        363, 374
Commodore, 66
Confederate States of America, 3, 4, 96,
        142
    U.S. blockade of, 13
Congress, Confederate, 12
Congress, U.S., 41, 55, 58, 128, 129,
        326, 332, 395
    conscription act passed by, 230
    see also House of Representatives,
        U.S.; Senate, U.S.
Constitution, U.S., 176, 211
    Thirteenth Amendment of, 395
Coon, S. Park, 24
Corcoran (Irish), Legion, U.S., 356
Corrick's Ford, Battle of, 30
Coster, Charles R., 281
Couch, Darius N., 38, 145, 154, 170,
        227, 253, 256, 257
    at Chancellorsville, 237, 244,
        250–51
    at Fair Oaks, 85–87
    at Fredericksburg, 188, 197, 201,
        221
    on Hooker at Chancellorsville, 237
    at Malvern Hill, 119, 121
Cox, Jacob D., 168–69
Crater, Battle of the, 380–85
Crawford, Samuel, 290–91, 336, 346,
        401–2
Crimean War, 29
Cross, Edward E., 88, 165–66, 182, 201,
        290, 412
Culpeper Court House, Battle of, 312
Cummings, Charles, 367
Curtin, Andrew Gregg, 4, 38, 146, 264
Curtin, Camp, 4
Custer, George A., 270, 301–3, 344,
        355, 361, 377, 399, 408, 411
Cutler, Lysander, 275, 276, 346

Dahlgren, John, 325
Dahlgren, Ulric, 325
Dana, Charles, 357, 393
Davis, Benjamin F., 261, 411
Davis, Jefferson, 1, 19, 62–63, 82, 92,
    95, 109, 142–43, 259, 315–16,
    325, 396, 404
Davis, Joseph, 276
Davis, William C., 212
Dawes, Rufus, 258, 283, 332, 372,
    378–79, 384
Dearing, James, 406
Deep Bottom, engagement at, 387–88
Delaware, 209
Democratic Party, 178, 179, 205
    1864, election and, 390–91
Dennison, William, 8, 29
Devin, Thomas, 272
Dilger, Hubert, 240–41
Dimmock Line, 371, 403–4
Dinwiddie Court House, engagement at,
    400
disease, 53, 80, 82, 91, 132
Dodge, Theodore, 113
Donaldson, Francis A., 214, 317
Donelson, Fort, 60, 327
Doubleday, Abner, 196–97, 276–77,
    278, 280, 283, 294, 326
draft riots, 311
Duffie, Alfred N., 261–62
Duryée, Hiram, 104

Early, Jubal A., 77, 196, 371, 395, 399
    at Chancellorsville, 235, 247–48
    at Gettysburg, 278, 281
    Shenandoah Valley Campaign of,
        386–87, 390
Edwards, Clark S., 27, 210
8th Illinois Cavalry, U.S., 261
8th New York Cavalry, U.S., 261
8th New York State Militia, 22
8th Ohio Regiment, U.S., 164, 191,
    197–99, 354 367
8th Virginia Regiment, C.S.A., 25
Eighteenth Corps, Army of the James,
    361, 365, 370, 371, 375, 382,
    394

18th Massachusetts Regiment, U.S., 36
18th North Carolina Regiment, C.S.A.,
    241
18th Virginia Regiment, C.S.A., 25
82nd Ohio Regiment, U.S., 240
83rd Pennsylvania Regiment, U.S., 105,
    289, 412
88th New York Regiment, U.S., 88
89th New York Regiment, U.S., 190,
    396
elections, U.S.:
    of 1862, 178, 179
    of 1864, 327, 332, 368–69, 387,
        390–91
Elements of Military Art and Science (Hal-
    leck), 130
11th Connecticut Regiment, U.S., 168
Eleventh Corps, Army of the Potomac,
    144, 147, 185, 221, 226, 232,
    239–41, 255, 271, 281–83, 314
11th Massachusetts Regiment, U.S., 21,
    390
11th New Jersey Regiment, U.S., 183
11th New York Regiment, U.S (Fire
    Zouaves), 9, 23
11th Pennsylvania Reserve Regiment,
    U.S., 105, 196
Elliott's Salient, 382
Ellsworth, Elmer, 9
Emancipation Proclamation, 138, 173,
    178, 205, 220, 227, 395
    Lincoln's proposal of, 128–29
    reactions to, 176–77, 179, 211–12
    and recruitment of African-Ameri-
        cans, 382–83
    signing of, 208–9
Emerson, Horace, 54
Englis, George, 396
English, Samuel J., 20
Evans, Nathan, 47
Ewell, Richard S., 96, 160, 335, 336,
    340, 341
    at Gettysburg Battle, 277, 282, 295,
        304
    in Gettysburg Campaign, 262–64,
        273
Excelsior Brigade, U.S., 39, 78, 222, 380

Fair Oaks, Battle of, 84–90, 217
Faller, John, 132
Falling Waters, Battle of, 308
Farnsworth, Elon, 270, 303
Ferrero, Edward, 382–83
Field, Charles, 340
5th Cavalry Regiment, U.S., 105
Fifth Corps, Army of the Potomac, 181,
    266, 271, 366, 370, 410
  at Antietam, 156, 157
  in Appomattox pursuit, 406, 408
  at Bethesda Church, 364
  in Burnside's reorganization, 185
  at Chancellorsville, 232–33, 235,
    238, 243, 254
  corps badge of, 226
  creation of, 80
  draft riots and, 311
  at Fredericksburg, 201
  in Grand Review, 412
  at Hatcher's Run, 396
  at Laurel Hill, 345, 346, 351, 354
  in McClellan's reorganization, 146
  in Meade's reorganization, 329–30
  at North Anna, 358
  in Overland Campaign, 335, 336,
    345, 346, 351, 354, 358, 364
  in Peninsula Campaign, 83, 84, 91,
    94, 98, 103, 106, 109, 114, 119,
    123–24
  at Petersburg, 372, 376, 384, 389,
    396, 399, 400
  Sykes appointed commander of, 270
  Warren appointed commander of,
    330
5th Maine Regiment, U.S., 25, 27, 254
5th Massachusetts Regiment, U.S., 21
5th New Hampshire Regiment, U.S., 52,
    88, 122, 158, 165–66, 201, 290
5th New York Regiment, U.S. (Duryée's
    Zouaves), 7, 104–5, 132, 412
5th Pennsylvania Reserve Regiment,
    U.S., 324
5th United States Artillery, 23
5th Vermont Regiment, U.S., 111
5th Wisconsin Regiment, U.S., 90

15th Massachusetts Regiment, U.S., 47,
    108, 116, 123, 163, 192, 214
15th New Jersey Regiment, U.S., 214
15th New York Engineers, U.S., 81, 189
50th New York Engineers, U.S., 81,
    189–90
51st New York Regiment, U.S., 168
51st Pennsylvania Regiment, U.S., 168
54th New York Regiment, U.S., 240
55th Ohio Regiment, U.S., 282
57th Massachusetts Regiment, U.S., 398
57th New York Regiment, U.S., 304
58th New York Regiment, U.S., 240
59th New York Regiment, U.S., 347
1st Connecticut Regiment, U.S., 14
First Corps, Army of Northern Virginia,
    C.S.A., 184, 234, 262, 312, 335,
    340, 344
First Corps, Army of the Potomac, 181,
    193, 213, 271, 294, 412
  at Antietam, 156–58, 161–62, 170,
    172
  in Burnside's reorganization, 185
  at Chancellorsville, 232, 239, 242,
    246, 254, 255
  corps badge of, 226
  at Fredericksburg, 195
  at Gettysburg, 275, 278, 280–83
  Hooker named commander of,
    144–45
  in McClellan's reorganization, 144,
    146
  in Meade's reorganization, 329
  in Rappahannock Department, 68, 70
  at South Mountain, 151–52
First Corps, Army of Virginia, U.S., 144
First Defenders, 4
1st Delaware Regiment, U.S., 197–99,
    373
1st Maine Cavalry, U.S., 261–62
1st Maine Heavy Artillery, U.S., 356,
    372
1st Maryland Cavalry, U.S., 261
1st Massachusetts Cavalry, U.S., 223
1st Massachusetts Regiment, U.S., 17,
    367

1st Michigan Cavalry, U.S., 301
1st Minnesota Regiment, U.S., 6, 23, 71, 111, 125, 286, 291, 299
1st New Jersey Brigade, U.S., 39, 75
1st New Jersey Cavalry, U.S., 261
1st New York Regiment, U.S., 230
1st Ohio Light Artillery, U.S., 240–41
1st Pennsylvania Cavalry, U.S., 261
1st Pennsylvania Reserve Regiment, 114
1st Rhode Island Cavalry, 229
1st South Carolina Rifles, C.S.A., 104
1st Texas Regiment, C.S.A., 160
1st United States Artillery, 23
1st United States Sharpshooters (Berdan's Sharpshooters), 91, 119
1st Vermont Cavalry, U.S., 355
Fisher's Hill, Battle of, 390, 412
Fisk, Wilbur, 394
Fiske, Samuel, 322
Five Forks, Battle of, 399–402, 414
Flint, Dayton E., 214
Flynn, James B., 5–6
Fort Donelson, 60, 327
Fort Gregg, 403–4
Fort Haskell, 397
Fort Henry, 60, 327
Fort Magruder, 76, 77
Fort Monroe, 64, 66, 68, 94, 133, 135, 386
Fort Sedgwick, 378
Fort Stedman, 397–98
Fort Sumter, 3, 5, 45
Fort Whitworth, 403–4
Fourth Corps, Army of the Potomac, 83–86, 89, 98–99, 108–9, 113, 119, 133, 135, 145
4th Maine Regiment, U.S., 25, 78
4th Michigan Regiment, U.S., 104, 412
4th New Jersey Regiment, U.S., 105
4th Ohio Regiment, U.S., 197–99, 367
4th Pennsylvania Regiment, U.S., 6, 19, 20
14th Brooklyn Regiment, U.S., 22, 23–24, 276
14th Connecticut Regiment, U.S., 322
14th Indiana Regiment, U.S., 164, 367

14th New York Regiment, U.S., 323
42nd New York Regiment, U.S., 214
44th New York Regiment, U.S., 289
48th Mississippi Regiment, C.S.A., 403–4
48th Pennsylvania Regiment, U.S., 382
49th Pennsylvania Regiment, U.S., 50
Fowler, Patrick K., 132
Fox, Gustavus, 55, 59
France, 96
Franklin, Battle of, 395
Franklin, William B., 11, 19, 79–80, 127, 131, 157, 185, 186, 222, 387, 412
    at Antietam, 166–67, 170–71
    in effort to undermine Burnside, 206–7, 213, 215–16
    at First Bull Run, 21, 27, 38
    at Fredericksburg, 193, 194–97, 203, 218
    Hancock praised by, 167
    in Peninsula Campaign, 70, 73, 111–13, 119, 124, 127, 131
    in Second Bull Run Campaign, 135–37, 147
    at South Mountain, 153–54
Fredericksburg, Battle of, 184–204, 198, 333, 334, 411–12, 416
    army reorganization and, 185
    army's reaction to defeat at, 209–10
    Burnside's confusing orders in, 194–95
    casualties in, 196, 202, 204
    Confederate deployment in, 192–93
    crossing of Rappahannock in, 187–91
    Marye's Heights assaults in, 197–202
    planning of, 184–85
    pontoon train fiasco and, 186, 187
    Prospect Hill assaults in, 195–97
    Union reaction to defeat at, 205–8
    Union withdrawal from, 203–4
French, William H., 38, 40, 87, 106, 145, 164, 197, 238, 307, 320, 329
Frontier Guard, 4
Fuller, Charles A., 201

Gaines's Mill, Battle of, 103–6, 122, 123–24

Galena, 113, 118, 121

Galwey, Thomas F., 354

Gates, Theodore B., 212

Geary, John, 293, 303

General Orders No. 8, 215–16

General Order No. 35, 413

General Orders No. 47, 29

General Orders No. 115, 329

General Orders No. 182, 174

Georgia, 95

Gerrish, Theodore, 391

Getty, George W., 201, 335, 336, 337, 340

Gettysburg, Battle of, 274–308, 279, 333, 334, 366, 411, 414
  assessment of, 304–5
  casualties in, 280, 283, 292, 296, 303–4
  cavalry engagements in, 300–302
  Cemetery Ridge fighting in, 291–93
  Confederate cannonade in, 297–98
  Confederate retreat in, 305–6
  Culp's Hill fighting in, 292–93, 295–97, 314
  Devil's Den fighting in, 287–88, 291
  Falling Waters engagement and, 308
  first day of, 274–83
  Lee-Longstreet conflict in, 285–86, 296–97
  Lee's attack decisions in, 285, 295
  Little Round Top fight in, 287, 288–89, 291, 293
  McPherson's Ridge fight in, 275–77
  Oak Ridge fight in, 277–80
  onset of, 274–77
  Peach Orchard fighting in, 287–88, 291
  Pickett's Charge in, 296–99, 304
  Reynolds's battle decision in, 275
  second day of, 284–94
  Sickles's salient in, 286–88
  terrain of, 274, 284–85
  third day of, 295–303
  Union council of war in, 293–95
  Union failure to counterattack in, 300
  Union pursuit in, 306–8
  Wheatfield fighting in, 287–91, 412

Gettysburg Campaign, 259–73, 310, 325–26
  Brandy Station Battle in, 260–62, 264
  casualties in, 262
  cavalry battles in, 260–62, 264
  Confederate spy in, 272–73
  Hooker's resignation in, 265–66
  Lincoln's call for volunteers and, 264–65
  Pipe Creek Line in, 271
  Stuart's absence from, 273
  Union command crisis in, 265–67
  Union march in, 263, 270–71
  Winchester Battle in, 262, 264
  see also Gettysburg, Battle of

Gibbon, John, 29, 157, 159, 248, 255, 261, 268, 286, 287, 307, 338, 351, 365, 376, 394, 404, 412
  at Brawner's Farm, 153
  as brigade commander, 152–53
  on Burnside, 193
  Emancipation Proclamation reaction of, 177, 180
  at Fredericksburg, 196
  at Gettysburg, 294–95
  Hancock's relationship with, 389, 393
  on Overland Campaign losses, 366–67
  at Ream's station, 388–89
  wounded, 299–300

Glendale, Battle of, 114–16, 122, 124, 125, 414

Globe Tavern, Battle at, 388

Goodyear, Robert B., 227

Gordon, John B., 353, 397–98, 403, 406, 408

Gorman, Willis A., 39

Gove, Jesse, 105

Grand Army of the Republic, 413

Grant, Julia, 398

Grant, Ulysses S., 60, 130, 220, 308,
    322, 330, 369, 375, 393, 411
  appointed general-in-chief, 326–27
  on art of war, 331–32
  background and personality of,
    327–28
  at Cold Harbor, 361, 362, 364–65
  generalship of, 326–27
  Lee's surrender to, 406–9
  Lincoln's meetings with, 386–87,
    389, 398–99
  Meade on, 327–28
  Meade's command relationship with,
    328, 342, 357, 373–74
  in Overland Campaign, 334–36,
    338–39, 345, 346, 348–51, 353,
    355, 357, 358–62, 364–65, 367
  at Petersburg, 371, 373–74, 376–78,
    380, 383, 385, 396–97, 400–402
  Sherman on, 326, 327
  at Spotsylvania, 350–51, 353
  at Wilderness, 338–39, 342–44, 345,
    346, 348–51, 353, 355, 357, 359
Great Britain, 96, 222
Greene, George S., 162, 292–93
Green Mountain Boys, 6
Gregg, David McM., 224, 261–62, 271,
    301, 377, 411
Gregg, Fort, 403–4
Gregg, Maxcy, 169
Griffin, Charles, 23, 147, 201, 335,
    336–37, 345–46, 402
Griffith, Paddy, 304
Groveton (Brawner's Farm), Battle of,
    134, 153
Guiney, Patrick R., 84, 220

habeas corpus, suspension of, 178
Haley, John W., 244, 250, 353–54, 396,
    409–10
Halleck, Henry W., 49, 148, 177, 180,
    209, 213, 215, 306, 322, 350, 364,
    369
  Fredericksburg Campaign and,
    184–85, 186
  Hooker disliked by, 28, 253, 256

Hooker's resignation and, 265–66
Lincoln's criticism of, 207
McClellan-administration interac-
    tions and, 132–33, 135, 138, 139,
    147, 173, 182
Meade-administration interactions
    and, 308–9, 317–18
Meade's appointment and, 267, 269
named general-in-chief, 130–31
post-Gettysburg operations and,
    312–15
Hamilton, Charles S., 76
Hamlin, Hannibal, 368
Hampton, Wade, 377
Hampton Roads Conference, 395–96
Hancock, Winfield Scott, 38, 50, 180,
    256, 267, 307, 316, 317, 318, 324,
    326, 347, 357, 412
  at Antietam, 167
  assessment of, 392
  at Chancellorsville, 236, 238, 245
  Franklin's praise of, 167
  at Fredericksburg, 188–89, 197, 200
  at Gettysburg, 281–82, 284, 285,
    289, 290, 292, 299–300, 304, 392
  Gibbon's relationship with, 389, 393
  leaves Army of the Potomac, 392–93
  in Overland Campaign, 335, 337–38,
    340–41, 348, 350–51, 353, 360,
    362
  at Petersburg, 370–72, 374, 376, 383,
    388–89
  at Wilderness, 337–38, 340–41
  at Williamsburg, 77–78
  wounded, 299–300, 304
Hardie, James A., 194, 266, 268
Hardin, Martin D., 290
Harper's Ferry, 12, 148, 169, 261, 265,
    269, 307
  in Maryland Campaign, 149–51, 153,
    155
Harris, Nathaniel, 403–4
Harris Farm, Battle of, 356
Harrison, Henry, 272–73
"Harrison's Landing Letter," 127–28
Harrow, William, 286

Harsh, Joseph L., 148, 150

Hartranft, John F., 19, 397–98

Haskell, Fort, 397

Haskell, Frank A., 158, 159, 272, 365

Hatch, John, 140

Hatcher's Run, engagement at, 396

Haupt, Herman, 184–85, 187, 305–6, 308

Haw's Shop, Battle of, 361, 411

Hay, John, 49, 137–38, 139, 179, 308, 369

Haydon, Charles B., 92, 184

Hays, Alexander, 115–16, 119, 205, 220, 291, 299, 307, 316, 337, 412

Hays, William, 307, 316

Heffelfinger, Jacob, 196

Heintzelman, Samuel P., 11, 61, 62, 72, 77, 121, 134, 147, 415
   at Bull Run, 18, 20–21, 37
   Kearny's confrontation with, 118–19
   in Peninsula Campaign, 65–66, 68, 76, 78–80, 85–86, 89–90, 108, 111, 113, 118–19, 124, 127, 131, 133
   at Williamsburg, 78–80

Hennessy, John, 330

Henry, Fort, 60, 327

Henry, Judith, 21

Heth, Henry, 273, 274–75, 277, 278, 337–38, 340, 387–88

Hill, Ambrose P., 29, 96, 102, 103, 169, 171, 196, 244, 260, 262, 264, 273, 277, 290, 296, 304, 316, 335, 338, 403

Hill, Daniel Harvey, 85, 96, 119, 120, 148, 150, 164–65
   at South Mountain, 151–52

Hincks, Edward, 382

Hitchcock, Ethan Allen, 64

Hitchcock, Frederick, 199

Holmes, Theophilus H., 109

Hood, John Bell, 96, 160, 285, 287–88, 292, 300, 395

Hooker, John, x, 38, 46, 87, 89, 146, 174, 178, 185, 186, 203, 213, 215, 228, 230, 260, 306, 314, 325, 326, 329, 337, 345, 411, 414–15
   aggressiveness of, 76

   at Antietam, 159–60, 172
   army reorganization and reforms of, 220–26
   assessment of, 266
   background and personality of, 74–75
   at Chancellorsville, 232, 233–37, 241, 243–45, 246, 248–55
   corps badges invented by, 226
   Couch on, 237
   "dictator" remark of, 216
   in Gettysburg Campaign, 263–66
   Halleck's antipathy for, 218, 253, 256
   on McClellan, 124
   Meade's confrontation with, 257
   Meade's replacement of, 266–69
   named army commander, 216–19
   named commander of First Corps, 144–45
   nickname of, 79
   at Oak Grove, 98–99
   in Peninsula Campaign, 78–79, 98–99, 113, 116–18, 124
   personality of, 218–19
   resignation of, 265–66, 268–69
   Sedgwick's confrontation with, 255
   at South Mountain, 151
   at Williamsburg, 78–79

Hopkins, Charles, 75

Houghton, William, 164

House of Representatives, U.S., 37, 179

Howard, Charles, 283

Howard, Oliver Otis, 11, 25, 39, 201, 221, 233, 256–57
   at Chancellorsville, 239–41, 250–51, 254–55
   at Fair Oaks, 87–88
   at Gettysburg, 277, 281–82, 283, 294

Howe, Albion P., 248

Hubbell, John T., 107, 112, 113

Huger, Benjamin, 98–99, 109, 114, 116

Humphreys, Andrew A., 93, 104, 117–18, 145, 170, 180, 201, 288, 306–7, 324, 326, 329, 372, 385, 389, 399–400, 406, 412
   assessment of, 393

as chief-of-staff, 306–7, 324
on McClellan, 117–18
Warren and, 104
Hunt, Henry J., 39–41, 45, 146, 189, 190, 245, 268, 326, 384
at Gettysburg, 284, 297–98, 306
at Malvern Hill, 118, 121
Hunter, David, 11, 18, 20, 371, 377, 386
Hyde, Thomas W., 91

Illinois, 30, 179
Illinois Central Railroad, 29
Indiana, 30, 145, 179
Ingalls, Rufus, 93
Irish Brigade, U.S., 227, 228, 380
at Antietam, 164–65
composition of, 39
demise of, 367
at Fair Oaks, 88–89
at Fredericksburg, 200–201
at Gaines's Mill, 185–86
Iron Brigade, U.S., 194, 412
at Antietam, 157–58, 159
demise of, 380
at Gettysburg, 275–80
headwear of, 152
in Overland Campaign, 337, 346, 348, 358
at South Mountain, 152–53
at Wilderness, 337
Irwin, William H., 50

Jackson, Conrad F., 204
Jackson, Thomas J. "Stonewall," 21, 22, 29, 82–83, 148, 150, 184, 285, 341, 415
at Antietam, 156, 159–60, 163, 166, 172
at Chancellorsville, 235–40, 241, 249
at Fredericksburg, 188, 192, 193, 194, 195, 196
in Peninsula Campaign, 94, 96–97, 99, 101–3, 109, 116
in Second Bull Run Campaign, 133–34, 136, 137

Valley Campaign and, 82–83
wounding and death of, 241, 258
Jameson, Charles, 86
Jenkins, Micah, 86
Johnson, Andrew, 368, 411
Johnson, Edward, 293, 320, 336, 353
Johnston, Joseph E., 12, 13, 42, 46, 59, 60, 69, 70, 73, 76, 81, 95, 397, 399, 405, 412
Davis and, 62–63
in move to Bull Run, 18–19
in Peninsula Campaign, 84–85, 87
wounded, 87
Joint Committee on the Conduct of the War (JCCW):
Ball's Bluff inquiry of, 58–59
Chancellorsville and Gettysburg inquiries of, 325–26
creation and purpose of, 58
Fredericksburg inquiry of, 206, 208
Meade's testimony to, 325–26
Jones, Archer, 107

Kautz, August, 376–77
Kearny, Philip, 38, 59, 121, 128, 226, 367, 412, 415
background and personality of, 74, 75–76
death of, 137
at Glendale, 115–16
Heintzelman's confrontation with, 118–19
leadership of, 115
McClellan confronted by, 124
McClellan criticized by, 97, 128
at Malvern Hill, 118–19
at Old Tavern, 98–99
in Peninsula Campaign, 72–79, 86–87, 89, 97–99, 108, 113, 115–16, 118–19
at Seven Pines, 89
on Stone's arrest, 59
at Williamsburg, 77–79
at Yorktown, 72–73
Kelly's Ford, engagement at, 228–29
Kentucky, 209

Kernstown, Second Battle of, 386
Kershaw, Joseph, 289, 340
Key, Francis Scott, 222
Key, Philip Barton, 222
Keyes, Erasmus D., 11, 23, 25, 38, 61, 62, 79–80, 85–86, 89, 108, 109, 127, 131, 415
Kilpatrick, Judson, 270, 271, 303, 317
    Dahlgren affair and, 324–25
Kingsburg, Charles P., 93
Knickerbocker, 66
Knipe, Joseph, 241

Lane, James, 4
Laurel Hill, Battle of, 345–47, 348, 357
Ledlie, James H., 359, 383–85
Lee, Elizabeth Blair, 222
Lee, Fitzhugh, 228, 344
Lee, Robert E., x, 9, 82, 84, 131, 132, 133, 134, 136, 175, 184, 186, 213, 230, 232, 258, 259, 269, 308, 310–11, 320, 334, 369, 415
    at Antietam, 156–57, 163, 167, 168, 170, 172
    appointed general-in-chief, 397
    at Appomattox, 405, 406–9
    attempted resignation of, 315–16
    Bristoe Campaign and, 316–17
    at Chancellorsville, 234–35, 238, 243–44, 246, 247–50, 254
    at Cold Harbor, 362, 364
    Dahlgren affair and, 325
    at Fredericksburg, 188, 192, 201
    at Gettysburg Battle, 276–78, 282, 285, 292, 294, 295–99, 301
    in Gettysburg Campaign, 259–60, 266, 272–73
    invasion of Maryland advocated and, 142–43, 148–51, 153
    Johnston replaced by, 95–96
    Longstreet's disagreement with, 285–86, 296–97
    on loss at Malvern Hill, 121–22
    "Lost Order" of, 148–50
    Meade letter of, 325
    at North Anna, 359
    in Overland Campaign, 335, 342–44, 353, 357, 359, 362, 364, 366, 367
    in Peninsula Campaign, 95–96, 101–2, 103, 106, 107, 109, 111, 113–14, 116, 119, 121–22, 125
    at Petersburg, 370–71, 375–76, 387, 397, 400, 404
    surrender of, 406–9
    at Wilderness, 342, 343–44
Left Grand Division, Army of the Potomac, U.S., 185, 193
Leister, Lydia, 294
Lemont, Frank L., 15, 36
Letterman, Jonathan, 225
Libby Prison, 325, 404
Lincoln, Abraham, x, 7, 9, 11, 12–13, 29, 36, 48, 75, 92, 135–36, 147, 150, 183, 184, 187, 213, 222, 223, 225, 256, 306, 313, 321, 322, 375, 409
    administration of, x, 42, 43, 68–71, 82–84, 94, 107, 132–33, 135, 138, 139, 147, 173, 182, 308–9, 317–18
    Antietam battlefield visited by, 175–77
    army corps reorganization and, 61–62
    Army of the Potomac visited by, 226–27
    assassination of, 410–11
    Burnside's resignations accepted by, 215–16, 385–86
    and calls for volunteers, 3–4, 5, 129, 144, 244–45
    Chancellorsville defeat reaction of, 252–53
    common soldiers and, 3, 14–15, 175–76
    descriptions of, 44–45, 175–76, 206, 368
    1864 election and, 368–69, 390–91
    Emancipation Proclamation proposed by, 128–29
    Emancipation Proclamation signed by, 208–9
    First Bull Run aftermath and, 26–27

Fredericksburg aftermath and, 206–8, 219–20

Fredericksburg Campaign and, 186

General War Order No. 1, 59–60

Gettysburg Campaign and, 260, 264–65

in grand review of army, 50

Grant appointed general-in-chief by, 326–27

Grant on military strategy of, 331–32

Grant's meetings with, 386–87, 389, 398–99

Halleck criticized by, 207

Halleck named general-in-chief by, 130–31

in Hampton Roads Conference, 395–96

in Harrison's Landing visit, 126–27

Hooker appointed army commander by, 216–19

McClellan removed by, 174–75, 177–81

McClellan restored to command by, 138–41, 143–44

McClellan's relationship with, 44, 45, 46, 49, 54–55, 58, 63–64, 69–71, 126–27, 414

military strategy of, 313–14, 331–32

Peninsula Campaign and, 69–71, 82, 83, 99, 117, 126–27

Petersburg visited by, 378, 398–99, 405

post-Gettysburg operations and, 313–14

and reaction to Gettysburg outcome, 308–9

Reynolds's meeting with, 257

Richmond visited by, 405

Scott's relationship with, 3, 8

Second Bull Run Campaign and, 137–41

Willie Lincoln's death and, 60–61

Lincoln, Edward, 61

Lincoln, Mary Todd, 61, 129, 226, 398

Lincoln, Robert, 308

Lincoln, Tad, 226, 398

Lincoln, William "Willie," 60–61, 138

Livermore, Thomas, 290

Longstreet, James, 17, 76, 78, 89, 96, 114, 115, 116, 119, 134, 136, 148, 152, 156, 165, 172, 184, 186, 201, 234, 250, 260, 262–64, 312, 316, 415

at Chickamauga, 313

at Gettysburg, 285–86, 287, 295, 296–97, 304

Lee's disagreement with, 285–86, 296–97

in Overland Campaign, 335, 340–41, 344

spy employed by, 272–73

wounded, 341

Lost Order (Special Order No. 191), 148–50

Louisiana Tigers, 318

Lyman, Theodore, 359, 362, 380, 392

McAllister, Robert, 106, 183

McCall, George, 38, 46, 94, 101, 103, 106, 109–10, 113, 114–16

McClellan, Ellen Marcy, 29, 30–31, 35, 44, 49, 51, 69, 71, 78, 84, 92, 94, 138, 144, 171–72, 180–81

McClellan, George B., x, 42–45, 105, 129–30, 134, 183, 186, 205, 208, 210, 215, 218–19, 223, 227, 249, 266, 267, 306, 310, 314, 315, 345, 385

administration's conflict with, 68–71, 82–84, 107

at Antietam, 156–57, 161, 166–67, 168, 170–73

army addressed by, 64–65

Army of the Potomac reorganized by, 32–37, 39–41, 61–62, 143–47

assessment of, 167, 172–73, 182, 414–15

background of, 29–30

Ball's Bluff fiasco and, 46, 47–48

battlefields avoided by, 106, 112, 113

Burnside's replacement of, 174–75, 179–81, 183

McClellan, George B. (*continued*)
 and contempt for authority, 43–44
 as derelict of duty, 118, 124–25
 in 1864 election, 390–91
 enemy strength overestimated by,
  42–43, 99, 182
 in grand review of army, 43–51
 "Harrison Landing Letter" of, 127
 Hooker on, 124
 Humphreys on, 117–18
 illness of, 54–55
 insubordination telegram of, 107
 Kearny's criticism of, 97, 128
 and legacy of cautious mindset, 336,
  339–40, 343, 357, 414–15
 Lincoln described by, 44–45
 Lincoln's Harrison Landing meeting
  with, 126–27
 Lincoln's reinstatement of, 138–41,
  143–44
 Lincoln's relationship with, 44, 45,
  46, 49, 54–55, 58, 63–64, 69–71,
  126–27, 414
 Lincoln's removal of, 174–75, 177–81
 Lost Order and, 148–50
 McDowell replaced by, 28–29
 in Maryland Campaign, 148–50,
  153–54, 155
 in Peninsula Campaign, 64–66, 68,
  76–78, 82–84, 87, 89–93, 95–96,
  98, 99, 102–3, 106–9, 112, 113,
  116–18, 121, 123, 124–25,
  131–33
 poor leadership of, 68, 94–95, 106–7,
  112, 113, 118, 124–25, 131–32,
  181, 414–15
 Pope's Bull Run Campaign and,
  134–36
 restored to command, 138–41
 Scott's conflict with, 44, 45, 48–49
 soldiers' bond with, 36–37, 92–93,
  122–23, 140–41, 143–44, 181–82
 staff of, 93
 Stanton and, 57, 64, 137
 Urbanna Plan of, 60, 61, 63
 war goals of, 57–58
McClellan, Henry, 262

McClintock, Andrew, 14
McClure, Alexander K., 182
McDowell, Irvin, x, 13, 37, 55, 59, 61,
 62, 68, 69, 70, 82, 83, 94, 101,
 124, 140, 144, 415
 army organized by, 11–12
 background and personality of, 8–9
 at Bull Run, 16–20, 21, 23, 24, 26–27
 McClellan's replacement of, 28–29
McIntosh, John, 301–3
McLane, John W., 105
McLaws, LaFayette, 120, 153, 238, 243,
 285, 287–88, 292, 300
McLean, William, 409
Magruder, Fort, 76, 77
Magruder, John Bankhead, 68, 109, 111,
 114, 119
Mahone, William, 388
Maine, 230
Malvern Hill, Battle of, 117, 118–21,
 122, 123–24, 125, 146, 412, 414
Manassas Gap, engagement at, 311
Manassas Gap Railroad, 12, 19
Mansfield, Joseph K. F., 8, 9, 144, 162,
 172, 178
"March to the Sea," 395
Marcy, Randolph B., 29, 93
Marshall, Charles, 409
Martin, Henry L., 1–2
Maryland, 4, 209, 265
 confederate invasions of, *see* Gettys-
  burg Campaign; Maryland Cam-
  paign
Maryland Campaign:
 Battle of South Mountain in, 151–54
 Harper's Ferry captured in, 149–51
 "Lost Order" and, 148–50
 see also Antietam, Battle of
Massachusetts, 4, 5, 37
Maycock, James J., 157
Meade, George (son), 268, 269, 283
Meade, George G., x, 35, 37, 38, 48,
 56–57, 58, 59, 61, 94, 101, 146,
 178, 180, 214, 215, 218, 220, 221,
 233, 316, 319, 324, 349, 387, 391,
 392, 393, 409, 411, 414–15
 appointed army commander, 266–69

Army of the Potomac reorganized by, 328–30
background and personality of, 367–68
Bristoe Campaign and, 317
at Chancellorsville, 235–38, 343–44, 250–51, 252, 254
Dahlgren affair and, 324–25
Doubleday and, 294
at Fredericksburg, 195–96, 197
at Gettysburg, 275, 281, 283–85, 287, 292, 293–96, 297, 300, 304–9
in Gettysburg Campaign, 268–70
on Grant, 327–28
Grant's command relationship with, 328, 343, 357, 373–74
Halleck and, 308–9, 317–18
Hooker confronted by, 257
JCCW testimony of, 325–26
Lee's letter to, 325
in Overland Campaign, 334–35, 338, 340–41, 343–44, 345, 346, 347, 354–55, 359, 360, 364–65
at Petersburg, 372, 373–74, 377, 378, 380, 383, 396, 400, 402
post-Gettysburg operations and, 310–15, 320–22
Sheridan's conference with, 354–55
Sherman's "inspiration" letter and, 360
Sickles and, 318, 329
Warren's dispute with, 357, 374
at Wilderness, 338, 340–41
wounded, 114–15
Meade, Margaret, 267, 327
Meagher, Thomas, 25, 39, 87, 88–89, 200
Mechanicsville, Battle of, 101–2, 122, 123–24, 412
Medal of Honor, 105, 245
Meigs, Montgomery, 8–9, 64, 131, 132, 133, 184
Meredith, Solomon, 277, 283
Merritt, Wesley, 270, 377, 387, 399, 411
Meter, Henry, 245
Mexican War, 7, 30, 317

Michie, Peter S., 68, 106
Michigan, 145
Michigan Brigade, U.S., 344, 355, 361, 377
Middleburg, engagement at, 264
Middle Military Division, U.S., 393
Miles, Dixon S., 11, 26
Miles, Nelson A., 245, 388–89, 404
Military Order of the Loyal Legion of the United States, 413
Miller, David R., 158
Miller, James T., 54, 225
Miller, John A., 367
Miller, Michael, 114
Mine Run, engagement at, 320–22
Mississippi Department, U.S., 130
Missouri, 209
Monitor, USS, 62, 66, 81
Monocacy, Battle of, 386
Monroe, Fort, 64, 66, 68, 94, 133, 135, 386
Morell, George W., 80, 103, 106, 119
Mott, Gershom, 337, 349, 376
Mountain Department, U.S., 68, 129
Mud March, 214–15, 218, 225
Mulholland, Clair A., 204
Murray, Williamson, 414, 415

Nashville, Battle of, 395
National Union Party, 368
Neill, Thomas, 342
New Jersey, 145, 179, 230
New Jersey Brigade, U.S., 39, 75, 367, 380
New Market, Battle of, 364
Newton, John, 38, 206–7, 215, 294, 329
New York, 5, 145, 179, 230
New York Times, 215, 386, 413
New York Tribune, 12
Ninth Corps, Army of the Potomac, 215, 370, 384, 412
at Antietam, 156, 157, 167–68, 172
in Appomattox pursuit, 406, 408
at Bethesda Church, 364
Burnside's resignation from, 385–86
creation of, 130
at Fredericksburg, 191, 201, 203

Ninth Corps, Army of the Potomac,
    (*continued*)
    in Grand Review, 411–12
    in McClellan's reorganization
        146–47
    in Meade's reorganization, 329–30
    at North Anna, 358, 359–60
    in Overland Campaign, 334, 340,
        341–42, 347, 350–51, 354, 358,
        359–60, 364
    at Petersburg, 371–72, 388, 397, 400,
        403
    rejoins army of the Potomac, 329–30
    Reno named commander of, 147
    in Second Bull Run Campaign, 134,
        137
    at South Mountain, 151–52
    at Spotsylvania, 350–51, 354
    transferred to Western Theater, 220
    at Wilderness, 334, 340, 341–42, 347
9th Massachusetts Battery, U.S., 288,
    291
9th Massachusetts Regiment, U.S., 7,
    84, 220, 367
9th New York Cavalry, U.S., 261
9th Pennsylvania Reserve Regiment,
    U.S., 116
19th Indiana Regiment, U.S., 63, 152,
    176
19th Maine Regiment, U.S., 406
19th Massachusetts Regiment, U.S., 354
19th Mississippi Regiment, C.S.A.,
    403–4
93rd New York Regiment, U.S., 141,
    176
95th New York Regiment, U.S., 276
North Anna, Battle of, 333, 358–60,
    359
North Carolina, 60, 61
Northwestern Virginia Department,
    U.S., 9, 29, 30, 37
Nye, George H., 154–55, 160

Ohio, 30, 145, 265
Ohio Department, U.S., 28, 29–30
100th Pennsylvania Regiment, U.S., 398

101st New York Regiment, U.S., 113
105th Pennsylvania Regiment, U.S.,
    288
111th Pennsylvania Regiment, U.S., 54,
    225
114th Pennsylvania Regiment, U.S.,
    288
116th Pennsylvania Regiment, U.S.,
    204
118th Pennsylvania Regiment, U.S.
    (Corn Exchange Regiment), 147,
    171, 214, 317, 412
119th Pennsylvania Regiment, U.S.,
    410
120th New York Regiment, U.S., 229
121st New York Regiment, U.S.
    (Upton's Regulars), 348
124th New York Regiment, U.S. (Or-
    ange Blossoms), 288
130th Pennsylvania Regiment, U.S.,
    164
132nd Pennsylvania Regiment, U.S.,
    157, 199
140th New York Regiment, U.S., 188,
    412
140th Pennsylvania Regiment, U.S.,
    286, 290
145th Pennsylvania Regiment, U.S.,
    245
148th Pennsylvania Volunteer Infantry
    Regiment, U.S., ix–x, 245, 367
151st Pennsylvania Regiment, U.S.,
    258, 280
153rd Pennsylvania Regiment, U.S.,
    240, 281
Orange & Alexandria Railroad, 12, 130,
    134, 184–85, 311–12, 316, 323
Ord, E. O. C., 394, 400
O'Rorke, Patrick H., 188, 289
Osborn, Thomas, 212
Overland Campaign, 333–73, 385, 412
    assessment of, 334, 367
    Bethesda Church engagement in,
        364
    casualties in, 350, 354, 356, 362, 364,
        365, 366, 373

Cold Harbor in, *see* Cold Harbor, Battle of
entrenchments in, 366–67
Grant-Meade command relationship in, 328, 342, 357, 373–74
Grant's turn south in, 345, 415
Harris Farm fight in, 356
Laurel Hill Battle in, 345–47, 348, 357
"Lee to the rear" incident in, 340
North Anna Battle in, 333, 358–60, 359
onset of, 333–34
Sheridan's raid in, 355–56, 361
Spotsylvania in, *see* Spotsylvania Court House, Battle of
Todd's Tavern incident in, 344, 354–55
Union morale in, 357–58, 364–65
Union reinforcements in, 356
Wilderness in, *see* Wilderness, Battle of the
Yellow Tavern fight in, 355

Paine, William, 284
Palmer, Oliver H, 192, 199, 209
Parke, John G., 385, 388
Patrick, Marsena, 142, 181, 225, 234, 239, 252, 264, 315, 321, 389
Patterson, Robert, 12, 13, 19, 27
Pattison, Alexander B., 334
Paul, Gabriel, 283
Payne's Farm, Battle of, 320
Peabody, Miles, 52–53
Pelham, John, 195, 229
Pender, William D., 278
Peninsula Campaign, 64–133, 67
    and administration-McClellan conflict, 68–71, 82–84, 94, 107
    army transported to, 65–66
    assessment of, 123–25
    Casey's Redoubt in, 85
    casualties in, 78, 89, 102, 106, 116, 121, 122–23
    Confederate forces in, 71–72
    Confederate reinforcements in, 96–97, 99

defense of Washington issue in, 69–70, 83–84
disease in, 80, 82
Fair Oaks Battle in, 84–90
Gaines's Mill Battle in, 103–6
Glendale Battle in, 114–16
Jackson's Valley Campaign and, 82–83
Lincoln's approval of, 64
McClellan-commanders conflict in, 77–80
McClellan's address to army and, 64–65
McClellan's withdrawal decision in, 106–9
Malvern Hill Battle in, 117, 118–21, 122
Oak Grove fight in, 98–99
Savage Station Battle in, 111–12
Seven Days' Battles in, *see specific battles*
Seven Pines Battle in, 84–90
siege of Yorktown in, 68, 70–73
Stuart's Ride in, 95, 99–101
Union reinforcements in, 93–94
Williamsburg fight in, 76–78
withdrawal decisions in, 106–9, 123, 131–33
Pennsylvania, 4, 5, 6, 30, 145, 178, 230, 265
    Confederate invasion of, *see* Gettysburg Campaign
Pennsylvania Department, U.S., 12
Perkins, Charles E., 90, 409
Perkins, Hugh C., 159
Petersburg, siege of, 368–405, 412
    African-American troops in, 382–84
    attrition strategy of, 375
    "Barlow's skedaddle" in, 376
    casualties in, 372, 376, 377, 385, 389, 396, 398
    cavalry engagement in, 376–78
    Confederate abandonment of, 404
    Confederate strength in, 395, 397
    Crater debacle in, 380–85
    Deep Bottom assault in, 387–88

Petersburg, siege of (*continued*)
    Dimmock Line in, 371, 403–4
    early Union assaults in, 372, 376
    Five Forks offensive in, 399–402
    Fort Stedman assault in, 397–98
    Globe Tavern fight in, 388
    Grant-Meade command relationship
        in, 373–74
    Hampton Roads Conference and,
        395–96
    Hatcher's Run fight in, 396
    Lincoln-Grant meetings in, 386–87,
        389
    Lincoln's visits to, 378, 398–99, 405
    mid-August offensives in, 387–88
    railroads and, 375–77, 387–88, 394,
        404
    River Queen conference in, 398–99
    Shenandoah Valley Campaigns and,
        386–87, 390
    Sheridan's raid and, 376–78
    Sherman's operations and, 389–90,
        395, 397
    "squibbling" practice in, 379
    trench life in, 378–79
    Union breakthrough in, 403–5
    Union-Confederate trades in, 379–80
    Union corps commanders in, 374–75
    Union morale in, 372–73
    Union move to, 369–70
    Union reinforcements in, 395
    Warren-Meade dispute in, 374
Petersburg & Weldon Railroad, 376–77,
    387–88, 394
Pettigrew, J. Johnston, 273
Philadelphia *Inquirer*, 78
Phillips, Wendell, 138
Pickett, George E., 29, 89, 294, 296,
    400, 401
Pingree, Samuel E., 350
Pinkerton, Allan, 43, 59, 229
Pipe Creek Line, 271, 283
Pleasanton, Alfred, 147, 150, 256, 264,
    270, 287, 307, 324, 325, 326, 330
    appointed cavalry commander, 146
    assessment of, 223–24
    at Brandy Station, 260–62

Pleasants, Henry, 380, 382
Plumb, Isaac, 323
Poffenberger, Joseph, 157
Pope, John, 129–30, 133–38, 139, 140,
    142, 144, 152, 183, 220, 221, 232,
    313, 316, 328
Porter, Andrew, 20–21, 32
Porter, David, 196
Porter, David D., 398
Porter, Fitz John, 38, 134, 170, 147, 171,
    216, 412
    court-martial of, 185–86
    in Peninsula Campaign, 72–73,
        79–80, 97, 98–99, 101, 102–3,
        105, 106, 108, 109, 118, 121,
        123–24, 127, 133
    at Yorktown, 72–73
Porter, Horace, 370, 400
Potomac Department, U.S., 37, 63
Potter, William W., 304
Provisional Division, U.S., 413
Pry, Philip, 166

Quaker guns, 63

Rable, George C., 195
Radical Republicans, 57, 128, 205,
    207–8, 218–19, 325–26, 329
Rappahannock Department, U.S., 68, 129
Rappahannock Station, engagement at,
    318–19
Raymond, Henry J., 215–16
Ream's Station, Battle of (June 1864),
    376–77
Ream's Station, Battle of (August 1864),
    388–89, 393
"Rebel Yell," 98
Regis de Trobriand, Philippe, 124, 137,
    288
Reno, Jesse, 29, 147, 152
Republican Party, 179, 206, 368
Reserve Division, Pennsylvania, 38, 39,
    83, 94, 101, 105, 109–10, 124, 146,
    195, 265, 267, 290, 346, 367, 412
Reynolds, John F., 38, 41, 102, 114, 146,
    180, 221, 267, 268, 270, 283, 285,
    294, 329, 412

at Chancellorsville, 239, 243–44, 246, 250–51, 252
death of, 276, 303–4
described, 101
at Fredericksburg, 193, 195–96
at Gettysburg, 275–76, 277, 281, 283
Lincoln's meeting with, 257
as prisoner of war, 106
on training of volunteers, 41–42
Rhea, Gordon, 123, 334, 343
Rhode Island, 5
Rice, James C., 350
Richardson, Israel B., 11, 113, 167, 412
at Antietam, 164, 165–66
at Bull Run, 17, 26, 39
at Fair Oaks, 87–88
soldiers's confidence in, 87–88
wounded, 166
Richmond and York River Railroad, 81–82, 95, 109
Rich Mountain, Battle of, 30
Ricketts, James B., 23, 24, 28
Right Grand Division, Army of the Potomac, U.S., 185, 186, 191, 194, 195, 197
River Queen, 395, 398
Roanoke Island, 60
Roberts, Richard P., 286
Robertson, Robert, 176
Robinson, John C., 276–77, 283, 345–46
Rodes, Robert E., 240, 277–78, 280, 336, 346–47
Rodman, Isaac, 168
Roebling, Washington, 373
Rollins, George, 20
Rosecrans, William S., 28–29, 220, 313
Rosser, Thomas, 344
Roulette, William, 164
Rowley, Thomas A., 276–77, 283
Rummel, John and Sarah, 301
Runyon, Theodore, 11, 26

Sanford, Edward S., 107
St. Clair, John W., 211
Sanitary Commission, 56, 179, 369
Savage Station, Battle of, 111–12, 114, 124

Sayler's Creek, Battle of, 406
Schimmelfennig, Alexander, 240
Schurz, Carl, 221, 239–40, 277, 281, 283
Scott, Winfield, 1–2, 4, 11, 12, 13, 14, 18–19, 27, 29, 30, 38, 39, 64, 75, 95, 130
background of, 7
Lincoln's relationship with, 3, 8
McClellan's conflict with, 44, 45, 48–49
resignation of, 49
Sears, Stephen W., 43–44, 123, 139, 182, 237, 320
Second Confiscation Act, 128
2nd Connecticut Heavy Artillery, U.S., 362
Second Corps, Army of Northern Virginia, C.S.A., 184, 262, 335, 356, 386, 397–98, 406, 408
Second Corps, Army of the Potomac, 135, 181, 188, 192, 221, 256, 271, 284, 320, 370, 392, 399, 405
at Antietam, 156, 157, 161–62, 164, 166, 167, 168, 170
in Appomattox pursuit, 406, 408
at Bristoe Station, 316
in Burnside's reorganization, 185
at Chancellorsville, 232, 233, 236–37, 243, 245, 248
at Cold Harbor, 362, 365–66
corps badge of, 226
at Fredericksburg, 191, 197
at Gettysburg, 286, 289, 292, 294, 307
in Grand Review, 412
in McClellan's reorganization, 145
in Meade's reorganization, 329
at North Anna, 360
in Peninsula Campaign, 81, 83, 85–86, 87, 98–99, 105, 106, 108, 110–12, 119, 133, 217
at Petersburg, 371–72, 373, 376, 387–89
at Savage Station, 110–12
at Spotsylvania, 347, 349, 350–51, 354
Warren named commander of, 316
at Wilderness, 335, 337, 340

Second Corps, Army of Virginia, U.S.,
    144
2nd Maine Regiment, U.S., 23, 210
2nd Maryland Regiment, U.S., 168
2nd Massachusetts Cavalry, U.S., 261
2nd Massachusetts Regiment, U.S., 170
2nd Michigan Regiment, U.S., 17, 77,
    92, 122, 184
2nd New Jersey Brigade, U.S., 39
2nd New York Cavalry, U.S., 261
2nd New York Heavy Artillery, U.S., 356
2nd Rhode Island Regiment, U.S., 20,
    90, 409
2nd Vermont Regiment, U.S., 25, 350,
    394
2nd Wisconsin Regiment, U.S., 13, 24,
    33, 54, 152–53, 225, 275–76, 280,
    367
Sedgwick, Fort, 378
Sedgwick, John, 38, 87, 88, 144, 254, 256,
    268, 324, 326, 330, 348, 357, 412
    at Antietam, 161–63, 164, 221–22
    at Chancellorsville, 234, 243–44,
        246–48, 250
    death of, 347
    at Gettysburg, 284, 294
    Hooker confronted by, 255
    in Overland Campaign, 335, 337,
        338, 340, 341, 342, 346–47
    promoted to corps commander,
        221–22
Senate, U.S., 179, 205, 222
Seven Pines, Battle of, 83, 84–90
7th Maine Regiment, U.S., 91
7th Massachusetts Regiment, U.S., 365
7th Michigan Cavalry, U.S., 301
7th Michigan Regiment, U.S., 190
7th New York Heavy Artillery, U.S.,
    356
7th New York Regiment, U.S., 5
7th Pennsylvania Reserve Regiment,
    U.S., 132
7th Wisconsin Regiment, U.S., 53, 140,
    152, 159, 214, 280, 357
17th Maine Regiment, U.S., 209,
    243–44, 250, 288, 290, 353, 376,
    409

17th Pennsylvania Cavalry, U.S., 261
17th Vermont Regiment, U.S., 367
70th New York Regiment, U.S., 78, 116,
    120, 137, 188, 222, 226
71st New York Regiment, U.S., 21
71st Pennsylvania Regiment, U.S., 367
79th New York Regiment, U.S.
        (Cameron's Highlanders), 6,
        24–25, 26
Seward, Frederick, 208
Seward, William, 44, 49, 55, 129, 207,
    208, 395
Seymour, Truman, 101, 342
Shaler, Alexander, 342
Sharpe, George H., 229, 234
Sharpsburg, Battle of, see Antietam, Bat-
    tle of
Shaw, Robert G., 170
Shenandoah Department, U.S., 69, 129
Shenandoah Valley, 12, 13, 82, 331, 411
    Early's campaign in, 386–87, 390
    Jackson's campaign in, 82–83
    Sheridan's campaign in, 387, 390
Shepherdstown, Battle of, 171
Sherfy, John, 288
Sheridan, Philip H., 344, 358, 361, 369,
    371, 377, 383, 391, 394–95, 399,
    411
    appointed cavalry commander, 330
    in Appomattox pursuit, 405–6, 408
    at Five Forks, 400–402
    Shenandoah Valley campaign of,
        387, 390
    Warren removed by, 401–2
    at Yellow Tavern, 354–55
Sherman, William T., 11, 37, 331, 360,
    386, 391, 397, 398–99, 411,
    412–13
    in Atlanta Campaign, 389–90
    at First Bull Run, 17, 21, 24–25
    on First Bull Run outcome, 24–25
    on Grant, 326, 327
    in March to the Sea, 395
Shiloh, Battle of, 327
Sickles, Daniel E., 38, 244, 307, 318,
    326
    background of, 222–23

at Chancellorsville, 250–51
at Gettysburg, 284, 286–88, 304
Meade and, 318, 329
wounded, 288, 304
Sickles, Teresa Bagioli, 222, 237, 239, 256–57
Sigel, Franz, 144, 147, 185, 221, 331, 364
Simmons, Seneca G., 114
Sixth Corps, Army of the Potomac, 5, 7, 216, 271, 320, 386, 389, 394–95, 412
at Antietam, 156, 166
in Appomattox pursuit, 406, 408
in Burnside's reorganization, 185
at Chancellorsville, 232, 234, 243, 246–49
at Cold Harbor, 361–62, 365
corps badge of, 226
creation of, 80
at Gettysburg, 284, 285, 294, 300
in McClellan's reorganization, 145
in Meade's reorganization, 329, 330
at North Anna, 358
in Overland Campaign, 334, 335, 337, 340, 342, 346, 347, 349, 351, 354, 358, 361–62, 365
in Peninsula Campaign, 83, 108, 110–12, 119, 133
at Petersburg, 398, 400
at Savage Station, 110–12
Sedgwick appointed commander of, 221–22
at Spotsylvania, 346, 347, 349, 351, 354
at Wilderness, 334, 335, 337, 340, 342
6th Massachusetts Regiment, U.S., 4
6th Michigan Cavalry, U.S., 361
6th New Hampshire Regiment, U.S., 168
6th New York Cavalry, U.S., 261
6th Pennsylvania Cavalry, U.S., 261
6th Wisconsin Regiment, U.S., 33, 152, 158, 180, 211, 258, 276, 332, 372, 378
16th Connecticut Regiment, U.S., 169

16th Maine Regiment, U.S., 278, 336
16th Michigan Regiment, U.S., 289, 412
16th Mississippi Regiment, C.S.A., 403–4
60th New York Regiment, U.S., 293
61st New York Regiment, U.S., 88, 165, 201, 245
63rd New York Regiment, U.S., 165
63rd Pennsylvania Regiment, U.S., 115, 337
69th New York Regiment, U.S., 7, 24–25, 88
slaves, slavery, 56, 57, 81, 127, 312
Emancipation Proclamation and, 128–29, 173, 176, 208–9, 211–12
peace talks and, 395–96
proposed Amendment on, 368
see also United States Colored Troops
Slocum, Henry W., 39, 80, 105, 106, 110, 113, 114, 221, 268
at Chancellorsville, 233, 235, 237–39, 251
at Gettysburg, 282–83, 295
Small, Abner, 336–37
Smith, Gustavus, 87, 95
Smith, William F., 38, 62, 80, 113, 193, 213, 370, 375
in attempt to undermine Burnside's authority, 206, 215–16
at Cold Harbor, 361–62
Smyth, Thomas A., 406
Sommers, Richard J., 415
South Carolina, 95, 397
South Mountain, Battle of, 151–54, 411
Southside Railroad, 375–76, 404, 408
Spaulding, Ira, 190
Special Order No. 191 (Lost Order), 148–50
Spotsylvania Court House, Battle of, 333, 343, 345–57, 352
Bloody Angle in, 353–54, 357–58, 412
casualties in, 350, 354, 356
Harris Farm action in, 356
Mule Shoe salient in, 348–54
Stahel, Julius, 270

Stanton, Edwin McM., 48, 61, 62, 69, 70, 79, 82, 99, 129, 130, 131, 133, 135, 177, 180, 182, 207, 209, 222, 255, 266, 270, 308, 314, 329, 330
  Lincoln's working relationship with, 56
  McClellan's insubordinate telegram to, 107
  McClellan's relationship with, 57, 64, 137
  named War Department secretary, 56–57
  Porter's court-martial and, 185
Stedman, Fort, 397–98
Stephens, Alexander H., 395
Stephens, Thomas, 366
Stevens, Isaac, 38, 137
Stevenson, Thomas G., 350
Stickney, Clifford, 405
Stillwell, A. W., 90
Stone, Charles P., 38, 46–48, 58–59, 87
Stone, Roy, 278, 280, 283
Stoneman, George, 29, 41, 223, 224, 228, 230, 232, 238, 255
Stones River, Battle of, 220
Stonewall Division, C.S.A., 351
Strong, George Templeton, 5
Stuart, J. E. B., 23, 95, 96, 109, 148, 150, 151, 154, 178, 192, 195, 223, 229, 238, 239, 244, 250, 260, 271, 304, 307, 312, 317
  at Brandy Station, 261–62, 264
  death of, 355
  at Gettysburg, 300–303
  Gettysburg Campaign and, 273
  Ride exploit of, 95
Sturgis, Samuel D., 201, 215
Sturgis Rifles, 33
Sumner, Edwin V., 37, 61, 62, 113, 147, 185, 186, 222, 412
  at Antietam, 157, 161–63, 164, 166–67, 170, 172, 217
  assessment of, 217
  at Fair Oaks, 85–87, 89
  at Fredericksburg, 187, 188–89, 191, 194, 195, 197, 201, 203

  at Glendale, 116
  retreat in Peninsula opposed by, 112, 121, 124, 127, 131
  at Savage Station, 111–12
  in Second Bull Run Campaign, 136, 137
Sumter, Fort, 3, 5, 45
Susquehanna Department, U.S., 256
Sutherland Station, engagement at, 404
Swinton, William, 215, 216, 413
Sykes, George, 103, 104, 106, 119, 235, 236, 237, 330, 412
  assessment of, 270

Taggart, Robert, 116, 196
Tarleton, J. B., 213
Tennessee, 60, 61, 220, 312, 314, 316, 322
Tenth Corps, Army of the James, 375, 387, 392, 393, 394
10th Maine Regiment, U.S., 154
10th New York Cavalry, U.S., 261
10th New York Regiment, U.S., 104
Texas, 4
Texas Brigade, C.S.A., 340
Third Cavalry Division, U.S., 270, 303, 408
3rd Connecticut Regiment, U.S., 23
Third Corps, Army of Northern Virginia, 262, 273, 296–97, 316, 335, 403
Third Corps, Army of the Potomac, 124, 147, 271, 304, 318, 337, 393
  in Bristoe Campaign, 320
  in Burnside's reorganization, 185
  at Chancellorsville, 232, 233, 239, 241, 244
  corps badge of, 226
  at Fredericksburg, 196
  at Gettysburg, 275, 286–88, 289, 292, 307
  in Meade's reorganization, 329
  in Peninsula Campaign, 65, 83–86, 89, 98–99, 108, 110–11, 113, 118, 119
  at Savage Station, 110–11, 113

in Second Bull Run Campaign,
    133–34, 136
Third Corps, Army of Virginia, U.S., 144
3rd Maine Regiment, U.S., 20, 25
3rd New Jersey Regiment, U.S., 5
Thirteenth Amendment, 395
13th New Hampshire Regiment, U.S.,
    213
13th New York Regiment, U.S., 24
33rd Virginia Regiment, C.S.A., 23–24
37th Massachusetts Regiment, U.S., 354
38th New York Regiment, U.S., 15, 25,
    68, 91, 122
39th New York Regiment, U.S.
    (Garibaldi Guards), 6–7, 14, 16
Thomas, George H., 395
Todd's Tavern, engagement at, 344,
    354–55
Toombs, Robert, 168
Townsend, Frederick, 243
Trevilian Station, Battle of, 377, 411
Trostle, Abraham, 288
Twelfth Corps, Army of the Potomac,
    254, 265, 271
    at Antietam, 156, 157, 160, 161–62,
        166, 170, 172
    in Burnside's reorganization, 185
    at Chancellorsville, 232, 235–36,
        238–39, 241, 243
    corps badge of, 226
    creation of, 144
    at Gettysburg, 282, 292–93, 296
    transferred to Western Theater,
        314–15
12th Mississippi Regiment, C.S.A.,
    403–4
12th New Hampshire Regiment, U.S.,
    365
12th New York Regiment, U.S., 17
12th Pennsylvania Reserve Regiment,
    U.S., 290
12th United States Infantry Regiment,
    141, 236, 372, 416
20th Indiana Regiment, U.S., 91–92,
    115, 122
20th Maine Regiment, U.S., 289, 412

20th Massachusetts Regiment, U.S., 47,
    163, 255
22nd Massachusetts Regiment, U.S.,
    105, 188, 378, 390, 412
23rd Pennsylvania Regiment, U.S., 78
Twenty-Fourth Corps, Army of the
    James, 394
24th Michigan Regiment, U.S., 215,
    229, 278–80, 312, 332
Twenty-Fifth Corps, Army of the James,
    394, 404–5
26th North Carolina Regiment, C.S.A.,
    278–80
26th Pennsylvania Regiment, U.S.,
    367
26th Wisconsin Regiment, U.S., 240
27th Connecticut Regiment, U.S., 227,
    245
27th Indiana Regiment, U.S., 148, 336
27th New York Regiment, U.S., 22
28th Massachusetts Regiment, U.S., 227
29th Massachusetts Regiment, U.S., 191
200th Pennsylvania Regiment, U.S.,
    398
208th Pennsylvania Regiment, U.S., 398
209th Pennsylvania Regiment, U.S., 398
Tyler, Daniel, 11, 17–18, 20, 21
Tyler, Robert O., 356

United States Colored Troops (USCT),
    331, 393, 404–5, 412
    in Crater debacle, 382–84
United States Engineer Battalion, 189
Upperville, engagement at, 264
Upton, Emory, 349–50, 362
Urbanna Plan, 60, 61, 63

Van Vliet, Stewart, 93
Vermont Brigade, U.S., 337, 340–41,
    394
Veteran Volunteer Corps, U.S., 393
Vicksburg Campaign, 220, 308, 327
Vincent, Strong, 288–89, 293
Virginia, 13, 30, 42, 45
    secession of, 3
Virginia, CSS, 62, 66, 81

Virginia Central Railroad, 369, 377
Volunteer Engineer Brigade, U.S., 81
volunteers:
    arrival in Washington, 1–2, 4–6
    discipline of, 34–36
    ethnic diversity of, 6–7
    expired enlistments of, 12–13, 19,
        20, 36, 229–30, 265
    in first advance to battle, 12–14
    Lincoln's calls for, 3–4, 5, 129, 144,
        244–45
    motivation of, 2–3, 34–35
    reenlistment of, 323–24, 393
    spying on, 1–2
    uniforms of, 6

Wade, Benjamin, 58–59
Wadsworth, James, 39, 275, 276, 283,
    294, 336–38, 340, 341
Wainwright, Charles S., 213, 217, 250,
    251, 255, 347, 372, 374, 410, 413
Walker, John, 168
Ward, J. H. Herbert, 243, 342
War Department, U.S., 5, 19, 26, 28,
    29–30, 60, 80, 82, 84, 85, 93–94,
    99, 107, 129, 138, 146, 175, 217,
    230, 253, 265, 270, 311, 321, 329,
    330, 350, 368, 391, 393, 414
    Bureau of Colored Troops of, 382–83
    Porter court-martialed by, 185–86
    Stanton named secretary of, 56–57
War of 1812, 7, 12
Warren, Gouverneur K., 104, 268, 370,
    396, 412
    appointed Fifth Corps commander,
        330
    appointed Second Corps commander,
        316
    at Chancellorsville, 243–44, 246,
        248
    at Five Forks, 399, 400–402
    at Gettysburg, 288–89, 306, 307
    at Globe Tavern, 387–88
    Humphrey and, 104
    JCCW testimony of, 326
    at Laurel Hill, 351, 354
    Meade's dispute with, 357, 374

    at Mine Run, 320–21
    at North Anna, 358, 359
    Pope criticized by, 140
    Sheridan's dismissal of, 401–2
    at Spotsylvania, 345–46, 351, 354
    at Wilderness, 335–36, 338, 340, 341
Washington, D.C., 32, 269
    C.S.A. spies in, 1–2
    Early's Valley raid and, 386, 390
    security of, 4, 33, 42, 45–46, 60–61,
        64, 69–70, 83–84, 269
    volunteers' arrival in, 1–2, 4–6
Washington, George, 59, 66, 326
Washington Department, U.S., 9, 29,
    30, 37, 39, 41
Washington Territory, 4
Waynesborough, Battle of, 399
Webb, Alexander, 252, 254, 257, 409
Weed, Stephen, 289
Weed, Thurlow, 129
Weigley, Russell F., 125, 172, 182, 257
Weitzel, Godfrey, 394, 404–5
Weldon Railroad, see Petersburg &
        Weldon Railroad
Welles, Gideon, 8, 130–31, 135, 139,
    140, 253, 266, 267, 308, 313
Welsh, Peter, 227–28
West Virginia, 265
Whipple, Amiel W., 250
Whitworth, Fort, 403–4
Wilcox, Cadmus M., 291, 338, 340
Wilderness, Battle of the, 333–42, 339
    Brock Road fight in, 341–42
    casualties in, 342
    Plank Road fight in, 340–41
    Saunders's Field fight in, 337–38
Wiley, William C., 116, 120, 137, 188,
    226
Wilkes, Charles, 35
Willard, George, 291
Willcox, Orlando B., 11, 17, 24, 169,
    384, 398
Williams, Alpheus, 162, 172, 183, 235,
    239, 240, 241, 243–45, 269, 296
Williams, Seth, 93
Willoughby, John, 324
Wilson, Hiram S., 141

Wilson, James A., 370, 376–77, 387
Winchester, Second Battle of, 262, 264
Winchester, Third Battle of, 390, 412
Woodbury, Daniel, 189
Wright, Ambrose R., 291–92
Wright, Horatio G., 351, 357, 361, 386, 406, 412

Wright, James A., 71, 111, 125
Wyman, Arthur, 347

Yellow Tavern, Battle of, 355, 411
Young, Frank, 123

Zook, Samuel K., 200, 290